Institute for
Research on
Public Policy

Institut de
recherche
en politiques
publiques

Founded in 1972, the Institute for Research on Public Policy is an independent, national, nonprofit organization.

IRPP seeks to improve public policy in Canada by generating research, providing insight and sparking debate that will contribute to the public policy decision-making process and strengthen the quality of the public policy decisions made by Canadian governments, citizens, institutions and organizations.

IRPP's independence is assured by an endowment fund, to which federal and provincial governments and the private sector have contributed.

Fondé en 1972, l'Institut de recherche en politiques publiques (IRPP) est un organisme canadien, indépendant et sans but lucratif.

L'IRPP cherche à améliorer les politiques publiques canadiennes en encourageant la recherche, en mettant de l'avant de nouvelles perspectives et en suscitant des débats qui contribueront au processus décisionnel en matière de politiques publiques et qui rehausseront la qualité des décisions que prennent les gouvernements, les citoyens, les institutions et les organismes canadiens.

L'indépendance de l'IRPP est assurée par un fonds de dotation, auquel ont souscrit le gouvernement fédéral, les gouvernements provinciaux et le secteur privé.

Copyright ©
The Institute for Research on Public Policy (IRPP) 2007
All rights reserved

Printed in Canada
Dépôt légal 2007

National Library of Canada
Bibliothèque nationale du Québec

LIBRARY AND ARCHIVES CANADA CATALOGUING IN PUBLICATION

A Canadian priorities agenda :
policy choices to improve economic and
social well-being / edited by Jeremy Leonard,
Christopher Ragan, France St-Hilaire.

Includes bibliographical references
ISBN 978-0-88645-203-2

1. Political planning—Canada. 2. Canada—Social policy.
3. Canada—Economic policy—1991-. I. Leonard, Jeremy, 1967-
II. Ragan, Christopher III. St-Hilaire, France
IV. Institute for Research on Public Policy

JL86.P64C369 2007   320.60971   C2007-905768-3

PROJECT DIRECTORS
Jeremy Leonard
Christopher Ragan
France St-Hilaire

COPY EDITORS
Barry Norris
Mary Williams

PROOFREADER
Barbara Czarnecki

EDITORIAL COORDINATOR
Francesca Worrall

COVER DESIGN
SCHUMACHER DESIGN

INTERIOR DESIGN
Anne Tremblay
Schumacher Design

PRODUCTION AND LAYOUT
Chantal Létourneau

PUBLISHED BY
The Institute for Research on Public Policy (IRPP)
l'Institut de recherche en politiques publiques
1470 Peel Street, Suite 200
Montreal, Quebec H3A 1T1

A Canadian Priorities Agenda

Policy Choices to Improve Economic and Social Well-Being

Edited by
Jeremy Leonard,
Christopher Ragan and
France St-Hilaire

CONTENTS

Foreword   xi

Acknowledgements   xiii

Setting the Stage
Jeremy Leonard, Christopher Ragan and France St-Hilaire   1

PART I
THE POLICY CHALLENGES

HUMAN CAPITAL
Investing in Human Capital: Policy Priorities for Canada   13
W. Craig Riddell

Comments
Smart Human Capital Policy: An Alternative Perspective
Serge Coulombe   57

Education and Human Capital: Reconciling Policy Imperatives
and Policy Design
Jane Gaskell   67

CLIMATE CHANGE
Canadian Policies for Deep Greenhouse Gas Reductions
Mark Jaccard and Nic Rivers   77

Comments
Slowing, Then Reducing, Greenhouse Gas Emissions Is
Important but Will Not Be Easy
Christopher Green   107

Time to Actually Begin
James Meadowcroft   115

NATURAL CAPITAL
Securing Natural Capital and Ecological Goods and Services
for Canada
Nancy Olewiler   125

Comments
Innovative Conservation Policies for Canada That Really
Integrate the Environment and the Economy
Wiktor Adamowicz   161

Nature as Capital: Concerns and Considerations
Peter A. Victor   171

POPULATION AGING
Some Economic and Social Consequences of Population Aging
David K. Foot   181

Comments
Population Aging: The Risk of Tunnel Vision
Peter Hicks   215

Population Aging: Better than the Alternative
Susan A. McDaniel   223

ECONOMIC SECURITY
A Better Income Security System for All Canadians
Jean-Yves Duclos   233

Comments
An Alternative Proposal on Income Security
David A. Green   267

The Practitioner's Perspective on Income Security Reform
Kathy O'Hara and Allen Sutherland   277

HEALTH OUTCOMES
Improving Health Outcomes in Canada
Robert Evans, Clyde Hertzman and Steve Morgan   291

Comments
Next Steps in the Health Policy Wars?
Raisa Deber   327

Canada's High Poverty Rate Is the Greatest Impediment
to Better Health Outcomes
Dennis Raphael   337

PRODUCTIVITY
Three Policies to Increase Productivity Growth in Canada
Andrew Sharpe   353

Comments
An Alternative Policy Script to Boost Canadian
Productivity Growth
Don Drummond   389

The Canadian Productivity Conundrum
Richard G. Harris   397

TRADE AND GLOBALIZATION
Canadian Engagement in the Global Economy
Michael Hart   405

    Comments
    Constructing Constructive Engagement
    Jonathan T. Fried   435

    Engage the United States, Forget the Rest?
    Keith Head   445

PART II
THE POLICY CHOICES
Rising to the Challenges of Economic Transformation
Wendy Dobson   457

Drawing a Policy Road Map for Canada
Alain Dubuc   473

Choosing Policies to Build and Sustain Well-Being
John F. Helliwell   487

Navigating the Shoals: The Search for Canadian Policy Solutions
Richard G. Lipsey   499

Policy Priorities for Canada: Making Choices
Carolyn Hughes Tuohy   515

Think Small and Do No Harm
William Watson   533

PART III
THE IMPLICATIONS
Epilogue: Some Reflections on the Judges' Policy Choices
Jeremy Leonard, Christopher Ragan and France St-Hilaire   549

Notes on Contributors   563

FOREWORD

The people behind large and path-breaking projects often claim that the idea originated on the back of a cocktail napkin, but the Canadian Priorities Agenda (CPA) is one of those rare examples that actually did begin this way. On a June 2005 flight from Washington, DC, to Montreal, returning from an IRPP-sponsored conference, Chris Ragan broached to IRPP vice-president of research France St-Hilaire the idea of embarking on a project that would allow meaningful and informative prioritization of specific public policy proposals across a wide range of issues. Intrigued, France spent the rest of the flight with Chris jotting down names, notes and questions on an Air Canada beverage napkin.

The scope of the project was daunting, even by the IRPP's ambitious standards. Not only would the CPA, whose process was inspired by the Copenhagen Consensus, entail commissioned research in multiple areas across the policy spectrum, but, more important, it would develop a consistent framework for prioritizing policy choices and ask a panel of judges to choose the better policy proposals. In doing so, it would accomplish what is so difficult in making policy: it would respect the fact that public resources are scarce, and some proposals, however desirable, must be de-emphasized or left behind altogether. In this spirit, Nancy Olewiler, one of the participants, jokingly referred to the exercise as a sort of *Policy Idol*.

Needless to say, many thorny issues had to be ironed out as the project evolved. How should the areas of research be determined, and who should determine them? What was meant by a "better" policy proposal? What ground rules, if any, needed to be imposed on the authors and judges? These and countless other questions were asked and answered over the course of the project, leading to a refined and improved (though admittedly not perfect) version of the original idea.

The value of the CPA project is twofold. First, the research papers addressing each of the eight broad challenges that were ultimately chosen are valuable in and of themselves, because each diagnoses a critical policy challenge facing Canada and offers three specific and well-defended proposals for addressing them. The second value lies in the process of the CPA project itself, which is unique among recent contributions to Canadian policy research. By presenting and evaluating policy options within a consistent framework, it departs from the standard "silo" approach to policy analysis, encouraging consideration of a wide range of issues in order to set priorities and make informed choices across policy areas, as well as fleshing out linkages and relationships among those areas.

The policies examined in this volume are not necessarily "right." But they do have the legitimacy of having survived this process. The IRPP will be presenting these proposals to political leaders and their policy advisers in order to spark debate about the long-run strategic challenges faced by Canada and to spur appropriate action. I would encourage them to consider the proposals seriously.

After two years of hard work on the part of the 45 participants in the project and numerous others both inside and outside the Institute, the fruits of the ideas scribbled on that cocktail napkin are spread before you in the pages that follow. I hope you will find them as interesting, provocative and useful as I have.

Mel Cappe
President and CEO
October 2007

ACKNOWLEDGEMENTS

A project of this scope and complexity could not have been completed, much less gotten off the ground, without the determined efforts of countless individuals.

A special word of appreciation is due Senator Hugh Segal, who was at the helm of the IRPP at the inception of the Canadian Priorities Agenda (CPA) project and who provided encouragement and enthusiasm throughout his tenure. His successor, Mel Cappe, has been equally determined to see this project through to a successful conclusion. The IRPP's board of directors, which always provides wise counsel with regard to the Institute's research directions, was also supportive of the venture from the outset. The advice of board members to proceed with caution proved perspicacious and resulted in important adjustments and improvements to the process along the way.

The concept and substance of the CPA project took the IRPP into uncharted territory, and we bounced questions large and small off numerous policy experts throughout the exercise. In particular, the attendees of an August 2005 planning dinner in Montreal — Keith Banting, Thomas J. Courchene, Don Drummond, Janet Ecker, Janice MacKinnon, Lars Osberg, Hugh Segal, Jim Stanford, Denis St-Martin and William Watson — provided guidance that was pivotal to finalizing the project's overall structure and organization.

Once the project was underway, virtually the entire IRPP staff had some degree of involvement in it, but special gratitude is due Suzanne Lambert, who organized the agenda-setters' meeting in January 2006 and the CPA conference in March 2007; L. Ian MacDonald, who, as editor of *Policy Options*, devoted the entire April-May 2006 issue to the agenda-setters' texts; Suzanne Ostiguy McIntyre, who handled the administrative end of the entire project; Francesca Worrall, who managed with grace the gargantuan task of coordinating the editing, layout and proofreading; and Chantal Létourneau, for her tireless energy, skill and attention to detail in laying out the texts. Their efforts and dedication were instrumental in bringing this book to fruition in record time. In addition, we thank Barry Norris and Mary Williams for excellent copy-editing, Barbara Czarnecki for meticulous proofreading, Anne Tremblay for layout assistance, and Jenny Schumacher of Schumacher Design for the distinctive cover concept and photo illustrations.

Finally, our heartfelt thanks go to the 45 individuals (agenda-setters, analysts, critics and judges) who accepted the challenge of writing papers and playing their assigned roles in the CPA process. Their cooperation and patience with our many requests for elaboration, clarification and all other manner of editing changes to their texts under very tight deadlines reflect their professionalism and their commitment to open and informed policy debate in Canada.

Jeremy Leonard
Christopher Ragan
France St-Hilaire

SETTING THE STAGE
Jeremy Leonard, Christopher Ragan and France St-Hilaire

Since the work of the Macdonald royal commission was concluded over 20 years ago, there have been few occasions for Canadians to engage in a comprehensive discussion of the country's economic and social prospects and which policies we could pursue to improve them. Even in the 2006 federal election campaign, the policy debate focused on a few specific, short-term issues and offered little in the way of competing views on the major policy challenges facing Canada in the years ahead.

The IRPP created the Canadian Priorities Agenda (CPA) to contribute to a broad-based and informed public debate on the economic and social policy choices and priorities for Canada. The central theme of the project is scarcity of resources and the need for choice: the everyday reality for policy-makers is that governments have limited means at their disposal — be it revenue, manpower or political capital — and must therefore choose carefully which policies to pursue and which to leave behind.[1] In making these choices, governments are understandably drawn to what is expedient and popular, but they should also consider the overall costs, benefits and distributional effects of various policies. Policies that offer genuine net benefits to society, even if they are somewhat complex, can be clearly explained to the electorate by a government that is prepared to expend sufficient effort.

Policy-makers also need to think carefully about the time horizons for various policies. Governments, especially minority governments, often appear to have planning horizons no longer than the next election, and this myopia may lead them to implement only those policies that promise quick results. Many worthwhile policies, however, stand to offer large net benefits to society only after incurring upfront costs, and thus are likely to be ignored by a short-sighted government. Throughout the Canadian Priorities Agenda project, our focus has been on the policy challenges and implications over the medium term in an attempt to counter the prevailing policy-making myopia.

The CPA is a three-act play that has been two years in production. In act 1, the lead roles are played by a dozen agenda-setters, whose individual and collective views have a profound influence on what follows. In act 2, 11 analysts take centre stage, proposing and examining the likely effects of a wide range of specific policies; crucial supporting roles are played by 17 critics. Finally, act 3 highlights the sage choices of 6 judges, who assemble their packages of preferred policies from the large menu set before them. The necessity for policymakers (and policy advisers) to make difficult choices while constrained by limited resources is the overarching theme that permeates each act of the Canadian Priorities Agenda.

ACT 1: SETTING THE AGENDA

It is one thing to choose a few policies from a list of possible alternatives. But where does such a list come from in the first place? As with any sensible policy-making process, the CPA began with a structured "blue sky" session designed to identify the broad economic and social issues — what we call the "broad policy challenges" — that are likely to matter most to Canada and Canadians over the medium term.

To identify these challenges, the IRPP brought together 12 agenda-setters — a group of academics, analysts and practitioners with wide-ranging expertise in Canadian public policy. In assembling this group, we strove for a balance among people from academia, government and independent research institutions whose views span the political spectrum.

Each agenda-setter was assigned the task of identifying the three broad policy challenges that, in his or her view, are most likely to affect Canada's economic and social prospects over the medium term. They were asked to make their selections based on two general criteria: the relative importance of the challenge, and whether it can be addressed through specific policy initiatives. They were also asked to write a short paper outlining their choices[2] and to defend their selections to the other agenda-setters at a one-day workshop, which took place in Montreal in January 2006.

As can be seen from the complete list of agenda-setters' priorities on page 4, there were considerable overlaps among the broad policy challenges tabled for consideration at the CPA workshop. In some cases, several participants identified nearly identical challenges, such as addressing the implications of an aging population; in others, several challenges had common themes, such as improving human capital, but they were articulated in different contexts and with different emphases. Therefore, the next step for the 12 agenda-setters was to agree on a streamlined list of challenges that did not overlap but nonetheless accurately reflected their divergent views. This required a great deal of discussion, argument and even horse-trading at times, and eventually culminated in a shortened list of 14 broad policy challenges that was deemed to fully reflect the ideas presented by the participants. As a final task, each agenda-setter had

THE CPA AGENDA-SETTERS

Ken Battle — President of the Caledon Institute

Pierre Fortin — Professor of Economics, Université du Québec à Montréal; policy advisor to René Lévesque

Anne Golden — President of the Conference Board of Canada; former president of the United Way of Greater Toronto

Jane Jenson — Professor of Political Science, Université de Montréal; Fellow, Trudeau Foundation

Tom Kent — Founding Editor of *Policy Options*; policy advisor to Lester B. Pearson

Robert Lacroix — Professor of Economics and Fellow, Center for Interuniversity Research and Analysis on Organizations; former rector, Université de Montréal

Kevin Lynch — Clerk of the Privy Council; former federal deputy minister of finance; former director, International Monetary Fund

Janice MacKinnon — Professor of Public Policy, University of Saskatchewan; IRPP Chair; former finance minister of Saskatchewan

Judith Maxwell — Senior Fellow and former president of Canadian Policy Research Networks; former chair of the Economic Council of Canada

Nancy Olewiler — Professor of Economics and Director of the Public Policy Program, Simon Fraser University

Lars Osberg — McCulloch Professor of Economics, Dalhousie University

Jim Stanford — Economist, Canadian Auto Workers; columnist for the *Globe and Mail*

to select a subset of 8 challenges from the shortened list. Thus, not only was each agenda-setter forced to make tough choices early in act 1 by selecting three policy priorities from a nearly infinite range of possibilities, but each was also required to choose his or her top 8 from the winnowed list of 14. The results of this vote are shown on page 5: the figure in the right-hand column indicates the number of agenda-setters who selected the policy challenge named in the left-hand column.[3]

Given the range of expertise and perspectives around the table, we were not surprised that the agenda-setters held strong and often divergent views on the most important policy challenges facing the country. Yet a number of overarching themes emerged. The concept of capital was raised often, and the importance of protecting Canada's natural capital and developing its human capital was emphasized by many. Equity was also a key consideration for most of the agenda-setters — in terms of young and old, rich and poor, and current and future generations — as indicated by widely shared concerns over the impact of economic insecurity and population aging on social cohesion. Of course, health care was also the focus of much discussion, and

CANADA'S ECONOMIC AND SOCIAL POLICY CHALLENGES: THE AGENDA-SETTERS' TOP THREE

Ken Battle
1. Reform adult benefits to improve assistance to the unemployed and the working poor
2. Enhance the economic security of families with children
3. Increase the availability and quality of early learning and child care

Pierre Fortin
1. Improve education by focusing on the acquisition of basic skills
2. Address the intergenerational and fiscal implications of an aging population
3. Rebuild national cohesion and strengthen Canadians' sense of national identity

Anne Golden
1. Improve Canada's global competitiveness
2. Address the labour force and fiscal implications of an aging population
3. Develop a climate change strategy and improve management of natural resources

Jane Jenson
1. Increase the availability of good-quality nonparental child care
2. Enable parents with young children to make full use of their education/skills
3. Enhance intergovernmental cooperation to better address policy challenges

Tom Kent
1. Establish a youth charter to improve the health, education and living standards of children
2. Encourage smarter work to improve Canadian productivity
3. Enhance equality of opportunity and ensure fairer rewards

Robert Lacroix
1. Increase investment in post-secondary education and university research
2. Redesign the equalization system and review other aspects of fiscal federalism
3. Fulfill Canada's Kyoto commitments while minimizing the associated distributional effects

Kevin Lynch
1. Increase Canadian productivity growth to close the gap vis-à-vis the United States
2. Improve human capital through education and training
3. Improve Canada's global reach (attract foreign direct investment and deepen trade links)

Janice MacKinnon
1. Reduce the growth rate of health care spending and invest in the long-term determinants of health
2. Promote innovation and increase productivity
3. Address the labour force and fiscal implications of an aging population

Judith Maxwell
1. Establish a social care system for seniors
2. Improve services and child care choices for families with young children
3. Provide alternative pathways from school to work for young adults

Nancy Olewiler
1. Ensure the sustainability of Canada's natural capital stock
2. Address insufficient and ineffective education and skills development
3. Improve Canada-US relations and economic cooperation

Lars Osberg
1. Reduce poverty and social exclusion to maintain social cohesion
2. Improve Canadians' sense of personal security over their economic futures
3. Enhance a sense of common citizenship among all Canadians

Jim Stanford
1. Reduce the concentration and depth of poverty to prevent social exclusion
2. Reduce greenhouse gas emissions to stabilize global climate change
3. Manage trade liberalization with emerging markets to sustain Canadian jobs

THE AGENDA-SETTERS' POLICY CHALLENGE SELECTIONS	
Enhance learning in Canada and the conditions under which investments in skills and learning pay off, from early childhood through adulthood	12
Improve the economic and environmental sustainability of Canada's natural capital in the global environment	10
Achieve effective intergovernmental relations within the federation	10
Address the economic and social implications of an aging population	8
Improve labour market opportunity and economic security for working-age adults	7
Improve economic security for families with children	7
Improve the health outcomes of the Canadian population	7
Improve Canada's absolute and relative productivity performance	6
Maximize the net benefits of Canada's active engagement in the global economy	6
Enhance Canada's capacity to create, transfer, commercialize and use knowledge	6
Improve the performance and sustainability of the health care system	5
Reduce poverty and social exclusion	5
Reduce economic disruptions from growing trade imbalances with emerging economies	4
Enhance Canadians' sense of common citizenship	3

familiar concerns about the sustainability of the current system were raised. Ultimately, a greater number of participants chose improving the health outcomes of Canadians as the more important challenge. Enhanced productivity performance was another strong theme — not surprisingly, since many other policy challenges become easier to address when overall long-term living standards are improved. Indeed, the same argument applies to another top-of-mind issue: Canada's ability to position itself amid rapidly changing trade and investment patterns in the global economy.

The agenda-setters' workshop concluded act 1 of the Canadian Priorities Agenda, but it was the starting point for act 2. The agenda-setters exit stage left, while the analysts and critics enter stage right.

ACT 2: CONDUCTING THE POLICY ANALYSIS

Mindful of the need to make choices and establish priorities, we decided to restrict the scope of our project to the detailed examination of eight of the broad policy challenges identified by the agenda-setters. We did so by following their preferences, starting at the top of their selected list and working our way down. We also modified the list in three ways. First, we recognized that the environmental challenge really contains two quite distinct issues — protecting Canada's natural capital and dealing with global climate change — and that a serious analysis of both would be beyond the scope of a single paper. For this reason, we split that challenge into two. Second, we omitted the third challenge (achieving effective intergovernmental relations), because such governance and institutional issues, as important as they are, actually pertain to the political environment within which all of the other policy challenges are to be addressed. It would therefore be difficult, if not impossible, to compare specific policies related to this challenge with those related to the other challenges. Put slightly differently, we judged that the CPA project would have a sharper and more useful focus if we restricted our attention to specific economic and social policies, taking as given Canada's existing governance structure.[4] Finally, since the fourth and fifth broad policy challenges both focus on economic security, and there was likely to be significant overlap in the specific policies proposed to address them, we combined them into one.

Armed with this final list of eight broad policy challenges, our next step was to find a cast of analysts capable of digging deeper and carefully examining and comparing policies to address each of them. Since we knew that we would need detailed analyses of specific policy alternatives, we searched for people who possess a combination of solid analytical skills, considerable policy savvy and expertise in the particular policy area. Moreover, since the task would involve identifying the overall costs and benefits of each policy proposed, it was clear to us that we needed economists, whose training encourages them to think precisely in these terms.

THE CPA POLICY CHALLENGES AND ANALYSTS

Human capital — W. Craig Riddell, University of British Columbia

Climate change — Mark Jaccard and Nic Rivers, Simon Fraser University

Natural capital — Nancy Olewiler, Simon Fraser University

Population aging — David K. Foot, University of Toronto

Economic security — Jean-Yves Duclos, Université Laval

Health outcomes — Robert Evans, Clyde Hertzman and Steve Morgan, University of British Columbia

Productivity — Andrew Sharpe, Centre for the Study of Living Standards

Trade and globalization — Michael Hart, Carleton University

We assigned all the analysts the same tasks: first, they had to present their perspectives on the broad policy challenge and articulate its importance to Canadians' economic and social well-being; second, they had to identify three policies that would be most effective in addressing the challenge; third, and most important, they had to analyze the effects of each policy — costs, benefits, distributional aspects — as precisely as possible and consider other relevant factors, such as the policy's political feasibility. In short, we asked them to make the best evidence-based case they could for their three chosen policies, almost as if they were trying to convince a skeptical prime minister or cabinet why the policies should be implemented.

The first part of this book contains the analysts' papers on the eight policy challenges and their policy proposals. It also includes the critics' assessments of the proposals (two for each challenge). Since we had intentionally solicited analyses from economists, we tried to counterbalance this bias by choosing several critics from a different background. But, in all cases, we chose academics or practitioners with considerable experience in either the design or the implementation of Canadian policy and with expertise in the particular area.

ACT 3: MAKING DIFFICULT CHOICES

If the analysts did their job well, then all 24 of the policies they selected would appeal to an ambitious government wishing to reach out to various voter constituencies. But resource constraints force any government to narrow its policy priorities. To capture this important aspect of real-world policy implementation, the third and final phase of the CPA project entailed a process of selection among the 24 policies recommended by the analysts.

In an ideal world, such choices — whether from among policies aimed at quite different challenges or policies aimed at the same challenge — would be made by experienced individuals who had wisdom acquired over years of observing which policies succeeded and which failed, and why. Such individuals could objectively assess the available evidence and, if that evidence was sufficiently compelling, alter their beliefs accordingly. They would also have the breadth of vision to predict how various policies might interact, and thus understand how the case for a specific policy in isolation could be altered by the simultaneous consideration of other policies.

The six individuals we asked to play the role of judge for the Canadian Priorities Agenda have contemplated, analyzed, explained and debated policy in the

---

THE CPA JUDGES

Wendy Dobson — Professor and Director, Institute for International Business, Rotman School of Management, University of Toronto; former federal deputy minister of finance

Alain Dubuc — Syndicated columnist for *La Presse* (Montreal)

John F. Helliwell — Professor Emeritus, University of British Columbia; Fellow, Canadian Institute for Advanced Research

Richard G. Lipsey — Professor Emeritus, Simon Fraser University; former fellow, Canadian Institute for Advanced Research

Carolyn Hughes Tuohy — Professor Emeritus, University of Toronto; Senior Fellow at the School of Public Policy and Governance at the University of Toronto

William Watson — Associate Professor of Economics and Chair of the Department of Economics, McGill University; columnist for the *National Post* and the *Gazette* (Montreal)

Canadian context for many years. Most have experience either in government or in advising government at the highest levels. Their mandate was to examine the evidence presented by the analysts, weigh the arguments of the analysts' critics and assemble from among the set of 24 policy recommendations their own packages of five preferred policies.

The full cast of players (analysts, critics and judges) came together for a two-day "performance" in Toronto in March 2007. In eight conference sessions, the analysts presented their cases for three specific policies. It was clear from the outset that some had a harder task than others, as their policy recommendations were less familiar to some of the judges. Creative policy recommendations — and many of the CPA policy recommendations are quite creative — are often greeted warily by decision-makers. The judges asked clarifying questions, but held their cards close to their chests.

As the critics rose to present their views, the real disagreements began to appear. Like the analysts, the critics were also specialists in the policy area being discussed, but their perspectives — often those of practitioners or academics with very different professional training — sometimes led them to offer contrasting views of the analysts' chosen policies. While these competing views were being aired before the entire group, one could see judges jotting down notes and sorting out their own thoughts.

The judges were then free to question the analysts and raise any concerns they had about what they had heard. Finally, the floor was opened to general discussion and debate among all participants. At this point, many commented on the interaction of individual policies, and it became clear that the case for any given policy would depend on which other policies were also chosen. Such interaction naturally makes the policy selection process more difficult, and we were glad we had chosen a panel of judges who were up to the task. During these discussions, a few of the judges revealed their cards, but surprisingly few, and never a complete hand. Each judge knew that it would take some time to clarify his or her thoughts. Making difficult choices is…well, difficult.

As the CPA conference ended, after an intense but fascinating two days, the real work for the six judges was just beginning. Though they were free to use whatever selection criteria they thought most appropriate, each agreed to write a paper clearly explaining his or her choices and rationale. The second part of this book contains their verdicts, and the reader will not be surprised to find that each judge has strongly held views about many things, including the appropriate role of public policy in a mixed economy; which criteria matter most in setting policy priorities and choosing from among them; and which policies are likely to work and which are likely to fail. In all cases, the judges have taken the time to seriously ponder the choices put before them and to present carefully reasoned policy packages.

In the third and final part of the book, we offer a brief analysis of the six judgments, and point to some overarching themes as well as potential directions for Canadian policy coming out of this unique exercise in policy research and deliberation.

The goal of this IRPP initiative was to bring together some of the best policy minds in the country to examine and discuss Canada's top economic and social policy priorities and choices over the medium term. We are confident that the ideas, insights and analyses generated by this impressive group of experts within the context of the Canadian Priorities Agenda will make a valuable contribution to policy debate in Canada. We hope you agree.

NOTES

1   We are pleased to acknowledge our intel-
    lectual debt to the Copenhagen
    Consensus, a project designed in a similar
    way to highlight the need for policy choice
    in a world of scarce resources (see
    www.copenhagenconsensus.com). But
    the contexts for the two projects are quite
    different. Whereas the Copenhagen
    Consensus project focuses on how the
    developed world should collectively
    choose and support policies to promote
    better living conditions within the develop-
    ing world (see Lomborg 2004), our focus
    is on how one country (Canada) should
    choose policies to promote better internal
    economic and social well-being.

2   Their essays appear in the April-May 2006
    issue of *Policy Options*.

3   In the April-May 2006 issue of *Policy
    Options*, we provided an interpretation of
    this list based on the workshop discus-
    sions and the views underlying the policy
    priorities, drawing out central themes
    where we thought they had begun to
    emerge. For this reason, in this introduc-
    tion we confine ourselves to only a few
    brief observations.

4   The IRPP has a long-standing interest in
    the evolution of Canadian federalism, con-
    stitutional reform and federal-provincial fis-
    cal arrangements, and it has published
    numerous reports and studies on these
    issues over the years. For more informa-
    tion about the IRPP's research projects
    and publications, see the Web site at
    irpp.org.

REFERENCE

Lomborg, Bjørn, ed. 2004. *Global Crises,
    Global Solutions*. Copenhagen
    Consensus 2004. Cambridge: Cambridge
    University Press.

HUMAN CAPITAL

INVESTING IN HUMAN CAPITAL: POLICY PRIORITIES FOR CANADA

W. Craig Riddell

Human capital refers to the skills, competencies and knowledge individuals possess. These skills and competencies include both cognitive skills such as literacy and numeracy and noncognitive skills such as self-discipline and perseverance. Human capital is the outcome of many influences, both hereditary and environmental, and makes an important contribution to individual and social well-being.

In this chapter, I first describe the challenges that Canada faces with respect to human capital. I then outline three specific proposals to address these challenges, and present a detailed assessment of each proposal. My intention is not to make the case for each policy proposal as an advocate would do, but to provide an objective assessment of the likely benefits and costs of each. To the extent possible with current knowledge, this assessment is evidence-based.

THE POLICY CHALLENGE

Although an individual's skills, knowledge and competencies are determined by many factors, in this chapter I pay particular attention to those, such as formal education, that public policy can influence. Policy might improve the contributions families and communities make to the skills and competencies of their members, and influence the effect of the workplace on the skills of employees.

Why human capital matters

Human capital exerts a major influence on individual well-being over the life-cycle. Three important factors that contribute to an individual's human capital are the nurturing, nutrition and stimuli received in the early years of life; formal education; and skills and knowledge acquired by work experience, other life experiences and adult education and training. There is considerable evidence that each factor contributes to an individual's cognitive and noncognitive skills and to overall well-being. For example, many studies have documented that formal schooling is one of the best predictors of who gets ahead. Better-educated workers earn higher wages, have greater earnings growth over their lifetimes, experience less unemployment and work longer. Higher education is also associated with longer life expectancy and better health. These labour market and health consequences constitute a major part of the private benefits from education; they also might imply social benefits associated with less reliance on publicly funded health care and social programs.[1] As well, for many people, education has consumption value in addition to the investment value associated with improved earnings — humans are curious creatures and enjoy learning and acquiring new skills.

The correlation between education and economic and health outcomes has been known for some time. Many social scientists, however, have been unwilling to attribute higher earnings and improved health to the acquisition of additional education. A positive correlation between education and labour market and health outcomes could arise because both are related to unobserved factors such as innate ability, motivation and personal characteristics such as the extent to which a person's behaviour is "forward looking." Consequently, many observers have (appropriately) been cautious about interpreting these associations as causal relationships. There is growing evidence from recent research, however, that these links are to an important extent causal in nature. This evidence implies that changes in educational attainment lead to increases in individual earnings, improvements in health and changes in other outcomes.

Education and other forms of human capital formation play important roles in society and the economy in addition to their labour market and health consequences. These nonmarket and social benefits include increased civic participation, reduced participation in criminal activities and higher rates of innovation and the associated increased growth in living standards. There are also important intergenerational effects associated with educational attainment. Especially noteworthy are improved child health, education and economic well-being. The existence of significant social benefits from human capital formation, in addition to private benefits, constitutes a primary rationale for government intervention in skills formation.

The emergence of the knowledge society and the growing demand for skills

Education, training and skills formation have become prominent public policy issues. Several factors account for this increased attention. Technological change — especially advances in information and computer technologies — and the globalization of production have resulted in growing demand for highly skilled workers and changes in workplace skills requirements. These same forces also appear to have contributed to widening inequality between more- and less-skilled workers in employment, wages and other labour market outcomes. In addition, there is growing concern about future skills shortages, in part due to the fact that the baby boom generation is approaching retirement age and is being replaced by much smaller cohorts. Finally, as part of a resurgence of interest in the determinants of long-term growth, new growth theory emphasizes the importance of human capital for the creation of new knowledge and growth of living standards over time. These factors explain the increased emphasis on skills and knowledge in economic policy.

As economic activity becomes more knowledge-based and less dependent on natural resources and physical capital, human capital is also increasingly viewed as central to social policy. Many current social programs were shaped during the expansion of the welfare state that took place after the end of the Second World War. With substantial changes to the economic and social environment in recent years, a reassessment of these programs has been underway. Governments have been moving away from passive income maintenance programs toward active policies that facilitate adjustment to change, assist the jobless to find work and encourage labour force participation. Associated with this shift is greater emphasis on individual responsibility and on providing those in need of assistance with the opportunity to improve their situation — providing a hand up rather than a handout. Investing in the human capital of those with limited skills is a key component of such an approach.

Distributional consequences and equality of opportunity

The increased emphasis on human capital in social policy also reflects the view that education and training could ameliorate widening income inequality. According to this view, investment in education should increase the supply of skilled workers, thus reducing upward pressure on their wages, and reduce the supply of the less skilled, thus reducing downward pressure on their earnings and employment opportunities. In periods in which the demand for skilled workers is growing rapidly, making higher education more accessible could prevent increases in income inequality that would otherwise occur.

Education is also a mechanism for promoting equality of opportunity and social mobility. Productivity and economic growth are enhanced if the population's talents are effectively used. The efficient allocation of talent requires that those with high ability be able to pursue productive and rewarding careers, whatever their family background. Thus, promoting equality of opportunity should be an objective of economic policy, especially in an environment in which success is increasingly dependent on human resources and knowledge. From the perspective of social policy, equality of opportunity contributes to social cohesion and common interests among citizens.

Key features of human capital investment decisions

Although, as noted, there might be some "consumption value" in learning new skills, choices relating to human capital are principally investment decisions. Individuals incur costs in the present in return for future benefits. The benefits of human capital acquisition typically accrue over a long period, in the form of a higher earnings stream (and other outcomes such as improved health) over many years. For this reason, in making such decisions, individuals need to compare the present value of the gradual accumulation of future benefits with the current costs. In order to make good investment decisions, individuals need to be far-sighted, rather than myopic. They also need to finance the investment, by either borrowing or running down existing assets.

A major component of the cost of acquiring human capital is the opportunity cost — the income forgone by not working. The more education an individual acquires, the higher the opportunity cost; thus, the cost of an additional year of schooling increases with the amount of schooling one has already obtained, suggesting that individuals face diminishing returns to investing in education. At the same time, there is evidence that those with a good base of skills can more readily acquire additional skills — in other words, that those who master competencies at an early age can more easily learn additional skills at later ages (Knudsen et al. 2006). These considerations imply that the return on human capital investments will be larger if the investments are made early in life, rather than later (see Carneiro and Heckman 2003).

Two additional features of human capital choices are worth noting. Because the benefits accrue in the future, typically there is uncertainty about the extent to which the investment will pay off: human capital investment is risky. Finally, as I discuss later, the benefits of human capital investments are transferred across generations. The payoffs thus persist for many decades.

Is government involvement in human capital formation warranted?

As is the case in most countries, all Canadian jurisdictions are characterized by extensive government involvement in the provision and financing of education. This involvement may be justified on both efficiency and equity grounds. Efficiency gains result in an increase in society's total income, and lead to higher average living standards. Equity considerations relate to how society's total income is distributed among citizens.

Efficiency rationales involve potential market failures in the provision of education. One rationale is based on the presence of benefits to society as a whole in addition to private benefits that accrue to those who receive education. Because they are not taken into account in the decision on how much schooling to acquire, such external benefits could result in underinvestment in education in the absence of government intervention.

Many observers suggest that education has substantial social benefits and advocate government involvement in its financing and provision. Indeed, when discussing education, many market-oriented economists depart from their usual laissez-faire position on the appropriate role of government. An illustration is Milton Friedman's position on the role of government in schooling:

> A stable and democratic society is impossible without widespread acceptance of some common set of values and without a minimum degree of literacy and knowledge on the part of most citizens. Education contributes to both. In consequence, the gain from the education of a child accrues not only to the child or to his parents but to other members of the society; the education of my child contributes to other people's welfare by promoting a stable and democratic society. (Friedman 1955, 23).

A second argument for intervention arises because of credit market failures that inhibit people from making productive investments. Individuals who might benefit from higher education but who do not have the resources to finance the investment typically are unable to use their potential human capital as collateral for a loan. This feature of credit markets makes investments in human capital fundamentally different from those in physical capital. As a consequence, there might be a case for government involvement in financing education, especially for those from disadvantaged backgrounds.

Not only is it difficult to collateralize human capital investments, the risks associated with these investments, unlike those of physical capital investments, are inherently nondiversifiable. An individual who chooses to become a pilot cannot diversify the risk associated with this occupation by selling claims on future income and purchasing claims on the future income streams of alternative occupations such as electricians and geologists.

A different type of market failure arises from imperfect information. Romer (2000) argues that the market for education suffers from pervasive problems of incomplete information. Students and parents, for example, face difficulties in judging the quality of educational programs, while evidence suggests parents find it difficult to evaluate the quality of child care (Helburn and Howes 1996). Government intervention could improve the quantity and quality of information, enabling individuals to make more informed decisions. Similarly beneficial might be government involvement in developing, publicizing and enforcing standards.

A final efficiency rationale arises from the fact that parents play a major role in financing and encouraging their children to acquire skills. Even altruistic parents might not take into account the consequences of their child-rearing decisions for those outside the immediate family — the so-called Samaritan's dilemma (Coate 1995). Yet these choices have implications for the broader society as well as for one's children.

Although it does not fit well with models of rational decision-making, another rationale for government intervention is based on the view that youths often make poor or myopic decisions that they later regret and that imply social costs as well as private costs (see the later discussion on policies to reduce the high school dropout rate).

Government intervention is also often justified on equity grounds: the promotion of equal opportunity, social mobility and a more equal distribution of economic rewards. Promoting equal opportunity could contribute to social cohesion and common interests among citizens, while increased skills formation could ameliorate widening income inequality.

Evidence on rates of return to human capital investment

An important distinction is that between private and social returns to human capital formation. Private returns are those based on the costs incurred and the benefits — both the consumption and investment consequences — received by the individual who acquires the skills and knowledge. Social returns are based on costs and benefits for society as a whole. There might be differences between private costs and social costs, as well as between private and social benefits. This distinction is important because individuals can be expected to base their decisions on private costs and benefits, whereas it is in the public interest to have decisions based on social costs and benefits.

Private returns

Many studies in Canada and elsewhere, using conventional multivariate methods that control for other observed factors that influence earnings, estimate the economic return to schooling to be approximately 8 to 10 percent, a rate that compares favourably with those on physical capital investments. Many social scientists are skeptical about these estimates, however, because they do not control for unobserved factors — such as ability, motivation and perseverance — that might influence both educational attainment and labour market success. Such unobserved factors are likely to imply that conventional estimates of the return to schooling are biased upward. Furthermore, if employers use education as a predictor of productivity and, in order to signal their ability, high-ability individuals acquire more schooling than do low-ability individuals, then one might observe a positive correlation between education and earnings even when education has no causal effect on individual productivity (Spence 1974). These concerns raise questions about whether large public investments in education are warranted.

Important advances have recently taken place in our understanding of the relationship between education and labour market success. These advances have occurred because of the use of natural experiments and instrumental variables (IV) methods that employ variations in educational attainment brought about by policy changes or unique events — variations that are arguably unrelated to unobserved factors that influence both schooling and labour market outcomes.[2] Such variations allow one to identify the causal impact of education. A large number of such studies have now been carried out in numerous countries — see Card (1999, 2001) and Riddell (2007) for surveys of these advances.

Three recent Canadian studies provide good illustrations of the natural experiment approach. Lemieux and Card (2001) study the impact of the *Veterans Rehabilitation Act* — the Canadian version of the US "G.I. Bill."To ease the return of Second World War veterans to the labour market, the federal government provided strong financial incentives for veterans to attend university or other educational programs. Because many more men from Ontario than from Quebec served as soldiers, those from Ontario were significantly more likely to be eligible for these benefits. Lemieux and Card estimate that the act increased the educational attainment of Ontario male veterans by 0.2 to 0.4 years. Further, using IV methods — which look only at the subset of the population whose education increased because of the intervention — they estimate the rate of return from the additional education to have been between 14 and 16 percent. In contrast, using the conventional ordinary least squares (OLS) method — which looks at the population as a whole — the estimated rate of return was just 7 percent.

Sweetman (1999), investigating the effect on education and earnings of Newfoundland and Labrador's raising the years of schooling required for high school graduation from 11 to 12, estimates that the change increased the educational attainment of the Newfoundlanders to whom it applied by 0.8 to 0.9 years. Moreover, estimated rates of return to the additional schooling are substantial: 17.0 percent for females (versus an OLS estimate of 14.6 percent) and 11.8 percent for males (compared with an OLS estimate of 10.8 percent). Perhaps the most compelling evidence comes from research on the effects of changes in compulsory schooling laws in the various provinces over the past century, which reveals that they have been large, with associated rates of return in the 12 to 15 percent range (Oreopoulos 2006a).

Research thus seems to confirm that, for certain groups, the returns to education are particularly high, and policy interventions that raised the educational attainment of certain groups many years ago had large beneficial effects on the subsequent lifetime earnings of these individuals.

Two principal conclusions follow from this recent research. First, rates of return on investments in education that certain groups make are high — higher than previous studies of the average effect of education on earnings for the population as a whole seemed to suggest. Second, the payoff to incremental investments in education could exceed the average rate of return in the population. In the past, interventions that raised educational attainment among individuals with relatively low levels of schooling yielded above-average returns. This finding is consistent with the view that these individuals stopped their schooling because of myopic decision-making or because they faced above-average costs in acquiring additional education, rather than below-average expected returns. Although there is no guarantee that the future will be like the past, these results suggest that investments at the margin in education need not yield below-average returns, as would be the case if there were diminishing returns to all human capital investments.

Nonmarket and social returns

In addition to the private benefits associated with increased employment and higher earnings, there is some consumption value associated with learning and with acquiring skills. Private benefits also come in the form of improved health and increased well-being of one's children.

Important advances have taken place in our knowledge of the nonmarket and social consequences of education. Central to the public funding — and often also the provision — of education is the belief that schooling provides major social benefits. Policy interventions designed to raise educational attainment are often justified on this basis. Until recently, however, evidence of the magnitude of these benefits has been lacking. Many studies confirmed that educational attainment is correlated with outcomes such as improved health and civic participation and reduced criminal activities. It remained unclear, however, whether these correlations reflect a causal effect of education or are due to both education and individual outcomes being related to unobserved factors. It was crucial to find the answer, since the case for public intervention would be much stronger if education was found to lead to social as well as private benefits.

Recent research using natural experiments and IV methods has indeed strengthened the case for believing that the nonmarket and social benefits of education are substantial (see Riddell 2005, 2007) with the evidence yielding the following estimates: innovation, knowledge creation and economic growth — 1-2 percentage points; knowledge spillovers — 0-1 percentage points; nonmarket benefits — 3-4 percentage points; and social benefits associated with taxation of higher incomes — 2 percentage points, for a total rate of return of 6 to 9 percent.

Knowledge spillovers arise if more education raises not only the productivity of those receiving the education but also the productivity of those with whom they work and interact through the exchange of ideas, imitation and learning-by-doing. Nonmarket benefits include social benefits associated with reduced crime, increased civic participation, improved health and longevity and intergenerational effects. Some of the intergenerational effects and the effects of education on health are private in nature, but in both cases there are social as well as private benefits. These estimates suggest that social benefits of education could be similar in magnitude to the private benefits associated with higher lifetime earnings (see also Wolfe and Haveman 2001; and Davies 2002). If so, the social returns to education are substantial and justify significant public subsidization of education.

Several additional observations are warranted. First, considerable uncertainty remains about the magnitude of the social benefits of schooling. In contrast to the substantial research effort on the relationship between schooling and earnings, much less is known about the causal effect of education on other outcomes, and what little is known comes from US studies, not Canadian. Some effects of schooling might be universal in nature, but others likely depend on the social and institutional setting. In the case of civic participation, for example, education appears to have a much larger effect on voting behaviour in the United States than it does in Canada or the United Kingdom, perhaps for reasons related to systems of voter registration in the respective countries (Milligan, Moretti, and Oreopoulos 2004). As another example, it is quite possible that the effects of education on criminal activity and health outcomes in Canada and the United States differ in size, even if the direction of influence is the same in both countries.

Second, little is known about the size of the social benefits associated with post-secondary education. Most studies use changes in compulsory school attendance and child labour laws to examine the causal effects of schooling, and thus provide evidence of such effects only at the secondary level.

Third, in estimating the nonmarket and social benefits of education, I did not try to separate private and social benefits associated with intergenerational effects — such as the effects of educational attainment of parents on the development, health and education of their children. I also did not separate the beneficial effects on individuals' health into their private and social components. To an important extent, one should appropriately view these consequences as private benefits, but it is unclear whether individuals take these consequences into account when they choose how much education to acquire. Whether one treats intergenerational effects on health and longevity as being mainly private benefits or as having a large social component, these consequences should be included in the overall return to education.

In summary, nonmarket and social benefits of education appear to be substantial, perhaps as large as private market returns to education from higher lifetime earnings. Public policies relating to education thus should take social and nonmarket benefits into account.

The current state of human capital in Canada

In examining briefly the current state of Canada's human capital, it makes sense to look at how the country compares with other industrialized nations with respect to the amount of money that is spent, publicly and privately, on education; educational attainment levels; measures of student achievement; and the cognitive skills of the adult population.

Public and private expenditure on education

Canada invests a substantial amount in formal education, traditionally ranking near the top of the developed countries in terms of spending per student from both public and private sources at all educational levels — albeit substantially below the top-ranked United States (for recent data, see table A-1, panel a; for earlier data, see Riddell 2004). In terms of the percentage of gross domestic product (GDP) devoted to education — a measure that reflects both spending per student and the number of students — Canada is about average among the developed countries (table A-1, panel b). Within Canada, the provinces differ considerably in spending per student, especially at the elementary and secondary levels (table A-1, panel c).

Over the past decade, however, Canadian expenditure on education has declined relative to that of other developed countries. For example, Canada's public and private spending per student at all levels of education fell from 35 percent above the average of member countries of the Organisation for Economic Co-operation and Development (OECD) in 1995 to 25 percent above the OECD average in 2003. Similarly, Canada's educational spending as a percentage of GDP dropped from 25 percent above the OECD average in 1995 to equal the OECD average in 2003. (See Riddell 2004 and table A-1.)

Provincial government transfers to universities and colleges have also signifi-cantly declined in recent years, whether measured in real per student terms, per capita terms or relative to GDP (Canadian Association of University Teachers 2007). Since the early 1980s, real per student funding has fallen by approximately 30 percent in Canada, while increasing by about 20 percent in the United States. The proportion of post-secondary education that Canadian governments finance is now well below the OECD average (OECD 2006a). Moreover, with increases in tuition fees during the 1990s, individuals now bear more of the costs of higher education, raising concerns about student debt loads and reduced access to post-secondary education.

Another noteworthy feature of Canadian education spending is the limited amount of public expenditure on the early years, prior to the beginning of formal schooling, with Canada ranking at the bottom of a recent survey of OECD countries (OECD 2006b).[3]

Educational attainment

One consequence of Canada's long-standing relatively high levels of expendi-ture on education is a population that is well educated by international standards. For example, 84 percent of Canadians have completed high school, well above the OECD average and similar to the level of Germany, Japan and the United Kingdom but mod-estly below that of the United States (table A-2, panel a). The average number of years of completed schooling by Canadians is also reasonably high by international standards, slightly below the level of Americans and Germans and more than a full year above the OECD average (table A-2, panel b).

Compared with that of Americans, the educational attainment of Canadians is lower at both the bottom of the education distribution (more of the population has not completed high school) and the top (less of the population has a university degree). Canada stands out, however, in the middle of the distribution — that is, in the pro-portion of the population that has completed high school or a nonuniversity post-sec-ondary program (Riddell 2004). Indeed, a unique feature of Canada's education system is the substantial investment of resources in nonuniversity post-secondary educational institutions, with the proportion of the population having received an education from such an institution being about triple the OECD average (table A-2, panel a).[4] Although the overall educational attainment of Canadians is impressive, high school completion has been a weak spot for many years, with graduation rates well below the OECD aver-age (see table A-2, panel c). In 2001, a quarter of all Canada's 18-year-olds had not graduated from high school. The rate is much higher among males (29 percent) than among females (20 percent) and is especially high in rural areas and among Aboriginal students (Canadian Council on Learning 2005). Completion rates tend to increase over time, however, thanks to the second chances many education jurisdictions provide. In addition, some high school dropouts subsequently obtain post-secondary schooling in the form of college diplomas and trade certificates.[5] Furthermore, the dropout rate has fallen over time, including some noteworthy declines in the Atlantic provinces over the past two decades (Bowlby 2005). Nonetheless, data from the 2001 census reveal that about 20 percent of Canadians in their 20s have neither completed high school nor obtained any post-secondary education (Oreopoulos 2005). The secondary school dropout rate, therefore, remains a real policy concern.

Student achievement

Canada has made important advances in providing information on the achievement of students. In 1985, the report of the Macdonald royal commission expressed considerable frustration with the lack of relevant data on education, concluding that "there is a need for a national body to develop achievement-testing procedures and to monitor standards of achievement across Canada" (Royal Commission on the Economic Union and Development Prospects for Canada 1985, 739-40). The situation today, however, contrasts sharply with that of 20 years ago: measuring student achievement has been a growth industry, and considerable information is now available, both across jurisdictions within Canada and across countries, so that students, parents, teachers, school administrators and policy-makers now can base their decisions on a much improved information base.

Recent international data on Canadian student achievement paint a mixed picture. Results from the Trends in Mathematics and Science Study (TIMSS) of curriculum-based tests of achievement in mathematics and science indicate that student achievement is satisfactory but not as good as one might expect given Canada's expenditure on elementary and secondary schooling (see table A-3). Overall, Canadian students rank somewhat above the middle of the pack, well below Japanese students, above Italians, and close to US and UK students. Achievement trends are also mixed, with some evidence of declining performance in Quebec but improvement in Ontario. In contrast, in the 2000 and 2003 Program for International Student Assessment (PISA) tests — which assess the ability to apply knowledge in reading, mathematics and science — 15-year-old Canadians performed well, ranking at or near the top among students in the Group of Seven (G7) major industrialized countries (see table A-4, panel a).

Among the provinces, substantial variations in student achievement exist (table A-4, panel b). Students in some provinces — such as Alberta and British

Columbia — achieve at high levels, while those in other provinces, especially in Atlantic Canada, achieve relatively low levels by international standards.

Canada thus appears to obtain reasonably good value for money from its elementary and secondary school system — at least as measured by student achievement in reading, mathematics and science in the PISA tests. The TIMSS results, however, lead to a less favourable assessment.

Cognitive skills

Data on student achievement provide information about the skills of the future labour force. Until the International Adult Literacy Survey (IALS) of the 1990s, however, no nationally representative measures of the skills of the adult population were available. In 2003, the International Adult Literacy and Skills Survey (IALSS), an assessment of literacy, numeracy and problem-solving skills, was carried out in Canada. Table A-5 summarizes key findings of the 1994-8 IALS.[6]

The literacy skills of Canada's adult population were above average among the G7 countries that participated in the IALS. In Canada, as in the United States and the United Kingdom, the population exhibits a high variance of literacy skills compared with European countries such as Germany. For example, individuals in the top 25 percent of the Canadian literacy distribution have higher skills than their German counterparts, but those in the bottom 25 percent of the Canadian literacy distribution have lower skills than their German counterparts.

From their analysis of the IALS and IALSS data, Green and Riddell (2003, 2007b) conclude that formal education is a key determinant of literacy and numeracy skills. This finding, together with the above-average skills of Canada's adult population compared with those of other G7 populations, suggests that Canada's education system is doing a reasonably good job of enhancing cognitive skills — a conclusion consistent with the PISA findings for 15-year-olds.

At the same time, the surveys find that a disturbingly large proportion of Canada's population has low levels of literacy and numeracy (see table A-5, panel b). By international standards, older and less-well-educated Canadians have relatively poor literacy skills, whereas younger and well-educated Canadians have relatively good literacy skills compared with their counterparts in other countries. Two groups with low literacy and numeracy skills are immigrants and Aboriginal people. Ferrer, Green and Riddell (2006) and Bonikowska, Green and Riddell (2007) find that immigrants who completed their education prior to arriving in Canada have substantially lower skills than either the Canadian-born or immigrants who completed their education in

Canada, even after controlling for such factors as educational attainment, age and work experience. Similarly, Green and Riddell (2007a) find that Aboriginal Canadians have much lower literacy, numeracy and problem-solving skills than other Canadian-born people, even after controlling for such factors as educational attainment.

Implications for policy

The challenges relating to human capital formation and the salient features of Canada's approach to them raise key issues for policy-makers.

One distinguishing feature of existing policy is the significant public investment in human capital, especially in elementary, secondary and post-secondary education. Individuals and families also make substantial private investments of time and money in acquiring skills and knowledge. The empirical evidence indicates that, on average, the private return to these investments is high. Furthermore, there are important social benefits from investments in education and skills formation. It is important to recognize, however, that substantial average returns to existing expenditures do not imply that additional public investments are warranted. What matters for such decisions is the return at the margin — the return on additional expenditures — which is likely to be highest in areas in which we currently devote relatively limited resources to skills formation. In addition, as I noted earlier, the return to marginal expenditures is more likely to be high for investments made early in the lifecycle.

Also noteworthy is the decline in public expenditure on formal education in recent years. Despite widespread agreement that human capital should receive greater emphasis as Canada evolves toward a knowledge-based society, public expenditure on skills formation has been losing out to other priorities. As a result, Canada risks falling behind other countries. One consequence of reduced public expenditure is a decline in the quality of education, most evident at the university level. Another is a widening of earnings differentials by educational attainment, which would suggest that the supply of highly educated workers is not keeping up with demand.

Another distinguishing feature of Canada's situation is the presence of important gaps in the skills of particular groups. Overall, the achievement levels of students and the cognitive skills of adults are reasonably good, but the inadequate skills of some groups present a barrier to their maintaining a decent standard of living and participating fully in society. For both efficiency and equity reasons, these gaps need to be addressed.

Because there are substantial private benefits to education and skills, individuals have powerful incentives to invest in human capital. Thus, public subsidies will displace, to some extent, private expenditures that would otherwise occur. To be most effective, public expenditures should be targeted toward activities that would not otherwise receive sufficient private investment. At the same time, it is important to achieve the right balance between private and public investment in human capital: the accumulating evidence on the social benefits of education indicates that, in the absence of government support, there would be significant underinvestment. In addition, although public support for elementary and secondary education remains substantial, this is not the case for early childhood education. The share of higher education that governments finance might also have fallen too far.

Three key dimensions of the policy challenge thus deserve emphasis. One is to increase the resources devoted to human capital at a time when the need is growing and yet the national willingness to respond to the need appears to be diminishing. The second is to direct additional effort to areas that have high potential returns (both private and social) and that would otherwise receive insufficient private investment. The third is to narrow gaps in educational attainment and skills among key subsets of the population.

These policy challenges could be addressed by increasing public resources devoted to human capital in three specific areas, which are promising for several reasons. First, the return to additional investments is likely to be high. Second, all three interventions would address important gaps in human capital formation that result in low skills among some groups or that reflect unequal opportunity. Third, these areas appear unlikely to receive sufficient attention in the absence of government intervention.

POLICY PROPOSALS

Policy recommendation 1: Increase public support for early childhood education and care

Many children start school with significant academic disadvantages. In addition, many social and emotional problems develop prior to school entry. Evidence suggests that it is important for children to get off on the right foot in school (Furstenberg, Brooks-Gunn, and Morgan 1987), that many skills are best learned early in life, that academic skills at school entry are related to subsequent school achievement (Entwisle and Alexander 1993), that those with a good skills base are better able to acquire additional skills (Knudsen et al. 2006) and that early interventions result in a long period over which benefits can accrue.

Thus, early childhood education and care (ECEC) programs targeted toward those who would not otherwise get a good start could be very beneficial, not only for participants but also for society.[7] Yet, as noted earlier, Canada invests relatively few public resources in this area, which suggests that potential returns from investments at the margin might be high. It is important, however, to note the large amount of existing private investment in the area. More than half of Canadian preschoolers are enrolled in some form of child care, and some of these programs have a significant educational component. In addition, parents invest substantial time and money in enhancing the skills and competencies of their children, as do various community organizations. Nonetheless, even taking this private component into account, investment in early childhood in Canada is insufficient.

Another potential benefit of enhancing investment in ECEC is that improved school readiness could raise the return to existing investments in education. In particular, ECEC might reduce the variability of readiness for school for children of school-entry age and increase the effectiveness of elementary and secondary schooling. Belfield (2007), for example, finds that the reading and mathematics achievement of kindergartners is positively related to the proportion of students in the class that participated in pre-kindergarten education.

Finally, there is considerable evidence that it is difficult to fix problems later. For example, most employment and training programs that focus on youths and young adults who are experiencing labour market difficulties have been found to be relatively ineffective (Lalonde 1995; Heckman, Lalonde, and Smith 1999).

Most of the available research on early childhood interventions — which comes from the United States and might not be readily transferable to the Canadian setting — points to both negative and positive consequences of such policies. Evidence is available on two broad types of programs: small-scale model programs that focus on specific target populations, and publicly funded, large-scale programs such as Head Start. Both types of programs are restricted to children from disadvantaged backgrounds.

Several excellent reviews of the literature on ECEC programs are available (Barnett 1995; Karoly et al. 1998; Currie 2001; Karoly, Kilburn, and Cannon 2005). The most convincing evidence comes from small-scale demonstration projects with randomized research designs. Random assignment ensures that the characteristics of those receiving the intervention (the treatment group) and those not receiving the intervention (the control group) are statistically indistinguishable. This property is crucial to obtaining credible estimates of the effect of the intervention on subsequent behaviour, because it ensures that the control group provides a suitable estimate of the counterfactual — the outcomes that would have been observed in the absence of the intervention.

Barnett (1995), Karoly et al. (1998) and Currie (2001) summarize evidence from numerous ECEC interventions. Some studies are of limited value because they suffer from attrition bias (due to nonrandom dropouts from treatment and control groups) or from limited follow-up. Other interventions, such as the Perry Preschool program, have limited attrition and follow members of both the treatment and the control groups into adulthood.

Overall, the evidence from small-scale programs with randomized research designs indicates that ECEC programs targeted toward disadvantaged families can have long-lasting and large beneficial effects. Although only one intervention (the Milwaukee Project) was found to have had long-term effects on IQ, early childhood education programs typically have positive effects on measures of scholastic success, with evidence of increased student achievement, improved behaviour and attitudes, decreased grade retention, less use of special education, less crime and delinquency and a higher probability of completing high school. The Perry Preschool program, which has now followed participants to age 40, has had statistically significant effects on adult income, home ownership, welfare receipt and arrests.

Given the magnitude of the estimated effects, the benefits of model ECEC programs can be substantial relative to their costs. In a cost-benefit analysis of the Perry Preschool program, Belfield et al. (2006) estimate the return to the public to be substantial: approximately $7 for every dollar invested. An important part of the social benefits arises from the reduction in crime and the associated benefits to victims of crime. But even without accounting for reduced criminal activity, the benefits to the public from reduced welfare receipt, less grade retention and use of special education, less use of the justice system, taxes on the higher earnings of those receiving the intervention and other outcomes are more than double the costs of the preschool program. There might also be other benefits, which the cost-benefit analysis does not include, such as improved well-being, life satisfaction, health status and mortality rates, as well as intergenerational effects in that women in the treatment group had fewer abortions and lower rates of teenage pregnancy and were more likely to form a two-parent family.

A recent cost-benefit analysis of the Carolina Abecedarian program also finds evidence of public benefits in excess of the cost of the intervention (Barnett and Masse 2007). Unlike the Perry Preschool program, which was a half-day educational program for children ages three and four during the academic year (and included home visits in which teachers provided tutoring and worked with parents), the Abecedarian program was a full-day, year-round child care program with an intensive education component. The intervention was long lasting, offering eight hours per day of educational experiences to children from early in their first year of life until they entered kinder-garten. The demonstration project also employed random assignment and followed par-ticipants into early adulthood at age 21. Barnett and Masse conclude that the net benefits of the Abecedarian program were positive over a range of reasonable discount rates, and included increased maternal earnings (associated with the full-time child care component), decreased schooling costs, increased earnings of children receiving early childhood education and decreased health care costs from reduced smoking. Effects on criminal activity were not important, although that could be because the Abecedarian program was undertaken in a setting with much less crime than that of Perry Preschool.

The evidence from such small-scale demonstration projects, however — even those with the benefit of random assignment — needs to be interpreted with care. Not all features of model programs, such as quality of staff and intensity of services, can be replicated in large-scale, publicly funded programs. In addition, even if the conclusions of studies based on model programs are valid for the specific site and target groups, they might not generalize to other locations and participant groups.

For these reasons, it is important also to assess evidence from larger-scale ECEC programs. The leading example is the US Head Start program, which has been in operation since the mid-1960s (see Currie 2001; Garces, Thomas, and Currie 2002; Ludwig and Miller 2006; and Currie and Neidell 2007). Because they generally pro-vide less-intensive services, have fewer teachers per child and hire less-qualified staff, Head Start and other publicly funded programs might be expected to provide fewer benefits than small-scale model programs do. Nonetheless, publicly funded programs do show evidence of short- and medium-term benefits, although initial program gains tend to fade throughout the course of elementary school — apparently because of low subsequent school achievement on the part of Head Start participants (Currie 2001). Thus, the longer-term benefits of ECEC might depend on the subsequent education that children receive.

Using evidence from studies of Head Start, Currie (2001) estimates the costs and benefits of operating a publicly funded, large-scale program full-time. She suggests that the more readily measured short- and medium-term benefits would equal between 40 and 60 percent of the program costs; estimates of the long-term benefits are more speculative. Currie concludes that such a program would pay for itself in terms of cost savings for government even if it produced only one-quarter of the long-term gains of model programs. In subsequent research, Garces, Thomas and Currie (2002) find evidence of long-term positive effects of Head Start. White children who attended Head Start are more likely to complete high school and attend college than siblings who did not participate. African-American children who attended Head Start are less likely than their siblings to have been booked or charged with a crime.

Another large-scale, ongoing program is the Chicago Child-Parent Centers, a federally funded program located in that city's high-poverty neighbourhoods. These centres offer educational interventions to children from preschool through grades 2 and 3. Using various methods to deal with the absence of random assignment, Temple and Reynolds (2007) find that children who participated in the program at ages three or four were less likely to require school remediation services such as special education and grade retention, more likely to complete high school and, as with the experience of the Perry Preschool project, less likely to commit crimes as juveniles and young adults. The authors also conclude that the program's benefit-cost ratio ranges from 6 to 10, depending on the assumptions made.

A number of additional findings from the US experience are worth noting. For one, the magnitude of the short-term effects on cognitive development appears to be related to the intensity, breadth and amount of involvement of educators with children and their families (Barnett 1995). There is also evidence of heterogeneity in the magnitude of beneficial effects — for example, in the Carolina Abecedarian project, the beneficial effects are often greater for the more disadvantaged children in the treatment group; in some other projects, greater benefits are experienced by children whose mothers are the least educated. Beneficial effects might be greater for children from families with low income or socio-economic status, but there is no evidence that meaningful effects cease if a child's family moves above the poverty line. Finally, long-term benefits tend to be greater for girls than for boys.[8]

The US evidence on ECEC, however, needs to be interpreted in a Canadian context with care. For example, a significant part of the high benefit-cost ratios of the Perry Preschool program and the Chicago Child-Parent Centers is associated with the reduction in criminal activity among young African-American men. It seems unlikely that these benefits would be as large in Canada, where the incidence of crime is much lower.[9]

Another important consideration is that some negative effects have been reported for centre-based care — the form of most early childhood education interventions — relative to care in the home. Studies from several countries and settings conclude that ECEC has positive effects on children's cognitive skills but negative effects on their behavioural skills. Belsky (2001) surveys earlier literature and concludes that early, extensive and continuous nonmaternal care is associated with less harmonious parent-child relations and elevated levels of aggression and noncompliance. A number of subsequent studies support this general finding. A comprehensive US study by the National Institute for Child Health and Human Development Early Child Care Research Network (NICHD 2003) finds that the cumulative time spent in child care during the first four years of life is associated with problem behaviour at ages four and a half to five — although the magnitude of the association is not as large as some other correlates, such as family income and maternal sensitivity. Watamura et al. (2003) find physiological evidence that child care environments are stressful for children — specifically, that patterns of cortisol production differ in children when at child care than when they are at home. Using US data from the Early Childhood Longitudinal Study, Loeb et. al (2007) also find that, although centre-based child care has positive effects on reading and mathematics scores, it has negative effects on various socio-behavioural measures. More intensive centre-based care leads to greater academic benefits but also to an increase in negative behavioural consequences. Magnuson, Ruhm and Waldfogel (2007) find a similar pattern for pre-kindergarten programs, which raise mathematics and reading performance at school entry but also increase aggression and reduce self-control.

In one of the few Canadian studies, Baker, Gruber and Milligan (2005) analyze the experience with provincially subsidized child care in Quebec. After the program was introduced in 1997, there was a dramatic increase in the use of child care, and in two-parent households subsidized child care led to more mothers taking on paid work outside the home. The authors also find that, relative to children in the rest of Canada, where no major expansion of child care took place, the well-being of Quebec children deteriorated in terms of increased anxiety and hyperactivity and reduced social and motor skills. Reported fighting and aggressive behaviour increased substantially. Some measures of parental well-being, such as maternal depression and the quality of the relationship with their partner, also declined in Quebec relative to the rest of Canada.

Evidence of negative behavioural effects from child care is by no means universal: studies of child care in Australia, Israel and the United States find no adverse behavioural effects (Love et al. 2003), which suggests that quality matters, and that high-quality child care can improve both cognitive and behavioural outcomes. There is also evidence that when child care is combined with early childhood education, the curriculum matters.

On balance, an early childhood education program targeted at disadvantaged children and their families seems to bring substantial benefits relative to the costs of the program. The negative behavioural effects that also appear to be associated with child care suggest, however, a cautious approach and a careful monitoring and evaluation of the effects of ECEC interventions.

Should ECEC programs be universal or targeted toward disadvantaged families? The principal advantage of targeting is that it focuses public resources on the children who are most likely to fall behind in the absence of the intervention — that is, on those for whom the program is likely to have the greatest benefits relative to costs. A universal program, in contrast, would spend public resources on a substantial number of children who would benefit only modestly from the intervention because they already receive significant amounts of early childhood education from parents and/or high-quality preschool programs. In other words, a universal program would result in "windfall beneficiaries" — families that would benefit from subsidized ECEC but that would have enrolled their children in such a program even in the absence of a government subsidy.[10]

Targeting, however, also has some disadvantages, such as the cost of determining eligibility and the negative work incentives that would apply to families with incomes on the borderline of eligibility. Also, participants in ECEC programs that are offered only to the disadvantaged could feel like a segregated group, unable to benefit from interaction with children from more enriched educational backgrounds. In addition, programs targeted at disadvantaged families might lack widespread public support and, as a consequence, tend to be of low quality. Furthermore, there is no simple dividing line in terms of family income or other observable factors that enables us to distinguish between children with low levels of school readiness and those with high levels. Measures of school readiness appear to increase approximately linearly with family income (Barnett 1995). Thus, many children from middle-income families might benefit from such a program, even though the proportion who would do so is smaller than that of children from low-income families.

Some of these disadvantages, such as negative work incentives, are inherent to targeting on the basis of family income. Others, such as segregation and lack of public support, arise when the services are provided only to disadvantaged families. These latter drawbacks could be minimized by a judicious choice of program design.

I conclude that Canada should introduce an ECEC program targeted toward children at risk of developmental and education failure. The arguments for doing so seem quite strong and the social benefits are likely to be larger than the costs. The case for going further and providing ECEC on a universal basis is not as compelling on benefit-cost grounds because more public expenditure would go to windfall beneficiaries.[11]

Space does not permit me to provide a detailed design and costing of such a program, but one can note some desirable design features, some of which are incorporated in the Georgia Pre-K program and appear to perform well (Levin and Schwartz

2007).[12] First, parents should be able to choose among alternative forms of ECEC, which argues for allowing many providers to emerge and for a mix of public and private providers or private providers alone. Competition among providers would also help to maintain quality and ensure the cost-efficient provision of services. Second, governments should set standards for quality ECEC and regulate providers to ensure that standards are met. Third, government support should be paid directly to families in the form of vouchers that could be redeemed for ECEC from an approved provider. The value of the voucher could be a function of family income and/or other indicators. For example, low-income families could receive a voucher to pay for high-quality ECEC services, while moderate-income families would receive a voucher sufficient to partially, but not fully, subsidize ECEC from an approved provider — in effect, the higher the family income, the lower the value of the voucher and the larger the family's co-payment.

This design would ensure that approved ECEC services were provided not just to disadvantaged families; indeed, it would provide an incentive for moderate- and middle-income families to purchase ECEC from an approved provider. It would also encourage the participation of families with a range of educational and income characteristics and should have broad public support.

Given Canada's limited experience with ECEC, there is a great deal yet to be learned about how best to design and operate such programs. Thus, there is considerable scope for experimentation and for the careful assessment and evaluation of the consequences of policy interventions in this important area.

Policy recommendation 2: Increase the compulsory school attendance age and improve programs in secondary school for those at risk of dropping out

Canada invests substantial public resources in elementary and secondary schooling. There is also considerable private investment in the form of student effort, parental inputs and expenditure on private schools. By international standards, average outcomes on participation and completion rates and student achievement are good, as would be expected given the resources devoted to formal schooling. Results in the lower tail of the distribution of student achievement and adult literacy, however, are problematic, with some students finishing their formal schooling with limited cognitive skills. A related concern is the high school dropout rate, which, despite gains over recent decades, remains too high at about 20 percent.

The trend over the past several decades has been toward declining opportunities for those with less than high school education, while most employment growth has occurred among those with post-secondary education. The current resource boom has provided increased employment opportunities for those with limited formal education, but this reversal of the trend is likely to be temporary. The long-term prospects for those with limited formal education are poor. As a consequence, Canada's high secondary school dropout rate represents an important policy challenge.

Canada invests relatively little in those who do not complete secondary school. To illustrate this point, consider a world in which every student, at the end of grade 10, received a voucher with which to purchase additional formal education or invest as a form of insurance against a future setback in the labour market. Further suppose that students were charged the full cost of the remaining two years of high school and for all their post-secondary education, and that the value of the voucher was sufficient to subsidize fully an additional four years of schooling — that is, enough to pay for the remaining two years of high school and the first two years of post-secondary education. In these circumstances, those who left high school after grade 10 would have a substantial nest egg to use as insurance against future unemployment or to acquire additional skills at a later stage. In sharp contrast, such individuals now walk away from additional formal education at highly subsidized rates.

Although Canada does not invest much *ex ante* in those who do not complete high school, society does bear some of the subsequent costs associated with limited education. As I noted earlier, it is difficult to fix problems associated with limited skills at a later stage. Employment and training programs that focus on youths and young adults who are experiencing labour market difficulties have been found to be relatively ineffective, as have programs for disadvantaged adult men (Lalonde 1995; Heckman, Lalonde, and Smith 1999).

Here, I focus principally on high school completion, but I should emphasize that *any* additional secondary school education yields substantial benefits, both private (such as higher earnings) and social (such as increased civic participation and reduced crime). High school completion is an important variable because potential employers can use it as a screening device and because it opens doors to additional educational opportunities. There is also evidence that completing high school is a key educational milestone that has significant consequences for subsequent outcomes.[13]

Because of declining opportunities for those with less than high school education, stay-in-school initiatives were introduced in Canada during the 1990s. These relied largely on moral suasion — that is, on attempting to convince teenagers that staying in school is in their long-run interest. Unfortunately, none of these initiatives was carefully evaluated to assess its effects. It is possible that these initiatives had some effect on high school completion, as the dropout rate did decline during the 1990s, but it is also possible that the decline was caused by the poor labour market opportunities that high school dropouts faced and by growing opportunities for those with post-secondary education.

A number of policy interventions could improve Canada's high school completion rates:

/ Raise the school-leaving age from 16 (as it is in most provinces) to 17 or 18.[14]

/ Devote more resources to vocational and technical programs in high school, and encourage those at risk of dropping out to enter these programs.

/ Devote more resources to cooperative education programs in high school, targeted toward those at risk of dropping out.

/ Pay teenagers from poor families to stay in school, as the United Kingdom does.

/ Mount stay-in-school campaigns to convince potential dropouts to remain in school.

Research from various countries indicates that past increases in the school-leaving age produced large benefits not only for individuals who were obliged to remain in school longer but also for society as a whole. In contrast, little is known about the consequences of stay-in-school programs that rely on information campaigns and moral suasion. There is also limited evidence on the effectiveness of the UK policy of paying 16-to-18-year-olds from low-income families a maintenance allowance to remain in school; moreover, despite having some attractive features, such an approach also has potential disadvantages.[15]

In examining the effects of compulsory schooling laws in Canada over the 1920-90 period, Oreopoulos (2006a) finds that, as adults, those who were compelled to remain in school longer had higher incomes, less unemployment and a lower incidence of poverty. They were also more likely to speak two languages and less likely to work in a manual occupation. Indeed, the effects of extra schooling on income were substantial: completing an extra grade produced an average increase of between 9 and 15 percent in annual income, representing a substantial increase in income and wealth over the lifecycle.

Angrist and Krueger (1991) and Acemoglu and Angrist (2001) estimate that, in the United States, annual earnings are approximately 10 percent higher for students who were compelled to remain in school an additional year; in the United Kingdom, earnings are about 14 percent higher (Harmon and Walker 1995). Other benefits from additional compulsory schooling are also evident from US studies, including a substantial reduction in mortality (Lleras-Muney 2005), a lower likelihood of committing a crime and a lower probability of incarceration (Lochner and Moretti 2004) and a reduction in teenage pregnancy rates (Black, Devereux, and Salvanes 2004). Recent increases in the school-leaving age to 17 or 18 in a number of US states also suggest that the effects on educational attainment, youth unemployment and annual earnings are similar in magnitude to those from past changes in compulsory schooling laws (Oreopoulos 2005).

Perhaps the most compelling evidence comes from a study of changes in the legal school-leaving age in the United Kingdom and Ireland during the early postwar period (Oreopoulos 2006b). Because many students left school as soon as they were legally able to do so, increases in the minimum school-leaving age from 14 to 15 years of age affected a large proportion of the school-age population. Oreopoulos finds that the additional required education not only had a large effect on adult earnings, but also resulted in a lower incidence of unemployment, improved health and greater satisfaction with life.

These gains from increasing the school-leaving age occurred when a much larger proportion of students did not finish secondary school; we cannot be certain that such a policy would have similarly large beneficial effects today. The rationale for raising the school-leaving age, however, remains the same as in the past: the need to increase the skills and knowledge of individuals to allow them to participate more meaningfully in society and the workforce.[16]

Increasing the minimum school-leaving age might seem inexpensive. To be effective, however, such a policy would have to be enforced and its associated enforcement costs considered; additional resources also would be needed in the later years of secondary school, otherwise the presence of additional students would result in a decline in the quality of education.[17] Furthermore, students who would otherwise have chosen to drop out of school would probably benefit from programs — including vocational/technical and cooperative education programs — designed with their characteristics in mind. During the 1980s and 1990s, Finland, Norway and Sweden introduced educational reforms along these lines and achieved significant reductions in the high school dropout rate (OECD 2000). Indeed, the availability of such programs could improve options for potential dropouts even if the legal school-leaving age were unchanged.

The costs of these changes would not be trivial. Moreover, some people would find the element of compulsion in such a policy change distasteful. But the evidence indicates that these investments would produce substantial benefits for individuals and for society — not the least important of which would be to help offset widening earnings inequality.

Policy recommendation 3: Increase merit-based post-secondary scholarships for students from low-income families

In a recent summary of key challenges facing post-secondary education (PSE), Beach, Boadway and McInnis note:

> Higher education has been under strain for a number of years in Canada and has reached the point where the system is fraying. Years of underfunding have threatened the quality of university education and research. Large increases in student tuition levels have threatened access to a university education in Canada and dramatically increased student debt levels upon graduation. And there is a looming shortage of new faculty to sustain the system as large numbers of older faculty retire over the next ten years. (2005, 1)

These strains are particularly evident at the university level. Furthermore, compared with those of other countries, Canada's mix of expenditure and participation is unusual, with its much greater share devoted to non-university PSE and smaller share devoted to university programs. At the margin, it is arguably the case that the returns per dollar invested are higher at the university level.

The pressures on higher education are not likely to abate. On the one hand, the demand for post-secondary, especially university, education probably will continue to grow. On the other hand, provincial governments appear unwilling to provide additional funding to PSE because of budgetary pressures from other priorities, especially health care. At the same time, because of concerns about limiting access to PSE, provincial governments are also unwilling to allow universities and colleges to address underfunding by further increasing tuition fees.

The private benefits of higher education in the form of greater earnings and employment opportunities exert an important influence on the demand side. As discussed earlier, the estimated real rates of return from investment in education are substantial. Changes over time in the returns from PSE are informative about the growth in demand for highly educated workers relative to the growth in supply. In periods when demand growth exceeds growth in supply, the relative earnings of PSE graduates rise and the earnings gap between high school and PSE graduates widens. The reverse occurs when the growth in supply of PSE graduates exceeds the growth in demand. The returns to PSE basically reflect the outcome of a race between growth in demand and growth in supply.

In the 1970s, the returns from a university degree fell in both the United States and Canada, suggesting that the supply of university graduates (from the large cohort of baby boomers) grew faster than demand. In the United States since the early 1980s, however, the earnings differential between those with high school education and those with university education has increased dramatically. In Canada over the same period, the returns from higher education did not increase as much as in the US (Murphy, Riddell, and Romer 1998; Burbidge, Magee, and Robb 2002), but they remained substantial despite rapid growth in supply, suggesting that growth in demand for PSE was at least as great.[18] However, since the mid-1990s, the returns from university education have increased relative to those from high school and college (Boudarbat, Lemieux, and Riddell 2006). This might indicate that the supply of university graduates is no longer keeping pace with growth in demand. And most forecasts predict continued strong growth in the demand for PSE graduates.

Recent analysis by Fortin and Lemieux (2005) raises questions about the extent to which Canada has responded to this increased demand. Their analysis shows that the size of the 18-to-24-year-old cohort is an important determinant of university enrolment rates, as is the level of provincial funding to universities per person in that cohort. In particular, they find that the percentage of successive cohorts of baby boomers with a university education did not increase significantly, which they attribute to a limited supply of university places for those who wish to attend. Their projections indicate that, unless enrolment rates grow more rapidly than their historical trend, wage differentials between high school and university graduates, especially men, will increase significantly.

A significant portion of the benefit of PSE accrues to the individuals who acquire the additional education. Thus, if the differential between the earnings of university and high school graduates continues to rise, as Fortin and Lemieux (2005) predict, the demand for university entry is likely to increase. The supply response, however, depends to an important extent on provincial government budgetary decisions. In the absence of a market mechanism for determining the appropriate level of university enrolments, increased demand for university education might not lead to increased supply of places, despite the declining size of the youth cohorts that are reaching university age (Fortin 2005).

One major obstacle to increasing the supply of places is the restrictions on the tuition fees that PSE institutions can charge. Tuition fees in Canada increased substantially in percentage terms during the 1990s, but remain fairly low relative to the cost of providing PSE of adequate quality. Provincial governments have been reluctant to remove restrictions on fees, however, because of concerns of access to PSE by students from low-income families. Indeed, equity considerations are important to policy-makers, as higher education is a tool for promoting equality of opportunity and social mobility. In fact, however, the long-term trend in Canada has been for increasing percentages of children from lower-income families to obtain PSE (Christofides, Cirello, and Hoy 2001; Riddell 2001), despite the steep increases in tuition fees in the 1990s (Corak, Lipps, and Zhao 2005).[19]

In addition to equity concerns about access to PSE, the country's standard of living will suffer if talented individuals do not invest in higher education that has high expected returns.

For these reasons, I recommend improving access to PSE, especially university, among children from low-income families. Two principal approaches appear attractive. One way would be to replace existing student loan programs with an income-contingent loan system that provided students with sufficient funds up front to finance their education and that based repayment on income after graduation (see, for example, West 1993; Riddell 2003).[20] A key advantage of this approach is that it would reduce the risk of investing in higher education: graduates with above-average earnings would pay back more than those with below-average earnings, and repayment would be scheduled in a manner that reflected the evolution of the individual's ability to pay. Australia, New Zealand and the United Kingdom have recently introduced income-contingent loan systems.

The second approach — which I prefer — would be to expand the program of grants to students from low- and moderate-income families. Here, Canada could draw lessons from US experience. Starting in the early 1990s, a number of states introduced merit scholarship programs that are broadly based, require relatively modest academic credentials (such as a B average) and are often targeted to students from low-income families. These programs have increased enrolment overall, and some have disproportionately increased enrolment of black and Hispanic students relative to whites, thus reducing the large college attendance gap among these groups (Dynarski 2004).

Either approach — an income-contingent loan system or expanded scholarships — should be accompanied by deregulation of tuition fees, allowing universities and colleges to reverse the slide in the quality of higher education. Allowing tuition revenue to become a more important part of university and college income would also foster competition among institutions to provide high-quality programs and reduce their reliance on government and business (Riddell 2003; Laidler 2005). By affecting the incentives to study, broadly based merit scholarship programs might also raise student achievement at the elementary and secondary school level.

A number of considerations would need to be addressed in designing such programs, although space permits only a brief comment. Design would be complicated by the fact that multiple levels of government, as well as the universities themselves, provide funding for students in coexisting but independent programs. The response of these institutions to new programs initiated at other levels could alter the programs' intended effects. For example, the Canadian Millennium Scholarship Foundation bursary funds could displace provincial spending on existing grants and loan remissions programs, thus having questionable effects on access. Similarly, merit-based state scholarships in the United States have displaced at least some university-level financial aid for low-income students without actually increasing the funding available to the poorest qualified students.

CONCLUSION

Many countries are placing greater emphasis on improving the skills and knowledge of their citizens and on the role of such human capital formation in achieving economic prosperity and social objectives. Canada is no different in facing these challenges. Skill formation has received considerable attention from social scientists in recent years. Because of this research, we can now be more confident than in the past about the causal effects of education on individual and social outcomes. Two key lessons emerge from these recent advances. One is that past policy interventions that raised educational attainment typically had large beneficial effects on the affected individuals — effects that are generally larger than previously believed. The second lesson is that human capital investments yield important nonmarket and social benefits — benefits that warrant substantial public subsidy of these activities.

The policies I have suggested in this chapter build on current knowledge about the consequences of human capital for achieving economic and social objectives. The recommendations would increase the public effort devoted to skills formation at a time when the need is growing yet the national willingness to respond appears to be diminishing. They would also direct additional resources to areas that have high potential returns (private and social) but that would otherwise receive insufficient private investment. Finally, the proposed policies would narrow gaps in educational attainment and skills among key subsets of the population.

APPENDIX

TABLE A-1. COMBINED PUBLIC AND PRIVATE EXPENDITURE ON EDUCATION, BY LEVEL OF EDUCATION, CANADA AND SELECTED DEVELOPED COUNTRIES, 2003.

(a) Per student (based on full-time equivalents), Canada and selected developed countries, in US dollars (converted using purchasing power parity exchange rates[1])

	Canada[2]	France	Germany	Italy	Japan	UK	US	OECD average[3]
Preprimary (ages 3 and older)	–	4,744	4,865	6,166	3,766	7,153	7,755	4,508
Elementary	–	4,939	4,624	7,366	6,350	5,851	8,305	5,450
Secondary	6,482	8,653	7,173	7,938	7,283	7,290	9,590	6,962
Post-secondary	19,929	10,704	11,594	8,764	11,556	11,866	24,074	11,254
All levels[4]	8,641	7,807	7,368	7,963	7,789	7,376	12,023	6,827

(b) As a percentage of GDP, Canada and selected developed countries

	Canada[5]	France	Germany	Italy	Japan	UK	US	OECD average[3]
Preprimary (ages 3 and older)	–	0.7	0.5	0.5	0.2	0.4	0.4	0.5
Elementary and secondary	3.6[6]	4.2	3.4	3.6	3.0	4.6	4.2	3.9
Post-secondary	2.4	1.4	1.1	0.9	1.3	1.1	2.9	1.4
All levels[4]	5.9	6.3	5.3	5.1	4.8	6.1	7.5	5.9

(c) Per student (based on full-time equivalents),[7] Canada and the provinces (in constant 2001 Canadian dollars)

	NL	PE	NS	NB	QC[8]	ON	MB[9]	SK[9]	AB	BC	CA
Preprimary, elementary and secondary	6,503	6,239	7,072	7,239	7,333	8,130	8,432	7,293	7,401	7,905	7,607
Post-secondary	15,455	17,615	18,925	17,247	17,769	19,065	22,930	23,790	20,461	21,025	19,253
All levels[4]	8,141	8,057	9,407	8,848	9,537	9,930	10,157	9,378	9,387	9,851	9,714

Sources: Council of Ministers of Education, Canada, and Statistics Canada (2006); OECD (2006a).

[1] The actual exchange rate might understate or overstate differences in purchasing power. Purchasing power parity exchange rates equalize the purchasing power of different currencies and are based on the cost of a fixed basket of goods and services in different countries.

[2] Public institutions only; data are from 2004.

[3] Unweighted country average.

[4] Includes preprimary (pre-elementary) and undistributed expenditures.

[5] Data are from 2002.

[6] Includes preprimary education as well as post-secondary nontertiary education.

[7] Trade-vocational programs are excluded because of poor quality of the estimation of full-time equivalent students.

[8] Full-time equivalent students at the elementary-secondary level in Quebec include trade-vocational enrolments administered through the elementary-secondary system.

[9] The higher cost per students at the post-secondary level could be explained by higher federal government expenditures for community colleges operated by Aboriginal people, for which enrolment data are missing.

TABLE A-2. EDUCATIONAL ATTAINMENT, CANADA AND SELECTED DEVELOPED COUNTRIES, 2004

(a) Proportion of the population ages 25-64 by highest level of educational attainment (percent)

	Canada	France	Germany	Italy	Japan[1]	UK	US	OECD average[2]
Less than upper secondary	16	35	16	51	16	15	13	30
Upper secondary graduate	27	41	52	36	47	56	49	44
Nonuniversity post-secondary	34	10	16	–	17	9	9	–
University graduate	22	14	15	12[3]	21	20	29	25[3]

(b) Average completed years of schooling, population ages 25-64

	Canada	France	Germany	Italy	Japan	UK	US	OECD average
Number of years	13.2	11.6	13.4	10.1	12.4	12.6	13.3	11.9

(c) Ratio of upper secondary graduates to population at a typical graduation age, 2001

	Canada	France	Germany	Italy	Japan	UK	US	OECD average
Both sexes	75	85	92	82	93	–	72	82
Males	71	82	89	79	91	–	70	78
Females	80	87	94	85	95	–	73	85

Sources: OECD 2003, 2004, 2006a; Council of Ministers of Education, Canada, and Statistics Canada 2006.
[1] Data are for 2003.
[2] Unweighted country average.
[3] Includes non-university post-secondary education; disaggregated data were not available.

TABLE A-3.   STUDENT ACHIEVEMENT IN MATHEMATICS AND SCIENCE, CANADA AND SELECTED DEVELOPED COUNTRIES, 1995, 1999 AND 2003

(a) Student achievement in mathematics and science[1]

	Canada	Japan	US	England	Italy	International mean
Grade 4 math 1995	–	567 (1.9)	518 (2.9)	484 (3.3)	–	–
Grade 4 math 2003	–	565 (1.6)	518 (2.4)	531 (3.7)	503 (3.7)	495 (0.8)
Grade 8 math 1995	521 (2.2)	581 (1.6)	492 (4.7)	498 (3.0)	–	–
Grade 8 math 1999	531 (2.5)	579 (1.7)	502 (4.0)	496 (4.1)	479 (3.8)	487 (0.7)
Grade 8 math 2003	–	570 (2.1)	504 (3.3)	498 (4.7)	484 (3.2)	467 (0.5)
Grade 4 science 1995	–	553 (1.8)	542 (3.3)	528 (3.1)	–	–
Grade 4 science 2003	–	543 (1.5)	536 (2.5)	540 (3.6)	516 (3.8)	489 (0.9)
Grade 8 science 1995	514 (2.6)	554 (1.8)	513 (5.6)	533 (3.6)	–	–
Grade 8 science 1999	533 (2.1)	550 (2.2)	515 (4.6)	538 (4.8)	493 (3.9)	488 (0.7)
Grade 8 science 2003	–	552 (1.7)	527 (3.1)	544 (4.1)	491 (3.1)	474 (0.6)

(b) Student achievement in mathematics and science, Quebec and Ontario

	Quebec	Ontario
Grade 4 math 1995	550 (4.2)	489 (3.5)
Grade 4 math 2003	506 (2.4)	511 (3.8)
Grade 8 math 1995	556 (5.9)	501 (2.9)
Grade 8 math 1999	566 (5.3)	517 (3.1)
Grade 8 math 2003	543 (3.0)	521 (3.1)
Grade 4 science 1995	529 (4.8)	516 (3.7)
Grade 4 science 2003	500 (2.5)	540 (3.7)
Grade 8 science 1995	510 (6.9)	496 (3.7)
Grade 8 science 1999	540 (4.8)	518 (3.1)
Grade 8 science 2003	531 (3.0)	533 (2.7)

Sources: TIMSS (2000a, 2000b, 2004a, 2004b).

Note: Numbers shown are mean scores for the country, year and subject. Standard errors are in parentheses. TIMSS scores in each subject are expressed on a scale adjusted so that the unweighted average score for all countries was 500 and the standard deviation was 100 in 1995.

[1] Because of differences in population coverage, 1995 data are not shown for Italy. England did not satisfy the guidelines for sample participation rates for some grades and years. France and Germany participated only in grade 8 tests in 1995. Canada did not participate in the 2003 round.

TABLE A-4. ACHIEVEMENT OF 15-YEAR-OLDS IN READING, MATHEMATICS AND SCIENCE, CANADA AND SELECTED DEVELOPED COUNTRIES, 2000 AND 2003

(a) Program for International Student Assessment (PISA) results

Reading 2003		Reading 2000	
Canada	528 (1.7)	Canada	534 (1.6)
Japan	498 (3.9)	UK	523 (2.6)
France	496 (2.7)	Japan	522 (5.2)
US	495 (3.2)	France	505 (2.7)
OECD average	**494 (0.6)**	US	504 (7.0)
Germany	491 (3.4)	**OECD average**	**500 (0.6)**
Italy	476 (3.0)	Italy	487 (2.9)
UK	–	Germany	484 (2.5)

Mathematics 2003		Mathematics 2000	
Japan	534 (4.0)	Japan	557 (5.5)
Canada	532 (1.8)	Canada	533 (1.4)
France	511 (2.5)	UK	529 (2.5)
Germany	503 (3.3)	France	517 (2.7)
OECD average	**500 (0.6)**	**OECD average**	**500 (0.7)**
US	483 (2.9)	US	493 (7.6)
Italy	466 (3.1)	Germany	490 (2.5)
UK	–	Italy	457 (2.9)

Science 2003		Science 2000	
Japan	548 (1.9)	Japan	550 (5.5)
Canada	519 (2.0)	UK	532 (2.7)
France	511 (3.0)	Canada	529 (1.6)
Germany	502 (3.6)	France	500 (3.2)
OECD average	**500 (0.6)**	**OECD average**	**500 (0.7)**
US	491 (3.1)	US	499 (7.3)
Italy	486 (3.1)	Germany	487 (2.4)
UK	—	Italy	478 (3.1)

(b) PISA results for Canadian provinces

Reading 2003		Reading 2000	
Alberta	543 (4.3)	Alberta	550 (3.3)
British Columbia	535 (2.5)	British Columbia	538 (2.9)
Ontario	530 (3.5)	Quebec	536 (3.0)
Quebec	525 (4.3)	Ontario	533 (3.3)
Newfoundland & Labrador	521 (3.2)	Manitoba	529 (3.5)
Manitoba	520 (3.3)	Saskatchewan	529 (2.7)
Nova Scotia	513 (2.3)	Nova Scotia	521 (2.3)
Saskatchewan	512 (4.2)	Prince Edward Island	517 (2.4)
New Brunswick	503 (2.1)	Newfoundland & Labrador	517 (2.8)
Prince Edward Island	495 (2.3)	New Brunswick	501 (1.8)

TABLE A-4.   ACHIEVEMENT OF 15-YEAR-OLDS IN READING, MATHEMATICS AND SCIENCE, CANADA AND SELECTED DEVELOPED COUNTRIES, 2000 AND 2003 (CONT'D)

Mathematics 2003		Mathematics 2000	
Alberta	549 (4.3)	Quebec	550 (2.7)
British Columbia	538 (2.4)	Alberta	547 (3.3)
Quebec	537 (4.7)	British Columbia	534 (2.8)
Ontario	530 (3.6)	Manitoba	533 (3.7)
Manitoba	528 (3.1)	Saskatchewan	525 (2.9)
Newfoundland & Labrador	517 (2.5)	Ontario	524 (2.9)
Saskatchewan	516 (3.9)	Nova Scotia	513 (2.8)
Nova Scotia	515 (2.2)	Prince Edward Island	512 (3.7)
New Brunswick	512 (1.8)	Newfoundland & Labrador	509 (3.0)
Prince Edward Island	500 (2.0)	New Brunswick	506 (2.2)

Science 2003		Science 2000	
Alberta	539 (5.6)	Alberta	546 (3.5)
British Columbia	527 (2.8)	Quebec	541 (3.4)
Quebec	520 (5.2)	British Columbia	533 (3.2)
Ontario	515 (3.9)	Manitoba	527 (3.6)
Newfoundland & Labrador	514 (2.9)	Ontario	522 (3.4)
Manitoba	512 (3.7)	Saskatchewan	522 (3.0)
Saskatchewan	506 (4.6)	Newfoundland & Labrador	516 (3.4)
Nova Scotia	505 (2.4)	Nova Scotia	516 (3.0)
New Brunswick	498 (2.2)	Prince Edward Island	508 (2.7)
Prince Edward Island	489 (2.6)	New Brunswick	497 (2.3)

Sources: Bussiere, Cartwright, Corcker et al. 2001; Bussière, Cartwright, and Knighton et al. 2004.

Note: Numbers shown are mean scores for the year and jurisdiction shown. Numbers in parentheses are standard errors. PISA scores in every subject area are expressed on a scale adjusted so that the OECD unweighted country average is 500. Reading scores for 2003 are evaluated at a scale developed for PISA 2000, which had a mean of 500 for the 27 countries that participated in the 2000 test. Because three additional OECD countries were included in the 2003 reading test, the overall OECD mean for PISA 2003 is 494. The United Kingdom participated in PISA 2003, but because of technical problems with its sample, the results are not reported or analyzed.

TABLE A-5.   LITERACY SKILLS IN CANADA AND SELECTED DEVELOPED COUNTRIES, 1994-8

(a) Mean score and score at the 25th and 75th percentiles of the prose, document and quantitative literacy scales

Literacy scale	Canada			Germany			UK			US		
	25th	Mean	75th	25th	Mean	75th	25th	Mean	75th	25th	Mean	75th
Prose	243	279	322	245	276	308	233	267	311	237	274	320
Document	243	279	326	256	285	318	230	268	314	230	268	316
Quantitative	247	281	323	265	293	324	231	268	314	237	275	322

(b) Adults with low literacy skills[1] (percent)

Age group	Literacy scale	Canada	Germany	UK	US
16-65	Prose	42	49	52	47
16-65	Quantitative	43	33	51	46
16-65	Document	43	42	50	50
16-25	Document	33	34	44	56
46-55	Document	54	42	53	50

(c) Mean document literacy score and educational attainment

Education	Canada	Germany	UK	US
Less than high school	227	276	247	200
High school graduate	288	295	286	266
Post-secondary graduate	318	315	312	303
All adults	279	285	268	268

Sources: OECD (1998); OECD and Statistics Canada (2000).
[1] Low literacy skills are defined as literacy levels 1 or 2 on document literacy. Literacy is measured on a scale from 1 to 5 with levels 1 and 2 being the lowest.

NOTES

I thank Iglika Ivanova for excellent research
assistance, David Card, Damon Clark,
David Green and Kevin Milligan for helpful
discussions, and Jeremy Leonard, Chris
Ragan and France St-Hilaire for comments on an earlier version.

1   Private benefits are those received by the
    individual in acquiring the skills and knowl-
    edge. Social benefits are those received
    by society as a whole. I discuss the dis-
    tinction between private and social bene-
    fits and costs later.

2   An instrumental variable is one that is cor-
    related with the independent variable of
    interest (in this case, education) but uncor-
    related with unobserved factors that influ-
    ence the outcome (in this case, earnings).

3   See, in particular, OECD (2006b, figure 5.3),
    which provides data on public expenditure
    on early childhood education and care ser-
    vices in the 14 OECD countries that partici-
    pated in the study. Canadian expenditure is
    about one-half that of other "low-expenditure"
    countries such as Australia, Italy, Germany,
    the Netherlands, the United Kingdom and
    the United States, and far below that of
    "high-expenditure" countries such as France,
    Finland, Norway, Sweden and Denmark.

4   Standard measures might overstate
    Canadian educational attainment in this
    dimension to some extent because not all
    those with a college diploma or trade cer-
    tificate have completed high school and
    because of the unique features of
    Quebec's system of junior colleges,
    known as CEGEPs (Collèges d'enseigne-
    ment général et professionnel).
    Nonetheless, even adjusting for these fac-
    tors, Canadian expenditure on and partici-
    pation in nonuniversity post-secondary
    education is much greater than that of
    other OECD countries (Riddell 2004).

5   Ferrer and Riddell (2002) find that
    between a quarter and a third of those
    who have completed a nonuniversity
    post-secondary education program did
    not graduate from high school.

6   To date, only a few other countries have
    participated in the current round of skills
    assessment; thus the scope for interna-
    tional comparisons is limited.

7   The term ECEC is used because early child-
    hood education interventions are typically
    centre-based and also provide child care.

8   In a re-analysis of the original data for the
    Perry Preschool, Carolina Abecedarian and
    Early Training projects, Anderson (2006) finds
    that girls received substantial short- and long-
    term benefits from the interventions but there
    were no long-term benefits for boys.

9   The absence of any effect on criminal
    activity in the Carolina Abecedarian pro-
    gram is consistent with this conjecture.

10 Some windfall beneficiaries could respond
    to the subsidy by purchasing higher-
    quality ECEC than they would otherwise.
    In this case, government support would
    not simply displace private support.

11 Another option would be a program that
    provided a basic level of services (essen-
    tially good-quality child care with an
    emphasis on developing cognitive and
    noncognitive skills) on a universal basis,
    but also more intensive services to chil-
    dren and families with characteristics that
    suggest they would benefit substantially
    from ECEC. Having most Canadian chil-
    dren enrolled in the basic services would
    also help to identify those who would
    most likely benefit from more intensive
    services. This option, however, seems like
    a very expensive way of identifying chil-
    dren in need of assistance.

12 Studies that discuss design features of uni-
    versal and targeted programs in the
    Canadian context include McCain and
    Mustard (1999); Friendly (2004); Richards
    and Brzozowski (2006); and Milligan (2007).

13 Ferrer and Riddell (2002) find that a major part of the economic return to finishing high school results from opening doors to post-secondary education. Coelli, Green and Warburton (2007) find that high school completion plays a major role in reducing welfare use among children whose parents are welfare recipients, thus breaking the intergenerational cycle of welfare receipt.

14 In most provinces, such a policy would require school attendance to age 18 or to high school graduation, whichever came first. In Quebec, the policy should reflect the fact that most students graduate from high school at age 17. New Brunswick increased the school-leaving age to 18 in 2000; Ontario has recently followed suit.

15 The effects of the UK Education Maintenance Allowance, introduced as a national program in 2004, have not yet been evaluated. Prior to its national rolling out, the program was piloted in several areas where it was believed it would have the greatest impact. An evaluation of the pilot (available at www.ifs.org.uk) suggests that it increased education participation past age 16, especially for males from low-income families. It is unclear, however, whether the pilot program had longer-term effects, as no significant difference in educational participation or employment was found between participants and non-participants at age 19.

   A key advantage of this approach is that it reduces the opportunity cost of remaining in school and provides funding for school-related expenses. The program is also designed to reward high attendance. It has, however, produced resentment among parents with incomes slightly above the eligibility cut-off, who argue that recipients of funding use the money for luxuries, rather than for school-related expenses, and that they cannot provide such pocket money for their children. Critics also argue that the program encourages students to select easy courses, since bonus payments are contingent on meeting predicted grades and passing exams.

16 Ontario premier Dalton McGuinty, for example, has stated: "We've got a law on the books that says you can quit school when you're 16. Think about it. This is the knowledge economy — that no longer makes sense. So we're going to require that young people be in school or learning outside school...until they reach the age of 18" (*National Post*, September 28, 2002).

17 One would also need to be concerned about the negative peer effects that would arise from the presence of poorly motivated students who would rather not be in school.

18 Murphy, Riddell and Romer (1998) conclude that the evidence is consistent with a steady growth in demand of similar magnitude for highly educated workers in both countries, but more rapid growth in supply in Canada.

19 During the 1980s and 1990s, university participation rates trended upward among youths in all family income groups, with the greatest growth — from 8 percent in 1979 to 21 percent in 1997 — among those from families with income below $25,000. Among youths in the highest family income category (over $100,000), participation increased from 30 percent to 38 percent. The gap in university participation between the highest- and lowest-income groups thus narrowed over this period, even though the latter years were characterized by steep increases in tuition fees. The gap, however, remains substantial (Corak, Lipps, and Zhao 2005).

20 A similar proposal, recommended by Carmichael (2005), is a graduate tax accompanied by upfront grants.

REFERENCES

Acemoglu, D., and J. Angrist. 2001. "How Large Are Human Capital Externalities? Evidence from Compulsory Schooling Laws." In *NBER Macroeconomics Annual 2000*, edited by B.S. Bernanke and K. Rogoff. Cambridge, MA: MIT Press.

Anderson, M. 2006. "Multiple Inference and Gender Differences in the Effects of Preschool: A Reevaluation of the Abecedarian, Perry Preschool, and Early Training Projects." Working paper, University of California at Berkeley.

Angrist, J.D., and A.B. Krueger. 1991. "Does Compulsory School Attendance Affect Schooling and Earnings?" *Quarterly Journal of Economics* 106 (4): 979-1014.

Baker, M., J. Gruber, and K. Milligan. 2005. "Universal Childcare, Maternal Labor Supply and Family Well-Being." NBER Working Paper 11832. Cambridge, MA: National Bureau of Economic Research.

Barnett, W.S. 1995. "Long-Term Effects of Early Childhood Programs on Cognitive and School Outcomes." *Long-Term Outcomes of Early Childhood Programs* 5 (3): 25-50.

Barnett, W.S., and L.N. Masse. 2007. "Comparative Benefit-Cost Analysis of the Abecedarian Program and Its Policy Implications." *Economics of Education Review* 26 (July): 113-25.

Beach, C.M., R.W. Boadway, and R.M. McInnis. 2005. "Introduction." In *Higher Education in Canada*, edited by C.M. Beach, R.W. Boadway, and R.M. McInnis. John Deutsch Institute for the Study of Economic Policy, Queen's University.

Belfield, C. 2007. "The Fiscal Impacts of Universal Pre-K Programs: Case Studies for Three States." *Economics of Education Review* 26 (1).

Belfield, C., M. Nores, S. Barnett, and L. Schweinhart. 2006. "The High/Scope Perry Preschool Program: Cost-Benefit Analysis Using Data from the Age-40 Follow Up." *Journal of Human Resources* 41 (1): 162-90.

Belsky, J. 2001. "Developmental Risks (Still) Associated with Early Child Care." *Journal of Child Psychology and Psychiatry* 42 (7): 842-59.

Black, S.E., P.J. Devereux, and K.G. Salvanes. 2004. "Fast Times at Ridgemont High? The Effect of Compulsory Schooling Laws on Teenage Births." NBER Working Paper 10911. Cambridge, MA: National Bureau of Economic Research.

Bonikowska, A., D.A. Green, and W.C. Riddell. 2007. "Cognitive Skills and Immigrant Earnings." Working paper, University of British Columbia.

Boudarbat, B., T. Lemieux, and W.C. Riddell. 2006. "Recent Trends in Wage Inequality and the Wage Structure in Canada." In *Dimensions of Inequality in Canada*, edited by D.A. Green and J. Kesselman. Vancouver: University of British Columbia Press.

Bowlby, G. 2005. "Provincial Drop-out Rates — Trends and Consequences." *Education Matters: Insights on Education, Learning and Training in Canada* 2 (4).

Burbidge, J.B., L. Magee, and A.L. Robb. 2002. "The Education Premium in Canada and the United States." *Canadian Public Policy* 28 (June): 203-17.

Bussière, P., F. Cartwright, R. Crocker, X. Ma, J. Oderkirk, and Y. Zhang. 2001. *Measuring Up: The Performance of Canada's Youth in Reading, Mathematics and Science. OECD PISA Study — First Results for Canadians Aged 15*. Cat. 81-590-XPE No. 1. Ottawa: Human Resources Development Canada, Statistics Canada, Council of Ministers of Education.

Bussière, P., F. Cartwright, T. Knighton, and T. Rogers (special contributor). 2004. *Measuring Up: Canadian Results of the*

OECD PISA Study. The Performance of Canada's Youth in Mathematics, Reading, Science and Problem Solving 2003. First Findings for Canadians Aged 15. Cat. 81-590-XPE No. 2. Ottawa: Human Resources Development Canada, Statistics Canada, Council of Ministers of Education.

Canadian Association of University Teachers (CAUT). 2007. *CAUT Almanac of Post-Secondary Education in Canada 2007.* Ottawa: CAUT.

Canadian Council on Learning. 2005. "Good News: Canada's High School Dropout Rates Are Falling." Ottawa: Canadian Council on Learning. www.ccl-cca.ca/ CCL/Reports/LessonsInLearning/ LiL-16Dec2005.htm.

Card, D. 1999. "The Causal Effect of Education on Earnings." In *Handbook of Labor Economics*, vol. 3A, edited by O. Ashenfelter and D. Card. Amsterdam: North-Holland.

————. 2001. "Estimating the Return to Schooling: Progress on Some Persistent Econometric Problems." *Econometrica* 69 (September): 1127-60.

Carmichael, H.L. 2005. "How Best to Fund Postsecondary Education: A Graduate Tax?" In *Higher Education in Canada*, edited by C.M. Beach, R.W. Boadway, and R.M. McInnis. Montreal; Kingston, ON: Queen's University, John Deutsch Institute for the Study of Economic Policy.

Carneiro, P., and J.J. Heckman. 2003. "Human Capital Policy." NBER Working Paper 9495. Cambridge, MA: National Bureau of Economic Research.

Christophides, L.N., J. Cirello, and M. Hoy. 2001. "Family Income and Post-secondary Education in Canada." *Canadian Journal of Higher Education* 31 (1): 177-208.

Coate, S. 1995. "Altruism, the Samaritan's Dilemma and Government Transfer Policy." *American Economic Review* 85 (March): 46-57.

Coelli, M.B., D.A. Green, and W.P. Warburton. 2007. "Breaking the Cycle? The Effect of Education on Welfare Receipt among Children of Welfare Recipients." *Journal of Public Economics* 91 (7-8): 1369-98.

Corak, M., G. Lipps, and J. Zhao. 2005. "Family Income and Participation in Postsecondary Education." In *Higher Education in Canada*, edited by C.M. Beach, R.W. Boadway, and R.M. McInnis. Montreal; Kingston, ON: Queen's University, John Deutsch Institute for the Study of Economic Policy.

Council of Ministers of Education, Canada, and Statistics Canada. 2006. *Education Indicators in Canada: Report of the Pan-Canadian Education Indicators Program 2005.* Toronto; Ottawa: Council of Ministers of Education, Canada, and Statistics Canada.

Currie, J. 2001. "Early Childhood Education Programs." *Journal of Economic Perspectives* 15 (Spring): 213-38.

Currie, J., and M. Neidell. 2007. "Getting Inside the 'Black Box' of Head Start Quality: What Matters and What Doesn't." *Economics of Education Review* 26 (July): 83-99.

Davies, J. 2002. "Empirical Evidence on Human Capital Externalities." Department of Economics, University of Western Ontario. Mimeographed.

Dynarski, S. 2004. "The New Merit Aid." In *College Choices: The Economics of Where to Go, When to Go, and How to Pay for It*, edited by C. Hoxby. Chicago: University of Chicago Press.

Entwisle, D., and K.L. Alexander. 1993. "Entry into School: The Beginning School Transition and Educational Stratification in the United States." *Annual Review of Sociology* 19: 401-23.

Ferrer, A., D.A. Green, and W.C. Riddell. 2006. "The Effect of Literacy on Immigrant Earnings." *Journal of Human Resources* 41 (Spring): 380-410.

Ferrer, A., and W.C. Riddell. 2002. "The Role of Credentials in the Canadian Labour Market." *Canadian Journal of Economics* 35 (November): 879-905.

Fortin, N.M. 2005. "Rising Tuition and Supply Constraints: Explaining Canada-US Differences in University Enrolment Rates." In *Higher Education in Canada*, edited by C.M. Beach, R.W. Boadway, and R.M. McInnis. Montreal; Kingston, ON: Queen's University, John Deutsch Institute for the Study of Economic Policy.

Fortin, N., and T. Lemieux. 2005. "Population Aging and Human Capital Investment by Youth." Working paper, Department of Economics, University of British Columbia.

Friedman, M. 1955. "The Role of Government in Education." In *Economics and the Public Interest*, edited by R.A. Solow. New Brunswick, NJ: Rutgers University Press.

Friendly, M. 2004. "Strengthening Canada's Social and Economic Foundations: Next Steps for Early Childhood Education and Care." *Policy Options* 25 (3): 46-51. Montreal: IRPP.

Furstenberg, F., J. Brooks-Gunn, and S.P. Morgan. 1987. *Adolescent Mothers in Later Life*. New York: Cambridge University Press.

Garces, E., D. Thomas, and J. Currie. 2002. "Longer-Term Effects of Head Start." *American Economic Review* 92 (September): 999-1012.

Green, D.A., and W.C. Riddell. 2003. "Literacy and Earnings: An Investigation of the Interaction of Cognitive and Unobserved Skills in Earnings Generation." *Labour Economics* 10 (April): 165-85.

_____. 2007a. "Literacy and Its Consequences among Canada's Aboriginal Population." Working paper, University of British Columbia.

_____. 2007b. "Literacy and the Labour Market: The Generation of Literacy and Its Impact on Earnings for Native Born Canadians." Working paper, University of British Columbia.

Harmon, C., and I. Walker. 1995. "Estimates of the Economic Return to Schooling for the United Kingdom." *American Economic Review* 85 (5): 1278-86.

Heckman, J.J., R. Lalonde, and J. Smith. 1999. "The Economics and Econometrics of Active Labor Market Programs." In *Handbook of Labor Economics*, edited by D. Card and O. Ashenfelter. Amsterdam: North-Holland.

Helburn, S., and C. Howes. 1996. "Child Care Costs and Quality." *The Future of Children* 6 (2): 62-82.

Karoly, L., M. Kilburn, and J. Cannon. 2005. *Early Childhood Interventions: Proven Results, Future Promise*. Santa Monica, CA: Rand Corporation.

Karoly, L., P. Greenwood, S. Everingham, J. Houbé, M. Kilburn, C. Rydell, M. Sanders, and J. Chiesa. 1998. *Investing in Our Children: What We Know and Don't Know about the Costs and Benefits of Early Childhood Interventions*. Santa Monica, CA: Rand Corporation.

Knudsen, E.I., J.J. Heckman, J.L. Cameron, and J.P. Shonkoff. 2006. "Economic, Neurobiological and Behavioral Perspectives on Building America's Future Workforce." NBER Working Paper 12298. Cambridge, MA: National Bureau of Economic Research.

Laidler, D. 2005. "Incentives Facing Canadian Universities: Some Possible Consequences." In *Higher Education in Canada*, edited by C.M. Beach, Robin W. Boadway, and R. Marvin McInnis. Montreal; Kingston, ON: Queen's University, John Deutsch Institute for the Study of Economic Policy.

Lalonde, R. 1995. "The Promise of Public Sector-Sponsored Training Programs." *Journal of Economic Perspectives* 9 (Spring): 149-68.

Lemieux, T., and D. Card. 2001. "Education, Earnings, and the 'Canadian G.I. Bill'." *Canadian Journal of Economics* 34 (2): 313-44.

Levin, H.M., and H.L. Schwartz. 2007. "Educational Vouchers for Universal Pre-Schools." *Economics of Education Review* 26 (July): 3-16.

Lleras-Muney, A. 2005. "The Relationship between Education and Adult Mortality in the United States." *Review of Economic Studies* 72 (January): 189-221.

Lochner, L., and E. Moretti. 2004. "The Effect of Education on Crime: Evidence from Prison Inmates, Arrests and Self-Reports." *American Economic Review* 94 (March): 155-89.

Loeb, S., M. Bridges, D. Bassok, B. Fuller, and R.W. Rumberger. 2007. "How Much Is Too Much? The Influence of Preschool Centers on Children's Social and Cognitive Development." *Economics of Education Review* 26 (1): 52-66.

Love, J.M., L.Harrison, A. Sagi-Schwartz, M. van IJzendoorn, C. Ross, J. Ungerer, H. Raikes et al. 2003. "Child Care Quality Matters: How Conclusions Vary With Context." *Child Development* 74 (July/August): 1021-33.

Ludwig, J., and D.L. Miller. 2006. "Does Head Start Improve Children's Life Chances? Evidence from a Regression Discontinuity Design." NBER Working Paper 11702. Cambridge, MA: National Bureau of Economic Research.

Magnuson, K.A., C. Ruhm, and J. Waldfogel. 2007. "Does Prekindergarten Improve School Preparation and Performance?" *Economics of Education Review* 26 (1): 33-51.

McCain, M., and F. Mustard. 1999. *Reversing the Real Brain Drain: The Early Years Study.* Toronto: Government of Ontario.

Milligan, Kevin. 2007. "Of Beer and Popcorn: Federal Policy on Childcare and Child Benefits." In *The 2006 Federal Budget:*

Rethinking Fiscal Priorities, edited by C.M. Beach, M. Smart, and T.A. Wilson. Montreal; Kingston, ON: McGill-Queen's University Press.

Milligan, K., E. Moretti, and P. Oreopoulos. 2004. "Does Education Improve Citizenship? Evidence from the U.S. and the U.K." *Journal of Public Economics* 88 (August): 1667-95.

Murphy, K.M., W.C. Riddell, and P.M. Romer. 1998. "Wages, Skills and Technology in the United States and Canada." In *General Purpose Technologies and Economic Growth*, edited by E. Helpman. Cambridge, MA: MIT Press.

National Institute for Child Health and Human Development (NICHD). 2003. "Does Amount of Time Spent in Child Care Predict Socioemotional Adjustment during the Transition to Kindergarten?" *Child Development* 74 (July/August): 976-1005.

Oreopoulos, P. 2005. "Stay in School: New Lessons on the Benefits of Raising the Legal School-Leaving Age." *C.D. Howe Institute Commentary* 223. Toronto: C.D. Howe Institute.

_____. 2006a. "The Compelling Effects of Compulsory Schooling: Evidence from Canada." *Canadian Journal of Economics* 39 (February): 22-52.

_____. 2006b. "Estimating Average and Local Average Treatment Effects of Education When Compulsory Schooling Laws Really Matter." *American Economic Review* 96 (March): 152-75.

Organisation for Economic Co-operation and Development (OECD). 1998. *Human Capital Investment: An International Comparison*. Paris: OECD.

_____. 2000. *From Initial Education to Working Life*. Paris: OECD.

_____. 2003. *Education at a Glance: OECD Indicators 2003*. Paris: OECD.

_____. 2004. *Education at a Glance: OECD Indicators 2004*. Paris: OECD.

_____. 2006a. *Education at a Glance: OECD Indicators 2006*. Paris: OECD.

_____. 2006b. *Starting Strong II: Early Childhood Education and Care*. Paris: OECD.

Organisation for Economic Co-operation and Development and Statistics Canada. 2000. *Literacy in the Information Age*. Paris and Ottawa: OECD and Statistics Canada.

Richards, J., and M. Brzozowski. 2006. "Let's Walk before We Run: Cautionary Advice on Childcare." *C.D. Howe Institute Commentary* 237. Toronto: C.D. Howe Institute.

Riddell, W.C. 2001. "Education and Skills: An Assessment of Recent Canadian Experience." In *The State of Economics in Canada: Festschrift in Honour of David Slater*, edited by P. Grady and A. Sharpe. Montreal; Kingston, ON: McGill-Queen's University Press.

_____. 2003. "The Role of Government in Post-secondary Education in Ontario." Background Paper for the Panel on the Role of Government in Ontario.

_____. 2004. "Education, Skills and Labour Market Outcomes: Exploring the Linkages in Canada." In *Educational Outcomes for the Canadian Workplace*, edited by J. Gaskell and K. Rubenson. Toronto: University of Toronto Press.

_____. 2005. "The Social Benefits of Education: New Evidence on an Old Question." In *Taking Public Universities Seriously*, edited by F. Iacobucci and C. Tuohy. Toronto: University of Toronto Press.

_____. 2007. "The Impact of Education on Economic and Social Outcomes: An Overview of Recent Advances in Economics." In *Fulfilling Potential, Creating Success: Perspectives on Human Capital Development*, edited by G. Picot, R. Saunders, and A. Sweetman. Montreal; Kingston, ON: McGill-Queen's University Press.

Romer, P.M. 2000. "Should the Government Subsidize Supply or Demand in the Market for Scientists and Engineers?" NBER Working Paper 7723. Cambridge, MA: National Bureau of Economic Research.

Royal Commission on the Economic Union and Development Prospects for Canada. 1985. *Report*. Ottawa: Minister of Supply and Services Canada.

Spence, A.M. 1974. *Market Signaling: Informational Transfer in Hiring and Related Screening Processes*. Cambridge, MA: Harvard University Press.

Sweetman, A. 1999. "What If High School Were a Year Longer? Evidence from Newfoundland." Western Research Network on Education and Training Working Paper 00-01. Vancouver: Faculty of Education, University of British Columbia.

Temple, J.A., and A.J. Reynolds. 2007. "Benefits and Costs of Investments in Preschool Education: Evidence from the Child-Parent Centers and Related Programs." *Economics of Education Review* 26 (1): 126-44.

Trends in Mathematics and Science Study (TIMSS). 2000a. *TIMSS 1999 International Mathematics Report: Findings from IEA's Repeat of the Third International Mathematics and Science Study at the Eighth Grade*. Chestnut Hill, MA: International Study Center, Lynch School of Education, Boston College.

_____. 2000b. *TIMSS 1999 International Science Report: Findings from IEA's Repeat of the Third International Mathematics and Science Study at the Eighth Grade*. Chestnut Hill, MA: International Study Center, Lynch School of Education, Boston College.

_____. 2004a. *TIMSS 2003 International Mathematics Report: Findings from IEA's Trends in International Mathematics and*

Science Study at the Fourth and Eighth Grades. Chestnut Hill, MA: International Study Center, Lynch School of Education, Boston College.

_____. 2004b. *TIMSS 2003 International Science Report: Findings from IEA's Trends in International Mathematics and Science Study at the Fourth and Eighth Grades*. Chestnut Hill, MA: International Study Center, Lynch School of Education, Boston College.

Watamura, S.E., B. Donzella, J. Alwin, and M.R. Gunnar. 2003. "Morning-to-Afternoon Increases in Cortisol Concentrations for Infants and Toddlers at Child Care: Age Differences and Behavioral Correlates." *Child Development* 74 (July/August): 1006-20.

West, E.G. 1993. *Ending the Squeeze on Universities*. Montreal: IRPP.

Wolfe, B., and R. Haveman. 2001. "Accounting for the Social and Non-Market Benefits of Education." In *The Contribution of Human and Social Capital to Sustained Economic Growth and Well-Being*, edited by J. Helliwell. Vancouver: University of British Columbia Press.

SMART HUMAN CAPITAL POLICY: AN ALTERNATIVE PERSPECTIVE

Serge Coulombe

After decades of debates about the business cycle, macroeconomists turned to the study of long-run growth and development following the pioneering works of Romer (1986), Lucas (1988), and Mankiw, Romer and Weil (1992). Along with institutional differences, human capital accumulation turned out to be one of the fundamental determinants of the wealth of nations (see Glaeser et al. 2004). Other candidates such as technology and physical capital (machinery) are mobile and flow to countries where institutions are good and human capital abundant.

I have devoted a substantial part of my research since 1995 to the study of Canadian provincial economic disparities using this new growth approach, and I have been able to verify the central role human capital accumulation plays.[1] Consequently, the growth economist in me has been consistently arguing that policies oriented at promoting human capital formation should be at the forefront of the Canadian policy agenda (Coulombe and Tremblay 2005).

Of course, the million-dollar question in economics is not usually what to do but how to do it. In "Investing in Human Capital: Policy Priorities for Canada," Craig Riddell bravely steps in the right direction with three separate proposals on how to improve human capital formation: (1) increase targeted early childhood education intervention; (2) raise the compulsory school-leaving age to 18 and improve secondary school vocational programs; and (3) establish a national university scholarship program targeted at youths from low-income families.

In this commentary, I explain the economic rationale for public intervention in education and argue that, since the Canadian education system is already very good, the benefit-cost ratio of Riddell's proposals (mainly his first and third) actually might be quite low. Instead, an efficient, or a smart, human capital policy already at our disposal might well be to adjust Canada's international immigration selection process toward selecting those with skills that are valued in the Canadian labour market. In the conclusion, I briefly mention other possible smart human capital interventions.

THE ECONOMIC RATIONALE FOR GOVERNMENT
INTERVENTION IN HUMAN CAPITAL DEVELOPMENT

From the point of view of an economist, government intervention in public education, as in any other area of human activity, should be motivated by concerns about efficiency and equity. Riddell does a good job in describing and synthesizing these traditional arguments. Such analysis is important since it can identify the channels through which economic returns can emerge.

The efficiency argument is mainly grounded on two market imperfections: externalities and failure of credit markets. For economists, an externality occurs when private action provides benefits to others at no cost to them. In the case of public education, externalities take the form of greater public participation in the democratic process, reduced crime and a lower demand for social assistance. As Psacharopoulos and Patrinos suggest, however, the empirical evidence of positive and significant externalities from education is "scarce and inconclusive" (2004, 117). Krueger and Lindahl (2001, 1130) conclude that empirical evidence for externalities from higher education is "fragile," and that, in developed countries, the potential for externalities (such as reduced crime) is larger for investments in disadvantaged, rather than advantaged, groups. The efficiency (externalities) and equity (equal opportunity) arguments for public intervention in education in developed countries thus appear to be tied together.

Credit market failures result when potential students cannot use their human capital as collateral for financing their education. This is probably the best argument for public investment in primary and secondary schooling. Although Canada already has an excellent and comprehensive public system of primary and secondary education, post-secondary education is not free. Moreover, despite the existence of government financial assistance, Canadians might not have equal access to post-secondary education. Again, one comes back to the equity argument.

In my view, the returns from further public spending on education in Canada depend critically on the need to promote equal opportunity, which raises the question: Does Canada have a problem in promoting equal opportunity? The answer may in fact be no.

CANADA'S EDUCATION SYSTEM: A GOOD REPORT CARD

In 2004, Statistics Canada summarized the results of the 2003 Program for International Student Assessment (PISA), in which 41 countries participated, by noting:

"Canadian 15-year-old students are among the best in the world when it comes to mathematics, reading, science and problem solving" (Statistics Canada 2004). Indeed, Canadian students clearly outperformed those in France, the United States and Italy.

The 2003 PISA results also indicate that Canada's primary and secondary education system is near the top of the world in terms of equality of opportunity. Evidence for this performance comes from the effect of socio-economic status on skills. In all 41 participating countries, students from families with high socio-economic status outperformed those from families with low status. This gap, however, typically is smaller in Canada than in other industrialized countries (Bussière et al. 2004, 65). Thus, it appears that the Canadian school system does a relatively good job of improving the skills of students with a low socio-economic background and, therefore, of reducing socio-economic disparities.

Additional evidence on the performance of Canada's school system comes from the small proportion of its students ranked at a low level of proficiency in mathematics.[2] With just 10 percent of its students ranked at the lowest skills level, Canada ranks second behind only Finland (7 percent), but higher than Japan (13 percent), Australia (14 percent), New Zealand (15 percent) and France (17 percent), and much better than the United States (26 percent), Portugal (30 percent), Italy (32 percent) and Mexico (66 percent).

Overall the PISA results suggest that Canada might well have one of the best public education systems in the world for primary and secondary schooling. On average, Canada's 15-year-old students outperform those of most developed countries and its education system appears especially effective at promoting equal opportunity.

The PISA results also confirm other evidence on the success of the Canadian education system in promoting equal opportunity. Results from the intergenerational mobility literature indicate that, in Canada, the relative incomes of parents and children are only loosely correlated (20 percent — see Corak and Heisz 1999; Corak 2001). This implies that the children of poor parents in Canada have a very good chance of earning more than their parents and escaping poverty. From the point of view of intergenerational equity, Canada ranks with Finland, Sweden and Denmark among the top countries. In contrast, a much larger proportion of relative income is transmitted to the next generation in France (40 percent), the United States and the United Kingdom (both with a correlation around 50 percent). Thus, Canada seems to offer much better opportunities for human capital development among poor children than does the United States or the United Kingdom. Given that most studies of the returns from early childhood education programs, such as Head Start, are from the United

States, it is important to keep in mind that their results might not apply to Canada, which is at the other end of the spectrum regarding equality of opportunity.

Finally, Corak, Lipps and Zhao (2005) find a long-lasting tendency for children from higher-income families to be more likely to attend university. From a historical point of view, however, the participation gap between those from the highest-income and those from the lowest-income families has tended to narrow — except during the early to mid-1990s, a period characterized by increases in tuition fees.

EVALUATING RIDDELL'S PROPOSALS

The main economic motivation for Riddell's three proposals is grounded in the equity argument: to promote equal opportunity for all Canadians with targeted investments in disadvantaged groups. And, in a developed country such as Canada, these are precisely the types of investments that have the potential to generate some kinds of externalities. In my view, all three policy proposals are likely to generate benefits for disadvantaged groups and, potentially, other Canadians as well.

My main concern about Riddell's first and third proposals is that they would require substantial public funding. Consequently, they might have a low benefit-cost ratio given the already excellent performance of Canada's education system in promoting equal opportunity. When a policy is targeted at an area where the needs are low, the returns are likely to be low. Both proposals, however, would have a higher benefit-cost ratio if implemented in the United States, since that country's system lags behind Canada's in promoting equity.

Furthermore, regarding Riddell's proposal on early childhood education, I would recommend a wait-and-see approach. Early childhood interventions are not easy to target, and the only reasonable way to get effective help to the disadvantaged might be to set up a costly universal basic program. This is what Quebec has done, and we should wait for further evidence on the effectiveness and policy design of its program. From the current perspective, however, Quebec's experiment appears to suffer from curriculum problems, high costs and uncertain returns.

Riddell's second proposal is worth considering. Keeping students at school and improving vocational training are two good objectives for any government. The two goals might also be complementary, since improved vocational training might help to keep 17- and 18-year-olds in school. But how should this be done? Keeping 17- and 18-year-olds in school against their will might create other problems, especially for teachers — although this is not a policy design issue that an economist is competent to tackle.

An economic point could be raised regarding increasing the school-leaving age by noting that increases in the school-leaving age during the period from the 1920s to the 1970s yielded quite spectacular returns. As Riddell points out, however, we should not expect the same benefits today since we would not be working from the same base. Nevertheless, Riddell argues that the net benefits from increasing compulsory schooling based on experiences since the 1970s are substantial enough to warrant policy action.

But in my view, other policies might have a higher benefit-cost ratio in Canada from the point of view of human capital — policies that could improve economic efficiency without requiring new funding. The area where there is more potential for improving human capital is one where the federal government already plays a key role: the selection of immigrants.

IMMIGRATION AND HUMAN CAPITAL

From the point of view of policy, Canadians should be concerned about the substantial deterioration in the relative earnings of immigrants in the 1990s (see Corak 2006). Ferrer, Green and Riddell (2006) find, after controlling for education, that immigrants have lower skills than the Canadian-born population; Coulombe and Tremblay (2007b) show that the skills gap between immigrants and native-born Canadians with the same level of education corresponds to three years of formal education in Canada. Furthermore, the gap is greatest in the case of immigrants who come from the least-developed countries. One-third of the gap can be attributed to lower language proficiency and the remaining two-thirds to the relatively low quality of schooling in the source countries. These findings seem to validate the notion that assessing the quality of foreign educational credentials has become a critical policy goal in Canada.

A growing literature in economic growth recognizes differences in educational attainment in cross-country comparisons. The general consensus is that, within a country, educational attainment is a good proxy for human capital but that, in cross-country analyses, educational attainment appears to be a biased indicator of human capital.

Since 1967, Canada has used a point system for selecting immigrants. Since 2002, education has been worth 25 points on a 100-point scale, but as the pass rate is 67 points, education could represent more than a third of the score for successful immigrants. Yet this selection procedure might not be the best way to maximize human capital; instead, it could be biased in favour of selecting immigrants from countries where degrees are easy to get — in effect, where education quality is low. The federal government has responded to the problems faced by immigrants with lower-quality education by creating the Foreign Credential Recognition program. In my view, it would be more efficient from an economic perspective to change the selection process — although, of course, from a political point of view, it would be unpalatable to select immigrants based on the development level of their country of origin.

I propose instead a policy that is smart from both an economic and a political perspective: select immigrants with skills that are valued in the domestic labour market. This policy follows the approach that both Australia and Quebec have recently adopted. In October 2006, Quebec modified its immigration selection criteria, which, like those of the federal government, are based on a point system for such factors as schooling achievement, language proficiency and age. The recent revision gives a substantial point premium for candidates with a valid employment offer, who hold a diploma from a Quebec university, or who have a foreign diploma recognized by a Quebec professional regulatory authority.[3] The premiums for these characteristics are substantial, and are likely to be a decisive factor in the evaluation process. With these changes, the Quebec selection process provides a better match between the credentials of international immigrants and the domestic labour market.[4]

CONCLUSION

In my view, the key issue with Riddell's proposals to increase early childhood education intervention and to establish a scholarship program for youths from low-income families is that they imply putting substantial public resources into areas in which Canada already performs quite well — ranking near the top among industrialized countries in promoting equality of opportunity for its citizens and in the quality of its public education system.

Better advice would be to apply efforts where the problem is real. I believe that one area in need of change is the way Canada selects its immigrants. We are choosing more and more immigrants with high educational attainment in their home countries but with low levels of skills. The cumulative diluting effect of such immigration on Canada's human capital stock is evident: Coulombe and Tremblay (2007b) show that, in 2003, immigration decreased Ontario's mean skills level by an amount corresponding to one and a half years of education in Canada.

Canada's immigration policy was designed decades ago, when the sources of immigration were very different than they are today. Adjusting the selection process to the new reality is an example of smart human capital policy. The potential return is high, since there is a real problem (bias in selecting immigrants) and the cost is small — hardly on the same scale as that of fulfilling any of Riddell's proposals.

Finally, I do not think that the possibilities for smart policies regarding human capital formation in Canada have been exhausted — for examples, see Coulombe and Tremblay (2005). One good direction might be for provincial governments to promote competition among schools, as does Alberta, the highest-ranked province for skills acquisition in the 2003 PISA results. Competition among schools could be encouraged by the production of publicly accessible data on school performance based on standardized tests and by increasing school choices for parents. Another example of smart policy might be to link federal social transfers to university enrolment, to mitigate the incentives of have-not provinces to underinvest in education because of interprovincial outmigration.

Human Capital: Comments

NOTES

I benefited from discussions with Daniel Boothby, Pierre Brochu, Miles Corak and Ruth G. Kane. I also thank Jeremy Leonard, Christopher Ragan and France St-Hilaire for their helpful suggestions.

1 Having documented the economic convergence of provinces (Coulombe and Lee 1995), I identified human capital accumulation as one of the key determinants of provincial relative growth (Coulombe and Tremblay 2001; Coulombe 2003; and Coulombe and Tremblay 2007a).

2 In the PISA results, students are ranked from level 1 (low skills) to level 6 (high skills). Students at level 1 in mathematics are unlikely to know enough mathematics for day-to-day purposes.

3 The recognition of foreign diplomas is a stated objective, but it has not yet been fully implemented, since the mechanisms are just now being put into place.

4 Other revisions are less appealing from an economic point of view. Quebec now gives additional points for selected occupations, such as biochemistry and meat-cutting. Yet picking future winners based on actual shortages in the domain of training is hazardous — the tech bubble prior to 2001 well illustrates this danger.

REFERENCES

Bussière, P., F. Cartwright, T. Knighton, and T. Rogers. 2004. *Measuring Up: Canadian Results of the OECD PISA Study*. Cat. 81-590-XPE No. 2. Ottawa: Statistics Canada.

Corak, M. 2001. "Are the Kids All Right? Intergenerational Mobility and Child Well-Being in Canada." In *The Review of Economic Performance and Social Progress 2001 — The Long Decade: Canada in the 1990s*, edited by K. Banting, A. Sharpe, and F. St-Hilaire. Montreal: IRPP.

———. 2006. "Do Poor Children Become Poor Adults? Lessons from a Cross Country Comparison of Generational Earnings Mobility." *Research on Economic Inequality* 13 (1): 143-88.

Corak, M., and A. Heisz. 1999. "The Intergenerational Earnings and Income Mobility of Canadian Men: Evidence from the Longitudinal Income Tax Data." *Journal of Human Resources* 34 (3): 505-33.

Corak, M., G. Lipps, and J. Zhao. 2005. "Family Income and Participation in Post-Secondary Education." In *Higher Education in Canada*, edited by C. Beach, R. Boadway, and M. McInnis. Montreal; Kingston, ON: Queen's University, John Deutsch Institute for the Study of Economic Policy.

Coulombe, S. 2003. "Human Capital, Urbanization and Canadian Provincial Growth." *Regional Studies* 37 (3): 239-50.

Coulombe, S., and F.C. Lee. 1995. "Convergence across Canadian Provinces, 1961 to 1991." *Canadian Journal of Economics* 28 (4): 886-98.

Coulombe, S., and J.-F. Tremblay. 2001. "Human Capital and Regional Convergence in Canada." *Journal of Economic Studies* 28 (3): 154-80.

———. 2005. "Public Investment in Skills: Are Canadian Governments Doing Enough?" *C.D. Howe Institute Commentary* 217. Toronto: C.D. Howe Institute.

———. 2007a. "Skills, Education and Canadian Provincial Disparity." *Journal of Regional Science*. Forthcoming.

———. 2007b. "Migration and Skills Disparities across the Canadian Provinces." *Regional Studies*. Forthcoming.

Ferrer, A., D.A. Green, and W.C. Riddell. 2006. "The Effect of Literacy on Immigrant Earnings." *Journal of Human Resources* 41 (2): 380-410.

Glaeser, E.L., R. La Porta, F. Lopes-de-Silanes, and A. Shleifer. 2004. "Do Institutions Cause Growth?" *Journal of Economic Growth* 9 (3): 271-303.

Krueger, A.B., and M. Lindahl. 2001. "Education for Growth: Why and for Whom?" *Journal of Economic Literature* 39 (4): 1101-36.

Lucas, R.E., Jr. 1988. "On the Mechanics of Economic Development." *Journal of Monetary Economics* 22 (1): 3-42.

Mankiw, N.G., D. Romer, and D.N. Weil. 1992. "A Contribution to the Empirics of Economic Growth." *Quarterly Journal of Economics* 107 (2): 407-37.

Psacharopoulos, G., and H.A. Patrinos. 2004. "Returns to Investment in Education: A Further Update." *Education Economics* 12 (2): 111-34.

Romer, P.M. 1986. "Increasing Returns and Long-Run Growth." *Journal of Political Economy* 94 (5): 1002-37.

Statistics Canada. 2004. "Performance of Canada's Youth in Mathematics, Reading, Science and Problem-Solving." *The Daily*, December 7. Accessed September 6, 2007. www.statcan.ca/Daily/English/041207/d041207a.htm

EDUCATION AND HUMAN CAPITAL: RECONCILING POLICY IMPERATIVES AND POLICY DESIGN
Jane Gaskell

Craig Riddell makes a powerful argument for increasing investment in Canadian education. He demonstrates that, despite Canada's historical commitment to education, its spending has declined over the past decade relative to that of other industrialized countries. Canada's investment in early childhood education is particularly low, secondary school dropout rates are high and participation rates in university education are relatively low.

Riddell's chapter, "Investing in Human Capital: Policy Priorities for Canada," makes the case that education has a causal effect on outcomes — that it is not simply a signalling device — and that Canadian schools are doing a good job in producing literate students with knowledge of mathematics and science.

Riddell also discusses the effects of education not just on student achievement and labour market outcomes, but on a wide range of indicators of individual and social well-being: health, prosperity, civic participation, democracy, social cohesion, inequality. A scarcity of highly skilled people increases inequality by raising their wages relative to the larger population. Broadly available, high-quality education makes good on Canada's promise of equality of opportunity for all. A strong educational system can provide the specialized skills and knowledge Canadians need, and can ensure citizens are well equipped to debate which policy initiatives will matter 10, 20 and 50 years from now.

Given that Riddell exhibits a strong concern for educational investment, what about the particular policies he recommends? Although he identifies three general areas where intervention would pay off and outlines some useful approaches, he does not dwell on the design of specific policies, their institutional forms or accountability. Rather, he approaches these issues almost entirely within the framework of economics — and as such it is a valuable contribution. But a discussion of the sociological, historical, educational and political context would also inform Canadians' ability to come up with effective policy initiatives in education. Successful policy interventions are those that take into account the complex politics of education and the large institutional framework that manages it. Successful policy interventions must resonate in the political landscape and provide incentives for institutions to change.

Given this, I thought a series of discussions was missing. All three of Riddell's policy proposals aim to increase the amount of education young people receive, but they skim over the questions of content and quality. How we decide what students should learn and how we foster better quality, not just quantity, of education deserves a fuller discussion. A discussion of governance and jurisdiction in education is also missing. Too many proposals for educational change in Canada degenerate into a debate about provincial and federal jurisdiction; an effective intervention has to address and finesse that question.

Each area that Riddell addresses has specific contextual issues that must inform policy development. In the field of early childhood education, we need to understand the variation in existing forms of provision, the reasons parents choose the providers they do, the cost drivers for different settings, the effects that regulation, unionization and price have on quality and Canadians' attitudes and beliefs about the role of women, the state and the family in the care of young children.

In the field of secondary education, policy must take account of teachers' unions, accountability systems and school board financing. Keeping students in school means increasing the flexibility of the curriculum and the possibilities of choice within the public school system. It need not mean charter schools, voucher systems or tax credits for private schools, although these options are likely to be on the table.

In the university sector, financial aid might increase the demand for university education, but its effects on supply are mediated by provincial funding formulae and tuition policies.

Canada has provisions for student financial aid at the federal, provincial and institutional levels, but they are complicated and poorly understood. Student financial aid is a significant part of university budgets, and changes in this area would have an effect on tuition, student politics, university autonomy, research and regulatory systems.

Space does not allow me to take up all of these issues, but let me look a bit more closely at each policy proposal and add some observations from the point of view of an educator.

EARLY CHILDHOOD EDUCATION

Riddell proposes to increase state intervention, in the form of funding targeted at programs for disadvantaged families. He does not, however, provide much detail about how this would work. The Liberal government of Paul Martin worked out with all the provinces a major initiative to fund early childhood education; the Conservative government of Stephen Harper replaced that initiative with a universal but taxed child care payment to all families. Both were attempts to increase funding for early childhood education, and in both cases the government claimed that equity would be enhanced. They are, however, dramatically different in their assumptions and effects. Indeed, the merits and problems of different schemes are absolutely central to any policy discussion.

Riddell cites several studies of whether what is described as "nonmaternal care" is a good thing for children. This is not the question on which I think we need to gather evidence. There are large differences among maternal care settings and among child care settings. If a study showed that the well-being of children deteriorated in a particular setting, whether at home or out of the home, I would conclude that the quality of that setting is poor — not that we should not provide child care outside the home or that children do not fare well in the home. The research leaves no doubt that the early experiences of children have dramatic long-term effects, both for good and for not so good (McCain and Mustard 1999).

Women with young children increasingly work outside the home. Bushnik (2006) reports that, in 2002-03, 64 percent of two-parent families with young children reported that both parents worked, up from 59 percent eight years earlier, while 68 percent of single parents with young children worked, compared with 51 percent eight years earlier. In the same year, 54 percent of preschool-age children were reported as enrolled in some form of child care, up from 42 percent eight years earlier. Allowing parents to work with confidence that their children are well looked after is in itself a positive impact. Participation rates are highest for children in families with the highest income levels.

We need evidence about what kind of nonparental care has the most benefit for children and their families, and how it can be increased. It is important to look within the black box of child care because of the enormous variability in forms of child care. There is no clear distinction between child care that has an educational component, such as the Montessori or Head Start programs, and other forms of child care. Bushnik (2006) reports that just under 30 percent of children in nonparental care are enrolled in a child care centre, which is likely to have some educational component. Only 24 percent of children are in the care of a trained caregiver; 30 percent are cared for by a relative, and about 20 percent are cared for in their own homes. McCain and Mustard (1999) find that children from low socio-economic backgrounds do better in early child development programs outside the home.

McCain and Mustard also conclude that programs for quality early child development and parenting "must apply to all sectors of society if we wish to decrease the steepness of the socio-economic gradient" (1999, 9). Labelling and stigma become a critical problem when programs are targeted only at disadvantaged families. Differential subsidies related to income, as Riddell suggests, are appropriate, but creating quality care for young children is a public good that benefits the society as a whole. Certainly, provincial governments believe this to be the case, at least beginning with six-year-olds, since all provide free public education for such children. Some provinces provide a half day for five-year-olds and some provide a full day; some provide free public schooling for four-year-olds. What is at issue is the age at which public funding is appropriate, not the value of publicly funded education for all children.

Many countries, including Canada, have experience with intergovernmental agreements on early childhood education. In Canada, until the 1960s, municipal authorities were the primary funders of child care; the federal and provincial governments began their support only in 1966 with the Canada Assistance Plan. The experience with such agreements offers lessons about how to frame an effective policy that balances equity and decentralization, garners public support and does not degenerate into constitutional bickering (Jensen and Mahon 2002). Any new program must ensure cooperation among different levels of government — not an easy achievement.

REDUCING THE DROPOUT RATE

In proposing to reduce the high school dropout rate by introducing compulsory schooling to age 18 and improving vocational programs for those at risk, Riddell notes that "results in the lower tail of the distribution of student achievement and adult literacy…are problematic" (34). Increasing high school graduation rates is important, but will laws about compulsory attendance change things? My suspicion is that such laws are less important than establishing schools and programs that engage students to stay involved in learning. And this is a more complicated policy challenge.

Compulsory schooling laws were enacted in Canada long before farm children actually stayed in school (Katz 1975). Criminalizing students who leave school early, especially when the cost of enforcement is high, seems unfortunate. Many students who leave school early do eventually return to complete their secondary education or to attend some form of post-secondary education (Bowlby and McMullen 2002). Statistics Canada's 1999 Youth in Transition survey reported that, although 11 percent of students left high school without a diploma, over the next two years 14 percent of those students returned (Bushnik, Barr-Telford, and Bussière 2004); moreover, 7 percent of students in Ontario schools were suspended in 2005-06, so dropouts are sometimes "push-outs." Anecdotal evidence also suggests that some time outside the school might not be a bad idea for students who are dissatisfied with the institution (Kelly and Gaskell 1996). That said, Ontario is now trying the policy Riddell recommends: students who leave school without graduating before age 18 will lose their driver's licences.

Disputes over federal and provincial jurisdiction have hampered efforts by the federal government to affect secondary schooling. Federal interventions in school initiatives of the 1990s, which Riddell mentions and which grew out of a series of Economic Council of Canada reports (Economic Council of Canada 1992), were scattered across the country and not well coordinated with provincial policy. Although the specific interventions were appreciated by the schools that were involved, they were not sustained and did not have a lasting effect on school retention or provincial policy (Renihan et al. 1994). Even the related research agenda was dropped partly because of concern about provincial cooperation.

Policy initiatives in relation to secondary schooling must be driven by provincial governments and produce a wider variety of secondary school programs that engage young people with different interests and needs. An emphasis on streaming and vocationalism is too narrow an approach. Although more and better programs closely linked to work would be an excellent thing for all kinds of students, streaming does not increase the achievement of students who are at risk of leaving school. Rather, research suggests that at-risk students respond to personal attention by a responsible adult, small alternative programs, culturally appropriate learning environments and relevant curriculum (Wehlage et al. 1989). The system needs to target specific groups of youth, among them Aboriginal and black students, students from families in poverty, gay and lesbian students and rural students. And it must create programs that are safe, supportive and nurturing, as well as academically rich. Studies of alternative programs that work, such as the Pathways program in Toronto or some Aboriginal programs in Manitoba, will encourage this kind of thinking. Governance changes that allow alternatives within the public system will encourage such initiatives, and funding formulae that target resources at students who are underperforming will sustain them. School choice is a controversial policy, but it need not mean charters and vouchers; school boards can encourage diversity and pluralism instead of looking for the one best system (Gaskell 2001).

MERIT-BASED SCHOLARSHIPS FOR LOW-INCOME STUDENTS

As for Riddell's suggestion that national, merit-based scholarships be targeted at low-income families, the policy problem of increasing access to university education is a critical one, but is a federal scholarship program the way to make a difference?

The federal government has made student aid available since the creation of the Canada Student Loans program in 1964 (see Fisher et al. 2006; Shanahan and Jones 2007). In the late 1990s, the Registered Education Savings Program and the Canada Millennium Scholarship Foundation were established, as the issue of student debt became politically important. Increased tax credits and targeted funding through the Canadian Opportunities Strategy have also been put in place federally. The Millennium Scholarship program is at arm's length from government and uses provincial infrastructure to distribute its scholarships. As a result, it has less visibility than it might, serving as a formulaic top-up to provincial programs — arguably displacing provincial dollars, rather than adding to them (Fisher et al. 2006, 67-8).

Current programs in Canada are complicated, putting together money at the federal, provincial and institutional levels, relying on loans, grants, tax deductions and rebates. A recent analysis of the various schemes concludes that, over the past 10 years, the trend has been away from needs-based financial aid — meaning that, despite increased spending on students by Canadian governments, "it is unclear to what extent the new universal investment has improved access to affordable higher education in Canada" (Berger, Motte, and Parkin 2007, 13).

Given the current complex array of programs, the design of any new initiative is critical. What we know about student aid is that it should be simple, transparent and well understood at the point when a student is making a decision. Students think university is more expensive than it actually is, and they are not as aware of the financial payoffs as they should be. Canadian parents and students think the cost of tuition is twice as high as it is. Part of what we face is an information problem (Canada Millennium Scholarship Foundation 2006).

Access trumps quality politically, but we must worry about sustaining the quality of university education as well as providing access. Tuition wars have been fought over quality and access, and quality has lost ground where tuition freezes have been imposed. The two can work together if targeted student aid enables tuition rises and protects families who cannot afford them. Low tuition merely subsidizes wealthy families who can afford to pay more. Federal support can also ensure quality through support of research and through transfers to the provinces for post-secondary education. A balance of types of government support should be maintained.

CONCLUSION

Although economic models provide important information about what pays off in general, contextually specific policy analysis is required to design effective Canadian interventions in education. We must worry about quality, not just quantity, and about a governance system that allows new policies to take hold and flourish in a complex political environment.

Investments in Canadian early childhood education are badly needed, and the "desirable design features" Riddell suggests are appropriate. Careful assessment of Canada's existing, varied system can teach us a lot, and we need more research on how it works and whom it serves. While increasing high school graduation rates is important, I do not believe that compulsory attendance laws are the answer. The creation of small, integrated, knowledge-rich, responsive and caring communities at the secondary school level would go a long way toward keeping students in school. Targeting programs at Aboriginal students is also important.

Deregulating tuition and substantially increasing needs-based financial aid in the post-secondary sector is appropriate in my view. However, doing so without putting in place a simple, transparent system that is widely understood by students, parents and voters would neither increase access nor succeed politically.

Human Capital: Comments

REFERENCES

Berger, J., A. Motte, and A. Parkin. 2007. *The Price of Knowledge 2006-07: How Governments Support Students*. Ottawa: Canadian Millennium Scholarship Foundation.

Bowlby J., and K. McMullen. 2002. *At a Crossroads: First Results for the 18-20-Year-Old Cohort of the Youth in Transition Survey*. Cat. 81-591-XIE. Ottawa: Statistics Canada.

Bushnik T. 2006. *Child Care in Canada*. Children and Youth Research Paper Series. Cat. 89-599-MIE — No. 003. Ottawa: Special Surveys Division, Statistics Canada.

Bushnik, T., L. Barr-Telford, and P. Bussière. 2004. *In and Out of High School: First Results from the Second Cycle of the Youth in Transition Survey, 2002*. Cat. 81-595-MIE — No. 014. Ottawa: Statistics Canada.

Canada Millennium Scholarship Foundation. 2006. *Closing the Information Gap: Does Information Matter?* Ottawa: Canada Millennium Scholarship Foundation.

Economic Council of Canada. 1992. *A Lot to Learn: Education and Training in Canada*. Ottawa: Economic Council of Canada.

Fisher, D., K. Rubenson, J. Bernatchez, R. Clift, G. Jones, J. Lee, M. MacIvor, et al. 2006. *Canadian Federal Policy and Postsecondary Education*. Vancouver: Alliance for International Higher Education Policy Studies and The Centre for Policy Studies in Higher Education and Training, Faculty of Education, University of British Columbia.

Gaskell, J. 2001. "Constructing the 'Public' in Public Schools: A School Board Debate." *Canadian Journal of Education* 26 (1): 19-37.

Jenson, J., and R. Mahon. 2002. *Bringing Cities to the Table: Child Care and Intergovernmental Relations*. Ottawa: Canadian Policy Research Networks.

Katz, M.B. 1975. "Who Went to School?" In *Education and Social Change: Themes from Ontario's Past*, edited by P. Mattingly and M.B. Katz. New York: New York University Press.

Kelly, D., and J. Gaskell. 1996. *Debating Dropouts: Critical Policy and Research Perspectives on School Leaving*. New York: Teachers College Press

McCain, M., and F. Mustard. 1999. *Reversing the Real Brain Drain: The Early Years Study*. Toronto: Government of Ontario.

Renihan, F., E. Buller, W. Desharnais, R. Enns, T. Laferrière, and L. Terrien. 1994. "Taking Stock: An Assessment of the National Stay-In-School Initiative." Hull, QC: Youth Affairs Branch, Human Resources Development Canada.

Shanahan, T., and G. Jones. 2007. "Shifting Roles and Approaches: Government Coordination of Post-Secondary Education in Canada 1995–2006." *Higher Education Research and Development* 26 (1): 31-43.

Wehlage, G., R. Rutter, G. Smith, N. Lesko, and R. Fernandez. 1989. *Reducing the Risk: Schools as Communities of Support*. London: Falmer Press.

CLIMATE CHANGE

CANADIAN POLICIES FOR DEEP GREENHOUSE GAS REDUCTIONS

Mark Jaccard and Nic Rivers

THE POLICY CHALLENGE

The litany of potential impacts associated with climate change is becoming familiar to anyone who regularly reads a newspaper or watches the news on television. Global average temperatures are expected to increase by between 2 and 6°C over the coming century. Temperature increases will continue to melt glaciers throughout the world as well as increase the rate of evaporation and precipitation, which will reduce water availability in many areas already facing potable water shortages. Melting glaciers and the thermal expansion of sea water are expected to gradually increase sea levels and potentially damage cities, infrastructure and populations worldwide. Rapid changes in temperature are also expected to significantly affect biological diversity and distribution, with as many as 20 to 50 percent of all species potentially facing extinction. While many species may be negatively impacted, others may thrive as a result of a warming climate; thus, many scientists foresee expansion in the range of tropical diseases like malaria and dengue fever as a result of climate change.

In addition to these and other gradual changes, scientists are particularly worried about abrupt, nonlinear changes resulting from increases in average global temperature. Key among these is the potential for rapid, irreversible melting or collapse of the Greenland and West Antarctic ice sheets. In 2002, part of the Antarctic ice shelf known as Larsen B, an area over half the size of Prince Edward Island and 200 metres thick, collapsed into the ocean, likely as a result of warming temperatures. Although the direct effects of this "small" collapse were limited, a similar collapse of larger parts of the West Antarctic and Greenland ice sheets could catastrophically raise sea levels by over 1 metre this century and up to 12 metres over several centuries. Researchers have also examined the possibility of dramatic changes in ocean circulation as a result of climate change. New evidence suggests that ocean circulation patterns can change very quickly (on the order of decades), and that this can dramatically alter land temperatures.

Although many impacts of climate change are expected to be felt most strongly in low-lying and developing countries, Canada is by no means immune from direct impacts. Temperature changes will likely be most significant at the earth's poles, which are predicted to warm at about double the average rate. A 4°C average global warming, near the central estimate for 2100, would therefore be expected to warm northern Canada by roughly 8°C. Such a change would obviously have dramatic effects on natural systems and on the human inhabitants of Canada's North. Other parts of Canada would probably suffer more prolonged water shortages and extreme weather events. Smog could be exacerbated due to higher temperatures in urban areas, and some pests, like the mountain pine beetle, could become endemic. Over the long term, agricultural and forestry output would likely suffer, even though productivity could actually increase in the short term.

Because of the emissions that have already been released, and because the greenhouse gases (GHG) that cause climate change stay in the atmosphere so long, the planet will be subjected to significant climate warming over the coming century unless technological advances enable us to extract GHGs from the atmosphere. The Intergovernmental Panel on Climate Change (IPCC) reports that to stabilize emissions at 550 parts per million (ppm) — roughly double the earth's pre-industrial concentration, and at the upper end of what most scientists consider acceptable — global GHG emissions have to reach their peak by 2020 to 2030 and decline quickly thereafter (IPCC 2007). With global emissions growing, and with the rate of growth increasing in step with rapid economic growth, particularly in developing countries, the global community will have to make a significant effort to stabilize emissions at 550 ppm. Some economists project that such an effort will impose costs of 1 to 3 percent of gross world product (Stern 2006).

Compounding the technical difficulty and high costs of action are the long time scale and global nature of climate change. While costs of climate change abatement are borne today by whatever party undertakes an action, most benefits of abatement are decades or even centuries away and would be spread throughout the entire world. Seen in this light, climate change is the ultimate public-good problem, which explains the effort that has been invested in coordinating international action and also helps explain negligible progress by national governments in the absence of an effective and truly global agreement (the current Kyoto Protocol to the United Nations Framework Convention on Climate Change [UNFCCC] sets targets for 2008 to 2012 that do not include the developing countries).

Canada produces over 2 percent of global GHG emissions, more than all but six other countries in the world, and it produces more emissions per capita than virtually any other country (UNFCCC 2005; Marland, Boden, and Andres 2006). Canada's emissions are also growing faster than those of most other industrialized countries —

they rose by 27 percent between 1990 and 2004 (Environment Canada 2006), primarily as a result of an expanding population, economic growth and increasing fossil fuel production (Rivers and Jaccard forthcoming). Since these are all expected to increase substantially over the coming decades, Canada's emissions will continue to rise quickly in the absence of strong policies designed to increase energy efficiency, prompt the switch to nonemitting fuels, and encourage the capture and storage of emissions resulting from continued fossil fuel production and use.[1]

The challenge of dramatically changing the course of GHG emissions, given the growth of these factors, is substantial. Politically, Canada is in a difficult situation in that jurisdiction over environmental problems is ambiguously divided between the provinces and the federal government. As an export-driven economy, Canada also faces pressure from business not to adopt environmental regulations that will place its companies at a competitive disadvantage compared with other commodity producers. And because of Canada's cold climate and vast territory, reducing its space-heating and transportation emissions even to current European levels presents a formidable challenge (Bataille et al. 2007).

Despite such challenges, any international agreement designed to tackle climate change will certainly require Canada to make substantial GHG reductions. If rich countries such as Canada do not take action, it will be impossible to convince poorer countries like China and India to do so. In this chapter, we therefore analyze a scenario in which, by 2050, Canada reduces its domestic GHG emissions by about 60 percent from today's level. This reduction is roughly consistent with emissions targets articulated by all of Canada's main political parties; with recent analysis conducted by the National Round Table on the Environment and the Economy; and with national targets set by the United Kingdom, Sweden, the European Union, California and other jurisdictions. The objective of this chapter is to describe a set of appropriate domestic policies for meeting this long-term goal of deep GHG reductions.

WHAT IS THE APPROPRIATE POLICY RESPONSE?
Criteria for choosing climate change policies

Climate change policy must provide strong long-run signals to motivate technological innovators, companies and consumers while avoiding unnecessary economic costs (Jaccard, Nyboer, and Sadownik 2002). The relative emphasis on certain policy tools to achieve this end and the ultimate design of a policy package involves many considerations and trade-offs. For instance, what may be most economically efficient or effective in realizing environmental benefits may be difficult from a standpoint of administrative feasibility or political acceptability.

Policy evaluation criteria have been forwarded in different contexts and by different organizations to assist environmental policy design (Department of Finance Canada 2005; IPCC 2007; Jaccard, Rivers, and Horne 2004). In this chapter, we evaluate policies based on the following criteria, which are common to most evaluative frameworks:

Effectiveness at achieving an environmental target

/ To what extent will the measure deliver its environmental objective? More specifically, how will the measure result in long-term sustainable reductions in GHG emissions by 2050?

/ Does the policy target the generation of GHGs directly, or does it do so indirectly — that is, by improving energy efficiency?

Economic efficiency

/ To what extent, from the perspectives of the government administrator and the firms/households subject to the measure, will emissions reductions be achieved at the lowest economic costs? Does the response to this question include a realistic consideration of consumer preferences (which are often ignored in cost analyses)?

Political acceptability

/ Will politicians find sufficient support to implement a policy?

/ Will Canada maintain the international competitiveness of industries producing goods that are traded in the international marketplace?

Administrative feasibility

/ Is the burden of administration, reporting, monitoring and enforcement acceptable?

In addition to these criteria, there are other important factors that should be considered in the context of GHG policy development in Canada. First, policy development will evolve from the interests and rights of multiple players within the political system and their relative power or influence in shaping policy. In the Canadian context, this is critical because multiple jurisdictions must be involved in enacting climate change policy (Bell et al. 2005). Of particular relevance is provincial jurisdiction over natural resources such as oil and gas, energy, mining, forestry and agriculture. A realistic assessment of policy must involve this dimension, and it should also include consideration of the options available for developing buy-in and of mitigating transitional impacts that may accompany policy implementation.

Second, while the focus of this chapter is on domestic policies, Canadian policies will be more effective if they are consistent with those of other countries and with international coordination mechanisms. The relationship to developments in the US is especially important. While ambitious policies in Canada may be hampered by the absence of such efforts in the US, innovative policy design and careful target setting may reduce the importance of this constraint.

Third, setting GHG policy is a classic case of decision-making with uncertainty, and this reality should be embraced instead of ignored or used as an excuse for inaction. This means that policies should be selected based on how well they perform (their robustness) under highly variable outcomes, and even highly variable reference cases. How might the economy evolve? What kind of international agreement might eventually follow the Kyoto Protocol? What will the US do, and how will its economy be affected? How will the pace and character of technological evolution change? How will our understanding of the costs and benefits of abating climate change evolve? Policies must be well positioned to incorporate unexpected technologies, to adapt to shifting targets, and to anticipate and mesh with international policy instruments. There is a great likelihood that policies developed today will need to be changed sometime in the future to accommodate an unexpected event or development, and they should be designed with this in mind.

Degrees of compulsoriness of environmental policies

Environmental policies should be chosen from the suite of available options based on their ability to satisfy each of these criteria. Policy options can be categorized in different ways. In this chapter, we describe policies in terms of their degree of compulsoriness — an important consideration, because it addresses the extent to which certain behaviour is required by government, which in turn helps to determine the efficiency, effectiveness and political acceptability of a policy. Policies that are noncompulsory involve government providing information or using moral suasion to encourage behaviour changes, while policies that are compulsory involve government mandating a particular choice or outcome, or using fiscal measures to change the market incentives for businesses and consumers. The following survey of policy options starts with the most compulsory and progresses toward less compulsory policies. Each policy is briefly described, and a discussion follows about how it performs relative to the policy evaluation criteria described in the previous section.

Command-and-control regulations are technology or performance standards enforced through stringent financial or legal penalties. This approach dominated environmental policy in the 1970s, and it is still important, although economists critique the regulations on the grounds of economic efficiency (Hausman and Joskow 1982). In particular, command-and-control regulations can be costly when they require identical equipment choices or management practices by firms or individuals whose costs of compliance differ considerably. Also inefficient are regulations that provide no incentive for companies or individuals to achieve emissions reductions beyond the legal requirement (Newell and Stavins 2003; Millman and Prince 1989). This traditional regulatory approach is therefore not ideal for stimulating large emissions reductions throughout the economy. Regulations that eliminate a subset of equipment choices may be justified where information or search costs are particularly high, and research has found that application of this type of regulation can deliver net benefits to consumers and to society in certain situations (Moxnes 2004). Regulations are often used to address market conditions associated with a lack of information; for example, over 50 countries, including Canada, use appliance efficiency standards that are periodically reviewed to account for new technological developments (Nadel 2002).

Market-oriented regulations impose an aggregate regulatory requirement on the entire economy or on a sector of the economy. Unlike traditional command-and-control regulations, however, this policy approach allows individual participants to choose whether they will take action or whether they will pay others to take action on their behalf. This negotiation is conducted through a permit or certificate market, and it can have an economically efficient outcome if the permit market works smoothly. We can distinguish two general types of market-oriented regulation based on the breadth of the policy and the focus of the regulation: emissions cap and permit trading; and obligation and certificate trading.

Emissions cap and permit trading was first proposed as an environmental policy instrument in the 1960s, and it has recently been used in several countries for control of local air pollutants, GHGs and other contaminants (Stavins 2001). An emissions-trading system sets an aggregate cap on emissions from a sector or multiple sectors of the economy and allocates tradable emission permits to all emitters covered by the program. The total number of permits allocated to emitters is equal to the overall cap on emissions. Permits are allocated by government, via either auction or free distribution to emitters.[2] At the end of each period (usually a year), each emitter must remit permits to the government sufficient to cover all the GHG emissions for which it was responsible. Emitters can trade permits (and, in some designs, they can purchase permits from entities outside the covered sectors), which will result in cost-effective emissions reductions if transaction costs are not prohibitively high and the market functions well.

Emissions cap-and-trade schemes are a form of regulation in that the aggregate emissions cap cannot be exceeded, participation is compulsory and penalties for noncompliance are severe. Unlike traditional command-and-control regulations, however, they allow participants to determine their level of emissions and whether they will buy or sell in the emissions permit market. In theory, emissions trading should result in exactly the same cost as a GHG tax for a given level of emissions reduction. In practice, it guarantees a certain amount of emissions, while costs are uncertain — in contrast to a GHG tax, which guarantees a certain maximum cost, while the level of emissions reduction is uncertain. Like a tax, a GHG emissions-trading system that focuses on carbon dioxide (CO_2) emissions from the fossil fuel industry can be applied upstream, on fossil fuel producers according to the carbon in the fuels they produce, or downstream, on CO_2 emissions at the point of end-use technologies.

An obligation and certificate trading system sets an aggregate obligation for a sector of the economy to produce a minimum amount of some desirable good — for example, a low-GHG technology, like a zero-emission vehicle or a process that captures and stores carbon. Certificates are earned by firms for units of the desirable good that are produced in each period. Certificates are tradable between firms, and the system can be designed to allow certificates to be banked for use in a future period or borrowed from a future period for use in the present; a safety valve can also be integrated to allow unlimited certificate purchases from government at a certain price, thereby ensuring an upper limit for the cost of this policy. At the end of each period, each firm must remit enough certificates to government to meet its obligation. This approach to environmental policy is very similar to an emissions cap-and-trade system, except while the latter regulates a maximum amount of an undesirable product (emissions), the obligation and certificate trading system requires a minimum amount of a desirable product or process.

Examples of obligation and certificate trading include the California vehicle emissions standard, which specifies a minimum aggregate level of zero- and low-emission vehicles in the California vehicle fleet but allows vehicle manufacturers to trade certificates among themselves in meeting the targets. Similarly, renewable portfolio standards for electricity, which exist in Australia, many European countries and about half the states in the US, require a minimum market share for certain forms of renewable energy production and allow trading between electricity generators to achieve the aggregate outcome. While both the emissions cap-and-trade system and obligation and certificate trading should cost-effectively meet their goals because of the flexibility resulting from trading provisions, there are notable differences between the two systems. First, while an emissions cap-and-trade system allocates emission permits to emitters at the beginning of each period in correspondence with the emissions cap, no certificates are allocated to firms in an obligation and certificate trading system — certificates are earned by firms when they produce a unit of the desirable good. Consequently, the obligation and certificate system avoids the politically sensitive issue of permit allocation, which can stall the implementation of an emissions cap-and-trade system. However, it also means that revenue is not generated for government through permit auction, which reduces potential government revenue but may improve political acceptability. Second, while the emissions cap-and-trade system necessarily focuses on emissions, the obligation and certificate system can focus on other targets. If the policy objective is emissions reduction, this may be less efficient, but it may also more effectively address market failures and barriers in particular markets.

GHG taxes require domestic emitters to pay a fixed fee per unit of GHG (measured in CO_2) released into the atmosphere. The emitter's response to the tax is to either pay the fee or reduce emissions to avoid it. In this sense, a GHG tax is not as binding as a regulation because it does not specify a particular action: the business or consumer chooses between taking no action to reduce emissions and reducing emissions. In theory, emitters will reduce emissions up to the point where the marginal abatement cost is equal to the tax. Since every emitter covered by the tax faces a uniform fee per tonne of CO_2, a tax system theoretically results in the lowest cost to the economy for a given level of emissions reduction (Baumol and Oates 1988). An emissions tax, unlike emissions trading, does not guarantee a particular level of emissions because emitters have flexibility to pay the tax or to reduce emissions (Weitzman 1974). As a result, it will likely be necessary to adjust the level of the tax to meet a given emissions target. A key economic advantage of GHG taxes is that they limit costs by allowing overall emissions to rise if abatement costs are higher than expected. GHG taxes can be applied upstream (on producers and importers of fossil fuels and other GHGs) or downstream (on final consumers of fossil fuels that produce emissions). GHG taxes raise government revenue, and government can use that revenue to offset other taxes. Alternatively, it could transfer the revenue to other regions or governments, increase spending or pay the revenue back in a lump sum to emitters. If government uses GHG tax revenue to offset other taxes that distort the economy (for example, income taxes or corporate taxes), the economy could benefit while GHGs are reduced. GHG taxes (and other green tax variations, such as environmentally motivated energy taxes) have been instituted in a number of European countries and are considered to have played a role in, for instance, the development of carbon capture and storage technologies in Norway. In practice, tax design has included refunds of taxes to vulnerable industries, differentials in the tax rates applied to industry and households, and exemptions to address equity and competitiveness concerns. Although most economists consider GHG taxes to be the optimal policy for deep GHG reductions in terms of economic efficiency, the Canadian public has to date been reluctant to consider new taxes (although there has been little opportunity for real public debate on GHG taxes). Even propositions to impose a revenue-neutral GHG tax — using the revenue from the GHG tax to offset other taxes — have been successfully portrayed by opponents as a government attempt to increase the overall tax burden (Svendson, Daugbjerg, and Pederson 2001).

Subsidies such as rebates, grants, low-interest loans and tax credits improve financial returns to businesses and consumers who take specified actions to reduce emissions. While this approach appears noncompulsory, governments generally acquire their funds from various types of compulsory taxes. As a result, while subsidies to low-emission technologies can influence the behaviour of consumers and businesses, governments generally lack the financial resources to induce large changes in GHG emissions through this method alone. Also, it is difficult to design subsidy programs to exclude free riders — participants who qualify for the subsidy even though they would have undertaken the action anyway. When free-rider effects are calculated, some subsidy programs prove to be much less effective, and thus much more expensive, than anticipated (Loughran and Kulick 2004). Finally, subsidies do nothing to discourage the development and dissemination of new technologies and products that emit GHGs, so this approach cannot be successful by itself.

Voluntary programs based on labelling and other forms of information provision, moral suasion and voluntary agreement allow individual companies and consumers to determine their own level of effort in the area of environmental protection, and they cast government in the role of information provider, facilitator, role model and award giver. Voluntary programs for GHG reduction and energy efficiency have formed a major part of past policy efforts, with programs directed at public outreach, industry energy efficiency and information provision to consumers and businesses. However, while the use of voluntary programs has been widespread, and while participating industry offers much anecdotal evidence of voluntary actions to improve the environment, it is difficult to estimate the aggregate effect of such programs (IPCC 2007; Harrison 1999). Recent empirical reviews of voluntary programs suggest that both their environmental effectiveness and their economic efficiency are poor (Organisation for Economic Co-operation and Development [OECD] 2003).

Using the criteria to choose policies from the menu

Each of these policies performs differently in relation to the criteria listed earlier. While no policy performs perfectly against all criteria, some do better against the suite of criteria than others. In developing GHG policy for Canada, it is important to choose policies that do not fare badly against any single evaluation criterion. In this vein, voluntary policies in general do not satisfy the environmental effectiveness criterion. Significant research has been conducted to determine the cost of deep GHG reductions, both in Canada and internationally (Energy Information Administration 1998; M.K. Jaccard and Associates 2003). Most peer-reviewed models predict long-run marginal costs of at least C$100 per tonne of CO_2 for deep emissions reductions. The cost is substantial, and so it is extremely unlikely that businesses and consumers will voluntarily reduce emissions on a large scale, even with government-provided information, education or moral suasion (Jaccard and Bataille 2003).

Even for small GHG reductions, we conclude — based on international and Canadian experience — that voluntary policy is relatively ineffective. For example, the Voluntary Challenge and Registry used in Canada in the 1990s to encourage businesses to reduce GHG emissions has been criticized for being ineffective (Bramley 2002; Takahashi et al. 2001). In Europe, the EU negotiated a modest voluntary agreement with automobile manufacturers, but these manufacturers are now falling short of their commitment (OECD 2005).

Like voluntary policies, subsidies are inappropriate for achieving deep GHG reductions. First, it is impossible to exclude free riders from a subsidy program, and they often represent more than 60 percent of total subsidy recipients (Loughran and Kulick 2004). Cost-effectiveness is further compromised by the rebound effect. By making a service cheaper, subsidies encourage increased consumption, which can off-set some of the energy-efficiency gains (Greening, Greene and Difiglio 2000). Subsidies to energy efficient or low-emission technologies also fail to curtail the development of new technologies, products and services that produce GHG emissions. New products and services are appearing at an accelerating rate. Finally, a subsidy approach generally places government in the position of having to choose specific technologies to support, and most analysis suggests that government has a poor track record in this.

Canada's GHG policy approach has thus far been dominated by voluntarism and subsidies — an approach that, while politically attractive, has been largely ineffective at stemming fossil fuel exploitation and the consumption of fossil fuel products (natural gas, gasoline, diesel, jet fuel, heating oil) that emit GHGs. Figure 1 matches the evolution of Canada's emissions since 1990 with the voluntary and subsidy policy initiatives launched by a succession of Canadian governments, including the most recent ecoENERGY initiative of the Harper government. Independent research suggests that past policies had little or no effect; the figure clearly shows that they did not lead to declining emissions. The figure also shows the emission levels that Canadian governments were trying to achieve with their policies. An important lesson is that government statements about emissions targets are not credible if they are not accompanied by policies that have a high probability of being effective in reducing emissions — namely, policies that include substantial financial penalties or regulatory constraints on emissions.

In order to assess the likely effect on emissions of a continued reliance on the voluntary approach, we used the CIMS energy-economy model to simulate rising subsidy levels for GHG emissions reduction actions across the Canadian economy. This model uses empirical estimates of how firms and households respond to the financial costs, risks and qualitative attributes of technology options for energy services. Subsidies reduce financial costs of low-emission technologies, which should reduce emissions. But, as noted, there are important countervailing effects. First, a large proportion of the subsidies is captured by free riders. Second, efficient technologies have lower operating costs, which can cause some increase (rebound) in the demand for certain energy services and, more generally, a

FIGURE 1. ACTUAL AND PROJECTED GREENHOUSE GAS EMISSIONS, CANADIAN POLICIES AND INTERNATIONAL TARGETS

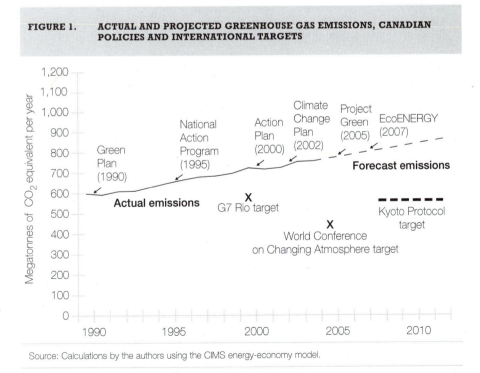

Source: Calculations by the authors using the CIMS energy-economy model.

long-term development of energy-using devices whose proliferation is in part stimulated by the gains in energy productivity from the subsidy programs.

The parameters in the CIMS model are based on 25 years of empirical research into government and energy utility subsidy programs in North America. Figure 2 provides the simulation of ever-higher subsidy levels on GHG emissions in the Canadian economy over the 45-year period 2005 to 2050. The simulation shows that even with a massive annual expenditure of $21.2 billion (1995 Canadian dollars), Canadian emissions are unlikely to fall below their 1990 levels by 2050. Even this level of reduction might not be achieved, since the simulation does not include a full estimate of the development and penetration of new energy-using and GHG-emitting technologies and services — like backyard patio heaters and roof de-icers. Yet this is a likely development in the absence of emissions caps, GHG taxes or regulatory prohibition of these technologies, especially as subsidy programs improve the rate of energy productivity innovations.

In designing our set of three key policies to meet the terms of this policy exercise for the Institute for Research on Public Policy, we therefore exclude voluntary and subsidy policies because they are largely ineffective.[3] We also rely only to a minor extent on traditional command-and-control regulations, as these would prove administratively

FIGURE 2. PROJECTED IMPACT OF SUBSIDIES ON CANADA'S GREENHOUSE GAS EMISSIONS, 1990-2050[1]

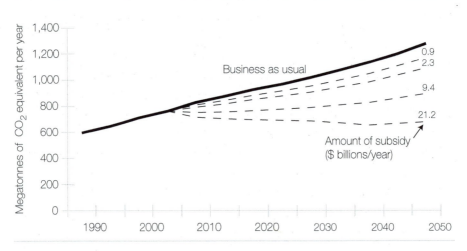

Source: Calculations by the authors using the CIMS energy-economy model.
[1] The broken lines show projected GHG emissions corresponding to different levels of government subsidy for emissions reductions. Monetary values are presented in 1995 Canadian dollars and costs are discounted using a social discount rate of 7 percent.

infeasible and economically inefficient when applied to a myriad of technologies across the economy. By imposing particular technologies and processes on all firms and consumers despite significant differences in their costs of abatement and preferences, government imposes disproportionately high costs on some. This can significantly reduce the political acceptability and increase the cost of command-and-control regulations. In addition, specifying regulatory standards for thousands of products throughout the economy is an enormous administrative task. Finally, command-and-control regulations provide little incentive for firms to develop innovative new technologies with dramatically lower GHG emissions, which will be critical in the future.

Although traditional command-and-control regulations are not appropriate to serve as the dominant policy approach for dramatic GHG reductions throughout the economy, some of these regulations can be cost-effective, administratively feasible and politically acceptable when they are used to consolidate gains achieved through other policies (Moxnes 2004). As a result, they play only a minor role in the policy package we describe here.

The policy approaches that perform best in terms of effectiveness and economic efficiency are ones that prohibit or financially penalize technologies and activities that emit GHGs. In other words, the only hope for substantially reducing GHG emissions in a market economy is to ensure that the atmosphere can no longer be treated as a free waste receptacle. The atmosphere must be valued. The policy options of interest, therefore, are either GHG taxes or market-oriented regulations on emissions, technologies and processes that force reductions in GHG-emitting activity.

There are many design options for these policy approaches. A GHG or carbon tax could be applied at the point of emission. GHG emissions from both large and dispersed sources can be accurately estimated based on the amount of fossil fuel consumed, since there is a direct chemical relationship between the amount and type of fuel and the GHG emissions released when it is burned. Instead of the carbon tax, an emissions cap and tradable permit system could be applied to large industries and energy supply facilities like oil refineries, thermal electricity generating stations and natural gas processing plants. This, in effect, is the "large final emitters" policy that Canada's previous, Liberal government tried to negotiate for almost 10 years and that the Conservative government resurrected in 2007 and presented as proposed new emission regulations for industry. Since large final emitters are responsible for about 50 percent of Canadian GHG emissions, the application of a cap-and-trade policy for these industries would raise the question of how to send the equivalent financial or regulatory signal to smaller emitters in light industry, the commercial sector, the residential sector and the transportation sector. One option is a GHG tax for smaller emission sources. Again, it would be fairly easy to link a tax to the carbon content in fuels used in smaller devices. And, possibly, the cap-and-trade system might be extended to all energy-related carbon emissions and perhaps even to other nonenergy GHG emissions. Yet another way to apply the cap-and-trade approach is to place a cap on the carbon content in fuels used and produced by the fossil fuel industry. This is referred to as "upstream cap and trade," since the regulatory constraint is applied to the upstream components of the fossil fuel industry. The advantage of this approach is that the costs of constraining carbon flows are passed down through the economy, so that the cap-and-trade system simultaneously affects large final emitters and all smaller emitters. This means, however, that the price of fossil fuel products would rise, just as they would with the carbon tax, and this would pose a political acceptability challenge.

Although these policies could cover all energy-related GHG emissions in Canada, there is evidence that the political acceptability (and perhaps even the economic efficiency) of such a profound, long-term technological transformation would increase if these economy-wide policies were complemented with sector-specific, market-oriented regulations to support the development of key technologies, energy forms and processes that need to be commercially available as businesses and consumers confront the rising costs of GHG emissions. There is also evidence that even some well-designed command-and-control regulations would improve consumer welfare in some circumstances.

Finally, another objective in policy design is to ensure that the policy does not force the premature retirement of existing infrastructure, buildings and equipment, as this would expose firms and individuals to substantial costs (Jaccard and Rivers 2007). To minimize these costs, policies should be designed to send long-run signals that will stimulate low-GHG innovations and technology adoption without significantly changing the operating costs of buildings and equipment, which, in any case, are likely to be renewed over the coming decades.

OUR POLICY PROPOSALS AND SIMULATIONS OF THEIR IMPACT

While other policy packages could certainly also be effective, we believe that the package we present here best satisfies the criteria we outlined earlier. It involves only three key policies: a carbon management standard that is very similar to the upstream cap-and-trade approach, a vehicle emissions standard and a limited application of appliance and building regulations. We will describe each in some detail and provide simulation of its impact on emissions.

A carbon management standard for fossil fuel producers and importers

The central policy requirement is an economy-wide instrument that imposes on GHG emissions a financial charge (a tax) or a regulatory constraint (a market-oriented regulation). While the options for this have their pros and cons, our position is that it is more important to emphasize the need for at least one of these options than to argue excessively about the relative superiority of one or the other. Canadian policy-makers do not appear to have learned this lesson, in spite of all the evidence of past policy failures. The recent Liberal federal government, the current Liberal opposition and the current Conservative federal government support the imposition of some form of emissions cap-and-trade regulation on large industrial and electricity generation sources, but none of them has considered deploying effective and efficient market-based mechanisms like GHG taxes or cap-and-trade regulation against the remaining 50 percent of emissions in the economy (the proportion not created by the large final emitters). And the cap-and-trade policies have numerous loopholes that allow industries to do something other than reduce emissions.

We believe that a GHG tax is the best policy to promote environmental effectiveness and economic efficiency, so this is our default policy recommendation. However, North American economists have been suggesting GHG taxes for 15 years with absolutely no success — emissions keep rising. If a carbon tax is simply unacceptable for political reasons, then some form of market-oriented regulation should be designed that approximates the environmental and economic effects of a GHG tax. Therefore, this is what we focus on in our proposal.

While major effort has been expended trying to establish a large final emitters cap-and-trade system over the last eight years, an effective market-oriented GHG regulation has yet to be implemented in Canada. In April 2007, the Conservatives proposed yet another version of the large final emitters regulation, but this latest incarnation contains several so-called flexibility mechanisms that allow industries to do something other than reduce their emissions. The policy gives emitters the opportunity to pay into a technology fund (which may or may not succeed in lowering the cost of future emissions reductions); it also subsidizes the efforts of unregulated emitters to reduce their emissions (an offsets program) and subsidizes emissions reductions in other countries using the flexibility mechanisms of the Kyoto Protocol. It is our assessment that the flexibility mechanisms in the initial Liberal version and the subsequent Conservative version of the large final emitters policy will severely limit the emissions reduction that occurs in Canada. Industry will look to emissions reduction actions elsewhere in the economy if these prove to be the cheaper option. However, while these actions may appear cheaper, given that they rely on subsidies (from large final emitters to smaller firms and individuals), they are still subject to the same ineffectiveness challenges that we have already described in relation to subsidy programs.

For these and other reasons, our key policy proposal is a variant of the upstream emissions cap-and-trade policy — with a wrinkle. Our policy borrows from the philosophy of other obligation and certificate trading programs, such as the vehicle emission standard and the renewable portfolio standard. We call this policy a carbon management standard.

Our carbon management standard is a form of market-oriented regulation that would require fossil fuel producers and importers to ensure that a growing fraction of the carbon they extract from the earth's crust does not reach the atmosphere.[4] This obligation would increase over time according to a preset schedule designed to allow the economy enough time to adopt the technologies required to achieve the standard. It would apply to fossil fuel producers and importers, and it would likely be based on measures and estimates from oil, gas and coal extraction activities; it would also apply directly to importers when their fossil-fuel-based product entered Canada.[5] (Fossil fuel exporters could receive partial exemptions from the obligation for exported carbon in order to limit the impact on their international competitiveness.)

The carbon management standard is different from an upstream cap-and-trade system in that it sets an obligation for a growing share of processed carbon to be captured and safely stored; a conventional cap-and-trade system for fossil fuel producers sets a cap on the overall amount of carbon-based fuels producers can sell. Rather than allocating permits to emitters in accordance with the cap, government would collect certificates from firms, and these would have to match the firms' aggregate obligations. At the end of every year, each producer and importer of fossil fuels would be required to remit certificates to the government in accordance with its overall obligation to ensure that a percentage of the carbon it has extracted from the earth is permanently stored. Substantial financial penalties would be levied on firms that failed to comply with the system. Firms participating in the system would be able to trade certificates in an established market. For increased efficiency, the system would allow firms to bank certificates acquired in one period for use in a future period and claim certificates from a future period for use in the present.[6]

By using this obligation and certificate approach rather than the conventional cap and permit approach, government would avoid politically and economically complex negotiations over initial permit allocation. Unlike a carbon tax, the policy would generate no revenue for government, and this would increase its political acceptability. But, like the upstream cap-and-trade system, the policy would cover all carbon flows in the economy. There are no loopholes that would allow regulated entities to subsidize unregulated entities; all carbon emissions in the economy would be covered by the policy.

Table 1 presents the carbon management standard in terms of the percentage of carbon that must be prevented from entering the atmosphere. Expressed in percentages, the carbon management standard functions, in one sense, as an intensity target. Rapid growth of the fossil fuel industry could offset in whole or in part the fact that a growing percentage of the carbon it processes is captured and stored. Only when the standard approaches 100 percent would its effect be closer to that of an absolute cap.

Using the figures in table 1 as an example, consider a coal-mining company that extracts 1,000 tonnes of coal per year. In each year of the period 2011-15, it must remit certificates to the government to indicate that 6 percent of the carbon in the coal it produces will never reach the atmosphere. (If the coal were pure carbon, the certificates would be for 60 tonnes of carbon.) The company could get these certificates by capturing some or all of the carbon as a solid or as CO_2 gas. More likely, it would purchase certificates from a coal-fired electricity plant, which would use coal for thermal purposes, or perhaps, in the future, from a coal-to-hydrogen gasification plant. These latter industrial activities tend to create lower costs for capturing carbon in solid or gaseous form and then permanently storing it. In any case, if the costs of capturing carbon are high relative to energy efficiency and fuel-switching alternatives (to nuclear or renewables), then the coal-mining industry will gradually lose market share over the coming decades. Society will gradually determine that shifting away from fossil fuels is cheaper than using fossil fuels without emissions, but the outcome will vary according to the resource endowments of each particular region.

The carbon management standard would cover all carbon contained in fossil fuels, and it could also directly cover emissions of HFC (hydrofluorocarbon), SF_6 (sulphur hexafluoride) and PFC (perfluorocarbon) on the basis of their equivalent global-

| TABLE 1. | PERCENTAGE OF CARBON THAT MUST BE PREVENTED FROM ENTERING THE ATMOSPHERE UNDER THE CARBON MANAGEMENT STANDARD, 2010-50 |

2010	2011-15	2016-20	2021-25	2026-30	2031-35	2036-40	2041-45	2046-50
0	6	11	17	25	34	43	52	56

warming potential (the values presented in table 1 would change if these gases were included). The system could also allow noncovered sources to sell project-based certificates to firms directly covered by the carbon management standard. Potential projects would include carbon capture and storage projects throughout the economy, as well as projects to reduce fugitive emissions from oil and gas wells and to reduce methane emissions from the coal-mining and agricultural sectors. Projects would need to be certified through government or third-party audits, and certificates could be

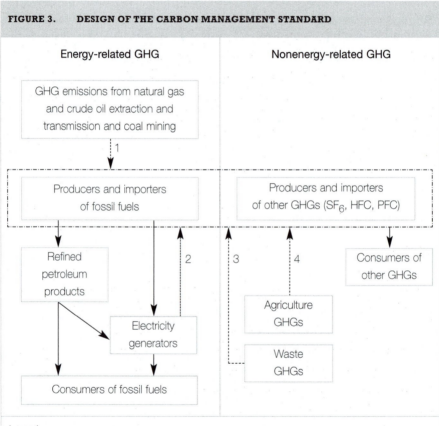

FIGURE 3.   DESIGN OF THE CARBON MANAGEMENT STANDARD

Energy-related GHG   Nonenergy-related GHG

GHG emissions from natural gas and crude oil extraction and transmission and coal mining

Producers and importers of fossil fuels

Producers and importers of other GHGs (SF$_6$, HFC, PFC)

Refined petroleum products

Electricity generators

Consumers of fossil fuels

Agriculture GHGs

Waste GHGs

Consumers of other GHGs

Legend

⌐:⌐:⌐⌐ Sectors covered by carbon management standard
-------▶ Project-based emissions reduction certificates
———▶ Flows of energy/products
⁞⁞⁞⁞⁞⁞⁞⁞ Separation between energy-related and nonenergy-related systems with trade in certificates between systems

Sample project-based certificates
1 Fugitive emissions management (e.g., capture, flaring, leak detection and repair)
2 Carbon capture and storage
3 Landfill gas capture and flaring or generation
4 Low-tillage agriculture

marketed through a central emissions exchange. Figure 3 shows the basic design features of the carbon management standard.

Careful design of the carbon management standard, including incorporation of a safety valve, monitoring, and certificate banking and borrowing, is critical if the policy is to function effectively and efficiently.[7] We do not address these issues in detail, but significant experience with design issues for economy-wide market-oriented regulations is available to draw upon through, among many other sources, the Emissions Trading Scheme of the European Union, the sulphur dioxide (SO_2) trading provisions under the US *Clean Air Act*, the California RECLAIM program for nitrogen oxides and SO_2 emissions, and the phase-out of lead from gasoline. In addition, there is a large theoretical and applied treatment of emissions-trading programs in the economics literature. As discussed earlier, the carbon management standard and emissions cap-and-trade systems applied to fossil fuel producers have many similarities.

A zero-emission vehicle standard for vehicle manufacturers

A vehicle emission standard (VES) is an obligation and certificate trading system that requires vehicle manufacturers and importers to sell a minimum number of zero-emission vehicles by a target date as a percentage of total vehicle sales. This market share percentage grows over time, thus creating and expanding an artificial niche market for low- or zero-emission vehicles. The goal is to reach a critical threshold at which the cost of producing the vehicles falls significantly and consumer acceptance becomes widespread. A VES, therefore, accelerates the process of developing, commercializing and disseminating low-emission vehicles, while letting industry pick technologies to meet the emissions criteria that are in accord with customer preferences. A per-vehicle penalty is charged to manufacturers who do not sell the required number of zero-emission vehicles, but manufacturers can trade among themselves to meet the overall target. A VES is therefore designed to give manufacturers significant flexibility in meeting the aggregate market outcome while bringing down the cost of innovative low-emission vehicles.

The development of zero-emission vehicles is critical for generating deep GHG reductions over a long period. Incremental price signals, as generated by the carbon management standard, are unlikely to quickly stimulate demand for zero-emission vehicles. The VES policy is designed to create a market for zero-emission secondary sources of energy in the transportation sector — namely, electricity and hydrogen, as well as biofuels like ethanol, methanol and biodiesel. The VES ensures that vehicles with engine platforms that use these sources of energy become available to consumers, as a policy like the carbon management standard gradually increases the cost of using fossil-fuel-based energy sources, like gasoline and diesel, to power vehicles.

California has had a VES in place since 1990 — the Zero-Emission Vehicle (ZEV) program. As part of the state's larger Low-Emission Vehicle (LEV and LEV II) programs to reduce smog-causing emissions, the ZEV program has aimed to commercialize vehicles with zero exhaust emissions under all operating conditions (a vehicle with zero local air emissions would also have zero GHG emissions at the point of end use). Although the California program has been amended several times and has faced legal challenges from vehicle manufacturers, the ZEV requirements still exist. In fact, they have been increased: by 2018, zero-emission vehicles must account for 16 percent of new vehicle sales (California Air Resources Board 2003, sec. 1962, title 13). Because a VES is already in place in California, and in a number of northeastern US states that automatically adopt California's regulations, the introduction of a Canadian VES should not cause competitiveness problems with the US. California, New York, Massachusetts and Vermont alone represented 18 percent of the US auto market in 2000, and vehicle manufacturers are already required to produce low- and zero-emission vehicles to meet the VES in those states (Larrue 2003).

Based on our simulations with the CIMS model, we present a schedule for specific requirements under the VES in table 2. For the policy simulated here, an aggregate target was set for vehicle manufacturers; in practice, government may distinguish between classes of vehicles (for example, cars and light trucks) in setting the standard. The VES could also be designed to allow manufacturers of low-emission vehicles to qualify for partial ZEV credits. This is done in California, where exceedances of the Ultra-Low-Emission Vehicle (ULEV) requirements are granted partial VES credit. The VES we design and model in this chapter applies only to passenger transportation, because experience exists with passenger transport VES in the US; in a comprehensive policy approach, the standard should also be applied to freight transportation, especially since zero-emission freight transportation vehicles may be more easily achieved in the medium term (Keith and Farrell 2003).

TABLE 2.   SALES OF ZERO-EMISSION VEHICLES AS PERCENTAGE OF NEW VEHICLE
            SALES UNDER THE ZERO-EMISSION VEHICLE STANDARD, 2010-50

2010	2015	2020	2025	2030	2035	2040	2045	2050
0	1	5	10	20	35	50	65	80

Residential and commercial building codes and appliance and equipment standards

The application of the carbon management standard will result in relative price increases for carbon-intensive energy forms, which in turn will motivate more efficient buildings and equipment, as well as a switch to cleaner fuels for end uses in the residential and commercial sectors. However, the existence of an incentive split in residential and commercial rental and leasing (a split between those who would pay the investment costs of efficiency improvements and those who would receive the operating cost benefits via lower energy bills), as well as incomplete information on consumer decision-making, provides the rationale for a more targeted approach to improving energy efficiency and reducing emissions.

The most cost-effective way to lower GHG emissions in the building stock (through energy efficiency and fuel choice) is by means of design and construction, which strongly influence energy use in space heating, lighting, cooling, ventilation and water heating during the life of a building. Currently, Canadian provinces have a diversity of energy-related requirements in their building codes, but some of these are quite lax.

In our policy proposal, new buildings are required to meet strengthened performance standards, in terms of either energy efficiency or GHG emissions (table 3). Both could be related to other "green" building requirements.[8] Standards would either eliminate the least energy-efficient (or GHG-intense) new buildings or encourage a shift across the entire market. Flexibility mechanisms could also be used to set average sales standards for developers or to specify shares of sales that must meet a desired performance level, with trading between developers permitted to meet the requirement.

TABLE 3. REDUCTION IN ENERGY USE REQUIRED BY STRENGTHENED RESIDENTIAL AND COMMERCIAL BUILDING CODES

Building type	Energy reduction by 2050 relative to current building practices (percent)
Residential buildings	
Apartments and attached buildings	40
Single-family detached buildings	35
Commercial and institutional buildings	55

The federal government stipulates minimum energy performance standards under the *Energy Efficiency Act* for more than 30 products. Because standards restrict consumer choices, an important consideration in policy development is whether given standards lower consumer utility. However, if research indicates that consumers would make different decisions if they had additional information, there can be a social benefit to eliminating the least energy-efficient products (Moxnes 2004).

Canada has relatively strong efficiency standards for some equipment — for instance, cooking appliances, commercial cooling equipment, refrigerators and freezers. However, we see from the examples of the European Union and Australia that there is substantial opportunity to achieve stronger standards in washing machines, dishwashers and commercial lighting while still achieving political acceptance. No mandatory standards have been introduced in relation to domestic electronic equipment and lighting. Energy consumption related to the former has grown considerably in Canada (and other countries), and there is some momentum internationally to develop limits for standby power use in small appliances. Table 4 shows the representative appliance and equipment efficiency standards that we propose for adoption over the coming decades. The standards as presented will not drive

TABLE 4.   MINIMUM EFFICIENCY REQUIRED UNDER ENHANCED EQUIPMENT AND APPLIANCE STANDARDS

Equipment and appliances	Minimum efficiency by 2050
Furnaces (annual fuel utilization efficiency)	92
Gas water heaters (energy factor)	0.86
Water fixtures	Low flow
Air-conditioning systems	
Central (seasonal energy efficiency rating)	15.5
Room (energy efficiency rating)	10.8
Clothes washers (modified energy factor)	46
Freezers (efficiency improvement)	
Upright	10%
Chest	50%
Minor appliances	1 kW standby loss
Lighting (overall luminous efficiency)[1]	6%

[1] "Luminous efficiency" refers to the percentage of lighting flux in total power (incandescent lighting is typically about 2 to 3 percent; compact fluorescent lamps, 7 to 9 percent; and prototype LEDs, 25 percent).

technological changes, since regulations are inefficient in that role, but they will follow and consolidate changes pushed by market conditions.

We used the CIMS energy-economy model to quantitatively estimate the effects of the policy package because it integrates three key dynamics: it makes technologies compete to provide end-use services based on realistic consumer and company decision-making; it integrates the energy demand and supply sides of the economy; and it estimates changes in the demand for final goods and services based on changes in energy prices and production costs (Bataille et al. 2007; Nyboer 1997). CIMS also allows modelling of sector- and technology-specific policies, unlike more aggregated models.

In a business-as-usual simulation, CIMS projects that energy-related GHG emissions will rise from over 700 million tonnes in 2010 to almost 1,200 tonnes in 2050 — an increase of 65 percent (see table 5).[9] Much of the increase comes from the oil and gas industry and is especially due to surging exports of crude oil from the oil sands. The transportation sector is also expected to grow significantly by 2050, primarily as a result of increased population and demand for mobility.

Table 5 also shows projected emissions in Canada in 2050 based on the implementation of our policy package. A few sectors make major contributions to the 60

TABLE 5. **ENERGY-RELATED GREENHOUSE GAS EMISSIONS, BY SECTOR, BUSINESS AS USUAL AND POLICY SIMULATION, 2010 AND 2050 (MEGATONNES OF CO_2 EQUIVALENT)[1]**

Sector	Business as usual		Policy simulation
	2010	2050	2050
Electricity generation	127	178	23
Oil and gas production	176	325	117
Energy-intensive industry	112	194	59
Non-energy-intensive industry	23	66	22
Residential	41	19	7
Transportation	193	272	95
Services	42	102	33
Total	713	1,157	357

Source: Calculations by the authors using the CIMS energy-economy model.
[1] Only energy-related GHG emissions are included; total GHG emissions are about 20 to 25 percent higher.

percent reduction in GHG emissions from 2010 levels. The electricity sector is highly responsive to GHG policy over the long term; CIMS projects an emissions reduction of almost 90 percent from 2010 levels. This conclusion is similar to those of other analyses, and it reflects the relatively low-cost opportunities for dramatic GHG reductions in the electricity sector. Oil and gas production is also quite responsive to aggressive GHG policy over the long term; emissions fall by about two-thirds compared with business as usual. Other sectors reduce emissions to a relatively lesser degree, because the cost of doing so for them is somewhat higher.

Figure 4 presents the results, in the form of wedges, of emissions reduction actions that would occur under the policies but not under business as usual. There are many actions, but they can be assembled into three main categories and a catch-all category. GHG emissions will fall for these reasons only: using less energy (efficiency and conservation) where fossil fuel use is substantial (as it is in most locations); switching from fossil fuels to renewables and nuclear power; and preventing emissions from the use of fossil fuels by implementing carbon capture and storage. The fourth action

FIGURE 4. PROJECTED CANADIAN GREENHOUSE GAS EMISSIONS UNDER THE BUSINESS-AS-USUAL AND THE PROPOSED EMISSIONS REDUCTION POLICIES, 2005-50

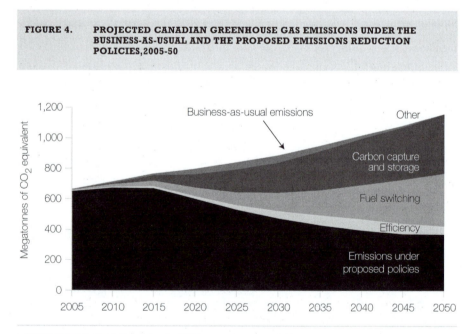

Source: Calculation by authors using the CIMS energy-economy model.
Note: The upper line shows projected business-as-usual GHG emissions (in the absence of policies specifically designed to control them). The bottom line shows projected GHG emissions with application of the proposed carbon management standard, the vehicle emission standard and the appliance and equipment standards. The wedges between the two lines show the emissions reductions that would occur as a result of actions under the policy proposals. Only energy-related emissions are shown.

category includes things like methane capture and use from landfills. Because the modelling conducted for this chapter covers only energy-related GHG emissions, actions related to afforestation and waste management are not included in the figure.

It may seem surprising that the contribution of energy efficiency is small compared with those of fuel switching and carbon capture and storage. There are two reasons. First, when risk and consumer preferences are accounted for, energy efficiency can be more expensive than its advocates suggest, so its contribution is diminished in comparison with the other main options. Second, the figure shows net energy efficiency. Expanded use of oil sands and coal, on the one hand, and the extra energy needed for carbon capture and storage, on the other, will tend to increase energy use in the economy. The net effect is that much of the improvement in end-use energy efficiency is offset by declining energy efficiency in the energy supply industry.

Implementation of our three major GHG reduction policies would impose costs on the Canadian economy. Cost increases would be highest by far in the industrial minerals sector, whose significant process-related GHG emissions are hard to reduce. The pulp and paper sector and the chemicals sector, both of which are energy-intensive, would also face increases in the cost of production. Other industrial sectors would face fairly minor cost increases.

The ability of firms to pass these cost increases on to consumers would depend heavily on how exposed the sector is to international competition and whether other countries impose policies to curtail GHG emissions on a scale similar to that of the policies proposed here. In a sector that faces large cost increases because emissions controls are expensive or impractical and that is exposed to competition from other countries (for example, the industrial minerals sector), leakage of firms to other countries would be likely if Canada's GHG policy were much more aggressive than those of other countries and offered the sector no partial exemptions. If, however, Canada's trading partners impose GHG policies of similar stringency, costs would likely be passed through to final consumers, and leakage of industrial activity to other countries would likely be minimal.

The economic impacts are also not distributed evenly by region. Although this is certainly not a prerequisite for cost-effective emissions reduction, the federal government has made it a priority throughout the process of developing climate change policy that no region should bear a disproportionate share of the cost of reducing emissions. To satisfy this self-imposed requirement, the federal government would have to design compensatory mechanisms to at least partially share nationally the cost burden of GHG emissions reduction.

CONCLUSIONS

Climate change policy in Canada to date has failed because it has relied primarily on voluntary and subsidy policies, which, although politically acceptable, are ineffective in producing substantial emissions reductions (Jaccard, Rivers, and Horne 2004). In the absence of a dramatic shift in approach, it is very likely that GHG emissions in Canada will continue to increase quickly, especially as a result of the combined effect of population growth, economic growth and growth in production of crude oil from Alberta's oil sands (Rivers and Jaccard forthcoming).

This chapter outlines three policies that could reverse the trend of increasing GHG emissions in Canada. The main policy proposed is an economy-wide market-oriented regulation, which we call a carbon management standard. It sets an obligation for the fossil fuel industry to prevent a growing percentage of the carbon it processes from reaching the atmosphere, eventually leading to intensified production of zero-emission forms of energy, such as electricity and hydrogen. This policy is supplemented with a zero-emission vehicle standard, which requires vehicle manufacturers to produce a minimum number of zero-emission vehicles to account for a percentage of total sales; the policy will eventually be applied to other forms of transportation as well. The carbon management standard is also supplemented with building and equipment standards, which require improvements in energy efficiency and emissions reductions in buildings throughout the economy.

We estimate that implementation of these three policies over a 45-year time frame would reduce energy-related GHG emissions to roughly 60 percent below current levels by 2050, a rate of reduction that may be required of industrialized countries such as Canada if humanity is to avoid dangerous anthropogenic interference with the climate system. Along with substantial GHG reductions, these policies are certain to have economic impacts; they will result in higher energy services costs to households and firms, and some loss of industrial output if Canadian firms are hit harder than their international competitors. But careful policy design can reduce these impacts significantly.

One of the key attributes of the policy package is that it explicitly targets the penetration of zero-emission technologies through the creation of artificial niche markets for these technologies (for example, zero-emission vehicles and zero-emission fossil fuels) rather than just seeking incremental improvement in current practices. As a result, industry and consumers gain experience with these revolutionary technologies while avoiding large cost increases in the near term. This experience is expected to drive down costs in the longer term, easing the pursuit of the dual goals of economic growth and environmental protection.

NOTES

1   Changing agricultural, forestry and land-use practices could also help to reduce emissions, but we do not address these here.

2   Economists who study emissions-trading systems generally favour distribution of at least some of the permits by auction as opposed to 100 percent free allocation, since an auction system reduces windfall profits to particular firms, barriers to entry and opportunities for gaming (Grubb and Neuhoff 2006).

3   Subsidies could be used, to a limited extent, as a complementary measure to help fund key public infrastructure, for building retrofits (particularly for low-income households) and possibly for research and development. Because of the scope of this chapter, we do not provide a discussion of these policies, which are less important to GHG emissions than the ones we do cover.

4   Other GHGs could also be covered by the carbon management standard — including HFCs (hydrofluorocarbons), PFCs (perfluorocarbons) and SF_6 (sulphur hexafluoride) — by using a project-based approach: projects proving emissions reductions would be given government-allocated certificates that could be sold in the certificate market. In total, 80 to 90 percent of Canadian GHG emissions would be covered by the carbon management standard, depending on how effectively fugitive emissions from the upstream oil and gas sector and other key sectors were addressed.

5   Applying the carbon management standard at bulk collection and shipment points would be less economically desirable than applying it at the wellhead, since a significant and rising amount of fugitive emissions (about 70 tonnes in 2004) is released at wellhead and would be outside the scope of the system. However, because of the large number of oil and gas wells in Canada (over 100,000 and counting) and because of the difficulty in measuring fugitive emissions, it would be administratively more feasible to apply the system at bulk collection and transshipment points. Firms undertaking verified emissions reduction upstream from the carbon management standard certificate requirement points could be given certificates that they could sell to firms directly regulated by the carbon management standard. For a discussion of the point of application of an upstream system in Canada, see National Roundtable on the Environment and Economy (1999).

6   The borrowing of permits or certificates is contentious, and a credible institutional arrangement is required to ensure that future permit or certificate deficits are not forgiven by the regulator. However, certificate borrowing is likely to significantly lower compliance costs (Richels and Edmonds 1995).

7   The safety valve is a guarantee by government to sell an unlimited number of permits or certificates at a predetermined price and to ensure that market prices for permits or certificates never exceed that price. It can be used in a cap-and-trade system or an obligation and certificate system to limit the exposure of sectors affected by the policy to very high abatement costs.

8   In this regard, interest has grown in the LEED (Leadership in Energy and Environmental Design) rating system, which ranks a building's environmental performance in different categories and awards points for achieving specific goals.

9   This chapter considers only energy-related emissions, thereby excluding emissions associated with agriculture, various kinds of urban and industrial waste, and certain chemicals. Energy-related emissions represent just over 80 percent of total Canadian emissions.

REFERENCES

Bataille, C., N. Rivers, P. Mau, C. Joseph, and J. Tu. 2007. "How Malleable Are the Greenhouse Gas Emission Intensities of the G7 Nations?" *Energy Journal* 28 (1): 145-69.

Baumol, W., and W. Oates. 1988. *The Theory of Environmental Policy*. 2nd ed. New York: Cambridge University Press.

Bell, W., J. Van Ham, J. Parry, J. Drexhage, and P. Dickey. 2005. *Canada in a Post-2012 World: A Qualitative Assessment of Domestic and International Perspectives*. Winnipeg: International Institute for Sustainable Development. Accessed June 12, 2007. www.iisd.org/pdf/2005/climate_can_post_2012.pdf

Bramley, M. 2002. *The Case for Kyoto: The Failure of Voluntary Corporate Action*. Drayton Valley, AB: Pembina Institute.

California Air Resources Board (CARB). 2003. "California Exhaust Emission Standards and Test Procedures for 2005 and Subsequent Model Zero-Emission Vehicles, and 2001 and Subsequent Model Hybrid Electric Vehicles, in the Passenger Car, Light-Duty Truck, and Medium-Duty Vehicle Classes." *California Code of Regulations* sec. 1962, title 13.

Department of Finance Canada. 2005. *The Budget Plan 2005: Supplementary Information and Notices of Ways and Means Motions Included. Annex 4: A Framework for Evaluation of Environmental Tax Proposals*. Ottawa: Department of Finance Canada.

Energy Information Administration (EIA). 1998. *Impacts of the Kyoto Protocol on the US Energy Markets and Economic Activity*, October. Washington, DC: EIA, Office of Integrated Analysis and Forecasting, US Department of Energy.

Environment Canada. 2006. *Canada's Greenhouse Gas Inventory, 1990-2004*. Ottawa: Environment Canada.

Greening, L., D. Greene, and C. Difiglio. 2000. "Energy Efficiency and Consumption: The Rebound Effect. A Survey." *Energy Policy* 28:389-401.

Grubb, M., and K. Neuhoff. 2006. "Allocation and Competitiveness in the EU Emissions Trading Scheme: Policy Overview." *Climate Policy* 6:7-30.

Harrison, K. 1999. "Talking the Donkey: Cooperative Approaches to Environmental Protection." *Journal of Industrial Ecology* 2 (3): 57-72.

Hausman, J., and P. Joskow. 1982. "Evaluating the Costs and Benefits of Appliance Efficiency Standards." *American Economic Review* 72 (2): 220-5.

Intergovernmental Panel on Climate Change (IPCC), Working Group III. 2007. *IPCC Fourth Assessment Report*. New York: Cambridge University Press.

Jaccard, M., and C. Bataille. 2003. "If Sustainability Is Expensive, What Roles for Business and Government?" *Journal of Business Administration and Policy Analysis* 30:149-83.

Jaccard, M., J. Nyboer, and B. Sadownik. 2002. *The Cost of Climate Policy*. Vancouver: University of British Columbia Press.

Jaccard, M., and N. Rivers. 2007. "Heterogeneous Capital Stocks and the Optimal Timing for CO_2 Abatement." *Resource and Energy Economics* 29 (1): 1-16.

Jaccard, M., N. Rivers, and M. Horne. 2004. "The Morning After: Optimal Policies for Canada's Kyoto Commitment and Beyond." *C.D. Howe Institute Commentary* 197. Toronto: C.D. Howe Institute.

Keith, D., and A. Farrell. 2003. "Rethinking Hydrogen Cars." *Science* 301 (5631): 315-6.

Larrue, P. 2003. "Lessons Learned from the Californian ZEV Mandate: From a 'Technology-Forcing' to a 'Market-Driven'

Regulation." *Cahiers de Gres* 2003-7. Bordeaux and Toulouse: Groupement de Recherches Economiques et Sociales.

Loughran, D., and J. Kulick. 2004. "Demand Side Management and Energy Efficiency in the United States." *Energy Journal* 25 (1): 19-43.

Marland, G., T.A. Boden, and R.J. Andres. 2006. *Global, Regional, and National CO_2 Emissions.* In *Trends: A Compendium of Data on Global Change.* Oak Ridge, TN: Carbon Dioxide Information Analysis Center, Oak Ridge National Laboratory, US Department of Energy.

Millman, S., and R. Prince. 1989. "Firm Incentives to Promote Technological Change in Pollution Control." *Journal of Environmental Economics and Management* 17 (3): 247-65.

M.K. Jaccard and Associates. 2003. "Construction and Analysis of Sectoral, Regional, and National Cost Curves for GHG Abatement in Canada," March 29. Report submitted to the Office of Energy Efficiency, Natural Resources Canada.

Moxnes, E. 2004. "Estimating Customer Costs or Benefits of Energy Efficiency Standards." *Journal of Economic Psychology* 25 (6): 707-24.

Nadel, S. 2002. "Appliance and Equipment Efficiency Standards." *Annual Review of Energy and Environment* 27:159-92.

National Roundtable on the Environment and Economy (NRTEE). 1999. *Canada's Options for a Domestic Greenhouse Gas Emissions Trading Program.* Ottawa: NRTEE. Accessed June 12, 2007. www.nrtee-trnee.ca/Publications/PDF/ Report_Emissions-Options_E.pdf

Newell, R., and R. Stavins. 2003. "Cost Heterogeneity and the Potential Cost Savings of Market-Based Policies." *Journal of Regulatory Economics* 23 (1): 43-59.

Nyboer, J. 1997. "Simulating the Evolution of Technology: An Aid to Energy Policy Analysis. A Case Study of Strategies to Control Greenhouse Gas Emissions in Canada." Ph.D. diss., Simon Fraser University.

Organisation for Economic Co-operation and Development (OECD). 2003. *Voluntary Approaches for Environmental Policy: Effectiveness, Efficiency, and Usage in the Policy Mixes.* Paris: OECD.

_____. 2005. *Act Locally, Trade Globally.* Paris; OECD.

Richels, R., and J. Edmonds. 1995. "The Economics of Stabilizing Atmospheric CO_2 Concentrations." *Energy Policy* 23 (4-5): 373-8.

Rivers, N., and M. Jaccard. Forthcoming. "Talking without Walking: Canada's Ineffective Climate Effort." In *Governing the Energy Challenge: Germany and Canada in a Multi-level Regional and Global Context,* edited by B. Eberlein and B. Doern. Toronto: University of Toronto Press.

Stavins, R. 2001. "Experience with Market-Based Environmental Policy Instruments," November. *Resources for the Future Discussion Paper* 01-58. Washington, DC: Resources for the Future. Accessed June 12, 2007. www.rff.org/documents/ RFF-DP-01-58.pdf

Stern, N. 2006. *Stern Review: The Economics of Climate Change.* London: HM Treasury, Government of the United Kingdom. Accessed June 12, 2007. www.hm-treasury.gov.uk/media/8AC/F7/Executive_ Summary.pdf

Svendson, G., C. Daugbjerg, and A. Pederson. 2001. *Consumers, Industrialists, and the Political Economy of Green Taxation: CO_2 Taxation in the OECD.* Cheltenham, England: Edward Elgar.

Takahashi, T., M. Nakamuro, G. van Kooten, and I. Vertinsky. 2001. "Rising to the Kyoto Challenge: Is the Response of Canadian Industry Adequate?" *Journal of Environmental Management* 63:149-61.

United Nations Framework Convention on
Climate Change (UNFCCC). 2005. *Key
GHG Data*. Bonn: UNFCCC. Accessed
June 12, 2007. unfccc.int/resource/docs/
publications/key_ghg_execsum.pdf
Weitzman, M. 1974. "Prices vs. Quantities."
Review of Economic Studies 41 (4): 477-91.

SLOWING, THEN REDUCING, GREENHOUSE GAS EMISSIONS IS IMPORTANT BUT WILL NOT BE EASY

Christopher Green

Climate change is an important, long-term issue of public policy — arguably a dominating and defining one for the twenty-first century. Given what we are learning about the science of climate change, we can anticipate that the issue will be of increasing public concern and a thorn in the side of those charged with creating Canadian public policy. Presently, all five federal parties (including the Green Party) rank climate change high on their political agendas.

Unfortunately, Canadian public policy has failed to come to terms with the fact that stabilizing climate is a truly daunting, long-term energy technology problem. The blind adherence of the previous Liberal government to Kyoto targets — which were both unachievable and, in climate change terms, essentially meaningless — has continued to infect climate change debate.

These opening remarks reflect what I bring to an assessment of "Canadian Policies for Deep Greenhouse Gas Reductions," Mark Jaccard and Nic Rivers' contribution to this volume. I will argue that the package of proposals vetted by the authors, while not without its faults, is one of the more sensible — and, in some respects, novel — to be suggested in the Canadian context. But I will also argue that although these proposals, if enacted, would undoubtedly make a huge dent in emissions from a correctly specified emissions baseline, it is important not to overstate what they can actually do to reduce emissions from current levels.

CRITERIA AND INSTRUMENTS

After offering a brief introduction to the climate change issue, Jaccard and Rivers set out criteria for choosing among climate change policies and several possible instruments for implementing policy actions. The criteria include the usual suspects: effectiveness, efficiency, acceptability and administrative feasibility. But the authors wisely warn that other considerations must not be overlooked, including Canada's multiple jurisdictions over the environment and the need to account for decision-making with uncertainty.

With regard to policy instruments, the authors' list amounts to the regular litany: command-and-control regulations, emissions cap and permit trading, greenhouse gas (GHG) taxes, subsidies and voluntarism. For all the right reasons, Jaccard and Rivers rule out subsidies (a costly method of accomplishing very little, or even doing the wrong thing) and voluntarism (we've tried that, and it doesn't work). As they make clear, we need a positive price for carbon, not a neutral (voluntarism) or negative (subsidies) one. However, I would have liked the authors to explain that their discussion of subsidies really applies to production subsidies. The emphasis on these types of subsidies (for example, to wind power and ethanol production) is as opportunistic — and scandalous — as the subsidies themselves are popular. In contrast, certain subsidies may be justified on the grounds that they promote a traditional public good or externality: subsidies to basic research and development for new energy technologies and sources; subsidies to the development of enabling technologies, such as storage for intermittent wind and solar energies, and smart grids to handle variable supplies as well as demands for electricity; and even some capital subsidies.

One novel inclusion in Jaccard and Rivers' list of instruments is a system of obligation and certificate trading (OCT). Although superficially similar to the emissions cap and tradable permit (ECTP) system, the two are quite different. Jaccard and Rivers point out that whereas ECTP "regulates a maximum amount of an undesirable product (emissions)," OCT "requires a minimum amount of a desirable product or process" (83) (presumably emissions reduction). Avoiding the highly controversial and inevitably political issue of how to allocate permits to produce a "bad," OCT instead grants certificates to firms when they produce a "good." But OCT does not wholly avoid the high costs of administration, monitoring and enforcement to which ECTP is subject. These costs would increase as the number of units with obligations rises. The discussion of this issue is not an idle one: Jaccard and Rivers propose to employ OCT as an integral part of two of their emissions-reducing initiatives. In my view, an initially low, gradually escalating carbon tax, combined with a research and development energy technology policy, would surpass by a wide margin either ECTP or OCT.

POLICY ACTIONS

Jaccard and Rivers propose three policies to reduce GHG emissions by 2050: a carbon management standard for fossil fuel producers and importers; a vehicle emission standard; and strengthened appliance and building standards. Before discussing these, I would like to register my support for the approach the authors have taken. With its focus on important potential undertakings, it stands in contrast to Canadian climate policy through 2005. The focus of that policy was on hard, near-term, quantitative emissions reduction targets — a legacy of our obsession with Kyoto. That obsession with targets led us to make commitments that Thomas C. Schelling has described as not generally "credible" (1992, 2005). At the same time, for all intents and purposes we have ruled out price-based instruments (for example, carbon taxes) as opposed to quantity-based instruments (emission permits, tradable or not). In contrast, Jaccard and Rivers suggest policy actions — commitments that may be credible in Schelling's terms and that could have important emissions-reducing impacts over time (although they would not likely meet hard, near-term targets).

A carbon management standard

Jaccard and Rivers would require fossil fuel producers and importers to "ensure that a growing fraction of the carbon they extract from the earth's crust does not reach the atmosphere" (92). To achieve this goal, the authors would employ an OCT system. Instead of allocating permits to firms, government would collect from firms certificates that matched their emissions reduction obligations. Those obligations would be measured in terms of a percentage of carbon fuels, rather than in absolute terms, thus relaxing the emissions constraint somewhat if consumption of fossil fuels grows (as it will). Firms that failed to comply would be subject to stiff penalties, but a safety valve would be added in the form of government-issued certificates sold at a predetermined price if the fossil fuel growth rate was faster than anticipated, or if abatement costs were significantly higher than expected.

The authors' approach to implementing a carbon management standard is novel, and it would seem to be a workable means of inducing carbon capture and storage (CCS) at electricity generating plants and fossil fuel production sites such as the Alberta oil sands. But it is less easy to discern how it could be applied to fossil fuel producers who sell (mainly oil and natural gas) downstream to final energy users — homes, buildings and factories — that employ these energy sources for heating, transportation and various industrial functions. One may reasonably ask how upstream producers and importers can be held responsible for the downstream use of their fuels. To be sure, the authors appear to be mainly considering CCS at power plants and plants in energy-intensive industries, and the capture of fugitive emissions from coal mines, oil and gas wells and natural gas pipelines. But then why do they include importers, and why do they limit certification to fossil fuel producers and ignore those whose activities directly generate fossil fuel emissions? In some cases, it would make more sense to move certification responsibility downstream to the power plant and pipeline levels.

A zero-emission vehicle standard for vehicle manufacturers

The second initiative that Jaccard and Rivers suggest is a vehicle emission standard (VES) that "requires vehicle manufacturers and importers to sell a minimum number of zero-emission vehicles by a target date as a percentage of total vehicle sales" (95). Again, the instrument of choice is obligation and certificate trading. The minimum market share of zero-emission vehicles (ZEVs) would rise over time. The authors argue that the VES "accelerates the process of developing, commercializing and disseminating low-emission vehicles" (95), and they cite the VES policies of California as a model.

Jaccard and Rivers make a strong case that we need to tackle the transportation vehicle sector if we are to see significant emissions reductions by 2050. Nevertheless, I have some reservations about their approach. The most important of these is that "zero-emission vehicle" is a misnomer if we consider the life-cycle, or well-to-wheels, analysis. Electric cars or plug-in hybrids require recharging, which would increase emissions if the electric power was generated by fossil-fuel-fired plants. If the authors are assuming that the generating-plant emissions would be subject to CCS, then they should make it clear that their ZEV proposal depends heavily on the viability of their proposed carbon management system and its unlimited capacity to scale up.

Moreover, if the ZEV proposal is based on ethanol and other biofuel usage, or on hydrogen, then life-cycle analysis takes on added importance. In the case of biofuels, a great deal of energy is needed to produce the inputs that go into ethanol and bio-diesel and then to convert these into liquid fuels. Some evidence suggests that the energy required to produce ethanol (including the energy used in the production of the input — corn) actually exceeds the energy content of the ethanol, resulting in negative net energy (Pimentel and Patzek 2005), while others have found slightly positive net energy (Farrell et al. 2006; Tilman, Hill, and Lehman 2006). In any case, if fossil fuels are used in the life-cycle biofuel production process, then the resulting emissions must be taken into account, or else somehow captured. If the fuel of choice is hydrogen, it is important to consider how the hydrogen is produced. If it is produced by reforming natural gas or by a process that gasifies coal, then emissions will be created unless the CO_2 (carbon dioxide) is captured. Thus, a ZEV is much better described as a low-, or lower-, emission vehicle.

Frankly, I would place greater emphasis on enhanced vehicle fuel efficiency standards. Presumably, Jaccard and Rivers have, like almost all economists, rejected fuel efficiency standards because they do not focus on emissions reduction and create a rebound effect — by increasing fuel efficiency, they lower the cost of vehicle use and increase kilometres driven, thus cutting into the emissions reduction effect. While this is quite true, a fuel efficiency standard (such as the US Corporate Average Fuel Economy, or CAFE) has legs: it is more easily administered and enforced than a VES (assuming the light-truck loophole in CAFE is closed); and it can largely preclude the rebound effect if accompanied by a low, but increasing, carbon tax.

Building and appliance standards

The third set of policies that Jaccard and Rivers propose are residential and commercial building codes and appliance and equipment standards. The authors argue that the "most cost-effective way to lower GHG emissions in the building stock (through energy efficiency and fuel choice) is by means of design and construction" (97). Their assumption is that design and construction influence the amount of energy used in heating and air conditioning, lighting, water heating and the like. I believe they are right, and a corollary to this (which they do not mention) is that it is much more cost-effective, and probably more energy-effective, to apply building standards when constructing new buildings, just as setting standards for new appliances and equipment is much more cost-effective than retrofitting existing ones.

As my final comment regarding the VES proposal suggests, I support the use of efficiency standards, including those for new buildings and appliances. Jaccard and Rivers note that although "Canada has relatively strong efficiency standards for some equipment" (98), there is still much room for improvement. Let me highlight two initiatives that the authors do not mention. One involves washing machines. Currently, most washing machines are top-loaders, although a growing number are front-loaders. Front-loaders are more energy-efficient because they use 30 to 40 percent less hot water. If Canada simply legislated that after, say, 2009, no top-loading washers could be sold in Canada, a small but important improvement would be made in the energy efficiency of household appliance use. The second initiative would be to require that when new buildings are under construction, pipes be sunk into the ground to facilitate geothermal means of climate control (heating in winter, cooling in summer). Of course, neither initiative allows us to predict emissions reduction over the short term, which is one reason why such obvious contributors to long-term emissions reduction get short shrift now that the pressure is on to achieve Kyoto-type targets.

RESULTS

In the final pages of their chapter, Jaccard and Rivers project the impact of their proposed policies. They detail their results in table 5 and summarize them in figure 3 — in both cases dealing exclusively with energy-related emissions. In the table and the figure, the authors make comparisons for both business-as-usual (BAU) and policy-related GHG emissions for 2050, using 2010 as a base year. The projected reductions are large, regardless of base or baseline. Table 5 indicates that the authors believe that especially large reductions can be achieved in the sectors of electricity generation, oil and gas production, energy-intensive industry and transportation. The estimated reductions are great enough to suggest the possibility of overstatement. Setting this concern aside, I nevertheless have reservations about the way in which Jaccard and Rivers calculated the BAU 2050 emissions level in their policy scenario.

According to the authors, emissions in 2010 will be 713 megatonnes of CO_2 equivalent, which implies an average annual growth rate in energy-related emissions of 2 percent from 1990 to 2010. They estimate that BAU emissions will be 1,157 megatonnes in 2050. That implies a 1.2 percent average annual rate of GHG emissions growth from 2010 to 2050 (using the authors' base of 713 megatonnes in 2010). What is not clear is why the no-policy growth rate of energy-related GHG emissions is so much lower for 2010-50 than the 2 percent rate for 1990-2010, a rate that would have raised energy-related emissions to around 1,574 megatonnes in 2050 as compared with Jaccard and Rivers' 1,157 megatonnes.

The authors imply that their policies can reduce energy-related GHG emissions in Canada to 357 megatonnes by 2050 — that is, by 356 megatonnes from their 2010 base of 713, and by 800 megatonnes from their 2050 BAU baseline of 1,157. Even assuming that their policy actions are capable of reducing GHG emissions by 800 megatonnes from baseline in 2050, the foregoing analysis suggests that there is plenty of room for doubt that energy-related emissions will be reduced to 357 megatonnes by that time.

Since Jaccard and Rivers are attempting to estimate the emissions reductions that flow directly or indirectly from energy technology changes, they would have done better to employ a "frozen technology" baseline (Edmonds and Smith 2006) — that is, a baseline that indicates emissions in the absence of energy technology change. A frozen technology BAU emission baseline for 2050 also avoids inadvertent double-counting of technologies (once in the baseline, and once in the policy emissions scenario). By using such a baseline, we would see emissions grow roughly at the rate of GDP. (I say "roughly," because changes in industry structure can alter somewhat the energy intensity of the economy. Calculations suggest that, on a trend basis, the structural factor constitutes 10 to 30 percent of trend energy intensity decline.) If the trend rate of GDP for the period 2010 to 2050 were 2.5 percent, and frozen technology emissions grew at a rate of 2 percent (allowing for structural factors to contribute 20 percent of the differential between GDP and GHG emissions growth), BAU emissions in 2050 would be 1,567 megatonnes. An 800-megatonne reduction (if achievable) from a 1,567-megatonne baseline would imply energy-related emissions in 2050 of 767 megatonnes — almost 24 percent higher than the 2004 level of 620 megatonnes, and more than double the 357-megatonne level that the authors say their policies can achieve.

CONCLUSION

Jaccard and Rivers have provided us with a useful set of policies with which to tackle a very important long-term problem. I think that their focus on appropriate policy actions rather than targets is a breath of fresh air. While I have raised some concerns with aspects of two of their policy actions, I think their determinations of where Canada can make important contributions to GHG reduction are good ones. However, I believe that their projections of where GHG emissions will be in 2050 are rather optimistic. Be that as it may, climate change deserves a high rank in the Canadian Priorities Agenda, and the policy actions presented by Jaccard and Rivers, with some modifications at the margin, could put us on a path to GHG emissions reduction.

REFERENCES

Edmonds, J.A., and S.J. Smith. 2006. "The Technology of Two Degrees." In *Avoiding Dangerous Climate Change*, edited by H.J. Schnellnhuber, W. Cramer, N. Nakicenovic, T. Wigley, and G. Yohe. Cambridge: Cambridge University Press.

Farrell, A.E., R.J. Plevin, B.T. Turner, A.D. Jones, M. O'Hare, and D.M. Kammen. 2006. "Ethanol Can Contribute to Energy and Environmental Goals." *Science* 311 (5760): 506-8.

Pimentel, D., and T.W. Patzek. 2005. "Ethanol Production Using Corn, Switchgrass, and Wood; Biodiesel Production Using Soybean and Sunflower." *Natural Resource Research* 14 (1): 65-76.

Schelling, T.C. 1992. "Some Economics of Global Warming." *American Economic Review* 82 (1): 1-14.

_____. 2005. "What Makes Greenhouse Sense?" *Indiana Law Review* 38:581-93.

Tilman, D., J. Hill, and C. Lehman. 2006. "Carbon-Negative Biofuels from Low-Input High-Diversity Grassland Biomass." *Science* 314 (5831): 1598-600.

TIME TO ACTUALLY BEGIN
James Meadowcroft

Mark Jaccard and Nic Rivers' chapter in this volume, "Canadian Policies for Deep Greenhouse Gas Reductions," is divided into three main sections. The first introduces the challenge of climate change policy. The second discusses criteria for selecting policies, the menu of available instruments and parameters for composing a preferred policy package. And the third describes, and then considers the combined impact of, three key policies: a carbon management standard for fossil fuel producers and importers; a zero-emission vehicle standard for vehicle manufacturers; and strengthened residential and commercial building codes and appliance and equipment standards.

After commenting briefly on the opening sections of the paper, I will focus on the three selected policies and then offer some concluding observations.

THE APPROACH TO CLIMATE CHANGE POLICY

Jaccard and Rivers provide an excellent introduction to the challenge of climate change policy in Canada, the criteria for selecting policies and the range of available instruments. The most important practical conclusion to be drawn from their opening discussion is that voluntary programs and subsidies will not prove effective in securing significant long-term greenhouse gas (GHG) emissions reductions. Instead, market-oriented regulations, supplemented by some more traditional command-and-control initiatives, will be required.

The necessarily synthetic presentation of the Jaccard and Rivers chapter causes some nuances to be lost, particularly with respect to the political complexity of the climate change file and the comparative costs and benefits of policy alternatives. To the points made in the chapter, it is worth adding several observations.

First, climate change policy requires both adaptation and mitigation. Neither of these can be avoided, because we are already fated to experience substantial climate change due to GHG releases that have already occurred, and because GHGs will continue to accumulate in the atmosphere (provoking still further warming) until global emissions are radically curtailed.

The authors' proposal of Canadian emissions reductions of 60 percent from current levels by 2050 provides a convenient basis for discussion, but deeper reductions with an earlier onset may be desired. European Union environment ministers recently agreed to a target reduction of 20 percent from 1990 levels by 2020 — that target would increase to 30 percent if other countries join the effort. Recent studies suggest that to reach stabilization in the range of 450 to 550 parts per million of carbon dioxide (CO_2), emissions from developed countries (as a group) would need to fall 70 to 90 percent below 1990 levels by 2050 to allow for emissions growth in developing countries (Stern 2006).

Canada's response over the past decade to the climate change issue represents a major policy disaster. The story is complex and has yet to be told in full. It includes a serious failure of political leadership and deliberate obstruction by vested interests. In policy terms, we lag perhaps a decade behind more innovative jurisdictions (such as the United Kingdom, Sweden, Germany and the European Union as a whole), and this will have political, diplomatic and economic consequences.

Although large distances and cold winters contribute to Canada's comparatively high energy intensity per unit of GDP and elevated GHG emissions per capita, the long-term historical development of the economy and earlier rounds of policy choice also play a significant role. Low-cost resource inputs have been a cornerstone of Canadian economic development — and note, for example, that gasoline taxes in Canada are less than half the levels in most other Organisation for Economic Co-operation and Development (OECD) countries.

Finally, while Jaccard and Rivers are correct that long-term price signals (which can be generated by environmental taxes or market-oriented regulations) provide an effective stimulus for technological innovation, there is evidence that other forms of government intervention can also encourage the development and diffusion of new technologies (Vollebergh 2007).

THE THREE POLICY OPTIONS

A carbon management standard for fossil fuel producers and importers

The authors' first proposed policy would require fossil fuel producers and importers to demonstrate over time that a growing proportion of the carbon in the fuel they sell did not reach the atmosphere. Each year, firms would submit to regulators certificates demonstrating that they had met the obligation. Regulated firms could trade certificates with each other and buy project-based certificates from upstream and downstream GHG abatement efforts (such as carbon capture and storage at power plants, and the reduction of emissions at the wellhead, in refineries, in pipelines and so on). The system could be designed to cover other GHGs in the energy sector, as well as producers and importers of nonenergy-related GHGs. It could incorporate a safety valve and/or the banking and borrowing of certificates. A partial exemption for fossil fuel exports would limit impacts on international competitiveness in this sector.

This is an innovative policy proposal with several appealing features. First, it focuses attention on the core of the mitigation issue: GHG releases associated with the production, distribution and use of fossil fuels. Second, it embodies the "polluter pays" principle and some notion of extended product liability. Companies that produce and import fossil fuels will ultimately be held accountable for the emissions generated from the products they bring to market. Third, it covers fossil fuel usage throughout the economy, in contrast to a downstream cap-and-trade system (like the European Union Emission Trading Scheme or the original Canadian large final emitters program), which deals only with large industrial emitters. Finally, it avoids problems associated with the distribution of permits under emissions cap and permit trading systems.

But there are also some difficulties. First, we have limited practical experience with upstream obligation and certificate trading systems; we know more about the actual operation of emissions cap and permit trading systems and tax-based instruments. In addition, most other jurisdictions have adopted (or appear to be gravitating toward) these alternative designs for GHG abatement. Selecting a policy design that is different from those of other industrialized countries involves some risks. It could, for example, make it somewhat more difficult to engage in international emissions trading.

Moreover, it is not clear whether this proposal would easily win political acceptance. Politicians and the public are just beginning to come to terms with the idea of a downstream cap-and-trade system. Might this proposal further complicate debate and delay action? Some will argue that it unfairly shifts the whole burden of responsibility for adjustment onto fossil fuel producers and importers. Paradoxically, removing the problem of permit allocation associated with emissions cap and permit trade systems might be perceived as a negative by some political and economic actors who would have decreased opportunities to "game" with the system.

A number of issues appear to merit further consideration. To begin with, it would be nice to see a more detailed comparison between this policy option and two others: a downstream cap-and-trade system supplemented by a downstream carbon tax (the latter applicable to the economic sectors, such as households and transport, not covered by the cap); and an upstream carbon tax (that is, one levied at the point of production or import). Such a comparison should not only deal with economic effects, but it should also consider how the rival systems would actually be experienced by different economic actors and perceived by different political actors.

Linkage to international GHG trading systems is important if Canadian companies are to have access to the most advantageous cost abatement options. Modalities for linking the proposed system to other trading systems (and for avoiding double counting) should be explored.

In the longer term, if highly localized options for GHG mitigation emerge, the carbon management standard trading system could be expanded to include emissions reductions secured by consumers of fossil fuels — extending the potential reach of the scheme as delineated in figure 3 of Jaccard and Rivers' chapter.

A zero-emission vehicle standard for vehicle manufacturers

The second policy establishes an obligation and certificate trading system for vehicle manufacturers and importers that requires an increasing percentage of total sales to be made up of zero-emission vehicles. The focus on zero (tailpipe and evaporative) emissions is intended to encourage technological system change rather than incremental improvements to fossil fuel engine efficiency. Although the proposal is centred on passenger vehicles, the policy could be extended to freight transport.

Among the advantages of this proposal are that it would create a protected niche to encourage the development of zero-emission vehicles (which are important for long-term GHG abatement), and that it would leave it to firms and markets to determine the best technologies to meet the mandated goal. Yet this approach raises some concerns.

First, from the perspective of long-term GHG abatement, it is important to minimize total emissions reaching the atmosphere. Other things being equal, policy-makers should be relatively agnostic about which technologies will deliver the required level of aggregate GHG reductions. Hydrogen, electricity, biofuels and hybrid technologies may all play a role in the solution. Zero-emission vehicles will be important, but so will low-GHG-emission vehicles. After all, a low-GHG-emission vehicle running on fossil fuels might be associated with lower-life-cycle GHG emissions than a zero-emission vehicle running on hydrogen or electricity derived from fossil sources. Moreover, it is unclear what the costs of the different technological options will be. For this reason it would seem prudent to link low-GHG-emission and zero-emission vehicles in the standard, an option the authors themselves raise.

Second, considering the international character of the auto industry, it may not make sense for Canada to pursue a technology-forcing policy in isolation from initiatives in other jurisdictions. The policy would be most effective if implemented in step with initiatives in other countries. Third, questions may be asked about the phasing and range of the obligation. For example, if the policy is promoted on the grounds of niche protection, why does it end by mandating 80 percent compliance in 2050?

Residential and commercial building codes and appliance and equipment standards

The third policy involves regulations designed to raise standards for the construction of residential and commercial buildings and for the energy efficiency of equipment and appliances. Strictly speaking, this is not one policy but a series of related policies involving carefully designed instruments enacted by different levels of government. These policies are intended not to drive technological innovation but rather to encourage the diffusion of existing technologies by prohibiting the least efficient products from entering the market and so gradually raising the average efficiency of the overall stock.

This policy strand is important in overcoming barriers that discourage groups and individuals from making more energy-efficient choices. It is also important because it creates the possibility of making relatively substantial short- to medium-term gains. Measures that reduce (or slow the growth of) aggregate electricity demand help postpone the need for additional generation capacity to a time when prices and technologies presumably will be more favourable to GHG abatement. Short-term reductions in GHG emissions are particularly desirable because they (modestly) contribute to slowing the rate of warming. More crucial are their potential political and diplomatic impacts at a time when Canada is failing to meet agreed international GHG reduction targets.

In developing such regulations, it is important to set them in a context of continuous improvement: there should be a commitment to periodic revision (perhaps every five years) and a strong signal that regulations will become ever more stringent.

ADDITIONAL OBSERVATIONS

The three policy proposals assessed here constitute a useful package of measures to pursue long-term abatement of Canada's GHG emissions. The first engages with the most important framework issue by driving up the price of carbon emissions. The second addresses the critical transport sector, where emissions are rising rapidly and fossil fuel dependence is most complete. The third involves regulatory initiatives to secure significant energy efficiency gains.

The assumption behind the Jaccard and Rivers proposal is that a long-run price signal is required to orient investment decisions toward GHG abatement and to stimulate the technological innovation required to achieve significant reductions. The real impact of the carbon management standard will be that it will progressively drive up the price of fossil fuels as it becomes necessary to prevent an ever-greater share of associated GHG emissions from entering the atmosphere.

However, as the Stern report has forcefully argued, carbon pricing is not enough. Other policy instruments must be invoked to accelerate technological invention, innovation and deployment, and to encourage behavioural change (Stern 2006). Public policy can help breach the barriers (including information issues, transaction costs, and behavioural and organizational inertia) that prevent smooth adjustments to rising carbon prices. Varied policy tools can be applied across the innovation chain to speed up the emergence and deployment of new technologies (Geels 2002). Although subsidies do have a place here, there is also a major role for government as a catalyst for innovation networks. Some of these issues have begun to be discussed in the emerging literature on transition management (Rotmans, Kemp and van Asselt 2001; Kemp and Rotmans 2003; Kemp and Loorbach 2005).

Although trajectories for GHG abatement are typically discussed in terms of environmental risks and economic costs, it is important to note that political factors should be accorded independent weight. Building successful international collaboration — and this would include inducing the large developing countries to achieve an appropriate level of participation — is essential if dangerous climate change is to be avoided. By securing emissions reductions in the short to medium term, developed countries can establish the seriousness with which they view this issue and thus encourage others to act. Given that Canada has taken no meaningful steps to achieve its agreed-upon (Kyoto) abatement target, an effort to secure some early emissions reductions (either domestically, or through the use of international mechanisms) is important politically — even if these reductions turn out to be somewhat more costly than they would have been had they been undertaken earlier (or would be if they are deferred).

One of the difficulties of approaching climate change by isolating one or two headline policies is that there is no magic bullet to be found. A mature policy framework must include initiatives related not only to mitigation but also to adaptation. An advantage of bringing forward the discussion of adaptation is that it makes more real the emerging costs of dealing with a changing climate. On the broad scale, initiatives in public education, science policy and industrial policy are also important dimensions of climate policy.

Nevertheless, at present, in order to advance climate change policy in Canada it is critical that government take action to end the free use of the atmosphere as a GHG dump. This could be done through a carbon tax, some form of emissions cap and permit trading system or the carbon management standard described by Jaccard and Rivers. In April 2007, the Conservative government announced a new regulatory framework, including a baseline and credit trading system involving intensity targets and a series of flexibility mechanisms (including contributions to a technology fund and offsets). The government objective is to reduce GHG emissions by 20 percent from 2006 levels by 2020, but the information released so far on the derivation of the intensity targets and the design of the scheme makes it unclear how far the system could actually contribute toward such a goal. After so many delays, some form of binding controls in this area would at least be a beginning. And the regime could be tightened in the future. But, to be effective, the initiative should ultimately be complemented with measures that apply to parts of the economy that fall outside the regulated sector, such as a downstream carbon tax.

Notwithstanding the recent federal announcements, the carbon management scheme presented by Jaccard and Rivers deserves consideration. It should be examined by a wider audience in Canada, including stakeholders in government, business and the environmental sector. And it should be considered among the options for post-Kyoto international efforts. Of course, changing policy designs at some point in the future (say from one market-oriented regulatory mechanism to another) would incur costs. But it is not impossible. Indeed, we should probably expect such shifts as countries learn more about GHG abatement over the coming decades.

REFERENCES

Geels, F. 2002. *Understanding the Dynamics of Technological Transitions: A Co-evolutionary and Socio-technical Analysis*. Enchede, the Netherlands: Twente University Press.

Kemp, R., and D. Loorbach. 2005. "Dutch Policies to Manage the Transition to Sustainable Energy." In "Innovationen und Nachhaltigkeit," *Jahrbuch Ökologische Ökonomik* 4. Marburg, Germany: Metropolis-Verlag.

Kemp, R., and J. Rotmans. 2003. "Managing the Transition to Sustainable Mobility." In *System Innovation and the Transition to Sustainability: Theory, Evidence and Policy*, edited by B. Elzen, F. Geels, and K. Green. Cheltenham, UK: Edward Elgar.

Rotmans, J., R. Kemp, and M. van Asselt. 2001. "More Evolution than Revolution: Transition Management in Public Policy." *Foresight* 3 (1): 15-31.

Stern, N. 2006. *Stern Review: The Economics of Climate Change*. London: HM Treasury, Government of the United Kingdom. Accessed June 15, 2007. www.hm-treasury.gov.uk/media/8AC/F7/Executive_Summary.pdf

Vollebergh, H. 2007. *Impacts of Environmental Policy Instruments on Technological Change*. Paris: Organisation for Economic Co-operation and Development (OECD).

NATURAL CAPITAL

SECURING NATURAL CAPITAL AND ECOLOGICAL GOODS AND SERVICES FOR CANADA

Nancy Olewiler

A STRATEGIC GOAL FOR CANADA

Canada is facing a crisis due to the loss of its natural areas. Southern Ontario has lost 70 percent of its wetlands; less than 3 percent of British Columbia's coastal and interior old-growth Douglas fir forests remains; and 65 percent of Atlantic Canada's marshes have vanished (Natural Resources Canada 2007; British Columbia Ministry of Forests and Range 2004). Canada's natural areas — its natural capital — are essential for wildlife habitat and biodiversity, and they absorb carbon dioxide, purify water and provide raw materials for all aspects of our lives, to name just some of their functions. We are losing these areas to urbanization, industrial activity, resource extraction and pollution. Much of the loss may be irreversible, yet we are not fully aware of this threat to our natural heritage. One reason for this general lack of awareness is that the destruction and degradation of natural areas due to human transformation is incremental. A forest is cleared to build a housing development, a wetland is drained to construct a greenhouse, wild fish are harvested, a road is built to access a new ski development.

Canadian governments are becoming increasingly aware of the need to protect our natural capital. The 2007 federal budget committed $250 million to protecting our natural heritage. "Securing Canada's natural capital is essential to ensure Canada's long-term competitiveness and environmental sustainability"(Ambrose 2006, 46): so begins a section of Environment Canada's 2005-06 *Departmental Performance Report*, a review of the ministry's strategic objectives and accomplishments. The term "natural capital" appears frequently in the report, predominantly in the sections devoted to conservation and biodiversity protection. Natural capital is the planet's stock of renewable and nonrenewable natural resources (forests, minerals, oil, plant and animal species), environmental resources (atmosphere, water) and land. The planet's ecosystems — combinations of plant and animal communities on land or in water — use these components of natural capital to create habitats capable of sustaining life. Land, natural resources and environmental resources are capital in that they can produce a steady flow of goods and services if depreciation or degradation is offset. Reserves of nonrenewable natural resources such as oil and gas will ultimately be exhausted through continued extraction, but the renewable forms of natural capital can, in principle, serve as substitutes for nonrenewable ones and be sustained as long as the sun produces the solar energy essential for life on this planet.

The goods and services that flow from natural capital are called ecological goods and services (EGS). EGS can be produced using human and physical capital — think of timber harvesting, natural gas extraction and capture, and fish farming. Some EGS require few if any inputs to produce value to society; natural landscapes with scenic views and recreational uses are one example. Some forms of natural capital are essential to sustain life: energy, water, atmosphere, land and the many (seen and unseen) plant and animal species that provide food for humans and other species. If we are to sustain complex ecosystems, we may have to leave them intact; however, we may find substitutes for individual forms of natural capital. Solar energy is essential for life on earth, but we can generate electricity from a host of natural resources. The box on the next page illustrates types of natural capital and the EGS that flow from them.

To secure natural capital is a strategic goal of the Government of Canada, one that is likely shared by most Canadians. What stakeholders disagree about is how much natural capital we need to secure, what type we should be focusing on and within what time frame we need to act. I see two major policy challenges here. The first is related to the question of whether we have enough natural capital to sustain our planet's ecosystems and our societies. From the Canadian viewpoint, this means not only domestic natural capital, but also that which we share beyond our borders — for example, the atmosphere and oceans. Canada has vast amounts of land and water relative to its population, and we need to ask ourselves whether we should secure another particular unit of natural capital or allow that capital to be degraded, destroyed or converted to another use. We must also consider whether each of our regions is protecting the best (in terms of both economic and ecological costs and benefits) natural capital. We need to be able to measure the value of EGS from natural capital and assess the costs of losing or finding substitutes for specific EGS.

The second policy challenge is to determine how to protect the natural capital that is located on private lands. It is estimated that in the United States, 95 percent of species identified under federal legislation as threatened and endangered can be found in habitats on private land, 19 percent of which (262 species) survive only on private lands (Merenlender et al. 2004).[1] Private lands contain significant habitat, such as wetlands, grasslands and forests. While much of Canada's land is held by the Crown, there are significant tracts of private land under threat of conversion to uses that destroy or degrade natural capital. Examples are massive urbanization in southern Ontario, the Fraser and Okanagan valleys of British Columbia, and the prairies and foothills surrounding Calgary. Golf courses and recreational homes are being built in natural areas of the Maritime provinces. Energy development in northern Canada threatens watersheds, wildlife and the livelihoods of Aboriginal peoples. A fundamental question is who should pay for conserving needed EGS on private land. Should

TYPES OF NATURAL CAPITAL, THEIR FUNCTIONS AND THE ECOLOGICAL GOODS AND SERVICES THEY PROVIDE

Type of natural capital

Atmosphere; lakes, rivers and riparian zones; forests; wetlands; grass and rangelands; cropland and soils; undeveloped lands; minerals, oil and gas resources; wild plant and animal species

Functions	Ecological goods and services
Regulation: maintain essential UVB ecological processes and life support systems (traded and nontraded ecological goods and services [EGS])[1]	Atmospheric regulation (ozone layer — protection); climate regulation; storm and flood protection; water regulation (drainage); water supply; soil retention; nutrient regulation (soil fertility); waste treatment (absorption, neutralization, filtration); pollination; biological control of pests and diseases
Habitats: provide living space for wild plant and animal species (primarily nontraded EGS)	Sustainable species populations; biological and genetic diversity
Production: used with other factor inputs (primarily traded EGS)	Food; raw materials for buildings; fuels and energy generation, fertilizers; genetic resources for crop protection, pesticides; medical resources (pharmaceuticals, chemicals); ornamental resources (jewellery)
Contribution to human well-being (traded and nontraded EGS)	Aesthetic (scenery); recreational uses; cultural and artistic; spiritual and historic; science and education

Source: Adapted from Potschin and Haines-Young (2003, 97); and de Groot, Wilson, and Boumans (2002, 396).
[1] Traded EGS are those that are bought and sold in markets for observable prices; nontraded EGS have implicit prices.

private landowners incur the cost of protecting natural capital on their lands while society reaps the benefits? Or should landowners be required to compensate society if they degrade or destroy natural capital? If society was to share the cost of protection, what policies are available to regulate this, and how would governments or non-governmental organizations finance compensation to landowners?

The goals of this chapter are to identify the factors that contribute to the decline in the quantity and quality of Canada's natural capital and to develop and assess three policy proposals that will help secure natural capital. These proposals are: first, to create a conservation plan to collect natural capital and EGS data, to produce natural capital indicators and to standardize approaches across the country to estimating target levels of natural capital; second, to establish funds for voluntary natural capital acquisition from public and private lands; and third, to introduce new, incentive-based policies to secure natural capital cost-effectively.

THREATS TO NATURAL CAPITAL IN CANADA

The casual observer might be surprised to learn that a country as rich in land and natural resources as Canada is concerned about securing its natural capital. Indeed, land cover maps of the country show that almost 82 percent of Canada's roughly 10 million square kilometres has some form of cover (forests, grassland, cropland, shrubland); the balance consists of water, urban and built-up areas, snow and ice, and forest that has been disturbed by harvesting or natural events and phenomena such as fire, weather or insects (Statistics Canada 2006, 40, table 2.1). Canada's waters cover almost 1.2 million square kilometres. Canada has 20 percent of the world's remaining natural areas, 25 percent of its wetlands, 10 percent of its forest and 20 percent of its fresh water (World Wildlife Fund Canada 2003, 6). These numbers mask two important characteristics of natural capital. The first of these is its quality — its ability to produce EGS over time. For example, consider a river system that is used for irrigation, domestic and industrial water supply, habitat and water for multitudes of species, waste disposal, transportation, commercial fishery and so on. If the quality of its water is degraded by pollutants, or if its flows are reduced by withdrawals, then its EGS will decline. It is not enough for us to know the quantity of natural capital; it is vital that we measure its ability to sustain production of EGS over time. The second important characteristic of natural capital is its location. This affects the value of its EGS — value that derives from both human use and ecosystem integrity. For example, natural areas located near urban areas (think of Stanley Park in Vancouver) can be much more valuable to Canadians than natural areas located far from where they live. A grassland area remote from roads or railway lines is less valuable for grazing than one near transportation. Ecosystem integrity is the complex set of relationships among organisms and habitat needed to sustain species. For example, a sufficient land area with ground cover for migrating animals (such as caribou) or foragers (such as bears) is an integrated ecosystem. One cannot simply substitute a nature preserve in southern Alberta for Arctic ice flows in Nunavut and thereby protect populations of polar bears and seals.

Concern about Canada's natural capital thus centres on the quantity, quality and location of that natural capital. Threats to natural capital emanate from five main problems: lack of knowledge about our stocks and flows of natural capital and how much of it we need to protect; the failure of markets to price nonmarket EGS; competing priorities of governments; financial constraints; and insufficient long-term planning by public decision-makers. I will now briefly discuss these threats, and this discussion will serve as a basis for selecting three policy proposals.

Knowledge gaps and identification of natural capital targets

No government in Canada has a comprehensive database related to the amount and quality of natural capital within its jurisdiction and how it changes over time. At best, estimates exist of the stocks of particular resources, only occasionally augmented by estimates of their quality. Statistics Canada has a natural capital program to develop estimates of natural capital stocks and EGS flows, particularly in forest and energy resources. Annual data exist for fisheries (landed catch statistics, and values for capture fisheries and aquaculture production), forests (volume of harvests, hectares of forested area harvested, productive forest land burned), mineral and energy reserves, and stream flows.[2] The data represent flows of EGS, but they tell us little about remaining stocks of natural capital or their quality. Timber stocks and mineral reserves are estimated. Environment Canada measures threats to natural capital in the form of air pollutants, greenhouse gas emissions and invasive species; and the agency identifies species at risk of extinction or extirpation. Agriculture and Agri-Food Canada has a number of initiatives to measure the EGS from agricultural lands. With the help of remote sensing, one could also calculate the growth in urban land use and the corresponding reduction in natural areas. Nongovernmental organizations (NGOs) such as the World Wildlife Fund Canada produce estimates of biodiversity loss; Ducks Unlimited Canada monitors wetlands and waterfowl populations; local NGOs, such as the Fraser Basin Council, map out land uses in their regions. What we are missing is comprehensive information for each province and territory on how the amount of resource extraction and production and the levels of threat posed by pollution, urbanization and invasive species affect the ability of natural capital to maintain EGS flows over time.

In terms of Canada's 8.2 million square kilometres of natural areas plus croplands, we cannot say precisely which portions are at risk of losing a significant share of their natural capital or of seeing it degraded; neither do we know what exact percentage of the total these at-risk portions represent. Without this information, it is difficult to establish targets for securing natural capital. Estimates are that as of 2003, Canada was protecting through legislation approximately 8.2 percent of its total area (81.9 million hectares) from logging, mining, hydroelectric power generation, oil and gas extraction and other large-scale operations (Statistics Canada 2006, 143, table 4.2).[3] This area is to be protected in perpetuity (or, more accurately, as long as the legislation does not change). A further 185,500 hectares (approximately) are protected through private initiatives in the form of either land trusts held by nonprofit conservation organizations (137,462 hectares) or eco-gifts (48,000 hectares), bringing the total to about 82 million hectares (which is still 8.2 percent of Canada's total area).[4]

Is protecting 8.2 percent of the total area of Canada anywhere close to sufficient, and do the areas chosen to be protected maximize the EGS from natural capital? The World Wildlife Fund Canada (WWFC) calculates that, on average, 44 percent of the country's 35 conservation planning regions need to be accorded protected reserve status if we are to achieve adequate biodiversity (WWFC 2003). Figure 1 shows the WWFC's identification of conservation planning regions using shades of grey to indicate that organization's recommended conservation strategies. The regions are ecologically based, but they are also defined by the types of human development and economic activity they contain. The identification process focuses on species at risk within the regions and thus represents one attempt to respond to the question of what to protect. The WWFC looks as well at the impacts of land use — forestry, fishery, agriculture, transportation and urbanization — on biodiversity to come up with a threat index that ranks the impacts on a scale from "negligible" to "critical." The latter describes critical disruption of habitat and ecosystems with only small fragments of baseline (before settlement) habitat remaining. The WWCF methodology is similar to one used by the United Nations Environment Programme.

This sort of exercise can be very helpful in identifying risks to natural capital from a biological perspective, but it does not reveal any of the trade-offs in terms of opportunity cost. Mark Shaffer, Michael Scott and Frank Casey provide a back-of-the-envelope calculation to determine the land values forgone if a country protected a percentage of its land area from any sort of development. The World Conservation Union

FIGURE 1. CONSERVATION REGIONS THAT REQUIRE PRIORITY ATTENTION ACROSS CANADA AND PARTS OF THE ADJACENT UNITED STATES

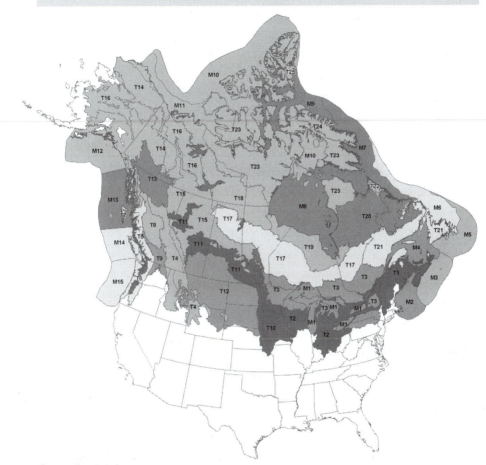

Conservation strategies

░ Conservation first: outstanding opportunities remain to protect intact habitats and species groups

▓ Time limited conservation opportunities remain to protect intact habitats and species groups

░ Priority conservation actions need to focus on the protection of remaining large habitat blocks and ensure the viability of wildlife populations

▒ Priority conservation actions need to focus on the protection of remaining natural areas with urgent conservation attention directed at the highest quality sites. Comprehensive management and intervention is required to protect some wildlife populations

▒ A comprehensive set of conservation actions is required, including protection of remaining natural areas, adoption of best management practices for natural resource-based industries, and significant efforts to restore habitat and recover species

▓ Protection of remaining natural areas is a high priority, but must occur in tandem with significant habitat restoration and species recovery efforts. Urban growth and/or industry practices must be managed to reduce the human footprint in these regions

Source: Map © WWF-Canada. World Wildlife Fund Canada. 2003. "The Nature Audit: Setting Canada's Conservation Agenda for the 21ˢᵗ Century." *WWFC Report* 1-2003. Toronto: World Wildlife Fund Canada.

recommends that 10 percent of each ecosystem within a country be strictly protected, with an additional 5 percent reserved as a buffer zone. Shaffer, Scott and Casey recommend 25 percent (2002). And, as I mentioned earlier, the WWFC suggests that 44 percent of each conservation region be protected.

Suppose the natural capital protection target is an additional 100 million hectares on top of the 82 million hectares now protected in Canada. Protected areas would then total approximately 18 percent of Canada's area.[5] Assume that 4 million hectares will be acquired each year for 25 years. The land can be purchased outright (fee-simple ownership) or can entail a conservation easement where specific land uses are prescribed. Ownership, however, remains in private hands; renting is permitted. Assume a purchase price of $2,000 (in current dollars) per hectare, $1,400 for a conservation easement and $100 per year for rent. The first year's payment for conservation easements is $5.6 billion; it costs $8 billion for fee-simple purchase, or $400 million to rent. While the rental option is by far the cheapest in the early years, recall that all 100 million hectares must be rented each year in perpetuity. If the amount of land, and hence rental values, escalate over time, the rental option looks less attractive. It is also the least secure in terms of ensuring that the natural capital is protected.

We can put these hypothetical conservation expenditures into perspective by comparing them with annual expenditures made by all levels of Canadian government related to pollution abatement and control. The most recent data available are from 2002-03, and in that fiscal year, governments spent $4.6 billion. In 2002, Canadian industries spent $3.6 billion on environmental protection. Thus we see that the cost of securing 18 percent of Canada's natural capital over 25 years is no greater than these annual expenditures.

More sophisticated approaches could be taken in assessing the amount of natural capital we should protect in Canada. David Newburn, Peter Berck and Adina Merenlender note that there will never be enough money to protect all the biologically valuable lands. They combine ecological and economic methodologies to try to optimize the acquisition of land to protect natural capital.[6] Their methodology takes into account land-acquisition costs, EGS and the likelihood of the land being used for a purpose inimical to conservation. Site selection is modelled as a process in which, each period, a planner decides what parcels of undeveloped land will be purchased for conservation easements, subject to a fixed budget for acquisition. Land not purchased for conservation easements might be developed for alternative uses. If this should occur, then environmental benefits would be permanently lost. Newburn, Berck and Merenlender compare their technique with two other decision-making tools. The first is standard (static) benefit-cost analysis that ignores the vulnerability of EGS to future land-use changes. This approach tends to result in the selection of low-cost sites in more remote areas because the decision method maximizes land-acquisition area for a given budget. Some of the sites chosen may never have been developed, hence the planner has spent funds to purchase land on which there was little threat of EGS loss. The second decision-making tool that Newburn, Berck and Merenlender present for comparison is the selection of sites with the greatest amount of EGS (for example, biodiversity measures). In settled areas of a country, this approach tends to be biased toward protecting the most vulnerable sites, which are frequently found on the urban fringe and are high-priced. Due to the cost of acquiring such land, only a relatively small amount of it can be protected. Newburn, Berck and Merenlender's approach combines the expected EGS with the probability of land conversion, and in their simulation of the three factors — land-acquisition costs, EGS and the likelihood of the land being used for a purpose inimical to conservation — for Sonoma County, California, they found that their methodology maximized the amount of land protected and minimized expected loss of EGS over time (Newburn, Berck and Merenlender 2006).

Market failure, land use and EGS from private lands

Market failure is very familiar territory to economists. The EGS from natural capital may have well-defined markets. Timber from forests, crops from fertile farmlands, electricity from dams or generated by fossil fuels are all sold at prices that more or less reflect the marginal costs of production, including the value of the natural capital inputs.[7] Many EGS have poorly defined markets or no markets at all in which to establish unit prices. A classic example of this absence of established value is the fact that individuals and industry use the natural environment as a free waste depository, discharging compounds that contaminate water, atmosphere and soil. Recreational users of natural capital rarely pay an established price for the privilege, one that fully reflects the value to the consumer of the EGS enjoyed. Markets don't account for damages to wildlife habitat due to road and residential construction. If EGS are exchanged without a full costing of all the impacts that production and consumption may have on natural capital, society risks overconsumption of EGS and not enough protection of natural capital. Private initiatives to establish prices (through bargaining, for example) typically do not address most of these market failures. Governments need to step in to help protect natural capital stocks.

EGS can flow from private as well as public lands. Suppose I own a private woodlot. I can harvest the timber and produce revenue from sales. That woodlot provides habitat for a variety of species, but the habitat will be lost when the timber is harvested. The value to society of habitat protection may exceed the market value of the timber, and I may even want to protect the forest from harvest, but I am dependent on the timber income. The policy problem is that there is no easy way to get society to pay for the ecological attributes of the woodlot. Ecological value is not traded in the marketplace.

Competing priorities of governments

Government policy must satisfy a number of objectives, some of which are in conflict. For example, the federal government has long provided tax expenditures to nonrenewable resource industries in the form of accelerated depreciation for exploration and development of mineral, oil and gas deposits, differential corporate income tax rates and so on. Renewable resource sectors such as fisheries receive labour subsidies in the form of more generous employment insurance coverage. These policies distort the extraction or harvest of natural resources and may tilt production to the present — that is, they may produce too much in early periods, leaving less for the future. Governments lease forest lands to timber harvesters without adequate provision for reforestation or habitat protection; they promote this inefficient use of natural capital to facilitate regional development and reduce income inequality. However, the result will be the loss of natural capital for future generations and a reduction in the sustainability of our environment and economy. The economic significance of natural capital loss depends on whether there are good substitutes: other types of natural capital, or capital and labour inputs. However, it may cost society a lot more to make such substitutions. The ecological costs may be the loss of habitats and species, and ultimately the sustainability of whole regions.

Human population growth involves significant land-use trade-offs. People need places to live and work. Conversion of natural areas to residential, commercial and industrial sites destroys and degrades natural capital. What land uses take priority in community development? Some of our most valuable natural capital is threatened by urbanization — for example, the Fraser Valley in BC, and the Oak Ridges Moraine in Ontario. Governments have to balance urbanization with protection of natural capital, a difficult task made more so by lack of knowledge and financial constraints.

A related issue is that natural capital may also transcend jurisdictional boundaries, requiring multiple governments and levels of government to decide jointly how best to manage their shared natural capital. Examples are watersheds and ecosystems that span municipal or provincial boundaries.

If local governments have the autonomy to set natural capital policy within their jurisdictions, then a beggar-thy-neighbour problem can emerge. Vancouver has a plan that promotes densification and restricts incremental building on natural areas. Land prices in Vancouver have soared, putting development pressure on municipalities removed from the city core. A municipality with a relatively small tax base will find it difficult to resist development pressure and may be less willing or able to implement policies to protect its natural areas. Provincial governments have not yet addressed this issue comprehensively other than to set aside Crown land as protected areas or to purchase natural areas for protection.

Financing constraints

The pressure to develop land for housing, commerce and industry is high. The market value of a given piece of land may exceed the community's ability to pay for its EGS. Local governments are faced with having to approve development to generate property tax revenue to pay for public goods even though natural capital may be lost as a result. There are other options: governments could compensate private landowners for protecting natural capital through financial incentives. Alternatively, they could levy fines if landowners do not protect natural capital. Not surprisingly, there is no consensus on this issue. Clearly, landowners would prefer positive to negative incentives, but the public, which pays to protect natural areas, would like to see the price remain as low as possible. If positive incentives are to be provided, where will the funds come from? Municipalities in Canada have a limited capacity to increase their revenues or reduce municipal goods and services to support conservation.

Long-term planning for development

Natural capital, like all capital, requires investment over time to offset depreciation (degradation) and to ensure that there are substitutes for nonrenewable forms. Governments have difficulty with long-term planning due to election cycles. Intergenerational planning of any sort — private or public — is hard for the current generation. One only need look at the statistics on how much Canadians have saved for their retirement to be convinced that no matter how many sophisticated models one produces to determine how much natural capital we should sustain, the choice between consumption today and investment in the future will be a very tough one.

Policies for long-term planning include zoning and myriad restrictions on land uses; set-asides of agricultural lands; and environmental impact assessment for major new capital projects. The pattern of land-use development across the country suggests that these policies have met with many challenges, which has resulted in the loss of significant natural capital, especially at the urban-rural fringes and in many ecosystems.

POLICIES TO SECURE NATURAL CAPITAL

In this section, I identify and classify policy options currently in use in Canada and other countries. Protection of natural capital can be accomplished in a number of ways, and many of these policy options are not mutually exclusive; they address different aspects of the policy challenge. Figure 2 classifies policies according to whether they are regulatory (command and control) or incentive-based. While the former place direct constraints on the use of natural capital, the latter make it more expensive to engage in activities that damage or degrade natural capital or reduce the cost of investing in activities that enhance it. These policy instruments can be compulsory (such as taxes) or voluntary (such as optional tax credits). All policies have the same opportunity cost; some call this the "baseline cost" — the difference between land's best private use and its value when it is used in ways that protect natural capital

FIGURE 2.   EXAMPLES OF POLICIES TO SECURE NATURAL CAPITAL

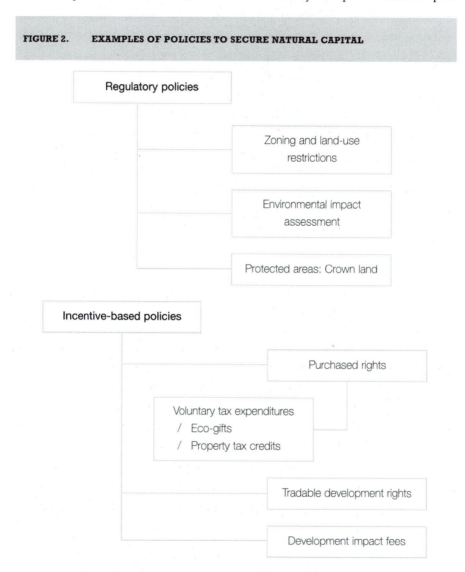

(Boyd, Caballero and Simpson 1999). A piece of land's private value is determined by the present value of its flow of goods and services. Once restrictions are placed on the land to protect its EGS, its private value will diminish. This is the opportunity cost of the policy. The benefits of the policy are the value of the EGS from the property to which it applies. Policies that protect natural capital differ in several areas: effectiveness in securing EGS, transaction and administration costs, political feasibility and determination of who will pay for securing EGS.

This section is organized by policy type: regulatory versus incentive-based. It examines specific examples of each type and provides an assessment of their strengths and weaknesses. This assessment sets the stage for the policy proposals put forth in the next section.

Regulatory policies

Regulatory policies prescribe actions that occur on privately owned property and Crown land. They control development through site-specific prescriptions and restrictions. The main strength of these policies is that they make compliance mandatory; conservation requirements will be met as long as monitoring and enforcement occur and legal challenges do not reverse the regulations. These policies can also be tailored to meet the needs of the jurisdiction. Zoning, environmental impact assessment (EIA) and the establishment of protected areas on Crown land represent the status quo in Canada; hence their characteristics are well known. I have already discussed the issue of whether we have enough protected areas, so I focus here on disadvantages of zoning and EIA.

The disadvantages of zoning are:

/ It lacks effectiveness in protecting natural capital in rapidly growing metropolitan areas.

/ It can give rise to "downzoning"— the rezoning of land so that it will have less-dense uses. This lowers the value of that property and creates incentives to seek variances to municipal plans. Variances cost society time and money and put pressure on decision-makers to change the rules.

/ It may promote urban sprawl by pushing housing development and other activities out to regions where restrictions are lighter and land is cheaper and more abundant. Sprawl exacerbates degradation of natural capital by increasing automobile use (with its adverse environmental impacts), reducing land cover and increasing septic system use (with its adverse impacts on water quality and supply). (Walls and McConnell 2004)

The disadvantages of EIA are:

/ It is project-driven rather than part of an overall framework for securing natural capital.

/ It fails to assess alternatives to a proposal. Decisions are made on an accept-or-reject basis; or modifications to an existing project are recommended.

/ It typically comes at the middle or end of a process rather than at the beginning, and this reduces its ability to have a significant impact on a project.

/ Regulators and project proponents may not be sufficiently independent of one another. (Potschin and Haines-Young 2003)

Incentive-based policies

Here we examine three types of policy: purchased property rights, tradable property rights and development impact fees. The first two compensate landowners for protecting the EGS on their property. The third requires landowners to pay for any impact their land use has on natural capital (and on other public goods and services). Methods of financing also differ.

Purchased property rights

The concept is simple: a government or other organization acquires either a piece of land outright (fee-simple title) or the attributes of the land that provide EGS (conservation easements). The acquisition can be accomplished by direct cash transfer from the buyer to the seller or via donations facilitated by tax incentives. "A conservation easement is a contract that divides portions of the land title between the landowner, or fee holder, and an easement holder" (Merenlender et al. 2004, 67).[8] The easement is legally binding on both parties and specifies conditions — such as limits on type of land use and land cover, setbacks from streams, distance between buildings, where cattle are allowed to graze and so on. The landowner retains the right to use the land in specified ways — to farm segments of it, to construct a certain number and particular types of buildings, to build roads. Conservation easements are typically held by governments or nonprofit conservation organizations. The holder has access to the land in order to monitor and enforce the easement. Such agreements often last in perpetuity; however, they can be made to cover a given period, and amendments are possible with the agreement of both parties.

A land trust is a nonprofit organization that acquires land or conservation easements and acts as a steward of a piece of land, enhancing the protection of its EGS. The land trust may hold the rights in perpetuity or for a specified period. The land may be donated or purchased. There are thousands of land trusts in the United States, and close to 100 in Canada. They range from small local organizations to large entities with thousands of employees (for example, Ducks Unlimited and the Nature Conservancy).

Conservation easements are a major factor in securing natural capital on private land in the United States, and they are supported by a wide variety of public policies at the state and federal levels.[9] The policies use tax incentives, like reducing capital gains taxes for donated lands (as does Canada's Ecological Gifts Program, described in the next section); providing funding through state and federal government agencies for the protection of specific types of natural capital (as does the US Department of Agriculture's Conservation Reserve Program); and offering local conservation bond issues. In 2006, $6.7 billion in state and local conservation funding was passed by voters in 133 different measures (Land Trust Alliance 2006). The Land Trust Alliance's 2005 census of protected areas notes that 37 million acres are under NGO- or government-run trusts, and of these, 6.2 million acres are held as conservation easements. There has been tremendous growth in the number of acres converted to trusts in recent years: from 338,000 acres annually in 1995-2000, to 1.2 million acres annually in 2000-05 (Land Trust Alliance 2006). This growth reflects the maturity of US incentive programs and the size of the financial incentives offered by governments and NGOs.

The Ecological Gifts Program — Federal programs in Canada to acquire conservation easements and land trusts began in earnest in 1995, with amendments to the *Income Tax Act* providing tax incentives for ecological gifts. Environment Canada has determined that land qualifies as an eco-gift if it is ecologically sensitive and important to the preservation of Canada's environmental heritage. The eco-gift recipient must be a government or a registered charitable conservation organization.[10] The recipient is responsible for monitoring and enforcing any provisions of the easement and ensuring compliance with government land-use regulations. Eco-gifters receive a charitable donation receipt equal to the fair market value of the gift. Between 1995 and 2000, eco-gifters had to include one-half of the accrued capital gains for the property in their taxable income for the year of the donation. The inclusion rate was reduced to one-quarter in 2000, and the spring 2006 budget eliminated capital gains tax on all ecological gifts made after May 2, 2006.

Between 1995 and March 2003, 325 gifts were made, totalling 24,000 hectares, at a market value of $67 million. Environment Canada indicates that more than 560 eco-gifts, valued at over $182 million, have been donated across the country; these gifts protect 48,000 hectares of wildlife habitat ("Ecological Gifts Program: History" 2007). Consider this: first, if one compares the hectares donated to the total hectares deemed at risk in Canada, it is clear that eco-gifts represent a minuscule percentage of Canada's 82 million hectares of protected land; second, the average value of the land is well over $3 million per hectare. The opportunity cost in terms of tax revenue forgone is thus not trivial — we must therefore question whether we are paying too much for the land. The Ecological Gifts Program to date has provided only a small incentive to secure natural capital, and, by itself, it will not have a large impact on the amount of land protected.

The literature on donated conservation easements and land trusts suggests they have the following advantages (see, for example, Land Trust Alliance 2006; Walls and McConnell 2004; McConnell, Kopits and Walls 2003; Duke and Lynch 2006):

/ A concrete monetary value is established for the EGS on the property with conservation easements (CEs).

/ CEs are typically cheaper than full acquisition of the land because only some of the characteristics of the land are transferred.

/ CEs represent a voluntary exchange between the landowner and the purchaser; hence any transaction must maximize the well-being of both parties.

/ CE and land trust programs do not penalize landowners for past conservation activities; land value is based on the current market value of all the land's attributes.

/ The portion of the land not covered by the CE remains on the tax rolls, thus reducing the fiscal costs to the community of conservation and improving community support for conservation.

/ The priorities of the local community are likely to be represented with these programs, as the CE must satisfy criteria of the purchasing party (government or an NGO).

/ CEs may be more flexible than land management by government agencies because they do not impose regulations.

/ CEs may be the only way that owners of family farms, ranches and private woodlots can afford to sustain their productive activities and still conserve their land.

Disadvantages or challenges of CEs include the following:

/ NGOs may have trouble raising funds to purchase CEs or land; and governments will have to face the problem of forgone tax revenue.

/ The cost of the CEs may be high relative to other policy options due to the difficulty of land valuation.

/ Land acquired may not be the most valuable in terms of EGS protected due to the voluntary nature of CE and land trust programs and the lack of a comprehensive plan and targets for protecting natural capital across Canada.

/ Participation rates in voluntary programs tend to be low.

/ Marginal EGS within a property are typically not priced; the land value is a composite.

Property tax credits for EGS — Property tax credits for protecting EGS on private lands have been employed widely by local governments in Canada and the United States. This tax policy creates a conservation easement by which the landowner voluntarily agrees to manage the property in a way that protects natural capital in exchange for financial compensation — a credit on his or her property taxes. The difference is twofold. First, the credit is generally calculated according to a fixed dollar amount assigned to each acre/hectare or type of EGS. This effectively puts a price on CEs, but it is an administrative price, not one determined in any sort of exchange process. The landowner simply takes it or leaves it. If the government adjusts the dollar credit in response to take-up, then this iterative process would mimic a market. Second, the duration of the agreement is usually only one year, whereas CEs or land trusts often last in perpetuity.

While techniques for defining the EGS characteristics for which government is willing to offer tax credits differ among the various schemes, the basic concept is that government assesses the ecological characteristics of the property and determines whether protecting the natural capital is in the interests of the municipality. On agricultural lands, for example, the landowner may have to agree to maintain a buffer zone around riparian areas in which no livestock can graze and no crops can be grown. Or it may be stipulated that a wetland cannot be drained or reduced in size. Implementation of the property tax credit thus requires data collection and assessment of the natural capital targets (as described in the earlier section entitled "Knowledge Gaps and Identification of Natural Capital Targets"), as well as ongoing monitoring to ensure compliance with the provisions of the plan.[11]

Advantages of property tax credits include the following:[12]

/ Property tax credits necessitate the establishment of a concrete monetary value for the EGS on the property.

/ They can be a very low-cost method of protecting natural capital; response to even small credits in some jurisdictions has exceeded expectations.

/ Property tax credits represent a voluntary exchange between the landowner and the municipality.

/ The tax credit program does not penalize landowners for past conservation activity; it specifies the types of activity that qualify for the tax credit. Compliance is ensured through annual surveillance; it does not matter when the landowner undertook the conservation activities.

/ The program improves awareness of the value of EGS to the community and may lead landowners to undertake more private initiatives for conservation without compensation.

Challenges related to property tax credits include the following:

/ The municipality does not know the precise monetary value of the EGS; it only knows that the private value of the EGS to the landowner cannot be greater than the value of the tax credit (otherwise the landowner would not seek the tax credit). The landowner might be willing to sell the rights to the land for a smaller tax credit, and hence the government will have paid "too much" for the EGS.

/ The municipality does not know how much land will be protected or for how long (unless the tax credits have minimum time requirements).

/ Landowners may be unwilling to participate because they don't know whether the tax credit will be available from year to year.

/ Governments have to estimate the tax credit level that will induce the participation target. If the tax credit is "too low," conservation targets will not be met.

/ The program may give rise to free riders: those who were already planning to protect natural capital without the subsidy will take advantage of it.

/ It may compel the municipality to forgo revenues (and hence goods and services).

/ The administrative costs of tax collection are higher with this program than they are with ordinary property tax collection.

We can make several general observations about property tax credits.[13] While most property tax credit programs offer only a modest incentive, they do assist landowners to use their land in a way that helps protect natural capital. Programs with clear eligibility requirements, low compliance costs and flexibility (in that they allow participation with small acreages) tend to have respectable participation rates and deliver the most valuable EGS. Key challenges are funding the tax credit and dealing with free riders, low uptake of the programs and lack of cost-effectiveness. On the funding issue, a number of hedonic studies of the impact on property values of proximity to natural capital in the form of greenbelts, open spaces, parks, forests and water bodies have found a positive and significant relationship.[14] For example, Moura Quayle and Stan Hamilton, in a study of Greater Vancouver and other BC municipalities, report a 10 to 15 percent increase in property values in residential areas close to riparian greenbelts (1999).[15] The increase in property values due to preservation of more natural capital mitigates the loss in property taxes due to withdrawals of property from the tax rolls. In some US examples, the creation of conservation easements has had a negligible effect on property tax revenues — and it may even have increased them.[16]

Tradable development rights

Development permits are common in most urban areas. They implement land-use plans; give permission for residential, commercial and industrial construction; and specify conditions governing that construction (such as building height, green space and setback requirements). A development permit specifies how a piece of land can be used — in essence, it defines land ownership in terms of the right to do particular things on that land. Tradable development rights (TDRs) are similar in that they sever the right to develop the land from the land itself, but they also allow that right to be bought and sold (McConnell, Kopits and Walls 2003). The theory is that the market value of a piece of land, if it is used for conventional development (residential, commercial or industrial), will exceed the market value of the EGS on it because so many of the EGS are not traded. Hence the value of the EGS is not reflected in the market price of a property. A tradable permit for EGS on the land establishes a market value for them. If the value to the landowner of sustaining the EGS on his or her land exceeds the value that could be derived from converting the land to another use, then the landowner will sell the permit. The rights thus price the EGS and compensate the owners for them.

Markets for TDRs can be quite complex to set up and operate. For example, governments need to establish the number of permits to be allocated, whether the rights are for a fixed period or perpetual, how the rights will be defined in relation to EGS and what sort of rules govern trades (for instance, it must be decided whether each permit can be traded one-for-one across the entire region, or whether there is a transfer ratio that sets the number of permits required based on land uses within the district).

The advantages of TDRs are similar to those of the property tax credit for conservation, but they also offer other benefits:

/ Trading establishes a price on the margin rather than an arbitrary price that may or may not represent marginal willingness to accept compensation.

/ Once transferred, rights in perpetuity provide predictable long-term protection of natural capital.

/ TDRs incorporate the benefits of regulation; they involve a fixed number of permits and zoning compliance.

/ The government may buy the rights and permanently retire them, thus protecting EGS in perpetuity.

The challenges of TDRs include the following:

/ The decision to develop is largely irreversible; by contrast, in a tradable pollution permit market, the flows can be turned off and on. Natural capital is a stock, the EGS are flows, but most schemes involving TDRs target land use.

/ The supply of rights offered for trade in each year is unpredictable and dependent on landowners' personal circumstances, price expectations and so on. This makes it difficult for municipalities to plan development over time.

/ Markets for TDRs are complicated to design, and they promote high transaction costs through their search, decision-making and bargaining functions.

/ Market efficiency may be challenged by noncompetitive behaviour (for example, there may be few developers in a given region).

/ TDRs can give rise to free riders (a problem shared with property tax credit programs).

/ Markets for TDRs may cause development hot spots — areas where, if permits can be traded one-for-one, there is overdevelopment.

Development impact fees

Development impact fees (DIFs) are upfront charges applied to new development to cover the incremental public infrastructure costs generated by the development — for example, costs related to schools, roads and sewers. In practice, however, DIFs tend to target average costs: they increase the cost of the development of greenfield properties versus the densification of existing properties.[17] If the developer pays the incremental costs incurred by the municipality when EGS are reduced — for example, when construction or upgrading of water and sewage treatment plants is required to offset the loss of purification services provided by forests and wetlands — then EGS are effectively priced by DIFs. In the US, 28 states have legislation that permits DIFs; few of these cover natural capital, but they could be extended to do so. In some cases, proxies for natural capital are covered — for example, scenic views.

The advantage of DIFs is that they raise revenue for the municipality, which the municipality can use to fund the protection of natural capital. The disadvantage is that we have little if any practical experience with them. It is difficult enough to compute the marginal costs of public physical infrastructure, let alone those of natural capital. In the US, some courts have ruled that the fees can be used only for physical infrastructure, so it is not even certain that they could be used to secure EGS. If DIFs are used without other natural capital policies, there is no guarantee that natural capital will be preserved if the substitutes for natural capital are imperfect or cannot be found. If all municipalities in a region do not charge DIFs, the impact will be similar to that of zoning; it will cause development to shift to regions that apply lower fees or none at all (Walls and McConnell 2004).

A POLICY AGENDA TO SECURE NATURAL CAPITAL

I posed these questions at the outset of the chapter: Are we securing enough natural capital on our lands and waters? Are we securing the most ecologically valuable natural capital? How do we finance the protection of natural capital? Are the means by which we protect natural capital cost-effective? The policies I now propose will help to address these questions. My policy proposals are not mutually exclusive. Securing natural capital for generations to come is a daunting task, and it requires a broad suite of instruments. I believe my first proposal is a necessary condition, regardless of what additional policies we implement. The second proposal addresses the funding issue, and the third is a compilation of the two explicit policies discussed in the earlier section entitled "Policies to Secure Natural Capital." I present the characteristics of each policy proposal and then assess each against a number of criteria.

Policy proposal 1: Canada's conservation plan

The federal government takes the lead in collecting data, producing natural capital indicators and standardizing approaches to estimating target levels of natural capital to be secured.

There are hosts of government agencies (from municipal to federal), conservation organizations and research groups engaged in valuing natural capital and its EGS, deciding what policies and legal frameworks will best protect natural capital, and securing funding to accomplish their goals. While these activities are laudable, my concern is that more time and money will be spent on this exercise than is warranted. Conversion of natural areas to other uses may be irreversible or impractical. Converting a channelized river back to a meandering one can cost in the neighbourhood of $1 million per linear mile. Recreating a wetland of one hectare on the prairies can cost many thousands of dollars. Separate and uncoordinated efforts may also result in the utilization of different processes for determining how much natural capital to secure in different parts of the country. While regional variation may be desirable, too much may lead to uncertainty and increase costs for property owners and governments. The federal government could coordinate the funding and examination of best practices for compiling natural capital data and developing practical models for application to land-use decisions across jurisdictions.

Goals
/ Identify and delineate targeted protected areas, ecosystems and EGS
/ Produce meaningful indicators for natural capital stocks and EGS flows
/ Estimate values of EGS
/ Assist governments, from local to federal, in land-use planning decisions
/ Assist stakeholders and the public to understand the trade-offs related to land-use decisions

Policy mechanisms
/ *Data collection* — Coordinated by Statistics Canada in cooperation with line ministries (Environment Canada, Natural Resources Canada, Agriculture and Agri-Food Canada, the Department of Fisheries and Oceans), provinces, territories and municipal governments
/ *Natural-capital-targeting* (ecological-economic) *model development* — Coordinated by Finance Canada[18] in cooperation with Environment Canada, Industry Canada and independent researchers (academic and NGO)
/ *Pilot studies* — Collate information on existing pilot studies valuing EGS and develop additional pilot studies (case/controls) using the ecological-economic models

Stakeholders
/ Federal government departments
/ Provincial and territorial governments
/ Municipal and regional governments
/ Industry
/ Conservation organizations
/ Research communities

Timelines

/ Short term (one to five years): Develop indicators in a framework, such as Driving Force, Pressure, State, Impact, Response (DPSIR),[19] which also incorporates existing environmental sustainability indicators. Develop a natural capital target model (or models) through the Department of Finance Canada, Industry Canada and Environment Canada with assistance from conservation organizations (like the Nature Conservancy of Canada, Ducks Unlimited Canada and World Wildlife Fund Canada) and academic researchers. Apply the model(s) in pilot programs in selected regions of the country to identify natural capital targets in land-use planning. Convene state-of-the-art working groups involving provincial, territorial and municipal governments, as well as conservation NGOs and academics.

/ Long term (five-plus years): Based on the outcome of the pilot programs, extend the model to all federal land-use decisions and replace the existing environmental impact analysis process. Urge provincial, territorial and local governments to adopt the natural capital target models in their land-use planning and EIA processes and to report their natural capital indicators annually.

Measures of successful implementation

/ Annual publication of municipal, provincial/territorial and national data to illustrate the progress that has been made toward meeting EGS targets

/ Deployment of working models for DPSIR indicators and natural capital targeting

/ Adoption of standard frameworks for analysis across jurisdictions

/ Implementation and analysis of pilot studies

Policy proposal 2: Canada's conservation fund

The federal government increases or levies taxes on activities that degrade natural capital and uses the tax revenue to secure natural capital on public and private lands. The candidate taxes are the GST and a new tax on carbon and air pollutants — the CAP tax. The tax revenue will be dedicated to purchasing strategic natural capital as identified by the first policy proposal and to covering the costs of voluntary incentive-based policies such as the eco-gift program and property tax credits for conservation.[20]

Economists and policy researchers have examined the concept of tax shifting, whereby activities that contribute to environmental degradation are taxed, providing the incentive to curtail those activities and thus to help correct the market failure created from pollution externalities.[21] The revenue this yields is used to reduce taxes on activities that contribute positively to the economy. Traditional models of environmental tax shifting involve taxes on pollution, with revenues recycled by lowering income or payroll taxes. Tax-shifting policies can be made revenue-neutral so that there is no net change in government revenues.

My policy proposal is to use revenues generated from the increase in the GST and from the introduction of the CAP tax to fund activities that furnish goods the market undersupplies. The policy proposal thus differs from pure tax shifting — it is not revenue-neutral. Given the many competing demands on government revenues, I believe that a policy that generates revenue to acquire and protect natural capital is more appealing to government and the public; other programs would not have to be cut, and income taxes would not have to be raised to fund natural capital protection.

Goals

/ Tax bads, subsidize goods
/ Obtain a steady flow of funds to secure and protect natural capital that are not dependent on annual budget allocations
/ Provide incentives to reduce emissions of greenhouse gases and air pollutants and thus lessen the adverse impacts of these emissions on natural capital
/ Increase the use of voluntary policies to secure natural capital

Policy mechanisms

/ *Raise the GST rate by 1 percentage point* — This would reverse the previous reduction; rebrand this as Canada's conservation tax; and/or
/ *Introduce a CAP tax* — The tax base would consist of emitters of greenhouse gases plus the major air pollutants (sulphur dioxide, nitrogen dioxide, particulate matter, volatile organic compounds and carbon monoxide). Environment Canada already collects data on the emissions of all these compounds from industry and other major sources (transportation, for example). For emitters who are currently most able to control their emissions, the tax rate could initially be set to cover the costs of controlling or neutralizing emissions. A low rate will be an incentive to reduce emissions while giving

those producers with high abatement costs time to find cheaper alternatives. Another option is to set the CAP tax rate at the current price of carbon permits in international markets. That rate can be raised or lowered over time, as monitoring of emissions determines the impact on emissions.

/ *Earmarking* — Revenue collected from the GST and/or the CAP tax would be earmarked for the conservation fund and is spent on acquiring protected areas (fee-simple title, conservation easements) and offsetting tax credits offered by two voluntary programs: eco-gifts[22] and municipal property tax credits.[23]

/ *Introduce municipal property tax credits for conservation easements* — This would be a comprehensive grants program for municipalities where threats to natural capital are the most severe (rural municipalities, or those on the urban/rural fringe). The grants would offset property tax losses due to the tax credits, thereby eliminating the disincentive to protect natural capital in the jurisdiction. The commitment period of property owners could be expanded from one year to, say, five years to increase the security of rights acquisition and decrease administrative costs.

Stakeholders

/ Finance Canada
/ Environment Canada
/ Provincial and territorial governments
/ Municipal and regional governments
/ Industries emitting greenhouse gases and air pollutants
/ Nonprofit conservation organizations
/ Property owners

Timelines

/ Short term (one to two years): The GST can be raised on very short notice. The CAP tax can be implemented within a year (after determination of the tax base and rates by the Department of Finance Canada in cooperation with Environment Canada). The GST revenues will provide immediate funding for tax credits to initially offset eco-gifts, and to develop the municipal property tax credit for conservation programs. Review the cost-effectiveness of eco-gifts. While undertaking the first policy proposal, expand/introduce pilot programs for property tax credits.[24]

/ Long term (two-plus years): Extend the municipal tax credit program to more municipalities to meet recommended targets for natural capital acquisition. Increase the CAP tax rate in accordance with an announced schedule to allow emitters time to adjust their processes and adopt less emissions-intensive technologies. If the CAP tax succeeds in reducing emissions over time, revenues for natural capital acquisition will decline; this is acceptable if the program to secure natural capital is successful in phasing in acquisition, and if target levels are obtained. Integrate eco-gifts with the first policy proposal's modelling exercise to ensure cost-effective acquisition of the best properties.

Measures of successful implementation

/ The GST is raised; the CAP tax is introduced and its rates are raised over time

/ Targeted natural capital is secured through expansion of voluntary programs

/ Reduction is achieved in the degradation of natural capital due to lower carbon and air pollution emissions

/ Alberta is still in the federation

Policy proposal 3: Provincial incentive-based policies to secure natural capital

Provincial and territorial governments require municipalities to introduce one of these incentive-based policies to secure natural capital: tradable development rights (TDRs) or development impact fees (DIFs).

The objective of these policies is to ensure that natural capital is part of all development plans and that there is a tangible, mandatory way to secure it. The policy may require a change in legislation to allow municipal governments to include costs of protecting/securing natural capital in development charges and to permit more provincial oversight of local development plans to ensure province-wide consistency. An important aspect of these policies is that they are largely self-financing and eliminate the burden on governments to fund acquisition of natural capital. TDRs require governments to set up and monitor the program. The market will take care of the rest. DIFs generate revenue that is recycled into the protection of natural capital and hence could be revenue-neutral.

Goals

/ Secure and protect targeted natural capital from incompatible development and land uses

/ Introduce mandatory policies that provide incentives on the margin to secure and protect natural capital

Policy mechanisms

/ *Provincial review of all land-use plans* — Each municipality files a land-use plan that also applies to adjacent municipalities (for example, in southern Ontario or Greater Vancouver) and that explicitly incorporates targets for natural capital protection using the natural-capital-targeting models developed as part of my first policy proposal. Zoning remains the regulatory framework, but it may need to be altered in light of the plans.

/ *Introduction of TDRs or DIFs in each municipality* — An empirical study of the impact of TDRs helps to determine whether offering them is a viable policy. TDRs are likely to be efficient where the market is large enough to ensure a sufficient number of trades. Large metropolitan areas are more likely to be able to implement TDRs than smaller ones. DIFs are introduced if TDRs are not viable.

Stakeholders

/ Provincial and territorial governments

/ Municipal and regional governments

/ Property developers

/ Property owners

Timelines

/ Short term (one to five years): Develop or modify land-use plans to incorporate natural capital targets (if this has not already been done). Explore the appropriate policy to implement; study potential markets for TDRs and comparative experience in US jurisdictions.

/ Long term (five-plus years): Implement TDRs or DIFs and monitor them, adjusting the fees or the market as necessary.

Measures of successful implementation

/ Land-use plans with natural capital targets are in place

/ Targeted natural capital is secured through programs

ANALYSIS OF THE POLICY PROPOSALS

In table 2, I compare the three policy proposals with major components of the status quo (continuation of zoning, EIA and current programs to acquire natural capital) using criteria and measures for each that are shown in table 1. Table 2 also presents estimates of the measures for each of the policies and my subjective assessment of the degree to which the policies meet the criteria.

All of my policy proposals rank above the status quo, but none of the alternatives clearly dominates the other. There are trade-offs. This is good news, as my policy approach allows governments to offer jurisdictions a range of policy options. The absolute values of these rankings are merely illustrative, and they represent equal weighting of the criteria. Government decision-makers would undoubtedly have a different weighting scheme. Policies such as the CAP tax are a hard sell politically, but perhaps less so in the current climate. Equity concerns may trump efficiency. The public has repeatedly favoured voluntary policies over mandatory ones — but, again, given the current heightened concern for the environment, people might be more willing to accept policies that are binding, particularly with earmarking.

My policy proposals attempt to address public and political concerns by focusing on such actions as sustaining voluntary programs, introducing mandatory policies and earmarking revenues for conservation. The proposals do not involve throwing out existing programs; they augment them to increase the probability of Canada securing natural capital in cost-effective ways. The proposals are designed to meet these important policy challenges: to provide the data and analysis needed to set targets for the protection of natural capital; and to introduce realistic policies that will help secure Canada's natural heritage for generations to come.

TABLE 1.   CRITERIA AND MEASURES FOR POLICY EVALUATION

Criterion	Measures/indicators for criterion	Metrics	Source of data
Political feasibility	Constitutional conflicts present or absent; number of agencies or ministries involved in decision-making	Fewer is better	Qualitative; literature/media
Economic efficiency	Does the policy establish a unit price for pollution? Does the price reflect some recognition that marginal benefits equal marginal costs?	Yes/no/maybe	Theory
Public acceptance	Public feedback on policy proposal; experience with similar policies in the past or in other jurisdictions	Qualitative	Polls; literature
Cost-effectiveness	Cost per hectare protected or per unit of ecological goods and services secured; elasticity of hectares added per dollar expended	Dollar estimates	Case studies from literature
Financial outlays	Public or private funds; capital versus operating costs	Expenditure levels	Policy design; nature of policy
Stakeholder acceptance	Landowner support for conservation and land acquisition	High for voluntary policies; low for coercive policies	Literature; theory
Impact on EGS	Total number of hectares protected	Prediction and evaluation of previous programs	Case studies from literature
Free riders	What proportion of ecological goods and services would have been protected without the policy?	High to low	Theory/guess
Equity effects	Intergenerational (who pays/who gains); intragenerational	Qualitative	Theory
Probability of sustained protection	Long-term versus temporary security of property rights; governments' commitment to fund programs; survival of nonprofit conservation organizations, continuance of programs	Temporary versus permanent	Theory and experience

TABLE 2.	ANALYSIS AND EVALUATION OF POLICY PROPOSALS[1]			
Criterion	Status quo (zoning, EIA,[2] protected areas)	Canada's conservation plan	Tax shift: GST and CAP[2] tax to fund tax credits	Incentive-based policies (TDRs and DIFs)[2]
Political feasibility				
Intergovernmental conflict	Already resolved (5)[2,3]	Unlikely with data collection, more likely with models (4)	None with GST (5); huge with CAP (1)	Federal-provincial: negligible (5); provincial-municipal: medium (3)
Number of agencies involved	Varies with policy (4)	Many, complex (1)	GST: Dept. of Finance (5); CAP: Dept. of Finance and others (3)	Provincial-municipal (4)
Economic efficiency	Low; pricing implicit, and some perverse incentives (1)	N/A for data collection; high (in theory) for models (5)	GST as revenue source is not efficient (1); CAP tax (5), tax credits = average prices (3)	Theory predicts economic efficiency (5), in practice it may be less efficient (4)
Public acceptance	People are used to the policy framework (3)	Helping the environment by measuring it is hard to oppose (5)	Tax shifting may initially be a hard sell until the public sees results, but it favours the polluter-pays principle (3, rising to 4)	If programs work, there will be a positive public response (4)
Cost-effectiveness	To be estimated: for EIA (2) zoning (3)	N/A – has to flow through policies	Eco-gifts (3); property tax credits (4)	TDRs (4), DIFs (5)
Financial outlays	Government expenditures for ongoing administration; legal costs to be estimated (3)	Government expenditures to establish the program are higher than ongoing costs (3)	Should be made revenue neutral at first; administration costs are low for GST, higher for CAP tax (4)	Small set-up costs, then the market for TDRs and DIFs raises revenue (5)

TABLE 2.	ANALYSIS AND EVALUATION OF POLICY PROPOSALS[1] (CONT'D)			
Criterion	Status quo (zoning, EIA,[2] protected areas)	Canada's conservation plan	Tax shift: GST and CAP[2] tax to fund tax credits	Incentive-based policies (TDRs and DIFs)[2]
Stakeholder acceptance				
Property owners	Zoning mandatory (1)	Most likely to be supported (if recognized at all) (4)	Voluntary for tax credits (5); taxes are broad based, but benefits are as well	TDRs voluntary for sellers (5), but buyers must have permits (1); DIFs mandatory (1)
Other sectors affected	EIA project developers (3); communities affected are often divided (3)	Most likely to be supported (if recognized at all) (4)	CAP-taxed entities (1); others (5)	Other sectors likely unaffected
Impact on ecological goods and services (EGS)	Low in urban/ rural boundary areas (2); better in protected areas, but still below suggested targets (4)	Will help protect EGS because it will better delineate amounts, quality and targets (5)	Impact of tax credits is low, but with greater funding from property tax credits, could rise; eco-gifts rising, too soon to tell (3)	TDRs are a cap-and-trade system, so it depends on the cap (4); DIFs are a tax, but with no flexibility in the amount paid (5)
Free riders	N/A	N/A	Empirical evidence for some (3)	Less of a problem than for tax credits (4)
Equity effects				
Intergenerational	Future deterioration relative to present (2)	Neutral — all should benefit (5)	Future may gain more than present if tax shifting is effective (3)	Neutral: all should benefit through increased EGS now and in future (5)

TABLE 2.   ANALYSIS AND EVALUATION OF POLICY PROPOSALS[1] (CONT'D)

Criterion	Status quo (zoning, EIA,[2] protected areas)	Canada's conservation plan	Tax shift: GST and CAP[2] tax to fund tax credits	Incentive-based policies (TDRs and DIFs)[2]
Intragenerational	Hard to assess (3)	Neutral — all should benefit (5)	Heavily taxed sectors are harmed relative to less heavily taxed ones; those with high incomes benefit more from tax credits (2)	Developers and buyers of TDRs lose (3)
Probability of sustained protection	Permanent in theory, but in practice they are subject to zoning variations and changes in government policy on allowed uses in protected areas (3)	Depends on certainty of government funding; once in place, it still needs continued government funding (3)	Tax rates can change, but once introduced, taxes are rarely removed; donated conservation easements and trusts are seen as having a very high probability of permanence (4)	Property-rights-based policies with high probability of sustained protection (5)
Overall ranking[4]	42/15 = 2.8	44/11 = 4.0	63/20 = 3.2	72/18 = 4.0

[1] Evaluations are subjective and range from 1 (unfavourable) to 5 (highly favourable).
[2] CAP = carbon and air pollutants tax; DIF = development impact fees; EIA = environmental impact assessment; TDR = tradable development rights.
[3] In the 1980s and early 1990s, conflicts erupted between the federal and provincial governments over particular applications of EIAs.
[4] The overall ranking is defined as the ratio of the total score to the number of measures for which a score is given.

NOTES

1. I could not find comparable information for Canada.

2. See Statistics Canada (2006) for annual statistics. The time series for each type of natural capital is variable — some go back many years, others just a few.

3. Data for this Statistics Canada table came from World Wildlife Fund Canada (2003).

4. The later section of this chapter titled "Policies to Secure Natural Capital" provides more details on land trusts and ecogifts. The data for land trusts were obtained from a survey of Canada's 82 land trusts; the response rate to the survey was 71 percent (see Watkins and Hilts 2001).

5. I have chosen the conservative figure of 18 percent because I do not have figures for the land area within each conservation zone shown in figure 1, and I base my calculation on Canada's total area (land plus water). This is simply an order-of-magnitude estimate of the costs of meeting a conservation target.

6. Economists have offered a number of methods for targeting lands for protection. For example, Paul Ferraro suggests combining distance functions with ecological characteristics to minimize costs when allocating conservation funds (2004). Ivan Hascic and JunJie Wu take an empirical look across the US at how three different measures of ecological stress (conventional water-quality measures such as eutrophication and dissolved oxygen; heavy metal toxicity; and species at risk) are affected by different types of land use. Their analysis also yields estimates of the elasticity of water-quality measures with respect to land use (Hascic and Wu 2006).

7. Natural capital inputs (mineral deposits, forests, water) may not have well-defined market values. The producer will, however, value them implicitly. An example of how implicit values are determined is found in timber harvesting. If a hectare of forested land is cut today, the producer has to wait, say, 30 years before new growth is ready for harvest. If the harvest is delayed one year, the trees will grow in volume, but future harvests will also be delayed. The producer must weigh the cost of waiting one year against the value of the incremental wood volume over that period.

8. Other names include "conservation covenants" and (in Quebec) "servitudes." I will refer to all such encumbrances of land as "easements."

9. Due to space constraints, I focus here on US policies, although I do recognize that there are incentive-based policies in other countries.

10. The national criteria for eligibility are broad and focus on ecological values with no economic criteria. Environment Canada's specification includes areas designated as ecologically significant, sites that contain biodiversity and/or species at risk, natural buffers around riparian areas, sites that encompass our environmental heritage and so on. A list of eligible charitable conservation organizations is available on the Ecological Gifts Program Web site (www.cws-scf.ec.gc.ca/egp-pde/). They include national organizations such as the Nature Conservancy of Canada and Ducks Unlimited Canada, as well as small regional organizations such as the Ruiter Valley Land Trust in Quebec, the Kettle Creek Conservation Authority in Ontario and the Bowen Island Conservancy in British Columbia.

11. Monitoring has been done in some cases by satellite imaging, a method that does not require incremental local resources and personnel.

12. The assessment of advantages and challenges is derived from the study of a number of the programs listed in table 2.

13. See Olewiler (2001) for an analysis of conservation property tax credit programs in Canada and the US (this unpublished paper is available from the author).

14. There are many US studies. See, for example, Geoghegan, Lynch and Bucholtz (2006) and King and Anderson (2004).

15 The property did not have to be immediately adjacent; people reported that they liked being near the greenbelt for recreational purposes.

16 One study found that in two Maryland counties, the elasticity of property values with respect to a 1 percent increase in the number of acres of open space meant that property values rose by 0.59 to 0.71 percent. The incremental property tax collected, assuming no change in mill rate, more than offset the total cost of the CEs (Geoghegan, Lynch and Bucholtz 2006).

17 A theoretical model by Jan Brueckner shows that development fees are efficient, assuming that the prices do reflect marginal costs and that the fees discourage sprawl if applied to all municipalities in the region (1997).

18 The Department of Finance is the coordinating agency for the development of the ecological-economic model for two reasons: its strength in the economic part of the modelling, and to tie into the subsequent policies that may involve fiscal instruments in its mandate: Environment Canada cannot levy taxes.

19 See Olewiler (2006) for a synopsis of a DPSIR framework and examples of indicators that can be incorporated into the framework.

20 The National Round Table on the Environment and the Economy (NRTEE) has proposed the creation of a similar fund: the National Conservation Fund. Its policy proposal differs from mine in that it suggests the funds be raised through a reallocation of general revenues from the federal government, to be matched by contributions from provincial and territorial governments (NRTEE 2003).

21 For examples of how tax shifting could work in Canada, see National Round Table on the Environment and the Economy (2001) and Jaccard, Olewiler and Taylor (1999). The theoretical literature is too large to cite; see Goulder (1995) for a review of the basic concepts.

22 The eco-gift program is sacred to nonprofit conservation organizations, and although I

am concerned about its cost-effectiveness, it would be politically unwise to tamper with it at this time. Analysis of the program's unit costs is needed. Integration with the guidelines and targets for natural capital laid out in my first policy proposal may increase cost-effectiveness.

23 Over time, CAP tax revenues should decline in response to higher prices for pollution-intensive activities. If the fund is used to purchase and protect natural capital, it will be like creating an annuity or an endowment, and the diminution in tax revenues will be of less concern than it would be if the funds were used to reduce taxes in a pure tax-shifting application. The mechanics of distributing the GST or CAP tax revenues across the levels of government is an important factor, and it would have to be worked out by the federal and provincial governments.

24 A number of earlier pilot programs were not continued due to lack of funding rather than lack of success.

REFERENCES

Ambrose, R. 2006. *Environment Canada 2005-2006 Departmental Performance Report*. Ottawa: Environment Canada. Accessed June 19, 2007. www.tbs-sct.gc.ca/dpr-rmr/0506/EC-EC/ec-ec_e.pdf

Boyd, J., K. Caballero, and R.D. Simpson. 1999. "The Law and Economics of Habitat Conservation: Lessons from an Analysis of Easement Acquisitions." *RFF Discussion Paper* 99-32. Washington, DC: Resources for the Future. Accessed June 27, 2007. www.rff.org/rff/Documents/RFF-DP-99-32.pdf

British Columbia Ministry of Forests and Range. 2004. *The State of British Columbia's Forests, 2004*. Accessed July 31, 2007. www.for.gov.bc.ca/hfp/sof/sof.htm.

Brueckner, J. 1997. "Infrastructure Financing and Urban Development: The Economics of Impact Fees." *Journal of Public Economics* 66:383-407.

de Groot, R.S., M.A. Wilson, and R.J. Boumans. 2002. "A Typology for

Description, Classification and Valuation of Ecosystem Functions." *Ecological Economics* 41 (3): 393-408.

Duke, J.M., and L. Lynch. 2006. "Farmland Retention Techniques: Property Rights Implications and Comparative Evaluation." *Land Economics* 82 (2): 189-213.

"Ecological Gifts Program: History." 2007. Ottawa: Environment Canada. Accessed June 24, 2007. www.cws-scf.ec.gc.ca/egp-pde/default.asp?lang=En&n=3DA67F34-1

Ferraro, Paul J. 2004. "Targeting Conservation Investments in Heterogeneous Landscapes: A Distance-Function Approach and Application to Watershed Management." *American Journal of Agricultural Economics* 86 (4): 905-18.

Geoghegan, J., L. Lynch, and S.J. Bucholtz. 2006. "Are Agricultural Land Reserves Programs Self Financing?" In *Economics and Contemporary Land Use Policy: Development and Conservation at the Rural-Urban Fringe*, edited by R.J. Johnston and S.K. Swallow. Washington, DC: RFF Press.

Goulder, L.H. 1995. "Environmental Taxation and the 'Double Dividend': A Reader's Guide." *International Tax and Public Finance* 2:157-83.

Hascic, I., and J. Wu. 2006. "Land Use and Watershed Health in the United States." *Land Economics* 82 (2): 214-39.

Jaccard, M., N. Olewiler, and A. Taylor. 1999. "Environmental Tax Shift: A Discussion Paper for British Columbians." Accessed June 27, 2007. www.emrg.sfu.ca/EMRGweb/pubarticles/1999/EnvTaxShift5.pdf

King, J.R., and C.M. Anderson. 2004. "Marginal Property Tax Effects of Conservation Easements: A Vermont Case Study." *American Journal of Agricultural Economics* 86 (4): 919-32.

Land Trust Alliance. 2006. *2005 National Land Trust Census Report*. Washington, DC: Land Trust Alliance. Accessed June 24, 2007. www.lta.org/census/2005_report.pdf

"Major Threats to Biodiversity." 1995. *Wilderness Committee Educational Report*

14 (4). Accessed June 19, 2007. www.wildernesscommittee.org/campaigns/species/sara/reports/Vol14No04/threats

McConnell, V., E. Kopits, and M. Walls. 2003. "How Well Can a Market for Development Rights Work? Evaluation of a Farmland Preservation Program." *RFF Discussion Paper* 03-08. Washington, DC: Resources for the Future. Accessed June 27, 2007. www.rff.org/Documents/RFF-DP-03-08.pdf

Merenlender, A.M., L. Huntsinger, G. Guthey, and S.K. Fairfax. 2004. "Land Trusts and Conservation Easements: Who Is Conserving What for Whom." *Conservation Biology* 18 (1): 65-75.

National Round Table on the Environment and the Economy (NRTEE). 2001. *Ecological Fiscal Reform: Executive Brief, Ecological Fiscal Reform in Canada*. Ottawa: NRTEE. Accessed June 26, 2007. www.nrtee-trnee.ca/eng/programs/Current_Programs/EFR-Energy/EFR-Exe-Brief-26-09-2001.pdf

_____. 2003. *Securing Canada's Natural Capital: A Vision for Nature Conservation in the 21st Century*. Ottawa: NRTEE. Accessed June 26, 2007. www.nrtee-trnee.ca/Publications/PDF/SOD_Nature_E.pdf

Natural Resources Canada. 2007. *The Atlas of Canada*. Thematic Modules: Wetlands. Accessed July 31,2007. www.atlas.nrcan.gc.ca/site/english/learningresources/theme_modules/wetlands/index.html

Newburn, D.A., P. Berck, and A.M. Merenlender. 2006. "Habitat and Open Space at Risk of Land-Use Conversion: Targeting Strategies for Land Conservation." *American Journal of Agricultural Economics* 88 (1): 28-42.

Olewiler, N. 2001. "Property Tax Credits for Conservation." Paper presented to the National Round Table on the Economy and the Environment, Ecological Fiscal Reform Working Group.

_____. 2006. "Environmental Sustainability for Urban Areas: The Role of Natural Capital Indicators." *Cities* 23 (3): 184-95.

Potschin, M.B., and R.H. Haines-Young. 2003. "Improving the Quality of Environmental Assessments Using the Concept of Natural Capital: A Case Study from Southern Germany." *Landscape and Urban Planning* 63 (2): 93-108.

Quayle, M., and S. Hamilton. 1999. *Corridors of Green and Gold: Impact of Riparian Greenways on Property Values*. Report prepared for the Fraser River Action Plan. Vancouver: Department of Fisheries and Oceans. Accessed June 25, 2007. www.dfo-mpo.gc.ca/Library/241452.pdf

Shaffer, M.L., J.M. Scott, and F. Casey. 2002. "Noah's Options: Initial Cost Estimates of a National System of Habitat Conservation Areas in the United States." *Bioscience* 52 (5): 439-43.

Statistics Canada. 2006. *Human Activity and the Environment: Annual Statistics 2006*, cat. no. 16-201-XPE. Ottawa: Statistics Canada. Accessed June 20, 2007. www.statcan.ca/english/freepub/16-201-XIE/16-201-XIE2006000.pdf

Walls, M., and V. McConnell. 2004. "Incentive-Based Land Use Policies and Water Quality in the Chesapeake Bay." *RFF Discussion Paper* 04-20. Washington, DC: Resources for the Future. Accessed June 27, 2007. www.rff.org/documents/RFF-DP-04-20.pdf

Watkins, M., and S. Hilts. 2001. "Land Trusts Emerge as an Important Conservation Force in Canada: A Summary of the Land Protected by Land Trusts and the Current Issues and Challenges Facing the Growing Land Trust Movement in Canada." Accessed June 27, 2007. www.uoguelph.ca/~claws/conference/landtrustsincanada.doc

World Wildlife Fund Canada (WWFC). 2003. "The Nature Audit: Setting Canada's Conservation Agenda for the 21st Century." *WWFC Report* 1-2003. Toronto: WWFC.

INNOVATIVE CONSERVATION POLICIES FOR CANADA THAT REALLY INTEGRATE THE ENVIRONMENT AND THE ECONOMY

Wiktor Adamowicz

In her contribution to this volume, Nancy Olewiler has made a case for identifying the securing of natural capital and ecological goods and services (EGS) as a strategic goal for Canada, and she has provided three integrated policy options to address this goal. Overall, I believe that she has succeeded in proposing a suite of policies that are of critical importance to an issue that is top of mind for Canadians. While I agree in principle with the issues and approaches Olewiler presents in "Securing Natural Capital and Ecological Goods and Services for Canada," and while I enthusiastically support the concepts she presents, I will provide some alternative perspectives on the problem of securing natural capital.

NATURAL CAPITAL AND ECOLOGICAL GOODS AND SERVICES: CANADIAN CASES

Olewiler claims that depreciation of natural capital affects the well-being of Canadians. The cases she presents involve air, water and land. Investigation of a few case studies may provide some insight into the importance of natural capital in Canada. World Bank data on genuine savings (an index that contains information on savings in an economy, including investment in, or depreciation of, natural capital and human capital) show a declining trend for Canada (World Bank 2004). The economic impact of a depreciation in air quality is significant. An Ontario Ministry of the Environment evaluation concluded that the cost of achieving a 19 percent improvement in air quality over 20 years was $146 million annually, while the benefits — arising from reduced health risks — were $1,273 million annually (1999). As Olewiler suggests, the location of the natural capital improvements is very important; substantial net benefits would accrue in Ontario for improvements in air quality relative to other parts of the country (Hrudey et al. 2004). Similar issues arise in relation to water quality. Linkages between water quality and human health generate significant economic values associated with improvements in natural capital or avoided reductions in natural capital, and these are location-sensitive as well (Adamowicz, Dupont and Krupnick 2004). There is also some evidence that these nonmarket values (values for ecological goods and services that are not typically captured in markets) are growing (Costa and Kahn 2003).

The importance of natural capital is clear in cases linked to air or water quality, in which the impact upon health and economic activity is often measurable. While other forms of natural capital are not as closely associated with human health and well-being, they are nevertheless considered significant by the Canadian public. Depreciation of habitat and endangered species loss is a case in point. There are few direct linkages between species loss and human well-being, yet the irreversibility of such loss provokes concern, even though the cost of protecting threatened species can be high (Loomis and White 1996; Adamowicz et al. 1998). Measurement challenges in these cases include answering the question "How much is enough?" and determining the most cost-effective strategy for reaching the environmental goal.

THREATS TO NATURAL CAPITAL

Olewiler lists five threats to natural capital; I will deal briefly with each. First, there are significant knowledge gaps associated with natural capital. Even for air quality and water quality, monitoring data are sparse and difficult to obtain (Hrudey et al. 2004). Setting targets is even more challenging than filling data gaps. In principle, targets are best set when information is available on the costs and benefits of alternative levels of the target. Without data on baseline levels of natural capital or on the relationships between policy actions, costs, benefits and natural capital, it is difficult to set a target.

Olewiler discusses some approaches to setting targets for natural capital, including approaches to identifying protected areas. These approaches, designed to minimize the costs of achieving alternative levels of natural capital, tend to involve strategies that are more cost-effective than purely biologically based strategies for biodiversity conservation, as the latter typically do not incorporate the opportunity cost of purchasing or leasing property (Ando et al. 1998; Polasky et al. 2005; Hauer et al. 2007). It is important to recognize that the available spatial information on land attributes (ecological and economic) is sufficient to allow decision-makers, with the help of current computing technology, to devise cost-effective conservation strategies. However, we still require institutions and processes to establish and enforce the targets.

The second threat Olewiler discusses is market failure. This is clearly the root source of threats to natural capital, as the market usually does not capture the value or importance of natural capital. The lack of market signals for natural capital and ecosystem services affects resource use, and it also affects investment in technology development and innovation in environmental services provision. Investment in technologies that conserve natural capital or ecosystem services, for example, does not yield a market return and therefore does not appear to be as important as investment in cost-reducing or revenue-improving technologies.

Olewiler's third threat — competing priorities of governments — is illustrated by the fact that the trade-off between maintaining the tax base and protecting natural capital, in addition to the desire to be re-elected, can lead municipal governments to opt for conversion of natural capital to constructed capital. Municipalities are often subject to pressure from developers to convert lands, and the developments erected on these lands serve to improve the tax base. Protecting natural capital will not provide the municipality with tax revenues, and this can create political and economic difficulties for the community. At a provincial level, similar problems arise. In Alberta, for example, confronting the issue of land-use trade-offs has become a high priority in several government departments. Olewiler's fourth and fifth threats are financial constraints and long-term planning for development. These threats are clearly related to the previous three. Lack of financing is linked to competing priorities, and there is a lack of long-term planning because short-term priorities take precedence over long-term goals and objectives.

What needs to be more clearly identified here is the deficiency of incentives to protect or invest in natural capital. Regulatory mechanisms are typically based on command-and-control approaches that provide no incentive to improve natural capital beyond the level of the standard or regulation. Once compliance is attained, there is no motivation to improve performance. A price signal would constitute a clear and continuous incentive. Best available technology standards can also fail to protect natural capital, as again there is no incentive to improve beyond those standards. For example, water for many major uses is free, so there are no incentives for reduced use beyond private costs. Environmental taxes are rarely in use in Canada; they are more common in other member countries of the Organisation for Economic Co-operation and Development (Adamowicz 2007). The fact that we in Canada have failed to use incentive-based policies gives rise to one of the major challenges we face in natural resource management: our limited ability to adapt to shocks, like climate change. It also poses a major threat to natural capital.

POLICIES TO SECURE NATURAL CAPITAL

In her chapter, Olewiler outlines a number of market-based instruments that may be applied to protect natural capital; she emphasizes land use and the EGS that arise from land. As I stated earlier, the use of such instruments is highly desirable. In addition to the incentive-based policies that Olewiler outlines, let me point to some that are in use in other parts of the world (and sometimes in Canada as well). First, one variant of purchasing property rights to protect natural capital is the use of conservation auctions — as by, for example, the Conservation Reserve Program in the United States and the BushTender program in Australia (see also Stoneham et al. 2003; Baerenklau 2005). The improvements in cost-effectiveness deriving from such an approach can be significant (Baerenklau 2005); auction programs for conservation land are designed to identify landowners who offer the best package of conservation benefits at the lowest cost to the agency. Programs that offer the same compensation for land to all participants will be more expensive because the cost of achieving the conservation target will be higher.

Olewiler discusses tradable development rights as a viable strategy for protecting natural capital (for US examples, see Hellerstein et al. 2002). One item she does not address is how such mechanisms might work on public land. Significant effects are evident on public land and in marine areas. In Alberta, the impact on woodland caribou, a threatened species, is a case in point. Inefficiencies arising from overlapping tenures for use (for forestry, energy, mining and so on) and multiple governing agencies complicate the problem of setting objectives and conserving natural capital. One market-based approach similar to tradable development rights is tradable disturbance rights (Weber and Adamowicz 2002; see Farr et al. 2004 for additional mechanisms for public land cases). Under the tradable disturbance rights scheme, developers would own a limited number of rights to disturb a forest area. If they could reduce the amount of land they disturbed, they could then sell some of their rights to other agents. This approach would provide some of the same incentives — a price or cost signal that would encourage land conservation beyond a target or standard — that derive from transferable development rights on private lands.

A POLICY AGENDA FOR CANADA
Policy proposal 1: Canada's conservation plan

In her first proposal, Olewiler argues that targets for natural capital need to be established and that data and indicators associated with natural capital are required to develop these targets. She highlights the need to move beyond simple indicators and characterize the relationships between actions and outcomes and assess trade-offs to support the development of targets. This is an excellent proposal. Others have also identified the need to collect meaningful data on environmental quality to support policy decisions, given the importance of environmental control costs to the economy (Banzhaf 2004, 2003). I am also in favour of the phased approach, which starts with pilot programs in selected regions of the country.

However, I am somewhat concerned about Canada's capacity to support the type of analysis required. Data collection and monitoring can be carried out relatively easily, but our capacity to develop integrated ecological-economic models and estimate opportunity costs for EGS provision is limited. Our capacity to measure environmental values or benefits is also limited; and benefit transfer techniques (based on benefit estimates from other regions or countries) may not be applicable in some of the more challenging and controversial cases. In part, this limitation may be due to the fact that our institutional framework for natural capital does not typically involve examination of environmental costs or benefits and has not provided incentives for the development of such skills in research agencies. Yet it may be that by improving capacity we will also improve our institutional frameworks. Implementing this objective and Olewiler's first and second policies may help develop our capacity. Canada's limited capacity in this area means that it may take a little longer to achieve this objective.

We must also ensure that in developing databases and monitoring programs we emphasize the intended use in order to guide policy analysis and assessment of investment alternatives. There are examples of monitoring efforts in which the objective or the links back to policy actions were unclear. As a final point, we must collect data on human as well as ecological factors. There is no reliable source of information on touristic, recreational or other human uses of EGS. The national survey on the importance of nature to Canadians was terminated in 1996 after two decades of high-quality information collection. This type of information will be important for an improved understanding of the values of EGS.

Policy proposal 2: Canada's conservation fund

This is my favourite of the three policy proposals — an innovative twist on tax shifting. It is an appropriate time to consider tax shifting and reallocation of GST revenue of this nature. Olewiler's proposal to "[r]aise the GST rate by 1 percentage point (reversing the previous reduction)" could be quickly implemented, but there would be concerns about the negative effect of earmarking on flexibility. Her suggestion of a new tax on carbon and air pollutants — a CAP tax — is an excellent one. This would be a good way to begin tax shifting, but there would have to be a balance between recycling the tax revenue to fund investments in natural capital and recycling it for other purposes (distributional purposes, for example).

Two aspects of this issue require further investigation. First, the capture of 1 percentage point of the GST would be quite large — approximately $5 billion (the federal portion of the GST was approximately $45 billion in 2005-06 [Statistics Canada 2006]). In some US jurisdictions, a fraction of 1 percentage point of sales tax has been earmarked for habitat programs. Arkansas, for example, voted to approve the allotment of one-eighth of 1 percentage point for wildlife habitat. A half-of-1-percentage-point program would still be significant, and it would provide for the purchases/leases that Olewiler outlines and the data collection/analysis expenses.

The second aspect of the issue that needs to be examined more closely is how the funds are administered and who decides which natural capital programs merit investment. In the US, the Natural Resource Damage Assessment (NRDA) program (which falls under the *Comprehensive Environmental Response, Compensation, and Liability Act*, commonly known as Superfund) appoints trustees to administer funds earmarked for compensating the public for the loss of environmental services due to damage. The appeal of the NRDA trustee system is that trustees are somewhat arm's length and independent.

This program could be linked to Olewiler's first proposal. The agency responsible for that proposal could also take part in monitoring and evaluating returns generated by the investments in natural capital proposed in the program.

Policy proposal 3: provincial incentive-based policies to secure natural capital

Aspects of this proposal are linked to the previous proposal through the collection and administration of funds for the incentive-based programs. Two issues deserve additional comment. First, I would not limit the set of incentive-based tools to tradable development rights (TDRs) and development impact fees (DIFs). Experience has shown that different circumstances require different instruments. If there are few agents in a market, or if all the agents are similar, then a tradable rights scheme may not be effective, though a price or tax scheme will be. Second, it is not clear that a provincial scale is appropriate for all cases. Various ecological objectives would be more appropriately addressed on a bioregional scale, which may or may not exceed provincial boundaries.

POLICY ANALYSIS

Olewiler offers an excellent framework for the analysis of policy options. One element that I would include as a criterion is an incentive for innovation and technology development. This is embedded in the economic efficiency criterion, but it would be worthwhile to identify it separately. In many cases, even relatively weak signals of the importance of protecting natural capital have stimulated the development and/or adoption of improved technology. The change to low-impact seismic lines in the energy sector of western Canada is one example. Historically, the energy sector would create wide linear disturbances in forest areas when building seismic lines for energy exploration. Evidence that this was harmful to wildlife habitat and conservation objectives led the sector to develop methods that disturbed a much smaller area.

SUMMARY

Overall, I strongly support the framework that Olewiler has developed and the integration of her three policy proposals. These useful policy options can be phased in, gradually increasing our protection of, and investment in, natural capital. Returns on investment in such policies are potentially substantial, as they will make significant contributions to the well-being of Canadians and people around the world.

I wish to raise several issues for further consideration. First, Olewiler's emphasis is primarily on natural capital protection and EGS on private land. Her set of options could be expanded to include water and air aspects of natural capital as well as natural capital protection on public land. However, since the examination of private land-use issues often requires funding for data collection, integrated assessment and incentive systems, I can see why Olewiler has concentrated on this. Second, while Olewiler's focus is on policies for investing in natural capital, a reconsideration of policies that directly or indirectly depreciate natural capital (like inefficient resource pricing; for other policies that lead to inefficient land use, see Farr et al. 2004) or that increase the cost of conserving natural capital should also be considered an important aspect of policy reform (see Hauer et al. 2007 for a description of how changing the system of forestry quota allocations to allow a single management agent to provide wood to the highest-value uses reduces the costs of achieving natural capital improvements by up to 30 percent). Third, I am all in favour of incentive-based programs. There is considerable experience with them in various parts of the world. However, for a variety of reasons, Canada has opted to engage in voluntary schemes and negotiations rather than set targets and incentives (Adamowicz 2007). If we choose learning by doing through pilot programs, we may reverse this trend and move toward the implementation of focused and cost-effective mechanisms to protect natural capital. The benefits to Canadians will be significant: improved health and well-being, a reduced risk of irreversible losses of species and ecosystems, and an improved ability to adapt to changes in economic and natural systems.

REFERENCES

Adamowicz, W. 2007. "Reflections on Environmental Policy in Canada." *Canadian Journal of Agricultural Economics/Revue canadienne d'agro-économie* 55 (1): 1-13.

Adamowicz, W., P. Boxall, M. Williams, and J. Louviere. 1998. "Stated Preference Approaches for Measuring Passive Use Values: Choice Experiments and Contingent Valuation." *American Journal of Agricultural Economics* 80 (1): 64-75.

Adamowicz, W., D.P. Dupont, and A. Krupnick. 2004. "The Value of Good Quality Drinking Water to Canadians and the Role of Risk Perceptions: A Preliminary Analysis." *Journal of Toxicology and Environmental Health* A67 (20-22): 1825-44.

Ando, A., J. Camm, S. Polasky, and A. Solow. 1998. "Species Distributions, Land Values and Efficient Conservation." *Science* 279: 2126-8.

Baerenklau, K.A. 2005. "Cost-Effectiveness of the Conservation Reserve Program: Discussion." *American Journal of Agricultural Economics* 87 (5): 1256-7.

Banzhaf, S. 2003. "Accounting for the Environment." *Resources* 151:6-10. Accessed July 19, 2007. www.rff.org/Documents/RFF-Resources-151-Enviroacctng.pdf

———. 2004. "Creating a Bureau of Environmental Statistics." In *New Approaches on Energy and the Environment: Policy Advice for the President*, edited by R.D. Morgenstern and P.R. Portney. Washington, DC: Resources for the Future. Accessed July 19, 2007. www.rff.org/rff/RFF_Press/CustomBook Pages/NewApproachesonEnergyandthe Environment/loader.cfm?url=/commonspot/security/getfile.cfm&PageID=15574

Costa, D., and M.E. Kahn. 2003. "The Rising Price of Nonmarket Goods." *American Economic Review* 93 (2): 227-32.

Farr, D., S. Kennett, M. Ross, B. Stelfox, and M. Weber. 2004. *Conserving Canada's Natural Capital: The Boreal Forest, Al-Pac Case Study Report*. Ottawa: National Round Table on the Environment and the Economy. Accessed July 20, 2007. www.nrtee-trnee.ca/eng/programs/Current_Programs/Nature/Boreal-Forest/Documents/200407-AlPac-Case-Study/200407-AlPac-CS_Complete_E.pdf

Hauer, G., S. Cumming, F. Schmiegelow, W. Adamowicz, M. Weber, L. Foote, and R. Jagodzinski. 2007. "Modeling Biodiversity-Forest Products Tradeoffs: A Spatial Analysis of the Implications of Forest Policy Options on Conservation Tradeoffs." University of Alberta Working Paper, Department of Rural Economy, University of Alberta.

Hellerstein, D., C. Nickerson, J. Cooper, P. Feather, D. Gadsby, D. Mullarkey, A. Tegene, and C. Barnard. 2002. "Farmland Protection: The Role of Public Preferences for Rural Amenities." *Agricultural Economic Report 815*. Washington, DC: United States Department of Agriculture, Economic Research Service. Accessed July 20, 2007. www.ers.usda.gov/publications/aer815/aer815.pdf

Hrudey, S.E., B.A. Hale, V. Adamowicz, R. Dales, A. Krupnick, M. Lippman, J. McConnell, and P. Renzi. 2004. "Report of an Expert Panel to Review the Socio-economic Models and Related Components Supporting the Development of Canada-Wide Standards (CWS) for Particulate Matter (PM) and Ozone to the Royal Society of Canada." *Journal of Toxicology and Environmental Health* B7 (3): 147-266.

Loomis, J., and D.S. White. 1996. "Economic Benefits of Rare and Endangered Species: Summary and Meta-analysis." *Ecological Economics* 18:197-206.

Ontario Ministry of the Environment. 1999. "Compendium on Current Knowledge of Fine Particulate Matter in Ontario." Accessed July 17, 2007. www.ene.gov.on.ca/programs/3952e_3.htm

Polasky, S., E. Nelson, E. Lonsdorf, P. Fackler, and A. Starfield. 2005. "Conserving Species in a Working Landscape: Land Use with Biological and Economic Objectives." *Ecological Applications* 15 (4): 1387-1401.

Statistics Canada. 2006. *Public Sector Statistics: Financial Management System, 2005/2006*, cat. no. 68-213-XIE. Ottawa: Statistics Canada. Accessed July 19, 2007. dsp-psd.communication.gc.ca/Collection-R/Statcan/68-213-XIB/68-213-XIE2006000.pdf

Stoneham, G., V. Chaudhri, A. Ha, L. Strappazzon. 2003. "Auctions for Conservation Contracts: An Empirical Examination of Victoria's BushTender Trial." *Australian Journal of Agricultural and Resource Economics* 47 (4): 477-500.

Weber, M., and W. Adamowicz. 2002. "Tradable Land-Use Rights for Cumulative Environmental Effects Management." *Canadian Public Policy/Analyse de Politiques* 28 (4): 581-95.

World Bank. 2004. "Adjusted Net Savings Time Series by Country, 1970-2004." Accessed April 29, 2007. www.siteresources.worldbank.org/INTEEI/1105643-1115814965717/21000013/ANS_1970_2004_3(L1).xls

NATURE AS CAPITAL: CONCERNS AND CONSIDERATIONS
Peter A. Victor

Nancy Olewiler's interesting contribution to this volume, "Securing Natural Capital and Ecological Goods and Services for Canada," presents a conceptual framework and three policy proposals.[1] The framework and proposals are not as tightly connected as they might be, which is both good and bad. It is good because any problems with the conceptual framework may not have a bearing on the merits of the policy proposals. It is bad because a tighter link between concepts and policy would make it easier to assess the relative strengths and weaknesses of the policy proposals. In this commentary on Olewiler's chapter, I address the conceptual issues first and then the policy proposals.

THE CONCEPTUAL FRAMEWORK

Olewiler defines natural capital as "the planet's stock of renewable and nonrenewable natural resources (forests, minerals, oil, plant and animal species), environmental resources (atmosphere, water) and land." She explains that "the planet's ecosystems...use these components of natural capital to create habitats capable of sustaining life. Land, natural resources and environmental resources are capital in that they can produce a steady flow of goods and services if depreciation or degradation is offset" (125). Olewiler defines ecological goods and services (EGS) as "the goods and services that flow from natural capital...EGS can be produced using human and physical capital — think of timber harvesting, natural gas extraction and capture, and fish farming. Some EGS require few if any inputs to produce value to society; natural landscapes with scenic views and recreational uses are one example" (126).

These definitions represent the first component of Olewiler's conceptual framework. I will comment on the second — market failure — in a moment. The first thing to note about the definitions is that they are anthropocentric. Nature is regarded as a storehouse of resources for human use: "to produce value to society." If nature belongs to us, then managing it is like managing a bank account, or several bank accounts — hence the appeal of natural capital for describing nature. Keep the capital intact and live off the interest. From this perspective, capital and interest include all other species that also live on earth to which we have no obligations or responsibilities. Such an anthropocentric view is not universally held.

Olewiler states that resources are capital because "they can produce a steady flow of goods and services." This is what resources and other forms of capital have in common. She does not comment on how they differ, and the differences are many. I will describe a few. The first stems from the different meanings of capital within economics. One is the stock of buildings and machines that are made by humans — so-called manufactured capital. Capital in this form provides services, often involving the manipulation of materials driven by some form of energy to make products. To use terminology promoted by Herman Daly and Joshua Farley, such capital is a "fund" providing a "service": a fund-service resource (2004). Raw materials, including deposits of minerals in the ground, are a stock-flow resource. The difference between a stock-flow resource and a fund-service resource is that funds do not end up in the product. A lathe does not become part of a piece of furniture. Manufactured capital cannot be changed into another form. A lathe cannot become a tractor.

At the other extreme we have the fundist notion of capital, according to which capital is a fund that finances investments in buildings and machines. As a fund, capital is completely malleable as long as the fund is maintained through the reinvestment of profits or interest. A lathe can become a tractor eventually, if the profit from woodworking is invested in the purchase of a tractor.

Neither of these concepts of capital fits nature very well. Nature is not fixed and rigid, as is manufactured capital. Sometimes nature provides services, such as when a tree captures carbon dioxide and produces oxygen (that is, as a fund service). The same tree can also be embodied in a product if it is cut down and made into paper (that is, as a stock flow). While it is common in nature for the same entity to be a fund service and a stock flow, it is atypical of manufactured capital. Nature is not fixed in form, like manufactured capital; nether is it perfectly flexible, like a fund. An acorn becomes an oak tree, not a swallow. After a forest fire, another forest grows, not a marsh. So the fundist notion of capital is also limited for conceptualizing nature as capital.

Olewiler refers to the "steady flow of goods and services" that nature can provide, just like any type of capital. This does have validity in some settings. However, nature can also be understood as a complex system, or a set of systems nested inside one another, with nonlinearities, feedbacks, thresholds, irreversibilities, stochasticity and other characteristics that generate anything but a steady flow of goods and services (Holling and Gunderson 2002). These characteristics are not typical of capital, a concept designed to represent nonliving buildings and equipment, which can be increased or decreased at will. Manufactured capital is reproducible by human action and can be substituted. Referring to nature as capital may lead people to think that it too can be reproduced and substituted just as if it were manufactured.

Alfred Marshall, one of the truly great economists, cautioned against such an approach. He distinguished between land — including "all free gifts of nature, such as mines, fisheries, etc. which yield income" — and capital. After maintaining that "land is a permanent and fixed stock while appliances made by man…are a flow capable of being increased or diminished," he concluded that "a far-seeing statesman will feel a greater responsibility to future generations when legislating as to land than as to other forms of wealth; and from the economic and from the ethical point of view, land must every-where and always be classed as a thing by itself" (1920). We should heed Marshall's warning before fully embracing the idea of nature as just another type of capital.

The second part of Olewiler's conceptual framework is market failure. She notes, "the EGS from natural capital may have well-defined markets. Timber from forests, crops from fertile farmlands…are all sold at prices that more or less reflect the marginal costs of production, including the value of the natural capital inputs. Many EGS have poorly defined markets or no markets at all in which to establish unit prices…If EGS are exchanged without a full costing of all the impacts that production and consumption may have on natural capital, society risks overconsumption of EGS and not enough protection of natural capital" (133).

This is a concise statement of the standard economic explanation of the overuse of the environment or, in this case, the undersupply of EGS. It is based on the premise that decisions about human interactions with nature are made by profit-maximizing com-panies and utility-maximizing individuals, all of whom are guided in their decisions by market prices. Anything that does not have a market price is ignored. So if the actions of a farmer reduce the supply of EGS for which he or she neither makes nor receives pay-ment, then that farmer will not take the impact on EGS into account when deciding what to do. On the other hand, if the farmer has to pay to destroy EGS or is paid to supply them, EGS will enter into his or her calculation of profit and more EGS will likely result.

This economic analysis is helpful to the extent that the assumptions of profit and utility maximization apply. It works well for land that is privately owned, as is most agricul-tural and urban land in Canada. Farmers and land developers make decisions that they believe will maximize their profits. In agriculture, this means concentrating on the produc-tion of farm products that attract the highest prices on secure markets while minimizing the use of purchased inputs. Any adverse impacts on the supply of EGS that result from specific farming practices may be regretted, but unless a farmer can see how the provision of EGS will bring a financial return, EGS will almost always be a second-order consideration. Land developers face a similar and even more profound dilemma insofar as the destruction of productive land is often an unavoidable aspect of their work. Governments try to prevent these problems through land-use planning, regulations and subsidies, but there is considerable scope for more enlightened and effective policies, such as those proposed by Olewiler.

In the case of land not under private ownership — such as that which is publicly owned, or owned by Aboriginal communities — market failure may be less relevant when it comes to understanding and resolving problems related to the supply of EGS. We may gain important insights by examining other patterns of land ownership and other behavioural assumptions.

Of the three categories of land ownership — public, private and Aboriginal — the first two can be subdivided: public as federal, provincial and municipal; and private as corporate, individual and nonprofit. Each of the three categories of ownership confers a range of rights and responsibilities on the owner. We may presume that landowners will make decisions about land use that best serve their interests, as they define them. Private landowners may well choose to maximize their net income and/or capital gain. Public and Aboriginal landowners may have other, broader objectives, including some relating to the supply of EGS for which they do not expect any financial reward. This is not to say that they take all the necessary actions (or inactions) to protect nature and supply the "right" type and amount of EGS. But it does mean that the standard market failure analysis has to be modified to fit these cases. For example, the provinces own 92 percent of Canada's boreal forest and the federal government owns 5.2 percent.[2] It is within the power of these governments to regulate the use of this land to ensure the supply of EGS without paying users (for example, forestry companies and recreationists) to alter their behaviour. In fact, such an approach would seem bizarre.

I am sure that Olewiler understands all this. The problem is that she relies primarily on studies written in and about the United States, whose pattern of land ownership is very different from that of Canada: in the US, much more land is in private hands. It would be interesting to see how countries with land ownership patterns closer to Canada's have approached the problem of securing an appropriate supply of EGS. Australia is perhaps the country most similar to Canada in terms of public/private land ownership.[3]

There are other issues relating to the market failure aspect of Olewiler's conceptual framework that I can only touch on in passing. Environmental issues are seen by many as issues of equity rather than efficiency. Olewiler remarks that "equity concerns may trump efficiency" (152). Economists have more to say about efficiency than about equity, though the two are not as disparate as some suggest. For example, prices reflect the actual distribution of income and wealth, not the just or desired distribution. A different distribution would generate different prices, because rich people spend their money on different products than poorer people. Change the distribution of income and wealth and you change prices. The use of shadow prices — that is, prices estimated by economists when market prices are clearly inadequate or do not exist at all, as is the case with many EGS — does not overcome this problem, since shadow prices are also based on the existing distribution of income and wealth. So, if the distribution of income and wealth is not considered just, why use market-based measures of value that reflect this distribution to determine the value of EGS, which are public goods?

Another question is whether private landowners are net producers or consumers of EGS (pollination, for example); and whether, if they are to be paid for providing EGS, they should also be obliged to pay for using them. This raises distributional issues that should be addressed in the process of policy design but that lie outside the normal domain of economics.

THE POLICY PROPOSALS

Discussion of Olewiler's conceptual framework leads to the question of whether economics should be used to determine the optimal level and mix of EGS supplied in Canada or, more simply, to determine the best way of supplying a desired level and mix of EGS — or both.

The first option is the most ambitious. Olewiler asks, "Is protecting 8.2 percent of the total area of Canada anywhere close to sufficient, and do the areas chosen to be protected maximize the EGS from natural capital?" (130). She describes a few studies that have tried to value EGS in Canada and the cost of protecting additional areas without indicating whether the World Wildlife Fund Canada target is appropriate. Her policy proposals are designed primarily with the second, more modest task in mind: to influence behaviour in the direction of more EGS. In the chapter section entitled "Policies to Secure Natural Capital," Olewiler reviews several policies in place or contemplated in various jurisdictions.

Policy proposal 1: Canada's conservation plan

This proposal calls for federal government leadership in an area of considerable provincial responsibility. Many EGS are local, which suggests a role for municipalities as well. The intergovernmental dimension merits careful consideration.

Statistics Canada has begun to take the lead in improving the measurement of Canada's natural capital (Environment Canada and Statistics Canada 2006). The natural capital approach provides a conceptual framework for developing a statistical program of the sort suggested by Olewiler, but it is not entirely satisfactory for the reasons given. Data collection and modelling should also be informed by a systems approach, as I mentioned earlier.

Other issues that should be addressed are the relationship between data collection and models. Which should come first? How can one design a data collection program without having a model of the system the data are supposed to describe and measure? Very often, data collection does precede modelling — the danger is that the model will model the data rather than "reality." A related issue is whether the Department of Finance is best placed to coordinate the development of a natural capital targeting model. Does the department have the expertise, let alone the interest, to play this role, and would the provinces and municipalities use a model produced in this way? Much would depend on the involvement of these and other stakeholders.

Policy proposal 2: Canada's conservation fund

If the market system is working well, then one principle of taxation policy is that the best taxes are those that do not influence behaviour. Taxing bads and subsidizing goods is a departure from this principle. Such taxes (and subsidies) are intended to change behaviour. However, it complicates the task of estimating how much revenue will be raised, as taxpayers adjust their behaviour in response to the new taxes. The "steady flow of funds" to which Olewiler refers may be anything but steady, creating further problems if the funds are earmarked for environmental purposes. In any case, earmarking may generate too little or too much revenue for supporting EGS, and it should be adopted with care, even though it may make an environmental tax shift more acceptable.

A proposal for an environmental tax shift based on a 1 percentage point change in the GST is likely to meet opposition from municipal governments that have announced their own ideas for using 1 percentage point of the GST.

If the goal is to pay private landowners for the production of EGS, it may be better to focus on specific goods and services rather than on the protection of specific areas. Is it feasible to value EGS on a site-specific basis and pay private landowners for producing them, paralleling the market price of marketed goods and services?[4]

Policy proposal 3: provincial incentive-based policies to secure natural capital

The proposal for mandatory incentive-based policies to lessen the impact of development on natural capital is helpful but, as stated, it does not deal with threats to natural capital unrelated to urban sprawl. What is the link between this proposal and the proposal for environmental tax shifting? Olewiler describes the mandatory measures as "largely self-financing," but in all likelihood some funds from the public purse will be required.

THE POLICY EVALUATION SCHEME

Olewiler has developed an interesting scheme for evaluating policy proposals and has applied it to her three policy proposals and the status quo. She claims that all of her policy proposals "rank above the status quo, but none of the alternatives clearly dominates the other" (152). Is this a reflection of the evaluation scheme, or are the proposals really that close? One way to find out would be to engage a varied group of people in evaluating the alternatives and see what emerges.

Finally, what is the role of the three levels of government in providing EGS? Is there a place for subsidiarity — that is, should EGS be stimulated at a jurisdictional level defined by their geographic range? Since the value of many EGS is highly dependent on their location, this is an issue that certainly merits further investigation.

NOTES

1   I am grateful for the helpful remarks of Ed Hanna and Jeremy Leonard on an earlier draft of this commentary.
2   *Atlas of Canada*, "Pie Chart of Land Ownership in the Boreal Forest," www.atlas.nrcan.gc.ca/site/english/learningresources/theme_modules/borealforest/owncht.gif/image_view (accessed July 13, 2007).
3   Information regarding EGS and natural capital approaches in Australia can be found at www.napswq.gov.au/mbi/index.html.
4   These issues are touched on in Notman et al. (2006).

REFERENCES

Daly, H.E., and J.C. Farley. 2004. *Ecological Economics: Principles and Applications*. Washington, DC: Island Press.

Environment Canada and Statistics Canada. 2006. *Canadian Environmental Sustainability Indicators 2006*, Environment Canada cat. no. EN81-5/1-2006E-PDF; Statistics Canada cat. no. 16-251-XWE/XIE, issue 2006000. Ottawa: Minister of Public Works and Government Services Canada.

Holling, C.S., and L.H. Gunderson. 2002. "Resilience and Adaptive Cycles." In *Panarchy: Understanding Transformations in Human and Natural Systems*, edited by L.H. Gunderson and C.S. Holling. Washington, DC: Island Press.

Marshall, A. 1920. *Principles of Economics: An Introductory Volume*. 8th ed. London: Macmillan.

Notman, E., L. Langner, T. Crow, E. Mercer, T. Calizon, T. Haines, J. Greene, T. Browne, J. Bergstrom, J. Loomis, J. Hayes, and J. Call. 2006. "State of Knowledge: Ecosystem Services from Forests." Unpublished white paper, October. Washington, DC: USDA Forest Service. Accessed July 16, 2007. www.fs.fed.us/ecosystemservices/pdf/state-of-knowledge.pdf

POPULATION AGING

SOME ECONOMIC AND SOCIAL CONSEQUENCES OF POPULATION AGING

David K. Foot

Canada's population is aging: over the past 50 years, the median age of Canadians has risen from 27.2 to 38.8. Not surprisingly, aging is reflected in the growing share of seniors in the population, with those ages 65 and older increasing from 7.7 to 13.2 percent over the same period.

Population projections for the next 50 years show a continuation of these trends. Statistics Canada projects that by 2026, when many of the postwar baby boom generation — those born between 1947 and 1966 — will have become seniors, the median age of Canada's population will rise to 43.3 and the share of seniors will be 21.2 percent. By 2051, these numbers are expected to increase to 46.8 years and 26.4 percent, respectively. These projections include immigrants, who tend to be younger.

The first Canadian boomers will reach age 65 in 2012, marking the beginning of an accelerated aging trend. Between 2011 and 2031, when the last Canadian boomer reaches seniorhood, the median age will have risen by four years, almost as much as it did over the first 50 years of the twentieth century (five years).

Canada is not alone in experiencing population aging; this demographic trend has now become a well-recognized feature of all countries in the developed world and, increasingly, countries elsewhere. Currently, western European populations are aging more rapidly than Canada's, although each country's time path reflects its particular socio-economic and demographic history. Eastern Europe and southern Asia, including China, are also experiencing population aging, as are some countries in other parts of the world.

Is there a common characteristic that binds countries with aging populations? Although there are many determinants of population aging — such as better health and longer life expectancy — the common and most dominant characteristic is sustained below-replacement fertility. Replacement fertility requires that two parents replace themselves and, on average, contribute extra children to account for women who do not give birth — a figure of 2.1 children per woman is considered sufficient to sustain a population through internal growth. Yet fertility is below this rate in many countries: in Canada and western Europe, it is 1.5, while in eastern Europe and Japan, it is just 1.3

(Population Reference Bureau 2006). In the developed world, only the United States has a replacement fertility rate of 2.1 children per woman, but even this is not sufficient to prevent the US population from aging as rising life expectancy increases both the median age and the share of seniors in the population. Even accounting for possible delayed child-bearing, which would increase these fertility numbers slightly, the effects of population aging in much of the world are inevitable. Population aging in Canada is thus part of a global trend, and many other countries are experiencing and discussing its economic and social consequences (Turner et al. 1998).

The macroeconomic challenges

A useful framework to embed discussions of the consequences of population aging is the identity

$$Q = (Q/H)\,(H/E)\,(E/L)\,(L/W)\,(W/P)\,P, \tag{1}$$

where

Q	=	real output,
H	=	average hours per employee,
E	=	number of employees,
L	=	labour force,
W	=	working-age population and
P	=	population size.

This identity makes it clear that the annual output of any society can be broken down into productivity performance (measured as output per hour worked, Q/H), the effort of employees (defined as average hours worked per year, H/E), the employment rate (E/L, which is 1 minus the unemployment rate), labour force participation (the share of the adult population looking for work, L/W), the share of the adult population in the total population (W/P) and the size of the population (P). Consequently, countries with better productivity, higher work effort, lower unemployment rates, higher participation rates, lower shares of children in the population and larger populations will produce more output.

Output growth is the sum of growth of each of these components. Therefore, growth in output declines when productivity growth slows, employee effort decreases, unemployment rises, participation falls, fertility rises and population growth slows. These are not unconnected influences: capital (human, natural, physical and social) has an influence on all components, as do the choices of individuals.

A common measure of material living standards is output per person (Q/P). Equation (1) can be rewritten as:

$$Q/P = (Q/H) (H/E) (E/L) (L/W) (W/P). \qquad (2)$$

This identity shows that material living standards can be broken down into productivity performance, work effort, unemployment, labour force participation and the age structure of the population. Note that slower output growth does not automatically result in a decline in the material standard of living. So long as output growth exceeds population growth, even if both are negative, output per person increases. Countries with slower or even shrinking populations do not automatically suffer declines in material living standards.

This framework can be used to identify the role of population aging in determining output growth and material living standards, as well as to suggest some of the social implications of aging. The effects of aging on productivity performance are beyond the scope of this chapter, but they remain an area that is ripe for further research.

A second potential influence of population aging is on average hours worked, which varies with age over the lifecycle. Of particular relevance is the declining number of hours worked by older workers who may be semi-retired. The most important determinant of work effort, however, is the trade-off among work, family and leisure, which varies by country and community.

The third potential effect of aging is on the unemployment rate (and, hence, E/L). If younger workers are more likely to be unemployed than older workers, population aging can help reduce the unemployment rate. But if older workers are passed over in employment, the opposite will be true. Again, the more important determinant of unemployment is elsewhere — namely, the performance of the economy relative to its potential, which is also influenced by demographics.

The fourth potential effect of aging is more nuanced. An increase in the number of older people leads to a decrease in labour force participation, especially when the working-age population (W) is defined as the adult population — usually those ages 15 years and older (rather than the 15-to-64 age group that is used to calculate the demographic dependency ratio). The aging of the population leads to a larger share of the population in retirement, which depresses overall participation (L/W). Population aging can also result in more adults in the total population, however — thereby increasing W/P — which can increase economic growth and material living standards. Note that it is important to include seniors in W, since they constitute a potential source of labour force growth in aging populations.

Finally, population size and growth directly influence output levels and growth, but not material living standards, except indirectly through the determinants in equation (2). Therefore, population policies — on immigration and fertility, for example — have important consequences for economic growth, but they affect material standards of living only indirectly.

The sectoral challenges

Although this framework is useful in identifying the consequences of population aging for all sectors of the economy, it does not identify additional consequences for specific sectors. Population aging, in fact, can be expected to change the sectoral composition of the economy, because the requirements of older people differ from those of younger people. For example, younger people require more formal education, while older people require more health care. Aging populations, therefore, can be expected to lead to a reduced share of education and an increased share of health care in the economy's output (Foot and Gomez 2006). Many other examples abound throughout the economy in both the private and public sectors.

The effects of population aging can also be felt within sectors — for example, the move from gynecology to geriatrics within health care. Other examples might be less obvious — the move from running to walking or from inexpensive to luxury automobiles. Once again, age-based life-cycle analysis is useful in identifying these shifts and the likely effects on the products and services of all sectors of the economy (Foot and Stoffman 1996).

The path ahead

In this chapter, I draw on two relevant theories related to population change to present an integrated framework for assessing the consequences of population aging on economic performance and social choice. First, I review demographic transition theory to establish a demographic foundation and to identify the transitions observed in populations and societies, including the transition to population aging. I then extend the theory to labour force growth and, using the above framework, to output growth and material standards of living. Second, I outline lifecycle theory as a means to introduce age and economic behaviour explicitly into the analysis. All of the determinants of economic output and material living standards — equations (1) and (2) — are potentially influenced by individual behaviour over the lifecycle. I then combine the two theories to identify and isolate the effects of population growth and aging on economic performance and social choice.

With these theoretical foundations in place, I then review some consequences of population aging for economies and societies and identify some important challenges that this largely inevitable trend is generating. Although the challenges are global, each country faces its own particular demographic and behavioural patterns. As a useful illustration, I focus on the consequences for Canada over the 2006-26 period; since this period encapsulates the time during which the massive boomer generation retires, it provides a particularly poignant illustration of the challenges aging societies face.

I then identify three important consequences for detailed discussion, with particular attention on public policies. First, I consider population policies: population size and composition are the most obvious demographic effects of impacts on output and material living standards — of particular interest in Canada are fertility and immigration policies. Second, I examine the effects of population aging on the future workforce — the challenges posed by slower workforce growth (and possible decline) and the implications of population aging for retirement and pension policies. Of particular interest is ameliorating the effect of the retirement of the large boomer generation on Canada's economic (and social) performance. Third, I briefly review, through a demographic lens, the effects of population aging on the health care sector. Here, I limit attention to selective, demographically sensitive delivery, funding and staffing issues that have been ignored in the past. Managing the effects of aging boomers on a sector whose share of the economy will only increase as the population as a whole ages poses important economic and social challenges.

DEMOGRAPHIC TRANSITION THEORY

Demographic transition theory, based on the historical development of societies over the past millennium, provides an explanation of the general evolution of human populations. The theory also provides a link between population growth and economic growth and development (including material living standards). It provides a further link between population growth and population aging and, therefore, a foundation for the issues I discuss in this chapter.

Population mathematics

In any society, population size is governed by four determinants, births (B), deaths (D), immigration (I) and emigration (E), according to the following identity:

$$P = P(-1) + B - D + I - E, \qquad (3)$$

where P(-1) is the population in the previous period (year). The difference between births and deaths, B - D, is the net natural change in the population, and the difference between immigration and emigration, I - E, is net migration. These differences can be positive or negative. For many countries, net migration is quantitatively small, so population change is determined primarily by net natural change. This is certainly true for the population of the world as a whole, which, of course, has zero migration.

To determine whether a population is increasing or decreasing, equation (3) can be rewritten to show population change:

$$P - P(-1) = B - D + I - E. \tag{4}$$

Population growth requires that change be positive, or that $(B + I) > (D + E)$. In the simple case where migration is negligible, this requirement becomes $B > D$; that is, the number of births must exceed the number of deaths. If $B = D$, the population is stationary; otherwise the population will decrease in the absence of positive net migration.

Demographic transition theory, however, is usually expressed in terms of rates, rather than numbers, so it is useful to rewrite equation (4) in rate form. Thus, population growth (g) is

$$(P - P(-1)) / P(-1) = (B - D + I - E) / P(-1), \tag{5}$$

which can be written in alternative notation as

$$g = \beta - \delta + \iota - \epsilon, \tag{6}$$

where $\beta = B / P(-1)$, $\delta = D / P(-1)$, $\iota = I / P(-1)$ and $\epsilon = E / P(-1)$, respectively representing the birth, death, immigration and emigration rates for the population (usually measured as per thousand people).

Consequently, the population growth rate is the difference between the birth rate and the death rate plus the difference between the immigration rate and the emigration rate; that is, population growth is the rate of net natural change plus the net migration rate. Where net migration is zero (or quantitatively small), population growth is determined by the difference between the birth and the death rates. Note that this is positive, and the population is growing if the birth rate exceeds the death rate, and vice versa. Currently, the annual world birth rate is 21 per thousand and the death rate is 9 per thousand, so the world population growth rate is 12 per thousand, or 1.2 percent per year (Population Reference Bureau 2006). For countries with quantitatively significant annual net migration — such as Canada, at 7 per thousand — the net migration rate also must be included in determining population growth.

Table 1, which illustrates the dynamics of equation (6) in Canada over the 20th century, clearly shows that both the birth rate and the death rate have declined substantially, resulting in a slower rate of natural increase. Net immigration (the difference between ι and ϵ) historically has been a much smaller contributor to overall population growth, but over the 1996-2001 period, for the first time, it accounted for a larger share of population growth than did natural increase (28.4 versus 20.8 per thousand).

TABLE 1.   SOURCES OF POPULATION GROWTH, CANADA, 1901-2001

	Population change from previous period (g)	Births (β)	Deaths (δ)	Net natural increase (β - δ)	Immigration (ι)	Emigration (ε)	Net immigration (ι - ε)
1901-11	341.6	358.4	167.6	190.8	288.6	137.8	150.8
1911-21	219.4	324.7	148.5	176.2	194.3	151.1	43.2
1921-31	180.9	274.8	120.1	154.8	136.5	110.4	26.2
1931-41	108.9	221.1	103.3	117.8	14.4	23.2	-8.9
1941-51	186.1	276.9	105.5	171.4	47.6	32.9	14.7
1951-56	151.7	154.3	46.4	107.9	57.4	13.6	43.8
1956-61	134.1	146.9	42.7	104.2	47.3	17.3	30.0
1961-66	97.4	123.3	40.1	83.2	29.6	15.4	14.2
1966-71	77.6	92.7	38.3	54.5	44.5	21.3	23.1
1971-76	75.6	81.6	38.2	43.4	48.8	16.6	32.2
1976-81	62.7	77.6	35.9	41.7	32.9	11.9	21.0
1981-86	55.9	75.4	35.7	39.8	27.3	11.2	16.1
1986-91	74.3	74.1	36.2	37.8	44.6	8.2	36.4
1991-96	60.4	69.1	36.5	32.5	39.9	12.1	27.8
1996-2001	49.2	57.6	36.8	20.8	41.1	12.7	28.4

Source: Census of Population, various years, Statistics Canada.
Note: Because data after 1951 are presented as five-year totals, they are not strictly comparable to the ten-year total presented from 1901 to 1951.

The theory

Demographic transition theory is usually presented for the zero net migration case, where the sole determinants of population growth are birth and death rates. I use this simplification here, but the analysis can be easily extended to the non-zero migration case by including the immigration rate with the birth rate and the emigration rate with the death rate.

Current demographic transition theory identifies four stages of population and economic development. Under the theory, a population transitions from stage I through to stage IV over time, but the time spent in each stage can vary significantly depending on the particular population being considered. A country can even get trapped in one of the stages if conditions are not conducive for the next transition. The four stages are easily defined using equation (6) (with $\iota - \epsilon = 0$):

Stage I: High β and high δ, usually with small positive g;
Stage II: High β and falling δ, resulting in increasing g;
Stage III: Falling β and low δ, resulting in falling g;
Stage IV: Low β and low δ, usually with small positive g.

Recent historical events in some countries with advanced population aging suggest that it is now appropriate to identify an additional stage in the theory:

Stage V: Low β and increasing δ, resulting in negative g.

The theory posits that, in its early years, a population — typically in a preindustrial society — experiences a high birth rate and a high death rate, resulting in slow population growth (stage I). The first demographic transition associated with economic development is a reduction in the death rate associated with improved health conditions — for example, better water quality and sanitation — which reduces the death rate, so that population growth increases (stage II). Continued economic development usually produces better and more widespread education for both males and females, resulting in more widespread family planning and opportunities for employment, which, in turn, reduces the number of children per family; the consequence is slower population growth (stage III). It is at this stage, with fewer children and with people living longer, that population aging typically sets in. The next stage of development retains good living conditions combined with good education, resulting in low death, birth and population growth rates (stage IV). Under these conditions, especially if the birth rate falls below the replacement rate, the speed of population aging increases. Canada is an example of a country at this stage today. The continuation of below-replacement fertility and population aging ultimately results in an increasing death rate — because of the presence of more elderly people, whose mortality rates are high — and a decreasing population (stage V).

Demographic transition theory is a general description of typical or average population transitions, but there are variations and exceptions. For example, the theory does not encompass rising birth rates associated with the postwar baby boom in many countries, although it does describe the consequences. However, the postwar boom, while important, followed a period of population aging (in the 1930s) and was historically short lived, lasting between one and two decades, thus constituting a temporary, rather than permanent, transition in the population. Another exception might occur when economic development stalls or even reverses, resulting in a return to a previous stage. Some countries in eastern Europe, such as Russia, have experienced this situation recently as worsening economic conditions resulted in a decrease in life expectancy (especially for males) and a return to a higher death rate. Once again, time could prove this to be temporary.

Nonetheless, even with these exceptions, demographic transition theory provides a robust description of population change over time in many countries and a framework with which to identify population transitions in relation to economic development. In particular, it outlines the conditions for slower population growth and population aging that Canada and many other countries in the developed world are experiencing today.

The consequences

The rise and fall of a population and, therefore, of population growth over time can be understood within this theoretical foundation, which clearly links population aging with slower population growth beyond stage II. Low birth and death rates produce fewer young and more seniors in a population, thereby increasing the average or median age. This is the definition of population aging.

Even reintroducing migration into the analysis does not fundamentally change the conclusions. Immigrants tend to be concentrated in the younger working ages and, while they might bolster population growth and counteract increases in a population's average age, the quantitative effect is invariably too small to reverse trends from domestic sources. This is true even of Canada, for example, which has one of the highest immigration rates in the world (Guillemette and Robson 2006), so it certainly applies to countries where migration is less quantitatively important.

Perhaps the best way to communicate the demographic consequences visually is through population pyramids, which summarize the age and gender structure of a population. Figures 1 through 4 show population pyramids of countries in each stage of demographic transition superimposed on that of Canada. A stage I population structure (exemplified by Nigeria; see figure 1) is characterized by a flat pyramid with a wide base of young people and very few in the upper ages. In stage II (illustrated by Pakistan; see figure 2), decreasing mortality results in more people in the upper ages, but continued high fertility ensures that the base remains wide, so that the associated population structure becomes a tall pyramid. In stage III (exemplified by Thailand; see figure 3), declining fertility causes the base of the pyramid to shrink, so that it gradually becomes a tall diamond, with the bulk of the population in the middle ages; this is the period of slower population growth and the beginning of population aging. Progression into stage IV (illustrated by Finland; see figure 4) moves the bulk of the diamond into the older ages, resulting in the appearance of almost an inverted pyramid with most people in the older ages and few people in the younger ages. As these seniors die and the population decreases (stage V), the pyramid likely will revert to a more cylindrical shape — although no country has yet been at this stage long enough to verify the typical shape of the population structure in practice. Although this transition process is widespread, its timing and the duration of each stage vary.

In summary, as a result of improving life expectancy and continuing low fertility, Canada and most other developed countries have moved through stage III and are becoming ensconced in stage IV of the demographic transition, which inevitably means slower population growth and population aging.

Is the demographic transition inevitable? Could the process that demographic transition theory describes be reversed without also reversing economic development? This appears to be very unlikely, for several reasons. First, increasing life expectancy results in a growing number of people at the older ages; when these people die, the death rate (δ) increases, which contributes to slower population growth. Second, feasible levels of immigration can alleviate, but not offset, the inevitable effect of a slowing natural rate of change of a population. Moreover, if an increase in the level of immigration does not at least match the population growth rate, the immigration rate ($\iota = I / P(-1)$) will fall, contributing to slower population growth. Third, the only other way to increase population growth and counteract population aging is to increase fertility. Since demographic transition theory, however, posits an inverse relationship between fertility and education — especially female education — and since it is unlikely that a developed country would withdraw universal education, it would be very difficult to increase the birth rate. Indeed, to date, pro-fertility policies of many forms in many jurisdictions have had only a minimal permanent effect on fertility rates; in

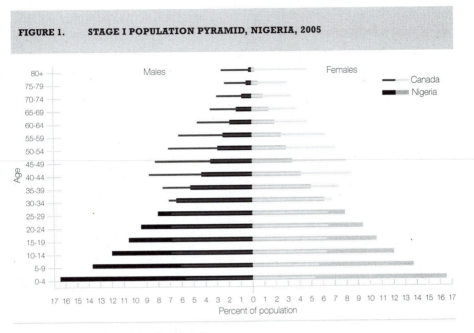

FIGURE 1.   STAGE I POPULATION PYRAMID, NIGERIA, 2005

Source: US Census Bureau, International Data Base.

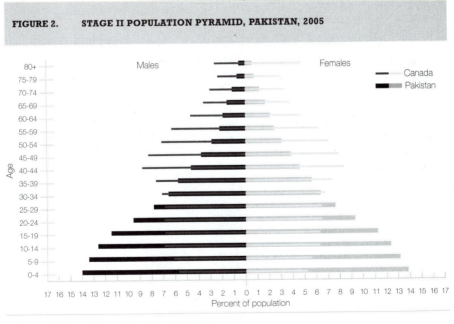

FIGURE 2.   STAGE II POPULATION PYRAMID, PAKISTAN, 2005

Source: US Census Bureau, International Data Base.

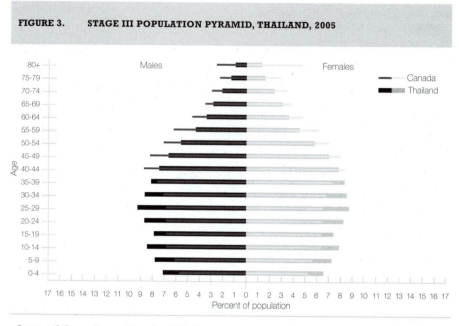

FIGURE 3.   STAGE III POPULATION PYRAMID, THAILAND, 2005

Source: US Census Bureau, International Data Base.

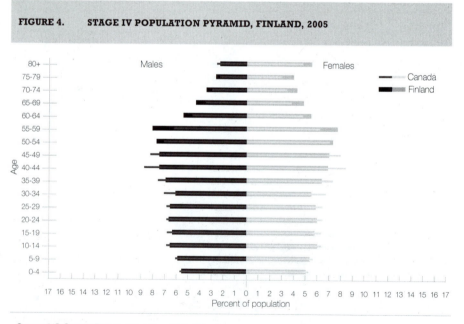

FIGURE 4.   STAGE IV POPULATION PYRAMID, FINLAND, 2005

Source: US Census Bureau, International Data Base.

general, they seem to be able only to lessen future decreases. In practice, the long-run inevitability of demographic transition is entrenched.

Of particular relevance to economic growth is the growth of the labour force (L = (L/W) (W/P) P in equation (1)). Having more people available to work can result in more output (providing they are employed). Population growth, however, usually translates into labour force growth only with a time lag. In the zero immigration case of traditional demographic transition theory, population growth is generated by the birth rate, but since it takes time for infants to grow into adults, births do not contribute to labour force growth — and thus to economic growth — for about two decades. In the interim, changes in demographic structure contribute to lower material living standards (a decrease in L/W in equation (2)) as the same output is spread over more people. This phenomenon occurred over the 1950s and early 1960s in Canada with the temporary effects of the postwar baby boom. The lag is not as relevant, of course, when population growth comes from increasing immigration, since most immigrants are of working age and are eligible for employment.

Subsequently, the effect of the lag reverses when declining population growth does not get translated immediately into lower labour force growth, and so maintaining output growth and temporarily increasing material living standards. Over the period in which boomers entered the Canadian labour force — from the mid-1960s to the mid-1980s — Canada experienced a declining population growth rate even as a higher rate of labour force growth resulted in a temporary economic dividend. This demographic dividend having now evaporated, another transition looms as the boomers gradually retire, thereby reducing the labour force participation rate (L/W in equations (1) and (2)). Understanding this behavioural transition requires a further theoretical foundation, to which I devote the next section.

LIFECYCLE THEORY

Lifecycle theory, with its particular emphasis on age, introduces economic and social behaviour into the analysis of the effects of population aging. The first formal use of the lifecycle approach in economics resulted from a puzzle concerning income and consumption. Although aggregate consumption expenditure appears to be proportionally related to aggregate income, the income profile of individual expenditure does not vary in the same way; rather, people use financial assets to smooth their expenditure by borrowing when young, repaying the loans in early middle age, then accumulating assets in later middle age to use in retirement when income falls. As a result, expenditure is proportional to permanent, not current, income.

Since its early application, lifecycle theory has permeated much decision theory in economics. Agents are presumed to have finite lifetimes over which they use capital markets to smooth revenue streams to match expenditure needs. A core premise of this research is the intertemporal budget constraint that requires the present discounted value of revenues from all sources to equal the present discounted value of expenditures (including inheritances) for all purposes over the lifetime of the agent. Lifecycle analysis also has been used in government decision theory, and has been extended to infinite horizon applications.

Applications of lifecycle theory in other disciplines have proved somewhat less pervasive. In sociology, it first found favour in gerontological analysis, where the life course is a foundation for understanding social behaviour and needs, especially among the senior population. This framework has since been incorporated into most other social analysis, and the theory is now a standard tenet of the discipline (Policy Research Initiative 2005).

Lifecycle mathematics

Since most empirical applications in lifecycle theory use discrete data, the mathematical framework I present here uses discrete mathematics. (For continuous applications, replace the summation sign, Σ, with an integral, $\int$.)

The theory can be illustrated by using labour force participation as an example. Aggregate labour force participation (L/W) is a weighted average of individual group (i) age-specific participation rates according to the following formula:

$$(L/W) = \Sigma_i \, (L/W)_i \, (W_i/W). \tag{7}$$

The age-specific participation rates of individual groups, $(L/W)_i$, are weighted by each group's share in the working-age population, (W_i/W), to obtain the aggregate participation rate, (L/W). (Equation (7) can easily be used to incorporate gender differences, and might need to be adjusted for groups, such as inmates of institutions, that cannot participate in the labour force.) Thus, the aggregate rate depends not only on individual behaviour, but also on the age structure of the working-age population. In this sense, changes in age structure are not just limited to the share of population of working age (W/P) but potentially permeate many other determinants of aggregate economic performance.

If the age-specific participation rate does not vary by age, population aging has no effect on the aggregate participation rate. Once the participation rate varies with age over the lifecycle, however, workforce aging can affect the aggregate participation rate even if age-specific behavioural rates remain unchanged. The same general conclusion also potentially applies to the rates of productivity (Q/H), effort (H/E) and employment (E/L) in equations (1) and (2), although the weights are the respective shares of each group in total hours, total employment and the labour force. Nonetheless, population aging can affect the shares of each of these determinants.

The theory

Lifecycle theory is important because economic and social behaviour changes with age over the lifecycle. The natural transitions from infancy through childhood into young adulthood bring changes not only in the human body but also in human needs. Expenditures and social behaviour change as the child grows, as do demands on educational and family support systems. Expenditures and needs change again when the young adult establishes a household and starts a family. Parenting is followed by grandparenting and retirement. Once again, economic and social behaviour changes as the adult transitions through the later stages of life. Many of these changes are precipitated by physical aging, which imposes constraints on individual choices. This changing economic and social behaviour over individual life transitions is the foundation for the importance of lifecycle theory in economic and social research.

The similarity between sequential societal demographic transitions and sequential individual life transitions provides a natural link between the demographic transition theory and the lifecycle theory. Since human lifetimes are much shorter than societal lifetimes, many individual behavioural changes occur within each stage of demographic transition. Nonetheless, the stage of demographic transition defines the societal context for individual decisions, and the aggregate of individual decisions determines the stage of demographic transition. For example, stages I and II are characterized by high birth rates, resulting in many children who need food and education but who are unable to participate as full workers in the economy. Stage III is characterized by fewer children and many workers, and by population aging. Stages IV and V lead to concerns about a lack of workers sufficient to support the requirements of the elderly.

The consequences

Demographic change affects macroeconomic performance in a variety of ways. Besides the obvious effect that a larger population provides more workers and consumers, the age structure influences the proportion of adults available to work. In addition, the determinants of macroeconomic performance also include behavioural rates — for example, participation and employment rates — that, in turn, are influenced by the age structure of the population, so that lifecycle behaviour affects economic performance. For example, if workforce aging puts more weight on groups with lower labour force participation, then population aging will result in a reduction in the aggregate participation rate, (L/W), in economic output and in material living standards even if individual age-specific behaviour remains unchanged.

Similarly, if employment rates fall (or unemployment rates rise) in the older age groups and more people enter these groups, the aggregate employment rate, (E/L), will fall even if there is no change in the age-specific employment (or unemployment) rates. If older employees work fewer hours and more people enter these age groups, the aggregate effort, (H/E), will decline even if there is no change in age-specific individual effort. In all of these cases, economic performance can suffer as a result of population aging even though age-specific behaviour remains unchanged.

The exact quantitative significance of each of these effects varies by country and over time. Nonetheless, in an aging population, the net effect of lifecycle behaviour is likely a reduction in economic performance and material living standards as the bulk of the population moves into older age groups — a situation that already characterizes Canada's population as well as those of many other developed countries. These effects will intensify as countries transition from stage III through stage IV. Thus, potential entry into a new stage V raises further concerns about the future of economies and, perhaps, even of countries, suggesting a multitude of economic and social issues.

POPULATION POLICIES

The future viability of countries is a major issue, especially for residents of those with a declining population. Japan and Russia have already reached this stage and a number of other countries — including Germany, Hungary, Italy, the Czech Republic and others in eastern Europe — are not far behind. The death rate is also closing in on the birth rate in Austria, Belgium, Greece, Poland, Portugal and Sweden (Population Reference Bureau 2006). A country with a decreasing market size not only potentially experiences diseconomies of scale in the provision of domestic output; it also gradually loses global importance from both economic and political perspectives and might even have more difficulty defending its sovereignty. In contrast, countries with growing populations are likely to take over global trade and affairs, with possible detrimental effects on those with decreasing populations. This scenario is increasingly becoming a reality for many countries in the developed world.

Can population decrease be prevented? Unfortunately, much future population growth is already predetermined by the current age structure of the population. Demographers refer to this phenomenon as population momentum: if most of a country's population is over age 40, then the birth rate will be low and the death rate will rise, inevitably resulting in slower population growth. If most of a country's females are over age 40, even a successful fertility policy that changes individual fertility behaviour will not result in many new births because older women increasingly do not conceive and bear children, underscoring the effect of aging on lifecycle choices.

For a population to grow, births plus immigration must exceed deaths plus emigration. Population increase is achieved by increasing births and immigration and reducing deaths and emigration. Few countries today are willing to contemplate policies that restrict emigration, although such policies have been widespread in the past. Keeping someone against his or her wishes is not likely to produce a desirable outcome for the individual or the society, so democracies, especially, tend to eschew such a policy. Similarly, most countries do not have a direct policy to influence deaths, although better health care can certainly prevent early death. Nonetheless, one certainty of life is death, so any policy in this regard is likely to have, at best, a temporary effect on the death rate.

That leaves births and immigration as the main components of a population policy. As I noted earlier, widespread education is an important determinant of the transition from stage II to stage III when birth rates decline. Yet, since few people in developed societies would argue for the withdrawal of education, especially for females, as a way to increase the birth rate, other pro-fertility policies must be contemplated. These can be described generally as family-friendly policies that reduce the cost and time of bearing and raising children. Usually, they vary from baby bonuses and subsidized daycare to improved maternity and paternity leave, although other strategies that provide appropriate and/or subsidized housing have also been used. Even if such policies successfully change individual fertility behaviour, however, demographic momentum will limit their impact on the birth rate of an aging population.

That leaves immigration, which has been Canada's main population policy in the postwar years. It is important to recall that the population growth rate is determined by the immigration rate, not just the number of immigrants (see equation (6)), so that the number of immigrants must grow by at least the same rate as the total population, otherwise immigration will act as a drag on population growth. In all cases, however, more immigrants are better than fewer immigrants as far as population growth is concerned.

Immigration policy in Canada

In most years past, Canada's natural increase has contributed more to population growth than has net migration. This is about to change (Statistics Canada 2005). In the years ahead, a decreasing number of births and an increasing number of deaths will slow population growth and reduce the domestic contribution to population growth. Under these conditions, immigration policy takes on a renewed role in Canada's demographic and economic future. Immigration, however, might slow down future population aging, but cannot prevent it (Guillemette and Robson 2006).

The simple case for immigration as an economically supportive population policy is that, *ceteris paribus*, a higher level of immigration leads to higher levels of population and output growth; moreover, since most immigrants are of labour force age, there is no time lag in translating population growth into workforce growth as there is with pro-fertility policies.

This case, however, comes with many caveats. First, keeping the immigration level unchanged in a growing population reduces the immigration rate (ι in equation (6)) and hence acts as a drag on population growth. For example, maintaining an annual intake of 250,000 immigrants while the population increases from 30 million (a rate of 8.33 per thousand) to 32.5 million (a rate of 7.69 per thousand) reduces annual population growth by 0.064 percent. To avoid this small negative effect, the immigration level could be linked to population growth. For maximum economic effect, however, immigration policy should be linked to the determinants of material living standards (see equation (2)). Within this framework, this means choosing immigrants who are

/ of working age, thereby contributing to W/P;
/ likely to participate in the workforce, thereby contributing to L/W;
/ likely to be employed, thereby contributing to E/L;
/ hard workers, thereby contributing to H/E; and
/ highly productive, thereby contributing to Q/E.

Of course, this is every employer's desirable potential worker, but there are many circumstances that impede an immigrant's ability to meet these requirements in Canada.

Canada's immigration policy for economic — as distinct from family and humanitarian — immigrants is based on a point system that appears to support each of these objectives, and is a sensible policy. Nonetheless, it has become clear that the policy intent and the realized outcomes have diverged for many immigrants to Canada over the past decade or more (Picot, Hou, and Coulombe 2007). In this regard, Canada's immigration system needs some retooling to maximize the economic benefit to immigrants and to the country.

First, under Canada's point system, the potential immigrant of working age receives maximum points, which satisfies the first requirement. Moreover, emphasis is on younger immigrants, who will live more of their lives in Canada and, therefore, will remain in the Canadian working-age population for a longer period, thus potentially contributing to output and material living standards for more years than would an older immigrant. This assumes that the immigrant does not emigrate sometime after arrival, so the likelihood of remaining in Canada is also a relevant consideration.

Second, the potential immigrant's willingness to actually enter the labour force — that is, to look for work — is desirable, and is assessed by the immigrant's past employment and the availability of work in Canada in the immigrant's chosen occupation. This satisfies the second requirement. Willingness to work and ability to work, however, might be quite different. Applying for work usually requires familiarity with the language of the workplace; thus, allocating points for proficiency in English or French is a supporting feature of Canada's immigration policy. However, since the workplace requires language proficiency in both oral and written form, inability in either one is likely to be detrimental to successful integration into the labour force. Accordingly, potential immigrants from countries in which neither English nor French is the first language would be at a disadvantage in their search for employment after arrival. Policies to remedy this disadvantage — such as English- or French-language training programs — would improve outcomes for immigrants and for the country.

The third issue is employability. The unemployment rate is higher in the immigrant population than in the general population, and considerably higher in some immigrant groups. There are many reasons for these outcomes, but a high unemployment rate (or low employment rate) does not contribute to material living standards for the immigrant or society. Policies to improve the employability of immigrants could range from eliminating discrimination in the workplace to building employment networks. Although a higher level of education — a core aspect of Canada's immigration policy — could improve employability, there are no guarantees, as many an immigrant can attest.

In fact, many immigrants have been blocked from employment in their chosen occupation by licensing authorities that refuse to recognize their professional or technical credentials and by employers who do not recognize their work experience. Health care workers, teachers, architects, engineers and many skilled trades have successfully blocked the entry of immigrants into occupations in which they have been trained and often have practised before coming to Canada. This has led to the incongruous policy of encouraging immigrants by giving them maximum points for education, then not allowing them to use their education in Canada's workplace after arrival. This policy must change. Every occupational licensing authority in Canada should be required to establish a procedure that allows immigrants to apply for certification through a timely, well-defined procedure of appropriate testing to ensure that their qualifications meet the current standards of the occupation. Moreover, each licensing authority should establish paths — such as apprenticeships and mentoring — through which immigrants can obtain the necessary qualifications with minimum dislocation of their careers. Such a policy might be limited, however, to immigrants whose occupations are in demand.

Work experience is more difficult to assess, but potential employers should be required to assess the foreign training and work experience of all job applicants, perhaps in consultation with the appropriate licensing or regulating authority.

An important example is health care. An aging population will need ever more health care workers, yet many immigrants with the appropriate training and experience are not working in that sector. They should be encouraged to become qualified to do so, for their benefit and that of Canada.

The fourth and fifth requirements (effort and productivity, respectively) are somewhat more difficult to access *a priori*. Both are dependent on good management skills to achieve the best results. This is true for all workers, not just immigrants. It is difficult to envision policies that are immigrant-specific in this context, with perhaps the exception of literacy, which is crucial for good productivity. The ability to read, understand and follow instructions, both oral and written, is often taken for granted. Increasingly, in an aging population, this is an issue for all workers: as new technologies and processes are introduced into the workplace, employers need to provide appropriate training and workers need to keep their skills up to current requirements. Literacy comprehension is even more difficult when the language of communication is not the immigrant's first language. Good literacy training in the workplace (and elsewhere) is essential if workers are to achieve their productivity potential, and good managers should be sensitive to the needs of workers when communicating in the workplace.

Finally, Canada's immigration strategy should be appropriate to the country's needs, both economic and demographic. On the economic front, however, this has not always been the case. From the 1950s through the 1980s, the immigration level generally varied inversely with the unemployment rate — when the unemployment rate rose, the immigration level fell, and vice versa. This relationship was broken in the early 1990s, when the immigration level was raised even as the unemployment rate increased (Foot 1994), making it difficult for immigrants to find jobs and placing them in direct competition with often-displaced Canadian workers. Canada is still paying for this misadventure, as unemployment has become entrenched among many who immigrated at that time, while domestic support for the immigration program suffered a setback. Thus, the national unemployment rate should remain a key determinant of Canada's immigration policy. Moreover, in considering the needs of employers, policymakers should recognize that employers benefit from a higher unemployment rate because it limits wage increases and, therefore, increases profits.

On the demographic front, Canada's immigration policy has become even less supportive of the country's needs, even though such consideration is required under the *Immigration Act*. Although population growth appears to be taken into account in setting policy, there is no linking of the age structure of immigrants with that of Canada's population. People are most mobile when they are in their 20s — that is, after completing their education and before starting families (a lifecycle effect). Yet, because of administrative delays in processing applications, most immigrants to Canada are now between ages 25 and 35. Meanwhile, the children of the boomer generation — the so-called echo generation — are now in their teens and early 20s, so increasing the immigration level (or rate) now runs the risk of placing new immigrants in competition for employment with the boomers' children. This is unwise. The immigration level (or rate) should not be increased substantially until the middle of the 2010s, to enable the echo generation to become established in the workforce. By then, the declining birth rate of the 1990s will have reduced workforce growth and increased labour market shortages, with a consequent reduction in the unemployment rate.

As a postscript, one should note that, like many younger workers, immigrants are drawn to locate in Canada's major urban centres (another lifestyle effect). A general policy of requiring immigrants to settle in smaller communities is unlikely to be successful, but a carefully targeted policy of inviting immigrants in their early 30s with young families to settle in smaller communities could have better success.

WORKFORCE POLICIES

Since employees are people, demographic change has a major effect on labour force growth and, hence, on output growth. As I noted earlier, changing age structure also affects the labour force participation rate, the employment rate and, perhaps, work effort and productivity, which are the determinants of economic performance. An increasing proportion of older workers in the population has important implications for Canada's future economic and social outcomes.

The massive postwar boom resulted in the rapid growth of the working-age population during the 1960s and 1970s. This growth, supported by increasing female labour force participation, was reflected in rapid economic growth. Thereafter, the effect of the birth control pill (and female education) led to a baby bust during the late 1960s and 1970s, resulting in a working-age population that grew more slowly and, together with a slower-growing labour force participation rate, a consequent reduction in labour force growth over the 1980s and 1990s. Output growth slowed accordingly. Other factors — such as the labour force participation rate and productivity performance; (see equation (1)) — also played a part, but much of the reduction in output growth in Canada since the 1970s can be attributed to demographic change.

Will this trend continue, or is Canada about to experience another demographic transition? The answers are yes and yes! Demographic transition theory teaches that slower population growth is entrenched; so are slower workforce and output growth. Recall, however, that this does not automatically mean falling material living standards, but the massive boomer generation, which is now in the working-age population, is poised to enter its next life transition.

Currently, boomers are in their 40s and 50s. If they begin to retire at the average Canadian retirement age of 62, the oldest boomers, born in 1947, reaches age 62 in 2009 and age 65 in 2012. The retirement of this massive generation of workers over the 2010s and 2020s will lead to even slower workforce growth and, *ceteris paribus*, output growth. Significant long-run improvement in productivity or other determining factors (see equation (1)) could lessen or perhaps even offset the demographic effect, but that appears unlikely to occur.

The expectation of slower future workforce growth and the possibility of emerging labour market shortages are thus creating concerns among economists, policy experts, business leaders and human resource management professionals. It has led to calls for increasing the level of immigration and for more creative workforce strategies. Policy proposals have proliferated, most of which focus on encouraging boomers to keep working beyond the traditional retirement age of 65 (Policy Research Initiative 2006). Mandatory retirement has been abolished in many jurisdictions to enable and encourage older employees to remain on the job (and to deal with human rights in the workplace). These concerns are timely and legitimate, although many of the proposals are incomplete or unrealistic.

Workforce mathematics

In terms of the mathematics I presented earlier, the retirement of the boomer generation will result in a reduction in the labour force participation rate (L/W) but not a change in the age structure of the population (W/P), since the adult working-age population (W) includes seniors. In fact, continued below-replacement fertility increases W/P as the pre-working-age share of the population continues to decrease. Unlike the usual definition of the working-age population as those between the ages of 15 and 64, this definition recognizes that, although most seniors retire fully from the workforce (a lifecycle effect), some continue to work into their later years. This expanded definition of W is increasingly appropriate as jurisdictions begin to remove mandatory retirement practices and as increasing life expectancy is creating more years of healthy, productive living for increasing numbers of people beyond age 64.

There is little evidence, however, that the average Canadian worker wishes to retire later. Rather, the evidence suggests that almost all workers who can afford to retire early do so. Better pensions (including public pensions) mean that an increasing share of the workforce is able to afford to retire earlier and chooses to do so (the lifecycle again), resulting in a downward trend in the average age of retirement over the 1980s and 1990s — although some recent evidence suggests that the downward trend might now have ended. Whether the average retirement age will start to increase depends on many factors, some of which I review later.

The labour force participation rate decreases among older Canadians (an inevitable lifecycle effect), so population aging will lead to slower labour force and output growth. Even if seniors decide to continue to work, thereby increasing the senior participation rate, it will still be well below that of the pre-senior ages, and an aging population inevitably leads to slower labour force growth. It is tempting to borrow from demographics and refer to this effect as "lifecycle momentum."

Moreover, lifecycle momentum is likely to affect other determinants of economic performance negatively as well. For example, older workers are more likely to work part-time than workers of prime working age. This means that an aging workforce reduces employees' average effort (hours per employee, H/E). Other effects are more conjectural but just as relevant. If, for example, older workers are discriminated against in the workplace or if an increase in structural unemployment affects older workers disproportionately, then a workforce with a larger share of older workers will lead to reductions in average employability (E/L). Also, if older workers are, on average, less technologically literate or slower physically or mentally than younger workers, then increasing the share of older workers in the labour force will lead to reductions in average productivity (Q/H). In short, all these effects of population aging have negative effects on economic performance.

At this stage, it is important to recall the role of capital markets in lifecycle theory. Under the conditions I have described, material living standards (Q/P) decrease, but the average person is not necessarily worse off, since leisure time increases and the assets the worker has accumulated over the lifecycle can be used to generate income in retirement. Lifecycle theory suggests that the composition of current income gradually shifts from labour income to capital income as more members of the aging population live off the stock of assets accumulated over their working years. This argument assumes, of course, that asset accumulation has taken place; in fact, there is evidence that debt/asset ratios are decreasing over the lifecycle in Canada, which suggests that boomers have indeed been accumulating a stock of assets. Whether this accumulation is sufficient to support the boomers' expected lifestyles in retirement remains to be seen, since economic growth and productivity will have an effect on the rates of return to these assets.

Workforce policies: boomer retirement

Demographic analysis indicates that, on average, the retirement of Canada's boomers will begin in the 2010s and be spread out over two decades. There is still some time, therefore, to prepare appropriate workforce policies to accommodate this demographic fact of life.

There are, however, exceptions to this trend. Some groups of workers with well-managed pension plans — such as teachers, police, military personnel and other public sector workers, along with many private sector employees, both unionized (including many in the skilled trades) and non-unionized (in the banking sector) — are being given opportunities for early retirement, and the effects of the retirement of boomers are already being felt in these areas. Indeed, to save on future pension payments, some employers are using early exit packages to encourage their boomer employees to retire early. Yet trends are driven by average, not exceptional, behaviour. In the meantime, the boomers' children — the echo generation — have been going through the education system — educational enrolment increased in many jurisdictions over the late 1980s and 1990s — and are now entering the workforce, causing a temporary increase in labour force growth.

What policies could encourage boomers to delay their retirement in order to offset slower workforce growth and labour market shortages in the 2010s? Some possible solutions are outlined in a recent report of the Canadian Senate (Senate Standing Committee 2006), which focuses on providing incentives to work, participating in lifelong learning, eliminating age discrimination in the workplace and devising a more effective immigration policy. It is hard to argue with these general recommendations, but the devil is in the details. For example, the best incentive to work is a decent wage, yet cost-cutting and global competition have limited real wage increases. Since business has an incentive to reduce wages to increase profits, it is not likely to champion such a solution. Another example is Ontario's recent elimination of mandatory retirement, which provides older workers with an incentive to work, yet employers are not required to provide workplace insurance for workers over age 65, which is a disincentive for older workers to keep working.

Somewhat more creatively, the Senate report (2006) includes recommendations to "enhance the labour force participation of older persons" through such measures as elder care, flexible working hours and pro-rated benefits for part-time workers. Over the next decade, although many boomers are likely to wish to continue working, they might prefer to do so only part-time. Thus, it might be useful to implement a flexible policy of phased retirement, whereby aging employees gradually reduce their workweek from five days to one, go on half-salary or half-time, or take on special projects that amount to a similar commitment of less-than-full-time employment (Foot and Venne 1998). Such flexible workplace policies are likely to be popular with boomers whose lifestyle needs mean travelling as well as spending more time with grandchildren or aging parents.

Flexible workplace policies have the additional advantage of facilitating workforce renewal, since a half-salary saved on an older worker could be used to hire a younger, echo generation worker full-time with no increase in the total salary bill. This workforce strategy would also allow cross-generational mentoring, whereby older workers share their experience with younger employees, who, in turn, teach older workers how to make efficient use of the latest technologies.

Of particular note are the 2006 Senate report's suggestions to eliminate the requirement that an individual must have ceased working before being able to collect retirement benefits, to allow pension credits to be accumulated on the basis of employment earnings after the normal retirement age of 65 and to permit an individual to defer receiving old age security benefits with appropriate actuarial adjustments. The essence of these recommendations is to allow workers both to draw from and to contribute to a pension plan at the same time, and they could be extended to any employee contemplating part-time retirement after age 55 or 60. Such a policy change would likely be effective in retaining boomers in the workplace.

Other workforce policies

The ability to save for retirement is crucial if workers are to avoid substantially reduced material living standards when they retire. Thus, the trend away from defined-benefit to defined-contribution pension plans in the private sector is a concern, since it transfers responsibility for pension management onto the person usually least equipped to handle it. The average employee is untrained to assume this responsibility, and has no opportunity to pool the risks and costs with other employees. Moreover, the expenses associated with individually managed investing are usually high and consume future pension income, and the risks of failure, either through oversight or lack of discipline, are also higher. As a result, tomorrow's seniors might not enjoy the income security that today's seniors do, which could increase poverty among the senior population.

One key policy change that the 2006 Senate report failed to recommend is the establishment of a new, optional private pension plan that would be managed in the same way as are contributions to the Canada Pension Plan (CPP) — namely, by an arm's-length public agency that would invest private pension contributions using appropriate expertise and that would pool risk in a cost-efficient manner. Under such a fund, an employee's account could accept registered retirement savings plan (RRSP) and employer contributions, as well as after-tax contributions for people who wanted their money managed professionally with appropriate risk sharing and a minimum of fees. Such a plan would make private pensions more portable and would facilitate saving for retirement by those who cannot contribute to an employer-sponsored pension plan. Although such a fund would have only a minimum effect on boomer retirement, since most of that generation's pension arrangements are already established, future generations of workers could benefit.

Also missing from the 2006 Senate report is an analysis of the fixed costs of employment created by the caps, or maximum limits, imposed on contributions to various government programs — for example, on CPP, employment insurance and, in some cases, workers' compensation. Such caps on contributions encourage employers to give current workers more hours, rather than spreading the work around to older part-time employees and hiring new, younger employees. Instead, caps on all employment-related programs should be replaced by a revenue-neutral rate — whether hourly, daily or weekly — to remove the disincentive to part-time and flexible work, especially by older workers.

Finally, it is worth noting that the federal government's recent decision to delay the age at which an individual must convert RRSP funds into income (from 69 to 71) is appropriate for a society that is experiencing increasing life expectancy.

Indeed, perhaps the conversion age should be linked explicitly to average life expectancy, with an opportunity for gradual conversion in cases where the holder can demonstrate that full retirement has not yet occurred. This deserves further study.

Policies to manage the effects on the Canadian workforce of the retirement of the boomer generation will be reflected in national economic performance and material living standards. The sooner they are discussed, evaluated and formulated, the better will Canada be positioned to face the economic challenges of an aging workforce. Demographic analysis that incorporates lifecycle behaviour thus provides a road map both for the most effective policies and for the timing of their implementation.

HEALTH CARE

The health care sector in all its manifestations is likely to be affected dramatically by Canada's aging population. Indeed, it has already experienced significant effects. Over the past decade, the boomers' aging parents — the relatively large generation born mostly during the Roaring 1920s — have been moving through the period of their most intensive use of the health care system, making increasing demands on physicians, hospitals, pharmaceuticals and home care services, stretching government-sponsored program budgets and service delivery to their limits.

Fortunately, demographic changes over the next decade could provide a respite for a health care system that has seemed unprepared for the inevitable effects of a rapidly growing population of aging seniors. The next generation to make intensive use of the system is the relatively small group born during the Great Depression of the 1930s, so growth in demand for health care could subside somewhat in the 2010s. This could provide a window of opportunity to develop effective and efficient health care delivery before the large boomer generation begins to make its highest demands on the system in the 2020s and 2030s.

The effect of future population aging on health care use, needs and finances is beyond the scope of this chapter; instead, I offer some observations on health care delivery, funding and staffing based on demographics and lifecycle analysis that the health care literature has largely overlooked.

Location

The first issue is people's access to health care where they live at different stages of life. According to lifecycle theory, young people tend to head to major cities for employment and entertainment. Thus, for example, boomers left Canada's small towns during the 1960s and 1970s, while the population of the downtown cores of Canada's three major cities grew rapidly. Then, in the 1980s and 1990s, the boomers started families and moved to the suburbs for the housing and space they needed in which to raise their children. In the past decade, the eldest boomers, reaching their 50s, began to inherit or purchase vacation properties — second homes that are located far from the major urban centres in which they spent their earlier years. In essence, then, population aging moves people away from downtown cores and back to smaller communities.

Yet hospitals and other health care providers are usually located in major urban centres where their older patients prefer not to be. Since the likelihood of disability or infirmity increases with age, distance from appropriate care can be debilitating for older patients. Even within major urban centres, transportation is often difficult for older people: important support and rehabilitation systems are disrupted when a 75-year-old woman has difficulty visiting her 77-year-old partner who has had a stroke or heart attack.

The response of boomers to this issue has been to place their aged and increasingly infirm parents in nursing homes located in suburban areas, which often disrupts the lifestyle of peace and quiet that their parents had become used to while living in smaller communities, further exacerbating their health care needs.

Canada thus needs to rethink the geographic delivery of health care services. At least for the needs of the aged, it makes little sense to locate hospitals, nursing homes and other health care facilities and services in the downtown cores of major cities. Instead, services and facilities should be located where the older population lives; the aged should not be expected to travel to the services. A more sensible policy would be to locate health care facilities on the suburban outskirts, where they would be more accessible to older adults from surrounding smaller communities. Younger downtown residents would still be able to access such facilities without undue imposition on their resources. In both cases, family and friends could more easily help with rehabilitation and other support services.

Another issue in the delivery of health care services is home visits, which are increasingly important for an aging and less mobile population. Because physical infirmity and disability increase with age, older patients often find it difficult to visit physicians, especially in winter, yet current policy discourages home visits by physicians or even nurses and nurse practitioners. An alternative delivery mode appropriate for an aging population should be considered — perhaps including the use of mobile nurse practitioners, which would improve service delivery and reduce waiting times in physicians' offices and hospital emergency wards. If the patient needed to see a physician or visit a hospital, the nurse practitioner could then advise and assist in the choice of facility and transportation, and provide a preliminary assessment to speed up diagnosis and treatment. In short, the use of nurse practitioners would improve the efficiency of the health care system by economizing on the use of scarce, more expensive physician and hospital resources. From the point of view of patients, it would also likely improve both service delivery and health outcomes.

Still another issue involves health outcomes. It is now widely recognized that increasing the volume of services generally improves the health outcomes of patients. Thus, for example, separate, stand-alone clinics that deliver specific health care services — such as cataract surgery, hip replacements and hernia operations — allow specialist physicians to increase the volume of their services in a single location. Such clinics also permit these specialists to create a work environment and manage a familiar caseload free from other pressures in the system. Relatively small clinics can also be less daunting and disorienting for older patients than large general hospitals, with staff who understand their needs, shorter corridors and more convenient parking for those who have difficulty walking, easier follow-up care and so on — all of which are important not only for older patients but also for their families and friends.

In general, the system should strive for the incorporation of best practices into all aspects of health care delivery. Undoubtedly, such a policy is more easily said than done, but appropriate geographic location needs to be better integrated into health care service delivery for Canada's aging population.

Funding and staffing

Health care is costly, but the future demands of an aging population are unlikely to bankrupt government. Indeed, Canada has a number of ways to fund future health care costs.

Given demographic changes that will see a declining share of children and young people and an increasing share of elderly in the population, one source of additional funding is to reallocate government funding away from education and toward health care.

Another source of funding is the boomers themselves, who will continue to pay taxes in their senior years. Robert Brown, an actuary from the University of Waterloo, contends that taxes on future pension withdrawals will finance all or most future health care needs of boomers (see Daw 2002). Currently, Canada's governments forgo more tax revenues from retirement savers than they collect from retirees, with boomers and other pre-retirement cohorts taking tax deductions on contributions and the tax-deferred accrual of investment gains. When boomers start withdrawing money from their pension sources, however, these tax deferrals will come due and government revenues will grow. Increases in contribution limits to RRSPs could provide even more tax revenues in the future. In short, the boomers will, in large part, self-finance their health care costs.

Governments also have other revenue options to finance future health care needs. For example, businesses operating in Canada benefit significantly from a public health care system that absolves them from the responsibility of providing health insurance for their workers. Recent events in the US steel, auto and airlines sectors have drawn attention to the high corporate costs of health insurance for workers in that country. Thus, in Canada, corporate and personal contributions to future health care costs could come, for example, from new, small employer and taxpayer health insurance taxes specifically earmarked for a health care fund, not from general government revenues.

The Achilles' heel of future health care delivery, however, is likely not to be Canada's ability to pay but its inability to find sufficient health care workers. By the 2030s, most boomers will have retired and begun to make significant demands on the health care system. Meanwhile, a declining birth rate will have resulted in a much smaller cohort on which to draw for new entrants into the labour market in general and the health care sector in particular. Moreover, since the boomers have had significantly fewer children than previous generations, they will have less family support on which to draw in their senior years. Thus, Canada cannot afford to wait: now is the time to recruit the echo generation into all health care occupations, to look after their aging parents when they need care the most.

CONCLUSIONS

The policies I have outlined in this chapter are examples of the larger generic policy challenge that an aging population poses. Canadian decision-makers, whether in the private or public sector, are largely rewarded for short-term decisions. In the private sector, executives focus on near-term stock prices and financial results; in the public sector, ministers (and many deputies and other officials) focus on results that will have a positive effect on the next election. Yet demographic change is gradual, seldom having any major effect in the short term, and is rarely considered in today's important policy decisions.

At one time, an advantage of tenure in the civil service was that it encouraged a focus on issues and solutions that transcended the current government's stay in power. This is no longer the case. The public sector has followed the private sector in introducing a focus on short-term incentives, and now even appointments below the deputy level typically are political, to provide better alignment with current government policies. Tenure is eroded as more public employees are replaced with each change of government, with the consequent loss of institutional memory and the effective discouragement of focus on longer-term issues and solutions. Policies with fast paybacks are favoured over those where results are delayed, especially if there are up-front costs, political or financial.

Although widespread, however, short-term thinking is not pervasive. In the late 1990s, for example, the solution to Canada's demographically driven pension crisis required a much longer-term time horizon. Alternative policies — increasing the retirement age (the US solution) or increasing contribution rates (ultimately the Canadian solution) — were considered. In addition, strategies to improve the rate of return on pension funds were discussed and implemented through the creation of an investment board. These difficult decisions subsequently removed the pension issue from public debate and private uncertainty.

Canada now needs to take the same approach to health care. Population aging inevitably is creating the perception of a looming health care crisis — an important economic and social issue that, like pensions, affects public budgets and private decisions. Piecemeal solutions with short-term political payback, such as reduced waiting times for selected operations or the delisting of certain procedures, cannot solve the problem or make it disappear from the public agenda. A more comprehensive, longer-term strategy is required.

Demographic momentum ensures the inevitability of population aging in Canada and elsewhere in the world. Slower population growth will result in slower economic growth, but not necessarily in declining material living standards. In this context, immigration policy will become even more important in the years ahead. Canada has a historical advantage in the global competition for immigrants, but its immigration program will have to be fine-tuned to yield the best results for both immigrants and the country.

A lifecycle approach can provide the foundation for determining the economic and social consequences of population aging. An aging workforce will produce slower labour force growth, while the impending retirement of the boomer generation will present a variety of human resource challenges, not the least of which will be in health care. Yet the ability to meet future health care needs does not have to founder on the shoals of inadequate funding; rather, the challenge is likely to be to devise an efficient and effective system of health care delivery and to find the staff necessary to deliver services. Now is the time to recruit and train the future health care workforce. Delay could have deleterious consequences both for the boomers and for Canadian society at large.

REFERENCES

Daw, J. 2002. "How Boomers Could Fund Future Health Care." *Toronto Star,* July 9.

Foot, D.K. 1994. "Canada's Unemployment-Immigration Linkage: Demographic, Economic and Political Influences." *Canadian Journal of Sociology* 19 (4): 513-23.

Foot, D.K., and R. Gomez. 2006. "Population Ageing and Sectoral Growth: The Case of the U.K., 2006-2026." *Oxford Journal of Business and Economics* 5 (1): 85-94.

Foot, D.K., and D. Stoffman. 1996. *Boom, Bust & Echo: How to Profit from the Coming Demographic Shift.* Toronto: Macfarlane Walter & Ross.

Foot, D.K., and R. Venne. 1998. "The Time Is Right: Voluntary Reduced Work Time and Workforce Demographics." *Canadian Studies in Population* 25 (2): 91-114.

Guillemette, Y., and W.B.P. Robson. 2006. "No Elixir of Youth: Immigration Cannot Keep Canada Young." *C.D. Howe Institute Backgrounder* 96. Toronto: C.D. Howe Institute.

Picot, G., F. Hou, and S. Coulombe. 2007. "Chronic Low Income and Low-Income Dynamics among Recent Immigrants." Research Paper 294. Ottawa: Statistics Canada.

Policy Research Initiative. 2005. *Encouraging Choice in Work and Retirement: Project Report.* Ottawa: Policy Research Initiative.

Population Reference Bureau. 2006. *World Population Data Sheet.* Washington, DC: Population Reference Bureau.

Senate Standing Committee on Banking, Trade and Commerce. 2006. *The Demographic Time Bomb: Mitigating the Effects of Demographic Change in Canada.* Ottawa: Senate of Canada.

Statistics Canada. 2005. *Population Projections for Canada, Provinces and Territories, 2005-31.* Ottawa: Statistics Canada.

Turner, D., C. Giorno, A. De Serres, A. Vourch, and P. Richardson. 1998. "The Macroeconomic Implications of Ageing in a Global Context." Economics Department Working Paper 193. Paris: Organisation for Economic Co-operation and Development.

POPULATION AGING: THE RISK OF TUNNEL VISION
Peter Hicks

Since there is so much in David Foot's chapter to agree with, I will follow the not-quite-honourable tradition of criticizing what is not there, and ignore many of the sensible and provocative things that *are* in "Some Economic and Social Consequences of Population Aging."

To begin, I would like to congratulate Foot for ignoring his mandate, at least in part. Authors were asked to propose three specific public policies and assess their effects. He wisely did not limit himself to three. I say "wisely" since, in my understanding, there are no big magic policy bullets to deal with the effects of Canada's changing demography. Many smaller changes and adaptations on many fronts are called for. If we were to pick only three, we would surely get it wrong.

IS "POPULATION AGING" A USEFUL WAY OF FRAMING THE POLICY AGENDA?

Indeed, I wish he had ignored the rest of his mandate as well. As he was asked to do, he limits the chapter to an examination of the effects of population aging — that is, the changes in the age structure of the population that flow from trends in fertility, mortality and immigration.

I would argue, however, that population aging is not a good way of framing discussions of specific policy responses. Other population characteristics, which Foot notes only in passing, are at least as important. Examples are changing educational and mobility profiles, changes in family formation, the increased participation of women in post-secondary education and in the labour market and the more recent changes in retirement patterns.

Moreover, changes in these other population characteristics — not to mention external changes in productivity, debt reduction or medical technology — can offset significantly the effects of population aging in a way that should not be ignored.

For example, increased employment rates by older workers can moderate greatly the economic effects of population aging, as shown by the Policy Research Initiative (2005). In reality, employment rates of older workers have been rising sharply in recent years.

Why, then, does population aging appear so often on lists of key policy challenges? When the 12 agenda-setters met in the earlier stage of this project, I noticed that population aging was mentioned only four times in the list of 36 policy challenges they identified, with fiscal and labour market implications getting the most attention. Yet, at the workshop, the agenda-setters gave a high score to addressing a range of social and economic implications of aging populations. What is going on?

In my view, population aging typically is identified as a priority because of the clear pressure it places on policies. It can be an important entry to policy discussions. It alerts us that something might need to be done. It is not, however, a helpful exit from those policy discussions, if the goal is to find specific proposals for change.

Let me put the case more strongly: population aging, taken in isolation, simply reinforces what we already know; it seldom leads to new policy directions. For example, studies typically argue that population aging means that pension financing should be sustainable, that governments should reduce debts (perhaps the societal analogy to individuals preparing for their old age by saving more when they are still working), that productivity should be increased to offset a reduced number of workers, that there should be less constrained choices in retirement transitions, that health care effectiveness should increase and that workplaces be more welcoming to older workers. These are all worthwhile policy directions, but they would all make sense regardless of the age structure of the population. An analysis of population aging adds little to shaping the design and implementation of such policies, although it might change priorities for action, and it does have something important to say about timing — that is, when policy action is needed.

Demographically based dependency ratios can be a good entry into discussions of, for example, changes in the numbers of children in school, employees in the workplace and beneficiaries of pensions. Yet when it comes to finding responses to the pressures imparted by these numbers, they are of little use. Indeed, they sometimes point us in the wrong direction. Let me give a couple of examples.

First, I think that dependency ratio analysis, based exclusively on the age structure of the population, which policy cannot change significantly, may well have encouraged us to look at ways of adjusting to seemingly inevitable trends, rather than at ways of fixing underlying problems that policy might be able to deal with — such as incentives that favour early retirement, lack of training to prepare people for working longer or improving workplace quality so that people will be less likely to leave. Second, dependency ratio analysis also may have invited us to underestimate the way in which people and employers adapt to changing situations even in the absence of specific policy action — as the large changes in the employment rates of older people suggest.

Yes, changes in the age structure of the population are important, but it is even more important to understand that people's activities do not depend only, or even primarily, on their age. A limited view of demographic change tempts us to overlook this fundamental policy message.

My main critique is not with Foot's chapter but with the starting premise that population aging is a good way of organizing our thinking about specific policy responses. Changing population characteristics are clearly important to policy, but even here I would have preferred a chapter based on an analysis of a broader range of changing population characteristics.

WHAT IS MISSING?

Foot does a fine job: there is much to agree with in his chapter and much that is controversial — just what is needed. Moreover, his exposition of the demography and economics of population aging is excellent, as one would expect from such a distinguished expert. Yet I think a few things are missing from his analysis.

Life course and lifecycle

I find it useful to distinguish between life course perspectives and lifecycle perspectives. Life course perspectives look at the main transitions and trajectories of life: early childhood; life in school, family, work and retirement (and in the giving and receipt of care); the transition from school to work; the transition from work to retirement; and so on. These transitions are not defined by age alone but happen at different times in the lives of real people. Lifecycle perspectives, on the other hand, are usually based on age, with the expectation, for example, that we save in our middle years and consume in our older years.

In my use of the terms, lifecycle analysis is mainly about age, while the life course encompasses (to use the language of demographers) cohort and period effects, in addition to age effects. It seems to me particularly important that we take the broader view in Canada, since life courses here tend to be less institutionalized and less age-dependent than in many other countries. For example, the timing and duration of the transition from work to retirement cannot be fully explained by age-based analysis alone.

Foot's analysis is mainly about age groups and lifecycles. That may be why he underplays a social change that I think might prove to be of great importance: the turn-around in the employment rates of older workers over the past decade. The upward trend might not continue on its present track, of course, but I think the rate is just as likely to accelerate as it is to fall back. As Foot points out, the eldest baby boomers will not reach 65 until 2012, and trends might well begin to change then. The baby boomers changed the nature of the education system when they moved through it; then they changed the nature of the workforce. Why should we assume they will not change the nature of retirement — possibly by demanding a much more active role in the workplace for longer? This discussion is important, since such trends could have deep effects in offsetting the negative consequences of population aging.

Economic, social and spatial effects

Foot limits his analysis to material living standards, defined as output per capita. Fair enough, but social consequences cannot be ignored when we move to policy implications. Most people would count it as a gain in well-being if, given real choices, they could choose more leisure and less time at work, even if this were to result in lower output per person. As well, productivity growth, which could have very large effects in lessening any adverse economic effects of population aging, deserves greater emphasis — as does the related subject of the productivity of an older workforce. (On a very minor note, I think that discussions such as this would be clearer if we cast them in terms of employment rates rather than labour force participation rates.)

Foot says little about social well-being, apart from its manifestations in economic well-being and health. Admittedly, the latter are major determinants of overall well-being, but I would have preferred some nod toward the broader dimensions of social well-being. In particular, I suspect that future generations might well wonder why we ordered policies and institutional arrangements in such a way that leisure is so heavily concentrated in the last third of life, with people out of contact with the workplace, one of the main institutions of our society.

With respect to economic effects, Foot says little about their spatial dimensions. Population aging might affect living standards by reducing labour force and economic growth, but, in addition to the sectoral challenges to which he alludes, there are also increased regional disparities. Aging, fertility and mobility patterns are expected to benefit the economies of western Canada and the larger urban areas but to hinder growth in the eastern and more rural parts of the country. Eastern Canada might even experience reductions in gross domestic product per capita because of population aging. In contrast, Ontario could see only small changes. Expected growth in the size of the younger Aboriginal population will also play a major role in some parts of the country.

WHAT ABOUT THE POLICY RECOMMENDATIONS?

Foot's chapter is rich with policy recommendations. There is lot here to like; there is also much that is quite controversial. I will duck commenting on which is which — for reasons that I hope will become apparent. Basically, I feel that discussion of particular program designs in response to population aging is premature.

I find Foot's discussion of the timing of reforms to be particularly helpful. He usefully reminds us that the baby boomers have not yet retired – and that the echo generation is currently entering the labour market. Too often, discussions of population aging forget that population aging is still working in the direction of a larger workforce, with more producers relative to consumers — the pressures toward a small workforce are still some years off. While I have expressed some doubts about the usefulness of population aging, by itself, as a driver of the policy agenda, it is still a most important dimension of that agenda — as Foot's insights on the timing of reforms make clear.

I am not sure that I agree, however, with all of the policy implications that seem to be drawn from Foot's discussion of the echo generation. In particular, there seems to be an assumption that quite a direct trade-off exists between older workers' working longer and the availability of jobs for the echo generation. Earlier analysis by the Organisation for Economic Co-operation and Development (OECD 1998), for example, found little evidence of a direct link between the employment and unemployment situations of young and old workers. It might be time to look at this again.

I also like the breadth of Foot's discussion. He covers policies related to the prevention of population decrease, the encouragement of continued (but flexible) labour force participation, improved income security in retirement and improved health care in terms of location, funding and staff. His chapter is thus in the tradition of the OECD and many other important studies of population aging that take a similarly broad approach.

It is worth noting, however, that the analysis in many of these earlier studies assumed that long-standing trends toward earlier retirement would continue into the future unless policy actions were taken, and that the most immediate challenges were on the fiscal front. In Canada today, things look a little different: instead, we have seen employment rates rise among older workers, action has been taken on the fiscal sustainability of public pensions, and Canada's fiscal house is generally in good order compared with that of other countries. I would like to see an exploration of the policy implications of these changed circumstances. Have things really changed? If so, what difference would that make to policy directions? Since we cannot predict the future well, what are the largest risks and uncertainties in thinking about policies that are intended to have their biggest effects many years from now? How do we mitigate those risks?

Foot was not asked to address these questions, and it would be unreasonable for me to criticize him for not having done so. Rather, he was asked to make specific policy proposals, and on this he certainly delivers. Specific proposals make sense when we are talking about policies that could be introduced soon and whose effects would be in the short and medium term. I wonder, however, if they really work in a policy area where the main effects will be felt only in the decades after 2012. Here, I think it would be better to deal with more general trends and directions for policy.

That being said, Foot has many useful ideas for specific policies that warrant serious discussion. In some cases, alternative proposals exist, and it might be interesting to see a comparative analysis. Assessing the merits of different proposals depends, of course, on the diagnosis of the problem; and, as I indicated earlier, I doubt we should frame that diagnosis in terms of population aging in isolation.

Foot's proposal to remove caps from social programs in order to increase hiring incentives is an example of the need to go beyond a population aging diagnostic. Such a change could have effects that go far beyond employment incentives — for example, removing the ceiling on the Canada/Quebec Pension Plan (CPP/QPP) could have a huge effect on the nature of Canada's public pension system, especially if it were done in a revenue-neutral way. The success of the pension system is often thought to reflect, in part, the fact that the combination of the various elements — the CPP/QPP, old age security, the Guaranteed Income Supplement and the tax system — means that people at all income levels receive about the same total amount of public pension. In other words, compared with that of many other countries, Canada's pension system is effective in reducing poverty among older people, while still involving citizens at all income levels in the system;

its public costs are relatively low; it contains relatively few work disincentives (at least for middle- and higher-income people); and it leaves room for a large private pension system, with a resulting diversification of risk. The CPP ceiling is one factor that ensures the system as a whole works in this manner. Thus, we simply must assess changes such as removing caps on these programs in a broader context.

This need to take account of a wide range of factors is still another reason I think that a discussion of the general policy directions that an aging society implies might make most sense, given where we are today.

Although I have argued that population aging, by itself, might not provide the best basis for framing a comprehensive policy agenda in today's environment, Foot should be congratulated for an excellent and thought-provoking chapter that addresses important issues which need to be taken into account in any policy agenda.

REFERENCES

Organisation for Economic Co-operation and Development (OECD). 1998. *Maintaining Prosperity in an Ageing Society*. Paris: OECD.

Policy Research Initiative. 2005. *Encouraging Choice in Work and Retirement: Project Report*. Ottawa: Policy Research Initiative.

POPULATION AGING: BETTER THAN THE ALTERNATIVE

Susan A. McDaniel

The elephant in the room in any discussion of population aging is that it is a triumph over premature death, killing childhood diseases, life-depriving poverty and unwanted pregnancies. It is a sign of progress and societal success. "Aging is better than the alternative," Mark Twain tells us, and it is certainly true for us as individuals who prefer not to die young. At the societal level, demographic aging is part of a socio-historical transition, an irreversible progression toward longer and better lives for the vast majority. David Foot's paper "Some Economic and Social Consequences of Population Aging" captures this essential insight exceedingly well.

Twenty years ago, I argued that population aging would become the popular policy paradigm of the 1990s and early 2000s, not for reasons of evidence but because it would serve as a politically palatable justification for restructuring social and health policies (McDaniel 1987). Everyone has to be right at least once, and I think I was — for the most part. Population aging has been seen as the culprit in rising health care costs, despite clear evidence to the contrary (see Evans et al. 2001) and the fact that the leading edge of the baby boom cohort — which hits age 60 in 2007 — is, for the most part, healthier than any previous cohort. Aging is also fingered in worries about the viability of pensions, productivity and the sustainability of many public programs. With respect to the Canada and Quebec Pension Plans, both the International Monetary Fund and the 2004 report of Canada's chief actuary find that long-overdue reforms in the late 1990s were sufficient to maintain a sound pension plan in Canada for the next 75 years (Office of the Chief Actuary 2004; International Monetary Fund 2005).

Some, however, seem mesmerized by the seeming logic of the link between population aging and the declining health of individuals with age. Thankfully, worries are proffered in somewhat less alarmist tones in the 2000s than they were in the 1990s. Nevertheless, demographic alarmism — or "the age quake" (Senate Special Committee 2007) — particularly about rising health care costs, seems reluctant to die a peaceful death. It is, as Evans et al. (2001) suggest, a "Zombie walking," a creature truly dead but still among us. Though tempered by recent evidence (see McMullin, Cooke, and

Downie 2004), population aging and its perceived negative policy implications remain, in some minds, a deep concern.

David Foot does not see population aging as the paradigm on which policy challenges pivot; in this, he is empirically well grounded (see Senate Special Committee 2007), and is also in the company of the best analysts in Canada (for example, Denton, Feaver, and Spencer 1998). Nor does he see the sustainability of government programs per se to be in doubt as a direct result of population aging. Nonetheless, there is room for useful innovation in the areas of population policy, workforce and retirement, and health care, as Foot outlines.

Foot clearly explains the complexity of issues and the demographic causal webs involved in population aging by reference to simple equations that he subsequently spells out in words. He carefully explores the consequences of population aging both with evidence and within the logic of demographic equations. Foot also considers factors and policies connected to population aging, such as immigration and labour market policies. He dismisses, gently but with strong analytical force, argumentation that is ungrounded in solid research, as well as alarmism about population aging. He admits that there remain unanswered research questions, such as the effects of population aging on productivity, about which not enough is yet known.

Foot's main analytical points can be handily summed up: trends and causes, effects, interpretation and policy implications. With respect to trends, Foot tells us that Canada's population is aging, largely because of below-replacement fertility, but other countries are aging more rapidly. He outlines effects as complex and interconnected with demographic momentum — that is, with trends that we cannot change with policy and should not try to change. For interpretation, Foot relies on demographic transition theory at the macro level and lifecycle (or what sociologists call life course) theory at the micro level, enabling deeper explanatory insights. Through demographic transition theory, we see the global historical sequencing of demographic changes that are not reversible without a reversal in economic development, which neither policy-makers nor the populace would accept. Increasing immigration and fertility rates, therefore, are not sufficient policy responses. Lifecycle theory reveals how individual behaviours and aggregate outcomes are separable. Workforce aging, for example, can affect aggregate labour force participation rates, even if age-specific rates (behaviour) remain unchanged.

As for policy implications, Foot focuses on three themes: immigration, retirement and health care. He is accurately concerned that, given Canada's aging population, policies that encourage the entry of skilled immigrants but then obstruct them from using their skills once in the country are incongruous. He cautions us not to overreact about the baby boomers' looming retirement, noting correctly that this will occur over a period of 20 years. Health care, however, will be a challenge, but not for the reasons typically cited. The essential policy challenges in health, Foot argues, are geographically appropriate delivery and the need to reallocate resources from education to health care.

With solid analysis, Foot comes to a number of policy recommendations. Worthy of emphasis is his crucial assertion that single policies are unlikely to be effective; rather, what are needed are coherent groups of policies that are based on the full recognition of what can and cannot be changed. With respect to population policies, for example, Foot argues that fertility policies are largely a dead end because of demographic momentum: the decline in the number of women of child-bearing age. His focus thus turns to immigration, where he argues that what is needed is to make maximum economic use of immigrants' skills for the benefit of both an aging Canadian population and the immigrants themselves: streamlining credentialing is good population policy and good economic policy.

With respect to workforce and retirement policies, Foot recommends planning for the retirement of the baby boomers over two decades (2011-31), with options for flexible retirement while working, as well as workforce succession by younger workers — another example of policies that cohere.

As for his third theme, health care, Foot recommends locating clinics and hospitals where the elderly live, not always in downtown city cores, reallocating funds from education to health care and investing in the recruitment and training of new health care workers.

Worthy of highlighting is Foot's explication of a counterintuitive disjuncture between individuals' behaviour and aggregate outcomes captured as rates. Planned parenthood, for example, is a choice many couples make, but it contributes, in aggregate, to population aging. Demographic processes have their own momentum, as Foot aptly shows. It is vital for policy to distinguish between the dynamics of individuals' life courses and the fundamentally different, often counterintuitive processes by which populations become older. Equating the two, as is often done, can be perilous. It is not the case, for example, that older populations are necessarily less productive or creative or more conservative socially or politically (Denton and Spencer 2003; Scarth 2003), although this may be true for some individuals as they age. Rather, the degree to which older people are integrated into the social and economic system is the key to their productivity. Foot shows this, but stops short of adding that myths about population aging can have self-fulfilling consequences.

As a second example, Foot notes that unemployment among older people might be hidden (see McDaniel 2003; and research in the Workforce Aging in the New Economy project, available at www.wane.ca). The policy inflexibility, for example, of public pensions that, unlike private pensions, require a one-way transition out of employment could exacerbate labour shortages. At present, involuntarily unemployed older workers lack access to their public pensions and face difficulties in finding suitable employment; they fall through the cracks and add to labour shortages, even if they want to work (McDaniel 2003).

Before I move to my additional policy recommendations, let me offer some quibbles about Foot's chapter. For one, his discussion of country viability is problematic: Japan and Russia are not parallel examples but demographically different, as well as economically and socially disparate. As a result of social and economic upheaval since the demise of the Soviet Union, Russia has experienced a stunning lowering of life expectancies to 59 years for men and 72 years for women. These declines are comparable in degree, if not level, to those seen in sub-Saharan Africa as a result of the HIV/AIDS pandemic. Japan's life expectancies, in contrast, are 79 years for men and 86 years for women; the country also has a low birth rate (9 per 1,000 population), a low death rate (8 per 1,000 population) and a highly productive economy (Population Reference Bureau 2007). Russia might be in peril as a country, but demographic change there flows from severe socio-economic problems. Japan is in far less peril, with a long-lived, relatively healthy, highly educated population on which to draw economically if labour market policies can adapt.

Foot also has some inaccurate expectations with respect to immigrants. A recent Statistics Canada study finds, for example, that family-class immigrants do better in the labour market than anticipated. The study also finds that visible minority women immigrants earn more than comparable men, but less than non-immigrants (2007). Thus, the policy challenge here is not the number of immigrants or their ages or qualifications, but the situations they face that prevent their full participation in Canada's society and economy.

With respect to health care, Foot counters many misperceptions about the consequences of population aging and makes innovative, timely and useful policy recommendations. The challenge of training new generations of health care workers is indeed upon us now, a crucial policy issue. This recommendation exemplifies the need for coherent policies — in this case, addressing labour market challenges for the so-called echo cohort while planning for future health care needs of the baby boomers. Attention to geographic dimensions of the provision of health care to seniors is another apt recommendation (see also Wilson and Rosenberg 2002, 2004; Moore and Pacey 2003).

Though he underemphasizes them, Foot does not overlook certain aspects of health care that provincial plans do not cover — namely, home care, long-term chronic care in extreme old age (85 and older) and palliative care in the last short period before death. Such care looms large in the future of an aging population in which many are likely to grow old in a healthy state but then decline rapidly.

Foot's introduction of demographic transition theory and lifecycle theory is most welcome. Theory situates policy challenges and helps to interpret needed policy action. The way in which individual life courses connect to policy shifts and changes in families and work matters to how society sees population aging and, subsequently, to how policies are shaped. For example, shifting entitlements and responsibilities among generations affect expectations from policy, from families and from employers. Those who expect a lot of support might be disappointed to receive an amount that another generation might see as generous. Growing diversity among the elderly and in the capacity of families to provide care across generations also affects how the policy implications of an aging population will play out. As John Helliwell's research (2002) tells us, trust, values and social participation matter greatly to the well-being of individuals and of societies.

Demographic analysis offers good evidence for policy, but, taken alone, it is limited — as is any unidisciplinary evidence in a global, complex world. Demographic changes are not removed from human actions but are aggregated human outcomes, connected with socio-economic and life course changes. Demography is not like the tectonic forces that cause earthquakes. Population aging, for example, is largely the overall outcome of a lot of people who are practising family planning. Understanding this point can lead to policy action. In the Population and Life Course project funded by the Social Sciences and Humanities Research Council, for example, population aging appears in all six strategic themes: family, work and work-life balance; immigrants and migrants; labour force, aging and life course flexibility; health: mortality, morbidity and the changing nature of the elderly population; education and lifelong learning; and income and inequality.

There is thus a strong need for integrated policy-illuminating analyses of demographic aging together with socio-economic and life course changes. We must, in effect, "walk the talk" of interdisciplinary policy-relevant basic research. Demographics are both cause and consequence of shifting socio-economic forces (both national and global) and changing individual choices.

What additional opportunities for policy research exist? I suggest there are four. First, issues of productivity and innovation should be connected to demographic aging, an area that Foot suggests is an open research question: how can the innovation agenda connect with productivity in an aging population? Second, since quality of life, education and literacy, information access, trust, values and social participation matter greatly to well-being as accumulated over the life course (Helliwell 2002), perhaps these areas could be nurtured fruitfully by policy. Third, policies still focus on age criteria even though labour markets are moving toward maximizing human capital through lifelong learning, which makes age increasingly irrelevant. Fourth, a preoccupation with demographic categories such as age veils deep connections across age groups, notably in generations, but also in communities.

I agree with Foot that flexible pension policies are needed (and soon) to reflect the changed behaviour of people who retire from one workplace but do not leave the workforce. I would add to his recommendation on health care my own recommendation for a registered aging savings plan to help individuals save for chronic care in their older years that public health insurance does not cover.

Lastly, in my view, Foot does not give enough attention to the need for home care, which has been recommended (and lobbied for) for decades. It is cost-effective and what seniors want, yet there has been little policy action so far.

As a final word, I recommend for future policy less tilting at nonexistent windmills (age quakes) and instead a sharper focus on developing more coherent groups of policies that address what is needed for an aging Canada, as Foot does in his chapter.

REFERENCES

Denton, F.T., C. Feaver, and B.G. Spencer. 1998. "The Future Population of Canada: Its Age Distribution and Dependency Relations." *Canadian Journal on Aging* 17 (1): 83-109.

Denton, F.T., and B.G. Spencer. 2003. "Population Change and Economic Growth: The Long-Term Outlook." SEDAP Research Paper 102. Hamilton, ON: McMaster University, Program for Research on Social and Economic Dimensions of an Aging Population.

Evans, R.G., K.M. McGrail, S.G. Morgan, M.L. Barer, and C. Hertzman. 2001. "APOCALYPSE NO: Population Aging and the Future of Health Care Systems." SEDAP Research Paper 59. Hamilton, ON: McMaster University, Program for Research on Social and Economic Dimensions of an Aging Population.

Helliwell, J. 2002. *Globalization and Well-Being*. Vancouver: University of British Columbia Press.

International Monetary Fund. 2005. *Canada: Selected Issues*. Country Report no. 05/16, March 29.

McDaniel, S.A. 1987. "Demographic Aging as a Guiding Paradigm in Canada's Welfare State." *Canadian Public Policy* 13 (3): 330-6.

_____. 2003. "Hidden in the Household: Now It's Men in Mid-Life." *Ageing International* 28 (4): 326-44.

McMullin, J.A., M. Cooke, and R. Downie. 2004. "Labour Force Ageing and Skills Shortages in Canada and Ontario." Research Report W24. Ottawa: Canadian Policy Research Networks.

Moore, E.G., and M.A. Pacey. 2003. "Geographic Dimensions of Aging in Canada 1991-2001." SEDAP Research Paper 97. Hamilton, ON: McMaster University, Program for Research on Social and Economic Dimensions of an Aging Population.

Office of the Chief Actuary. 2004. *Actuarial Report (21st) on the Canada Pension Plan*. Ottawa: Office of the Superintendent of Financial Institutions Canada.

Population Reference Bureau. 2007. *Datafinder*. Washington, DC. Accessed March 1, 2007. www.prb.org/Data Find/datafinder7.htm

Scarth, W. 2003. "Population Aging, Productivity, and Growth in Living Standards." SEDAP Research Paper 90. Hamilton, ON: McMaster University, Program for Research on Social and Economic Dimensions of an Aging Population.

Senate Special Committee on Aging. 2007. *Embracing the Challenge of Aging*. First Interim Report. Ottawa: Senate of Canada.

Statistics Canada. 2007. "Study: Low-Income Rates among Immigrants Entering Canada, 1992 to 2004." *The Daily*. January 30.

Wilson, K., and M.W. Rosenberg. 2002. "The Geographies of Crisis: Exploring Accessibility to Health Care Services in Canada." *The Canadian Geographer* 46 (3): 223-34.

_____. 2004. "Accessibility and the Canadian Health Care System: Squaring Perceptions and Realities." *Health Policy* 67 (2): 137-48.

PART I   THE POLICY CHALLENGES

ECONOMIC SECURITY

A BETTER INCOME SECURITY SYSTEM FOR ALL CANADIANS

Jean-Yves Duclos

Canada needs a modern income security system for a modern world. The country's economic and social fabric has evolved dramatically since the end of the Second World War, yet its income security system has not kept up. Canada's out-of-date system compromises our ability to achieve both a just and a productive society.

In designing a new income security system for Canada, two main challenges must be tackled. The first is the challenge of dealing with evolving sources and forms of economic insecurity. Canada's current social safety net has several important holes. During the past decade, thanks to relatively strong growth and favourable fiscal conditions, these flaws did not matter as much as they could have, and they did not seem to preoccupy policy-makers and analysts as much as they should have. Because of demographic pressures, however, fiscal determinants are likely to become more adverse in the near future, and the risk of economic downturn is always present. It is imperative to fix our income security system before the next recession occurs and to leave to the next generation a legacy of well-functioning economic and social security programs adapted to the determinants of modern insecurity.

The second challenge is to build an income security system that supports, rather than undermines, the strength of Canada's economy. In a world in which productivity and international competitiveness increasingly matter and Canada's labour markets are under demographic pressure, a healthy income security system matters even more. Concerns are rising about shortages of skilled labour, due in large part to the impending retirement of the massive baby boom generation. For Canada to prosper, all working-age adults should have the ability to contribute to our economy.

The two pillars of Canada's current income security system for working-age adults are employment insurance (EI) and social assistance. The original unemployment insurance program, introduced in 1941, targeted workers who were suffering from temporary, infrequent and unpredictable spells of unemployment. It excluded the majority of the workforce, mostly covering employees in industry and commerce. Since then, the program has grown into a complex system that severely distorts incentives for a significant segment of working-age adults and even contributes to increased economic insecurity in the long run. EI also covers an increasingly small proportion of the unemployed, and its financing and arcane benefit rules are inequitable in many ways.

Social assistance, intended to be only a marginal element in postwar Canada's conception of an income security system, was designed to serve as a last-resort safety net for the very small numbers of those who were in need of temporary assistance or who could not be expected to work. Today, however, the money Canadians receive through social assistance almost equals the amount paid in EI benefits (see table 1; see also Battle, Mendelson, and Torjman 2006, figure 12). Far from shrinking, social assistance has become a major social program of first (and only) resort for millions of Canadians, including many of the employable.

TABLE 1. **EXPENDITURES ON REGULAR EMPLOYMENT INSURANCE BENEFITS AND TOTAL PROVINCIAL/TERRITORIAL/MUNICIPAL EXPENDITURES ON SOCIAL ASSISTANCE, 1980-2002 (BILLIONS OF CONSTANT 2002 DOLLARS)**

	Employment insurance	Social assistance
1980	10.8	6.2
1982	17.7	7.5
1984	17.3	8.9
1986	16.9	9.3
1988	15.9	9.5
1990	19.2	11.0
1992	22.8	16.0
1994	17.7	16.6
1996	14.7	14.3
1998	13.9	12.1
2000	12.4	10.5
2002	13.5	10.3

Source: Battle, Mendelson, and Torjman (2006, figs. 4, 11).
Note: Prior to1996, employment insurance was called unemployment insurance.

Finally, access to a range of much-needed employment-related and skills development services — including training, upgrading, placement and counselling — is ill targeted and inefficient, and typically contingent on the recipient's being on either EI or social assistance. Moreover, for social assistance recipients, these services are typically of low quality. Good-quality training services are therefore mostly available to those with good jobs and to a few of the nonworking poor, but not to the rest, leading to uneven coverage and a lack of options to alleviate economic insecurity.

There is, fortunately, reason for hope as one ponders the future of Canada's income security system. With the implementation of the National Child Benefit (NCB) in the 1990s, the federal and provincial governments made some progress toward designing a system — albeit for children — that is more growth enhancing, more supportive of individual freedoms and capabilities and more inclusive of those in need of economic security and support. Such outcomes would certainly seem desirable in any reform of income security for working-age adults. The NCB also showed the way for a collaborative sharing of responsibilities and financing between the two levels of government.

This chapter has three main sections. In the first, I review quickly some of the issues that Canada faces with respect to growth, employment and security, and I discuss some of the associated policy challenges. In the next section, I describe three basic principles I believe a sound income security system should follow. In the last section, I present three policy proposals that aim at providing a better income security system for all Canadians. The first proposal is to implement a universal basic income for all Canadians. The second is to revamp the EI program to make it both more efficient and more equitable. The third is to put into place policies that will better promote and protect assets — in particular, human capital and savings.

In presenting this analysis, I draw from the existing literature and do not pretend to be original in my assessment and vision of Canada's income security system. Neither do I purport to cover in sufficient detail many of the difficult issues of program design, financing and jurisdictional division of responsibilities that must be tackled in making important policy changes. I hope, however, to convey a sense of how an improved system would better serve Canadians' well-being and security.

THE POLICY CHALLENGE: TO IMPROVE CANADIANS' SECURITY AND WELL-BEING

Canada's economic and social fabric has evolved significantly over the past two decades. The income security system, however, has not kept up with these changes, and that is posing increasingly important policy challenges.

Growth, employment and security

The performance of Canada's economy and labour market has been comparatively strong over the past decade. The unemployment rate is now below 7 percent, from a peak of above 11 percent during the early 1990s recession. Growth in incomes has also been strong, explained in good part by rises in educational attainment and labour market participation levels.

Set against this positive picture, however, are the emerging challenges that the Canadian economy and Canadian workers are facing. Globalization is making markets for goods and services ever more competitive, rewarding more flexible labour market practices — including those that encourage greater mobility, skills development, adaptability and pay-for-performance remuneration mechanisms. Technological change has also increased the relative rewards for more highly skilled work. A consequence of this has been a fall in the relative wages of younger, less educated, newly immigrated or newly hired workers (see Chung 2004). It has also meant an increased concentration of unemployment and time not spent working among the least skilled.

Nonstandard employment

Since the end of the 1970s, there has also been a fall in so-called standard employment, defined as "employment of individuals for wages and salaries by a single firm, where individuals work full-time on the employer's premises, and expect (and are expected) to be employed for an indefinite period of time" (Public Service Commission 1999, 2). The forms of nonstandard employment are growing and include part-time work, temporary employment and self-employment. Vosko, Cranford and Zukewich (2003) find that, in 2002, only 63 percent of Canadian workers were full-time, permanent and paid employees; of the remainder, 11 percent were permanent part-time, 11 percent were temporary and 15 percent were self-employed (see also Saunders 2003). Nonstandard employment is typically associated with lower wages, lower education and skills, no career path and no formal or on-the-job training (Battle, Mendelson, and Torjman 2006). Such employment is also associated with higher insecurity: a higher risk of unemployment, no occupational pensions and no disability benefits or supplementary medical and dental insurance plans. As I discuss later, most workers with nonstandard employment also cannot qualify for EI or benefit fully from public pension plans.

Low pay

Related to the growth of nonstandard employment is the growth in the proportion of working-age adults considered to be low-paid workers. One in six Canadians working full time currently earns less than $10 per hour (in 2001 dollars: this is the usual definition of low pay; see Saunders 2005b). Almost half of workers ages 15 to 24 are low paid, as are about 16 percent of those ages 25 to 34, about 13 percent of those ages 35 to 44 and 23 percent of single parents. In 2000, almost one-third of recent visible-minority immigrants were low paid, compared with one-sixth of Canadian-born workers. Although the incidence of low pay rose in all categories of educational attainment (particularly for men) between 1980 and 2000, low pay is four times as prevalent among those who lack high school completion as it is among university graduates (Chung 2004, chart B). This is another sign of the shift of labour market rewards toward the remuneration of more highly skilled work.

The effect of low pay is also reflected over the longer term: half of low-paid workers — especially women and those with lower educational levels — will still be on low pay in five years' time (see Janz 2004; Saunders 2005a). Furthermore, despite the rise in average educational attainment since 1981, the share of total jobs that pay less than $10 per hour (in 2001 dollars) has not fallen (Saunders 2005a). Compounding the effects of low pay among nonstandard workers is their lack of access to occupational pension benefits and insurance plans (see figure 1): only 12 percent of those who earn $10 or less per hour have a registered pension plan, compared with 74 percent of those who earn $20 or more. Similarly, only 13 percent of low-paid workers are covered by extended medical, dental and life/disability insurance, compared with 77 percent of those who earn $20 or more an hour.

FIGURE 1. PROPORTION OF WAGE EARNERS WITH ACCESS TO NONWAGE BENEFITS, 2000, BY HOURLY WAGE RATE GROUP (PERCENT)

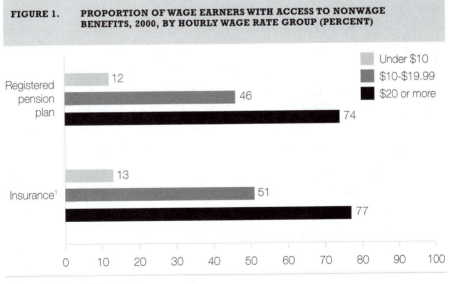

Source: Saunders (2005a, fig. 9).
[1] Refers to extended medical, dental and life/disability insurance.

Economic security

Adding to the challenges that low-paid workers face is the worrying prospect of substantial new economic risks. One such risk is increasing income volatility. In the United States, middle-class families faced annual income swings of about 15 percent a year in the 1970s, but during the 1980s and 1990s that volatility rose to between 25 and 30 percent a year (Bordoff, Deich, and Orszag 2006, fig. 1). About half of US families now experience a drop in real income over a two-year interval; moreover, the size of the median decline rose from around 25 percent of income in the early 1970s to around 40 percent by the late 1990s and early 2000s. The probability that an average working-age individual will experience at least a 50 percent drop in family income has also increased from 7 percent at the beginning of the 1970s to 17 percent in 2002 (Hacker 2006).

In Canada, the trend toward greater income volatility appears so far to be less pronounced than in the United States. One recent study finds no evidence of a widespread increase in earnings instability between 1980 and 2000, although the authors note that "year-to-year instability is consistently higher in the lowest third of earners, regardless of population group" and that it has grown substantially for lone parents (Morissette and Ostrovsky 2006, 15). Since 30 percent of low-paid workers and more than half of low-paid lone parents also live in low-income families (Chung 2004), this instability affects both their financial and economic security.

Sharpe and Osberg (2006) also report an increase in economic insecurity in Canada over the past two decades, despite the significant increase in consumption, income and wealth per capita since the middle of the 1990s. Economic insecurity is driven, in large part, by the increasing risk of financial loss and stress from illness — measured as the share of private personal disposable income going to health care — and by the increasing risk of financial loss from unemployment. Battle, Mendelson and Torjman (2006) report that, in recent years, one in eight Canadian workers was jobless at least once in the course of the year. When combined with the flatness of median wages, the increased duration of unemployment, the fall in the share of EI recipients among the unemployed and the greater uncertainty of pension benefits, this increased income volatility adds to the growing concerns about the effects of increased economic insecurity. This perspective is further reinforced by the effects of other important social and economic trends of the past few decades — deregulation, economic restructuring, globalization and family transformation — that are still underway.

Demography

Demographic changes have also exacerbated the effects of socio-economic trends. Apart from their effects on Canada's labour market and on governments' fiscal circumstances, one of the most important outcomes of these demographic changes is the increase in the number of years Canadians are now expected to live in retirement. Life expectancies have steadily increased, as David Foot notes in his chapter in this volume, while the average retirement age declined from 65 in the mid-1970s to 61 by the mid-1990s — although it has held fairly steady since then.

The need to encourage workers to secure sufficient retirement savings during their working-age years has therefore become a central issue. The shift in pension risk in recent decades — away from employers providing defined benefit pensions toward employees setting up defined-contribution retirement plans in the form of personal retirement savings accounts, usually with the help of employers — has also compounded the need to address the issue of retirement savings and financial security. In the United States, defined-contribution retirement plans accounted for more than 80 percent of contributions to pensions in 1998, compared with just over one-third in 1975 (Gale and Orszag 2003; Gale, Gruber, and Orszag 2006). While this change has been much less pronounced in Canada, there has also been a trend toward increased reliance on defined-contribution retirement plans: in January 2000, such plans accounted for about 14 percent of all pension plans, up from about 10 percent in 1996. Moreover, the percentage of paid workers covered by a registered pension plan has also trended downward, from 45 percent in 1991 to 41 percent in 1999 (Statistics Canada 2000).

Other socio-demographic changes such as increased family dissolution and single parenthood, which are important determinants of poverty and insecurity (see, for instance, National Council on Welfare 2006a), have also come into play. Finally, because of its low birth rate and aging population, Canada must increasingly rely on immigration for its labour supply. Although recent immigrants are generally as well educated as average Canadians, they have not been doing as well in the workforce in recent years and run a significantly higher risk of poverty and underemployment (Reitz 2005; Reitz and Banerjee 2007).

Policy challenges

This picture of increased income insecurity in Canada must be seen in the context of Canada's changing economic environment, which demands greater labour market flexibility and greater productive efficiency. The policy challenge that is central in assessing the pillars of Canada's current income security system is, therefore, the need to address both growth and security concerns.

Employment insurance

It has long been argued that Canada's employment insurance system has grown into a multipurpose, burdensome social program that is probably doing more harm than good, considering the disincentives it creates and their long-term effects on labour market behaviour (see, for instance, Lemieux and Macleod 2000; Gray 2006). EI distorts the labour force's incentives to adjust to economic and social changes by hampering individual and community initiative. EI also functions badly as an income support program in that it redistributes income poorly from the less to the more needy and fails to treat equals equally (see Battle, Mendelson, and Torjman 2006).

In a series of changes in the 1990s, leading to the newly named "employment insurance" program, the federal government attempted to tackle some of these difficulties by tightening access to the program and reducing benefits. Specific changes included disentitling workers who quit their jobs voluntarily, cutting the earnings replacement rate, increasing the minimum number of weeks required to qualify for benefits, raising work requirements for new workforce entrants and re-entrants as well as for repeat claimants and reducing the maximum duration of benefits. These changes were meant to encourage workers to attach themselves to the labour force before claiming EI benefits and to discourage repeat use (Gray 2004). The program changes, however, affected nonstandard workers disproportionately.

More recent changes to the EI system have somewhat undermined this earlier reform. Gray (2006, 8) notes, "The central thrust of all of these [recent] legislated and regulatory changes applied to the EI regime has been to accommodate sporadic, fragmented, interrupted, seasonal work patterns." Poschmann and Robson (2006, 2) also state that "recent new payments to workers who routinely work less than a full year are undermining a decade-old effort to remake EI as an insurance backstop against unexpected and temporary unemployment."

EI thus remains poorly designed to address the income insecurity and work support needs of many nonstandard and low-paid workers. As a result of changes in 1997, for instance, individuals who work fewer than 15 hours per week can apply for EI benefits, but there has also been a significant increase in the number of cumulative hours of work that are required to qualify for those benefits (see Fudge, Tucker, and Vosko 2002; Townson 2003; Task Force on Modernizing Income Security for Working-Age Adults 2006). Indeed, those who qualified for regular EI benefits fell from 74 percent of Canada's unemployed in 1990 to 39 percent in 2001 (Saunders 2005b). Part of this drop can be traced to the increase in nonstandard employment over that period, but much of it is due to design changes in the EI program, which effectively excludes the long-term unemployed, the underemployed, part-time workers, precarious workers, new workers and of course the self-employed.

Substantial differences in coverage also exist across provinces (see figure 2). In 2004, more than half the unemployed in Quebec and Atlantic Canada received regular EI benefits, with the proportion reaching 93.3 percent in Newfoundland and Labrador. In the rest of the country, the picture is quite different — in Ontario, for example, only 29.7 percent of the unemployed received benefits.[1]

Both work requirements and maximum duration of benefits also vary significantly by region. For instance, since the minimum hours of work required for EI eligibility varies between 420 and 700 hours depending on the local unemployment rate, the EI regime can treat two otherwise identical unemployed Canadians living in different regions very differently. Further inequity arises from the way in which the EI regime is financed: almost all employed workers pay EI premiums, but only a minority of premium-paying workers who lose their jobs actually receive any benefits. Non-eligibility is particularly a problem for low-wage and nonstandard workers.

Employment insurance — the first pillar of Canada's income security system — is thus filled with holes. Nationally, it covers little more than 40 percent of all the unemployed (and coverage rates are even lower in many provinces and regions), it is

FIGURE 2.   PERCENTAGE OF UNEMPLOYED RECEIVING REGULAR EI BENEFITS, BY PROVINCE, 2004

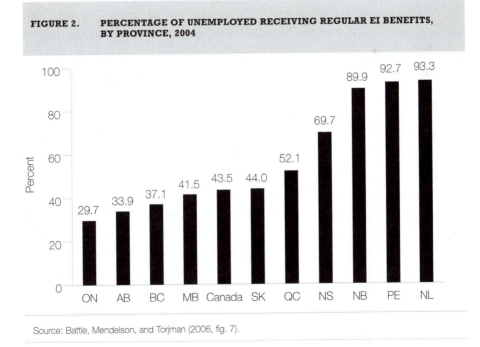

Source: Battle, Mendelson, and Torjman (2006, fig. 7).

horizontally and vertically inequitable, and it creates perverse incentives that distort labour markets in both the short term and, especially, the long term. EI is also complex and costly to manage. Few Canadians understand its rule-bound structure — well exemplified by the labyrinth of work requirements and benefit conditions that are differentiated according to individual and local characteristics. This lack of transparency has also undermined democracy, "providing 'regional' benefits that [have] little or nothing to do with the actual experiences of unemployed Canadians, and everything to do with regional politics" (Battle, Mendelson, and Torjman 2006, 23).

Social assistance

The original expectation for social assistance was that a recipient who managed to find work would simply forgo assistance altogether. Social assistance pays low benefits: their value has declined in real terms over time and is now at its lowest level since the mid-1980s and well below any reasonable poverty line. Yet it can still provide a better living standard than low-paid work, especially for families with children. Indeed, those who leave social assistance can incur a substantial financial penalty in the loss of cash (through child, spousal and single-parent benefits) and in-kind benefits (for instance, supplementary health and dental care) — a phenomenon the Caledon Institute has dubbed "the welfare wall" (Battle, Mendelson, and Torjman 2006).

In practice, the welfare wall is composed of several layers. One is the high clawback rate of social assistance benefits when recipients have income from employment. The taxback on employment earnings is usually as high as, and sometimes higher than, 100 percent above a small earnings exemption. In figure 3, which shows the marginal effective tax rates faced by a typical single parent in Quebec in 2002, the peaks and valleys are explained by the dismaying array and interaction of different elements of the tax and transfer system. The loss of in-kind benefits, such as supplementary health, dental and drug benefits, by recipients who move off social assistance produces another important layer. The removal of other forms of support — for example, child care subsidies, educational and training and retraining opportunities, support for persons with disabilities — adds a further layer to the welfare wall. A last important layer, and another perverse consequence of Canada's social assistance programs, is the typically prohibitive limit on recipients' liquid and fixed assets in order to qualify. Once they become recipients of social assistance, individuals are not permitted to accumulate assets, trapping many of them and their families in a system that not only provides them insufficient income to live on, but also impedes stable employment, social participation and asset protection and investment (see National Council on Welfare 2006b).

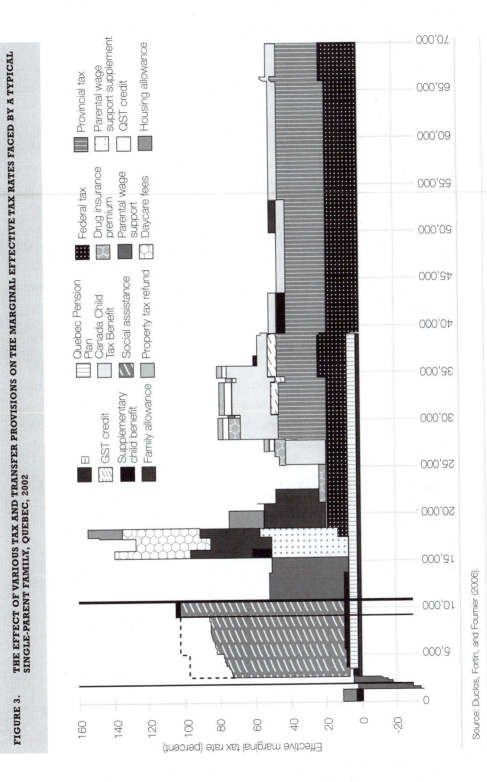

FIGURE 3. THE EFFECT OF VARIOUS TAX AND TRANSFER PROVISIONS ON THE MARGINAL EFFECTIVE TAX RATES FACED BY A TYPICAL SINGLE-PARENT FAMILY, QUEBEC, 2002

Source: Duclos, Fortin, and Fournier (2006).

The welfare wall also has dynamic and intergenerational trapping effects. Long-term and repeat use of social assistance can reinforce poverty and further risk eroding recipients' employment skills, lowering their aspirations and morale. This is also true in an intergenerational sense: parental use of social assistance can increase the probability that their children will also be recipients (see Beaulieu et al. 2005 for evidence in Quebec).

Social assistance thus builds on a model that entangles recipients in a web of liberty-restricting rules and restrictions, thereby limiting their ability to become independent of the system and improve their well-being. Social assistance is also full of holes. Many of the unemployed who do not qualify for EI are also ineligible for social assistance, or do not apply for it, because of stringent eligibility rules and demeaning conditions for the receipt of assistance. Only around 5 percent of those who exhaust their EI benefits receive social assistance benefits (Battle, Mendelson, and Torjman 2006). This leaves many low-income workers with no income security, an issue that has become more critical since access to social assistance was made more difficult in the 1990s — it would be even more problematic in a future economic downturn.

Recipients of social assistance are also victims of stigma and social exclusion. As Battle, Mendelson and Torjman put it, welfare is a "complicated, rule-burdened system that is secretive (very little information is made available to clients, researchers or the public), virtually impossible to understand, and often punitive and inconsistent in its treatment of recipients" (2006, 13), leading to inequitable administrative errors. The rules governing eligibility, benefit setting, monitoring and reporting are obtuse, even to the well-informed. Significant resources are also wasted on managing excessive complexity, rather than providing useful services to the population. The whole structure of social assistance is detrimental to the democratic, social and economic rights of Canadians, to the least privileged in our society in particular. The main reason social assistance benefits have not kept pace with Canadians' overall economic well-being may be explained as follows:

> In 1975 in Ontario, social assistance for a single person stood at 70 percent of the amount received by a single senior citizen without any other income. This same social assistance recipient now receives less than 45 percent of what the senior receives and the percentage is trending down...These ratios will continue to erode into the foreseeable future, as indexation remains the federal rule and the provincial exception. This is happening without public debate and without reference to the governance structures in Canada that gave rise to the programs in the first place. (Task Force on Modernizing Income Security for Working-Age Adults 2006, 26)

As Battle, Mendelson and Torjman put it, "The politics of welfare are simple: Governments typically win votes by cutting benefits, and lose votes by raising benefits" (2006, 12).

Training and education

Despite the need for skills development and employment services spurred by economic restructuring and the rise in structural unemployment, serious training and employment support is typically not offered to non-recipients of EI. Help is thus effectively denied to the many unemployed Canadians who do not meet EI's eligibility rules: basically all those in nonstandard employment and many of the working poor. Without access to formal on-the-job training, such workers can be stuck in low-paid jobs. Most nonstandard workers are left to fend for themselves to upgrade their skills: only 20 percent of those who were paid less than $10 an hour received employer-provided classroom training in 2001, compared with 45 percent of those earning more than $20 an hour (see Battle, Mendelson, and Torjman 2006). Because of the premium that technological change has placed on skilled work, many Canadians are getting left behind. In Ontario, for instance, almost three-quarters of young social assistance recipients have less than high school education versus one-third for all workers (Task Force on Modernizing Income Security for Working-Age Adults 2006).

BASIC PRINCIPLES FOR A BETTER INCOME SECURITY SYSTEM

Tying growth and security

An improved income security system would mean greater prosperity and better security for Canadians for several reasons. A better system could boost economic performance by encouraging Canadians to make investments — in entrepreneurship and physical and human capital, for instance — that foster growth. Without adequate protection, investors tend to be overly cautious from society's perspective, especially since the gains to risky investment can involve positive externalities — namely, they can benefit others. Better labour market and investment incentives could also help address the significant socio-demographic and economic challenges that Canada is facing and whose importance is almost certain to continue increasing in the foreseeable future. Addressing these challenges is, in fact, necessary if Canadians' living standards are to be maintained over time.

When hardship occurs — an inevitability in the context of a dynamic economy — a sound income security system can help individuals get back on their feet. Better financial assistance, training and education can then help protect and enhance the human and physical capital needed for individuals to thrive again. As Bordoff, Deich and Orszag put it, "Families with access to some form of financial assistance, educational and training opportunities, and basic health care are less likely to be permanently harmed by the temporary setbacks that are an inevitable part of a dynamic economy. For families experiencing short-term difficulties, a safety net can be a springboard to a better future and higher productivity" (2006, 7).

A sound income security system can also attenuate the usual demands for growth-impairing policies, such as protectionism and heavy-handed regulation of the economy. These demands are almost always formulated in response to fears that the benefits of technological change and competition may in fact harm particular industries or workers, which almost always leads to growth-reducing policies. A good income security system could help mitigate such harmful policy responses.

It should be clear, however, that the determinant of whether Canada's income security system will spur or hamper economic growth is not so much the extent of the economic security that is provided, but rather how it is provided. Careful attention thus needs to be paid to incentives and their effects on behaviour, in both the short and the long term. Only then can an efficient income security system be designed that will support economic growth, security and well-being. Indeed, in my view, it is this search for efficiency that should form the first principle to guide the design of a new system.

Enhancing capability and responsibility

The reform of Canada's income security system should also be inspired by a more modern view of individual well-being than that implicit in a "system that assumes anyone needing assistance is also in need of having their life supervised by government...[and that is] draining recipients of their confidence" (Battle, Mendelson, and Torjman 2006, 24).

One modern view is provided by focusing on the real freedoms or capabilities that individuals enjoy, not solely on the physical or financial resources they hold. To see this, it is important to distinguish between *formal freedom*, which consists of the formal or legal right to be or to do a particular thing, and *real freedom*, which is the actual capacity to be or to do something. Broadly speaking, the real freedoms one enjoys are a function both of formal freedoms and of the resources one controls. It is the set of real freedoms to which one has access that determines the extent of one's capability to be and to do as one wishes.

This conception of well-being also emphasizes the importance of individual freedom of choice as a determinant of well-being. In the words of two influential philosophers, "The 'good life' is partly a life of genuine choice, and not one in which the person is forced into a particular life — however rich it might be in other respects" (Sen 1985, 69-70); and "The minimal state...by respecting our rights... allows us, individually or with whom we choose, to choose our life and to realize our ends and our conception of ourselves" (Nozick 1974, 333-4). To be treated "with respect" and to lead a "good life" thus requires that we not be forced into lifestyle choices that are against our "conceptions of ourselves." The more important and broader freedoms appear to be as follows: to escape material destitution, to participate in social and public life, to enjoy self-esteem and to choose one's lifestyle.

A second objective of a sound income security system, then, is to maximize the extent of these freedoms and capabilities, especially for those who are initially more deprived of them. For policy design, this is an important change in outlook — instead of punishing low-income people for trying to improve their situation, a modern system should support their capacities and aspirations. In practice, such an approach would imply a number of reforms:

/ Make sufficient income support available so that all have the freedom to escape from material poverty, especially those who cannot reasonably be expected to be self-sufficient in terms of income generation.

/ Make work pay, by enhancing the freedom of all to become at least partly self-sufficient in terms of income generation; for example, the system should make it financially attractive to work and to move from social assistance to paid employment.

/ Provide opportunities for social participation, especially for those who cannot work.

/ Create opportunities — for example, through skills training and employment services, supplementary health and dental care and disability support — to enhance the security and well-being of those who are deprived of them. In particular, workers must be able to retrain and upgrade their skills if they are not to be left behind.

/ Eliminate the prohibitive penalties on private savings and human capital formation.

Associated with this vision of freedom and well-being is the important issue of personal responsibility. As the Task Force on Modernizing Income Security for Working-Age Adults states, "A modern income security system would expect and encourage individuals to assume personal responsibility for taking advantage of opportunities for engagement in the workforce or in community life" (2006, 16).

Promoting inclusion and equity

A sound income security system should include all Canadians, regardless of their attachment to the labour market. In the words of Vallée (2005, iii), "Providing access for all members of a given national community to a broad range of rights (retirement, illness, disability, drug insurance, occupational training, parental benefits) regardless of their participation in the labour market seem[s] particularly suited to the multitude of factors contributing to the vulnerability of these workers." Conversely, considering work as a basis for social rights seems increasingly inappropriate in the context of changing and more flexible labour markets. Similarly, with more diverse and more volatile social and family environments, individual rights, not family rights, should increasingly be the basis of social policy. In particular, an individual's income security entitlement should not be based on the characteristics and work status of another family member. Again quoting Vallée (2005, 4-5), "Societal changes argue in favour of changing this social protection model, which is based on the concept of the male breadwinner, through the individualization of rights, defined as the elimination of derived rights and the generalization of personal rights."

A more inclusive income security system would also lead to greater vertical and horizontal equity in its effects. Vertical and horizontal equity are the two traditional redistributive principles that serve to assess the effect of government policy. Vertical equity assesses the relative effects of policies across individuals with differing levels of income. Horizontal equity, in contrast, appraises the relative effects across individuals who are equal in all "ethically relevant respects" — in essence, those who have equal needs (see Duclos 2006 for a discussion).

Vertical equity usually requires that government policy disproportionately benefit the more deprived. In practice, this also implies that the greatest possible set of real freedoms be granted to those who have the least of them initially. Horizontal equity demands that the state treat individuals with equal real freedoms and/or well-being equally. Justice, indeed, would seem to require governments to avoid all forms of arbitrary discrimination — say, by gender, race, language, area of residence, religion and ethnicity — in their treatment of citizens. As we will see later, this third principle, inclusion and equity, has some important implications for the design of a new income security system for Canada.

SPECIFIC POLICY PROPOSALS

To improve Canada's income security system according to the basic principles of tying growth and security, enhancing capability and responsibility and promoting inclusion and equity, I propose a strategy based on three major components:

/ putting in place a system of basic income that would be available to all working-age adults;

/ establishing EI more firmly on social insurance principles; and

/ promoting investment in human and physical assets.

These components are strongly interlocked, so that, although it would be possible to implement them separately, they would be much more effective as a package.

A universal basic income

The first element of the strategy involves creating a basic income (BI) transfer, for which eligibility would be universal but whose net value would decline with rising levels of income, as does the Canada Child Tax Benefit. BI would cover all working-age Canadians, not only those currently entitled to EI or social assistance benefits. Depending on its precise form, BI would also substitute for several other benefits, such as social assistance, disability, parental and sickness benefits. BI would be available for an unlimited time and would be noncontributory — that is, it would be funded out of general revenues — unlike the current EI program, which taxes only certain sources of earned income and is subject to a ceiling. BI would be federally financed and administered through the personal income tax system.

To be fully effective, and in order to break through all the layers of the welfare wall, an effective new approach to income security would also require that in-kind supports such as supplementary health, dental care and prescription drugs — currently targeted to social assistance recipients — also be available to the working poor.

Such a strategy would produce a simpler and more integrated system than the current set of intricate and provincially differentiated social assistance programs. It would also be a more complete substitute for the current system than often-proposed alternatives. One such proposal is to add income supplements to current social assistance programs. Often referred to as "in-work benefits," such income supplements have become a major policy tool in a number of countries, including the United States (where it is known as the Earned Income Tax Credit), the United Kingdom (the Working Tax Credit) and France (Prime pour l'emploi). However, as add-ons to existing systems based on traditional social assistance, such income supplements can make them even more complex.

Consider, for example, the proposal of the Task Force on Modernizing Income Security for Working-Age Adults (2006) — which Saunders (2005b) also advocates — to provide a combination of a basic refundable tax credit and a working income benefit to all low-income working-age adults. This combination would offer a maximum benefit of around $4,000 per year, which would begin to be clawed back at an income of around $5,000 per year and would be reduced to zero when income reaches $21,000 per year. And the benefit would not be available to those without earnings.

Figures 4a to 4d provide a simple illustration of the effect of adding in-work benefits to a typical social assistance system and how that differs from BI under a flat tax regime. All four figures show after-tax and after-benefit income (disposable income) as a function of pre-tax and pre-benefit income (market income). In figure 4a, a typical social assistance program provides a basic benefit level, denoted by A, that is clawed back at a rate

FIGURE 4.   THE EFFECT ON DISPOSABLE INCOME OF VARIOUS TYPES OF SOCIAL PROGRAMS

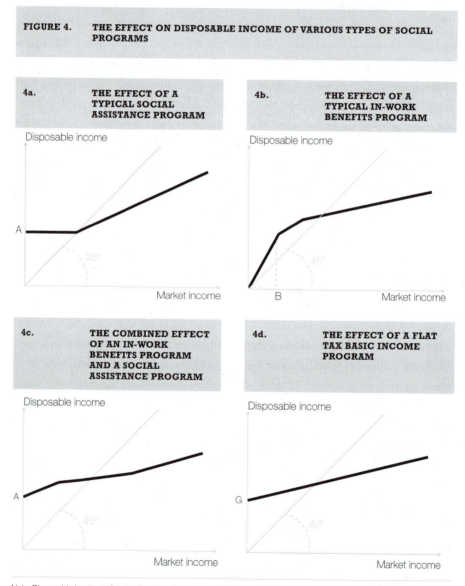

4a.   THE EFFECT OF A TYPICAL SOCIAL ASSISTANCE PROGRAM

4b.   THE EFFECT OF A TYPICAL IN-WORK BENEFITS PROGRAM

4c.   THE COMBINED EFFECT OF AN IN-WORK BENEFITS PROGRAM AND A SOCIAL ASSISTANCE PROGRAM

4d.   THE EFFECT OF A FLAT TAX BASIC INCOME PROGRAM

Note: Disposable income refers to after-tax, after-benefits income. Market income refers to pre-tax, pre-benefit income.

of approximately 100 percent until it is completely recuperated and disposable income equals market income. In figure 4b, in-work benefits are provided progressively to those receiving social assistance; once market income attains a level given by B, the benefits are clawed back until they are completely recuperated and disposable income equals market income. Figure 4c shows the combined effect of social assistance and in-work benefits, which introduces multiple kinks and marginal tax rates in the effective taxation of market income as it increases. As figure 4d shows, the effect of a flat tax BI is to remove the kinks and variability in effective tax rates; the impact is felt at all levels of market income.

Compared with other alternatives, therefore, BI has the advantage of greater simplicity. As was the case with the National Child Benefit, it would reduce overlap and duplication of government programs. And much like the temporary income support program that Battle, Mendelson and Torjman propose, BI would also be as "non-intrusive as possible and would have a simple, flat-rate benefit structure, income-tested through a straightforward income test" (2006, 26); as such, it would be very different from social assistance or EI. Perhaps more important, eligibility for BI would be universal and receipt would not depend on an individual's labour market status or type of income received, a feature that is not shared by in-work benefits schemes.

Araar, Duclos and Blais (2005) simulate the redistributive effect of alternative forms of BI in three different scenarios in the context of Quebec. All three scenarios are "budget neutral" (relative to the 1999 tax and transfer system, referred to as the base case scenario A) in the sense that they show the tax and expenditure changes for the combined provincial and federal budgets that would be required to implement each BI scenario without affecting the existing budget balance. Table 2 shows the income tax parameters for the three scenarios and the level of basic income provided.

/ Scenario B resembles the proposal of the Task Force on Modernizing Income Security for Working-Age Adults (2006) mentioned above. Marginal rates of personal income taxation do not change, but the BI transfers are nontaxable. The BI is financed by eliminating most refundable and nonrefundable tax credits — including those related to basic needs, age and family dependants — and by abolishing certain transfer programs, such as family allowances, old age security and the Guaranteed Income Supplement. Social assistance and EI are left unchanged under this scenario.

/ Scenario C replicates scenario B but introduces a more generous BI system, which is financed by changing the structure of marginal rates of personal income taxation and putting in place a flat tax rate of 53 percent on all income except the BI, which is nontaxable. Again, social assistance and EI are left unchanged.

TABLE 2. **BASIC INCOME TRANSFERS AND INCOME TAX RATES UNDER THREE SCENARIOS (COMPARED WITH QUEBEC'S TAX AND TRANSFER SYSTEM IN 1999)**

| Income bracket ($) | Marginal tax rate of personal income tax (%) | | | |
	Base case A	Scenario B[1]	Scenario C[1]	Scenario D[1]
0–15,000	37	37	53	60
15,000–25,000	37	37	53	60
25,000–29,590	40	40	53	60
29,590–50,000	49	49	53	60
50,000–59,180	52	52	53	60
59,180 and over	55	55	53	60

Family type	Level of nontaxable basic income transfer ($)			
Single parent	n/a[2]	3,640	6,300	9,100
Adult other than a single parent	n/a[2]	2,600	4,500	6,500
Child	n/a[2]	1,873	3,712	2,730
Senior citizen 65 +	n/a[2]	9,000	9,000	12,000

Source: Araar, Duclos, and Blais (2005, table 3).
[1] Under scenarios B and C, most tax credits and transfer allowances are replaced by a BI transfer; under scenario D, EI and social assistance benefits are also abolished. See text for more details.
[2] The base case is Quebec's tax and transfer system in 1999. For purposes of comparison, social assistance transfers in Quebec that year were around $6,223 for a nondisabled, single adult, $8,951 for a disabled adult, $12,957 for a one-child, single-parent family and $16,020 for a family of two adults and two children.

/ Scenario D corresponds to what can be referred to as a full BI — namely, one that pays as much as Quebec's current social assistance program for those with no market income. Scenario D replicates scenario C but, in addition, it eliminates Quebec's social assistance program as well as federal EI (both benefits and contributions) in order to substantially increase BI transfer levels. The personal income tax rate required under this scenario is a flat rate of 60 percent on all income, even for those in the lowest bracket. BI remains nontaxable.

Note that, under these three scenarios, other transfers, such as disability and parental leave benefits, are unaffected. They could, however, be part of a more comprehensive BI package. In scenarios B, C and D, therefore, disability and parental leave benefits would be added to the BI transfers.

As might be expected, the overall redistributive effect of the different scenarios varies significantly by family type and income level (see table 3). The most affected are single-parent families, whose average disposable income, relative to the base case A, falls by 7.2 percent in scenario B, but increases by 3.3 percent and 12.5 percent in scenarios C and D, respectively. Single adults lose, while couples with children gain on average in all three scenarios. The income of couples without children undergoes little change on average. Scenario B increases financial poverty for single adults and single parents; scenario C reduces it only for couples with children and single parents, but this translates into a net gain over the entire population; and scenario D reduces poverty overall and for almost all socio-demographic groups except single adults. Relative to the level of inequality in disposable income generated by the base case, inequality in disposable income increases substantially under scenario B, decreases slightly under scenario C and decreases significantly in scenario D.

Scenarios C and D, therefore, probably would be more acceptable on equity grounds, as well as more realistic in terms of redistributive politics. Although the concept of "political feasibility" is somewhat fuzzy, it would seem easier to defend the implementation of significant changes to the tax and transfer system if these changes could be shown to decrease both poverty and inequality. A partial BI (scenario B) would still offer some advantages in terms of simplicity and work incentives, but it would also imply a significant increase in inequality and poverty, and likely would be politically acceptable only as a first step toward the progressive implementation of a fuller BI.

The high rates of marginal income taxation in scenarios C and D (53 percent and 60 percent, respectively) could have potentially large effects on labour supply and savings. As Araar, Duclos and Blais (2005) point out, however, the scenarios are calculated on the basis of the income distribution in Quebec in 1999. All things being equal, each 1 percent growth in per capita income from the base year also increases the personal income tax base by about 1 percent, which, in turn, would allow the flat tax rate to be reduced by 1 percent. Therefore, assuming no change in other per capita budget expenditures, one would need total growth of only 20 percent in per capita income — for instance, 2 percent per year between 1999 and 2009, the rate Quebec actually experienced between 2002 and 2007 — to bring a flat tax rate of 60 percent down to a more reasonable 50 percent by 2009.

A basic income system would have several advantages. One is that it would encourage social inclusion by reducing the appeal of the underground economy. Because marginal effective tax rates would be lowered for many at the bottom of the income distribution (by eliminating clawbacks on various benefits), managing

TABLE 3.   CHANGES IN ADULT-EQUIVALENT INCOME[1] UNDER SCENARIOS B, C AND D

Type of house-hold	Number of individuals	Number of families	Average income				Variation (%)		
			A	B	C	D	(A,B)	(A,C)	(A,D)
Single parent	405,057	160,685	13,460	12,559	13,920	15,390	-7.2	3.3	12.5
Two parents	3,020,547	763,436	17,635	18,349	19,329	18,319	3.9	8.8	3.7
Single	800,105	800,105	12,850	12,115	11,810	11,454	-6.1	-8.8	-12.2
Couple	1,841,502	772,496	21,737	21,669	21,364	21,243	-0.3	-1.8	-2.3
Senior 65 +	1,088,435	711,757	15,536	15,638	14,489	16,419	0.7	-7.2	5.4
All	7,155,646	3,208,479	17,600	17,767	17,969	17,849	0.9	2.1	1.4

Source: Araar, Duclos and Blais (2005, table 7)
[1] Adult-equivalent income is a way to adjust income to take into account the needs of the family as a whole and reflect the well-being of each of its members.

BI through the personal income tax system would remove some of the incentives to stay out of the system. Another advantage of a BI is that it would facilitate EI reform by decreasing the relative importance of EI as a form of implicit social assistance, as opposed to social insurance. Reformers often advocate that EI should be broadened to cover not only single-employer, temporarily laid-off, full-time workers but also those facing permanent job loss and nonstandard work. Yet, given the equity and efficiency difficulties of the current EI program, it does not seem appropriate to extend its scope even more. An effective BI system would be a better alternative — among other things, it would address the needs of low-paid workers more equitably and efficiently.

Putting a BI transfer in place would also help to do away with much of the current intricate and nontransparent system of tax credits, social assistance and EI provisions. As Battle, Mendelson, and Torjman note,

> The fact remains that welfare — with all its rules and regulations and limitations on assets — is simply a poor program. It is an inadequate safety net for those who cannot work or cannot find work. It is also an inappropriate program to supplement the wages of the working poor. Piecemeal add-ons have not worked, and cannot work. The core design of welfare is not amenable to fixing up. (2006, 14)

As a substitute for social assistance, a BI system would make it unnecessary to design such "piecemeal add-ons."

A national BI transfer program would also be more appropriate than the regional and demographic redistributive transfers that are implicit in the current EI program. BI transfers would be more tightly linked to individual circumstances, and would thus be more equitable, both vertically and horizontally. Unlike EI, BI would be funded from broad-based general revenue, rather than from employer and employee contributions, so that its funding would also be more vertically and horizontally equitable.

In practice, a BI could also be considered a form of negative income taxation. A key issue is the marginal tax rates (implicit and explicit) that should apply to different income tax brackets and, more particularly, whether these rates should increase or decrease with income. The scenarios in Araar, Duclos and Blais (2005) broadly favour a constant marginal tax rate and, therefore, a flat tax system. Apart from the obvious advantages of greater transparency and simplicity, a flat tax system also has the advantage of being neutral as to the choice of individual income or family income as the tax base (see Kesselman 2000). It is also neutral with respect to the choice of accounting periods, even in the presence of income variability. In other words, with a constant marginal tax rate, the same total tax (positive or negative) applies whether it is monthly or yearly income that is taxed and whether or not there is variability in the flow of individual and family income over time. A system with varying marginal tax rates penalizes those — mostly low-income earners — with greater instability of income and family composition (see Saunders 2005a).

Thus, although a BI system would not also require a flat tax, a flat tax would add further advantages to such a scheme. Note also that, contrary to general perceptions, a flat tax combined with BI-type universal transfers would not necessarily move Canada away from a progressive tax and transfer system based on the principle of ability to pay, as shown by scenarios C and D, where disposable income inequality decreases relative to the present system. When coupled with universal transfers, a personal income tax system based on a constant rate of marginal taxation could indeed lead to greater inequality reduction than one with varying marginal tax rates.

Note also that negative income taxation — a BI transfer system, in particular — can be more vertically and horizontally equitable than social assistance in terms of real freedoms. For example, figures 5 and 6 show that marginal effective tax rates would be equalized by shifting from the current tax and transfer system to a full BI scenario. The incentives and the freedom to earn and to save, therefore, would be more equally distributed than is now the case, both vertically and horizontally. A significant BI transfer would not only make it possible for all Canadians to escape from material destitution, it would also lead to greater

FIGURE 5.   DISTRIBUTION OF MARGINAL EFFECTIVE INCOME TAX RATES, QUEBEC, 1999

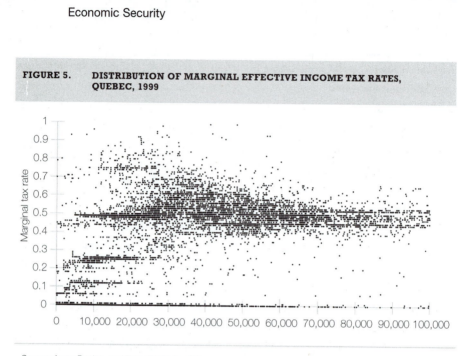

Source: Araar, Duclos, and Blais (2005, fig. 21).

FIGURE 6.   DISTRIBUTION OF MARGINAL EFFECTIVE TAX RATES UNDER A FULL BASIC INCOME (SCENARIO D), QUEBEC

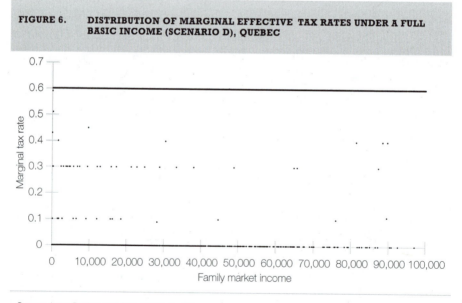

Source: Araar, Duclos, and Blais (2005, fig. 24).

self-esteem and a better distribution of the capacity to choose one's lifestyle, including the ability to make decisions concerning labour supply, savings, family composition and human capital investment, all of which can contribute to enhanced well-being and security. A BI system would facilitate individuals' participation in the economic and social spheres. A more transparent income security system would also further citizens' understanding of social policy and, presumably, strengthen democratic debate about its elements and objectives.

This is not to say that a BI would not create losers. Single adults, for instance, would lose on average under all three scenarios presented. In scenario D, the extent of redistribution from the richer to the poorer would amount to as much as 2 percent of per capita national income. In scenarios C and D, many in the middle class would face higher marginal tax rates. Moreover, implementing a universal and comprehensive BI (scenario D) would represent a gigantic fiscal venture. For instance, although the elimination of tax credits, social assistance and EI benefits and contributions would generate around $23 billion for Quebec alone (provincial and federal tax and transfer systems combined), that amount falls far short of the $35 billion it would cost to implement a full (nontaxable) BI system for the province (scenario D). A flat tax of the type shown in scenarios C and D, however, would have been enough to finance a comprehensive BI in Quebec in 1999. With continued economic growth, such an ambitious BI scenario would become increasingly feasible.

A better EI program

Implementing a universal basic income program would also facilitate, and provide a rationale for, the second element of the strategy: a fundamental reform of EI to have it conform more closely with social insurance principles.

The central principle to be applied in such a reform is that of experience rating, under which both contribution rates and benefit levels are continually adjusted to account for the risks that firms and workers transfer to the EI program. Firms that lay off fewer workers would face a lower EI contribution tax rate on their payroll; workers who make fewer and less frequent EI claims would receive greater EI benefits when they do claim them. This is analogous to how private insurance is provided, with the difference that EI would be administered publicly and uniformly across the country to maximize efficiency, ensure accessibility and facilitate the functioning of the labour market.

In practice, a better EI program would involve reinstating and reinforcing many of the provisions enacted in the *Employment Insurance Act* of 1996. Most changes to the EI regime since 2000, for instance, have involved increasing the generosity of EI benefits paid to seasonal workers, which has simply encouraged more seasonal employment. An overriding objective of reform, then, would be to facilitate the transition to full-year employment when possible and desirable, hence removing current built-in incentives for seasonal and temporary work (see, for example, Guillemette 2006; Organisation for Economic Co-operation and Development 2006; Orr 2006). For example, the intensity rule and other provisions intended to discourage repeat use of EI (see Gray 2004) would be reintroduced and reinforced, either by shortening bene-fit entitlement periods for repeat users or by increasing contribution rates as repeat layoffs are observed.

Because a reformed EI would operate on a strict insurance basis, it would finance itself over time as contributions equalize benefits. In this sense, it would con-trast markedly with the operation of EI in the 1990s, when changes to the program that increased eligibility requirements and reduced benefit payments led to record sur-pluses, which the federal government then used to fund other programs. Not only did this cause political difficulties, it also overtaxed labour income as a source of revenue for the federal government.

The immediate effect of such a reform, therefore, would be to reduce indi-viduals' incentive to resort to seasonal and unstable work and provide better labour market incentives overall, especially for younger workers and those with greater occu-pational and geographic mobility.

A second effect would be the removal from EI of the *ex ante* implicit redistribu-tive elements of the current program — stemming from, among other things, its built-in regional and industrial preferences and its failure to follow insurance rules. Such a reform would make EI less discriminatory and more equitable, both vertically and horizontally. The elimination of implicit subsidies probably explains the long-standing resistance to EI reform, since there has been no suitable alternative for regions and workers who use EI a great deal. However, it would be much better in terms of efficiency, equity and account-ability if subsidies were made more transparent by explicitly subsidizing employment cre-ation and regional development — rather than discouraging personal and community initiatives. Another effect of EI reform would be to significantly simplify the complex set of rules that currently govern the program (see Gray 2006).

Interestingly, a reformed EI could serve as a platform for improving its cov-erage and impact. With EI operating on a truer insurance basis, it would create fewer disincentives and moral hazard problems, and it would be fairer. It would then make sense to raise the earnings replacement ratio above the current level of 55 percent; decrease the eligibility requirements in low-unemployment regions, with a lower min-imum work requirement of, say, 360 hours everywhere; reduce the current extreme-ly high work requirement (910 hours) for new entrants; and improve access to other benefits and services that are currently accessible only to EI claimants — in particular, employment supports, training services and parental leave benefits. These extended benefits would be made possible by moving to experience rating.

Such enhancements to EI would have a particularly strong positive effect in Canada's cities, where there is a greater proportion of immigrants and a younger labour force that is not well served by the current structure of the program.

Promoting and protecting assets

Introducing a BI system and reforming EI would also help to implement other policy changes aimed at promoting and protecting assets. With a reformed income security system, Canadians would be more economically secure, more resilient to change and better able to improve their prospects for labour market participation and social inclusion provided they also have the capacity and freedom to build their human and financial capital in the form of skills development and savings.

Training and participation

Escaping from low pay and labour market insecurity depends, in the long run, on fostering productivity and human capital development in high-wage sectors of the economy. Given the dynamic nature of the economy, all Canadians, especially those with low incomes, need to be kept abreast of labour market changes, which would also help to sustain economic growth and social inclusion.

One way to achieve this goal would be to subsidize employment programs with clear labour market ties — in other words, programs that have been identified as most effective (see Task Force on Modernizing Income Security for Working-Age Adults 2006). In practice, of course, enhancing educational and training options should take many forms, depending on local and individual conditions. However they are designed, they should increase opportunities for occupational training in high schools, reduce high school dropout rates, support the development of literacy and essential skills, expand apprenticeships, provide recent immigrants with greater access to language training and help with the acquisition of Canadian credentials, and offer job protection for training and educational leaves.

Many such programs — those involving apprenticeships and on-the-job training, for example — are already oversubscribed, however, and others have been criticized for their lack of cost effectiveness. Thus, for efficiency and equity reasons, program designers need to address the supply, the demand and the quality of training and employment services.

Universal accessibility to training and employment services seems a promising avenue for resolving these issues, especially for workers who are difficult to employ or keep employed. A BI, acting as a form of guaranteed minimum income, and a reformed EI that reduced disincentives to work and training would help to reach that goal. Universal accessibility to training and employment services could take the form of partly subsidized and occupationally differentiated vouchers for services. Those who used their vouchers to obtain services would thus bear part of the cost; the federal government would cover the rest. Ottawa's share of the cost could vary according to the service provided and the nature and size of local labour market disequilibria. Their universality would mean that the use of vouchers would not compromise receipt of a BI or reformed EI benefits.

Because users would bear part of the cost, the demand for training and employment services would better reflect the true value workers place on such services. By setting the share of the cost that users bear, the federal government could also influence demand for these services to reflect local and national labour market conditions and priorities. To promote accountability and quality, the forces of choice and competition should be used to deliver the best results. That certainly could involve a mixture of public and private services. Designed in this way, training and employment services could advance efficiency and equity at the same time.

Note also that, with the elimination of social assistance and the proposed changes to EI, fewer public resources and less caseworkers' time would be spent on managing complex programs and more on assisting and advising workers who are difficult to employ or keep employed on how to build up their human capital and position themselves in the labour market.

Assets and savings

Another key part of the strategy is to enhance the financial assets of vulnerable Canadians, an important determinant of their overall well-being (see, for example, Maxwell 2002; Saunders 2005b). Feeling more secure encourages people to stay employed rather than resort to social assistance, and asset accumulation allows them to get more education rather than stay in a low-paying job. Better education lessens individuals' income instability. It also increases their ability to cope with economic shocks by shortening the time they can expect to be without work after displacement and by increasing the likelihood that they will find full-time, rather than part-time, employment. Asset accumulation also, of course, provides a financial cushion when shocks do hit.

Several ways exist to help enhance vulnerable Canadians' financial assets. One way would be to remove assets from the means tests imposed on social assistance recipients, as is implicit in the proposals for a BI and reformed EI presented earlier. Currently, asset tests often make it impossible for an individual with more than a few thousand dollars to receive social assistance. Without a significant easing of asset limits, recipients cannot accumulate savings that would help them when a financial setback occurs. Asset tests are effectively a tax on retirement savings, since accumulating such savings reduces social assistance benefits that otherwise would have been provided.

A second avenue is to provide low-income Canadians with the same incentives to build up and shelter assets from taxes that higher-income Canadians get from Registered Retirement Savings Plans (RRSPs). This policy — advocated by Gale, Gruber and Orszag (2006), among others — would replace current tax deductibility for contributions to tax-favoured retirement accounts with universal matching contributions by government on all registered deposits up to some maximum limit.

The structure of the current RRSP system is such that the incentive to save increases with the marginal personal income tax rates of individuals. The current tax system thus provides the smallest incentive to save to low- and middle-income individuals, as it is they who generally face the lowest marginal tax rate on their income. It is also they who most need to save to increase their economic security and meet basic retirement needs. In the words of Gale, Gruber and Orszag, "Current incentives for saving — which are overwhelmingly devoted to encouraging contributions to retirement accounts by high-income households, rather than contributions by households with low and middle incomes — are thus upside down" (2006, 23).

With this new policy, all individuals who make a contribution to a registered savings account would receive a related contribution from government. The current deduction for contributions to RRSPs would thus be replaced by a government contribution of approximately 30 percent of new savings. Gale, Gruber and Orszag (2006) estimate that, in the United States, the impact of such a scheme would be roughly revenue neutral for government. But it would significantly push up the share of tax subsidies accruing to the savings of middle- and low-income households: the authors estimate that 80 percent of US households would enjoy a stronger incentive to save under such a proposal. Once savings are eventually withdrawn from the registered accounts, the amount of the initial grant would be sent back to government and the interest accrued would be taxed as personal income. This would provide two types of saving incentives: first, the interest on the grant would accrue to savers; second, interest would be taxed only on the withdrawal of savings.

An alternative proposal, often suggested, is to increase the limit that individuals can contribute to their RRSPs. Such a change, however, would affect only those individuals who are constrained by the current limits and whose additional savings are thus stored in other, non-registered accounts. Indeed, raising the contribution limits would provide mostly windfall gains for such individuals, whose likely behavioural response would be to shift assets from nonregistered accounts to tax-favoured registered accounts — with little encouragement of new savings. Such a policy would improve neither economic security nor equity in the distribution of tax benefits.

A focus on children and the disabled

Two important groups of individuals to whom I have not given appropriate attention so far are children and the disabled. The same general principles of fostering growth, security, efficiency, capability, responsibility, inclusion and equity should also guide the design of Canada's income security programs for these two groups.

In a rapidly changing demographic and family environment, the costs of looking after the development of future citizens should be seen increasingly as a social responsibility. Not only would this lead to greater equality of opportunity for all children, but it would also provide greater vertical and horizontal equity and support to those Canadians who incur the burden of raising and supporting the development of the next generation.

Federal and provincial governments have tended to help families through a series of somewhat uncoordinated child benefits, entangled with social assistance and often excluding higher-income families. Horizontal and vertical equity, however, demand that support reflecting the responsibility of child rearing should be paid through a separate program on behalf of all children, whether their parents are on social assistance or not. To account for the costs of raising all children, a basic child benefit should be paid on behalf of all children, regardless of parental income. An example, which could certainly be made more generous and applicable to children of all ages, is the Universal Child Care Benefit of $100 per month for children under six years of age. The need to increase low parental income should and could be mostly addressed through the programs for working-age adults I discussed earlier. Thus, a BI transfer would provide universal benefits for the period during which parents wish to stay at home to look after young children. Parental benefits thus would no longer be handled as a separate entity — in contrast to the current structure of ill-targeted parental leave benefits that, except in Quebec, are linked to EI, even though child rearing has nothing to do with unemployment.

Fortunately, the basis for a universal child benefit already exists in the form of the National Child Benefit (NCB). Of little value to medium- and high-income families, the NCB should be expanded to better reflect the child-raising costs all Canadian families incur. The Caledon Institute for Social Policy estimates the annual cost of raising a child in Canada at around $5,000 and recommends raising the NCB to that level from a maximum of about $3,500 now, which should be possible, given the double objective of reducing child poverty and ensuring equity for those with child-rearing responsibilities (Mendelson 2005; see also Task Force on Modernizing Income Security for Working-Age Adults 2006; Canadian Policy Research Networks 2004; Saunders 2005b).

When it was introduced in 1998, an important objective of the NCB was to "make work pay" by providing government support to children whose parents have low-paid jobs or are moving from social assistance to employment. It would be much easier to achieve that objective by using a single federal-provincial platform to provide support to families with children, rather than embedding child benefits in social assistance or other adult transfers.

Many social assistance recipients face multiple barriers to finding and keeping a job, including mental health difficulties and barriers to skills development. Given these limitations, it would seem reasonable to have a separate national system of support for the disabled. A reasonable proposal is that of the Task Force on Modernizing Income Security for Working-Age Adults, which suggests that such a system "reinstate earlier provincial policies to set disability benefits at the same levels received by senior citizens who have no other source of income" (2006, 15). The national program of support for the disabled thus would work as a supplement to a BI transfer. The federal government would be responsible for funding and delivering the cash transfers component of the program, but the provinces and territories would manage the delivery of in-kind, long-term support services to help the disabled participate in the social and economic life of their community.

Implementation issues

The components and responsibilities of a new income security system could be divided between the federal and provincial governments in a number of ways. For reasons of efficiency, administration and equity, the federal government should take the main responsibility for the BI system and reformed EI. Constitutionally, nothing prohibits the federal government from making income transfers to Canadians — it already provides benefits to seniors and children. With a BI administered by Ottawa in the form of a refundable tax credit for all Canadians, the provinces would then be able to provide income supplements and supplementary social assistance as they wished.

The federal government should also take the lead in replacing tax deductions on RRSPs with matching contributions on registered deposits. For efficiency and accountability reasons, however, provincial and local governments should be responsible for providing educational and training vouchers and employment services.

If Ottawa were to take primary responsibility for what is now social assistance, provincial and local governments would save substantial costs. This could be viewed as a way to address the perceived fiscal imbalance between provinces and the federal government by shifting some of the provinces' financial burden to the more appropriate federal level. From an economic perspective, it is also more appropriate that the federal government bear more of the highly variable costs of income security, which are brought about by the inevitability of business cycles. Provinces could then use the savings to finance much-needed training and employment support.

The federal government should also provide financial support for Canadians with disabilities, as it does for senior citizens through old age security and the Guaranteed Income Supplement. Again, provincial governments would see considerable savings, since a substantial number of current social assistance recipients would be eligible for the new federal program. As Battle, Mendelson and Torjman argue, "The provinces and territories could use their savings to introduce a separate disability support program — which has been identified as a key priority by disability organizations in Canada — to provide a full range of employment and living supports to Canadians with disabilities" (2006, 29). As the authors also suggest, testing for disability could be done using the same administrative structure currently in place for the public pension plans.

CONCLUSION

I have outlined three proposals for a reform of Canada's income security system for all working-age adults. They are intended to alleviate some of the flaws of two pillars of Canada's current income security system, employment insurance and social assistance. The first proposal is to implement a universal basic income for all Canadians. The second is to revamp the employment insurance program to make it both more efficient and more equitable. The third is to put into place policies that will better promote and protect assets — in particular, human capital and savings. As a package, these reforms should make Canada's income security system more growth enhancing, more supportive of individual freedoms and capabilities, and more inclusive of those in need of economic security and support.

NOTES

1   Low and decreasing coverage is also the rule in the United States, where about 37 percent of unemployed workers receive unemployment insurance benefits; see Kletzer and Rosen (2006). Approximately one-third of US recipients exhaust their benefits before finding a new job.

REFERENCES

Araar, A., J.-Y. Duclos, and F. Blais. 2005. "Effets redistributifs d'un régime d'allocation universelle: une simulation pour le Québec." *L'Actualité économique* 81 (3): 421-84.

Battle, K., M. Mendelson, and S. Torjman. 2006. *Towards a New Architecture for Canada's Adult Benefits*. Ottawa: Caledon Institute of Social Policy.

Beaulieu, N., J.-Y. Duclos, B. Fortin, and M. Rouleau. 2005. "Intergenerational Reliance on Social Assistance: Evidence from Canada." *Journal of Population Economics* 18 (3): 539-62.

Bordoff, J.E., M. Deich, and P. R. Orszag. 2006. "A Growth-Enhancing Approach to Economic Security." The Hamilton Project Strategy Paper. Washington, DC: Brookings Institution.

Canadian Policy Research Networks (CPRN). 2004. *Kids Canada Policy Digest Annual: 2004*. Ottawa: CPRN.

Chung, L. 2004. "Low-Paid Workers: How Many Live in Low-Income Families?" *Perspectives on Labour and Income* 16 (4): 23-32.

Duclos, J.-Y. 2006. "Innis Lecture: Equity and Equality." *Canadian Journal of Economics* 39 (4): 1073-1104.

Duclos, J.Y., B. Fortin, and A.-A. Fournier. 2006. "Une analyse des taux marginaux effectifs d'imposition au Québec." Cahiers de recherche CIRPÉE 06-27. Montreal: Centre interuniversitaire sur le risque, les politiques économiques et l'emploi.

Fudge, J., E. Tucker, and L. Vosko. 2002. "The Legal Concept of Employment:

Marginalizing Workers." Report for the Law Commission of Canada. Ottawa: Law Commission of Canada.

Gale, W.G., J. Gruber, and P.R. Orszag. 2006. "Improving Opportunities and Incentives for Saving by Middle- and Low-Income Households." The Hamilton Project Discussion Paper 2006-02. Washington, DC: Brookings Institution.

Gale, W.G., and P.R. Orszag. 2003. "Private Pensions: Issues and Options." In *Agenda for the Nation*, edited by H.J. Aaron, J.M. Lindsay, and P.S. Nivola. Washington, DC: Brookings Institution.

Gray, D.M. 2004. "Employment Insurance: What Reform Delivered." *C.D. Howe Institute Backgrounder* 82.

———. 2006. "Has EI Reform Unraveled? Canada's EI Regime in the 2000s." *C.D. Howe Institute Backgrounder* 98.

Guillemette, Y. 2006. "Misplaced Talent: The Rising Dispersion of Unemployment Rates in Canada." *C.D. Howe Institute e-brief*. July 19.Toronto: C.D. Howe Institute.

Hacker, J.S. 2006. "Universal Insurance: Enhancing Economic Security to Promote Opportunity." The Hamilton Project Discussion Paper 2006-07. Washington, DC: Brookings Institution.

Janz, T. 2004. "Low-Paid Employment and Moving Up: A Closer Look at Full-time, Full-Year Workers 1996-2001." Income Research Paper Series. Cat. 75F0002MIE-No. 009. Ottawa: Statistics Canada.

Kesselman, J. 2000. "Flat Taxes, Dual Taxes, Smart Taxes: Making the Best Choices." IRPP *Policy Matters* 1 (7).

Kletzer, L.G., and H. Rosen. 2006. "Reforming Unemployment Insurance for the Twenty-First Century Workforce." The Hamilton Project Discussion Paper 2006-06. Washington, DC: Brookings Institution.

Lemieux, T., and W.B. Macleod. 2000. "Supply Side Hysteresis: The Case of the Canadian

Unemployment Insurance System." *Journal of Public Economics* 78 (1-2): 139-70.

Maxwell, J. 2002. *Smart Social Policy — "Making Work Pay."* Ottawa: Canadian Policy Research Networks.

Mendelson, M. 2005. "Measuring Child Benefits: Measuring Child Poverty." Ottawa: Caledon Institute of Social Policy.

Morissette, R., and Y. Ostrovsky. 2006. "Earnings Instability." *Perspectives on Labour and Income* 7 (10): 5-16.

National Child Benefit. n.d. Accessed September 7, 2007. www.nationalchildbenefit.ca/ncb/thenational1.shtml

National Council on Welfare (NCW). 2006a. *Poverty Profile, 2002 and 2003.* Ottawa: NCW.

———. 2006b. *Welfare Incomes 2005.* Ottawa: NCW.

Nozick, R. 1974. *Anarchy, State, and Utopia.* Oxford: Basil Blackwell.

Organisation for Economic Co-operation and Development (OECD). 2006. *Economic Survey of Canada 2006.* Paris: OECD.

Orr, D. 2006. "Moving to Where the Jobs Are: There Has Never Been a Time Like the Present." Commentary. Boston: Global Insight.

Poschmann, F., and W.B.P. Robson. 2006. "Lower Taxes, Focused Spending, Stronger Federation: A Shadow Federal Budget for 2006." *C.D. Howe Institute Backgrounder* 93. Toronto: C.D. Howe Institute.

Public Service Commission. 1999. "The Future of Work: Non-Standard Employment in the Public Service of Canada." Ottawa: Public Service Commission, Policy, Research and Communications Branch, Research Directorate.

Reitz, J.G. 2005. "Tapping Immigrants' Skills: New Directions for Canadian Immigration Policy in the Knowledge Economy." *IRPP Choices* 11 (1).

Reitz, J.G., and R. Banerjee. 2007. "Racial Inequality, Social Cohesion and Policy Issues in Canada." In *Belonging? Diversity,*

Recognition and Shared Citizenship in Canada, edited by Keith Banting, T.J. Courchene, and F.L. Seidle. Montreal: IRPP.

Saunders, R. 2003. "Defining Vulnerability in the Labour Market." Vulnerable Workers Series 1. Ottawa: Canadian Policy Research Networks.

———. 2005a. "Does a Rising Tide Lift All Boats? Low-Paid Workers in Canada." Vulnerable Workers Series 4. Ottawa: Canadian Policy Research Networks.

———. 2005b. "Lifting the Boats: Policies to Make Work Pay." Vulnerable Workers Series 5. Ottawa: Canadian Policy Research Networks.

Sen, A. 1985. *Commodities and Capabilities.* Amsterdam: North-Holland.

Sharpe, A., and L. Osberg. 2006. "New Estimates of the Index of Economic Well-Being for Canada." Paper presented at the annual meeting of the Canadian Economics Association, Concordia University, Montreal, May 26-28.

Statistics Canada. 2000. *Pension Plans in Canada.* Cat. 74-401-XIB. Ottawa: Statistics Canada.

Task Force on Modernizing Income Security for Working-Age Adults. 2006. *Time for a Fair Deal.* Toronto: St. Christopher House and Toronto City Summit Alliance.

Townson, M. 2003. "Women in Non-Standard Jobs: The Public Policy Challenge." Ottawa: Status of Women Canada.

Vallée, G. 2005. "Towards Enhancing the Employment Conditions of Vulnerable Workers: A Public Policy Perspective." Vulnerable Workers Series 2. Ottawa: Canadian Policy Research Networks.

Vosko, L., C. Cranford, and N. Zukewich. 2003. "Precarious Jobs? A New Typology of Employment." *Perspectives on Labour and Income* 4 (10): 16-26.

"What Is the Child Benefit (NCB)?" n.d. Accessed September 20, 2007. www.nationalchildbenefit.ca

AN ALTERNATIVE PROPOSAL ON INCOME SECURITY
David A. Green

In his chapter on economic security, Jean-Yves Duclos argues for replacing existing transfer systems with a multifaceted system that includes universal basic income (BI), a reformed employment insurance (EI) system that focuses more on insurance principles, a supplementary program for the disabled and a training system that permits wider access. I agree, in broad terms, with much of Duclos' description of the key problems facing us, but I would choose a different emphasis. I argue that problems of subsistence for people at the very bottom of the income distribution are currently more pressing than issues of security and incentives to work for people higher in the distribution. Based on this difference in emphasis and on a somewhat different analysis of existing policies, I argue for a different transfer and security system from the one Duclos proposes in "A Better Income Security System for All Canadians."

THE PROBLEMS WE FACE

Duclos' characterization of the current Canadian policy environment is one in which a social safety net full of holes and counterproductive incentives is matched against a workforce subject to increasing feelings of insecurity and (at the bottom end) declining incomes. His solution is to introduce a universal BI, replacing the entrapping rules of social assistance with simple, unconditional transfers and freeing up EI to act as true insurance for all.

While I agree with much of this characterization, there are several points on which I disagree. My first contention is that widespread insecurity is not our primary problem. Duclos points out that standard employment — full-time paid employment not being done on temporary contract — made up only 63 percent of total employment in Canada in 2002. This is not a new phenomenon, however: in 1993, standard employment made up 64 percent of total employment (Vosko, Cranford, and Zukewich 2003). Although this proportion represented a decrease from the 1980s,

Canada clearly is not facing a rapid increase in nonstandard employment, as some observers — although not, explicitly, Duclos — claim. Further, polls over a long period have asked Canadians a consistent question about whether they think their present job is safe. At the cyclically similar points of 1981, 1990 and 2000, the proportions answering yes were 79 percent, 74 percent and 80 percent, respectively (see CTV 2003). Thus, there is little evidence of a growing feeling of insecurity among Canadian workers. Clearly, workers in nonstandard employment are underserviced by the EI and social assistance systems. My point is that this does not constitute the defining problem of our times.

What, to my mind, deserves more emphasis is Duclos' description of falling incomes at the bottom end of the income distribution. Using census data from 1980 to 2000, Frenette, Green and Milligan (2007) show that the strong increase in inequality in market incomes (income before taxes and transfers) over that period was driven mainly by changes in the top and bottom ends of the distribution. The changes at the bottom end were also reflected in growing insecurity about access to food and trends in homelessness. The Canadian Association of Food Banks (2005) reports that 1.4 percent of Canadians used a food bank in a given month in 1989, and 2.6 percent did so in 2005. Estimates of the incidence of homelessness vary widely, but a conservative estimate for 2000 suggests the number was in the 35,000 to 40,000 range (Murphy 2000).[1] Between 2002 and 2005, the number of homeless people in Greater Vancouver roughly doubled to more than 2,000. Many of those who face homelessness and food insecurity also face multiple barriers to regular participation in work and society, including drug addiction, mental illness and criminal records (Goldberg et al. 2005).

We have thus reached a situation of extreme deprivation in parts of our society that social policy is not addressing. In their proposals, Duclos and others in this area treat the issues these unfortunate Canadians face as separate from the standard social security system, and to be addressed by a somewhat vague separate system. But attempts to address incentive problems in the main system through, for example, work and training requirements affect a range of people for whom such requirements are problematic. The design of the main social security system and the lack of support for people at the very bottom are not separate problems.

In this fundamental sense, Duclos' characterization of the policy problem is correct: our social transfer system is so distorted that it fails to address key problems. Pavoni and Violante (2007) argue that because skills deteriorate further the longer an individual is unemployed, the optimal sequence of transfer policies is to offer unemployed individuals EI benefits at the outset, when it is in their best interests to search for work, followed by a search monitoring period, during which benefits continue but are contingent on job search, followed by social assistance, with benefits but no requirement to search for work. Social assistance thus becomes the program of last resort, when the individual has reached the stage where further job search is unlikely to be successful. Our problem is that we have so unravelled the EI system in attempting to prevent people from abusing it that, for many people, the first two stages are no longer available. Instead, the social assistance system has become a de facto EI system, but one with punitive eligibility conditions that require people to divest themselves of their assets first.[2] In contrast to Duclos, who places primary emphasis on the failure of the EI system and the need to construct a transfer system that does not ensnare workers with work disincentives, I place primary emphasis in my characterization of the problems we face on the failure to help the least well off.

WOULD DUCLOS' PLAN SOLVE OUR PROBLEMS?

Duclos' description of the problems with current policies raises two questions. First, are incentives that entrap recipients a primary problem of the current system? This question must be addressed in the context of the strong declines in social assistance use that have occurred in most provinces since the mid-1990s. In British Columbia's case, social assistance recipients declined from approximately 11 percent of the population in 1996 to 3 percent in 2004; among young, single individuals without children, it is now on the order of 1 percent (Wallace, Klein, and Reitsma-Street 2006). The BC system has essentially been converted into a US-style system that covers lone parents but not employable singles. A decade ago, incentives to remain on social assistance were the prime problem; however, in an environment where many do not have access to social assistance at all, such incentives have ceased to be the welfare system's main issue. Work incentives are a worry, but the first-order problem now must be those who are living on the streets.

The second question that arises from Duclos' chapter is: Would the system he proposes solve the problems he describes? The key to his proposal is a universal BI, involving an income transfer to everyone in the economy combined with a flat income tax rate. His evidence in favour of a BI comes from an earlier paper (Araar, Duclos, and Blais 2005) in which he and his colleagues argue that such a scheme would reduce inequality. In both the earlier paper and Duclos' chapter in this volume, there appears to be an implicit assumption that no behavioural responses would occur in terms of the labour supply to the proposed changes to the tax and transfer system. This is somewhat odd given that a key rationale presented for reforming the system is its negative effects on the labour supply.

Duclos' main argument is that streamlining the tax and transfer system and using the liberated resources for an unconditional BI would yield an increase in income for most people at the bottom of the income distribution. Yet Araar, Duclos and Blais (2005) show that "single employables" would lose under such a shift, since providing even quite a low basic income would be expensive under a BI scheme. Having single employables receive less might not be considered a problem if we viewed this group's receipt of transfers simply as an attempt to obtain state-sponsored leisure; it would appear to be more of a problem, however, if one considered that many individuals in the "multiple barrier" group fit in this category.

Duclos also suggests that the current EI and social assistance systems contain incentives that trap workers in low-employment states. Note, though, that Duclos proposes a marginal tax rate of either 53 percent (scenario C) or 60 percent (scenario D), high rates by any standard. Moreover, if, as he suggests, the BI were reduced at higher incomes, then even higher marginal tax rates would be incurred at some point. Put another way, Duclos' proposal still contains substantial disincentives to work — it just moves them to a higher earnings range.

Duclos' suggestion to base the EI system more firmly on social insurance principles raises the information problems that governments perennially face in establishing transfer systems. In a standard description of the problem, governments want to transfer resources to individuals who lack skills and hence are needy while avoiding subsidizing individuals who simply do not want to engage in market employment by choice. Since governments cannot observe ability directly, they must make transfers conditional on, say, observed income or employment. The problem stems from the fact that more highly skilled workers then might choose to behave like the less able (by cutting back on work) in order to obtain the transfer, thus reducing output in the economy and making everyone worse off. Current social assistance programs address this problem by making the benefit small, requiring applicants to divest themselves of assets and imposing work requirements. Both the EI system created in 1996 and Duclos' reformed version address the problem by making benefits harder to access and by reducing repeated use of EI through experience rating. Essentially, the idea is to turn EI into a true insurance system and move away from using it to transfer income to individuals who might plausibly be of low ability (the long-term or chronically unemployed). Part of what a BI then would do is assume the task of transferring money to the less able.

Is Duclos' approach of splitting the social insurance and social assistance elements of the system the best way to address our problems? Beaudry and Blackorby (1997) argue that a scheme in which transfers are tied to work is optimal in this second-best world. High-ability, leisure-loving people would decline this type of benefit because obtaining it would require effort, but for less money than they could earn if they simply went to work; at the same time, low-ability individuals who found themselves without jobs or prospects would have access to some support. An EI scheme could fit these requirements for a transfer system.[3] The implication of these arguments is that a division of tasks — with EI providing only insurance and a BI providing income support — is not as obvious a solution as it might initially appear. Following the logic of Beaudry and Blackorby further, a negative income tax scheme, with more emphasis on an earnings subsidy that is reduced with rising income, might be preferable to a BI scheme based on unconditional income.

I should add, though, that neither of these approaches addresses how to deal with the homeless and individuals who face multiple barriers to employment. These people are unlikely to hold employment consistently enough for us to transfer income to them in an employment-tied form. Duclos' supplementary system for the disabled is also unlikely to be successful for this group, since some key barriers (such as drug addiction and a criminal record) would not be incorporated in any definition of the disabled. Moreover, we need to consider the dynamics of how individuals come to have multiple barriers in the first place. If lack of financial support exacerbates existing problems — if, for example, living on the streets because of a lack of resources reduces health — then failing to provide sufficient, non-employment-conditioned support at one point might lead an individual to need more help later. One might think that such a problem would point to the need for a BI. The reality is, however, that the level of BI that both is affordable and fits with incentive constraints would not be enough to provide adequate food and housing for a single person in a large Canadian city.

PHILOSOPHICAL ARGUMENTS

One of the strengths of Duclos' work, here and elsewhere, is his incorporation of arguments about justice based on political philosophy. In particular, following Amartya Sen (1999), he argues for a version of justice in which the goal is to maximize real freedom for the least well off. Real freedoms consist of both formal freedoms (where one is not legally restricted from carrying out an action) and capabilities (where one has the ability actually to be or do something). One of Duclos' strongest arguments in favour of a BI is that it would promote real freedom by providing everyone, regardless of their attachment to work, with the means to pursue their own conception of the good life. He also argues that a BI would incorporate a requirement of personal responsibility, since the individual would determine how to use the offered funds.

My opinion on these arguments is similar to that of Anderson (1999, 2005), who, also quoting Sen, argues for a notion of justice based on what might be called social equality, which dictates that we owe to all the citizens in society the wherewithal to act as equals in society. This notion differs from that of Duclos in a subtle but important way. While Duclos argues for providing monetary resources to all, Anderson favours a more direct solution:

> The preference for income rather than in-kind transfers reflects the commitment of real libertarianism to promoting freedom, conceived as a generic good; the real libertarian urges that we provide people with the resources they need to achieve their aims, whatever those aims are. Thus it gives no special priority to freedom from disease over the freedom to idle: freedom is freedom. As an account of what we owe to one another, that seems misguided. What we owe are not the means to generic freedom but the social conditions of the particular, concrete freedoms that are instrumental to life in relations of equality with others...A maximal [universal] BI risks overproviding optional freedoms at a substantial sacrifice — large enough to compromise social equality — to the particular freedoms we owe one another. (2005)

Complementing this argument is one by Blackorby and Donaldson (1988) that the provision of transfers in kind rather than in cash can be optimal in a second-best world. Moreover, while targeting resources to the truly needy, rather than giving income to all, might be more effective, providing resources in kind would allow for more substantial transfers. For example, transfers of cash to the sick might induce some healthy people to pretend to be ill to get the cash, but transfers in the form of medicine would not.[4] Thus, for both philosophical and efficiency reasons, in-kind transfers might be preferable.

Anderson (2005) also criticizes a BI because of its focus on an ideal world in which individuals are capable of taking full advantage of the money they receive and the real freedom it might provide. This perspective, however, overlooks the real-life constraints faced by many, if not most, individuals targeted by this approach. Clear examples are those affected by family circumstances and the need to care for dependants or, in terms of our discussion, those multiple-barrier individuals for whom a relatively small amount of money would not form the basis of real freedom. Rather than relying on a BI, a preferable starting point would be to consider how to provide these individuals with the basis of equal dignity and citizenship: secure housing, secure food, medical care and opportunities for literacy.

CONCLUSIONS

I do not want to overstate my criticisms of Duclos' proposals, many of which seem correct to me. In particular, the need for those who apply for social assistance to divest themselves of their assets before becoming eligible for benefits is clearly damaging, and Duclos is sound in concluding that the requirement should be jettisoned. Similarly correct is his argument that training policy is piecemeal and its delivery through the social assistance and EI systems suboptimal. My only concern is that his emphasis on individual-based training places too much of the risk of adjusting to changes in the economy on the shoulders of workers rather than on firms. Policies that encourage firms to invest in their workers and, thus, improve job security are worth considering.

I have a great deal of sympathy for Duclos' goals and his interpretation of the problems we face. My analysis, however, has led me to prefer a somewhat different program. Primarily, I disagree with his emphasis on a BI, since I do not see a feasible BI as being large enough to address our first-order problem: the burgeoning population of the homeless and the food-insecure. I also challenge the notion that the EI system should focus solely on insurance, rather than be acknowledged as an integral part of the income redistribution system. Duclos and I agree on the need for some in-kind transfers, but I would put more emphasis on this element. Thus, I would suggest a system with the following outline:

/ Provide certain fundamental goods as transfers in kind, including social housing, long-term care and rehabilitation for people with substance abuse problems. I view this part of the system as targeted primarily at individuals who face multiple barriers to employment.

/ Reinstate social assistance as a true program of last resort. This would mean turning the social assistance program into something like the BI system Duclos proposes, but without its being the centrepiece of the social safety net. Instead, it would be a program that individuals came to after moving through a fully functioning EI system, rather than a universal, unconditional transfer.

/ Expand access to EI to provide effective unemployment insurance to the large majority of people who now effectively have none.

/ Extend to all the earnings or wage subsidies now available to families with children under the National Child Benefit system. The key goal would be to "make work pay."

/ Make training accessible through other means in addition to the EI and social assistance systems.

Taken together, the last three items would help to support the working poor as they attempt to gain both a reasonable standard of living and income security.

I have made no attempt to price these suggestions. It seems clear that, taken as a whole, they would cost more than we currently spend on income security. It is equally clear to me, however, that although the current system might pass the test of fiscal minimalism, it does not pass the test of social justice.

NOTES

1   Murphy describes the pitfalls in defining and estimating the number of homeless nationwide. Similar problems exist in gauging the severity of problems related to food insecurity. The United Nations Economic and Social Council (2006) cites estimates in the range of 100,000 to 250,000 for Canada's homeless and 2.3 million (7.4 percent of the population) for those suffering from food insecurity.

2   Social assistance applicants must undergo a needs test, which entails a full review of their assets, income and basic needs. To qualify, they are usually required to convert any nonexempt fixed assets (excluding principal residence, vehicle and household effects) into cash to cover their spending needs before they qualify for welfare. All nonexempt liquid assets are also subtracted from budgetary needs for social assistance purposes (see National Council of Welfare, 2006, 1-3).

3   Extending this line of thought, Blackorby (2001) argues that one can view EI as a system that redistributes income to lower-ability individuals through a work requirement.

4   The argument here is that the size of the cash payment that could be provided without distorting the behaviour of the non-needy is limited. With in-kind transfers, government could provide benefits of greater value since, presumably, the non-needy would not change their behaviour to gain access to a good they do not want.

REFERENCES

Anderson, E.S. 1999. "What Is the Point of Equality?" *Ethics* 109 (2): 287-337.

———. 2005. "Optional Freedoms: A Response to 'A Basic Income for All' by Philippe van Parijs." *Boston Review*. bostonreview.net/BR25.5/anderson.htm

Araar, A., J.-Y. Duclos, and F. Blais. 2005. "Effets redistributifs d'un régime d'allocation universelle: une simulation pour le Québec." *L'Actualité économique* 81 (3): 421-84.

Beaudry, P., and C. Blackorby. 1997. "Tax and Employment Subsidies in Optimal Redistribution Programs." Discussion paper 97-21. Vancouver: University of British Columbia, Department of Economics.

Blackorby, C. 2001. "Canadian Unemployment Insurance as a Pareto-Optimal Policy Instrument." *Canadian Journal of Economics* 34 (4): 849-58.

Blackorby, C., and D. Donaldson. 1988. "Cash versus Kind, Self-Selection and Efficient Transfers." *American Economic Review* 78 (4): 691-700.

Canadian Association of Food Banks (CAFB). 2005. *HungerCount 2005*. Toronto: CAFB.

CTV. 2003. "Poll Finds Canadians Optimistic about Economy." July 7. www.ctv.ca/servlet/ArticleNews/story/ CTVNews/1057530975679_22/ ?hub=Canada

Frenette, M., D.A. Green, and K. Milligan. 2007. "The Tale of the Tails: Canadian Income Inequality in the 1980s and 1990s." *Canadian Journal of Economics* 40 (3): 734-64

Goldberg, M., Eberle Planning and Research, Jim Woodward & Associates, Deborah Kraus Consulting, J. Graves, Infocus Consulting, and John Talbot and Associates. 2005. "On Our Streets and In Our Shelters: Results of the 2005 Greater Vancouver Homeless Count." Vancouver: Social Planning and Research Council of BC.

Murphy, B. 2000. *On the Streets: How We Created Homelessness*. Ottawa: J. Gordon Shillingford.

National Council of Welfare (NCW). 2006. *Welfare Incomes 2005*. Ottawa: NCW.

Pavoni, N., and G.L. Violante. 2007. "Optimal Welfare-to-Work Programs."

Review of Economic Studies 74 (1): 283-318.

Sen, A. 1999. *Development as Freedom*. Anchor Books.

United Nations Economic and Social Council. 2006. "Concluding Observations of the Committee on Economic, Social and Cultural Rights — Canada." Thirty-Sixth Session, May 1-19. New York.

Vosko, L., C. Cranford, and N. Zukewich. 2003. "Precarious Jobs? A New Typology of Employment." *Perspectives on Labour and Income* 4 (10): 16-26.

Wallace, B., S. Klein, and M. Reitsma-Street. 2006. *Denied Assistance: Closing the Front Door on Welfare in BC.* Ottawa: Canadian Centre for Policy Alternatives.

THE PRACTITIONER'S PERSPECTIVE ON INCOME SECURITY REFORM

Kathy O'Hara and Allen Sutherland

In "A Better Income Security System for All Canadians," Jean-Yves Duclos briskly walks readers through their paces in outlining the importance of the income security system and the pressures affecting it. As Duclos suggests, an effective income security system is pivotal to Canada's being "both a just and a productive society." To aspire to income security reform is to dream big, and Duclos should be given full marks for audaciousness and degree of technical difficulty.

Duclos proposes three sweeping changes to Canada's income security system:

1) a universal basic income (BI) that would be "federally financed and administered" and, in tandem with his employment insurance (EI) proposal, would "break through all the layers of the welfare wall";

2) a better EI system, grounded in social insurance principles, to replace the "poorly designed" current system; and

3) initiatives to enhance assets, notably through training vouchers and incentives for asset building and protection.

Duclos' basic diagnosis is that the income security system transcends the economic and social spheres, with considerable effects both intended and unintended. His major points include the following:

/ In the context of globalization and increased competitiveness, the forms of economic insecurity are evolving, and our income security system must also evolve in light of these developments.

/ Some important gaps in the existing income security system for Canadians need to be addressed.

/ Elements of EI and social assistance act as disincentives to work.

/ Significant numbers of Canadians are low-wage workers: "One in six Canadians working full time currently earns less than $10 per hour (in 2001 dollars)" (236).

Although this diagnosis is sound, it could be strengthened in several areas related to the depiction of EI and the inefficiencies in the Canadian labour market. For example, Duclos notes that, since the 1970s, the percentage of nonstandard employment has crept upward. What should also be noted is that, since 1997, the proportion of the labour market in nonstandard employment has in fact remained stable at 37 percent. The evidence also suggests that the correlation between nonstandard work and labour market vulnerability is not clear: 35 percent of nonstandard workers (representing 9 percent of the workforce) are considered low-wage workers; a high proportion (59 percent) of nonstandard workers live in a family unit with another higher-income earner; and only 13 percent of nonstandard workers (representing 3.5 percent of the workforce) live in low-income households. The reality is that a number of forces — for example, the availability of more flexible hours and as a way to move to full-time employment — are making nonstandard employment more acceptable and even desirable for a growing number of individuals.

In this comment, we bring a practitioner's eye to Duclos' chapter and his main proposals. Our perspective is grounded in the practitioner's traditional concern about implementation: a world in which the "how" of policy development has at least equal standing with the policy pathfinder's concern for the "what" and the "why."

STARTING FROM FIRST PRINCIPLES

Principles, particularly rights, are clearly central to Duclos' assessment of the status quo and to his proposed policy prescriptions. This is a classic contribution that academics can make to the public policy debate: to set out a normative vision of a better future. It is with just such a vision that the modern welfare state was conceived and developed, including approaches that address both the economic and social dimensions of society through the work of such income security pioneers as Lord Beveridge and Leonard Marsh.

Duclos proposes three sets of principles:

/ tying growth and security;

/ enhancing capability and responsibility; and

/ promoting inclusion and equity.

It is striking that there is little discussion of how his double-barrelled principles are in tension or conflict, either internally or one to the other. For instance, policy dilemmas, trade-offs or conflicting notions of the good life might be expected to arise in tying growth and security or in promoting such broad concepts as choice, inclusion and equity, particularly horizontal and vertical equity. The tension between fiscal constraints and income security receives minimal consideration from Duclos.

Our experience is that cost often influences (and sometimes determines) policy choice, and that the extent of income security remains an important consideration.

Working with some of the principles Duclos cites, we note that a number of tensions and trade-offs emerge from a practitioner's perspective:

/ *Equity versus efficiency.* A ubiquitous tension surrounds the balance between adequacy and generosity and the potential effects on incentives to work and on dependency and cost. This dilemma pervades issues surrounding a guaranteed annual income, of which Duclos' proposed BI is one form. These trade-offs might help to explain why no industrialized country has been willing to embrace fully a no-strings-attached, fully developed guaranteed income.

/ *Universality versus targeting.* In a world of scarce resources, trade-offs pervade discussions of vertical and horizontal equity. For instance, horizontal equity drives us to universal programs (such as the Universal Child Care Benefit), but the level of absolute support such programs provide is limited due to cost considerations. In contrast, vertical equity allows for better targeting of scarce resources, but fails to include all (for example, the National Child Benefit). While the principles are important, it is again important to recognize that a range of approaches exists that can serve to balance interests effectively in a broad income security system.

/ *Rights versus responsibilities.* By making a bold case for placing rights at the centre of his proposed income security reform, Duclos is rowing somewhat against the current in several industrialized countries which, in recent years, has flowed toward a greater balance of rights and responsibilities across a broad range of policy issues. In particular, many provincial social assistance reforms of the mid-1990s tended to reduce benefit levels substantially and introduce more stringent eligibility criteria in order to set incentives and reduce moral hazard. The driving sentiment has not been friendly to the idea of unconditional benefits solely on the basis of income, as Duclos proposes, particularly if nonparticipation in the labour market is deemed a lifestyle choice that the taxpayer would be expected to underwrite.

/ *Types of fairness.* Discourse about rights tends to obscure other important principles. Citizens vary considerably in their needs, capacities and circumstances, of which income is only one dimension. Responsive public policy cannot be a matter of one size fits all. Fairer treatment often means tailoring public services to citizens' needs — in other words, complex and "unequal" treatment is required to address divergent needs.

THE POLICY SUITE

Some elements of Duclos' proposals occupy well-travelled policy ground — a fact that does not diminish their attractiveness as options. He could have strengthened his case, however, by drawing more directly on the state of debate in these areas and by showing how other countries that have sought to advance similar principles have struck different policy balances, with important implications for their income security and societal outcomes.

A comparative approach is a useful point of reference for practitioners. Carefully used, not only does it allow for learning from others' experiences, but it also enables benchmarking of practices and outcomes, which, in turn, helps to gauge the innovativeness and effectiveness of the Canadian policy mix. At the broad policy level, then, there has been a general trend away from passive measures and toward more active measures such as labour force training, which forms a part of Duclos' voucher and EI proposals. The shift to more active measures has occurred in large part to address the growing importance of human capital development in a global, knowledge-based society. New Zealand has gone the farthest in developing a focus on jobs, while Sweden and Denmark have been evolving toward innovative "flexicurity" approaches.[1]

To the extent that income measures have been advocated, the trend over the past decade has generally been toward *earnings* supplementation and, with some important exceptions — such as vulnerable groups, seniors and families with children — less *income* supplementation. For instance, the last major US income security reform, when President Bill Clinton famously declared "the end of welfare as we know it," led to the creation of the Temporary Assistance for Needy Families initiative.[2] Other complementary US policy changes reinforced welfare-to-work efforts — most notably, targeted human capital initiatives and a series of increases to the federal minimum wage and the Earned Income Tax Credit.

Around the same time, the Labour government in the United Kingdom committed itself to ending child poverty (by 2020) and reducing "worklessness." It has since introduced a broad range of measures, including a national minimum wage, the New Deals (targeted to groups such as youth and people with disabilities) and two new generous income-tested tax measures, the Child Tax Credit and the Working Tax Credit.

The reformer's dilemma: big bang or incremental change?

What lessons can we learn from these reform efforts? The sheer complexity of the modern welfare state can discourage broad-based reform. Changes in one area have ripple effects elsewhere. Moreover, the difficulties associated with developing consensus in an increasingly diverse Canadian society, the overall political calculus and the federal-provincial context can bedevil reform efforts. Certainly, recent Canadian experience with social security reform in the mid-1990s, as well as elsewhere, demonstrates the difficulties and perils of undertaking broad-based reform in this area.

We compliment Duclos for not succumbing to cynicism, but more stepping stones are needed from his vision to implementation. In providing them, he should be encouraged to deal with the skeptics head-on by addressing directly their concerns about feasibility and by assessing whether the conditions are ripe for large-scale reforms. Some key dimensions to be explored include:

/ Cost and sustainability
/ The distribution of winners and losers
/ Federal-provincial environment, dynamics and implications
/ Possible risks (in managing the transition to reform, for example) and unintended consequences
/ The development of a societal-political consensus

Were this to happen, two things might emerge. First, Duclos might find it worthwhile to add some water to his wine. The pragmatist school of thought argues that the better approach is to seek incremental change for more transformative ends. Second, and as a consequence, a more careful look at feasibility might cause him to look more generously at the status quo.

The existing income security foundations, including EI and social assistance, are continually built upon with a view to reforming the social security system for the modern era. Duclos correctly identifies and lauds the creation of the National Child Benefit; he might equally have cited recent tax measures, including the proposed Working Income Tax Benefit and the ongoing modernization of labour market programming, as well as provincial social assistance reform efforts. Indeed, antecedents for many of Duclos' proposals exist in nascent form within the current system.

THE POLICY PROPOSALS

Space does not permit us to assess fully Duclos' specific proposals, but we might make a number of initial observations.

A universal basic income

Duclos' proposal for a universal BI is an important contribution to what might be a growing debate within Canada. Some notable recent efforts to develop proposals to reform Canada's income security system include those by the Caledon Institute (Battle, Mendelson, and Torjman 2006) and the Task Force on Modernizing Income Security for Working-Age Adults (2006) — table 1 on page 284 sets out their respective recommendations. Duclos' proposals follow the main broad thrusts of the Caledon and Task Force work, though his, particularly the BI, appear to be more generous, largely due to his rights-based approach. In contrast, the other two approaches are more willing to differentiate among different types of recipients and their varied circumstances. All three present proactive visions, with the Caledon Institute providing, on balance, the most transformative vision, while the Task Force presents the most practical approach by proposing the most specific set of recommendations. Although Duclos' BI proposal has the benefit of simplicity, it appears to gloss over the importance of different types of support (short-term, long-term, active, passive). Since social assistance recipients have a variety of needs, minimal recourse to needs testing does not necessarily lead to fairer treatment and better outcomes.

In terms of next steps, assessment and modelling would be required to assess the implications of introducing Duclos' BI into the overall income security architecture — including its effect on federal expenditures, on in-kind benefits and services, and on incentives to work, and the need to adjust federal-provincial and territorial funding arrangements. In-kind benefits extend beyond the formal income security system to include nonmedicare health programs (drugs, vision and dental care, home care, long-term care); individual financing supports for post-secondary education (scholarships/bursaries, loans, tax credits); other employment and social services; child care; and Canada Pension Plan disability benefits and the Disability Tax Credit, as well as provincial programs supporting persons with disabilities. Most important, the federal-provincial ramifications of such reforms would be sweeping, with the need to factor in corollary reforms to transfer payments and existing funding agreements on interrelated issues, such as the Canada Social Transfer.

A better EI system

Duclos raises a number of considerations relevant to any insurance-based income replacement program: overall program effectiveness, broader adjustment issues and the effects of design on labour market participation. His assessment of EI is perhaps best summarized by his statement that the program is one that "is probably doing more harm than good" (240). In this regard, a more balanced assessment of the evidence might be warranted.

With the Canadian labour market performing exceptionally well, there seem to be many indications that the overall situation is much better than Duclos maintains and that EI is, in fact, serving its intended objectives. Unemployment is at historic lows, access for those who contribute to the program remains at high levels and premium rates have declined 30 percent in the past decade while program benefits have been significantly expanded.[3] At the same time, benefits levels have risen while exhaustion rates continue to fall (Human Resources and Social Development Canada 2007, 57). Frequent EI claimants, an area of concern for Duclos, are a declining proportion of the overall employed labour force.

There are also a number of instances where Duclos' specific criticisms of EI appear to contradict the solutions he offers. For example, he faults EI for not providing income support to those who do not qualify because they have worked too few hours or because they have never worked or contributed, yet he identifies an improved program as one based more firmly on an individual's unemployment and contributory record. Although the issues that vulnerable nonstandard workers face are certainly of concern with respect to any discussion of federal income support levers, Duclos' emphasis on EI might be overstated. Despite his criticism of current EI eligibility requirements, particularly as they apply to nonstandard workers, evidence indicates that reducing entrance requirements would lead to only a small increase in the number who would qualify for benefits. Further, only a small proportion of the unemployed (10 percent) is ineligible due to lack of hours. In the case of the self-employed, a population EI is not designed to serve, there are important challenges for coverage (such as how to determine job loss, moral hazard), which the literature documents well.[4]

Turning to the feasibility of Duclos' proposal, a number of practical considerations surrounding the implementation of such major changes to EI could have received more attention. For example, although he recognizes the challenges associated with reducing a pattern of reliance on EI, Duclos could have gone further in elaborating his rationale for the proposed income security architecture, including how the proposal would address the many recognized challenges associated with changing EI.

Incentives for asset building and protection

For his third policy proposal, Duclos provides a thoughtful, but brief, investigation of the potential role for training vouchers and the need to encourage asset building to improve Canadians' security and resiliency in the face of change. As these

TABLE 1.	INCOME SECURITY ARCHITECTURE PROPOSALS		
	Duclos' proposal	Caledon Institute of Social Policy (Battle, Mendelson, and Torjman 2006)	Task Force on Modernizing Income Security for Working-Age Adults (2006)
Proposed architecture	Refocus income security programs and introduce a new basic income (BI) to make the system more growth enhancing, more supportive of individual freedoms and capabilities, and more inclusive of those in need of economic security.	Replace current income security architecture with new three-tiered system (including scaled-down versions of some existing programs) to better support labour market participation and those who cannot be reasonably expected to work.	Recommends a broad range of changes (mostly incremental) to existing architecture to promote and sustain labour market participation by low-income, working-age Canadians and to better support those who cannot be reasonably expected to work.

Duclos' proposal

Universal basic income — federal
/ Universal, income-tested benefit to cover all working-age Canadians, broader than current employment insurance (EI) or social assistance coverage.
/ Flat rate structure.
/ Available for an unlimited time.
/ Noncontributory (funded through general revenues).
/ Administered as a refundable credit through personal income tax system.
/ Provide supports such as supplementary health, dental care and prescription drugs to working poor; offer universal access to training and employment services; enhance the financial assets of vulnerable Canadians; establish a federal disability benefits program.
/ No specific design recommendation, but a reference to three illustrative scenarios developed in a Quebec context: a limited base benefit; a more generous version using a flat tax; and a full BI that would replace welfare (and use a flat tax, but at a higher rate than the previous option). Depending on the scenario, benefits would be $2,600-$6,500 for a single individual and $3,640-$9,100 for lone parents.

A reformed EI
/ Simplify the system and base it more on insurance principles: a contributory program providing wage replacement based on individual unemployment and contributory record.

Caledon Institute of Social Policy (Battle, Mendelson, and Torjman 2006)

Tier 1: Two-part unemployment assistance — federal
/ Short-term, time-limited income support for the temporarily unemployed.
/ Introduce temporary income (TI), a noncontributory program paying income-tested benefits to working-age adults who are unemployed but actively seeking work and in financial need:
- simple, flat-rate benefit structure;
- could provide social benefits such as parental leave and sickness benefits;
- not accompanied by employment services; available for a limited time.
/ Reformed EI would act as complementary benefit for contributors, continuing to provide wage replacement for the unemployed, but based more firmly on contributory records.

Tier 2: Medium-term support through an employment preparation program — provincial/territorial
/ For working-age adults unemployed for longer than under tier 1 and in financial need.
/ Purpose is to prepare people for employment (including active job search, longer-term training).
/ Replaces social assistance for most employables.
/ Benefit structure could be much simpler than welfare and wage-like, with bi-weekly, flat-rate payments and, possibly, contributions to the Canada and Quebec Pension Plans to treat recipients as workers and link them to the public pension system.

Task Force on Modernizing Income Security for Working-Age Adults (2006)

Two-part refundable tax credit — federal
/ A basic refundable tax credit for all low-income, working-age adults (working or otherwise, including people with disabilities).
- Maximum benefit would be $1,800/year ($150/month). It would begin to be recovered at $5,000/year in household income, reducing to zero by $21,500/year.
- All adults, parents, singles and childless couples would get the same refundable credit on the same basis.
/ A new working income supplement called a working income benefit.
- Maximum benefit would be $2,400/year ($200/month), reducing to zero at $21,500 per year in household income.
- Minimum work hours to qualify would be 50 hours/month or a household income of $400/month or $4,800/year.
/ Cost: $8.5 billion, including a $1.7 billion offset from repurposing the Goods and Services Tax Credit.

A reformed EI
/ Decrease entrance requirements in low-unemployment regions as a first step toward uniform eligibility requirements.
/ Reduce the current hours for eligibility of new entrants and re-entrants.

TABLE 1.	INCOME SECURITY ARCHITECTURE PROPOSALS (CONT'D)

	Duclos' proposal	Caledon Institute of Social Policy (Battle, Mendelson, and Torjman 2006)	Task Force on Modernizing Income Security for Working-Age Adults (2006)
Proposed architecture (cont'd)	/ Introduce experience rating for firms and workers. / Remove incentives for seasonal/temporary work.	/ Could continue for several years for some recipients, but it would not be expected to provide permanent income support. Expectation would be that the recipient would get a job. / Limited, residual welfare system would remain as an ultimate fallback for those who can reasonably be expected to earn their living through work but do not. **Tier 3: Long-term support through a BI program — federal** / A long-term, non-contributory, income-tested benefit for those (such as people with severe disabilities) who cannot be reasonably expected to earn an adequate income from employment. Recommends a broad range of measures to make work pay (including improved minimum wages, working income supplements) and to better support the working poor (including adequate child benefits, supplementary health, prescription drugs, dental care).	/ Remove the current exclusion of "voluntary quits" and "dismissed for cause" and returning to former practice of imposing a penalty of a number of weeks' delay for benefit receipt. / Improve access to other benefits and programs that are only accessible to those eligible for EI, including employment supports, training and parental leave benefits. Also recommended is a broad range of complementary measures, including regular minimum wage improvements; a national disability income support program; integrated provincial and territorial child benefits systems; prescription drug, vision and dental care coverage for low-income workers; employment supports, training and upgrading for social assistance recipients and low-income workers; and ongoing disability/medical coverage for people with disabilities active in the labour market.
Implementation	/ For efficiency, administrative and equity reasons, Duclos suggests federal responsibility for BI and EI; provinces and territories could choose to implement income supplements and supplementary social assistance. / Having the federal government take over some or all of social assistance would result in substantial savings for provinces and territories. Duclos suggests that these savings could be used to finance training and employment supports and, implicitly, in-kind benefits and services for the working poor. / EI changes in many ways would be a return to 1996 reforms (fewer disincentives to work full time, full year).	The authors chose not to deal with the political and economic dimensions of their proposals or with policy and program design, financing, jurisdictional division of labour, implementation strategies. They do recommend roles for the federal, provincial and territorial governments.	/ Proposals target specific changes to particular elements of the employment and income security system across all jurisdictions. / Recommendations are positioned as having the potential to be segmented and implemented in a sequential manner.

represent a cutting-edge area of public policy, it would be interesting to see a more fully developed proposal.

Vouchers could be a way to develop skills and improve labour market outcomes as part of a broader jobs strategy. That said, vouchers are but one strand of what must inevitably be a multipronged effort to create robust labour market conditions. According to the Organisation for Economic Co-operation and Development (2006), a dynamic labour market policy mix requires a comprehensive approach marked by four pillars: setting an appropriate macroeconomic policy; removing impediments to labour market participation and job search; tackling labour and product-market obstacles to labour demand; and facilitating the development of labour force skills and competencies.

CONCLUSION

In his introduction, Duclos states that he does not "purport to cover in sufficient detail many of the difficult issues of program design, financing and jurisdictional division of responsibilities that must be tackled in making important policy changes" (235). As necessary as this might have seemed from the perspective of making this huge set of issues manageable, it is nevertheless a breathtaking statement for a public policy document aimed at agenda setting.

The result is an uneasy silence on many of the central considerations and conundrums that animate effective public policy development, from straightforward fiscal capacity issues and the federal-provincial environment to the changing Canadian citizen and society. John F. Kennedy's oft-quoted injunction that "to govern is to choose" applies. Nowhere is this clearer and more difficult than in the exercise of setting priorities amid fiscal, political and governance constraints. For practitioners, Duclos has defined away too much of what makes public policy reform the art of the possible.

As an exercise in setting out the broad directions of income security reform, however, Duclos sets a bountiful table of food for thought, from his contribution to the income supplementation debate to his championing of training vouchers. In doing so, he raises important and sometimes troubling questions for practitioners, who would do well to examine his vision of a better income security system for all Canadians.

NOTES

1   Although varying concepts of flexicurity exist across Europe, the approach supports forging a balance between flexibility (in employment relationships, as in the number of hours worked) and social security (including retraining and providing generous benefits during periods of unemployment) to support competitiveness and increased productivity and to enable both firms and workers to adapt to economic change.

2   These reform efforts, which shifted federal financing from an open-ended matching grant to fixed block allocations, allowed for increased state discretion in program design, added a five-year limit on the use of federal funds for benefits and raised federal requirements for the engagement of recipients in work and work-related activities (such as job search, community service and education and training).

3   The Employment Insurance Coverage Survey provides the most accurate measure of EI coverage, as it identifies and excludes from the calculation individuals for whom the EI program is not designed to provide coverage. By this measure, in 2005, among the unemployed in Canada who had a recent job separation that qualified under the EI program, 83 percent were eligible to receive EI benefits. Regarding the benefits themselves, significant changes were made in 2000 and 2001 to improve access and flexibility, including doubling benefit duration times, reducing the minimum hours needed to qualify for special benefits, permitting recipients to continue to work while on parental leave in order to maintain their attachment to the labour market and eliminating a benefit repayment provision for all special benefits claimants. Compassionate care benefits were expanded in 2004 and again in 2006 to help eligible families provide or arrange care for an ill family member.

4   See, for example, the federal government's response to the Standing Committee on the Status of Women on the issue of extending maternity and parental benefits to self-employed workers (Governement of Canada 2006).

REFERENCES

Battle, K., M. Mendelson, and S. Torjman. 2006. *Towards a New Architecture for Canada's Adult Benefits*. Ottawa: Caledon Institute of Social Policy.

Government of Canada. 2006. "Government Response to the Fifth Report of the Standing Committee on the Status of Women, Interim Report on the Maternity and Parental Benefits under Employment Insurance: The Exclusion of Self-Employed Workers." Ottawa: House of Commons Standing Committee on the Status of Women.

Human Resources and Social Development Canada (HRSDC). 2007. *Employment Insurance: Monitoring and Assessment Report 2006*. Ottawa: HRSDC.

Organisation for Economic Co-operation and Development (OECD). 2006. *OECD Employment Outlook 2006: Boosting Jobs and Incomes*. Paris: OECD.

Task Force on Modernizing Income Security for Working-Age Adults. 2006. *Time for a Fair Deal*. Toronto: St. Christopher House and Toronto City Summit Alliance.

HEALTH OUTCOMES

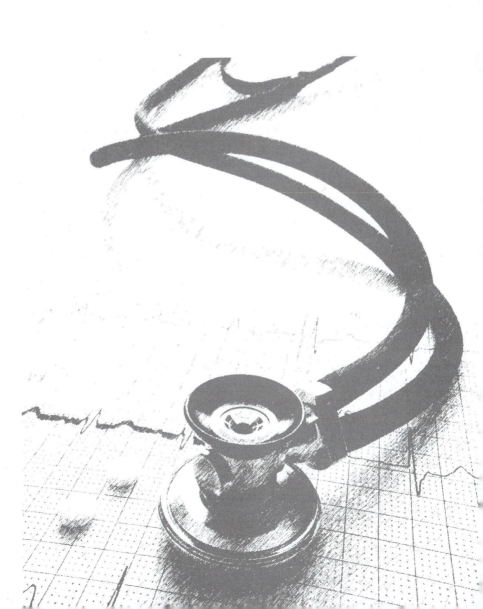

IMPROVING HEALTH OUTCOMES IN CANADA
Robert Evans, Clyde Hertzman and Steve Morgan

> The Health Department of a great commercial district which encounters no obstacles and meets with no opposition may safely be declared unworthy of public confidence; for no sanitary measure, however simple, can be enforced without compelling individuals to yield something of pecuniary interest or of personal convenience to the general welfare.
>
> (Metropolitan Board of Health of the State of New York, 1868)

Canadians would be virtually unanimous in supporting improving "the health outcomes of the Canadian population" as part of the Canadian Priorities Agenda, though on average Canadians are already among the healthiest people in the world. The persistence of large and socially graded inequalities in health, however, indicates that there is still considerable room for improvement. Improved health outcomes also contribute to the priorities of addressing "the economic and social implications of the aging population," and are also embedded in the top priority of enhancing "learning in Canada and the conditions under which investments in skills and learning pay off, from early childhood through adulthood" (5). Improved health is one of the potential payoffs from investment in skills and learning; for some it is also, particularly in early childhood, a precondition for improved learning.

The New York board of health (quoted in Duffy 1974, 1) reminds us, however, that any concrete proposals for pursuing these universally shared objectives will necessarily "[compel] individuals to yield something of pecuniary interest or of personal convenience to the general welfare." The benefits and costs of public policies are never spread equally across the population. General benefits will impose particular costs, and narrowly based but strategically placed interest groups can be counted upon to mount opposition to any policy that imposes (net) costs on them. Indeed, as the New York board of health recognized, the absence of opposition is a warning that a policy is unlikely to have any significant effect. The three policies we recommend here will not raise that warning.

Our proposals address both major categories of determinants of health: those that influence whether people become ill or injured, and those that support responses to those illnesses or injuries. The first proposal, an early childhood development

(ECD) program, draws upon a large body of evidence that "why some people are healthy and others not" is rooted in their social context, "the conditions in which they live and work" (Evans, Barer, and Marmor 1994; Heymann et al. 2006). While the contributions of modern health care are far from trivial, these social context factors are far more powerful in their effects on health status at the population level.

In particular, the experiences of early childhood become "embedded" in the form of patterns of response to later stresses, not only as healthy or unhealthy behaviours, but also as "learned" biological responses through the endocrine and cardiovascular systems that may support or damage health. This early embedding has identifiable health consequences over the whole life course.

A serious ECD program will be expensive. Our second proposal is for a major reorientation of the funding and regulation of pharmaceuticals in Canada that could dramatically reduce their public and private costs without threat to the health of patients. How this could be done administratively is not mysterious; the fundamental challenge is political. But it is important to be clear that the potential and the means are there.

The feasibility of a major ECD program does not, however, depend upon freeing up significant funds from the pharmaceutical sector — desirable as that might be. Figure 1 is a backdrop to all our proposals. The Canadian government is in the

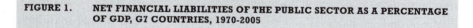

FIGURE 1. NET FINANCIAL LIABILITIES OF THE PUBLIC SECTOR AS A PERCENTAGE OF GDP, G7 COUNTRIES, 1970-2005

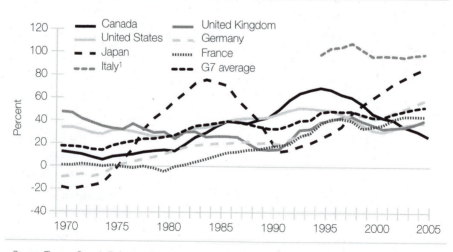

Source: Finance Canada Reference Table #57, 2006.
[1] Data for Italy not available prior to 1995.

strongest fiscal position among the Group of Seven countries and, barring a major recession or tax cuts, will continue to strengthen. We have the public means; action depends only on political priorities and will.

Our third proposal focuses on medicare — physicians and hospitals. Medicare has never been "managed" for effectiveness, much less cost-effectiveness. There are understandable political reasons for this, but it is also, we suggest, because the information systems required for such management are not in place. There is extensive evidence of large variations in clinical practice, with major cost implications, that are not linked to patient needs or outcomes. We argue that a comprehensive clinical information system, a universal electronic medical record (EMR), would provide the tools for such management, and we note that other countries are now moving rapidly down this road. A health care system that was managed for effectiveness might not necessarily achieve better outcomes for less money, but it could certainly reallocate the current very high level of resources to produce better health outcomes.

THE SOCIAL GRADIENT IN HEALTH

For virtually every measure of health, those lower down the socioeconomic scale have, on average, poorer health. This social gradient is universally observed and widely studied. Social status may be measured by income, or education, or occupational prestige, or whatever other characteristics (for example, accent or caste) correlate with respect. But higher is always healthier.

There are, however, significant differences among countries in the steepness of the health gradient, and these differences in average health are observed at the bottom of the scale, not the top. The degree of disadvantage is strongly influenced by differences in social context. The Scandinavian countries, for example, have relatively flat gradients, continental Europe's is steeper, and that of the United States is markedly steeper again. Canada's lies between those of Europe and the United States, depending upon the measure.

An obvious but incomplete explanation is the effect of poverty and deprivation. These are certainly harmful to health, but ill health is not simply concentrated among "the poor" and randomly distributed among the rest of us. Health and social status are correlated all the way along the social spectrum.

Some point to "unhealthy behaviours" — poor diet, smoking, lack of exercise — associated with lower income and education. But the health gradient remains after adjusting for specific unhealthy behaviours (Marmot et al. 1978). Moreover, the correlation of smoking or poor diets with social position in itself requires explanation.[1] "Tastes" for unhealthy behaviours do not arise randomly in a population; they emerge from a particular social context.

Much evidence, from human and particularly animal studies, shows that the way organisms respond to stress has significant effects on their long-term health. The endocrine system generates a "fight or flight" response to stress, but it must also turn that response off quickly when the threat is past. Chronic stress impairs the ability to turn the response off, and the result is damage to a number of body systems. This "learned" biological response thus parallels the equally "learned" behavioural response of smoking or heavy drinking, and is equally beyond the reach of well-meant exhortations to make healthier "choices." "Learned" unhealthy stress responses may include lighting up a fag or hitting the bottle, but they also include impaired ability to down-regulate the autonomic nervous system.

The impact of differences in social context has been brutally illustrated by the contrasting experience of people east and west of the Berlin Wall, not just after its fall, but in the 20 years prior. Working-age male life expectancy remained static or fell in every Soviet society between 1970 and 1990, and rose everywhere in the West.

Laboratory studies of 50-year-old males in Vilnius (Lithuania) and Linköping (Sweden) found that the much higher cardiac mortality rates in Lithuania were associated not with differences in the "usual suspects" — smoking, high blood pressure, elevated serum lipids — but with differences in the stress response. The unhealthy chronic low-level arousal and slow turning off of the response to laboratory stresses was more prevalent in Vilnius (referenced in Evans 2002).

POLICY PROPOSAL 1: IMPLEMENT A COMPREHENSIVE EARLY CHILDHOOD DEVELOPMENT PROGRAM TO REDRESS THE SOCIAL GRADIENT IN HEALTH

What has this to do with children? The "environments in which people live and work" become embedded, for good or ill, in their biology and behaviour, but the embedding process, in both cases, is most effective in early life (McCain and Mustard 1999; Keating and Hertzman 1999). Like language, resilience or vulnerability to stress is best learned early, and for the same reasons. The much greater plasticity of the young brain is a very effective evolutionary adaptation that permits rapid learning — for good or ill. But developmental windows missed do not open again. As with languages, later learning is possible, but is more difficult and rarely as effective.

The adult gradients in health are less pronounced among children or adolescents. Instead, one finds gradients in readiness to learn at school entry, in school performance, in post-secondary education, in contacts with the justice system, in attachment to employment and quality of jobs (in skills acquisition and productivity) and in later adult health status and mortality (Keating and Hertzman 1999). A good or bad start leads to a life trajectory in which good or poor performance at each stage reinforces the probability of success or failure at the next.

The fundamental idea is very old — as the twig is bent, so grows the tree; the Jesuits say, "Give me the child until he is seven, and I will give you the man." But in the last 20 years there has been an explosion of research, documentation and developing biological understanding of the pathways through which early life experience becomes embedded in "coping styles" or responses to the later opportunities and challenges of life.

FIGURE 2.   INTERNATIONAL ADULT LITERACY SURVEY SCORES FOR YOUTH AGES 16-25 RELATIVE TO PARENTS' EDUCATION, SELECTED COUNTRIES, 1994

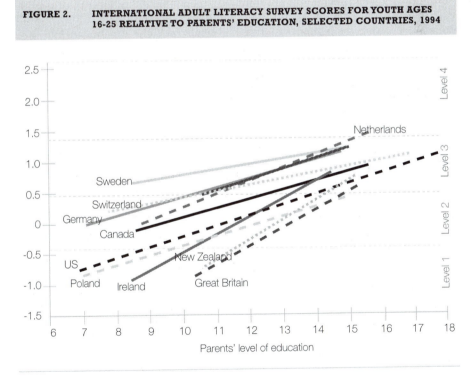

Source: Organisation for Economic Co-operation and Development (OECD), and Statistics Canada (1995,151).
Note: The left-hand side reports "Z scores," in which the individual scores on the literacy test have been standardized by subtracting the mean score for the tested group and then dividing by the standard deviation around the mean. These are then averaged for each level of parental schooling in each country. The right-hand side classifies these Z scores into broad categories, from a very crude level of literacy up to highly sophisticated skills. Level 3 skills are judged necessary for daily living in a modern society; literacy below that level represents failure.

Even the genetic endowment, once thought of as an immutable inheritance, now turns out to be expressed in different ways depending on early experience. The DNA sequence for a given gene may be present, but whether it is expressed depends on the pattern of attachment of methyl groups to those different genes, and that pattern is influenced by the early environment.[2]

The fact that social gradients in health, literacy, school and work performance are much steeper in some countries than in others (figure 2) shows that they can be modified. And the societies with flatter gradients are not only healthier but have higher educational attainment and literacy, lower poverty rates and smaller prison populations, and they just plain work better. The argument for a serious ECD program is supported not just by the research literature on the importance of the early years, but by the simple observation that other countries have such programs, and their population-level results are much better than those in Canada.

Our first policy proposal would therefore require that the federal government revitalize the National Children's Agenda for ECD. A national child care program could be the vehicle for bringing Canada's performance in ECD up to the best international standard. The benefits — in terms of education, health and economic performance — would ramify across all the objectives generated by the Canadian Priorities Agenda process, as one can see in those societies that have taken this issue seriously.

While it is true that a great deal, probably the majority, of successful early child development takes place in a well-ordered (and well-resourced) home, it is also true that more than 25 percent of Canadians reach adulthood without the competencies they need to cope in the modern economy. Many families are succeeding, but many are not.[3] Prime Minister Stephen Harper's dismissal of national child care — "We've offered a real choice to the real experts. And their names are mom and dad" — was at best ignorance and wishful thinking, at worst political cynicism (Office of the Prime Minister 2007). It does not have to be this way; international experience indicates that our 25 percent rate could be reduced to under 10 percent. Quite apart from improved heath and well-being, the implications for international competitiveness should be obvious.[4]

Change requires two things: institutions and money. Countries that outperform Canada have a national child care policy *and* a program. This was recognized by the broad coalition of ECD researchers, business leaders, economists, child care activists and antipoverty activists who supported the National Children's Agenda. A substantial range of initiatives have been consistent with our new understanding of ECD (Aboriginal Head Start, year-long parental leave benefits, the Quebec child care plan, hundreds of new, small, community-based and targeted programs for ECD around the country). But without a national power grid, "a thousand points of light" are simply swallowed up in the darkness.

Canada needs to reverse current policy trends and to establish a comprehensive system of ECD, care and education. This would provide but go well beyond universal daycare, to address the full range of factors shown to promote optimal child development, such as parental leave, newborn screening and follow-up, and so on. The experience of countries with better developmental outcomes than Canada indicates that a truly comprehensive system would require a commitment of $20 to $25 billion annually, or about 1.5 to 2 percent of current gross domestic product (GDP), compared with our present commitment of about 0.25 percent.[5] The principal aims would be:

/ to reduce from more than 25 percent to less than 10 percent the proportion of Canadians reaching adulthood without the competencies they need to cope in the modern economy, and thereby at the same time addressing an important determinant of health and well-being across the life course; and

/ to address simultaneously child poverty, a shrinking labour force and high levels of work-life/home-life conflict by facilitating female labour market participation.

In brief, the details of our first policy proposal are as follows:

/ The federal government should initiate negotiations with the provinces to reinstate the Early Learning and Child Care transfer payment program.

/ The negotiations should involve a 10-year plan to resource the contributory programs at a level that will eliminate all barriers to access.

/ The core model of direct service delivery should be the early childhood development and parenting centre proposed by the Council for Early Child Development. These would be nonprofit, community-based centres, created in unused school spaces whenever possible, that provide a flexible range of child care and family drop-in and support programs. These would follow the QUAD principles — quality, universality, accessibility, developmental focus — with at most nominal charges to families, so as not to deter any who wish to come.

/ The centre would also serve as a hub of access to recreation, library and health programs (for example, vision, hearing, dental, speech and language).

/ A legally incorporated intersectoral governance structure would exist at the level of the centre and also at the level of the region. This is because a variety of issues regarding accessibility, quality, inclusiveness and intersectoral collaboration need to be handled in overlapping ways at the local and regional levels. Regions may be defined according to school district or municipal boundaries. The core of federal-provincial negotiations on resource transfers would involve agreements on the standards against which funding for a full network of centres would flow.

In addition to the direct service delivery component, there would need to be a series of federal, federal-provincial and federal-provincial-municipal arrangements, funded from the 1.5 to 2 percent of GDP commitment, around nonservice delivery factors that influence ECD and access to programs. The principal issues are quality, affordable housing; flexible work arrangements; transportation; and aspects of neighbourhood character that influence ECD (safety, cohesion and socio-economic mix).

Federal funding would flow against a provincial commitment to collect data on ECD initiatives to assess the quality of nurturing environments for children and, most important, outcomes. Outcome measurement would be population-based and analyzable at the local community level. The Early Development Indicator, which has been applied population-wide in British Columbia and Manitoba and in many other local communities, would be the standard. These data would be used to fulfill seven purposes:

/ Assess the state of ECD at the population level

/ Judge the resilience of communities in supporting children's development

/ Evaluate change in ECD over time

/ Understand the state of ECD in special populations (for example, Aboriginal, special needs)

/ Monitor progress in meeting the "Rights in Early Childhood" provisions of the Convention on the Rights of the Child

/ Anchor developmental trajectories

/ Provide feedback on the effectiveness of the programs that form this agenda

It is critical that a national ECD program be adequately resourced. Countries with universal access to child care programs have found that 1.5 to 2 percent of GDP is sufficient to offer universal access to quality child care. Quebec has tried to offer Northern-European-style care with fewer resources, by cobbling together a system combining old, informal arrangements with newer, formal arrangements. The results fall short of universal, but there has been a marked increase in the proportion of low-income families with children getting access to licensed and/or regulated care. This proportion is now about 10 percentage points higher in Quebec than in the rest of the country; prior to the program the ratios were about equal.

One concern expressed with the Quebec program has focused on the finding (Lefebvre 2004) that it has been disproportionately used by children from middle- and upper-income families. Such a concern revives the ancient debate about universal versus targeted social programs in general. The argument that a more targeted program will cost less and be more effective in reaching those who can benefit most is in fact half right. It will cost less. Proponents of targeting tend to argue that they are seeking the most efficient use of scarce public funds, but behind that claim may lurk simple hostility to any public program.

In the first place, data on readiness to learn at school entry show that the problem of "unreadiness to learn," while more prevalent lower down the social scale, is by no means exclusively a problem of "the poor." Both the National Longitudinal Study of Children and Youth and population-based data using the Early Development Indicator consistently show that more than half of Canadian children not ready for school are found (spread more thinly) across the much more numerous middle and upper classes. Targeting not only tends to ghettoize the program participants as children of socially inadequate families; it also abandons significant numbers of children with problems whose families are not poor.

Perhaps most fundamentally, however, the observation that a program attracts middle- and upper-income participation is a mark of strength, not a reason for concern (Brownell, Roos, and Fransoo 2006). Targeting social programs leaves them with a very weak supportive constituency.[6] Contrast, for example, the marginal role of Medicaid for the poor in the United States with the broad and powerful public support for Canada's universal medicare — or for that matter America's universal Medicare for the elderly. Targeted programs lack broad public support and are always more vulnerable to political attack or simple neglect.

Sven Bremberg (2006) makes the point clearly in the Swedish context:

> For the family, day care is quite costly. In order to get a high coverage not only the parents but also other citizens have to contribute. We do it by means of taxes. To achieve that, support from the upper middle class is needed. That group can arrange day care for their children on their own. Thus, they do not need tax supported day care. Yet, if they can get as good quality of day care by means of a tax supported system they will support it. The group that will benefit most from the system is low income people. Yet, if that was an arrangement only for these groups, it would not get wide support. The Swedish system is built to benefit all families, including the upper middle class. (8)

Swedes see their program not as a cost drain to be minimized, but as a critical component of a more comprehensive integrated social welfare policy. The availability of high-quality daycare also underpins Sweden's low child poverty rate:

> When most parents work, relatively few will be poor. That is true in Sweden both for single mothers, which is a vulnerable group, and cohabiting or married women. The participation has been quite stable around 80 percent during the last decades...Explanation #1 for the low poverty rate in the Nordic countries is not the construction of the system for taxes and transfers but the high female participation in the workforce. (Bremberg 7)

The Swedish program is not only a mechanism to promote child development, with long-run benefits, it is also a component of labour market policy, expanding employment and reducing poverty. Nonetheless it is also, like our proposal, first and foremost a program to promote ECD, care and education, designed to produce healthier, better-educated and more productive citizens. This was the program, based on the QUAD principles, that was put forward by the Martin government. More recent proposals for targeted, voucher-based daycare, by contrast, amount to little more than subsidized babysitting for the poor that aim to push them into the job market at minimum cost in taxes. As Fraser Mustard has commented, they represent "a knee-jerk reaction, because you don't understand the subject" (quoted in Rushowy 2007, A1).

The importance of social policy in the high-tax, high-income Nordic countries has recently been emphasized by Sachs (2006), who contrasts their collective experience with that of the low-tax, high-income, so-called "Anglo-Saxon" countries: the United States, the United Kingdom, Canada, Australia and New Zealand. Sachs notes:

> [T]here is by now a rich empirical record...comparing a group of relatively free-market economies that have low to moderate rates of taxation and social outlays with a group of social-welfare states that have high rates of taxation and social outlays...On average, the Nordic countries outperform the Anglo-Saxon ones on most measures of economic performance. Poverty rates are much lower there, and national income per working-age population is on average higher. Unemployment rates are roughly the same. (42)

Failure to act on the ECD agenda simply means persistent untapped human potential. Our international performance will remain mediocre compared with better-organized societies but no worse than our usual comparators, the other Anglo-Saxon countries. A bronze medal performance — good enough for Canada.

A significant opportunity will continue to be ignored, but the burden of the loss will mostly fall on those at the lower end of the socio-economic scale, who have relatively few political resources. Meanwhile the public policy debate remains "clouded by vested interests and ideology" (Sachs 2006, 42). Well, the New York board of health might have told Sachs that.

COST TRENDS IN THE CANADIAN HEALTH CARE SYSTEM

While "an ounce of prevention is worth a pound of cure" is folk wisdom, the dependence of a population's health on the conditions in which they live and work, including the experiences of early childhood, is much less widely understood. By contrast, the conviction that the main road to health runs through health care is almost universal, and the derivative claim that health care is "underfunded" has powerful resonance everywhere.[7]

There is in fact no systematic relationship, at least among high-income countries, between the health of a population and its level of spending on health care. Indeed, within the United States, very detailed research has shown clear evidence that mortality rates are actually higher in high-spending regions even after adjusting for prices and population characteristics (Fisher et al. 2003a, 2003b), and the quality of care is lower (Baicker and Chandra 2004).

Nevertheless, all high-income countries spend far more on their health care systems than on upstream efforts to improve the health and resilience of their populations. As an old colleague once quipped, "The single redemptive act has always been more popular than the life of virtue." Overall health costs in Canada (about $150 billion in 2006) are toward the high end among Organisation for Economic Co-operation and Development (OECD) countries, at over 10 percent of national income (figure 3).

FIGURE 3.   NATIONAL HEALTH EXPENDITURES AS A PERCENTAGE OF GDP, SELECTED OECD COUNTRIES, 1960-2004

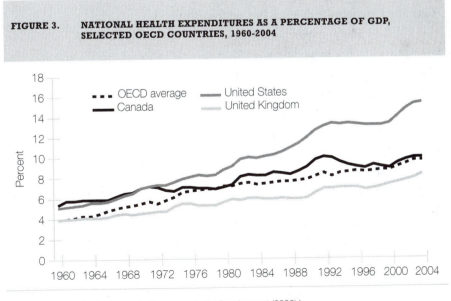

Source: Organisation for Economic Co-operation and Development (2006b).

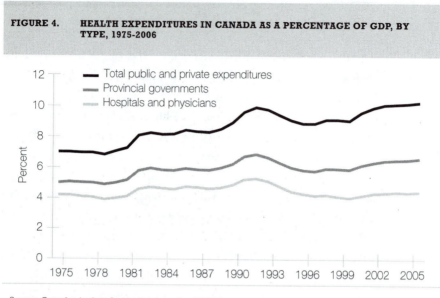

FIGURE 4. HEALTH EXPENDITURES IN CANADA AS A PERCENTAGE OF GDP, BY TYPE, 1975-2006

Source: Canadian Institute for Health Information (2006a).
Note: Data for 2005 and 2006 are forecasts

Frequent political claims of "cost explosions" and the "unsustainability" of Canada's public medicare system (dutifully amplified by the media) are, however, mythical. Spending on hospitals and physicians — the medicare program — takes roughly the same share of national income today as it did 30 years ago (figure 4).

There have also been claims, particularly from certain provincial governments, that rising health care expenditures are "crowding out" other public programs, including education and welfare programs that might in fact have a greater impact on population health. Most of this rhetoric, like claims of "unsustainability," emerges from a data-free (or carefully data-filtered) environment. It is primarily a smokescreen for ideological and interest-based attacks on the public health insurance system itself. The objective is not to contain health spending, but rather to transfer the cost burden from taxpayers to patients or private insurance, from the healthy and wealthy to the unhealthy and unwealthy. Overall health spending may then go where it will — that is, up — so long as public costs fall. Rarely noticed in the debates about public versus private health care financing is that Canada's proportion of private spending is among the highest in the OECD, and its reliance on private insurance is the 14th highest in the world (see figure 5).

Spending on medicare is not taking up an increasing share of provincial revenues (Evans 2005). Rather, several provincial governments have in the last decade made significant cuts to their income tax rates, and then cut expenditures to restore

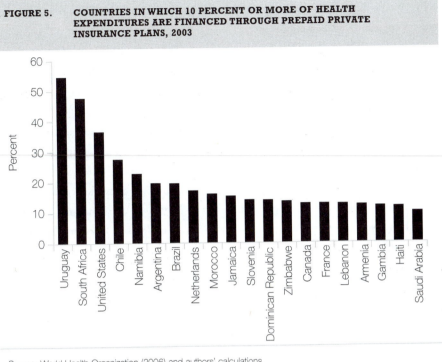

FIGURE 5. **COUNTRIES IN WHICH 10 PERCENT OR MORE OF HEALTH EXPENDITURES ARE FINANCED THROUGH PREPAID PRIVATE INSURANCE PLANS, 2003**

Source: World Health Organization (2006) and authors' calculations.

budget balance. Since cutting health spending is so politically charged, they have chosen to cut other programs more. The mathematical result has been an increase in the share of health in provincial spending (not revenues), but this is a "crowding out" manufactured by deliberate policy and driven by the tax-cut agenda.

All that said, however, 10 percent of national income is still an enormous commitment of resources, and should justify close attention to the efficiency and the effectiveness of the health care system, to assure value for money. In fact, detailed analyses show significant possibilities for increasing efficiency and reducing inappropriate servicing and costs. The opportunity costs of inefficiency are correspondingly high; a 10 percent saving in health care could fund over half the cost of a very broadly based national childhood development program.

Here again, however, we meet the New York board of health. Every dollar spent on health care, in Canada or anywhere else, is a dollar of someone's income. Whether the services provided are highly effective, or totally useless, or even harmful, if money is spent, money is received.[8] There is thus a built-in and very well-resourced constituency supporting every activity in the health care system, ready to challenge or subvert efforts to cut its funding and transfer the resources to other programs, and indeed constantly advocating for more.

The sheer scale of the health care sector and its insatiable appetite for more resources and money means that a great deal of time, effort and political capital must be used up in preventing it from crowding out every other public program and absorbing an ever-growing share of national income. When Aaron Wildavsky (1977) formulated his Law of Medical Money 30 years ago — "costs will increase to the level of available funds [so] that level must be limited to keep costs down" — he was generalizing from a wide range of international experience. There is no other way to contain health care costs, in any country, but to contain total funding. So while health care costs have not in fact been running away with public budgets, they constantly threaten to do so and to lay claim to every spare dollar in those budgets. As Fraser Mustard has remarked, "It is difficult to move forward while you have a hyena gnawing on your foot." All this leads to our second proposal.

POLICY PROPOSAL 2: IMPLEMENT A NATIONAL PHARMACARE PROGRAM TO CONTROL ESCALATING PHARMACEUTICAL COSTS

One component of the cost of Canada's health care system that is apparently escalating out of control is pharmaceuticals. Prescription drugs have long been a cornerstone of modern health care, but (outside hospitals) they have never been covered by Canada's universal, single-payer, federal-provincial medicare system. While Justice Emmett Hall (Royal Commission 1964) identified national pharmacare as an important policy goal, he recommended that it be deferred until such a time as rapidly escalating drug costs should reach a plateau. This was a fatal error, and Canadian policy-makers have been struggling with the anomaly ever since.

What Hall could not have known at the time (Wildavsky's Law drew on more than a decade of subsequent experience) but soon became clear was that there would be no plateau. Health care cost escalation continues until an external constraint is imposed. Universal sole-source funding is the only known mechanism for imposing such a constraint in high-income countries. The rapid growth in drug costs of the 1950s and 1960s accelerated in subsequent decades (figure 6) and continues, precisely because Canada has had no pharmacare plan. Hall's recommendations led Canada into a policy trap: no pharmacare without cost control; no cost control without (universal) national pharmacare. We are still in the trap.

The significance of sole-source funding is clearly reflected in figure 3 on page 301. Prior to 1970, the United States set the pace for cost expansion not only in Canada but in the rest of the OECD. Canada's trend line is virtually identical to that of the United States; the OECD average is lower but rises in parallel. The extension of Canada's medicare program to cover physicians was associated with a shift in public policy priorities from expanding the health sector to overall cost containment. Universal coverage provided the administrative and financing framework to pursue these priorities with considerable effect. In the United States, the enactment of national Medicare only for the elderly and state-based Medicaid for the poor, alongside a system of multiple, competing private insurers (with heavy public subsidies but minimal public control), was associated with continuing escalation. From 1970 on, cost trends in the two countries take markedly different paths, and the divergence is projected to continue. If Canada had continued to follow the American trend, we would have spent about $75 billion more on health care in 2006, or nearly $2,500 extra for every person in the country.

During the 1970s, all other high-income countries developed administrative mechanisms for cost containment, varying according to their specific institutional contexts. The trend for the average of OECD countries drops away from that for the United States and comes to parallel (from above) that for the United Kingdom. All these countries have either explicit single-payer systems, as in the United Kingdom and Sweden, or

FIGURE 6. **PHARMACEUTICAL EXPENDITURES PER CAPITA (INFLATION-ADJUSTED), CANADA, 1933-2005**

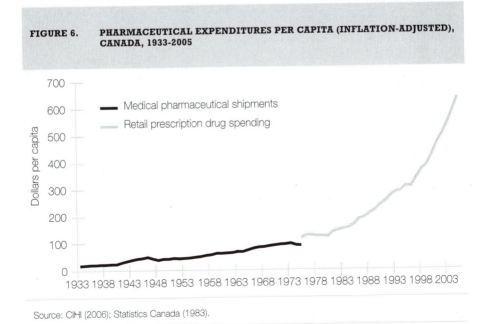

Source: CIHI (2006); Statistics Canada (1983).

multiple nonprofit payers with tight public coordination, as in Germany. The message that stands out so clearly in figure 3 corresponds with identifiable changes in financing patterns to achieve effective single-payer control. Everyone learned from Wildavsky's Law; or perhaps more accurately Wildavsky framed his law by learning from others' experience.

The United States, however, has resolutely rejected many years of calls for universal national health insurance, and instead has tried out a very imaginative array of policies to try to achieve cost containment in a context of multiple, largely independent payers. All have been discredited; figure 3 shows the result.

Of course cost containment is not an end in itself. The real question is the balance of costs and benefits. Do Americans get more for their money? The consistent answer from a growing body of research is "no." No better health, no greater satisfaction, no better quality of care and very much worse overall coverage. Extensive references can be found in Evans (2007a, 2007b), but the most succinct explanation for higher American costs is given by Anderson et al. (2003): "It's the prices, stupid!"

The overall pattern of pharmaceutical funding in Canada is similar to that for hospital and medical care in the United States: a mix of public and private insurance, and private out-of-pocket payment, with private insurance primarily purchased by

FIGURE 7.   HEALTH EXPENDITURES AS A PERCENTAGE OF GDP, BY CATEGORY, CANADA, 1975-2006

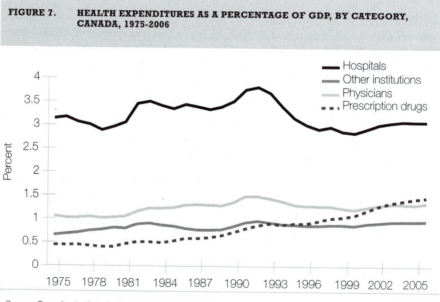

Source: Canadian Institute for Health Information (2006a).
Note: Data for 2005 and 2006 are forecasts.

employers but heavily subsidized through preferential tax treatment. It is thus hardly surprising that the pattern of Canadian pharmaceutical cost escalation parallels the overall American experience: fragmented funding supports uncontrolled cost escalation.

Between 1975 and 2006, per capita private and public expenditure on prescription drugs rose from $128 (in 2006 dollars) to $649, reaching a total of $21.1 billion (Canadian Institute for Health Information 2006). Drugs dramatically outpaced other forms of health spending over this period (figure 7); their share of total health costs rose from 6.3 percent to 14.3 percent. If expenditures on prescription drugs had risen since 1975 only at the same rate as costs in the rest of the health care sector, they would now be about $12.5 billion lower, and total health care costs in Canada would account for about 9.5 percent of national income instead of 10.3 percent.

The Canadian compulsory licensure program in the 1970s and early 1980s did introduce a degree of genuine price competition into the Canadian pharmaceuticals market, which considerably moderated the rate of escalation.[9] But for precisely that reason, heavy pressure from the industry (transmitted in part through the United States government) led to its abandonment. The program was politically vulnerable because the federal government bore no financial responsibility for pharmaceutical costs, and thus had no fiscal stake in defending it.

By the time the National Forum on Health recommended that Canada adopt a national pharmacare program (National Forum on Health 1997), Wildavsky's Law was well understood. The National Forum was explicit about the multiple goals attainable through universal pharmacare coverage, not the least of which was cost control. A single purchaser for pharmaceuticals can use a number of policy tools that are not available in a multi-payer system. Moreover, the payer in a single-payer system typically has a much greater incentive to manage expenditures than do those in a multipayer system — costs cannot be passed on to someone else.

The National Forum's proposal died quite rapidly in the face of intense hostility from the pharmaceutical industry — a hostility that reflected its clear understanding of the dynamics of single-payer financing. A naive economist might imagine that an industry would welcome a proposal for government to pay for its products, on behalf of users. But those in the pharmaceutical industry are not naive; they recognize, quite correctly, that a single government payer has countervailing power to balance the vast market power of the industry. Throughout the health care industry, negotiated prices are lower prices, and lower prices mean lower profits. Expenditures equal incomes — any form of cost containment means lower industry profits.

Uncontrolled cost escalation is not the only major problem with the present pattern of pharmaceutical reimbursement. It is inequitable in terms of both access to drugs and the distribution of financial burden. It is also inefficient in that it offers very few incentives to provide value for money, and thus generates a very high level of "cost without benefit." These weaknesses are also traceable to the fragmented funding system, and have their parallels in the equally fragmented American system of funding for health care more generally.

Inequity of access arises insofar as people without public or private coverage may be deterred from receiving necessary medicines because of out-of-pocket costs. Even those with coverage may face "deterrent" charges that deter both necessary and discretionary use of medicines; these impediments bear more heavily on those with lower incomes (Soumerai et al. 1990; Adams, Soumerai, and Ross-Degnan 2001; Tamblyn et al. 2001). Private, employer-based coverage is correlated with income; access to private insurance is least available to those with the lowest incomes and the greatest health needs.[10]

Inequity of financial burden is an inevitable consequence of out-of-pocket payment; this form of funding operates as a "tax on the sick." The sick pay and the healthy do not, and the amount the sick pay is related to their use but not their incomes. On average, then, the burden of user fees falls as income rises. A tax-financed system, by contrast, requires greater contributions from those with greater resources, regardless of their health status. Private insurance, for those who have access to it, does tend to equalize the financial burden between the healthy and the sick. But like out-of-pocket payments, and unlike taxation, private premiums are unrelated to income. Thus they take a larger share of the income of people with lower incomes. This is quite obvious a priori, but if empirical confirmation were needed, research has provided it.

The "cost without benefit" arises from two different sources. First, as is well documented (see, for example, Woolhandler and Himmelstein 1991; Woolhandler, Campbell, and Himmelstein 2003), the overhead costs of private health insurance systems are far greater than those of public systems. A much higher proportion of system revenue is absorbed in managing the payment process. But the second and larger generator of cost without benefit is payment for an ever-growing array of new drugs, most of which provide no evidence of superior therapeutic effect. More than 90 percent of new drugs introduced in Canada are either higher-priced replacements for drugs whose patent life is expiring, or simply "me too" drugs developed to share the market for a successful patented drug.[11] These absorb a high proportion of research effort, and an even larger share of drug costs is devoted to marketing them (Morgan, Bassett, et al. 2005).

This makes perfect sense from a corporate perspective; better to spend on competing for a share of an established market than to take a risk on some new and untried therapeutic agent. But for patients, and the Canadian public generally, the benefit of this activity approaches zero.[12]

Steady inflation of drug costs is not a law of nature. There are examples of countries that have developed sophisticated and successful national purchasing programs. But it does require a single entity to coordinate all purchases.

The case of New Zealand is particularly compelling because, beginning in 1994, with Wildavsky's Law in mind, that country centralized the management of drug purchases. New Zealand's approach was to "get a budget" — to create a national purchasing management agency (PHARMAC) tasked with keeping spending within budget targets (Brougham, Metcalfe, and McNee 2002).[13] PHARMAC has the mandate to provide New Zealanders with universal access to all medically necessary drugs; it covers about 80 percent of all pharmaceutical expenditures in the country. The results, and the stark contrast with Canada, are dramatic, even spectacular (figure 8).

PHARMAC's expenditure per capita grew at a rate of 0.15 percent per year (unadjusted for inflation) from 1996 to 2006. In contrast, public drug expenditure per capita in Canada grew 10.1 percent per year over that period. Had Canada's public drug costs grown at the same rate as PHARMAC's, public drug spending in 2006 would have

FIGURE 8. PUBLIC EXPENDITURES ON PRESCRIPTION DRUGS PER CAPITA, CANADA AND NEW ZEALAND, 1996–2006

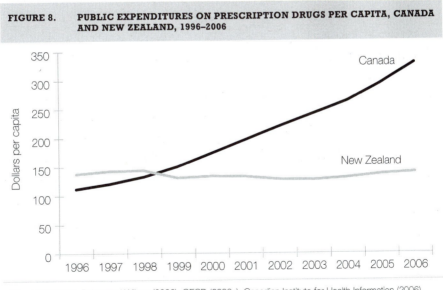

Sources: Morgan, Balma and Wilcox (2006); OECD (2006a); Canadian Institute for Health Information (2006). Figures for 2006 extrapolated based on five-year average annual growth rate.
Note: PHARMAC covers 80 percent of drug spending in New Zealand, whereas public plans cover about 50 percent of costs in Canada

been $114 per Canadian rather than the estimated $340. The implied savings to Canada's public sector would be approximately $5.9 billion per year. But PHARMAC covers 80 percent of all New Zealand drug costs, while Canadian public drug plans cover less than 50 percent of prescription costs. If total prescription drug costs in Canada had escalated only at the PHARMAC rate since 1996, the Canadian drug bill in 2006 would have been approximately $250 per capita instead of the estimated $648. Thus, a pharmaceutical purchasing agency — modelled on PHARMAC and covering the bulk of drug costs for the whole population — could by now be saving approximately $13 billion per year for Canadian governments, patients and employers. The stakes are not small. These savings alone could fund the expansion in ECD programs described above.

PHARMAC's multibillion-dollar secret? "It's the prices, stupid!" Control over national purchasing has enabled it to negotiate very significant price rebates from manufacturers, by steering purchases to the low bidders (often the leading brand-name manufacturers) and effectively forcing price competition. Large American buyers — state governments, private drug insurance plans and health maintenance organizations — have done the same, though typically a condition of the rebates is that they shall not be disclosed publicly.[14] The competitive market works, but in the pharmaceutical sector it must be created and protected by public initiative. And governments will not take on the political costs of confronting the pharmaceutical industry unless they are on the hook for all or most of the costs — single-payer.

The road to national pharmacare

As part of the 2004 Ten-Year Plan to Strengthen Health Care, Canada's first ministers agreed to develop a National Pharmaceuticals Strategy (NPS) (Health Canada 2004, 7). The first ministers provided an overarching principle that "no Canadian should suffer undue financial hardship in accessing needed drug therapies, and that affordable access to drugs is fundamental to equitable health outcomes for all our citizens." Decisions about what the NPS would actually become and what it would do to address priority issues were left to a ministerial task force made up of ministers of health from federal, provincial and territorial governments (except Quebec, which is not participating). In the 2006 progress report, the task force identified five priority areas for short- or medium-term focus:

/ Catastrophic drug coverage
/ Expensive drugs for rare diseases
/ Common national formulary
/ Pricing and purchasing strategies
/ Real-world drug safety and effectiveness

There appears little doubt that Canada will address regional disparities in drug coverage through the creation of a national standard for pharmacare programs. Income-based pharmacare has been proposed as the national standard (Federal/Provincial/Territorial Ministerial Task Force on the National Pharmaceuticals Strategy 2006). Experience in British Columbia suggests that income-based coverage has some benefits, but also significant limitations. More to the point, focusing on the "catastrophic" portion of drug coverage policy to the exclusion of the other goals of pharmacare policy will, in the long run, render national reform a costly failure. Justice Hall might have been excused for not knowing better, but we do not have that excuse today: "Costs will increase to the level of available funds [so] that level must be limited to keep costs down."

It is important to recognize that limiting only the public expenditures on pharmaceuticals — which income-based pharmacare is designed to do — does not save money for Canadians; it costs us money, and a great deal of it. Income-based pharmacare provides no mechanisms for cost containment. Continuing cost escalation will inevitably push provinces toward the easy option of increasing deductibles and co-payments. New Zealand's success rests on two pillars: universal coverage *and* a fixed budget from which to negotiate drug purchases. A similar strategy for Canada cannot be created overnight; it will have to proceed incrementally. But the incremental steps must generate momentum toward the ultimate objectives of universality and budget management. The dynamics of partial, catastrophic coverage lead in the opposite direction.

We therefore propose to retain comprehensive pharmacare for seniors and social assistance recipients. For the whole population, we would add full first-dollar coverage for drugs to treat specific health conditions: for example, diabetes, asthma, cardiovascular diseases and depression. A national, publicly accountable agency would manage benefits under the program to meet strict budget targets. This coverage would be within a framework that explicitly identifies and pays for only evidence-based and cost-effective treatment.[15] Manufacturers would have to compete on price (or rebates) to have their drugs covered. At current retail price levels, we estimate that a program covering five leading drug classes would cost about $10 billion nationwide (Morgan, McMahon, et al. 2005).

The initial diseases chosen would affect a large proportion of the population and demonstrate clear health system benefits from pharmaceutical management. Over time, savings similar to those achieved in New Zealand would permit expansion to other classes of drugs. The cost of the program should be borne evenly by federal and provincial governments, with patient co-payments (if desired) limited to the pharmacist's dispensing fee. We would also propose a separate federal fund — at $2 billion for 2008 — to cover the costs of costly drug treatment for very rare conditions. This budget would also be managed according to the benefit and cost of adding drugs to the list of treatments covered or removing them.

Unfortunately fiscal priorities in the 1990s and today have not permitted a meaningful policy debate on a comprehensive, national pharmacare program. Although such a program could significantly lower the overall cost, public and private, of pharmaceuticals in Canada, it would require the transfer of billions of dollars from private to public expenditure. Opponents of a national plan have been successful in keeping public attention focused on this fact, and obscuring the corresponding very large potential savings in total costs that could be achieved through this transfer.

Over the longer term, public expenditures on prescription drugs are likely to be much larger as a result of failure to adopt a national drug purchasing policy. Efforts by provincial governments to shift part of this escalating burden back onto patients or private insurers have had precisely the same effect as similar efforts in the United States. The dynamics are quite simple.

In reducing their share of the total expenditure, governments also divest themselves of the policy tools and leverage needed to rationalize the system. Rapid cost escalation continues, such that the smaller public share of a larger total quickly becomes a larger budgetary item for governments than before the shift. Limiting government's commitment then requires shifting an ever larger share of costs to private payers, with attendant threats to health and equity. At the same time, rising total costs make ever more costly the process of rationalization through universal public coverage and prudent purchasing.

International trade agreements pose a further threat. Any national strategy that builds in a role for the private insurance industry, bringing with it both high levels of administrative overhead and the inability to exert any effective control over cost escalation, may be irreversible under those agreements. Canadian patients, governments and corporate benefits departments may then be facing a permanent and steadily growing siphoning of wealth into the hands of multinational corporations that have successfully manipulated the domestic and international political process to their benefit, but not ours. Welcome to the real world.

THE COST OF A LAISSEZ-FAIRE APPROACH TO CLINICAL PRACTICE

Although pharmaceutical costs are rising much more rapidly than those in the rest of the health care system, hospitals and doctors still absorb half of all health care spending and two-thirds of public spending. Furthermore, the public debate is dominated by allegations and concerns about those sectors — waiting times, an alleged doctor shortage, inadequate public surgical capacity or inpatient beds — and the endless repetition of proposals for more private delivery and private payment.

While many of these claims are overblown or specious, a more explicitly evidence-based approach to clinical decision-making within the public system could considerably advance the health and well-being of Canadians. Our third proposal therefore addresses systemic problems that have been part of medicare since its inception. These problems may now be undermining the fundamental principles of that system in ways that could threaten Canadians' health and would certainly threaten their well-being.

Two strategic ideas — federal cost-sharing and the concept of "medical necessity" — are fundamental to medicare. But the concept of medical necessity has never been given explicit content, never translated into a guide for clinical decision-making or a tool for system management. It is explicit in the language of the *Canada Health Act* — all medically necessary services are to be free — but only implicit in the actual program.[16] In effect, any diagnostic or therapeutic intervention offered by a qualified physician and accepted by an insured patient is from the federal perspective assumed to be medically necessary. Provinces may limit the range of reimbursable interventions in minor ways — how far has never been tested — but the federal government has taken little interest in this.[17] In effect, medicare simply infers medical necessity from observed clinical practice, rather than using evidence of health outcomes to guide practice.

Individual physicians have thus preserved almost complete autonomy in deciding which interventions to recommend to which patients, subject only to their own collective self-government processes and the availability of associated public facilities and equipment. The implicit, and often explicit, conflict between physicians' right to determine medical necessity on a case-by-case basis and provincial governments' authority to set limits on total system cost is one of the twin roots of the claims of public "underfunding" that have marked the history of medicare. (The other root is the conflict between the income aspirations of physicians and other providers, and the constraints imposed by public financing.)

The national pharmaceuticals strategy we have proposed, by contrast, would include the principle that when two different drugs are available with equivalent effect but different prices, the higher-priced drug is not medically necessary, even if it is recommended by a duly qualified physician. A pharmaceutical intervention is implicitly presumed to be medically necessary, but the higher-priced drug is not, and the prescription will be reimbursed only at the lower price. This principle has long been accepted when chemically equivalent generic versions of patented drugs are available; the controversy emerges over the therapeutic equivalence of chemically different drugs.

The consequences of this laissez-faire approach to clinical practice emerge elsewhere in the system in the form of wide variations in patterns of care, across countries, large and small regions, and hospitals and individual clinicians, and over time — variations that cannot be linked to differences in patient needs or outcomes but have major significance for resource requirements and costs. There is now a very large research literature on practice variations from many countries and extending back over decades; for example, Vayda (1973), McPherson et al. (1982), Roos et al. (1986), Wennberg (1988) and, of particular importance, the studies by Fisher et al. (2003a, 2003b).

The significance of all these findings for Canada can be illustrated from the *Canadian Cardiovascular Atlas* (Tu et al. 2006), an extensive collection of papers by the Canadian Cardiovascular Outcomes Research Team.

Hall and Tu (2003) document very large regional variations across Canada in cardiovascular hospitalization rates for acute myocardial infarct, congestive heart failure, angina and chest pain. These range from 508.4 per 100,000 people in Vancouver to 1,929.6 in one specific region of New Brunswick. Rates were markedly lower in metropolitan areas, but there was also a pronounced east-west gradient; Winnipeg's rates were 30 percent higher than Vancouver's, while Toronto's, Ottawa's and Montreal's were 45 to 55 percent higher and rates in Halifax were 75 percent higher. The average rate for Canada as a whole was 93 percent above that for Vancouver. If Vancouver patterns of cardiac care could be replicated across Canada, hospital caseloads for these four conditions could be cut nearly in half. Inpatient bed use could fall by more than half, because average lengths of stay are also significantly lower in British Columbia. No one has offered evidence that these variations correspond to differences in patient needs or outcomes.

This is where the studies by Fisher and colleagues (2003a, 2003b) become so important. Thirty years of observation of clinical practice variations have had no observable impact on clinical practice. The typical response by clinicians (if they gave any) was, in effect: "Who knows which rates are right? Perhaps they all are, being based on patient differences not captured in available data, but known to individual clinicians." "Business as usual" gets the benefit of any possible doubt. But Fisher and colleagues, studying hundreds of thousands of American Medicare patients, carefully standardized for differences in health status and showed not only very large variations across regions in patterns of care and cost, but systematically worse outcomes —

higher mortality rates — in high-cost and high-intervention regions. High rates of intervention and expenditure are a threat to health as well as to wealth.

Although the regional variations in hospital use reported by Hall and Tu (2003) are variations around a stable or declining average rate, studies of cardiac care and costs in Ontario show similar wide and unexplained regional variations around rapidly escalating overall rates (see Alter, Przybysz, and Iron 2004). Total provincial expenditures for a set of six cardiac services rose from $206.9 million to $390.8 million between 1992 and 2001 (Alter, Stukel, and Newman 2006), an average increase of 7.3 percent per year. This is well above increases in cardiac disease prevalence or shifts in demographic structure and, the authors suggest, is "likely attributable to continued proliferation in cardiac technology and specialty physician supply, as well as to changes in physician referral behaviours" (383).

Particularly worrying for the longer term is that despite these increases, the capacity for and use of these procedures in the United States remain far above Ontario levels. There is thus the potential for considerable further seepage into Canada, more or less indefinitely, of the American disease of "cost without benefit" (except to providers). And this problem is not confined to cardiac care; the proliferation of magnetic resonance imaging, for example, not only has been costly but is the thin edge of the wedge for both private provision and private payment.

POLICY PROPOSAL 3: DEVELOP A STANDARDIZED ELECTRONIC MEDICAL RECORD TO IMPROVE THE COST-EFFECTIVENESS OF CLINICAL DECISION-MAKING

If you can't measure something, you can't understand it. If you can't understand it, you can't control it. If you can't control it, you can't improve it.
(Harrington and McNellis 2006)

So why has the evidence of large and unexplained clinical practice variations, accumulating over decades, had so little impact? Changes over time may be linked to the powerful financial incentives embodied in fee-for-service payment, backed up by the formidable and sophisticated marketing pressures from for-profit drug and equipment manufacturers. But these cannot explain regional variations; all physicians are exposed to these incentives. Varying degrees of capacity constraint across regions are also part of the story, but there is a more fundamental problem.

Physicians make decisions for individual patients, not for statistical averages, and in real time, not after the data have been collected. All of them believe that what they are doing is most likely right for *this* patient, under *these* circumstances. Their individual practices may differ — they do — but they typically have limited awareness of what their colleagues are doing, let alone what is going on in other regions or provinces. In any case such information is irrelevant — "*My* patients are different."

A firm belief in the fundamental value of physician autonomy supports an implicit view that whatever is done is right, regardless of how it compares with what is done by others. Clinical variations data have little meaning in this environment, whatever their implications for costs or patient outcomes at a system level. The result is that Canadians continue to pay more and more money for more and more services, while knowing little about what we are buying and less about why.

Patterns of care are very far from random; the economist's fantasy of individuals choosing to use ever more health care because it is free is just that, pure fantasy. Most of the care in our system, or in any other, is provided to sick people, often very sick people. It goes to the right people, but is it the right care? The clinical variations suggest strongly that frequently it is not. Yet our system lacks any information base sufficient to support the translation of these observations into changes in clinical practice. The development of a nationwide electronic medical record (EMR) would provide the information base from which medical necessity, or perhaps better evidence of health outcome, could drive clinical practice.

Is the Canadian information base uniquely inadequate? Ten years ago, no. Twenty years ago our databases — built up from physician billings per item of service according to standard fee schedules and hospital discharge abstracts containing diagnostic and procedural data — provided physician- and patient-specific data (after the fact) that was perhaps the best in the world. But there has been little progress since, and indeed some regress. Physicians are increasingly being reimbursed through programs not based on items of service, leaving no central record of the activities or procedures performed.

Other countries have now caught up and passed us. Schoen et al. (2006) report the results of a 2006 survey of primary care physicians in seven countries: Australia, Canada, Germany, the Netherlands, New Zealand, the United Kingdom and the United States. That survey "reveals striking differences in elements of practice systems that underpin quality and efficiency. Wide gaps exist between leading and lagging countries in clinical information systems and payment incentives" (555). The study goes on to say that "use rates in Canadian and US primary care practices are low — and well below those of the leading countries — for EMRs and for electronic prescribing and retrieval of test results" (558). It concludes: "Overall, findings highlight the importance of nationwide policies" (555). The laggards, Canada and the United States, have no nationwide policies.

Schoen et al. emphasize the importance of electronic medical records for improving the quality and effectiveness of physicians' practices, as monitoring and "decision support" tools for practitioners themselves. But they can also be powerful mechanisms for steering and managing clinical practice when they are used, most notably in the United Kingdom, as a basis for quite significant payment incentives for physicians.

The current slogan for the United Kingdom National Health Service is "an outcome-led service," drawing on many years of heavy investment in information technology to permit the linkage, system-wide, of clinical activities to health outcomes. But reform also builds on the principle of "a primary-care-led service." The large, capitated primary care trusts — which represent the current stage of evolution from capitated and then budget-holding general practitioners — are to be the institutional mechanism for aligning general and specialty practice with the vastly expanded evidence of outcomes emerging from electronic records.[18]

There is rapidly growing interest in the EMR in the United States — indeed, the March-April 2007 issue of the influential journal *Health Affairs* is entirely devoted to the subject. The principal focus is on the potential of the EMR for system-wide "rapid learning" through the on-line assembly and assessment of a vast array of clinical experience, and consequent significant improvement in health outcomes. Most contributors, however, are doubtful of significant cost savings from the EMR. By Wildavsky's Law, any savings from reduction of ineffective care will be absorbed in increases elsewhere (thus preserving incomes).

But to be useful, the EMR must be used, and so far uptake by clinicians has been limited and selective. "Pay for performance" (P4P) is also much discussed in the United States; this might motivate clinicians more strongly. As Aneurin Bevan said, "To send a message to doctors, write it on a cheque." That is a key component of the current United Kingdom approach.

It can be done in North America — the United States Department of Veterans' Affairs has revolutionized its hospitals and medical clinics through the introduction of a uniform electronic record that links clinicians, laboratory testing, diagnostic imaging and pharmaceutical prescribing and dispensing. The results have been dramatic improvements in the quality of care, lower rates of utilization and costs, and much greater patient and practitioner satisfaction. The leading American health maintenance organizations, such as Kaiser-Permanente and Seattle Group Health, have a long record of using advanced information technology to improve patient outcomes and satisfaction and pare down ineffective clinical activity.

But these are only a few bright lights in what Schoen et al. report to be a pretty dark world. Most important, in both the United Kingdom and the American examples, primary care physicians are organized into groups and reimbursed by capitation, not fees for items of service. Budgets place clinicians at collective financial risk for the costs of the care — drugs, specialty referrals — they order. Fee for service rewards doing, not thinking.

The effective use of information from the EMR in Canada will depend on major changes, particularly in primary care. Bonus fees for particular interventions with good evidentiary support might go some distance, but very little. As well expressed in the dedicated issue of *Health Affairs* noted above, the EMR is a vehicle, not a destination. To realize its potential will require agreement on a destination, and a driver (and fuel!).

On the other hand, the information that would emerge from a comprehensive, system-wide EMR could considerably reinforce other pressures for primary care reform. Patterns of interventions and associated outcomes could be observed in real time at the individual patient level, making very clear the diversity of interventions and the often tenuous linkage to evidence of effectiveness.

Change will require a national initiative and considerable amounts of money. The current Canada Health Infoway project — a federal-provincial EMR initiative — may cost $10 billion over a decade.[19] But this — less than 1 percent of current public outlays on health care — takes no account of the costs of changing the organization and reimbursement of clinicians to take advantage of the new information base. This will be a major task, and the federal government will have to offer significant leadership, perhaps on a province-by-province basis, not just sit back and send money.

CONCLUSION

Federal cost-sharing has always been the bedrock of national medicare, because the *British North America Act* (1867) placed health care firmly within provincial jurisdiction. Any national policy for health requires provincial cooperation, and that requires money. But the present dog's breakfast of pharmaceutical reimbursement shows what happens in the absence of a strong federal initiative. Medicare came into existence through federal cost-sharing and standards and began to unravel when cost-sharing was replaced by the Established Programs Financing legislation. The *Canada Health Act* (1984) reintroduced a backdoor form of cost-sharing by linking the federal cash transfers to provincial compliance with national standards.

In short, any national policy for health care requires federal cash and federal strings. Provincial governments prefer cash without strings, but that translates into no national policy. Trickling out relatively small amounts of federal money to buy short-term peace is a recipe for continuing drift.

Drift may not be fatal — medicare is not fiscally unsustainable nor on the verge of collapse.[20] It continues to do a remarkable job — ask patients, not the media! But the evidence of wide variations in clinical practice and a steady growth in increasingly expensive diagnostic interventions, both without any evidence of improved outcomes, represent significant opportunities for improving "value for money." We could do better; other countries seem to have figured this out. The bronze medal syndrome again?

And while the economic consequences of "business as usual" — for better or for worse, it is an option — are not catastrophic, the political consensus may not hold under the present sustained attack. The powerful propaganda on behalf of private delivery, private payment and private insurance — now encouraged by the courts — could lead to real and perhaps irreversible damage. "Little America" lies down that road, with major increases in "cost without benefit," which will be felt not only by those at the bottom of the social scale, but across the broad middle ranges as well. The benefits will be concentrated at the upper end, where the gains from lower taxation far outweigh the costs of private payment for health care.[21] But the net impact will be a substantial increase in the overhead burden of wasteful and useless activity, exactly where current pharmaceutical policy is taking us.

This chapter is orders of magnitude short of the scope and resources necessary to detail a national project to bring the information base for Canada's medicare system into the twenty-first century. What we hope to have made clear, however, is that our system has drifted from being a leader to being (along with the United States) a rather distant laggard internationally in the application of information technology in the management of clinical practice.

This is costing us. One cannot say a priori that a more evidence-based system would necessarily be less costly. Many commentators are skeptical. But there seems to be widespread agreement that better health outcomes can be had from the considerable sweat and treasure now absorbed in our health care system. That would be no small achievement.

NOTES

1   Some point to the correlation of unhealthy behaviour with lower education. But it is difficult to believe that anyone in the known world has not heard that smoking causes cancer.

2   Under normal circumstances, a given stretch of DNA will be translated into the formation of an enzyme that, in turn, will do cellular work. Methylation alters the active portion of the DNA (the nitrogenous base portion), interrupting the translation of the affected stretch to enzyme. This is currently the best studied of the pathways from early experience to gene expression, but the whole field is under very active investigation.

3   Brownell, Roos, and Fransoo (2006) found that as early as Grade 3, 15 percent of children in the poorest neighbourhoods in Winnipeg were no longer regularly attending a school and thus did not write the standardized educational tests. Researchers in BC have found similar non-attendance and "DNW" rates in Grade 4 in that province.

4   It might be argued that the Canadian economy is thriving, and unemployment is at historic lows. But it is also true that the income gap is widening steadily, and productivity growth is lagging. Improved well-being requires a more productive workforce, not more low-skill workers.

5   Using the OECD criteria for defining such spending.

6   The classic economic analysis is Hirschman (1970).

7   This asymmetry of concern may be a consequence of the very powerful bias in the public news media, featuring almost exclusively stories (usually negative) about the health care system (Hayes et al. 2007),

8   This accounting identity is sometimes confused with the observation that payments to personnel account for a relatively large proportion of health budgets. But all other payments also emerge, through different channels, as someone's income.

9   Under Canada's compulsory licensing program for drug patents, generic drug manufacturers could obtain a licence to sell copies of a patented drug subject to payment of a royalty to the patent holder, fixed by the commissioner of patents. Patent holders could not block the licence.

10   It is estimated that between 10 and 20 percent of Canadians are either uninsured or underinsured for pharmaceutical expenses (Applied Management, Fraser Group, and Tristat Resources 2000a, 2000b; Coombes et al. 2004). But one should not be lured into the trap of imagining that a low-budget, quasi-universal program could be created by cobbling together present public and private plans with a separate plan for the currently uninsured. As the analysis above emphasizes, and Quebec's experience confirms, this is a myopic approach that would yield the long-term pain of continuing uncontrollable cost escalation and associated pressures to shift costs to patients. User charges are universally recognized as the most inequitable way to finance health care.

11   Our naive economist might imagine that "me too" drugs would compete on the basis of price; but again, pharmaceutical firms are not naive. Barriers to development even of "me too" drugs are high, restricting entry, and sellers of these drugs, like sane oligopolists, compete on marketing expenses, not price.

12   This observation is neither idiosyncratic nor new; see, for example, Commission of Inquiry (1985).

13   The details of the New Zealand approach, which includes a variety of forms of direct negotiation between PHARMAC and phar-

maceutical firms, are described elsewhere (Braae, McNee, and Moore 1999; Davis 2004).

14 Available data, however, suggest that such negotiated purchases may secure discounts of at least 50 percent from average wholesale prices (von Oehsen 2001).

15 Patients would, of course, be free to purchase drugs outside the program at their own expense.

16 The obvious implication is that interventions by non-physicians, or prescription drugs, are not medically necessary — an unfortunate anomaly.

17 Certain elective cosmetic procedures are excluded from coverage by common agreement.

18 Capitated practices are reimbursed according to the number and characteristics of the patients for whose care they are responsible (payment per head or "capita"), not according to the numbers and types of services or procedures they provide. Historically, British general practitioners were paid this way for their own activities while specialty services were provided (on referral) by salaried hospital staff. Beginning at the end of the 1980s, "budget-holding" general practitioners were paid substantially larger capitation amounts, from which they paid for certain specialty and hospital services (and drugs). Primary care trusts are large groups of general practitioners and other staff, receiving still larger capitation payments, and financially responsible for all the costs of reimbursable care, by whomsoever provided, of patients in a defined geographic area.

19 The consultants' report prepared for Canada Health Infoway in March of 2005 (Booz Allen Hamilton 2005) estimated an "acquisition cost" for a "Pan-Canadian EHR" at $9.99 billion over 10 years, with a total "ownership cost," including recurrent costs, of $22.7 billion. Total cost savings, however, were projected at more than $60 billion over 20 years, for a net savings of about $40 billion and a return on investment of 8:1. It is important to note, however, that three-quarters of the estimated cost savings were from reduced adverse drug events, with further but much smaller gains from reduced duplicative laboratory testing and diagnostic imaging. No account was taken of the large potential for reductions in clinical variations and improved effectiveness of clinical practice emphasized in this paper. This is unfortunate, but may be realistic. The potential savings appear very large, but every dollar of these savings would represent a corresponding reduction in someone's income as well as a degree of threat to individual clinical autonomy. Hence the skepticism, even cynicism, about savings expressed by some EHR commentators. Still, reduced drug reactions represent a significant improvement in patients' health as well as costs.

20 Continuous tax-cutting could of course make it or any other public program "unsustainable."

21 At first. In the United States, however, mixed funding and uncontrollable costs have led to both high taxes *and* high private costs. As a result, access and quality of care are much more steeply graded by income level than in other high-income countries.

REFERENCES

Adams, A.S., S.B. Soumerai, and D. Ross-Degnan. 2001. "The Case for a Medicare Drug Coverage Benefit: A Critical Review of the Empirical Evidence." *Annual Review of Public Health* 22:49-61.

Alter, D.A., R. Przybysz, and K. Iron. 2004. "Non-Invasive Cardiac Testing in Ontario." ICES Investigative Report, October. Toronto: Institute for Clinical Evaluative Sciences.

Alter, D.A., T.A. Stukel, and A. Newman. 2006. "Proliferation of Cardiac Technology in Canada: A Challenge to the Sustainability of Medicare." *Circulation* 113 (3): 380-7.

Anderson, G.F., U.E. Reinhardt, P.S. Hussey, and V. Petrosyan. 2003. "It's the Prices, Stupid: Why the United States Is So Different from Other Countries." *Health Affairs* 23 (3): 89-105.

Applied Management, with Fraser Group and Tristat Resources. 2000a. *Canadians' Access to Insurance for Prescription Medicines.* Ottawa: Health Canada, Health Transition Fund.

_____. 2000b. *Canadians' Access to Insurance for Prescription Medicines: Volume 2.* Ottawa: Health Canada, Health Transition Fund.

Baicker, K., and A. Chandra. 2004. "Medicare Spending, the Physician Workforce, and Beneficiaries' Quality of Care." *Health Affairs* W4:184-97.

Booz Allen Hamilton. 2005. "Pan-Canadian Electronic Health Record: Executive Summary." Report prepared for Canada Health Infoway. McLean, VA: Booz Allen Hamilton.

Braae, R., W. McNee, and D. Moore. 1999. "Managing Pharmaceutical Expenditure while Increasing Access: The Pharmaceutical Management Agency (PHARMAC) Experience." *PharmacoEconomics* 16 (6): 649-60.

Bremberg, S. 2006. "Swedish Policies for Pre-school Children." Karolinska Institute, Stockholm. Accessed October 10, 2007. www.excellence-jeunesenfants.ca/documents/BrembergANG.pdf

Brougham M., S. Metcalfe, and W. McNee. 2002. "Our Advice? Get a Budget!" *Healthcare Papers* 3 (1): 83-5.

Brownell, M., N.P. Roos, and R. Fransoo. 2006. "Is the Class Half Empty? A Population-Based Perspective on Socioeconomic Status and Educational Outcomes." *IRPP Choices* 12 (5).

Canadian Institute for Health Information (CIHI). 2006. *National Health Expenditure Trends 1975-2006.* Ottawa: CIHI.

Commission of Inquiry on the Pharmaceutical Industry. 1985. *Report of the Commission of Inquiry on the Pharmaceutical Industry.* Ottawa: Supply and Services Canada.

Coombes, M.E., S.G. Morgan, M.L. Barer, and N. Pagliccia. 2004. "Who's the Fairest of Them All? Which Provincial Pharmacare Model Would Best Protect Canadians against Catastrophic Drug Costs?" *Longwoods Review* 2 (3): 13-26.

Davis, P. 2004. "'Tough but Fair'? The Active Management of the New Zealand Drug Benefits Scheme by an Independent Crown Agency." *Australian Health Review* 28 (2): 171-81.

Duffy, J. 1974. *A History of Public Health in New York City, 1866-1966.* New York: Russell Sage Foundation.

Evans, R.G. 2002. *Interpreting and Addressing Inequalities in Health: From Black to Acheson to Blair to...?* London: Office of Health Economics.

_____. 2005. "Political Wolves and Economic Sheep: The Sustainability of Public Health Insurance in Canada." In *The Public-Private Mix for Health,* edited by A. Maynard. Abingdon, UK: Radcliffe Publishing for the Nuffield Trust.

_____. 2007a. "Devil Take the Hindmost? Private Health Insurance and the Rising Costs of American 'Exceptionalism'." In *Health Politics and Policy,* 4th ed., edited by J. Morone, L. Robins, and T. Litman. New York: Delmar Publishers. In press.

_____. 2007b. "Extravagant Americans, Healthier Canadians: The Bottom Line in North American Health Care." In *Canada*

and the United States: Differences That Count, 3rd ed., edited by D.M. Thomas. Peterborough, ON: Broadview Press. In press.

Evans, R.G., M.L. Barer, and T.R. Marmor, eds. 1994. *Why Are Some People Healthy and Others Not?* Hawthorne, NY: Aldine De Gruyter.

Federal/Provincial/Territorial Ministerial Task Force on the National Pharmaceuticals Strategy. 2006. *National Pharmaceuticals Strategy Progress Report*. Ottawa: Health Canada.

Fisher, E.S., D.E. Wennberg, T.A. Stukel, D.J. Gottlieb, F.L. Lucas, and E.L. Pinder. 2003a. "The Implications of Regional Variations in Medicare Spending, Part I: The Content, Quality, and Accessibility of Care." *Annals of Internal Medicine* 138 (4): 273-87.

———. 2003b. "The Implications of Regional Variations in Medicare Spending, Part 2: Health Outcomes and Satisfaction with Care." *Annals of Internal Medicine* 138 (4): 288-98.

Hall, R.E., and J.V. Tu. 2003. "Hospitalization Rates and Length of Stay for Cardiovascular Conditions in Canada, 1994 to 1999." *Canadian Journal of Cardiology* 19 (10): 1123-31.

Harrington, H.J., and T. McNellis. 2006. "Mobilizing the Right Lean Metrics for Success." *Quality Digest* 26 (11).

Hayes, M., I.E. Ross, M. Gasher, D. Gutstein, J.R. Dunn, and R.A. Hackett. 2007. "Telling Stories: News Media Health Literacy and Public Policy in Canada." *Social Science & Medicine* 64 (9): 1842-52.

Health Canada. 2004. "A 10-Year Plan to Strengthen Health Care." Ottawa: Health Canada. Accessed September 5, 2007. www.hc-sc.gc.ca/hcs-sss/delivery-prestation/fptcollab/2004-fmm-rpm/index_e.html

Heymann, J., C. Hertzman, M. Barer, and R.G. Evans, eds. 2006. *Healthier Societies: From Analysis to Action*. New York: Oxford University Press.

Hirschman, A.O. 1970. *Exit, Voice, and Loyalty: Responses to Decline in Firms, Organizations, and States*. New York: Basic Books.

Keating, D.P., and C. Hertzman, eds. 1999. *Developmental Health and the Wealth of Nations*. New York: Guildford Press.

Lefebvre, P. 2004. "Quebec's Innovative Early Childhood Education and Care Policy and Its Weaknesses." *Policy Options* 25 (3): 52-7. Montreal: IRPP.

Marmot, M.G., G. Rose, M.J. Shipley, and P.J.S. Hamilton. 1978. "Employment Grade and Coronary Heart Disease in British Civil Servants." *Journal of Epidemiology and Community Health* 32 (4): 244-9.

McCain, M.N., and J.F. Mustard. 1999. *Early Years Study – Final Report*. Toronto: Children's Secretariat.

McNee, W. 2006. "Toward a National Pharmaceuticals Strategy." 18th Annual Health Policy Conference, UBC Centre for Health Services and Policy Research. Vancouver, Canada. Accessed August 30, 2007. www.chspr.ubc.ca/files/publications/2006/chspr06-10.pdf

McPherson, K., J.E. Wennberg, O.B. Hovind, and P. Clifford. 1982. "Small Area Variations in the Use of Common Surgical Procedures: An International Comparison of New England, England and Norway." *New England Journal of Medicine* 307 (21): 1310-4.

Morgan S.G., C. Balma, and M.-.E. Wilcox (eds.). 2006. *Toward a National Pharmaceuticals Strategy: A Summary of the 2006 Health Policy Conference of the UBC Centre for Health Services and Policy Research*. Vancouver, BC: Centre for Health Services and Policy Research. www.chspr.ubc.ca/files/publications/2006/chspr06-10.pdf

Morgan, S.G., K.L. Bassett, J.M. Wright, R.G. Evans, M.L. Barer, P. Caetano, and C. Black. 2005. "'Breakthrough' Drugs and Growth in

Expenditure on Prescription Drugs in Canada." *British Medical Journal* 331: 815-6.

Morgan, S.G., M. McMahon, J. Lam, D. Mooney, and C. Raymond. 2005. *The Canadian Rx Atlas*. Vancouver: Centre for Health Services and Policy Research.

National Forum on Health. 1997. *Canada Health Action: Building on the Legacy*. Ottawa: Health Canada.

Organisation for Economic Co-operation and Development (OECD). 2006a. Directorate for Employment, Labour and Social Affairs. *OECD Health Data 2006: Statistics and Indicators for 30 Countries*. Paris: OECD.

———. 2006b. *OECD Economic Outlook* 79 (June). Paris: OECD.

Organisation for Economic Co-operation and Development, and Statistics Canada. 1995. *Literacy, Economy and Society: Results of the First International Literacy Survey*. Paris: OECD and Industry Canada.

Office of the Prime Minister of Canada. 2007. "Prime Minister's address at Banquet de la Francophonie." Speech, March 24. www.pm.gc.ca/eng/media.asp?category=2&id=1600

Roos, N.P., G. Flowerdew, A. Wajda, and R.B. Tate. 1986. "Variations in Physicians' Hospitalization Practices: A Population-Based Study in Manitoba, Canada." *American Journal of Public Health* 76 (1): 45-51.

Royal Commission on Health Services. 1964. *Royal Commission on Health Services*, volumes I and 2. Ottawa: Queen's Printer.

Rushowy, K. 2007. "Canada Is Failing Its Kids, MD Says." *Toronto Star*, April 30.

Sachs, J. 2006. "The Social Welfare State: Beyond Ideology." *Scientific American* 295 (5): 42.

Schoen, C., R. Osborn, P.T. Huynh, M. Doty, J. Peugh, and K. Zapert. 2006. "On the Front Lines of Care: Primary Care Doctors' Office Systems, Experiences, and Views in Seven Countries." *Health Affairs* 25 (6): 555-71.

Soumerai, S.B., D. Ross-Degnan, S. Gortmaker, and J. Avorn. 1990. "Withdrawing Payment for Nonscientific Drug Therapy: Intended and Unexpected Effects of a Large-Scale Natural Experiment." *Journal of the American Medical Association* 263 (6): 831-9.

Statistics Canada 1983. *Historical Statistics of Canada* (2nd ed.). Accessed September 7, 2007. http://www.statcan.ca/english/freepub/11-516-XIE/sectiona/toc.htm

Tamblyn, R., R. Laprise, J.A. Hanley, M. Abrahamowicz, S. Scott, N. Mayo, J. Hurley, et al. 2001. "Adverse Events Associated with Prescription Drug Cost-Sharing among Poor and Elderly Persons." *Journal of the American Medical Association* 285 (4): 421-9.

Tu, J.V., W.A. Ghali, L. Pilote, and S. Brien, eds. 2006. *Canadian Cardiovascular Atlas*. Toronto: Canadian Cardiac Outcomes Research Team.

Vayda, E. 1973. "A Comparison of Surgical Rates in Canada and in England and Wales." *New England Journal of Medicine* 289 (23): 1224-9.

von Oehsen, W.H. 2001. *Pharmaceutical Discounts under Federal Law: State Program Opportunities*. Washington, DC: Public Health Institute.

Wennberg, J.E. 1988. "Practice Variations and the Need for Outcomes Research." In *Health Care Variations: Assessing the Evidence*, edited by C. Ham. London: King's Fund Institute.

Wildavsky, A. 1977. "Doing Better and Feeling Worse: The Political Pathology of Health Policy." *Daedalus* 106 (1): 105-24.

Woolhandler, S., T. Campbell, and D.U. Himmelstein. 2003. "Costs of Health Care Administration in the United States and Canada." *New England Journal of Medicine* 349 (8): 768-75.

Woolhandler, S., and D.U. Himmelstein. 1991. "The Deteriorating Administrative Efficiency of the U.S. Health Care System." *New England Journal of Medicine* 324 (18): 1253-8.

World Health Organization. 2006. *World Health Report 2006: Working Together for Health*. Geneva: WHO.

NEXT STEPS IN THE HEALTH POLICY WARS?
Raisa Deber

Robert Evans, Clyde Hertzman and Steve Morgan do not think small or short term. They begin by deciding that the best way to improve the health outcomes of the Canadian population is to focus on children and bring back the national child care program. Their second proposal is to reduce dramatically the costs of pharmaceuticals. Their third is to employ a universal electronic medical record (EMR) to provide the tools to manage physicians and hospitals for effectiveness.

These authors are not naive; they have been through the policy wars. They are among Canada's leading scholars of health policy and are recognized internationally. Yet their chapter "Improving Health Outcomes in Canada" — which presents some excellent ideas — seems strangely detached from current political reality. They pay some attention to ideology, but not much. Yet it was not by accident that the Harper Conservative government dismantled the federal-provincial agreements negotiated by its Liberal predecessor to implement the National Child Care Strategy. Even though the Organisation for Economic Co-operation and Development (OECD) has argued that Canada's public expenditure on early childhood education services for children up to age six is by far the lowest among 14 countries examined and has recommended that Canada implement a universal service with substantial public funding (OECD 2006), others use the language of "choice" to express their preference for giving tax cuts to individuals over funding daycare services (Kershaw 2004). This policy preference — shared by neo-liberal regimes in various countries — appears based on strongly held personal values about the appropriate role of government and on views about federalism (see Teghtsoonian 1993; Friendly 2000). As such, it is not a matter of evidence; it seems unlikely that this proposal, however well justified, would suddenly convert them or their supporters.

Evans, Hertzman and Morgan aptly note that "for virtually every measure of health, those lower down the socioeconomic scale have, on average, poorer health" (293). The steepness of the social gradient does vary, and reducing it seems wise on both moral and economic grounds. Yet how we can do this is far less clear. If chronic exposure to stress is a major culprit, it would not be easy to reduce stress levels in a globalized, dog-eat-dog world in which no one's job appears to be safe and there is constant pressure to reduce labour costs. Still, the evidence the authors cite does suggest that successful early development could mediate these stress responses. Accordingly, they suggest that we should put a lot of money — 1.5 to 2 percent of gross domestic product (GDP) — into a comprehensive system of early childhood development, care and education. This sounds like a fine idea, yet the ability of this proposal to achieve the desired outcomes for Canada seems somewhat problematic. If, as they suggest, "developmental windows missed do not open again" (294), it is not clear how this proposal could improve health outcomes for either those already past the critical years or those whose developmental windows were forged outside Canada. If the goal is to reduce the proportion of Canadians reaching adulthood without the competencies they need to cope in the modern economy from the current guesstimate of 25 percent to less than 10 percent, is it wise to restrict our focus to those born in Canada? At the time of the 2001 census, 18.4 percent of Canada's population — and more than 25 percent of those living in Ontario and British Columbia — were foreign-born. To the extent that their developmental windows were forged elsewhere, a policy concentrating only on educating those children living in Canada might have significant limitations.

The reward system for politicians is notoriously based on showing rapid results, with "the long term" referring to the time of the next election. Yet the authors' proposal to spend money to educate other people's children would not show results for decades. The top bureaucrats on the BBC comedy *Yes Minister* noted that

> there are four words to be included in a proposal if you want it thrown out — complicated, lengthy, expensive, controversial. And if you want to be really sure that the Minister doesn't accept it you must say the decision is courageous...Controversial only means this will lose you votes, courageous means this will lose you the election. (Lynn and Jay 1989)

That being said, I agree that restoring and resourcing such a program is a worthy — and courageous — priority, and one I strongly support.

Not content with taking on the Prime Minister, much of the national media and the family values coalition, the authors next turn their attention to the international pharmaceutical industry and recommend introducing a single-payer system. Pharmaceuticals constitute a large and growing proportion of health expenditures (Canadian Institute for Health Information 2007), and the authors correctly note that the pharmaceutical industry does not want countervailing power to balance its market power, and would oppose their proposal. Their research shows that greater government involvement in British Columbia has been effective in controlling costs while maintaining access to medicines and improving financial equity across income categories (Morgan, Evans, et al. 2006). Yet, as they clearly recognize, even a single payer would have a hard time negotiating lower prices for many drugs.

The pharmaceutical industry has another advantage: unless there are several competing, clinically identical products, it would be remarkably difficult for payers to exercise their ability to walk away and refuse to purchase them, which, in turn, would make it easier for the industry to hang tough. As Joseph Newhouse notes, there are particular problems relating to any "drug that is on patent, represents a major therapeutic advance, and has no close competitors" (2004, 91) — by definition, such a drug does not face competition, and the industry has not been reluctant to exploit the resulting monopoly power. It is remarkably difficult to convince patients or physicians to willingly forgo therapy they believe would be helpful, merely to save money. Indeed, policy-makers in most developed countries face what have been termed "Astroturf" groups — which purport to be grassroots organizations representing the general public, but which are often funded by corporations seeking to influence government policy (Lyon and Maxwell 2004). Backed by the media, such groups make an emotional case for paying whatever price manufacturers demand for the newest drug. Few governments have proven able to resist this pressure to help identifiable individuals who might — or might not — benefit. Centralized drug review processes might help, but they are not a panacea (Morgan, McMahon, et al. 2006). Focusing on "me too" drugs might achieve considerable savings (Morgan et al. 2005), but pharmaceutical companies have proven remarkably adept at arguing why their products represent improvements over cheaper alternatives. Indeed, in the United States, the suggestion that the federal government be allowed to use its bargaining power to negotiate lower prices for the new Medicare prescription drug program — an activity that had been explicitly banned in the 2003 legislation — led to immediate charges by opposing legislators that cost control necessarily would mean denial of needed care. This, in turn, suggests that having a single payer would not be enough to control costs.

Technology assessment presumes that decision-makers are rational and that they will not buy products that are not cost-effective. In this ideal world, decisions would be made on the basis of appropriateness, recognizing that there is a sliding scale of ability to benefit and a point at which costs (and risks) outweigh benefits. Treatments highly appropriate for certain subgroups of patients would not be indicated for others, with an inevitable grey zone in the middle (Deber 1992). Yet most people tend to presume that newer is better, and that treatment is always beneficial. Somehow, the lessons of Vioxx — a popular drug whose risks proved to be understated, leading to use by millions where the risks outweighed the benefits, scandals about whether the company withheld data, a recall by the US Food and Drug Administration and a series of lawsuits — have not yet sunk in (Karha and Topol 2004). Pharmaceutical companies are corporations; they unsurprisingly wish to maximize profits. In the absence of countervailing forces, they have an incentive to encourage marginally appropriate use, price their products as high as possible and spin research results to encourage physicians to prescribe their products and patients to "ask your doctor" about them. The results are often lose-lose.[1]

While agreeing with Evans, Hertzman and Morgan that our current system generates far too many costs without benefits, I am unconvinced that the fragmented funding system is the only culprit. Hope is important, and pharmaceuticals are not the only industry to profit from it. Indeed, if critics are correct regarding the extent to which the pharmaceutical industry is reaping large profits while de-emphasizing basic research in favour of marketing (see, for example, United States Office of Technology Assessment 1993; Angell 2004; Goozner 2004; Kalant and Shrier 2006), could one not make a case for setting up a nonprofit corporation to test new drugs and bring them to market, where the economic incentives to fudge results, inflate costs and market to marginally appropriate clients might be minimized?

The authors' third recommendation is an offshoot of their second: use EMRs to improve clinical practice to ensure that treatment is appropriate. Unfortunately, however, the assumption that electronic medical records could enforce evidence-based practice does not yet appear to be supported by the evidence. As Jaan Sidorov suggests,

> Electronic health record (EHR) advocates argue that EHRs lead to reduced errors and reduced costs. Many reports suggest otherwise. The EHR often leads to higher billings and declines in provider productivity with no change in provider-to-patient ratios. Error reduction is inconsistent and has yet to be linked to savings or malpractice premiums. As interest in patient-centeredness, shared decision making, teaming, group visits, open access, and accountability grows, the EHR is better viewed as an insufficient yet necessary ingredient. Absent other fundamental interventions that alter medical practice, it is unlikely that the U.S. health care bill will decline as a result of the EHR alone. (2006, 1079)

Many of the widely touted results come from a small number of "early adopters," and success appears to require, at minimum, organizational change, workflow redesign and careful attention to the incentives built into reimbursement systems (Chaudhry et al. 2006).

Again, political realities would seem to intrude. A disquieting feature of the wait-time debate that has dominated Canadian health policy in recent years is the relative lack of attention to outcomes and appropriateness. Although clinicians are making a valiant effort to make some wait-time standards evidence-based, the public assumption appears to be that no one should ever wait — that more is always better. But treatments have risks and benefits. Consider the priority categories and benchmarks for joint replacement agreed to by the Wait Time Alliance:

Priority 1: A situation that has the potential to deteriorate quickly and result in an emergency admission should be operated on within 30 days.
Priority 2: A situation that involves some pain and disability but is unlikely to deteriorate quickly to the point of becoming an emergency admission should be operated on within 90 days.
Priority 3: A situation that involves minimal pain, dysfunction or disability and is unlikely to deteriorate quickly to the point of requiring emergency admission should be operated on within 6 months. (Wait Time Alliance for Timely Access to Health Care 2005, 19)

Some might suggest that "minimal pain, dysfunction or disability" might not warrant surgery at all. That, however, was not the reaction of the Wait Time Alliance's focus groups: "While most people surveyed viewed these proposed benchmarks for joint replacement as a significant improvement over current wait times, some people found them to be too lengthy" (19-20). One participant was quoted as saying, "Six months is too long to wait if you think about anyone supporting a family. How can they wait that long?" (20).

Shortening waiting periods for unneeded therapy that causes harm seems counterproductive. Yet patients are not homogeneous, evidence is often lacking and treatment cannot wait. How much physician autonomy is appropriate? Who should decide? I agree with Evans, Hertzman and Morgan that improving the appropriateness of clinical practice, by a variety of methods, could pay enormous dividends. The quality improvement movement, which includes a strong focus on patient safety, has made many promising suggestions (see, for example, Baker and Norton 2001; Institute of Medicine 2001; Health Council of Canada 2006). The EMR could indeed be a tool, but it is unlikely to be the only one or even the most useful one. Again, however, that does not mean it should not be pursued.

These three priorities, then, seem promising, but in my view they are unlikely to deliver the promised results, at least in a politically salient time frame. Moreover, they are not self-evident to those whose support would be needed for action. Unfortunately, it is likely that even good evidence might not be sufficiently persuasive.

As Evans has so ably and repeatedly pointed out, Canadian health expenditures are not out of control (see, for example, Evans et al. 2001; Evans 2004). Yet the fact that, impervious to evidence, the myth continues to exist is itself evidence of the importance of ideology in making policy decisions.

There are also enormous structural barriers. Surprisingly, Evans, Hertzman and Morgan make little mention of federal-provincial issues or the unwillingness of many provinces to allow Ottawa to take the lead in an area under provincial jurisdiction. Neither do they make much mention of global trade agreements and intellectual property requirements, which constrain the ability of governments to act (see Epps and Flood 2002; Johnson 2004; Wilson, McDougall, and Upshur 2006). The most notorious examples — such as restricting access to essential drugs in poorer countries — have attracted international attention, if not full solutions (Westerhaus and Castro 2006), but other examples can be gleaned from the newspapers. In 2007, for example, stories in the *Globe and Mail* (Priest 2007a, 2007b) and the *Halifax Chronicle-Herald* (Smith 2007) revealed that changes to Canada's intellectual property rules would soon give the pharmaceutical company sanofi-aventis Canada an additional eight years of market exclusivity over the colorectal cancer drug oxaliplatin, even though its patent protection had long expired. This meant that three companies that had been offering the product as a generic (for $400 to $500 a vial) would no longer be able to do so, and the price would double to the $1,000 charged by sanofi-aventis. Cancer care providers were concerned about the implications for their budgets, but appeared resigned to the need to find the additional money.

Neither do Evans, Hertzman and Morgan give much consideration to the reaction of interest groups to their various proposals. The Canadian Institute for Health Information (2005) notes, for example, that perhaps only a third of Canadians even recognize population-level factors, including income and social support, as determinants of health, so there are not many votes to be found there. Instead, many Canadians focus on individual lifestyles, which often tend to be seen as individual choices and hence not a legitimate target for government intervention.

In practice, a host of other factors are also likely to make the authors' otherwise excellent ideas extremely difficult to implement and even harder to sustain. That does not mean such ideas are not worth trying, but there are few quick wins to be found here — and in their absence, there is little to help maintain the political consensus, particularly given what the authors correctly note is a sustained attack on what is still a pretty good system.

I am also somewhat surprised to see no mention of the environment. One is tempted to return to the language of the Lalonde report and its description of health fields (Lalonde 1974). Evans, Hertzman and Morgan speak about human biology and health care organization, and elsewhere have written about lifestyle — particularly obesity (Evans 2006; Heymann et al. 2006). Yet they do not discuss the environment, which Lalonde notes

> includes all those matters related to health which are external to the human body and over which the individual has little or no control. Individuals cannot, by themselves, ensure that foods, drugs, cosmetics, devices, water supply, etc. are safe and uncontaminated; that the health hazards of air, water and noise pollution are controlled; that the spread of communicable diseases is prevented; that effective garbage and sewage disposal is carried out; and that the social environment, including the rapid changes in it, do not have harmful effects on health. (1974, 32)

At a time when Health Canada is suggesting that canned tuna can be harmful to one's health, in part because of the detrimental effects of accumulated toxins on developing brains, it might be worth considering whether making more efforts to remove mercury, PCBs, lead and other toxins from the food supply is a priority. Similarly, might asthma rates — which are highly correlated with childhood ill health — decrease if air quality were better? Would rates of tooth decay — which are rising after years of decreases — be reduced if people, including yuppie parents, felt that their families could go back to drinking fluoridated tap water? Would diabetes and heart disease rates fall if food processors reduced the amount of salt and sweeteners in our diet? Would more attention to public health prevent outbreaks of water-borne disease (see Deber et al. 2006)?

Preventing disease is usually preferable to treating it, and it is not clear why the focus should only be on children, as Evans, Hertzman and Morgan suggest. There is considerable public support for such prevention efforts. Some could show quite rapid results, and the window of opportunity for action might be open. That being said, it is always a pleasure reading these authors.

NOTES

1   A recent example is Bayer's Trasylol, a drug
used to prevent blood loss during artery
bypass graft surgery. According to newspaper coverage, the drug cost roughly $1,300
per patient, compared with $11 and $44 for
its alternatives, but was nonetheless becoming popular. By some estimates, 246,000 US
patients received it in 2006 — most for uses
other than those formally approved by the
Food and Drug Administration. What did this
extra money buy? Nonrandomized studies
found the drug yielded higher death rates and
higher risks of such serious side effects as
kidney problems, heart attacks and strokes,
with no increase in effectiveness (Mangano,
Tudor, and Dietzel 2006). The total cost for
these worse outcomes was estimated at
$250 million in direct costs for the drug, plus
$1 billion in indirect costs just for dialysis treat-
ment of the additional cases of kidney failure
attributed to the drug's side effects. See the
Web site of the Food and Drug
Administration, http://www.fda.gov/cder/
drug/InfoSheets/HCP/aprotininHCP9_2006.
htm, which has issued an alert for the product. Personal injury lawyers are also eagerly
following the saga and launching lawsuits.

REFERENCES

Angell, M. 2004. *The Truth about the Drug
Companies: How They Deceive Us and
What to Do about It.* New York: Random
House.

Baker, G.R., and P. Norton. 2001. "Making
Patients Safer! Reducing Error in
Canadian Healthcare." *HealthcarePapers*
2 (1): 10-31.

Canadian Institute for Health Information (CIHI).
2005. *Select Highlights on Public Views of
the Determinants of Health.* Canadian
Population Health Initiative. Ottawa: CIHI.

_____. 2007. *Drug Expenditure in Canada,
1985 to 2006.* Ottawa: CIHI.

Chaudhry, B., J. Wang, S. Wu, M. Maglione,
W. Mojica, E. Roth, S.C. Morton, and
P.G. Shekelle. 2006. "Systematic Review:
Impact of Health Information Technology
on Quality, Efficiency, and Costs of
Medical Care." *Annals of Internal Medicine*
144 (10): 12-22.

Deber, R. 1992. "Translating Technology
Assessment into Policy: Conceptual
Issues and Tough Choices." *International
Journal of Technology Assessment in
Health Care* 8 (1): 131-7.

Deber, R., K. Millan, H. Shapiro, and C.W.
McDougall. 2006. "A Cautionary Tale of
Downloading Public Health in Ontario: What
Does It Say about the Need for National
Standards for More than Doctors and
Hospitals?" *Healthcare Policy* 2 (2): 56-71.

Epps, T., and C.M. Flood. 2002. "Have We
Traded Away the Opportunity for
Innovative Health Care Reform? The
Implications of the NAFTA for Medicare."
McGill Law Journal 47 (4): 747-90.

Evans, R.G. 2004. "Financing Health Care:
Options, Consequences, and Objectives."
In *The Fiscal Sustainability of Health Care
in Canada: Romanow Papers, Volume 1*,
edited by G.P. Marchildon, T. McIntosh,
and P.-G. Forest. Toronto: University of
Toronto Press.

_____. 2006. "Fat Zombies, Pleistocene
Tastes, Autophilia and the 'Obesity
Epidemic'." *Healthcare Policy* 2 (2): 18-26.

Evans, R.G., K.M. McGrail, S.G. Morgan,
M.L. Barer, and C. Hertzman. 2001.
"APOCALYPSE NO: Population Aging and
the Future of Health Care Systems."
SEDAP Research Paper 59. Hamilton,
ON: McMaster University, Program for
Research on Social and Economic
Dimensions of an Aging Population.

Friendly, M. 2000. "Child Care and Canadian
Federalism in the 1990s: Canary in a Coal
Mine." Occasional Paper 11. Toronto:

University of Toronto, Centre for Urban and Community Studies, Childcare Resource and Research Unit.

Goozner, M. 2004. *$800 Million Pill: The Truth behind the Cost of New Drugs*. Berkeley: University of California Press.

Health Council of Canada. 2006. *Health Care Renewal in Canada: Clearing the Road to Quality*. Toronto: Health Council of Canada.

Heymann, J., C. Hertzman, M.L. Barer, and R.G. Evans, eds. 2006. *Healthier Societies: From Analysis to Action*. New York: Oxford University Press.

Institute of Medicine. 2001. *Crossing the Quality Chasm: A New Health System for the 21st Century*. Washington, DC: National Academic Press.

Johnson, J.R. 2004. "International Trade Agreements and Canadian Health Care." In *The Fiscal Sustainability of Health Care in Canada: Romanow Papers, Volume 1*, edited by G.P. Marchildon, T. McIntosh, and P.-G. Forest. Toronto: University of Toronto Press.

Kalant, N., and I. Shrier. 2006. "Research Output of the Canadian Pharmaceutical Industry: Where Has All the R&D Gone?" *Healthcare Policy* 1 (4): 21-34.

Karha, J., and E.J. Topol. 2004. "The Sad Story of Vioxx, and What We Should Learn from It." *Cleveland Clinic Journal of Medicine* 71 (12): 933-9.

Kershaw, P. 2004. "Choice Discourse in BC Child Care: Distancing Policy from Research." *Canadian Journal of Political Science* 37 (4): 927-50.

Lalonde, M. 1974. *A New Perspective on the Health of Canadians: A Working Document*. Ottawa: Information Canada.

Lynn, J., and A. Jay. 1989. *The Complete Yes Minister*. London: BBC Books.

Lyon, T.P., and J.W. Maxwell. 2004. "Astroturf: Interest Group Lobbying and Corporate Strategy." *Journal of Economics and Management Strategy* 13 (4): 561-97.

Mangano, D.T., I.C. Tudor, and C. Dietzel. 2006. "The Risk Associated with Aprotinin in Cardiac Surgery." *New England Journal of Medicine* 354 (4): 353-65.

Morgan, S.G., K.L. Bassett, J.M. Wright, R.G. Evans, M.L. Barer, P.A. Caetano, and C.D. Black. 2005. "'Breakthrough' Drugs and Growth in Expenditure on Prescription Drugs in Canada." *British Medical Journal* 331:815-6.

Morgan, S.G, R.G. Evans, G.E. Hanley, P.A. Caetano, and C.D. Black. 2006. "Income-Based Drug Coverage in British Columbia: Lessons for BC and the Rest of Canada." *Healthcare Policy* 2 (2): 115-27.

Morgan, S.G., M. McMahon, C. Mitton, E. Roughhead, R. Kirk, P. Kanavos, and D. Menon. 2006. "Centralized Drug Review Processes in Australia, Canada, New Zealand, and the United Kingdom." *Health Affairs* 25 (2): 337-47.

Newhouse, J.P. 2004. "How Much Should Medicare Pay for Drugs?" *Health Affairs* 23 (1): 89-102.

Organisation for Economic Co-operation and Development (OECD). 2006. *Starting Strong II: Early Childhood Education and Care*, 2nd ed. Paris: OECD.

Priest, L. 2007a. "Trade Gambit Doubles Cost of Cancer Medicine." *Globe and Mail*, May 25.

_____. 2007b. "Monopoly on Drug Pricing Sparks Debate." *Globe and Mail*, May 26.

Sidorov, J. 2006. "It Ain't Necessarily So: The Electronic Health Record and the Unlikely Prospect of Reducing Health Care Costs." *Health Affairs* 25 (4): 1079-85.

Smith, Amy. 2007. "Cancer Drug Costs to Double." *Halifax Chronicle-Herald*, May 26.

Teghtsoonian, K. 1993. "Neo-Conservative Ideology and Opposition to Federal Regulation of Child Care Services in the United States and Canada." *Canadian Journal of Political Science* 26 (1): 97-121.

United States Office of Technology Assessment. 1993. *Pharmaceutical R&D: Costs, Risks and Rewards.* OTA-H-522. Washington, DC: US Government Printing Office.

Wait Time Alliance for Timely Access to Health Care. 2005. *It's about Time! Achieving Benchmarks and Best Practices in Wait Time Management.* Final report. Ottawa: Canadian Medical Association.

Westerhaus, M., and A. Castro. 2006. "How Do Intellectual Property Law and International Trade Agreements Affect Access to Antiretroviral Therapy?" *PLoS Medicine* 3 (8): 1230-6.

Wilson, K., C. McDougall, and R. Upshur. 2006. "The New International Health Regulations and the Federalism Dilemma." *PLoS Medicine* 3 (1): 1-5.

CANADA'S HIGH POVERTY RATE IS THE GREATEST IMPEDIMENT TO BETTER HEALTH OUTCOMES

Dennis Raphael

Canadian analysts trying to identify policy directions to improve health outcomes are faced with a profound conundrum: the primary determinants of health outcomes have little to do with the health care system (see Raphael 2004; Marmot and Wilkinson 2006). Although the health care system consumes a significant proportion of public monies, dominates the attention of the public, the media and policy-makers and draws the lion's share of health research dollars,[1] identifying the best policy directions for improving health outcomes could well exclude consideration of health care system issues (see McKeown 1976; McKinlay and McKinlay 1987). Indeed, the chapter by Jean-Yves Duclos elsewhere in this volume, in which he addresses the economic security challenge, might best identify the means by which Canadians' health outcomes could be improved (see Acheson 1998; Shaw et al. 1999; Auger et al. 2004).

Yet neglecting health care seems inconceivable considering its prominence in public policy debates. To deal with this problem, Robert Evans, Clyde Hertzman and Steve Morgan suggest one policy direction that addresses a key social determinant of health outcomes — early childhood development (ECD) — then direct their attention to two further policy courses concerning the organization and management of the health care system: developing a pharmacare program and an electronic medical record (EMR). These three recommendations — and the authors' analyses of their benefits — are compelling. In a rational policy-making environment free from ideological disputes about the role of the state versus that of the free market, the recommendations in "Improving Health Outcomes in Canada" would be implemented. Their potential benefits clearly exceed their costs, probably by a wide margin.

Instituting these three policy directions is important, but do they constitute the three primary policy directions toward improving health outcomes? To my mind, the authors' early ECD recommendation is more important for health outcomes than their two health care system proposals. But even the ECD recommendation — while central to improving health outcomes — would have modest effects without addressing what is known to be the strongest determinant of health outcomes: the incidence of poverty.

Canada's poverty rates are high and its health outcomes indicators — such as rates of infant mortality and low birth weight — are modest by international comparisons (Organisation for Economic Co-operation and Development [OECD] 2005). Moreover, the incidence of poverty — and its related health outcomes effects — is a reflection of numerous public policies that shape the distribution of economic resources among Canadians (Raphael 2007a).

To facilitate examination of the relevant public policies for health outcomes, I propose an additional — and to my mind essential — policy direction for improving health outcomes: reduce Canada's high poverty rates.

OPTION 1: REVITALIZE THE CANADIAN CHILDREN'S AGENDA

First and foremost, it all begins in early childhood. At this point, three factors are of crucial importance: health, income poverty, and "developmental priming mechanisms" such as reading to children, social stimuli, and guidance. Families with limited resources are likely to fall short on all three counts. A strong welfare state in the conventional sense can avert the first two factors, but if cognitive stimulation is key we must rethink policy. We cannot pass laws that force parents to read to their children, but we can compensate. One option is to ensure that parents of small children are given the possibility of low-stress employment and adequate time with their children. A second, perhaps more effective option, is to promote universal, high-quality day care. (Esping-Andersen 2002, 49)

The ECD program

When I am asked to name the one single policy direction that governments could immediately implement to improve the health outcomes of Canadians, I reply: a national program of licensed, regulated child care. A program such as detailed by Evans, Hertzman and Morgan would provide any number of benefits: promoting early childhood development, providing employment opportunities and boosting productivity, supporting gender equity for women and supporting community development in Canadian cities and towns, among others (Friendly 2004). Not surprisingly, nations with such programs have flatter health and literacy gradients, superior health outcomes and quality of life, lower unemployment rates and greater proportions of women gainfully employed in the labour force and serving in elected chambers (Innocenti Research Centre 2005).

The authors observe that "the argument for a serious ECD program is supported not just by the research literature on the importance of the early years, but by the simple observation that other countries have such programs, and their population-level results are much better than those in Canada" (296). This observation, however, must be placed in context. Nations with ECD programs have better indicators of health and quality of life, but they also have more developed welfare states associated with greater government transfers in support of programs, services and cash supports to citizens than does Canada, smaller gaps between rich and poor, and poverty levels that put Canada in a poor comparative light (OECD 2005). Moreover, the best examples of these nations — Sweden, Norway, Denmark and Finland — have policies shaped by decades of social democratic rule supported by the presence of proportional representation in the electoral process (see Esping-Andersen 1985; Navarro and Shi 2002).

The observation of this background context, however, does not detract from the basic thrust — namely, that implementation of a serious ECD program would have positive benefits across a whole range of health outcomes (see also Browne 2004). Among Canadian women with young children, about 75 percent are employed, yet only about 10 to 15 percent have access to licensed, regulated child care (Friendly 2004). The primary barrier to such a program appears to be resistance based on ideological opposition to state involvement in service provision. As I stated earlier, however, any such program needs to be supplemented by policies that reduce the incidence and health-related consequences of poverty.

Reducing the incidence and consequences of poverty

> Studies show that the living conditions experienced by those living in poverty are associated with a very wide range of health indicators. Poverty is a strong predictor of life expectancy and individuals' report of their quality of health. Poverty predicts the incidence of, and death from, a staggeringly wide range of diseases. Poverty also predicts incidence and death from injuries, levels of health literacy, and use of health services. And experiencing poverty during childhood is not just a good predictor of poor health in childhood but a good predictor of health problems during adulthood. (Raphael 2007c, 205)

Evans, Hertzman and Morgan are generally accurate in stating that "poverty and deprivation...are certainly harmful to health, but ill health is not simply concentrated among 'the poor' and randomly distributed among the rest of us" (293). But their analysis misses some key points.

First, poor health outcomes are indeed disproportionately concentrated among the poor. The gaps in health outcomes — life expectancy, rates of infant mortality and low birth weight, mortality from and incidence of chronic diseases such as diabetes and heart disease, and suicide rates, among others — are greater between the lowest income quintile and the next income quintile of Canadians than among the succeeding quintiles, as shown in figure 1 (Wilkins 1999; Wilkins et al. 2000; Wilkins, Berthelot, and Ng 2002). This is also the case for the use of health care services, hospital admissions and hospital day stays (Roos and Mustard 1997). The health of poor children is especially problematic (Canadian Institute of Child Health 2000), as figure 2 indicates.

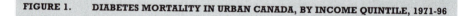

FIGURE 1.   DIABETES MORTALITY IN URBAN CANADA, BY INCOME QUINTILE, 1971-96

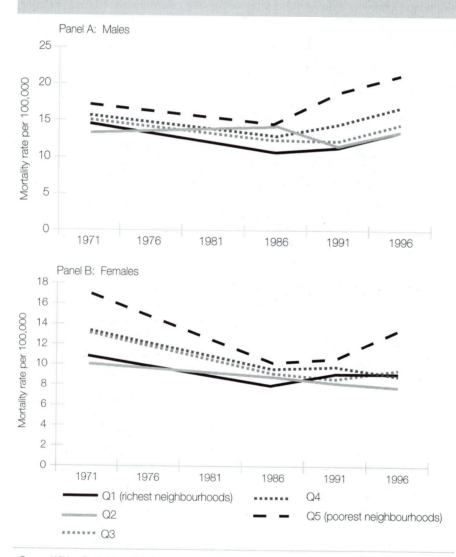

Source: Wilkins, Berthelot, and Ng (2002, 17).
Note: Data not available for 1976 and 1981.

Second, low-income Canadians have four times the risk of reporting poor or fair health as do those with higher incomes (Xi et al. 2005). They also have two and a half times the risk of achieving poor scores on a concrete index of functional health as do higher-income Canadians. In contrast, middle-income Canadians have only one and a half times the risk of reporting poor or fair health or showing poor functional health scores as do wealthier Canadians (see figure 3). As John Lynch notes, "The fact that health differences can be observed between the top of the social hierarchy and the next level down is surely important, but may be an incomplete basis for understanding why the largest burden of excess deaths occurs at the bottom of the social hierarchy" (2000, 1004).

Third, the life situations of people living in poverty are qualitatively worse — in terms of material and social deprivation, day-to-day stress and adoption of coping behaviours such as tobacco and alcohol use — than those of Canadians even slightly higher up in the income and wealth scale (Baxter 1995; Ocean 2005; Neysmith, Bezanson, and O'Connell 2005; Reid 2004). Researchers in the United Kingdom have demonstrated that material and social deprivation shows a nonlinear relationship with income such that the poverty line represents a situation whereby social exclusion — a result of significant material and social deprivation — is especially great (Gordon 2006).

FIGURE 2. PERCENTAGE OF CHILDREN WITH LOWER FUNCTIONAL HEALTH, BY INCOME LEVEL, TWO-PARENT FAMILIES, 1994-95

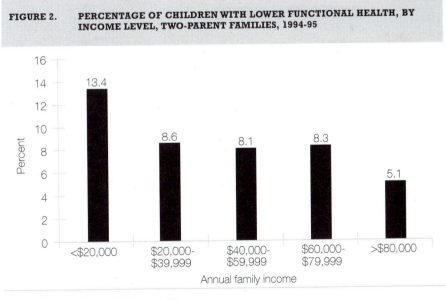

Source: Ross and Roberts (1999, chart 18).

Fourth, people who live in poverty are much more adversely affected by regressive public policy changes that weaken social infrastructure and the social safety net than are those higher up the income ladder (Davies et al. 2001; National Council of Welfare 2001; Neysmith, Bezanson, and O'Connell 2005). Moreover, the plight of poorer Canadians has become especially problematic as a result of the withdrawal of governments from the provision of housing, reduced eligibility for unemployment insurance benefits and failure to maintain social

FIGURE 3. ODDS RATIOS FOR RISK FACTORS ASSOCIATED WITH SELF-RATED POOR OR FAIR HEALTH AND POOR SCORES (50ᵀᴴ PERCENTILE) ON THE HEALTH UTILITIES INDEX

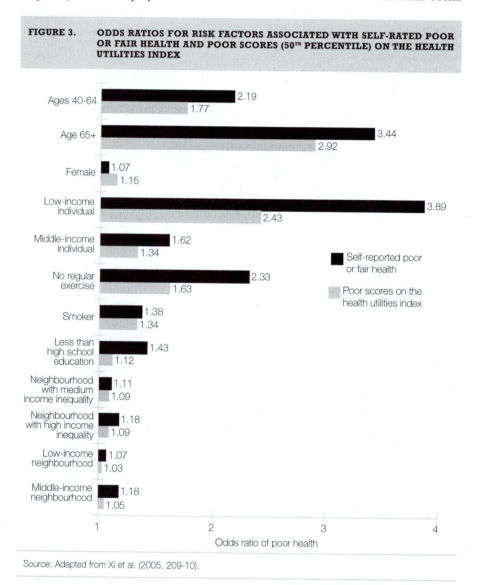

Source: Adapted from Xi et al. (2005, 209-10).

assistance and minimum wage levels adequate for health (National Council of Welfare 2004).

Fifth, the poor — both children and adults — are especially likely to experience stigma, aspersions on their morals and integrity, and denigration by governments, the media and the general public (Swanson 2001). The effects of these psychological insults have clear health outcome implications (McIntyre, Officer, and Robinson 2003; Chunn and Gavigan 2004; Mosher et al. 2004; Reid 2004; Neysmith, Bezanson, and O'Connell 2005; Robinson, McIntyre, and Officer 2005).

Finally, recent research suggests that high rates of poverty serve to weaken various determinants of health of other Canadians. The reason is that the presence of a significant labour pool of individuals desperate to acquire *any* gainful employment suppresses wages, makes the provision of employment security and benefits less likely for those already employed and weakens working-class solidarity (Wright 1994; Alesina and Glaeser 2004; Coburn 2004). Grace-Edward Galabuzi (2005) suggests that racism, sexism and other resentments become more likely in a highly stratified society that contains significant numbers of people living in poverty.

Poverty is associated with poor health outcomes because individuals are exposed to adverse living conditions (the materialist explanation), which are exacerbated by underinvestment by governments in social infrastructure — such as schools, services, programs and transfers to citizens — in support of health (the neo-materialist explanation) (see Raphael 2007d). It is beyond the scope of this commentary to provide a detailed presentation of policy directions that would reduce the incidence of poverty and weaken its association with adverse health outcomes, but a brief overview seems useful.[2]

Raising Canada's rather low minimum wage (by the standards of the OECD; see OECD 2005), reforming its inadequate social assistance benefits[3] and restoring unemployment insurance eligibility and benefits to previous levels would serve immediately to reduce the incidence of poverty and improve health outcomes. Combined with a longer-term commitment to providing a basic minimum income, these moves would allow all Canadians to achieve the prerequisites of health.

In terms of broader public policy related to investments in social infrastructure, Canada's spending on active labour policy, pensions and support to families generally lags behind that of most developed nations (Raphael 2007a). Increased support for housing, employment training and provision of early childhood education would have clear poverty-reducing implications that would serve to improve health outcomes (Bryant 2004; Friendly 2004; Jackson 2004; Tremblay 2004).

OPTION 2: A NATIONAL PHARMACEUTICALS STRATEGY

There is some evidence to support the contention that increasing the amount of spending on medications that comes from the public purse will help to control overall drug expenditures. However, just increasing public spending, while necessary, may not be sufficient. In addition to a national Pharmacare plan, whereby the government (federal, provincial or both) covers the bulk of the cost of prescription drugs, other measures should be considered in order to contain drug spending. (Lexchin 2007, 7)

Evans, Hertzman and Morgan note that, in 1997, the National Forum on Health recommended instituting a national pharmacare program, and they argue that such a program would result in profound cost savings and the potential for improved health outcomes. (Interestingly, Lexchin [2001] points out that the Royal Commission on Health Services recommended such a program as long ago as 1964!) In support of a national program, studies have found gross inequities among Canadians in their access to pharmaceuticals (Millar 1999; Kozyrskyj, Mustard, and Simons 2001). One study finds, for example, that Canadians with lower-than-average incomes were three times more likely, and those with average incomes were almost twice as likely, not to fill a prescription due to cost than Canadians with above-average incomes (Schoen and Doty 2004).

The authors note (as does Lexchin 2001) that the large pharmaceutical companies would likely mount strong resistance to a national pharmacare program. This would not be surprising considering how profitable such companies are — from 1996 to 2003, the rate of return on shareholders' equity among large pharmaceutical firms (those with sales in excess of $75 million) was nearly twice that of all large manufacturing firms (Lexchin 2007).

Moreover, according to Moynihan and Cassels (2005), the aggressive marketing of drugs by "Big Pharma" has contributed not only to out-of-control cost increases, but also to inappropriate prescribing of medication, resulting in numerous health issues. Even though the vast majority of new patented drugs are no better than existing ones, they are introduced at prices that are virtually identical (95.9 percent of the prices of existing drugs and 91.5 percent of the price of the most expensive drug) to prices of existing ones (Lexchin 2007). Similarly, brand-name companies do not compete — that is, lower their prices — on the introduction of generic drugs. New drugs, therefore, are allowed to enter the market at the same high prices as drugs that, in theory, compete with the generics. Thus, drug prices do not seem to operate as the classical economists suggest, and provide strong evidence for government intervention in the working of the marketplace.

The proposal of Evans, Hertzman and Morgan for a national pharmacare program, therefore, is consistent with what we know about improving the health outcomes of Canadians. Indeed, public control of drug expenditures would not be unusual: Lexchin (2007) reports that, in 2002, 37.2 percent of drug expenditures in Canada were public (in the United States, the figure was just 19.5 percent), but in other OECD countries the percentages are much higher, whether in social democratic political economies (Sweden, 71.5 percent; Finland, 53 percent; Denmark, 52.5 percent), in conservative political economies (Germany, 74.8 percent; Greece, 71.5 percent; both Switzerland and France, 67.0 percent) or other liberal political economies (Ireland, 84.2 percent; Australia, 53.8 percent).[4]

The authors thoughtfully propose not just increasing public responsibility for prescription medicine payments through the public purse to better control and reduce costs, but also imposing numerous controls and mechanisms to improve health outcomes by monitoring the use and effects of drugs. Primary resistance again would come from both Big Pharma and those who are ideologically opposed to government interference in the marketplace (Saint-Arnaud and Bernard 2003).

OPTION 3: A STANDARDIZED ELECTRONIC MEDICAL RECORD

It has long been argued that the Canadian health care system is in need of better management and organization (see, for example, Rachlis 2004). Clearly, Canada now lags behind many other nations in managing its health care system. It may well be that creation of an EMR, as Evans, Hertzman and Morgan propose, would facilitate such action, and some rather large initiatives along those lines are already underway.

The authors, however, point out some rather significant barriers to developing an EMR. These barriers include the fee-for-service processes associated with primary care in Canada, increasing calls for privatization of health care services and the resistance of established interest groups, from Big Pharma to physicians, to any significant reform of the health care system. This task, therefore, seems rather daunting. Nevertheless, the emerging literature the authors cite indicating profound variations in practice observed among jurisdictions, their associated financial costs and their potentially harmful health effects suggests pursuing this path would contribute to the maintenance of Canada's public health care system.

Improving the health outcomes of Canadians requires greater government involvement in issues related to child development, poverty reduction and the provision of health care and other services. The neo-liberal belief that an unfettered marketplace will provide improved health outcomes and a better quality of life for the majority of Canadians has been found to be lacking (see Coburn 2001, 2004, 2006). Recognizing the role that political ideology plays in shaping the perceived viability of various policy options related to promoting health outcomes is but a first step in instituting public policies in support of improving health outcomes (Raphael and Bryant 2006).

<dt>8</dt>

NOTES

1   The best estimates are that, of the 30 or
·   so years of improved life expectancy
    achieved by Canadians since 1900,
    about 10 to 15 percent can be
    accounted for by improvements in health
    care. The rest is a result of improved living
    conditions that now go under the rubric of
    the social determinants of health.

2   See Raphael (2007b) for policy prescrip-
    tions provided by the Association of
    Canadian Food Banks, the Caledon
    Institute, Campaign 2000, the Federation of
    Canadian Municipalities and the National
    Anti-Poverty Organization, among others.

3   The OECD (1999) identifies Canada's
    social assistance programs as *not* intended
    to provide an adequate quality of life.

4   In his influential work *The Three Worlds of
    Welfare Capitalism,* Esping-Anderson identi-
    fied a typology of three welfare states (1990).
    Social democratic nations such as Norway
    and Sweden are committed to having the
    state play a key role in promoting equity and
    social rights. Liberal political economies such
    as the United States, Canada and the United
    Kingdom have the business sector shape
    the allocation of economic and other
    resources. Conservative political economies
    such as France and Germany emphasize
    stability and security while maintaining status-
    related employment differences.

REFERENCES

Acheson, D. 1998. *Independent Inquiry into Inequalities in Health.* London: The Stationery Office.

Alesina, A., and E.L. Glaeser. 2004. *Fighting Poverty in the US and Europe: A World of Difference.* Toronto: Oxford University Press.

Auger, N., M. Raynault, R. Lessard, and R. Choinière. 2004. "Income and Health in Canada." In *Social Determinants of Health: Canadian Perspectives*, edited by D. Raphael. Toronto: Canadian Scholars' Press.

Baxter, S. 1995. *No Way to Live: Poor Women Speak Out.* Vancouver: New Star Books.

Browne, G. 2004. "Early Childhood Education and Health." In *Social Determinants of Health: Canadian Perspectives*, edited by D. Raphael. Toronto: Canadian Scholars' Press.

Bryant, T. 2004. "Housing and Health." In *Social Determinants of Health: Canadian Perspectives*, edited by D. Raphael. Toronto: Canadian Scholars' Press.

Canadian Institute of Child Health. (CICH) 2000. *The Health of Canada's Children: A CICH Profile*, 3rd ed. Ottawa: CICH.

Chunn, D.E., and A.M. Gavigan. 2004. "Welfare Law, Welfare Fraud, and the Moral Regulation of the 'Never Deserving' Poor." *Social and Legal Studies* 13 (2): 219-43.

Coburn, D. 2001. "Health, Health Care, and Neo-Liberalism." In *Unhealthy Times: The Political Economy of Health and Care in Canada*, edited by P. Armstrong, H. Armstrong, and D. Coburn. Toronto: Oxford University Press.

———. 2004. "Beyond the Income Inequality Hypothesis: Globalization, Neo-Liberalism, and Health Inequalities." *Social Science and Medicine* 58 (1): 41-56.

———. 2006. "Health and Health Care: A Political Economy Perspective." In *Staying Alive: Critical Perspectives on Health, Illness, and Health Care*, edited by D. Raphael, T. Bryant, and M. Rioux. Toronto: Canadian Scholars' Press.

Davies, L., J.A. McMullin, W.R. Avison, and G.L. Cassidy. 2001. *Social Policy, Gender and Poverty.* Ottawa: Status of Women Canada.

Esping-Andersen, G. 1985. *Politics against Markets: The Social Democratic Road to Power.* Princeton, NJ: Princeton University Press.

———. 1990. *The Three Worlds of Welfare Capitalism.* New York: Oxford University Press.

_____. 2002. "A Child-Centred Social Investment Strategy." In *Why We Need a New Welfare State*, edited by G. Esping-Andersen. Oxford: Oxford University Press.

Friendly, M. 2004. "Early Childhood Education and Care." In *Social Determinants of Health: Canadian Perspectives*, edited by D. Raphael. Toronto: Canadian Scholars' Press.

Galabuzi, G.E. 2005. *Canada's Economic Apartheid: The Social Exclusion of Racialized Groups in the New Century*. Toronto: Canadian Scholars' Press.

Gordon, D. 2006. "The Concept and Measurement of Poverty." In *Poverty and Social Exclusion in Britain: The Millennium Survey*, edited by C. Pantazis, D. Gordon, and R. Levitas. Bristol, UK: Policy Press.

Innocenti Research Centre. 2005. *Child Poverty in Rich Nations, 2005*. Report Card 6. Florence, Italy: Innocenti Research Centre.

Jackson, A. 2004. "The Unhealthy Canadian Workplace." In *Social Determinants of Health: Canadian Perspectives*, edited by D. Raphael. Toronto: Canadian Scholars' Press.

Kozyrskyj, A., C. Mustard, and F. Simons. 2001. "Socioeconomic Status, Drug Insurance Benefits and New Prescriptions for Inhaled Corticosteroids in Schoolchildren with Asthma." *Archives of Pediatrics and Adolescent Medicine* 155 (11): 1219-24.

Lexchin, J. 2001. *A National Pharmacare Plan: Combining Efficiency and Equity*. Ottawa: Canadian Centre for Policy Alternatives.

_____. 2007. *Canadian Drug Prices and Expenditures: Some Statistical Observations and Policy Implications*. Ottawa: Canadian Centre for Policy Alternatives.

Lynch, J. 2000. "Income Inequality and Health: Expanding the Debate." *Social Science and Medicine* 51 (7): 1001-5.

Marmot, M., and R. Wilkinson. 2006. *Social Determinants of Health*, 2nd ed. Oxford: Oxford University Press.

McIntyre, L., S. Officer, and L.M. Robinson. 2003. "Feeling Poor: The Felt Experience of Low-Income Lone Mothers." *Affilia* 18 (3): 316-31.

McKeown, T. 1976. *The Role of Medicine: Dream, Mirage, or Nemesis?* London: Neufeld Provincial Hospitals Trust.

McKinlay, J., and S.M. McKinlay. 1987. "Medical Measures and the Decline of Mortality." In *Dominant Issues in Medical Sociology*, edited by H.D. Schwartz. New York: Random House.

Millar, W.J. 1999. "Disparities in Prescription Drug Insurance Coverage." *Health Reports* 10 (4): 11-31.

Mosher, J., P. Evans, E. Morrow, J. Boulding, and N. VanderPlaats. 2004. *Walking on Eggshells: Abused Women's Experiences of Ontario's Welfare System*. Toronto: York University.

Moynihan, R., and A. Cassels. 2005. *Selling Sickness*. Toronto: Greystone Books.

National Council of Welfare. 2001. *The Cost of Poverty*. Ottawa: National Council of Welfare.

_____. 2004. *Income for Living?* Ottawa: National Council of Welfare.

Navarro, V., and L. Shi. 2002. "The Political Context of Social Inequalities and Health." In *The Political Economy of Social Inequalities: Consequences for Health and Quality of Life*, edited by V. Navarro. Amityville, NY: Baywood.

Neysmith, S., K. Bezanson, and A. O'Connell. 2005. *Telling Tales: Living the Effects of Public Policy*. Halifax, NS: Fernwood Publishing.

Ocean, C. 2005. *Policies of Exclusion, Poverty and Health*. Duncan, BC: WISE Society.

Organisation for Economic Co-operation and Development (OECD). 1999. *The Battle against Exclusion: Social Assistance in Canada and Switzerland*. Paris: OECD.

_____. 2005. *Society at a Glance: OECD Social Indicators, 2005 Edition*. Paris: OECD.

Rachlis, M. 2004. *Prescription for Excellence: How Innovation Is Saving Canada's Health Care System*. Toronto: HarperCollins.

Raphael, D., ed. 2004. *Social Determinants of Health: Canadian Perspectives*. Toronto: Canadian Scholars' Press.

———. 2007a. "Canadian Public Policy and Poverty in International Perspective." In *Poverty and Policy in Canada: Implications for Health and Quality of Life*, edited by D. Raphael. Toronto: Canadian Scholars' Press.

———. 2007b. "The Future of the Canadian Welfare State." In *Poverty and Policy in Canada: Implications for Health and Quality of Life*, edited by D. Raphael. Toronto: Canadian Scholars' Press.

———. 2007c. "Poverty and Health." In *Poverty and Policy in Canada: Implications for Health and Quality of Life*, edited by D. Raphael. Toronto: Canadian Scholars' Press.

———. 2007d. "Poverty and Health: Mechanisms and Pathways." In *Poverty and Policy in Canada: Implications for Health and Quality of Life*, edited by D. Raphael. Toronto: Canadian Scholars' Press.

Raphael, D., and T. Bryant. 2006. "Maintaining Population Health in a Period of Welfare State Decline: Political Economy as the Missing Dimension in Health Promotion Theory and Practice." *Promotion and Education* 13 (4): 12-8.

Reid, C. 2004. *The Wounds of Exclusion: Poverty, Women's Health, and Social Justice*. Edmonton: Qual Institute Press.

Robinson, L.M., L. McIntyre, and S. Officer. 2005. "Welfare Babies: Poor Children's Experiences Informing Healthy Peer Relationships in Canada." *Health Promotion International* 20 (4): 342-50.

Roos, N.P., and C.A. Mustard. 1997. "Variation in Health Care Use by Socioeconomic Status in Winnipeg, Canada: Does the System Work Well? Yes and No." *Millbank Quarterly* 75 (1): 89-111.

Ross, D.P., and P. Roberts. 1999. *Income and Child Well-Being: A New Perspective on the Poverty Debate*. Ottawa: Canadian Council on Social Development.

Saint-Arnaud, S., and P. Bernard. 2003. "Convergence or Resilience? A Hierarchical Cluster Analysis of the Welfare Regimes in Advanced Countries." *Current Sociology* 51 (5): 499-527.

Schoen, C., and M.M. Doty. 2004. "Inequities in Access to Medical Care in Five Countries: Findings from the 2001 Commonwealth Fund International Health Policy Study." *Health Policy* 67 (3): 309-22.

Shaw, M., D. Dorling, D. Gordon, and G. Davey Smith. 1999. *The Widening Gap: Health Inequalities and Policy in Britain*. Bristol, UK: The Policy Press.

Swanson, J. 2001. *Poor-Bashing: The Politics of Exclusion*. Toronto: Between the Lines Press.

Tremblay, D.G. 2004. "Unemployment and the Labour Market." In *Social Determinants of Health: Canadian Perspectives*, edited by D. Raphael. Toronto: Canadian Scholars' Press.

Wilkins, R. 1999. "Health Status of Children." *Health Reports* 11 (3): 25-34.

Wilkins, R., J.-M. Berthelot, and E. Ng. 2002. "Trends in Mortality by Neighbourhood Income in Urban Canada from 1971 to 1996." *Health Reports* 13 (Supplement):1-28. Accessed July 27, 2007. www.statcan.ca/bsolc/english/bsolc?catno=82-003-S20020016353

Wilkins, R., C. Houle, J.-M. Berthelot, and D.P. Ross. 2000. "The Changing Health Status of Canada's Children." *ISUMA* 1 (2): 57-63.

Wright, E.O. 1994. "The Class Analysis of Poverty." In *Interrogating Inequality*, edited by E.O. Wright. New York: Verso.

Xi, G., I. McDowell, R. Nair, and R. Spasoff. 2005. "Income Inequality and Health in Ontario: A Multilevel Analysis." *Canadian Journal of Public Health* 96 (3): 206-11.

PRODUCTIVITY

THREE POLICIES TO INCREASE PRODUCTIVITY GROWTH IN CANADA

Andrew Sharpe

Labour productivity growth in the Canadian economy has been weak since 2000. Yet increased productivity growth is by far the most important determinant of increased material living standards for Canadians. It is also the most important means by which any fiscal pressures arising from the demographic challenges associated with an aging population can be met. From this perspective, lagging productivity growth represents a serious economic problem that must be addressed for the sake of Canadians' future living standards (Lynch 2006).

My objective in this chapter is to suggest ways to improve the productivity performance of the Canadian economy. I set the stage by discussing the context of the productivity debate and by examining the optics of productivity policy in Canada. Then I present three concrete policy proposals to improve productivity:

/ foster the diffusion of best-practice technologies;

/ remove provincial sales taxes on purchases of machinery and equipment; and

/ promote interprovincial movement of workers by improving labour market information, removing professional barriers to labour mobility and establishing a tax credit for interprovincial job search.

THE CONTEXT FOR THE PRODUCTIVITY DEBATE IN CANADA

To engage in constructive and meaningful debate on effective policies to raise productivity levels in Canada, it is useful to have some background on the productivity issue. Accordingly, here I briefly discuss definitions of productivity measures and concepts; the relationship among productivity, material living standards and well-being; the main drivers of productivity growth; and Canada's recent productivity performance.

Basic productivity definitions and concepts

Economists define productivity as the ratio of output to inputs.[1] A partial measure of productivity can be obtained by dividing output (either value added or gross output) by a single input. The best-known partial productivity measure, and the one on which I focus, is the ratio of output to labour input — or labour productivity. Other partial productivity measures are capital productivity, energy productivity (or intensity) and materials productivity. A total factor or multifactor productivity measure is the ratio of output to two or more inputs that are combined in a composite input index — in effect, a measure of the efficiency with which inputs are used. Total factor productivity measures are most often based on capital and labour as inputs, but can also include energy, materials and purchased services. From the point of view of increasing material living standards and real wages, however, labour productivity is key, because real income can be increased in the long run only if more real output is produced, rather than by simply increasing the efficiency of production. Thus, in all references to productivity in this chapter, I mean labour productivity.[2]

Finally, it is important to distinguish between the *level* and the *growth rate* of productivity. The level of productivity is the measure of the ratio of output to input; the growth rate of productivity is the rate of change of the ratio of output to input. Thus, the level might be low even though the current growth rate is high, and vice versa. Business analysts tend to focus on the level of productivity in specific firms or industries because this concept is more closely aligned with the notion of the competitive success of the enterprises. Similarly, as we will see shortly, indicators of average material living standards are closely related to the level of aggregate productivity. The growth rate of productivity, in contrast, is reflective not of material living standards but of how quickly those living standards (high or low) are changing over time.

The contribution of productivity to economic growth, living standards and well-being

One way to decompose economic growth — that is, growth in real gross domestic product (GDP) or real output — is to look at the growth of labour inputs as measured by hours worked and the growth of labour productivity, defined as output per hour worked. As table 1 shows, productivity growth accounted for 63 percent of Canada's economic growth over the 1947-2006 period. Labour productivity's contribution to that growth was larger in the 1947-73 period (77 percent) than from 1973 to 2006 (45 percent).

TABLE 1. **THE RELATIONSHIP BETWEEN GDP AND PRODUCTIVITY IN CANADA, 1947-2006**

	GDP (millions of 1997 chained $)	Total hours worked for all jobs (millions)	Labour productivity (1997 chained $)
	A = B x C	B	C
1947	132,799	13,063	10.17
1973	457,766	17,349	26.39
1996	846,952	24,298	34.86
2000	1,020,488	26,607	38.35
2006	1,191,073	29,054	41.00
2026[1]	1,705,965	30,897	55.21

Compound average annual growth rates (percent)

	A ≈ B + C	B	C
1947-2006	3.79	1.36	2.39
1947-1973	4.87	1.10	3.74
1973-2006	2.71	1.48	1.22
1973-1996	2.94	1.57	1.34
1996-2000	4.77	2.30	2.42
2000-2006	2.61	1.48	1.12
2006-2026[1]	1.81	0.31	1.50

Relative contribution to GDP growth (percent)[2]

	A = B + C	B	C
1947-2006	100	36.0	63.1
1947-1973	100	22.5	76.6
1973-2006	100	54.4	44.9
1973-1996	100	53.6	45.7
1996-2000	100	48.1	50.7
2000-2006	100	56.6	42.8
2006-2026[1]	100	17.0	82.8

Source: Statistics Canada, CANSIM.
[1] From 2006 to 2026, labour productivity is assumed to grow by 1.5 percent per year; average hours worked per week are held at the 2006 level; employment is assumed to grow at the same rate as that of the labour force; and labour force growth is based on projected growth in the 15-64 age group with the 2006 labour force participation rate for this age group held constant.
[2] Numbers might not add up to 100 due to rounding.

The size of the working-age population (those ages 15 to 64) is the primary driver of the trend in hours of potential labour supply, which, in turn, is determined by employment trends. In theory, declines in the unemployment rate, higher labour force participation rates and increases in average annual hours worked could offset declines in the size of the working-age population. But the magnitude of changes from these sources is too small to offset demographic developments.

Consequently, with the aging of the baby boomers and their retirement from the workforce, which will start in a few years, labour force growth will fall significantly, turning negative around 2023 (figure 1).[3] Thus, as sources of economic growth, hours worked will also fall and productivity growth will assume a greater relative importance. It is estimated that, from 2006 to 2026, with employment growth expected to be only 0.3 percent per year, productivity growth will account for 83 percent of economic growth (see table 1). In effect, once employment growth disappears around 2023, economic growth will become synonymous with labour productivity growth. In the future, if Canada wants to increase GDP, it will have to increase labour productivity.

GDP per capita — the most widely used measure of material living standards — can be thought of as the product of labour productivity (defined as output per hour worked at the total economy level), the average number of hours each employed person works and the proportion of the entire population that is employed.[4] Likewise, the

FIGURE 1.   NET LABOUR FORCE GROWTH IN CANADA, 1977-2026

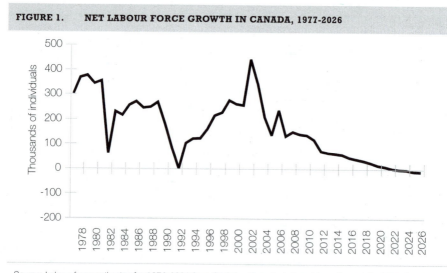

Source: Labour force estimates for 1976-2006 from Statistics Canada, Labour Force Survey; for 2007-2026 from Statistics Canada, Population Estimates and Projections.
Note: Projected labour force estimates are calculated by multiplying projected population by the 2006 labour force participation rate.

growth rate of real income, as proxied by the GDP per capita growth rate, can be approximately decomposed into the summation of the growth rates of these three variables.

As table 2 shows, over the 1947-2006 period, Canada's GDP per capita grew by 2.12 percent per year on average, driven entirely by productivity growth of 2.39 percent per year. In other words, productivity growth accounted for 113 percent of the increase in living standards over the period.[5] Strong productivity growth from 1947 to 1973, in particular, accounted for 146 percent of the growth in living standards over that period. In absolute terms, growth in GDP per capita fell from an average annual rate of 2.55 percent in the period 1947-73 to 1.79 percent in the 1973-2006 period. The 2.4 percentage point slowdown in labour productivity growth between these periods more than accounted for the deceleration in growth of income per capita.[6]

Demographic developments will mean that, in the future, productivity gains will be more important as a source of advances in living standards than they were in the 1973-2006 period. Between 2006 and 2026, the rapid growth in the population of those ages 65 and older will cause the employment-population ratio to fall, putting downward pressure on growth in material living standards. With no expected increase in average weekly hours, 143 percent of the growth in living standards could be attributed to increases in productivity.

In addition to its positive effect on living standards, productivity growth has a salutary effect on the broader concepts of economic and social well-being. In an earlier study (Sharpe 2002), I show that productivity growth can lead to improvements in a number of dimensions of economic well-being, including consumption flows, stocks of wealth, equality and economic security (see also Osberg and Sharpe 2001, 2002; Banting, Sharpe, and St-Hilaire 2002).

Productivity drivers

In developing policies to improve productivity performance, it is important first to identify the drivers of productivity growth (see Harris 2002). The standard starting point for the discussion of the dynamics of productivity growth is the simple neoclassical growth-accounting model. In this model, three key factors determine labour productivity growth. The first is investment in capital goods, which determines the size of the capital stock and, hence, the amount of machinery, equipment and structures available to each worker: higher ratios of capital to labour — capital intensity, to economists — boost labour productivity. The second factor is investment in human resources, which determines the quality of labour input: more human capital makes a worker more productive. The third key factor is the pace of technological progress, which is very roughly

TABLE 2.	THE RELATIONSHIP BETWEEN REAL PER CAPITA INCOME AND PRODUCTIVITY IN CANADA, 1947-2006			
	GDP per capita (1997 chained $)	Output per hour (1997 chained $)	Average work-week (hours)	Employment-population ratio
	A = B x (C x 52) x (D/100)	B	C	D
1947	10,586	10.17	50.50	39.60
1973	20,387	26.39	37.00	40.10
1996	28,642	34.86	34.80	45.40
2000	33,294	38.35	34.70	48.20
2006	36,557	41.00	33.90	50.60
2026[1]	45,040	55.21	33.90	46.30

Compound average annual growth rates (percent)

	A ≈ B + C + D	B	C	D
1947-2006	2.12	2.39	-0.68	0.42
1947-1973	2.55	3.74	-1.19	0.05
1973-2006	1.79	1.34	-0.27	0.70
1973-1996	1.49	1.22	-0.27	0.54
1996-2000	3.83	2.42	-0.11	1.50
2000-2006	1.57	1.12	-0.37	0.82
2006-2026[1]	1.05	1.50	0.00	-0.45

Relative contribution to the growth rate of GDP per capita (percent)[2]

	A = B + C + D	B	C	D
1947-2006	100	112.70	-31.80	19.60
1947-1973	100	146.40	-46.60	1.90
1973-2006	100	81.80	-18.00	36.00
1973-1996	100	75.30	-15.00	39.50
1996-2000	100	63.10	-3.00	39.10
2000-2006	100	71.10	-23.50	52.30
2006-2026[1]	100	143.00	0.00	-42.40

Source: Statistics Canada, CANSIM .
[1] From 2006 to 2026, labour productivity is assumed to grow by 1.5 percent per year; average hours worked per week are held at the 2006 level; employment is assumed to grow at the same rate as that of the labour force; and labour force growth is based on projected growth in the 15-64 age group with the 2006 labour force participation rate for this age group held constant.
[2] Numbers might not add up to 100 due to rounding.

proxied by the rate of total factor productivity growth: technological progress is affected by the development of new knowledge through research and development (R&D).

Capital investment, human capital and technological change might be the proximate sources of labour productivity growth, but by themselves cannot explain why productivity growth actually takes place. Rather, it is the decisions of businesses to invest and innovate and of workers to acquire human capital that drive advances in business sector productivity. These decisions are affected by many factors, such as the state of business confidence, the entrepreneurial spirit of the business class and — the focus of this chapter — government policies.

Government policies affect the environment in which businesses operate in myriad ways. The existence or absence of the rule of law is an obvious example, although of more relevance at the margin to developing than developed countries. Macroeconomic policies that affect the business environment include monetary policy, fiscal policy, tax policy and trade policy, among others. Policies of a more microeconomic nature that affect the business environment include competition policy, regulatory policies and intellectual property protection.

The magnitude of the effect of government policies on business sector productivity growth is difficult to gauge. There is no doubt that, through bad policy, government can have a significant detrimental effect on economic and productivity growth. Stagnant countries rife with corruption and lacking appropriate governance structures testify to the ability of government to kill the economy — recent developments in Zimbabwe drive home this point. Thankfully, such a situation is not relevant to Canada, with its democratic traditions, strong rule of law and professional public service.

Long-run business sector productivity growth in Canada is driven primarily by the pace of technological change, supported by human resource development, and is not impeded in a significant way by current government policies. In an ideal world, however, one would prefer government policies that were actively conducive to productivity growth. At the same time, one must be realistic about the potential for government policies to make a major difference. The Bank of Canada (Bank of Canada 2006) estimates Canada's potential labour productivity growth to be about 1.5 percent per year — it is unlikely that better government policies could, say, double that rate. Still, in my view, better policies might add as much as 0.5 of a percentage point per year over the medium term, although factors such as faster technological progress and capital accumulation would have a much greater effect. Indeed, few economists would argue that the rapid acceleration of labour productivity in the United States since 1995 has been driven primarily by improved public policy.

Although the effect of better public policies on productivity might seem small, in an economy the size of Canada's it would still amount to a large sum: an increase of half a percentage point in the nominal value of Canada's GDP in 2006 would have equalled $7 billion — well worth the search for and funding of public policies that could effectuate such an increase in income.

Two other factors also influence productivity growth and levels. One is the reallocation of labour and capital across sectors of the economy. As a general rule, workers leave firms, industries, sectors and regions characterized by below-average productivity levels and move to those characterized by above-average levels. This movement produces a bonus to aggregate productivity growth above the contribution from productivity gains within sectors — the postwar movement of Canadian workers out of low-productivity agriculture is the best-known historical example of this source of aggregate productivity growth.

The other factor that affects aggregate productivity relates to changes in relative prices — especially notable in the natural resource industries. Increases in resource prices increase the value of output produced in these sectors. Even if the volume of output is unchanged, real GDP (as conventionally measured) rises, and so does measured productivity. If the volume of resource output rises, then the effect is increased. Applying the argument in the current Canadian context, increases in the world price of oil over the past few years have increased measured GDP and

FIGURE 2.   PROVINCIAL GDP PER WORKER AS A PROPORTION OF THE NATIONAL AVERAGE, 2005

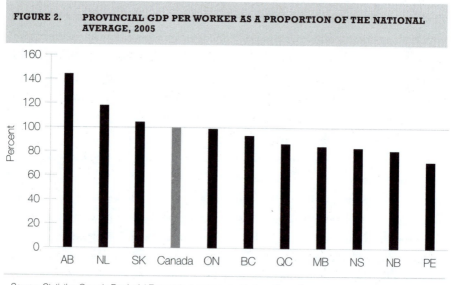

Source: Statistics Canada Provincial Economic Accounts and Labour Force Survey.

productivity in the oil-producing regions of the country — Alberta's GDP per worker increased from 111 percent of the national average in 1999 to 144 percent in 2005, largely as a result of increases in oil prices (figure 2).

Productivity trends

The Canadian economy has performed well on almost all indicators in recent years. Output and employment growth have been strong, inflation and unemployment are low, the federal government deficit has long since been eliminated, public debt is falling both in absolute terms and relative to GDP, and the Canadian dollar has appreciated. As the Organisation for Economic Co-operation and Development remarks in its 2006 country report on Canada (OECD 2006a, 9), "The Canadian economy has continued to deliver excellent results in nearly all respects." A recent report on Canada by the International Monetary Fund (IMF 2007) reaches a similar conclusion.

As both the IMF and the OECD point out, however, one area in which Canada has performed relatively poorly in recent years is productivity growth, despite its paramount importance to future living standards.[7] Between 1996 and 2000, business sector output per hour increased at an average annual rate of 2.9 percent, but between 2000 and 2006, that growth rate was just 1.1 percent. Moreover, Canada's productivity growth has also been weak relative to that of the United States, where the business sector's output per hour growth rate has averaged 3.0 percent per year since 2000 (figure 3). As figure 4 shows, Canada's lagging labour productivity growth has widened the business sector labour productivity gap between Canada and the United States from 17 percentage points in 2000, when it was 83 percent of the US level, to 26 points in 2006, or 74 percent of the US level (see also Rao, Tang, and Wang 2004).[8]

Canada's productivity performance has also been weak relative to the average of OECD countries. Over the 1973-2006 period, output per hour in Canada advanced at only a 1.2 percent average annual rate, one of the lowest in the OECD. During the 1950-73 period, in contrast, Canada's level of output per hour grew at an average rate of 3.0 percent per year, among the highest in the OECD (see table 3 and figure 5).

The causes of the fall-off in labour productivity growth in Canada after 2000 are still poorly understood. Possible explanations include sluggish investment in information and communication technology; failure to exploit advanced technologies; exploitation of poorer-quality resources in mining industries such as the oil sands; weak wage growth leading to a slower rate of substitution of capital for labour; and measurement problems (Rao, Sharpe, and Smith 2005). Indeed, the inability of productivity analysts to provide a definitive account of the reasons for Canada's poor

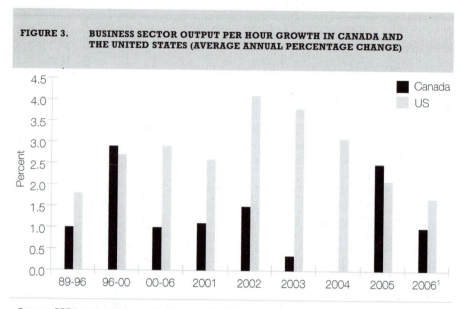

FIGURE 3.   BUSINESS SECTOR OUTPUT PER HOUR GROWTH IN CANADA AND THE UNITED STATES (AVERAGE ANNUAL PERCENTAGE CHANGE)

Sources: GDP in chained dollars and total hours worked from the Productivity and Costs Program of the Bureau of Labor Statistics for the United States, and annual averages of quarterly estimates from the Productivity Program Database of Statistics Canada for Canada.
[1] Canada's 2006 estimate is for the first three quarters only.

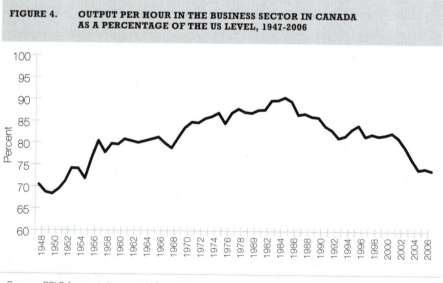

FIGURE 4.   OUTPUT PER HOUR IN THE BUSINESS SECTOR IN CANADA AS A PERCENTAGE OF THE US LEVEL, 1947-2006

Sources: CSLS Aggregate Income and Productivity Database.

TABLE 3.   RELATIVE OUTPUT PER HOUR IN SELECTED OECD COUNTRIES, 1950-2006

(United States = 100)

	1950	1973	1995	2000	2006
Australia	73.4	75.3	82.1	82.2	78.2
Austria	30.0	62.9	89.2	92.4	89.1
Belgium	49.1	79.7	105.2	102.6	95.7
Canada	81.0	88.5	85.5	83.2	78.1
Denmark	56.5	74.6	97.3	91.8	85.9
Finland	33.9	54.5	80.0	81.8	81.7
France	42.1	73.9	104.9	104.1	100.1
All Germany			88.2	87.0	82.5
West Germany	36.7	75.4	108.3		
Ireland	29.0	44.3	79.8	96.7	98.1
Italy	42.9	75.9	99.4	93.2	81.2
Japan	18.3	51.3	74.0	71.9	71.7
Luxembourg	66.7	84.7	106.6	107.2	102.4
Netherlands	56.8	84.6	98.9	96.4	91.1
New Zealand[1]	92.0	67.6	64.5	61.8	56.3
Norway	51.2	73.8	114.0	114.2	111.1
Portugal	18.1	43.3	51.5	54.4	48.3
South Korea[2]	17.8	17.0	38.4	41.2	44.6
Spain	21.2	44.5	80.1	71.1	60.7
Sweden	57.4	80.6	84.5	85.3	86.4
Switzerland	73.1	88.7	84.0	81.0	76.9
United Kingdom	61.9	66.0	86.6	86.4	84.4
United States	100.0	100.0	100.0	100.0	100.0
Unweighted average[3]	48.1	67.0	86.5	85.0	81.2

Source: Groningen Growth and Development Centre and the Conference Board, Total Economy Database, June 2007.
[1] Data for New Zealand shown for 1950 are actually for 1956, the first year for which data are available for both New Zealand and the United States.
[2] Data for South Korea shown for 1950 are actually for 1963, the first year for which data are available for both South Korea and the United States.
[3] The average excludes the United States for relative levels. For 1950 and 1973, West Germany is included and All Germany is excluded. For 1995, 2000 and 2006, All Germany is included and West Germany is excluded.

FIGURE 5.   AVERAGE ANNUAL GROWTH IN OUTPUT PER HOUR, SELECTED OECD COUNTRIES, 1973-2006

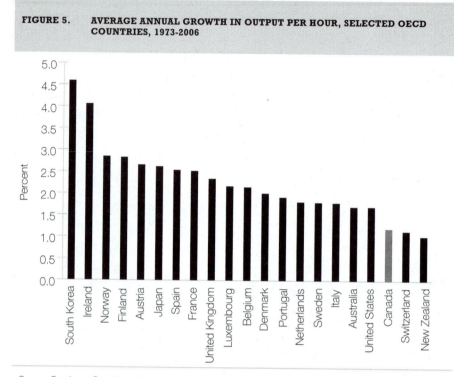

Source: Groningen Growth and Development Centre and the Conference Board, Total Economy Database, February 2007.

productivity growth makes the development of policies to reverse this situation more difficult: if we knew what was wrong, we could take appropriate action. But the historical and international data speak for themselves: Canada's productivity growth rate is sub-par, and is falling behind that of other OECD countries. We do know, however, that technological change and investment are fundamental drivers of productivity growth. Reviving that growth is the biggest economic challenge Canada faces.[9]

WHY PRODUCTIVITY IS A TOUGH SELL

Despite the consensus among economists about the importance of productivity to the Canadian economy, few governments or political parties are willing to address the issue.[10] Indeed, politicians tend to avoid the word, preferring euphemisms such as prosperity and innovation (Gardiner 2005), since they know that productivity does not poll well or resonate as an issue for Canadians. Why does the general public appear to be allergic to talk about productivity? What are the public's misconceptions of what productivity is all about?

Productivity myths and misconceptions

Public distrust or ambiguity about productivity stems largely from a number of misconceptions and a lack of knowledge about what productivity is and how it works.

First, people associate productivity increases with working longer hours. Indeed, a person who works longer hours might produce more than someone who works fewer hours, and might be considered more productive on that basis. But the relevant metric for productivity measurement is output per hour, not per person. Working longer hours does not represent an advance in productivity in this sense.

Second, workers sometimes regard exhortations by employers to improve productivity as a way to get them to work faster and harder. It is true that greater worker intensity is a potential source of productivity growth, although its sustainability is questionable. But few advocate this measure as a means to increase productivity. It is widely recognized that the key to productivity growth is to "work smarter, not harder."

Many also fear that higher productivity at the industry or firm level translates into layoffs — that striving for productivity advance just means working oneself out of a job. This can be true in an individual industry or firm characterized by strong productivity gains and limited potential for increases in demand for output — an example is agriculture, where productivity has soared and employment plummeted over the past half-century. At the level of the total economy, however, there is no long-run negative relationship between productivity and employment. Productivity growth increases potential real income, which, in turn, increases demand, resulting in employment opportunities in new industries. There is no reason, therefore, that productivity growth should have negative long-run consequences for total employment. Indeed, there is reason to believe that aggregate productivity growth actually drives increases in aggregate employment — as long as total hours worked increase with higher real wages (positively sloped labour supply curve). Individual workers are naturally concerned about the effects of productivity on their jobs, but they typically do not think about the employment opportunities created by rising aggregate productivity growth.

For some people, productivity growth is associated with economic growth, which they believe contributes to environmental degradation and climate change. Certain environmentalists regard the consequence of raising productivity and income as more spending, which means, for example, more and bigger cars and hence more greenhouse gas emissions. But it is not inevitable that increased production and consumption must harm the environment. With the appropriate tax and regulatory regimes, any negative environmental effects from productivity and economic growth can be minimized. Indeed, rich countries are better positioned to take the steps needed to preserve the environment than poor countries. Thus, productivity growth, by transforming poor countries into rich countries, could be more a part of the solution to environmental degradation than its cause.

These myths and misconceptions about productivity could pose a serious barrier to the development of effective policies to improve productivity. If the public feels that productivity advance is not in its interest or not important or does not understand what productivity is and why it is important, governments will have little political incentive to pursue the issue.

Productivity is a tough sell for another reason as well. Workers are encouraged to strive for more productivity on the premise that their wages and benefits will rise in tandem with productivity growth. Indeed, this has been the historical experience in Canada. In recent years, however, increases in median labour compensation have not kept pace with productivity gains. This bifurcation of productivity and wage growth reflects the increased share of nonwage components (such as profits) in national income and the increased inequality in labour income fuelled by strong gains in labour compensation for those in the top income brackets. If average workers benefit little from productivity growth, why should they care about productivity gains? If productivity is to resonate as an issue of importance with the public, productivity gains must be more equitably distributed. Productivity growth with equity must be the clarion call to build broad-based support for a productivity agenda.

In an ideal world, governments should strive to educate the public about the importance of productivity, to convince the public to see productivity as an opportunity, not a threat. But this is a long-term project. In the short to medium term, governments can still do much to improve productivity by highlighting policies to foster innovation, investment and human capital. These drivers of productivity have much better press than productivity itself, and the public will react more positively to actions that address problems or weaknesses in these areas.

There is more to life than productivity

For Canadians, the bottom line should be quality of life, measured in both objective and subjective terms. The economic dimensions of quality of life are but one aspect of overall well-being. Canadians do not have to — and do not want to; see Graves and Jenkins (2002) — pursue productivity and wealth creation to the detriment of other aspects of existence, especially since this is already a very rich country. Fortunately, no irreconcilable tradeoffs appear to be necessary between the pursuit of higher productivity — and hence a higher material standard of living — and the pursuit of other aspects of well-being, such as environmental quality.

In a critique of productivity as a social priority, Heath (2002) points out that certain types of goods — such as houses in desirable locations — are in such scarce supply that no amount of productivity growth could make them available to the general population. Indeed, one must closely assess the relative benefits of allocating scarce resources to programs and policies designed to enhance productivity as opposed to those meant to achieve other societal goals, and programs and policies to boost productivity might not have the highest return for society. But many measures that can be used to foster productivity could be implemented merely through changes in policy regimes, the costs of which are minimal. If more intelligent public policy can provide free lunches, why not pursue it?

Some skeptics of productivity growth suggest that, given the high standard of living Canadians have already achieved, further productivity gains might be less important than they once were, particularly if they involved significant short-term sacrifice or opportunity costs. According to this view, higher productivity and income do not lead to greater happiness, so why bother to expend effort to achieve it when there is so much else in life? It is, of course, true that productivity growth does not guarantee happiness. But productivity does lead to greater income, which in principle can be used to raise economic well-being, at least as measured objectively. Households can use increased income arising from higher productivity for private consumption; governments can use it to fund public services or to provide income support for the disadvantaged.

To sum up, the upcoming retirement of the baby boom generation will cause the growth of Canada's net labour force and employment to vanish. Instead, all economic growth and GDP per capita growth will come from productivity growth. Labour productivity growth of at least 2.0 percent per year over the next 50 years would be sufficient to manage the financial burden arising from the aging baby boomers. Such growth would mean significantly higher real incomes, which would generate greater tax revenues to pay for the additional health and pension costs of Canada's rising population of seniors.[11] Productivity growth that is significantly lower than this rate, however, could lead to sustainability problems for social programs.

In short, the message that Canadians must hear is that productivity growth is vital to their economic destiny.

POLICIES TO IMPROVE CANADIAN PRODUCTIVITY

As part of the effort to design intelligent public policy to improve productivity in Canada, I propose three specific policy changes: foster the diffusion of best-practice technologies; remove the provincial sales tax on purchases of machinery and equipment; and promote interprovincial movement of workers by improving labour market information, removing professional barriers to labour mobility and establishing a tax credit for interprovincial job search. Before I present the details of these three policies, it is useful to review some general principles for the application of productivity policy.

General principles for productivity policy

Productivity is determined, either directly or indirectly, by many factors, including the education and health of the workforce, the availability of all types of investment and technological change. Many public policies thus have some link to productivity, which interest groups often use in arguing for their own pet approaches to fostering growth. Such policies are not necessarily bad from the point of view of the overall societal interest, but any argument for a particular policy — such as lower taxes or more spending — that an interest group rationalizes or justifies by its effects on productivity should be viewed with suspicion: cloaking policy objectives in the blanket of the general interest in productivity growth can be an effective strategy for interest groups that seek primarily to promote their own narrow interests. Thus, in any assessment of policies to improve productivity, the general interest or benefits principle should be applied.

The private sector is directly responsible for the productivity performance of the business sector through its decisions on innovation and on investment in physical and human capital. Governments play a crucial role in setting the framework for these decisions, but there is little governments can do in the short to medium run to increase business sector productivity, since the effects of changes in framework policies take time to take hold. In the long run, of course, having the appropriate macroeconomic and microeconomic frameworks in place is essential for strong productivity performance.

As a general principle, the most important framework policy that governments can pursue to foster productivity growth is to ensure a competitive marketplace. There is much evidence from many countries that competition spurs productivity advance (Sharpe 2006b). A highly instructive example is the air passenger travel industry in Europe, deregulation of which led to the development of a number of low-cost, high-productivity airlines, such as Ryanair, that have revolutionized air travel. An example closer to home is the Canadian wine industry — the lowering of trade barriers meant that, to survive, the industry had to improve the quality of its product, a challenge the industry met. In a highly competitive environment, firms must invest, innovate and closely monitor costs to survive, with beneficial effects for productivity. Barriers to competition are the enemies of productivity growth.

Canadian governments have done much to provide a more conducive economic environment for productivity growth in the areas of monetary, fiscal and trade policy. Some segments of the economy are still protected from market forces, however, with negative implications for innovation, investment and productivity growth. Policies to enhance competition, in fact, might be more important for productivity growth than those directly aimed at improving productivity itself.

Policy proposal 1: Foster more rapid diffusion and adoption of best-practice technologies

Technological progress is the most important determinant of productivity advance. At any given time, only a few firms or countries are on the frontier of technologies that are the most advanced, efficient and cost-effective; the rest are left to play catch-up by adopting similar best-practice technologies. The rapid growth in Europe and Japan in the immediate postwar period in large part reflected their technological catching up or convergence with the United States, the world technology leader in most fields (Wolff 2000).

Canada, too, is playing catch-up relative to the United States: in 2001, Canada's level of labour productivity in the business sector, on average, was only 82 percent of that of the United States — labour productivity was below this average in 12 out of 27 Canadian industries (Rao, Tang, and Wang 2004, table 2).[12] The reasons for these large productivity gaps are complex.

One factor is that capital intensity — that is, capital per unit of labour — is lower in Canada than in the United States: total capital stock per hour worked in the Canadian business sector in 2001 was 85 percent of the US rate (Rao, Tang, and Wang 2004, table 4), while for machinery and equipment specifically, crucial for productivity growth, it was just 55 percent of the US rate in 2003 (Sharpe 2004, 22). This lower capital intensity reflects lower levels of investment. Indeed, investment in machinery and equipment in Canada as a share of GDP has considerably lagged behind that in the United States over the past half-century.

Investment is the vector through which most technological advances are manifested in the workplace — in effect, they are embodied in new capital goods. Canada's relatively weak investment in machinery and equipment, therefore, implies that the technology in use in Canada is, on average, older and therefore less advanced than that used in the United States. To the degree that Canadian firms in these industries are able to adopt advanced technologies through increased investment, some of the Canada-US labour productivity gap could be closed. From this perspective, public policies that foster the diffusion and adoption of best-practice technologies, largely through investment, have a significant role to play in improving Canada's productivity growth, in both absolute and relative terms. Yet Canada produces only a very small share of the world stock of new knowledge — it was responsible in 2004 for just 2.0 percent of total R&D spending and 2.9 percent of spending on R&D by OECD countries.

Some free-market economists argue that public policies to foster the adoption of new technologies are not needed because firms already have a huge economic incentive to adopt best-practice technologies: why should governments offer additional incentives for firms to do what is already in their interest? The counterargument is that certain types of firms, particularly small and medium-sized enterprises (SMEs), face barriers to the adoption of new technologies, which government policy can help them to overcome. The acquisition of information and the adoption of new technologies have a cost, and such firms might lack the time to keep abreast of new technological developments, the expertise to identify those that are potentially appropriate and to make effective use of them, as well as the financial resources to purchase the capital goods that embody the technology.

The federal and provincial governments devote significant resources to subsidizing private sector R&D activities, particularly through tax credits. Indeed, the federal Scientific Research and Experimental Development tax credit is projected to cost $2.7 billion in 2007 (Department of Finance Canada 2005). Very large subsidies (in the form of negative tax rates) for R&D are available at the provincial level as well, ranging in 2004 from a low of 40 percent in Alberta to a high of 202 percent in Quebec (Mackenzie 2005).

To be sure, R&D is important for innovation, particularly in high-technology sectors such as communications equipment and aeronautics. In 2002, however, only 12,272 Canadian firms — less than 1 percent of the total — actually reported performing R&D, with 100 firms accounting for 56 percent of all R&D (Statistics Canada 2006, 17). If the term "innovative" were reserved for firms that undertook R&D, few Canadian firms would qualify as innovative. An innovative firm is more appropriately defined, however, as one that introduces new production processes and products. By this criterion, 81 percent of manufacturing firms in Canada can be considered innovative according to the 1999 Survey of Innovation (Arundel and Mohnen 2003, 58). Thus, from the point of view of fostering productivity growth, R&D is not relevant for the vast majority of Canadian firms. More relevant is the adoption of best-practice technologies, yet this path to productivity improvement receives much less attention than R&D.[13]

A distinction thus needs to be made between innovation in the sense of knowledge creation (invention) and innovation in the sense of the adoption of existing technologies (diffusion). Lipsey, Carlaw and Bekar (2005, 518) suggest that economists have not appreciated the trade-off between invention and diffusion, as they assume that diffusion occurs instantaneously or costlessly. Innovators introduce new stand-alone technologies that diffuse through the economy in unchanged form. But invention and diffusion are separate activities. New technologies must be adapted for particular uses and require supporting technologies and facilitating structures. Lipsey, Carlaw and Bekar also point to sunk costs — defined as costs that have already been incurred and cannot be recovered to any significant degree — as a barrier to diffusion, a situation that, in their view, might justify public policy intervention:

> Sunk costs are important for the development of new products and processes; they are equally important for acquiring codifiable knowledge about new knowledge, as well as tacit knowledge about how to operate given technologies. One major policy implication is that governments can effectively disseminate technological knowledge by operating on a scale that makes the sunk costs bearable, or even trivial, where they would otherwise be prohibitively high for small firms. This is the objective of the Canadian Industrial Research Assistance Program…, which seeks, among other things, to help firms to identify existing technologies that are of potential value to them and to assist them in adapting these technologies to their specific needs. (2005, 520)

One could therefore make a case for rebalancing the relative efforts that Canadian governments devote to supporting private sector R&D activities and those supporting the adoption of best-practice technologies. To foster technological innovation and productivity growth, therefore, additional resources should be allocated to programs that assist SMEs to identify and adopt (or adapt) new technologies.

As Lipsey, Carlaw and Bekar (2005) note, a Canadian example of a successful technology transfer program is the National Research Council's Industrial Research Assistance Program (NRC-IRAP). The program provides a range of both technical and business-oriented advisory services, along with potential financial support to growth-oriented SMEs. The program is delivered by an extensive integrated network of 260 professionals in 90 communities across the country and serves over 12,000 firms annually. Working directly with these clients, NRC-IRAP supports innovative research and development and commercialization of new products and services. The IRAP portfolio of services has four main components: technology expertise and advisory services; financial assistance for R&D activities; networking; and partnerships.[14] IRAP's fiscal year 2005/06 budget was $216 million, up from $214 million in 2004/05 and $208 million in 2003/04 (Treasury Board of Canada 2006). In a 2002 evaluation, the NRC found that sales linked to IRAP-assisted innovations were 11 times the program's total contributions to clients, and concluded that IRAP had been successful in its mission of stimulating wealth for Canadians through technological innovation (NRC 2002). It should be noted, however, that no rigorous, independent evaluation of IRAP's activities has been undertaken in recent years, so definitive evidence of IRAP's cost-benefit ratio is absent.

Productivity advance in Canada could be fostered in a cost-effective manner by expanding existing technology transfer programs such as IRAP and by creating new programs with similar objectives. Specific initiatives to develop these types of programs merit serious attention.

Policy proposal 2: Remove provincial sales taxes on purchases of machinery and equipment

It has long been recognized that investment in machinery and equipment is a key driver of productivity growth, yet such investment historically has been weak in Canada relative to other OECD countries. According to the most recent OECD data, Canada devoted 6.3 percent of GDP to investment in machinery and equipment in 2004, ranking 20th out of 28 OECD countries (figure 6).

One important factor in the decision to invest is the cost of capital,[15] a proxy for which is the marginal effective tax rate (METR) on capital. Mintz (2006) finds that Canada's METR, at 36.6 percent, is one of the highest in the world; it is also third-highest among OECD countries, surpassed only by those of Germany and the United States (figure 7). Thus, one reason for the relatively lower level of investment in machinery and equipment in Canada might be the higher cost of capital in this country.

A key reason Canada's METR is so high is that five provinces — Ontario, British Columbia, Prince Edward Island, Saskatchewan and Manitoba — apply provincial sales tax (PST) to the purchase of capital goods, including machinery and equipment (which also includes information and communication technology goods). Because of this tax policy, these five provinces have much higher METRs than do the other provinces (see figure 8).[16] Federal Department of Finance analysis shows that, if

FIGURE 6.   MACHINERY AND EQUIPMENT INVESTMENT AS A PERCENTAGE OF GDP IN SELECTED OECD COUNTRIES, 2004

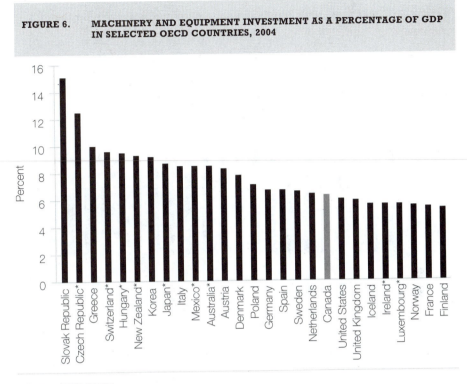

Source: OECD (2006b).
Data are not available for 2004, so data for the most recent year are used.

there were no PST on the purchase of capital goods, METRs in Canada would be approximately 5 percentage points lower than they are now (Department of Finance Canada 2005). Indeed, tax policy experts across the political spectrum are unanimous that the current PST regime's taxing of the purchase of new capital equipment is extremely bad policy — perhaps unique in its incompetence among developed countries. The effect of such a tax is to increase the price of capital relative to the price of labour, giving firms less incentive to substitute capital for labour and hence leading to slower growth in the capital-labour ratio, or capital intensity. Since capital intensity growth is a key driver of labour productivity, the latter suffers. Industry Canada economists estimate that Canada's lower level of machinery and equipment intensity relative to that of the United States accounted for 30.3 percent of the Canada-US labour productivity gap in the business sector in 2001 (Rao, Tang, and Wang 2004).

If Canada were a labour surplus country, there might be some justification for such a policy on the basis of fostering employment, at least in the short to medium term — although it is not clear that the long-run health of an economy is promoted

FIGURE 7. MARGINAL EFFECTIVE TAX RATE ON CAPITAL IN SELECTED OECD COUNTRIES, 2006

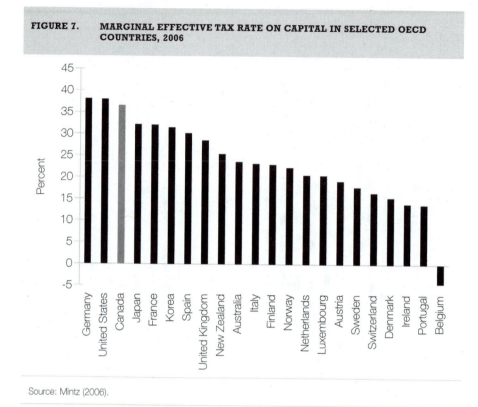

Source: Mintz (2006).

by subsidizing employment and taxing capital goods. But with the unemployment rate at around 6 percent, Canada should be encouraging substitution of capital for labour.

Evidence of the positive effect of removing the PST on capital investment comes from work by Michael Smart and Richard Bird (2006) and Smart (2007), who find that growth in investment per capita has been more rapid in the provinces that do not tax capital inputs than in the provinces that impose such a tax. Baylor and Beauséjour (2004) illustrate the inefficiency resulting from the PST on capital goods by finding that the marginal cost of a dollar of revenue that provincial governments raise through sales taxes on capital is $2.30, compared with $1.40 for corporate income taxes and $1.13 for consumption taxes such as the goods and services tax or harmonized sales tax (GST/HST).[17]

In reducing the METR, why cut the PST and not, say, the corporate income tax? The reason is that cutting the PST would have a greater incremental effect by reducing the relative price of capital goods to firms and making it more profitable to invest. Cuts to the corporate income tax, on the other hand, would increase after-tax profits but would have no effect on the relative price of capital goods; there is also no

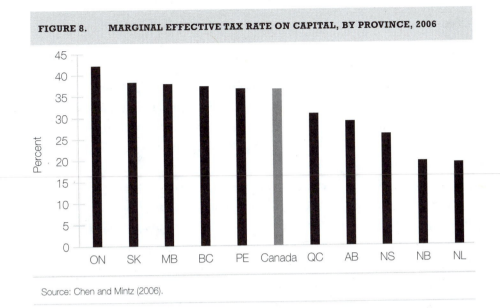

FIGURE 8.   MARGINAL EFFECTIVE TAX RATE ON CAPITAL, BY PROVINCE, 2006

Source: Chen and Mintz (2006).

guarantee that any *ex post* increase in after-tax profits would be invested. An additional reason to reduce the METR by removing the PST rather than by cutting the corporate income tax is that the latter's current rates ensure at least some of the resource sector's economic rents arising from higher commodity prices flow to governments as corporate taxes. It should also be noted that the PST affects short-lived assets such as information and communications technology investment goods — important for productivity growth — much more than long-lived assets such as structures since the former turn over, and hence are taxed, more frequently than the latter.

The federal government has long recognized the problems associated with the PST on capital goods, particularly in Ontario and British Columbia, which are responsible for the lion's share of the 5-percentage-point national gap between the METR with and without the PST. Ottawa would like to see all provincial sales taxes harmonized, as in most of Atlantic Canada, with the GST, which, as an input tax credit, would remove the PST from capital goods. But provinces are reluctant to drop the PST on capital goods since, for such a measure to be revenue neutral, they would have to increase taxes on consumer goods — a politically unpopular move.

A possible resolution would be for the federal government to provide financial assistance to provinces to encourage them to harmonize their PST with the GST, as it did in the early 1990s in the three Atlantic provinces that adopted the HST. For example, the federal government could offer the PST provinces some of the fiscal room that will be created by the planned 1-percentage-point reduction in the GST rate; Kesselman

(2006) provides some detailed suggestions along this line. Given the federal government's currently sound fiscal situation, this is the ideal time for such an initiative.

Policy proposal 3: Promote the geographical migration of workers

In addition to the three fundamental drivers of productivity growth (technological progress, physical capital and human capital), the reallocation of factors of production from low-productivity uses to high-productivity uses can also contribute significantly to aggregate productivity growth.

The provinces differ significantly in their levels of labour productivity, reflecting differences in resource endowments, industrial structure, human capital and demand conditions. In 2006, GDP per worker ranged from a high of $125,938 in Alberta to a low of $63,149 in Prince Edward Island, a difference of 2 to 1 (table 4). These productivity differences result in large differences in labour compensation, although these latter differentials are not as drastic (figure 9). This means that the national productivity level is boosted when a worker moves from a low-productivity province such as Prince Edward Island to a high-productivity province such as Alberta — if the worker performs at the higher productivity of the new province. Consequently, since interprovincial migration contributes to aggregate productivity growth, measures that increase interprovincial migration would increase productivity.

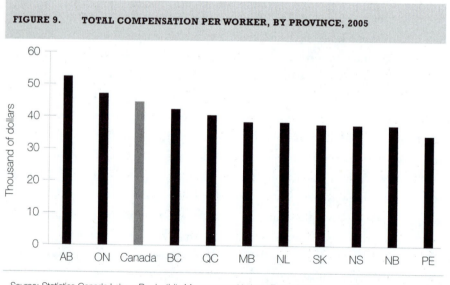

FIGURE 9.   TOTAL COMPENSATION PER WORKER, BY PROVINCE, 2005

Source: Statistics Canada Labour Productivity Measures and Labour Force Survey.

TABLE 4.	GDP PER WORKER IN CURRENT DOLLARS, BY PROVINCE, 1991-2006			
	1991	1996	2001	2006
Canada	53,305	62,353	74,136	87,313
Newfoundland and Labrador	46,834	55,557	69,573	115,424
PEI	42,228	47,929	53,947	63,149
Nova Scotia	46,374	51,770	62,401	72,354
New Brunswick	46,230	54,422	62,660	70,965
Quebec	50,303	57,680	67,329	75,466
Ontario	56,426	65,447	76,559	85,678
Manitoba	47,413	54,956	63,426	76,247
Saskatchewan	47,194	63,363	71,968	91,642
Alberta	56,752	70,197	92,755	125,938
British Columbia	51,885	59,934	69,481	81,850

Source: Statistics Canada, CANSIM.

In 2006, 370,791 persons moved between provinces (table 5), equivalent to 1.14 percent of the population, and an increase of 46 percent from the 2003 interprovincial mobility rate of 0.78 percent. In 1972, however, the rate was as high as 1.78 percent, which suggests that Canadian workers are less willing to seek economic opportunities in other provinces now than they were three decades ago. The much greater importance of dual-earner families, reflecting increased female labour force participation, is one factor that appears to have reduced geographical mobility; the aging of the population has also contributed somewhat.[18]

Canada's incidence of interprovincial labour mobility is not only falling, it is well below its counterpart in the United States, where the interstate migration rate in 2005 was 2.60 percent, nearly three times the Canadian rate (Sharpe and Ershov 2007). It would thus appear that US workers are significantly more mobile than their Canadian counterparts, a source of labour market flexibility and dynamism that likely contributes somewhat to the lower US unemployment rate.

Productivity gains from geographical mobility

It is difficult, for many reasons, to estimate the productivity gains from geographic mobility, and a full discussion of the issue is well beyond the scope of this chapter. Yet one can use two very crude methodologies to present estimates of the output and productivity gains arising from interprovincial migration.[19] The first methodology uses the effect of interprovincial migration on earnings to estimate the

TABLE 5. **TOTAL GROSS AND NET INTERPROVINCIAL MIGRATION, 1987-2006 (PERSONS)**

	Total gross migration	As % of the total population	Total net migration to positive-balance provinces	As % of the total population
1987	306,410	1.16	57,126	0.22
1988	311,501	1.17	40,639	0.15
1989	335,707	1.23	40,592	0.15
1990	320,900	1.16	50,066	0.18
1991	304,105	1.09	40,831	0.15
1992	297,868	1.05	40,511	0.14
1993	273,145	0.96	37,336	0.13
1994	276,222	0.96	34,532	0.12
1995	276,100	0.95	27,751	0.10
1996	274,115	0.93	32,428	0.11
1997	280,719	0.94	39,770	0.13
1998	286,380	0.95	49,833	0.17
1999	266,690	0.88	38,132	0.13
2000	280,645	0.92	46,619	0.15
2001	271,371	0.88	34,906	0.11
2002	271,738	0.87	22,622	0.07
2003	247,230	0.78	14,835	0.05
2004	260,532	0.82	26,216	0.08
2005	304,991	0.95	54,404	0.17
2006	370,791	1.14	69,740	0.21
Annual average	290,858	0.99	39,944	0.14

Sources: Statistics Canada, CANSIM.

gains from migration. The second methodology uses differences in interprovincial labour productivity.

People migrate largely for economic reasons; not surprisingly, therefore, migrants experience larger gains in earnings than do nonmigrants. Finnie (2001, table 1a) finds that interprovincial migrants experienced a 9.4 percent increase in earnings over a two-year period, compared with 4.8 percent for stayers and 0.8 percent for others — in other words, interprovincial migrants enjoyed a 4.6 percent wage gain relative to stayers.[20] According to the 2001 census, 82 percent of interprovincial migrants were of working age (15 and over) and the employment rate of working-age migrants was 66 percent. This implies that, of 370,791 migrants in 2006, 201,000 were employed in their destination province. In 2006, total employment in Canada was 16,484,000, so interprovincial migrants represented 1.22 percent of this total. Labour income, expressed in current dollars, was $737 billion, or 53 percent of GDP. Assuming that the labour income of migrants is the same as that of the average worker, the labour income of interprovincial migrants was $9.0 billion. If wages were 4.6 percent higher for this group due to interprovincial migration, their gain in labour income was $413 million and the gain in GDP was $779 million, equivalent to 0.05 percent of GDP.

Even larger gains to productivity growth are evident if one uses differences in interprovincial labour productivity, since this second methodology takes a broader, social approach to the concept of productivity by including the benefits for the economy from individuals moving from nonemployment to employment through migration.

Sharpe and Ershov (2007) quantify changes in aggregate output and labour productivity brought about by the interprovincial migration of workers. Total output gains are the result of two separate effects: the effect of employment gains as a result of interprovincial migration and the effect of the reallocation of workers between jobs with different productivity levels. The former effect occurs when people move from provinces with lower employment rates to provinces with higher employment rates, which results when some people who were unemployed or out of the labour force in their province of origin gain employment in their destination province, thereby creating output gains. The latter effect occurs when already-employed workers move from provinces with low average productivity levels to provinces with high average productivity levels. Assuming that workers, on average, adopt the average productivity level of their province of residence, they will become more productive as a result of migrating. Total national output then increases by the difference in average productivity between high- and low-productivity provinces for every worker who moves, also increasing aggregate labour productivity.[21] Sharpe and Ershov find that, in 2006, the total change in nominal output as a result of interprovincial migration was just under $2 billion, equivalent to 0.14 percent of GDP. About 70 percent of the gains ($1.4 billion)[22] were from the reallocation of workers and the remainder from employment increases.

It should be noted that the contribution of interprovincial migration to nominal output in 2006, at 0.137 percent of GDP, was more than three times the average contribution for the 1987-2005 period, and can be explained by three factors: the very large net interprovincial migration to Alberta in 2006 (62,291 people); the widening gap in nominal labour productivity levels between provinces with positive net migration and those with negative net migration, due to rising energy prices; and the widening gap in employment rates between provinces with positive net migration and those with negative net migration.

According to these methodologies, the gains to aggregate productivity from interprovincial migration are not huge, although they are likely underestimated for a number of reasons, including the fact that migrants self-select and likely have non-observable characteristics, such as drive, that distinguish them from nonmigrants and that lead them to have above-average productivity.[23] The inclusion of intraprovincial migration, nearly three times that of interprovincial migration, would also have greatly increased the gains to aggregate productivity from migration. Importantly, however, the estimated annual output gains from migration are positive and cumulate over time. For example, the gains to nominal output from the level effects of interprovincial migration from 1987 to 2006 add up to 0.75 percent of GDP, or over $11 billion in 2006 dollars.[24] Migration, clearly, is a significant contributor to aggregate productivity growth.

Policies to foster internal migration

Trends in interprovincial and intraprovincial migration are largely determined by market forces. Differences in employment opportunities, as evidenced by differences in unemployment rates and labour compensation between provinces and regions, are the main drivers of net internal migration in Canada. In most instances, government policies do not directly promote migration. Indeed, it is probably accurate to say that the net effect of government policies is to reduce migration. For example, the federal employment insurance (EI) program, which is more generous in regions of high unemployment than in regions of low unemployment, reduces the incentive for the unemployed to leave high-unemployment regions, although this disincentive effect might not be particularly large.[25] Provincial governments, which invest heavily in the human capital, naturally prefer to see their residents find employment in the province, and establish policies and programs to achieve this objective.

Nevertheless, from the pan-Canadian point of view of the federal government, policies that promote interprovincial migration by reducing barriers to mobility foster the national economic interest through their positive effect on output and productivity (see Gomez and Anderson 2007). One current initiative to promote interprovincial mobility is the labour market information (LMI) programs run by Human Resources and Social Development Canada. These programs, such as the National Job Bank and Job Futures, provide information on job vacancies and career and employment opportunities to all Canadians. One concrete suggestion thus would be to create an independent agency for the development and dissemination of LMI along the lines of the Canadian

Institute for Health Information. Both the federal and provincial governments play a role in the LMI area, but their efforts are often uncoordinated and duplicative. A nongovernmental agency funded by both levels of government could invigorate the LMI field and make Canadians more aware of employment opportunities throughout the country.

The federal government is also attempting to reduce barriers to labour mobility in provincially licensed professions through the Agreement on Internal Trade secretariat. Grady and Macmillan (2007) report that remaining interprovincial barriers related to licensing are limited, but measures to eliminate them would still have an economic payoff.

In terms of new policies to foster interprovincial mobility, I propose that the federal government establish a tax credit for expenses associated with looking for work in other provinces. Moving expenses are currently deductible from income, but not expenses associated with the initial job search, such as travel and accommodation. Adding such expenses to allowable deductions would reduce the after-tax cost of interprovincial job search and provide an additional fiscal incentive for workers to seek better employment opportunities in other provinces. The risk of such a mobility tax credit, however, is that it might encourage some people to claim a deduction for job search costs even though they were not genuinely looking for new work; thus, it might be a good idea for individuals to submit proof of job search, such as a form signed by employers approached, to claim the deduction.

The actual costs of such a program would be small. The federal Department of Finance estimates (2005) the cost of the moving expense deduction to the federal treasury to have been $88 million in 2002 and projects it to rise to $100 million in 2007. Considering this amount includes the cost of moving possessions and family members and that it applies to both interprovincial and intraprovincial moves, the cost of adding a deduction for interprovincial job search expenses for one family member would be much less — perhaps in the range of $15 to $25 million.

Another advantage of this proposal is that it would highlight the role of interprovincial mobility in a dynamic labour market. Such a tax credit would be a concrete manifestation of the importance the federal government attaches to workers' seeking employment opportunities where they arise throughout the country.

CONCLUSION

Productivity is Canada's economic destiny, yet, from both a historical and an international perspective, Canada's relatively dismal productivity performance represents the country's biggest economic challenge. Three specific policies to improve Canada's productivity performance are to foster the diffusion of best-practice technologies; remove the provincial sales tax on purchases of machinery and equipment; and promote interprovincial movement of workers by improving labour market information, removing professional barriers to labour mobility and establishing a tax credit for interprovincial job search. The short-term costs of these policies would be greatly outweighed by the long-term benefits.

NOTES

I would like to thank Chris Ragan for the invitation to prepare this paper. I would also like to thank project organizers Chris Ragan, France St-Hilaire and Jeremy Leonard and discussants Don Drummond and Rick Harris for their very useful comments. I would like to thank John Lester from Finance Canada and Robert Reichert from the National Research Council for assistance.

1   For more extensive discussions of productivity concepts and issues, including problems of measurement, see CSLS (1998); Rao and Sharpe (2002); Sharpe (2002); and articles published in the *International Productivity Monitor* (www.csls.ca/ipm).

2   The two productivity measures can give different signals. For example, on July 15, 2005, Statistics Canada released estimates showing that multifactor productivity in Canada since 2000 was growing at twice the rate of the 1990s. This development reflects the fall in the rate of growth of capital input, which is actually positive from the point of view of multifactor productivity. Yet Statistics Canada had earlier reported that labour productivity growth since 2000 was much worse than in the 1990s. The media ignored the report on multifactor productivity. This was fortunate, as a story about improved multifactor productivity would have confused Canadians about whether or not Canada is experiencing a productivity problem, as I believe it is.

3   Immigrants will account for a large proportion of the new entrants into the labour force.

4   Changes in the terms of trade can also contribute to changes in real income. Such changes were particularly important for Canada in the 2002-05 period, but their contribution over long periods is small (Kohli 2006); I therefore ignore terms-of-trade effects in the determination of GDP per capita.

5   The employment-population ratio grew modestly over this period on an annual percentage basis, making a small contribution to GDP per capita growth. Average hours of work, on the other hand, declined from 51 hours per week in 1947 to less than 35 hours per week in 2004, representing a serious drag on GDP per capita growth.

6   The negative effect of much slower productivity growth on GDP per capita was offset by an increase in the employment rate.

7   The OECD (2006, 10) says that the challenge for all levels of government is to raise productivity and that boosting productivity growth depends on improving the overall business environment. See also Cotis (2006).

8   The Canada-US labour productivity gap at the total economy level, however, is less than at the business sector level (Baldwin et al. 2005). See also Maynard (2007); and Isgut, Bialas and Milway (2006).

9   Space limitations prevent a more detailed analysis of Canada's productivity developments, such as trends in capital and total factor productivity, and productivity trends by industry and by province. For details, see the productivity database at the Web site of the Centre for the Study of Living Standards (www.csls.ca).

10   See Drummond (2006) for a discussion of the reasons for economists' lack of influence on the productivity agenda.

11   The long-term labour productivity growth base case assumption used by the chief actuary of Canada for the Canada Pension Plan (CPP) is 1.2 percent per year. If annual productivity growth were to accelerate to 2.0 percent, the future financial position of the CPP would improve dramatically: by 2050, the ratio of assets to expenditures in the CPP would be 9.4

(compared with 6.3 in the base case scenario); by 2075, it would be 13.7 (compared with 6.9 in the base case). See Office of the Chief Actuary (2004) and Sharpe (2006a).

12 The relatively poorly performing industries (with their productivity relative to their US counterparts in brackets) were: textile and clothing (62 percent); petroleum and coal (61 percent); plastic and rubber products (77 percent); fabricated metal (52 percent); machinery and computers (63 percent); electronic and electrical equipment (44 percent); furniture (73 percent); miscellaneous manufacturing (56 percent); utilities (75 percent); wholesale trade (69 percent); information and cultural industries (60 percent); and finance, insurance and real estate (55 percent).

13 For an overview of the issue of the diffusion and adoption of advanced technologies, see CSLS (2005).

14 The key elements of the four components are as follows. First, "Industrial Technology Advisors...help to identify and address the technical and research needs of SMEs...at each stage of the R&D development process and the innovation cycle." Second, "NRC-IRAP provides non-repayable contributions to Canadian SMEs interested in growing by using technology to commercialize services, products and processes in Canadian and international markets. NRC-IRAP also provides mentoring support and invests on a cost-shared basis for research and pre-competitive development technical projects." Third, "The NRC-IRAP Network [brings] together the key players in the Canadian Innovation System for the benefit of SMEs. This extensive network links entrepreneurs,...R&D institutions, technology brokers and technology transfer centres to those with knowledge and information about local sources of financ-

ing." Fourth, "NRC-IRAP maintains strong partner relationships with organizations at the regional, national and international level whose capabilities extend and complement NRC's contributions to the Canadian Innovation System for the benefit of SMEs" (IRAP 2007).

15 Ab Iorwerth and Danforth (2004) find increasing evidence that lowering the user cost of capital would have a significant effect on firm investment.

16 In New Brunswick, Nova Scotia and Newfoundland and Labrador, the PST was merged with the harmonized sales tax, while in Quebec, it was replaced with a value-added tax; Alberta has no provincial sales tax.

17 The marginal cost of a dollar of revenue is the cost of raising an additional dollar of revenue, which includes the direct cost (the dollar of revenue actually raised) plus any additional welfare costs resulting from the change in the tax structure.

18 While older workers have lower mobility rates than younger workers, the aging of the labour force accounts for only about one-eighth of this downward trend. If the 1972 age structure had prevailed in 2006, the incidence rate would have been 1.22 percent, only 0.08 percentage points higher than the actual rate of 1.14 percent.

19 I ignore the gains arising from intraprovincial migration, even though, in large provinces such as Ontario and Quebec, such migration is significant. The 2001 census estimates that the one-year intraprovincial migration rate, defined as migration between census divisions (Ontario has 47), was 2.76 percent, nearly three times the interprovincial migration rate of 0.97 percent.

20 In an earlier study on the economic returns to mobility, Lin (1995) finds that moving to another province pays off greatly. On average, male migrants' nominal earnings from

paid employment increased by $7,682, while those of nonmigrants increased by only $2,162, a net earnings return to mobility of $5,520, or nearly 26 percent of male migrants' pre-move earnings. The earnings return to female mobility was a bit smaller than that of males in magnitude ($5,220), but even higher (nearly 45 percent) when expressed as a percentage of female migrants' pre-move earnings.

21 In more concrete terms, gains in output due to employment changes are equal to the product of the number of new jobs gained as a result of migration between provinces with different employment rates (provinces with net gains will have higher employment rates) and the average productivity level of provinces with net migration gains. The gains in output due to reallocation are equal to the difference in average productivity between provinces with net migration gains and provinces with net migration losses, multiplied by the number of workers who leave provinces with net migration losses. Total gains in output due to interprovincial migration are equal to the sum of the two factors. Many assumptions had to be made concerning the migrants in order to quantify the effects of migration on output. It was assumed that the migrating workers have had, on average, the average productivity of their province and that when they moved to a new province, they obtained jobs with the average productivity of the new province. In addition, it was assumed that migrants had the demographic structure of their province of origin. The results obviously depend on the validity of the assumptions. The CSLS is currently examining interprovincial migration data to assess the realism of these assumptions.

22 This is double the contribution found through the productivity effect of inter-provincial migration as measured by the effect on wages.

23 On the other hand, the gains might be overestimated to the degree that the employment rate and the labour productivity level of interprovincial outmigrants and in-migrants differ from the provincial average.

24 The cumulative gains to real GDP from interprovincial migration over the 1987-2006 period were 0.66 percent of GDP, or $6.2 billion (in 1997 dollars).

25 Lin (1995) finds that receipt of employment insurance, on average, does not significantly increase the probability of interprovincial labour mobility, although he does note that specific aspects of the EI system might positively affect mobility. Duclos (elsewhere in this volume) proposes changes to EI that would eliminate the negative effect on mobility.

REFERENCES

Ab Iorwerth, A., and J. Danforth. 2004. "Is Investment Not Sensitive to Its User Cost? The Macro Evidence Revisited." Working Paper 2004-05. Ottawa: Department of Finance.

Arundel, A., and P. Mohnen. 2003. "Analytical Methods and Interpretation of Innovation Surveys." In *Understanding Innovation in Canadian Industry*, edited by F. Gault. Montreal; Kingston, ON: McGill-Queen's University Press.

Baldwin, J. R., J.-P. Maynard, M. Tanguay, F. Wong, and B. Yan. 2005. "A Comparison of Canadian and U.S. Productivity Levels: An Exploration of Measurement Issues." Economic Analysis Methodology Paper Series: National Accounts. Cat. no. 11F0026MIE-028. Ottawa: Statistics Canada

Bank of Canada. 2006. "Monetary Policy Report." October. Ottawa: Bank of Canada.

Banting, K., A. Sharpe, and F. St-Hilaire, eds. 2002. *The Review of Economic Performance and Social Progress*, vol. 2, *Towards a Social Understanding of*

Productivity. Montreal: IRPP; Ottawa: Centre for the Study of Living Standards.

Baylor, M., and L. Beauséjour. 2004. "Taxation and Economic Efficiency: Results from a Canadian CGE Model." Working Paper 2004-10. Ottawa: Department of Finance Canada.

Centre for the Study of Living Standards (CSLS). 1998. "Productivity: Key to Economic Success." Report prepared for the Atlantic Canada Opportunities Agency. Ottawa: CSLS.

————. 2005. "The Diffusion and Adoption of Advanced Technologies: An Overview of the Issues." CSLS Research Report 2005-05. Ottawa: CSLS.

Chen, D., and J.M. Mintz. 2006. "Business Tax Reform: More Progress Needed — Supplementary Information." *C.D. Howe Institute e-brief*. June 20. Toronto: C.D. Howe Institute.

Cotis, J.-P. 2006. "Benchmarking Canada's Economic Performance." *International Productivity Monitor* 13 (Fall): 3-20.

Department of Finance Canada. 2005. *Tax Expenditure and Evaluations*. Cat. no. F1-27/2005E. Ottawa: Department of Finance.

Drummond, D. 2006. "The Economists' Manifesto for Curing Ailing Canadian Productivity." *International Productivity Monitor* 13 (Fall): 21-6.

Finnie, R. 2001. "The Effects of Inter-Provincial Mobility on Individuals' Earnings: Panel Model Estimates for Canada." Research Paper 163. Ottawa: Business and Labour Market Analysis, Statistics Canada.

Gardiner, D. 2005. "The Missing Productivity Word." *Ottawa Citizen*, November 24.

Gomez, R., and M. Gunderson. 2007. "Barriers to Inter-provincial Mobility of Labour." Ottawa: Human Resources and Social Development Canada and Industry Canada.

Grady, P., and K. Macmillan. 2007. "Interprovincial Barriers to Labour Mobility in Canada: Policy, Knowledge Gaps and Research Issues."

Ottawa: Industry Canada and Human Resources and Social Development Canada.

Graves, F., and R. Jenkins. 2002. "Canadians' Attitudes toward Productivity: Balancing Standard of Living and Quality of Life." In *The Review of Economic Performance and Social Progress*, vol. 2, *Towards a Social Understanding of Productivity*, edited by A. Sharpe, F. St-Hilaire, and K. Banting. Montreal: IRPP; Ottawa: Centre for the Study of Living Standards.

Harris, R.G. 2002. "Determinants of Canadian Productivity Growth: Issues and Prospects." In *Productivity Issues in Canada*, edited by S. Rao and A. Sharpe. Calgary: University of Calgary Press.

Heath, J. 2002. "Should Productivity Be a Social Priority?" In *The Review of Economic Performance and Social Progress*, vol. 2, *Towards a Social Understanding of Productivity*, edited by A. Sharpe, F. St-Hilaire, and K. Banting. Montreal: IRPP; Ottawa: Centre for the Study of Living Standards.

Industrial Research Assistance Program (IRAP). "Mandate, Mission and Strategic Objectives." Accessed September 10, 2007. http://irap-pari.nrc-cnrc.gc.ca/aboutirap_e.html

International Monetary Fund (IMF). 2007. *Canada: Article IV Consultation – Staff Report*, IMF Country Report 07/51. Washington, DC: IMF.

Isgut, A., L. Bialas, and J. Milway. 2006. "Explaining Canada-U.S. Differences in Hours Worked." *International Productivity Monitor* 13 (Fall): 27-45.

Kesselman, J. 2006. "All Together Now." *National Post*, December 13.

Kohli, U. 2006. "Real GDP, Real GDI and Trading Gains: Canada, 1981-2005." *International Productivity Monitor* 13 (Fall): 46-56.

Lin, Z. 1995. "Interprovincial Labour Mobility in Canada: The Role of Unemployment

Insurance and Social Assistance."
Evaluation Brief 26. Ottawa: Insurance
Programs Directorate, Human Resources
Development Canada.

Lipsey, R., K. Carlaw, and C. Bekar. 2005.
*Economic Transformations: General
Purpose Technologies and Long Term
Economic Growth*. Oxford: Oxford
University Press.

Lynch, K. 2006. "Canada's Success Is No
Accident, and It Isn't Given." *Policy
Options* 27 (4): 12-7. Montreal: IRPP.

Mackenzie, K. 2005. "Tax Subsidies for R&D in
Canadian Provinces." *Canadian Public
Policy* 31 (1): 29-44.

Maynard, J.-P. 2007. "The Comparative Level
of GDP per Capita in Canada and the
United States: A Decomposition into
Labour Productivity and Work Intensity
Differences." Cat. no.15-206-XIE.
Ottawa: Statistics Canada.

Mintz, J. 2006. "The 2006 Tax Competitiveness
Report: Proposals for Pro-Growth Tax
Reform." *C.D. Howe Institute Commentary*
239. Toronto: C.D. Howe Institute.

National Research Council (NRC). 2002.
"Evaluation of NRC's Industrial Research
Assistance Program." Ottawa: Policy,
Planning and Assessment Directorate,
National Research Council.

Office of the Chief Actuary. 2004. *21st Actuarial
Report of the Canada Pension Plan as of
December 31st, 2003*. Ottawa: Office of
the Chief Actuary.

Organisation for Economic Co-operation and
Development (OECD). 2006a. *OECD
Economic Surveys: Canada*. Paris: OECD.
_____. 2006b. *OECD Factbook 2006:
Economic, Environmental and Social
Statistics*. Paris: OECD.

Osberg, L., and A. Sharpe. 2001. "Trends in
Economic Well-Being in Canada in the
1990s." In *The Review of Economic
Performance and Social Progress*, vol. 1,
*The Longest Decade: Canada in the
1990s*, edited by A. Sharpe, F. St-Hilaire,
and K. Banting. Montreal: IRPP; Ottawa:
Centre for the Study of Living Standards.
_____. 2002. "An Index of Economic Well-
Being for Selected OECD Countries."
Review of Income and Wealth 48 (3):
290-308.

Rao, S., and A. Sharpe, eds. 2002.
Productivity Issues in Canada. Calgary:
University of Calgary Press.

Rao, S., A. Sharpe, and J. Smith. 2005. "An
Analysis of the Labour Productivity Growth
Slowdown in Canada since 2000."
International Productivity Monitor 10
(Spring): 3-23.

Rao, S., J. Tang, and W. Wang. 2004.
"Measuring the Canada-U.S. Productivity
Gap: Industry Dimensions." *International
Productivity Monitor* 9 (Fall): 3-14

Sharpe, A. 2002. "Productivity Concept, Trends
and Prospects: An Overview." In *The
Review of Economic Performance and
Social Progress*, vol. 2, *Towards a Social
Understanding of Productivity*, edited by
A. Sharpe, F. St-Hilaire, and K. Banting.
Montreal: IRPP; Ottawa: Centre for the
Study of Living Standards.

Sharpe, A., and D. Ershov. 2007. "The Impact
of Interprovincial Migration on Aggregate
Output and Labour Productivity in
Canada, 1987-2006." CSLS Research
Report 2007-02. Ottawa: Centre for the
Study of Living Standards.
_____. 2004. "Ten Productivity Puzzles
Facing Researchers." *International
Productivity Monitor* 9 (Fall): 15-24.
_____. 2006a. "Future Productivity Growth in
Canada and Implications for the Canada
Pension Plan." CSLS Research Report
2006-01E. Ottawa: Centre for the Study
of Living Standards.
_____. 2006b. "Lessons for Canada from
International Productivity Experience."
CSLS Research Report 2006-02. Ottawa:
Centre for the Study of Living Standards.

_____. Forthcoming. "Internal Labour Mobility in the United States: Trends and Issues." Paper prepared for the Labour Market Policy Directorate, Human Resources and Social Development Canada. Ottawa: Centre for the Study of Living Standards.

Smart, M. 2006. "The Economic Impacts of Value Added Taxation: Evidence from the HST Provinces." Paper presented at the Workshop on Harmonizing the RSTs and GST in Canada: Arguments and Issues, November 17, John Deutsch Institute, Queen's University, Kingston, ON.

Smart, M., and R. Bird. 2006. "The GST Cut and Fiscal Imbalance." Paper presented at the Federal Budget Roundtable, June 21-22, School of Policy Studies, Queen's University, Kingston, ON.

Statistics Canada. 2006. *Industrial Research and Development: 2005 Intentions*. Cat. no. 88-202-XIE. Ottawa: Statistics Canada.

Treasury Board of Canada. 2006. "National Research Council of Canada: Departmental Performance Report, 2005-06." Ottawa. Accessed September 10, 2007. www.tbs-sct.gc.ca/dpr-rmr/0506/NRC-CNRC/nrc-cnrc04_e.asp

Wolff, E. 2000. "Productivity Convergence among OECD Countries: The Postwar Experience." *International Productivity Monitor* 1 (Fall): 17-22.

AN ALTERNATIVE POLICY SCRIPT TO BOOST CANADIAN PRODUCTIVITY GROWTH
Don Drummond

Andrew Sharpe correctly identifies productivity as a key determinant of a country's economic and social success. Strong productivity creates the private sector income and public sector revenues to pursue the choices a society wishes to make. As such, efforts to improve productivity should be viewed not as competing with other aspirations such as improving health care or the environment, but as a necessary precondition. Without adequate productivity, sacrifices on many fronts would be required because the society would not be able to afford the amenities its citizens desire.

In "Three Policies to Increase Productivity Growth in Canada," Sharpe provides a good discussion of Canada's productivity condition. The patient is not doing well: not only is productivity growth falling short of historical norms, but virtually every other nation of note is surpassing us. Output per hour worked in the business sector has grown just barely over 1 percent per annum so far this decade. If this anemic pace were to continue, Canada's living standards would fall still farther behind those of other countries and — especially with the impending retirement of the baby boomers — Canadians would find it increasingly difficult to obtain the quality of life to which they aspire.

My only quibble with Sharpe's data presentation is that he does not acknowledge the work of John Baldwin and others at Statistics Canada, who have identified many problems in comparing output per hour worked in Canada and in the United States (Baldwin et al. 2005). Instead, Sharpe focuses on Industry Canada data, which show that Canada's productivity, as measured by output per hour worked in the business sector, is now just below 75 percent that of the United States (Rao, Tang, and Wang 2004). Baldwin and his colleagues have not published recent comparable figures, but it is likely that their careful calculations to remove data inconsistencies on hours worked would show that, on this basis, Canada's productivity is around 80 to 83 percent of that of the United States. The gap remains very large, however, so the correction would not alter fundamentally Sharpe's conclusion that Canada's productivity record must be improved.

Sharpe suggests 0.5 of a percentage point as a realistic objective for policy-induced annual improvements to Canada's productivity growth rate. Yet he appears simply to pull this number out of the air. It is much smaller than the recent gap in Canada-US productivity growth or the gap between Canada's current productivity growth rate and the record of the 1960s or even the second half of the 1990s, so it may well be that Sharpe is selling short what we could achieve if we were determined. Further, he makes little attempt to explain that if the annual growth rate rose, the cumulative effect over time on the level of Canada's standard of living would be quite impressive.

The Institute for Competitiveness and Prosperity (2007) reports a gap in gross domestic product per capita of $9,200 between Canada and the United States; Canada's shortfall on productivity accounts for $6,800 of the gap. Closing the difference in output per capita would lift the annual personal disposable income for the average Canadian household by $11,900 and add $108 billion per year in revenues for the federal, provincial and local governments. Of course, it would not be realistic to presume Canada could close the gap in a short period of time. But such calculations do give a glimpse of the payoff for stronger Canadian productivity growth.

How, then, can Canada raise its productivity growth rate? Sharpe identifies three strategies: bolster the diffusion and adoption of best-practice technologies; harmonize the remaining provincial retail sales taxes with the goods and services tax (GST); and remove impediments to internal labour mobility across the country. Here, I comment on each initiative and then refer to some alternatives I think would be more effective.

Sharpe makes a very useful point that we are likely far too obsessed with promoting research and development. A lot of technological breakthroughs are being made around the world, and they can be adopted in Canada with short lags and reasonable costs. But, while many studies document Canada's shortcomings in research, Sharpe's assertion that Canadian companies are slow to adopt best-practice technologies is on more tentative ground. And even if there were a solid case, one has to wonder why the private sector does not see action as being in its own best interest. Sharpe makes reference to some possible elements of market failure for small and medium-sized enterprises, but he does not provide conclusive evidence. Finally, his only practical suggestion is to expand the Industrial Research Assistance Program (IRAP). The program is generally well regarded, but Sharpe makes no attempt to demonstrate that the benefits of expansion would exceed the costs. Further, an expanded program would simply become one more obstacle to the growth of smaller companies since it is not available to large companies. It has been suggested that IRAP needs to have greater private sector involvement, but Sharpe does not get into suggestions for improving the program. He also suggests that other programs could be designed with similar objectives, but why, when IRAP already exists?

Sharpe's suggestion that the five provinces that still impose a retail sales tax (RST) harmonize their tax with the federal government's GST is on more solid economic ground. The most recent and best analysis of the economic benefits of harmonization is Smart (2006), three of whose points are particularly relevant for Sharpe's proposal. First, using data from Baylor and Beauséjour (2004), to which Sharpe also refers, Smart calculates that harmonization could raise GDP by $1.75 billion; while he notes some important caveats to the calculation, it does give a feel for the magnitude of potential gain. Second, Smart's results on the effects of harmonization on provincial revenues and on consumers are diametrically opposed to Sharpe's: he finds they would be roughly revenue neutral for all provinces.

Third, under the assumption that taxes on business inputs are passed through to consumers, Smart demonstrates that harmonization would not have a large net effect on consumer finances, even though the experience of the three Atlantic provinces that harmonized their RSTs with the GST shows that the taxes were indeed fully passed through — as was the case when the GST was introduced. Sharpe goes wrong when he infers that the tax that falls directly on business inputs is borne by the corporate sector. There is ample evidence, augmented by Smart's work, that the business sector passes these costs onto consumers.

So, in two very important respects, harmonization is more powerful economically than Sharpe argues because two of the drawbacks he highlights — provincial revenue losses and negative effects on consumers — should not be of great concern. As harmonization would not lead to large provincial revenue losses at prevailing tax rates, it should not be conditional on federal financial assistance. Sharpe suggests that federal assistance should go to the five provinces that still have an RST because the federal government gave an upfront payment to the provinces that moved to a harmonized sales tax (HST). It should be noted, however, that, in order to receive the federal payment, the three HST provinces had to reduce their tax rates substantially; this would not be the case with the five RST provinces.

Removing impediments to internal labour mobility is unquestionably of economic benefit, but Sharpe's estimated economic effects are trivial — indeed, he says little about another element that would have a much more powerful effect: reform of Canada's employment insurance program, whose economic harm is well documented. Further, his claim that his main policy instrument, expanding the tax credit for moving expenses, would be a small cost to the treasury has a flip side: it would also be of small benefit to people in the labour force. It is quite possible that Sharpe has substantially underestimated the potential benefits of enhanced internal labour mobility. If that is the case then policy changes in this area could be deserving of greater priority than he suggests. However, as Sharpe says, the effects of both the disease and the suggested cure are so tiny that one wonders if he simply ran out of ideas — odd, since there are plenty of additional tools in the mainstream economics literature for improving productivity. Indeed, box 1 presents the elements of a consensus among Canadian economists on what we need to do to improve Canada's productivity (Drummond 2006). There is much to choose from to replace at least Sharpe's third pick. The absence of internal free trade is surely a national disgrace, but analysis suggests that the economic effect of removing remaining barriers would not be huge, so this might not make the cut (although it should be done nonetheless).

Many studies have demonstrated that competition is at the heart of productive economic performance. Statistics Canada has found that foreign companies are the most productive in Canada, followed by domestic companies that trade internationally, then domestic companies that do not trade (Baldwin and Gu 2003). So it is counter to productivity objectives to continue restrictions on foreign ownership in key Canadian sectors. Furthermore, large corporations have much higher productivity than small corporations; they also trade more, do more research and pay higher wages (see, for example, Baldwin and Gu 2004). Yet Canada has constructed numerous barriers to the growth of smaller corporations, including a huge jump in marginal corporate income tax rates when they pass the small business tax income threshold, loss of eligibility for all kinds of programs and the imposition of many new regulatory nets.

There are many factors driving up taxation of capital in Canada. Instead of just looking at RSTs, why not look at the economic damage caused by capital taxes (see Baylor and Beauséjour 2004)? Several provinces still impose such taxes, yet, as Sharpe identifies, one of the reasons Canada suffers on the productivity front is its relative lack of capital investment compared with other economies. So it makes absolutely no sense to tax capital directly. Canada's marginal effective personal income tax rates are also among the highest in the world. Factoring in the loss of various social benefits as income rises, the marginal effective rate for most families up to middle-income levels is typically 60 percent or more (see in this volume Duclos, figure 3). Reducing these rates would raise not just labour supply but also productivity, as the incentives to save and invest would be sharpened.

We are close to the point where in-migration will account for 100 percent of Canada's population growth. Yet, from an economics perspective, immigrants are not faring well. Their labour force participation rates are lower than those of the Canadian-born, their unemployment rates are higher and, even after they have been in Canada for

BOX 1.	ECONOMISTS' SCRIPT FOR STRONGER PRODUCTIVITY GROWTH

Attitudes
/ Recognize the problem and act upon it.

The macroeconomic environment
/ Low, stable inflation.
/ Reasonably low government debt-to-GDP ratios.

The business environment
/ Free trade (multilateral or bilateral agreements).
/ Internal free trade (and other aspects of improving the economic union, including getting rid of overlapping securities regulations).
/ Competition promotion, including removing foreign ownership restrictions.
/ Remove barriers to firms growing larger (such as the huge leap between the small and general corporate income tax rates, the eligibility of small companies only for many benefits and the inclusion of large companies only in certain regulations).
/ Remove labour mobility restrictions, by reforming employment insurance (through employer-employee experience rating, loosening the link between qualifications and local labour market conditions, and so on — see Duclos elsewhere in this volume), better information on job opportunities, recognition of credentials and perhaps more inclusive tax deduction of moving costs.
/ Reduce the regulatory burden.

Taxation
/ Cut the tax rate on capital — eliminate capital taxes, reduce provincial corporate income .tax rates, eliminate retail sales taxes on capital and reduce property taxes on industrial-commercial properties (which tend to far exceed residential rates).
/ Line up economic and taxation depreciation (such as on manufacturing plants, where capital cost allowance rates need to be enhanced).
/ Cut high effective marginal personal income tax rates, perhaps by making greater use of consumption taxation or environment taxes to finance tax shifting).

Immigration
/ Reform immigration design, administration and settlement services to increase the odds that those coming will be gainfully employed, and focus more attention on education issues of immigrants' children.

Education and training
/ Increase investment in post-secondary education, especially at the graduate level, and pay greater attention to the non-post-secondary stream through literacy programs, apprenticeships and training.

Infrastructure
/ Reinvest in key areas, including transportation, border crossings and so on, and use public-private partnerships and user-fee financing where feasible.

Private sector behaviour
/ Foster a more entrepreneurial spirit that leads to greater capital formation, exports, research, adoption and adaptation of technology and labour training.

a long time, their earnings are inferior (Aydemir and Skuterud 2005). In other words, immigrants are realizing lower productivity and, as their numbers grow, they will slow Canada's productivity growth unless the situation is turned around. Some greater attention is being paid to aspects of immigration, such as credit recognition and settlement services, but one could argue for a much more wholesale reform that would involve redesigning the selection process. As Serge Coulombe suggests elsewhere in this volume, perhaps we should go back to placing more attention on skills rather than general education, and also revamp the methods of administration — for example, by not considering applications in the order they are received and by accelerating acceptance of those most likely to find work.

Infrastructure got caught in the crossfire of the deficit reduction campaigns of federal, provincial and municipal governments. The gaps are starting to be addressed, but more could be done. The needs will not be met through conventional government financing, however, so more emphasis should be put on private sector involvement and user fees.

Finally, it must be recognized that governments are not solely accountable for Canada's lacklustre productivity performance. Companies and individuals need to modify their behaviour as well. In particular, they need to invest more in both capital and human capital development and be more entrepreneurial at home and abroad.

There is so much to choose from that it is difficult to narrow down the choice to three options. Nevertheless, that is the task at hand, so choices must be made. I would keep Sharpe's suggestion that the remaining RSTs be harmonized with the GST. My other two choices would be to reduce marginal effective personal income tax rates and reform most aspects of Canada's immigration program. Eliminating capital taxes would have made my list, but Ontario has already pledged to phase out its tax and Quebec is cutting its counterpart. Still, they should be struck from the tax arsenal more quickly.

REFERENCES

Aydemir, A., and M. Skuterud. 2005. "Explaining the Deteriorating Entry Earnings of Canada's Immigrant Cohorts, 1996-2000." *Canadian Journal of Economics* 39 (May): 641-71.

Baldwin, J.R., and W. Gu. 2003. "Participation in Export Markets and Productivity Performance in Canadian Manufacturing." Economic Analysis Research Paper Series. Cat. no. 11F0027 No. 011. Ottawa: Micro-Economic Analysis Division, Statistics Canada.

———. 2004. "Innovation, Survival and Performance Participation of Canadian Manufacturing Plants." Economic Analysis Research Paper Series. Cat. no. 11F0027 No. 022. Ottawa: Micro-Economic Analysis Division, Statistics Canada.

Baldwin, J.R., J.-P. Maynard, M. Tanguay, F. Wong, and B. Yan. 2005. "A Comparison of Canadian and U.S. Productivity Levels: An Exploration of Measurement Issues." Economic Analysis Methodology Paper Series: National Accounts. Cat. no. 11F0026MIE-028. Ottawa: Statistics Canada.

Baylor, M., and L. Beauséjour. 2004. "Taxation and Economic Efficiency: Results from a Canadian CGE Model." Working Paper 2004-10. Ottawa: Department of Finance.

Drummond, D. 2006. "The Economists' Manifesto for Curing Ailing Canadian Productivity." *TD Bank International Productivity Monitor*. Accessed September 18, 2007. www.td.com/economics/special/dd0906_prod.pdf

Institute for Competitiveness and Prosperity. 2007. *Report on Canada 2007: Agenda for Canada's Prosperity*. Toronto: Institute for Competitiveness and Prosperity.

Rao, S., J. Tang, and W. Wang. 2004. "Measuring the Canada-U.S. Productivity Gap: Industry Dimensions." *International Productivity Monitor* 9 (Fall): 3-14.

Smart, M. 2006. "The Economic Impacts of Value Added Taxation: Evidence from the HST Provinces." Paper presented at the Workshop on Harmonizing the RSTs and GST in Canada: Arguments and Issues, November 17, John Deutsch Institute, Queen's University, Kingston, Ontario.

THE CANADIAN PRODUCTIVITY CONUNDRUM
Richard G. Harris

Andrew Sharpe has written a thoughtful overview of the Canadian productivity debate and makes three specific proposals. Here, I offer my own view of the productivity debate; I then comment specifically on Sharpe's proposals in "Three Policies to Increase Productivity Growth in Canada."

THE DEBATE

The Canadian productivity debate was ignited around 1997. The spark undoubtedly was the remarkable increase in the US productivity growth rate, from the 1.0-1.5 percent range in the 1980s to the 2.5-3.5 percent range by the late 1990s. This increase, which coincided with the information and communication technology boom and the introduction of the "New Economy" paradigm, occurred after decades of relatively modest growth in US labour productivity. Canada did not experience the same increase, however, initiating a great deal of research and policy discussion on the reason for this lag. Further attention was devoted to measuring the gap in Canadian and US productivity levels, which by various estimates stood anywhere between 20 and 33 percent. This raised lots of red flags among economists. Not the least of the concerns was the implication this productivity gap might have for long-term material living standards in Canada, as well as the prospects for Canadian firms to compete in an increasingly integrated global economy.

By and large this debate took place among the business, academic and policy elites in Canada. For a number of reasons, it never really gained much resonance with either the public or politicians. Why? I think there are at least four reasons, all of which conspired to defuse public concern about or interest in productivity policy.

The first reason is simply an unfortunate association in the public's mind of some negatives with the term "productivity." Although it seems perfectly clear and almost policy neutral to economists, the public associates the term with either job cuts or corporate tax cuts. The association with job cuts results because much of the immediate effect of increased productivity is reduced use of labor and increased use of capital. The association with corporate tax cuts comes about largely because the business community argues that such cuts would enhance productivity by increasing incentives to invest. Groups opposed to tax cuts, therefore, are antagonistic to any policy that includes the term "productivity." In many countries, this state of affairs has led to the use of alternative language: "competitiveness" and "prosperity" are frequently used, as in "prosperity agenda." I think we economists should admit defeat and go even further. Familiar economic terms such as "total factor productivity index" should be replaced with "total factor prosperity index."

The second reason for the public's lack of interest in productivity is that, despite economists' claims that future prosperity is at risk, their warnings do not fit with the economic success that Canada has experienced in recent years: growth of gross domestic product has been strong, inflation low and employment growth exceptional. Due to sound macro policy, a booming global economy that has raised commodity prices very high and a strong US economy, the Canadian economy has been firing on all cylinders. Economic circumstances have not been this good since the boom period of the 1960s. It is hard in such circumstances to get people motivated about a measured Canada-US income gap when they do not relate to it. Moreover, concerns about future competitiveness problems — for example, in the auto industry — are at best regarded as academic speculation. Most people are not concerned, and they will remain unconcerned until they perceive that a threat to future growth is imminent. The global warming debate owes its front-page attention to extreme weather events; thus far, Canada has not experienced events in the arena of productivity growth analogous to extreme weather disturbances.

The third reason for the public's apathy toward productivity is that, for the most part, the attention in this country has been on Canada-US comparisons — in particular, the unusual way in which the results of the acceleration of productivity growth have been distributed in the United States. We now know that, since 1997, there has been virtually no improvement in the US median real wage. Moreover, according to Dew-Becker and Gordon (2005), virtually all of the productivity gains from 1997 to 2004 went to the top 2 percent of the income distribution. This is highly unusual: in past productivity booms, the gains have been much more evenly shared, with increases in real wages across the board. Why this is occurring is not well understood by economists and is the subject of a great deal of research. But this productivity outcome implies that the gap between the average Canadian worker and the average US worker is much less significant than the aggregate data would suggest. Moreover, Canadian professionals, including corporate managers, know they are not doing as well as their US counterparts, but this income gap simply reflects the current distributive outcome in the US economy. Canada has seen some increase in income inequality, but nothing similar to the extreme top-end loading that has occurred in the United States. The net result is that most Canadian voters do not view productivity comparisons with the United States as relevant. Indeed, many groups would take it one step further, arguing that attempts to induce US-type productivity growth in Canada might lead to the same distributive outcome. Thus, advocates of a productivity agenda for Canada most likely will have to provide some evidence that such an outcome, where the bulk of the gains accrue to the richest in society, would not be the result.

The fourth reason for the public's lack of interest is that there is no simple way to label one policy a "productivity policy" and another policy something else: virtually all government policies have productivity consequences. Sometimes we think of certain policies as having a more direct consequence for productivity growth, but everything from social policy to tax policy has both short- and long-run effects on productivity growth. Since these effects are both uncertain and difficult to quantify, most policy choices inevitably tend to focus on those that are both immediate and measurable. The net result is that, simply by omission, productivity growth can be compromised by a large number of small, unintended effects. Regulation is a perfect example. The Organisation for Economic Co-operation and Development has done a lot of work demonstrating the significant negative effect that the overall level of regulation can have on productivity growth (see Conway et al. 2006). Yet it is also true that most regulations are brought in for what seem at the time completely legitimate reasons.

Thus, raising productivity from the last to the first criterion by which policies are judged will require significant shifts in public and political priorities.

SPECIFIC PRO-PRODUCTIVITY POLICIES

Sharpe suggests three policies to improve Canadian productivity:

/ expand programs that promote the adoption of best-practice technology;
/ eliminate the provincial sales tax (PST) on the purchase of machinery and equipment in provinces where this tax remains (including British Columbia and Ontario); and
/ improve policies to support interprovincial labour mobility, particularly interprovincial job search.

Each of these policies, I believe, would have some modest effect on productivity growth. My strong preference, however, is for Sharpe's second policy proposal: elimination of the PST on machinery and capital good purchases. I concur with him that this policy has been well researched: he cites substantial evidence that the marginal effective tax rate (METR) on capital is high, and thus the level of investment in machinery and equipment is lower than it would otherwise be. Moreover, since new investment in machinery and equipment is critical to support the use of new technologies, we have every reason to believe that reducing the METR on machinery and equipment purchases by firms should raise productivity growth. The political barrier to changing these policies resides at the provincial level, but further efforts by the federal government to induce provinces to eliminate these capital taxes — for example, through harmonization of the PST with the goods and services tax — certainly would be welcome.

As for Sharpe's proposal of programs to support the adoption of best-practice technology, there is certainly evidence that programs such as the Industrial Research Assistance Program have worked in the past. Such programs were mostly justified, however, by the barriers to information that small and medium-sized Canadian firms once faced. With the advent of the Internet, these barriers now seem much less relevant than they once were. We know that Canada has too many small firms, which is one reason for the persistent Canada-US productivity gap in manufacturing. While I think Canada's inability to grow medium-sized firms into large firms remains one of the biggest policy challenges and puzzles, a focus on technology adoption per se is probably not the most relevant issue here, as I have argued elsewhere (Harris 2005).

Sharpe's third policy proposal is to improve labour mobility between provinces, specifically by effective tax subsidization of out-of-province job search. He cites the basic data on interprovincial labour mobility, which, in comparison with interstate mobility in the US, is low. Given significant differences in the levels of labour productivity across provinces, moving people from where productivity and wages are low to where they are high should increase the aggregate level of productivity. None of this is controversial. Sharpe cites some recent work that suggests there are some small positive benefits to increasing the overall degree of labour mobility between provinces. The only problem is that most studies suggest these effects are likely to be small. The issue seems to be not that productivity differences between regions are insignificant, but that, even in the absence of barriers, the number of people who would relocate in any year is quite modest. In Canada, formal barriers to interprovincial labour migration (except in a few professions and trades) are generally quite low. Therefore, additional policy measures to promote interprovincial mobility are not likely to have much growth impact on the margin. The European Union, for example, has tried to increase labour mobility between its member states, with surprisingly little success.

In summary, Andrew Sharpe's chapter is a useful review of the evidence on productivity, and it contains some interesting proposals. However, for the reasons outlined in these comments, they are issues and proposals which are unlikely to receive much policy attention in the short or medium term.

REFERENCES

Conway, P., D. De Rosa, G. Nicoletti, and F. Steiner. 2006. "Regulation, Competition and Productivity Convergence." Working Paper 509. Paris: Economics Department, Organisation for Economic Co-operation and Development.

Dew-Becker, I., and R.J. Gordon. 2005. "Where Did the Productivity Growth Go? Inflation Dynamics and the Distribution of Income." *Brookings Papers on Economic Activity* (2): 67-127.

Harris, R.G. 2005. "Canada's R&D Deficit — and How to Fix It." *C.D. Howe Institute Commentary* 211. Toronto: C.D. Howe Institute.

PART I THE POLICY CHALLENGES

TRADE AND GLOBALIZATION

CANADIAN ENGAGEMENT IN THE GLOBAL ECONOMY
Michael Hart

This chapter argues that Canada's principal priorities in getting more out of its international engagement are threefold. The federal government's first priority should be to pursue further domestic economic reforms that will allow market forces — that is, the choices made by Canadians as producers and consumers — to reach their full potential. Twenty years ago, Canadians accepted that they needed to banish the last vestiges of the National Policy. Remnants of the interventionist state, however, continue to limit the capacity of Canadian firms to compete in the global economy. These range from supply-managed agriculture to ownership restrictions in the financial services, telecommunications, transportation and energy sectors. Such policies may serve politically persuasive public policy goals, but they also limit Canadians' capacity to maximize benefits from their global engagement.

As a second priority, the federal government should reduce activities that provide the illusion of engagement but that lead, at best, to marginal results — from the Doha Development Round of World Trade Organization (WTO) negotiations and the pursuit of free trade agreements with minor markets to the promotion of more diversified trade patterns with new, emerging markets such as China and India. A successful Doha Round offers too few benefits to Canadians to be worth the considerable expenditure of political and human capital needed to bring these talks to a successful conclusion. Free trade agreements with minor trading partners such as Costa Rica and the Dominican Republic are marginal in their economic and commercial impact but large in their ability to gobble up political and financial resources. Government-led trade diversification has no basis in the real economy; in any event, governments agreed to eliminate or discipline the requisite instruments in multilateral and other trade negotiations because they accepted that such tools — from tariffs and quotas to subsidies and procurement preferences — were detrimental to global and national economic well-being. Trade missions and similar programs, while popular with ministers, have virtually no enduring impact on trade and investment patterns.

Finally, the federal government should make it a priority to strengthen the policy framework that governs cross-border trade and investment with the United States in order to enhance North America's — and Canada's — capacity to participate effectively in the global economy. Productive relations with the United States are the indispensable anchor of Canadian security and prosperity, and on both fronts there are important policy issues in which the two governments need to engage. Specifically on the economic front, the two governments must do more to address the dated, dysfunctional and intrusive nature of border administration, the haphazard process leading to deepening regulatory convergence and the frail institutional capacity to govern accelerating integration.

The analysis here proceeds on the assumption that Canadians do many things right as they work to maximize the benefits of engagement in the global economy, and they should continue to do these things — from participating actively in such international organizations as the International Monetary Fund (IMF) and the Organisation for Economic Co-operation and Development (OECD) to maintaining a strong domestic macroeconomic environment. The focus of this chapter is on two policy areas where the federal government can do more and one where it should do less; in all three cases, such an adjustment would have a material impact on the extent to which Canadians benefit from global engagement.

GLOBALIZATION, INDUSTRIAL FRAGMENTATION AND CROSS-BORDER INTEGRATION

If we are to maximize the economic benefits of international engagement, we must first recognize the tremendous changes in the global economy that have taken place over the past few decades: the rapid and pervasive diffusion of production, consumption and investment of goods, services, capital and technology. In response to developments in communications technology and transportation facilities, and to the progressive liberalization of global markets, production is steadily being reorganized on a global basis, and the nature of extranational economic transactions reflects this change. The global economy has been transformed into "a highly complex, kaleidoscopic structure involving the *fragmentation* of many production processes, and their *geographical relocation* on a global scale in ways which slice through national boundaries" (Dicken 2003, 9).

The fragmentation of production through a process of outsourcing and subsequent rebundling within large and technologically sophisticated supplier networks has become increasingly prevalent in, for example, food processing, aircraft and motor vehicle production and the manufacture of apparel, electronics and household products. Value-chain fragmentation and the sophistication of the firms that make up the fragments have made it easier to relocate specific nodes of production and to take advantage of a range of distant factors, from low-cost labour, specialized skills and attractive markets to access to critical inputs and public policy considerations. Fragmentation and integration combine to increase the extent and intensity of international transactions, encouraging the relocation of slices of the production process to the best possible site and allowing firms to specialize to a much greater degree and reap greater advantages from economies of scale and scope (Sturgeon 2006; Gereffi 2005).

Systematic data on the extent of this spatially dispersed integration are difficult to find, in part because conventional statistics fail to capture the full extent of trade in parts and components, the full value of cross-border service links or the input of services provided through proprietary and other networks — for example, design, engineering and marketing, whether done in-house, outsourced locally or outsourced internationally (Ridgeway 2006; Mandel et al. 2006). Statistical agencies cannot quantify the value of the Italian design and the German engineering of a toilet that is ultimately manufactured in Mexico and imported into Canada through a US distribution network. They count the computer on which this chapter is written as a Chinese import rather than the fruit of the design, engineering and marketing expertise at Apple's campus in Cupertino, California. In a world in which tariffs are low or nonexistent, customs officials are less interested in the origin or foreign value added of a particular cross-border transaction than in its final transaction price. The data these officials supply to statistical agencies often severely overstate the value contributed by the designated country of origin and undervalue the diverse inputs of other countries.

From a public policy perspective, governments are particularly interested in the intersection of firm-specific and location-specific value. Firms are now less constrained in their choice of geographic location by technology and policy, and they seek to increase value by dispersing their value-adding activities spatially. Governments, in the interest of attracting value-adding activity to their jurisdictions, now compete in promoting policy settings that are congenial to increasingly mobile slices of production by removing barriers and providing positive incentives. In this quest, they are learning that the trade agreements of the past may have been critical in providing the framework of rules that initially facilitated fragmentation and integration, but they are no longer sufficient to address contemporary policy challenges.

What is happening at the global level has a longer history at the bilateral Canada-US level. Proximity, history, technology, opportunity and policy have combined to create deep and irreversible ties between Canadian and American production and consumption patterns. Starting with US investment in Canadian mining and forestry through the establishment of tariff-jumping, miniature-replica branch plants, Canadian production has long been intimately tied to US production, trade and investment patterns, while Canadian consumers have long expressed a strong preference for American products. The implementation of the Canada-US Autopact (1965), followed by the Canada-US Free Trade Agreement (CUFTA, 1989) and the North American Free Trade Agreement (NAFTA, 1994), deepened the integration of the Canadian and US markets by accelerating the process of cross-border fragmentation and agglomeration. As US business economist Stephen Blank concludes, "Ottawa and Washington talk about the world's largest bilateral trading relationship. But we really don't trade with each other, not in the classic sense of one independent company sending finished goods to another. Instead we make stuff together...[We] share integrated energy markets; dip into the same capital markets; service the same customers with an array of financial services; use the same roads and railroads to transport jointly made products to market; fly on the same integrated airline networks; and increasingly meet the same or similar standards of professional practice" (2005).

FIGURE 1. **EXPORTS (X) AND VALUE-ADDED EXPORTS (VAX) AS A PERCENTAGE OF CANADA'S GDP 1988-99**

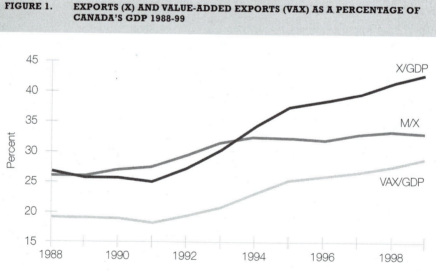

Source: Cross (2002).
Note: M/X is the import content of Canadian exports.

Philip Cross and his colleagues at Statistics Canada have done extensive work in an effort to understand the changing nature of cross-border production, trade and investment patterns. They have calculated that the import content of Canadian exports has risen steadily over the past two decades: it was 25.9 percent in 1988 and peaked at 33.5 percent in 1998 (see figure 1). The rapid rise in trade in the 1990s was in large part the result of rationalization; imported components replaced domestic components and the final product was exported to a broader market base. More significant than the rise in exports as a share of GDP was the rise in value-added exports in GDP — from 19.1 percent in 1988 to 28.8 percent in 1999 (Cross and Cameron 1999; Cross 2002). Economist Glen Hodgson concludes that "trade has evolved beyond the traditional exporting and importing of goods, and has entered the next generation of trade — integrative trade. Integrative trade is driven by foreign investment and places greater weight on elements like the integration of imports into exports, trade in services and sales from foreign affiliates established through foreign investment" (2004). Nowhere has this process of integration been more pronounced than between Canada and the United States.

High levels of both two-way intra-industry trade and foreign direct investment indicate continued cross-border integration and rationalization of production between Canada and the United States, as well as a deepening interdependence between manufacturing and service industries. Integration has allowed Canadian industry to become more specialized and has had a significant impact on the growth of value-added sectors. The changing intensity and composition of bilateral trade have contributed greatly to making Canadians better off both as consumers and as producers. Canadians employed in export-oriented sectors have consistently been better educated and better paid than the national average. As Cross and Cameron point out, "The importance of trade to the economy does not come from an excess of exports over imports: rather, it is from the productivity gains that accrue with increased specialization" (Cross and Cameron 1999, 3.3). Specialization, in turn, increases as markets expand in response to the openness fostered by trade agreements.

DOMESTIC IMPEDIMENTS TO CANADIAN GLOBAL ENGAGEMENT

Progress in reducing conventional barriers to trade and investment flows has now reached the point where, with a few exceptions, the Canadian economy is open to broad international competition and participation, as are most markets of interest to Canadian suppliers and investors. Canadian trade and investment patterns

TABLE 1.   **CANADIAN TRADE AND INVESTMENT PATTERNS, 2000-06 (BILLIONS OF CANADIAN DOLLARS)**

	2000	2001	2002	2003	2004	2005	2006
Exports of goods and services							
Total[1]	489.1	480.8	477.5	460.1	493.0	518.0	523.7
United States	394.3	387.9	384.4	363.9	386.8	404.4	397.6
European Union[2]	32.4	33.9	33.2	34.4	37.7	40.7	46.0
Japan	14.5	13.3	13.1	11.7	12.9	13.8	13.4
Rest of world	47.9	45.7	46.8	50.1	55.8	59.1	66.7
Imports of goods and services							
Total	427.8	417.9	427.4	415.7	440.2	466.9	486.5
United States	308.6	295.6	297.5	283.4	295.6	305.0	311.3
European Union	43.7	45.8	47.3	46.9	49.1	51.1	55.8
Japan	13.8	12.7	14.7	13.4	12.7	14.6	15.1
Rest of world	63.7	63.8	67.9	72.0	82.8	96.2	104.3
Outward FDI flows							
Total	66.3	55.8	42.0	30.1	56.3	41.3	47.8
United States	38.0	27.8	17.6	5.7	40.1	23.0	22.9
European Union	15.9	7.8	10.9	14.4	3.8	3.3	13.6
Japan	3.7	1.8	1.7	.3	1.3	.6	4.3
Rest of world	8.7	18.4	12.8	9.7	11.1	14.4	7.0
Inward FDI flows							
Total	99.2	42.9	34.8	10.7	2.0	41.0	75.6
United States	16.5	39.2	28.4	5.2	6.7	18.4	21.0
European Union	76.9	1.3	4.4	4.0	-14.3	8.5	29.5
Japan	.2	.2	.8	.5	.6	.7	1.2
Rest of world	5.6	2.2	1.2	1.0	10.0	13.4	23.9
Outward FDI stocks							
Total	356.5	399.3	435.5	411.9	451.4	465.1	n/a
United States	177.9	188.5	200.0	169.9	196.3	213.7	n/a
European Union	75.2	82.5	90.3	102.8	121.2	110.3	n/a
Japan	5.6	7.0	9.7	8.4	8.5	7.4	n/a
Rest of world	97.8	121.3	135.5	130.8	125.4	133.7	n/a
Inward FDI stocks							
Total	319.1	340.4	356.8	364.7	381.0	415.6	n/a
United States	193.7	219.9	231.6	235.6	248.5	266.5	n/a
European Union	96.0	92.1	94.3	97.3	96.6	104.4	n/a
Japan	8.0	7.8	9.3	9.9	10.3	10.8	n/a
Rest of world	21.4	20.6	21.6	21.9	25.6	33.9	n/a

Source: Foreign Affairs and International Trade Canada (n.d.).

FDI = Foreign direct investment

n/a = not available

[1] Totals may not add up due to rounding.

[2] EU-15 for 2000-01; EU-25 for 2002-06.

(see table 1) thus reflect increasingly the market choices of Canadian consumers, investors and traders and decreasingly the effect of Canadian and foreign government trade and investment policies. Nevertheless, there remain pockets of border protection — for example, for supply-managed dairy and poultry products and for a few consumer products, such as clothing and footwear. Eliminating tariffs in these pockets would reduce existing drags on the economy by allowing markets to determine areas of comparative advantage (see table 2).

Canada also maintains a variety of domestic policies that serve as reminders of an earlier era of regulatory zeal and nationalist foolishness. These include ownership restrictions in the telecommunications, energy and transportation sectors; subsidies to favoured sectors; restrictive banking regulations and tax policies that coddle some economic activities and shackle others; and competition policies that limit mergers and acquisitions and growth. More important, such policies impede Canadian participation in global value chains and North American integration. They belong to an era in which it was assumed that products and firms had clear national identities and benefited from policies that promoted national champions. But if Canadians want to get more out of their engagement in today's world of deep regional integration and complex global value chains, then they will have to be prepared to consign such policies to the dustbin of history.

TABLE 2.   SELECTED CANADIAN TARIFF LEVELS, 2006

Product	Rate (percent)	Product	Rate (percent)
Butter	298.5	Ships	25.0
Cream	292.5	Footwear	20.0
Cheese	245.5	Clothing	18.0
Milk	241.0	Cloth	14.0
Chicken	238.0	Knits	14.0
Yogourt	237.5	Carpets	12.5
Eggs	163.5	Leaf springs	8.0
Turkey	154.5	Yarns	8.0
Barley	94.5	Cotter pins	6.5
Wheat, other	76.5	Rivets	6.5
Wheat, durum	49.0	Crushed or ground spices	3.0

Source: Canada Border Services Agency (2006).

For example, Canada imposes severe restrictions on foreign ownership and control in selected sectors of the economy. There is no apparent reason why the standard rules of investment protection agreements should not be applied to foreign direct investment (FDI) in protected industries. Most FDI today originates with transnational corporations and involves large sums of money; it is often part of a larger regional or global strategy. The widely owned corporation is one of the distinguishing features of modern business, in terms of both its financial arrangements (the sharing of risk among a large number of otherwise unrelated investors) and its institutional arrangements (a hierarchically structured organization aimed at exercising efficient control over a large number of participants in the productive process). A variety of inter- and intracorporate arrangements now allow business to be pursued efficiently and effectively on a global basis, all of them involving some form of FDI.

The presumed benefit of linking ownership to the achievement of a range of regulatory objectives appears to be a holdover from a time when there were many more regulated industries — particularly so-called natural monopolies in, for example, fields related to the telephone, electricity and urban transit — and when there was a prevalent belief that such restrictions were needed to ensure effective public regulation. Over the years, economic theory and practice have demonstrated the benefits of competition, privatization and foreign investment even in these industries, as well as the capacity of governments to regulate in the public interest without regard for foreign or domestic ownership or control (Safarian 1993). Canadians would be better off if these lessons were applied across all sectors of the economy.

Ironically, some Canadians worry that Canada is not getting its fair share of NAFTA inward foreign direct investment. Putting aside the question of whether the idea of "fair share" has any merit, Canada lags in attracting FDI for a very simple reason: Canadians have chosen to hobble the most mobile and internationally active sectors of the global economy by limiting foreign participation in those sectors in Canada. As the annual *World Investment Report* catalogues, a large share of global investment activity involves mergers and acquisitions in the telecommunications, financial services and transportation sectors (United Nations Conference on Trade and Development 2004). Canada limits participation by foreign investors in all three sectors. Simply by changing these rules, Canada could increase the relative share of FDI it attracts and thereby improve the performance of its economy.

Similarly, subsidies help some industries while penalizing others. No matter how welcome any particular government grant or "investment" may be to individual firms, regions or industries, each involves a transfer of resources from one group of taxpayers to another. Jobs "created" or "saved" by such a program necessitate reduced opportunities for other firms or sectors. Whether a subsidy is delivered through a grant, a tax writeoff, a loan guarantee, a research and development incentive or any other government intervention, the result is the same: the substitution of political for market judgment. It may be theoretically possible for governments to make choices that over time prove wise and beneficial, but experience has not demonstrated the superiority of political over business judgment. The factors that are persuasive to governments are rarely those that are persuasive to private capital. The result is typically a misallocation of scarce resources, missed opportunities and reduced prosperity. In the long run, Canadians will see greater benefits from their engagement in the global economy if there are fewer programs that involve politically motivated investments of public funds in market-based activities.

As discussed in more detail in the chapter prepared for this volume by Andrew Sharpe and the commentaries contributed by Don Drummond and Richard Harris, there are many ways in which Canadian public policy creates a business environment that promotes private investment in productive, efficient and competitive economic activity in Canada. Nevertheless, as they also point out, there remains considerable scope for improvement. Such improvement should be undertaken not only for its own merit but also because it can strengthen Canadian engagement in the global economy and ensure greater benefits from that engagement for individual Canadians.

RETAIL TRADE POLICY AND CANADIAN GLOBAL ENGAGEMENT

Canada's self-image as a trading nation and its record of active and constructive international trade negotiations have created the inertia that is now controlling contemporary trade policy. As becomes evident when one reads the speeches of Trade Minister David Emerson and his immediate predecessors, officials busy themselves with a wide range of initiatives, from trade negotiations to export financing. To be sure, some problems are still amenable to negotiation. World agricultural markets, for example, remain deeply distorted by misguided subsidy, border and other measures; the markets of many developing countries are less open than those of developed countries; and the spread of trade remedy measures to an ever-increasing number of countries is a blight on the international trade regime. These policies may affect the interests of individual Canadian firms, but their impact on the Canadian economy as a whole is now marginal. The pursuit of trade, investment and other international economic arrangements will continue to preoccupy Canadian officials. Much of this activity, however, now serves what might be characterized as retail trade policy: it responds to the interests and complaints of individual Canadian firms rather than to the broader interests of the Canadian economy.

In the on-again, off-again Doha Round of WTO negotiations, Canada has found itself largely on the sidelines, unable to contribute constructively (Hart and Dymond 2006). In the not-too-distant past, Canada was a player and, together with the United States, the European Union and Japan, essentially determined the agenda and outcome of multilateral trade negotiations; but India, Brazil and Australia have displaced Canada. Convinced of the political weight of Canada's farm lobby, Canadian politicians of all stripes insisted that Canada make every effort to bring down trade barriers and subsidies on Canada's exports, but not at the expense of supply management and the monopoly marketing of wheat and barley. This posture left Canadian negotiators little room to manoeuvre. However, even if Canada had adopted a negotiating position consistent with its interests as a major net agriculture exporter and left the dwindling herd of dairy and chicken farmers to face up to reality, it would have remained a minor player because it now had little to contribute to or gain from multilateral trade negotiations. The simple fact is that Canada's most basic economic interests have become inextricably bound up with those of the United States and can no longer be addressed multilaterally in the WTO.

The fact that the WTO's role as a negotiating forum is diminishing does not mean that Canada should be indifferent to other developments at the WTO. The rules and procedures embedded in the WTO and its constituent agreements provide an essential basis for the conduct of world trade, including cross-border trade with the United States. Eventual success in concluding the Doha Round may be of marginal net benefit to Canada. That success is more important to the prosperity and welfare of developing countries, but as long as most of them persist in thinking that the rules of the game are stacked against them and that they need special treatment in the negotiation and application of the rules, the impact of multilateral negotiations will remain marginal for them as well (Hart and Dymond 2003). Canada is not well placed to effect a more productive approach to a revived Doha Round; as a result, both government and business have correctly concluded that Canada should maintain a relatively low profile in multilateral negotiations while remaining an active player in the day-to-day affairs of the WTO.

As indicated in table 1, Canada's trade beyond the United States is relatively modest and is concentrated in a limited number of markets. Taking into account the supply capabilities of the Canadian economy, the returns on extensive government trade and investment promotion programs beyond North America are likely to be fairly small. Much of this activity amounts to the provision of a service to individual firms — a service that makes very little difference to the level of Canadian economic activity or the prosperity of Canadians as a whole. Inertia, however, maintains the extensive array of programs and attitudes developed in an earlier era, and it contributes to the myth that they have an important role to play.

Most modern industries, from the automotive to the electronics and banking industries, have developed sophisticated global and regional supply and distribution networks and would be hard pressed to identify the national origin of their inputs and even of some of their final products. Individual firms are not averse to using Canadian commercial representation at embassies abroad, but few would be prepared to pay for the service, suggesting that its importance has become marginal to their interests. In these circumstances, it may be time for the government to reconsider the benefits Canadians derive from the extensive trade and investment promotion services offered at Canadian missions around the world. Many domestic services to Canadians have been placed on a cost-recovery basis, from access to all but the most basic statistics to passports and the delivery of the mail. Given the cost of maintaining trade promotion services at dozens of posts around the world and the limited number of Canadians who are dependent on such services, Canada could stretch its foreign representation activity by exercising part of it on a cost-recovery basis — as it has already done with certain aspects of Canadian immigration programs — and by reducing or eliminating other parts.

Some Canadians believe that the government must become more actively engaged in diversifying Canadian trading patterns. They are worried that the concentration of Canadian exports to the United States exposes the Canadian economy to serious risk should the US economy falter. This sentiment has a surface appeal, but it does not survive closer scrutiny. Canadian producers have long known that US customers offer the most profitable and constant opportunities. Some of their exports to the United States are incorporated into products that end up in other countries; others come back to Canada to be further processed or consumed by Canadians. In each case, markets determine the best use of scarce resources. In the other direction, US firms supply more than 60 percent of Canadian imports, roughly the norm for the past 150 years. As discussed earlier, modern manufacturing and distribution supply chains make it increasingly difficult for government statisticians to track the origin and destination of products with any precision. Many of these US-origin products may contain substantial foreign content. In the final analysis, however, none of this matters. What does matter is that the Canadian economy is functioning at a high level of productivity and efficiency, underwriting the prosperity and welfare of Canadians.

Who Canadians trade with is also of little import. Nevertheless, given current patterns of production, trade and investment, Canada's proximity to the United States and the extent to which Canadian firms are already part of US-based supply chains, Canadians will benefit the most from efforts to ensure that the Canada-US relationship is as good as it can be. In a world of disaggregated production and open markets, little trade now takes place among unrelated firms exchanging nationally identifiable products. Instead, modern trade involves highly complex exchanges within spatially disaggregated value chains dispersed not only within one national economy but also among many. The growth potential for Canadian firms relies on how well these firms are integrated into US-anchored value chains, rather than on policies based upon the false premises of national markets and products and on the assumption of a wise and all-knowing government.

Proponents of more diversified trading patterns insist that they do not want to reduce trade with the United States. Rather, they want to boost trade with the rest of the world. Again, serious analysis of this proposition suggests that the issue is political rather than economic. With the economy running at or near capacity and enjoying the fruits of a cyclical global resource boom, there is little room to produce more goods for export without setting off inflationary alarm bells at the Bank of Canada. As the Canadian dollar strengthens, particularly against the US dollar — another product of the resource boom — some Canadian manufacturers are having difficulty maintaining their competitive position. At the level of the individual and the firm, the resulting pressure can be very hard to bear. At the level of the economy as a whole, the disappearance of some manufacturing firms releases resources to shift to other areas of comparative advantage — for example, resource exploitation and processing. At some point in the future, the prospects for manufacturing and resource exports may reverse, as they did in the late 1970s and early 1980s. The result then was a change in the composition, direction and terms of Canadian trade, the opposite of what has happened in the last few years. In both instances, fundamental global economic forces fuelled the changes and thus contributed to the strengthening of the economy as a whole, although at the expense of some individuals and firms (Goldfarb 2006). Few if any of these changes in trade and investment patterns can be attributed to the success or failure of trade promotion or other government programs.

For the government to intervene in this process of market-based creative destruction in order to achieve more politically pleasing patterns of Canadian imports, exports and production would be highly detrimental to the long-term prosperity of most Canadians. To forestall such a development, governments, including the Canadian government, have spent the last 70 years devising rules and procedures that reward countries that abandon the instruments of protection and intervention and penalize those that maintain or reintroduce them. At one level, this is a difficult fact for some well-meaning politicians and lobbyists to accept. At another, most Canadians accept that the international trade regime has underwritten their prosperity and that only short-term gain and long-term pain would flow from undermining its principles. In this light, efforts to diversify Canadian trade patterns may remain an important part of Canadian political discourse, but they are unlikely to lead to any major policy initiatives.

Over the past decade, China has demonstrated that it is finally emerging from its long sleep, India has begun to dismantle the highly protectionist regime that has long shackled its economy, and Brazil has enjoyed sufficient stability in its politics and policies to allow some of its more adventurous entrepreneurs to look beyond its borders. Modernization, urbanization and marketization are now taking place at a dizzying pace in all three economies ("New Titans" 2006). Recent economic growth has averaged nearly 10 percent a year in China and a little less in India and Brazil. China can now be considered the workshop of the world, while India is becoming its call centre.

Some Canadians worry that unless we start trading more with these and other emerging economies, we will miss the boat and others will develop the relationships that will determine future trade and investment patterns. This is a highly overwrought concern. Should current patterns of growth and development in these markets continue, global economic activity will accelerate to an unprecedented degree, creating continuing strong demand for goods and services. Canada will be a major beneficiary of this growth, regardless of whether Canadian exporters are active in these markets or continue to concentrate on those markets with which they are most familiar. For Canadians, the potential for additional exports to emerging markets is modest. The real challenge lies in forging investment arrangements that will harness complementary strengths. Such arrangements will require cooperation between government and private investors that goes well beyond the hoopla of Team Canada missions. The increasingly integrated nature of North American production and investment patterns suggests that Canada must also work with the United States to ensure an enhanced North American platform for trade with emerging markets.

In recent years, the instrument of choice for pursuing trade diversification and strengthening trade and investment with new partners has been the free trade agreement. After the Mulroney government concluded CUFTA and NAFTA, the Chrétien government sought to establish its free trade credentials by concluding FTAs with smaller trading partners. This was an admirable policy impulse, and it signalled the extent to which free trade, rather than protection, had become the default position in Canadian trade policy. Experience has demonstrated, however, that it is difficult to conclude such agreements with minor partners. Negotiations with Chile and Costa Rica concluded successfully, but negotiations with the rump of the European Free Trade Association (EFTA) — Norway, Switzerland, Iceland and Liechtenstein — and the Central American four — Guatemala, El Salvador, Nicaragua and Honduras — proved difficult in the face of small pockets of politically significant opposition: shipbuilding in the former case and clothing in the latter. The current bilateral negotiations with South Korea — a market that is at least large enough to warrant some serious attention — similarly faces well-organized opposition from the auto sector and will experience an uphill struggle to conclude. Rumoured negotiations with other minor partners are likely to suffer similar fates. In the absence of strong support from the business community as a whole, such negotiations are easily derailed by entrenched import-competing interests concerned about the loss of a cherished remnant of the interventionist past. Ministers correctly conclude that the amount of political capital needed to reach such agreements is out of all proportion to the economic and commercial benefits. This leads to a willingness to initiate, but not conclude, such negotiations. The resultant misuse of resources signals a lack of seriousness that will not advance long-term Canadian trade and investment interests.

In sum, the best trade and economic policy for Canada in its relations with the rest of the world is one of benign neglect at the macro level and assistance to individual firms as needed. Government officials should be prepared to help individual Canadian firms with specific access or related issues. If a government-induced barrier prevents a Canadian firm from achieving its full potential, then the federal government should make every effort to negotiate its removal. Federal officials should insist that other governments live up to the rules and their commitments. They should use the dispute settlement provisions of international trade agreements to defend the trading rights of Canadians, and they should be equally prepared to live up to Canadian trade and investment obligations. Much of this activity, however, will have at most a marginal impact on the prosperity of Canadians as a whole. Billions of dollars in international transactions now take place daily without government direction or intervention due to the successful implementation of a sophisticated and mature global trade regime. In these circumstances, significant savings can be realized by reducing resources and programs devoted to marginal activities and redeploying them to areas of greater potential.

CANADA AND THE UNITED STATES

The area of greatest potential is the United States. Engagement with our southern neighbour is the indispensable foundation of any Canadian policy to maximize

418

benefits from international trade and investment. The key will be to achieve a seamless border embraced within an agreement implementing rules, procedures and institutions consonant with the reality of ever-deepening, mutually beneficial cross-border integration. To get there, Canadians will need to decide whether they want their government to help or hinder cross-border economic integration. While some might express horror at any policy explicitly aimed at facilitating integration, few would support the imposition of barriers to the millions of visits that Canadians make to the United States each year, to the thousands of trucks that cross the border every day, to the billions of cross-border phone calls, to the dozens of US TV channels beamed into Canadian homes, to the millions of US books, movies, CDs and magazines delivered to Canadian homes every year. The default position is integration, and the challenge for governments is to pursue the most effective measures to achieve that end.

The policy attitude of the past decade or more has been that such alterations as may be desirable to facilitate Canada-US trade and investment can be tackled through incremental improvements in discrete policies and programs, many of which can be made by Canada on its own. There are a number of problems with this approach. To begin with, incrementalism is slow and fails to take advantage of the synergies that may arise in dealing with related issues, particularly those that may be of interest to the United States and thus provide scope for trade-offs. Second, if the purpose of many of these programs is to strengthen US confidence in Canada as an economic and security partner, then bilateral engagement is critical. Third, experience tells us that Canadians are reluctant to do what makes sense unilaterally; they need the goad and reward of a trade or similar international agreement. Finally, given the forces of proximity and consumer and producer preferences, deepening integration is inevitable, but without bilateral engagement, it will happen on a basis that favours US default positions rather than jointly agreed-upon programs.

To reap the full benefits of deepening cross-border economic integration, Canada and the United States must engage in three fundamental and interrelated challenges: reducing the impact of the border; accelerating and directing the pace of regulatory convergence; and building the necessary institutional capacity to implement the results of the first two undertakings. Each will prove difficult, and solving the problems associated with either of the first two will prove illusory if we do not also address the others.

Border administration

The first challenge is to rectify the increasingly dysfunctional impact of border administration (Robson and Goldfarb 2005). Even after 15 years of "free" trade, the Canada-US border still bristles with uniformed and armed officers determined to ensure that commerce and interaction between Canadians and Americans comply with an astonishing array of prohibitions and restrictions. The list of rules and regulations for which the border remains a convenient, and even primary, enforcement vehicle has grown rather than diminished since the implementation of free trade, particularly in response to the new security realities created by 9/11. One study estimated that Canadian border officials are responsible for ensuring compliance with nearly 100 statutory instruments on behalf of several dozen federal departments and agencies; on the US side of the border, officials verify compliance with some 400 statutory instruments (Hart and Noble 2003). This has not created a single, integrated North American market but has instead produced two markets with many cross-border ties that are hostage to the efficiency and reliability of customs clearance, an issue of greater importance to Canadian-based firms than to US-based ones. The logic of the market dictates that new or expanded production facilities locate in the larger market and export to the smaller market. Canadian policy for the past 70 years has been geared toward reducing the impact of this logic. Much progress has been made, but as long as a border separates the two markets, firms that locate in the smaller market will start out with a distinct disadvantage.

Canada and the United States share three goals: a secure border; the rapid movement of legitimate travellers and efficient clearance of freight; and the interdiction of terrorism, illegal drugs, smuggling, illegal migrants, money laundering and other criminal activity. These goals are broadly shared by the two national governments — they differ only on matters of detail and emphasis. The clearance of a shipment of goods through either Canadian or US customs, for example, is contingent upon border officials being satisfied that the goods, the vehicle (truck, train, plane or ship) and the driver or operator are all eligible for entry. Establishing the eligibility of goods may involve, among other things, considerations related to customs (tariffs, rules of origin and similar issues), health, safety, labelling, government procurement, trade remedies, taxes and the environment. The vehicle must be certified to meet safety and similar requirements. The driver or operator must satisfy immigration requirements regarding citizenship, visas, criminal records, professional certification, labour regulations and similar matters. In each case, Canadian and US laws seek to safeguard security, health, safety, employment and other important policy goals.

Infrastructure investment that has failed to keep pace with the near tripling in Canada-US trade volumes since the mid-1980s has put additional pressure on border-crossing operations. In recognition of the extent of their shared objectives — as well as in an effort to reduce costs, facilitate legitimate travel and commerce and address pressure on infrastructure — Canadian and US officials over the course of the 1990s initiated a series of programs and dialogues aimed at making the border more open, effective and efficient. Such programs as CANPASS, FAST and INSPASS were designed to ease travel for frequent, low-risk border crossers. Other initiatives — from the Shared Border Accord, announced in 1995, to the Canada-US Partnership Forum, formed in 1999 — tried to make better use of emerging technologies, find ways to streamline the implementation of border policies, share information, coordinate activities and otherwise make existing laws and policies work more effectively.

Since 9/11, the two governments have incorporated these various initiatives into the broader program set out in the 2001 Smart Border Accord and subsequently encompassed in the 2005 Security and Prosperity Partnership. Both initiatives, however, have been limited by the decision to work within the confines of existing legislative mandates and by the lack of an intellectually coherent, strategic framework. Creating such a framework, investing in infrastructure and in technology (both at ports of entry and in the corridors leading to such ports) and targeting resources at pre-clearance programs for goods, vehicles and people are critical components of any comprehensive effort to improve the management of the border and reduce its commercial impact. Ultimately, the objective should be to create a border that is considerably more open and less bureaucratic within a North America that is more secure.

In considering ways and means to address the increasingly dysfunctional economic impact of border administration and remaining trade barriers, it is useful to distinguish between efforts to ensure compliance with a host of regulatory requirements and efforts to enforce laws and other matters that fall within the ambit of police and security considerations. Most of the requirements administered at the border involve regulatory matters and are secondary to the objective of maintaining a secure border. Therefore, a key aspect of any initiative to ensure the more efficient and effective operation of the border is the identification of those functions within the border clearance process that can be performed away from the border or — as discussed in more detail later — that can be eliminated altogether.

Much of the customs clearance of goods, for example, involves onerous information and reporting requirements — requirements that can be met in a way similar to that in which normal domestic reporting requirements for firms in both economies are met. Most of these reporting requirements operate as though the two economies were not joined by a free trade area. Additionally, most customs requirements — like origin certificates — can easily be streamlined by, for example, harmonizing most-favoured-nation tariff levels. A well-designed initiative to identify those remaining aspects of customs administration that can be either eliminated or addressed away from the border would contribute greatly to making the border function more effectively. The $430-million initiative announced by the government in January 2007 to strengthen electronic risk assessment procedures away from the border is a step in the right direction (Canada Border Services Agency 2007).

Similarly, virtually all travel across the border is undertaken by properly documented and eligible individuals in pursuit of legitimate objectives, from business to tourism. Much of the activity of immigration officers, therefore, is routine and makes at most a marginal contribution to safety and security. Attempts to cross the border by those who pose potential threats to either Canadians or Americans are rare and isolated, particularly relative to the huge number of crossings: about 400,000 every day. Every port of entry is, of course, vulnerable to penetration by undesirable elements, but experience indicates that those with serious criminal intent have ample space — and resources — to bypass port of entry controls without much effort. Again, a well-designed initiative to determine how these routine requirements could be eliminated, performed away from the border or satisfied by relying on more modern technologies would pay handsome dividends; it would create a more efficient, effective and secure border and a better-functioning North American economy. The solution to any real threat lies in directing more attention and resources to intelligence gathering, information sharing and entry by individuals and goods from non-North American points of origin, rather than to increasing routine inspections at the Canada-US border.

Some Canadians have expressed alarm at the idea of moving in this direction because they believe it would require the two countries to establish a "common perimeter." It is hard to take this concern seriously; a de facto North American perimeter is a matter of long standing. The decision to maintain a North American security perimeter and pursue a North American economic space was made many years ago and based on agreements ranging from NATO and NORAD to the Autopact and NAFTA. The issue today is how, in the face of heightened security concerns, the two countries can strengthen the perimeter that already exists and address security issues within their common economic and security space.

More resources at the border seem unlikely to achieve greater security, absent extraordinary further investments in human and physical infrastructure. Furthermore, to increase resources to such an extent is to risk causing considerable collateral damage to economic interests; solutions can be found more effectively and efficiently by other means. The two governments need to work with each other at every level, institutionalizing contacts, enhancing cooperation and sharing information on matters small and large. They could make much greater investments in intelligence gathering and gradually focus ever-larger parts of that effort on initial entries to North America. They could also make far larger investments in infrastructure and in technology. Both types of investment are critical to any comprehensive attempt to improve the management of the border. Such investments should not proceed on the basis of current inspection methodologies but should rely much more on risk assessments and random inspections. They should also focus more on targeting resources at preclearance programs for goods, vehicles and people. Finally, the two governments need to engage in discussions about increasing the level of convergence in US and Canadian policies governing such matters as cargo and passenger preclearance programs, law enforcement programs of all types, and immigration and refugee determination procedures.

Reducing border administration will have beneficial effects at three levels: it will decrease enforcement and administrative costs for governments and compliance costs for industry, and it will reduce trade and investment disincentives. Various attempts have been made to quantify these benefits. As Pierre Martin concludes, "Although the total costs are difficult to estimate with precision, they are significant and likely to become higher" (2006, 15). Perrin Beatty, then president of Canadian Manufacturers and Exporters, claimed that "border delays alone cost the Canadian and US economies an estimated C$12.5 billion annually. In the automotive industry alone, it is estimated that the additional reporting, compliance and delay costs translate into an estimated $800 Canadian per vehicle" (2005). Canada's former ambassador to the United States, Michael Kergin, has said that nontariff border costs add 5 percent to the invoice costs of most exports, and the figure could be as high as 10 to 13 percent for trade-sensitive products (2002). John Taylor and Douglas Robideaux have made the most detailed study of Canada-US border costs, and they estimate that direct costs — out-of-pocket costs to government and business of administering border requirements — add between US$7.5 and US$13.2 billion annually to cross-border trade, with a midpoint of US$10.3 billion (Taylor and Robideaux 2003). Indirect costs are even more difficult to estimate. Automotive industry analysts estimate, for example, that "a lost hour of assembly output due to a parts shortage costs approximately US$60,000 per hour in lost earnings" (Andrea and Smith 2002, 19). The impact that a more open border would have on either direct or indirect costs is equally difficult to estimate. The European Union experience, however, suggests that the move toward a more open border — the Schengen Agreement — both boosted commerce and reduced direct and indirect costs without any significant negative impact on security and regulatory objectives (Egan 2001; Hart 2004b; Hart 2006).

Regulatory cooperation

A key component of trimming border congestion is meeting the second challenge: reducing the impact of regulatory differences between Canada and the United

States. As Europeans have learned, regulatory cooperation and the reduction of border formalities are two sides of the same coin. There may be a long tradition of pragmatic, informal problem solving between the regulatory authorities of the two federal governments, as well as among provincial and state governments, but the time has come to ask how much regulatory enforcement needs to be exercised at the border and how much can be exercised behind the border. More fundamentally, as regulatory cooperation and convergence proceed, the two governments need to ask whether they are ready to proceed to a more formal, treaty-based process of regulatory cooperation aimed at eliminating, to the largest extent possible, what can be characterized as the tyranny of small differences. When those differences are eliminated, much of the rationale for border administration disappears.

The extent of regulatory convergence and cooperation today is largely determined by bureaucratic agendas and preferences. The results have been interesting: Canadian jurisdictions align their regulatory goals and objectives with those of their US counterparts, work with US regulators in many areas, but maintain sufficient regulatory autonomy to chart their own path. This has produced two very similar but autonomous regulatory regimes characterized by extensive duplication and redundancy. However, broader goals — from economic development to regulatory efficiency — remain of secondary importance. This default position also avoids confrontation with the two related issues: the border and institutional capacity.

The External Advisory Committee on Smart Regulation (EACSR), appointed by Prime Minister Chrétien, concluded that this model was no longer adequate and recommended that the federal government "work to: achieve compatible standards and regulation in areas that would enhance the efficiency of the Canadian economy and provide high levels of protection for human health and the environment; eliminate small regulatory differences and reduce regulatory impediments to an integrated North American market; move toward single review and approval of products and services for all jurisdictions in North America; and put in place integrated regulatory processes to support key integrated North American industries (e.g. energy, agriculture, food) and provide more effective responses to threats to human and animal health and the environment" (Canada, EACSR 2004, 17, 21).

The government broadly accepted the recommendations of the EACSR, and in the context of the Security and Prosperity Partnership adopted by the Presidents of the United States and Mexico and the Prime Minister of Canada in Waco, Texas, in March 2005 — confirmed by the three leaders a year later — it took important steps to move the agenda along. It appointed a group in the Privy Council Office (PCO) to pursue the path charted by the EACSR. Additionally, the federal government's Policy Research Initiative was charged with considering ways and means to implement the EACSR recommendations. What has emerged to date is a commitment to what might be characterized as accelerated incrementalism. The result is a higher level of awareness of regulatory developments in the US among Canadian policy-makers, leading to enhanced opportunities to align Canadian regulatory policy with developments in Washington. What is missing is a strong political commitment to regulatory cooperation and a plan to put it into effect. Not surprisingly, the pace in implementing this program has been glacial.

The current Canadian approach also appeals to American regulators, who have to date exhibited little appetite for more. The US decision-making system is extraordinarily resistant to centralized control and thus offers little more than piecemeal, regulator-to-regulator cooperation. The US president, for example, may appoint commissioners to the Securities and Exchange Commission, but once in office, the commissioners act with full independence. Nevertheless, in both Washington and Ottawa, regulatory reform and streamlining has a growing number of supporters. Congress in 1980 established the Office of Information and Regulatory Affairs (OIRA) in the Office of Management and Budget, and successive presidents have, through executive orders, set out the basis for OIRA to provide systematic, centralized review and appraisal of all federal regulations. Much of this initiative has been coordinated with broader international ones, particularly at the OECD. Canadian efforts parallel those of the United States. Since 1978, Canadian federal regulatory activity has been subject to a constant, comprehensive, centralized process of review, housed initially in the Treasury Board, subsequently in the PCO and now in Industry Canada, with a view to eliminating duplication and redundancy and promoting best international practice. The guiding policies developed in both capitals for rule making and review are remarkably similar in tone and intent and reflect the high level of ongoing discussions at the OECD and bilaterally. A sound foundation has, therefore, been created for a more formal program of cross-border regulatory cooperation and even coordination. But to go to the next level, the two governments will need to develop an enforceable agreement and the institutional capacity to make it work.

Initially, the two governments should build confidence and gain experience at the federal level, but given the federal structure of the two countries, the sooner they engage provincial and state regulatory authorities in a similar process of mandatory information exchange and consultations, the sooner they will arrive at a "North American" approach to meeting their regulatory goals and objectives. Because of the large number of jurisdictions involved, this is an area that will require some creative decision rules as well as institutions to make them work. Fortunately, as at the federal level, extensive regional networks of collaboration already exist between Canadian provincial and US state regulators. Any successful federal strategy on economic integration and regulatory convergence will need to both complement and take advantage of these existing cross-border institutions.

The benefits of further regulatory convergence lie in reducing costs and duplication. Lack of compatibility in various sectors — from transportation and food safety to telecommunications, pharmaceuticals, environmental protection, labour markets and professional services — adds to compliance and enforcement costs for both government and industry, continues to segment the two national markets and necessitates continued border administration. Lessons from Europe and elsewhere suggest significant benefits from cooperation leading to more effective regulation, higher levels of compatibility and reduced border administration (Egan 2001; Bermann, Herdegen, and Lindseth 2000).

As the Canadian beef industry learned in 2003-05, it does not take much to cause chaos: a single incident of BSE (mad cow disease) led to the closure of the border; it was not fully reopened for more than two years. Failure to pursue an integrated regulatory regime consonant with the integrated market proved costly, with estimates ranging from $4 billion and up (Moens 2006; Le Roy and Klein 2005). Other sectors of the economy could face similar problems as regulators on one side of the border or the other address issues without regard for the reality of integration. But, as the beef industry also learned, once the two sets of regulators develop the basis for an integrated approach, problems are quickly resolved. There was one incident of BSE in Canada in 2003, leading to more than two years of trade disruption. There were five cases in 2006, not one of which led to trade action.

For consumers, regulatory divergence is tantamount to a concealed "inefficiency tax" that citizens pay on virtually everything they purchase. This tax is the sum of the costs of duplicate regulations, border administration delays and other regulatory impediments. For businesses, higher costs of compliance hinder international competitiveness and complicate the efficient deployment of scarce resources. For governments, regulatory divergence increases risk, reduces efficiency and leads to less than optimum outcomes in achieving regulatory goals. Polling in both countries has suggested strong public support for regulatory convergence and more cohesive North American policies to improve living standards.

Compliance with different national and subnational rules, together with the redundant testing and certification of products, processes and providers for different markets, raises costs for manufacturers and providers operating in an integrated market. Complex and lengthy product- or provider-approval procedures can slow innovation, frustrate new product launches, protect domestic producers from foreign competitors and create a drag on competitiveness, productivity, investment and growth. In its latest survey, the Fraser Institute indicated that between 1975 and 1999, over 117,000 new federal and provincial regulations were enacted — an average of 4,700 a year. It estimated that administrative costs had reached $5.2 billion by 1997-98, compliance costs were $103 billion and "political" costs (regulation-related lobbying) were $10.3 billion, adding up to the equivalent of more than 12 percent of Canadian GDP (Jones and Graf 2001). The Canadian Federation of Independent Business (CFIB) estimates that Canadian business annually spends $33 billion, or 2.6 percent of Canada's GDP, complying with this profusion of regulatory activity (CFIB 2005). Producing such estimates is at best an inexact science, but the figures do provide an indication of orders of magnitude. Canada's Policy Research Initiative is looking at better ways to measure the extent and costs of Canada's regulatory regimes (Ndayisenga and Downs 2005; Ndayisenga and Blair 2006).[1]

While greater cross-border regulatory convergence would not eliminate these costs, it would certainly reduce duplication and overlap, particularly for the Canadian government. Even a 10 percent reduction in duplication would make an important contribution to reducing compliance and administration costs.

Institutional capacity

Progress in addressing the governance of deepening integration depends upon building sufficient institutional capacity and procedural frameworks to reduce conflict and provide a more flexible basis for dynamic rule making and adaptation for the North American market as a whole. It may well be necessary to overcome traditional Canadian and US aversion to bilateral institution building and look creatively to the future. While the European model of a complex supranational infrastructure may not suit North American circumstances, there are lessons Canadians and Americans can learn from the EU experience.

Rather than seeking to create structures where they are not needed, the two governments should focus upon the functions that must be performed for the efficient governance of deepening integration and create new institutions only where current arrangements are unsuitable. To some extent, this could be accomplished by making creative use of existing Canada-US cooperative arrangements, by vesting officials in agencies on both sides of the border with new responsibilities or by building on existing models that have worked well.

The two governments could, for example, stipulate that the Canada Border Services Agency and the US Customs Service coordinate their efforts to ensure efficient administration of third-country imports. Similarly, an appropriate understanding could be reached requiring Transport Canada and the US Department of Transportation to coordinate their efforts to ensure highway safety; for example, before any new rules and regulations were enacted, mandatory coordination efforts could be made to achieve compatible outcomes and recognize each other's approaches to the same problem. A good basis for this kind of cooperation already exists in informal networks among officials and in the relatively minor differences in regulatory approach. What is missing is an agreed-upon mandate to resolve differences and a more formal institutional framework with authority to ensure mutually beneficial outcomes. Establishing a bilateral commission to supervise efforts to establish a more coordinated and convergent set of regulations governing all customs or transportation matters could prove critical to providing the necessary momentum and political will.

In both countries, labour mobility is hampered by provincial and state labour laws and delegated professional accreditation procedures. NAFTA put in place a modest process to permit temporary entry for business and professional visitors and mutual recognition of professional accreditation. The latter has been hampered by the conflict of interest inherent in a system of self-regulation. As the EU learned, a more centralized approach was required to overcome conflicts of interest and bureaucratic inertia. From architects and accountants to doctors and dentists, there remains considerable scope for enhancing mutual recognition arrangements (Hart 2004b). An important step toward breaking the logjam would be to appoint a bilateral task force to develop model mutual recognition arrangements for consideration by state and provincial accreditation bodies.

Much can be achieved on the basis of existing networks of cooperation; specific joint or bilateral commissions can be added where existing networks are inadequate. More will be achieved, however, if the two governments commit to the establishment of a limited number of bilateral institutions with a mandate to provide government with the necessary advice and information to effect a more integrated North American approach to regulation. An independent Canada-US secretariat with a mandate to drive the agenda and report annually to the president and the prime minister on progress could, for example, prove critical to overcoming bureaucratic inertia. Similarly, a joint advisory board for the president and the prime minister could contribute some creative drive to the development of new bilateral initiatives. As numerous studies have demonstrated, regulatory agendas are prone to capture, geared to serving the narrow interests of regulator and regulatee. Bilateral initiatives limited to regulatory authorities are unlikely to be immune to this reality. Regular review by an independent advisory board of progress in implementing a bilateral program of guided regulatory convergence could thus prove valuable in the attempt to keep the program focused on broader objectives.

Governments must think carefully about any initiative that could compromise their ability to discharge their responsibility for the security and well-being of their citizens. Canadian experience in negotiating international rules and pursuing regulatory cooperation, both multilaterally and bilaterally, suggests that there is no inherent conflict between these responsibilities and such rule making and cooperation. Nevertheless, vested interests can mount emotional campaigns casting doubt on the idea that regulations made jointly can serve to fulfill Canadian responsibilities. Fortunately, it is not difficult to dispel such doubts. Canadians, for example, routinely travel in the United States, comfortable with the reliability of US safety regulations. They eat and drink as freely in the United States as they do at home, and if they fall sick, they can rely (although at considerable expense) on US medical advice and US-approved drugs. From almost any perspective, Canadians have few if any qualms about the goals and efficacy of US regulations when in the United States. There are few other countries in which Canadians routinely exhibit such confidence. The reason is simple: Canadian and US regulatory regimes are, in almost all respects, closely aligned. The differences are matters of detail that may matter to individual regulators but have little impact on residents of either country.

CONCLUSIONS: COSTS AND BENEFITS

More than ever, the two-way movement of goods and services across the Canada-US border is Canada's economic lifeline. The extent of economic integration or linkage between the two countries has reached the stage where Canada's economic well-being is directly tied to an open and well-functioning bilateral border. Failure to maintain or even enhance an open border will have a corrosive impact on Canada's continued economic prosperity. To that end, the federal government needs to mount a major initiative to conclude a treaty-based arrangement that addresses current impediments to a better-functioning, integrated North American economy (Gotlieb 2003). Fundamental to such a treaty are a better-functioning border, deeper regulatory convergence and enhanced institutional capacity.

The federal government is currently devoting considerable resources to activities that will have at best a marginal impact on the productivity and well-being of Canadians — from participation in the Doha Round of multilateral trade negotiations, to extensive trade promotion activities in obscure markets around the world, to negotiation of free trade agreements with minor trading partners. Most of these activities respond to the perceived needs of individual constituents, but at a much higher cost than is generally realized. For example, teams of up to 85 individuals representing 20 or more federal agencies routinely travel back and forth between Canada and South Korea in pursuit of a trade agreement that may never see the light of day. Dozens of officials scattered throughout Ottawa continue to participate in various aspects of the Doha Round, with a clear mandate to hold the line on a program — supply management — that costs Canadian consumers billions of dollars annually. Hundreds of trade commissioners deployed to European, African, Latin American and Asian countries dutifully fill in annual forms claiming the amount of business "influenced," even as trade with these places stagnates. Others are engaged in building "gateways" and organizing Team Canada missions that are big on photo ops and press announcements but not so big on measurable increases in trade and investment.

Meanwhile, a growing agenda with the United States languishes on the back burner as politicians and bureaucrats shrink from tackling "controversial" issues. In the absence of sufficient resources and a bureaucratic home with enough clout to move rent-seeking officials to engage the bilateral regulatory agenda, little will be accomplished that goes beyond Ottawa's commitment to incrementalism. Even a stealth agenda requires clear objectives and the resources to pursue them. Instead, the government maintains a trade department led by a senior minister saddled with an increasingly marginal mandate, and it has not been able to figure out how to organize the bureaucracy to prioritize Canada's most important trade and economic partner.

As a matter of priority, therefore, the government should take some of the resources now devoted to marginal trade negotiations and trade promotion activities and redeploy them to the Canada-US agenda. The resources needed to establish a department of North American integration can be found not only in the trade components of the Department of Foreign Affairs and International Trade, but also (and even more so) in the Departments of Finance, Industry, Natural Resources, and Agriculture and Agri-food. Led by a senior minister and an experienced deputy, such a department would have the authority to take on the dozens of small bilateral initiatives scattered throughout the bureaucracy, mould them into a coherent agenda and pursue them strategically and urgently.

As this department's work progressed, it would feed back into the domestic agenda and provide an intellectually and politically persuasive basis for tackling some of the remaining sacred cows of Canada's waning nationalist heritage, from provincial trade barriers to supply management and ownership restrictions. While each of these issues should be tackled on its own merits, experience demonstrates that success is more likely in the context of a broader initiative, in which politically persuasive gains can be used to offset the inevitable wailing from narrow but entrenched interests.

Ironically, building the basis for a deeper and more functional bilateral engagement will allow Canadian firms to strengthen their participation in US-based global value chains and thus increase their profiles in other markets. Modern trade and investment patterns reflect the critical importance to most firms of a strong regional base. For most Canadian firms, that base is North America. For those for whom diversification is the Holy Grail, deeper bilateral integration holds the key.

The benefits to Canadians of such a reordered agenda and redeployment of resources are potentially enormous. A reduction in the direct and indirect costs of administering the border would alone be worth the effort. Reducing overlap and duplication in Canada's increasingly costly regulatory regimes would put even more dollars in the pockets of Canadians and increase their capacity to pay for other priorities, from health care reform to education. The indirect benefits of redirecting private resources to more rewarding activities would be even larger —the Canadian economy would be strengthened, as would the ability of Canadians to focus on other important matters. The only cost that would arise would be political — that is, Canadians' exaggerated preoccupation with ephemeral concepts of sovereignty and nationhood. As the past two decades of experience with bilateral free trade has demonstrated, however, these concerns have no basis in reality. Canada is a stronger country now than it was 20 years ago, not despite but because of bilateral free trade. The time has come to complete the project and reap its full advantages.

Reordering the agenda along these lines inevitably raises serious political concerns, including Canadian sovereignty and engagement with the rest of the world. To each of these concerns, there are serious responses, which need to be discussed frankly and openly. Such concerns have been used instead to shut off debate, resulting in the drift that now characterizes Canada's engagement with the United States and the rest of the world. Canadians deserve more from their analysts and scholars.

NOTES

1   These costs are consistent with other
national estimates. The Adam Smith
Institute, for example, reports that British
estimates of the costs of compliance with
national and EU regulatory requirements
annually add up to 10 to 12 percent of
GDP (2007). An extensive survey of
these costs in the United States has
been catalogued by the Cato Institute. In
a 2004 report limited to federal regulations, it reported:

- The *Federal Register* contained 71,269
pages in 2003 and a record 75,606
pages in 2002.

- Regulatory agencies issued 4,148 final
rules in 2003 and in the Unified Agenda
reported on 4,266 regulations that were
at various stages of implementation
throughout the 50-plus federal departments, agencies and commissions —
an increase of 2 percent from the previous year.

- Of the 4,266 regulations in the regulatory pipeline, 127 were "economically significant" rules that would have at least $100
million in economic impact — that is, they
would create at least $12.7 billion yearly in
future off-budget costs.

- The five most active rule-producing agencies, which accounted for 46 percent of the
rules under consideration, were Treasury,
Transportation, Homeland Security,
Agriculture and Environmental Protection.

- Regulatory costs of $869 billion are
equivalent to 7.9 percent of US GDP;
these added up to more than twice the
$375-billion budget deficit and exceed-
ed all corporate pretax profits, which
totalled $665 billion in 2002 (Crews
2004).

Mark Crain calculates that the total cost of
the federal regulatory burden had risen to
US$1.1 trillion by 2004 (Crain 2005; see
also Crain and Hopkins 2001).

REFERENCES

Adam Smith Institute (ASI). 2007. *The Adam Smith Regulatory Monitor*. London: ASI. Accessed May 2, 2007. www.adam smith.org/index.php/main/individual/regu latory_monitor

Andrea, D. J., and B. C. Smith. 2002. *The Canada-U.S. Border: An Automotive Case Study*. Ann Arbor, MI: Center for Automotive Research; Ottawa: Foreign Affairs and International Trade Canada. Accessed May 2, 2007. www.cargroup.org/pdfs/The%20Canada-U.S.%20Border.pdf

Beatty, P. 2005. "Speaking Notes for the Hon. Perrin Beatty, President and CEO, Canadian Manufacturers and Exporters, to the US Senate Committee on Foreign Relations, July 12, 2005, Washington, D.C." Accessed May 2, 2007. www.cmemec.ca/pdf/US_Senate.pdf

Bermann, G. A., M. Herdegen, and P. L. Lindseth, eds. 2000. *Transatlantic Regulatory Co-oper-ation: Legal Problems and Political Prospects*. Oxford: Oxford University Press.

Blank, S. 2005. "Three Possible NAFTA Scenarios: It Is Time for Canada to Think Carefully about North America." *Embassy*, September 7. Accessed May 2, 2007. www.embassymag.ca/html/index.php?display=story&full_path=/2005/september/7/blank/

Canada. External Advisory Committee on Smart Regulation (EACSR). 2004. *Smart Regulation: A Regulatory Strategy for Canada*. Ottawa: EACSR. Accessed May 2, 2007. www.bradford.ac.uk/irq/ docu ments/archive/Canada_Smarter_Regulation _Report.pdf

Canada Border Services Agency (CBSA). 2006. *Customs Tariff, Departmental Consolidation 2006*. Accessed April 26, 2007. www.cbsa-asfc.gc.ca/general/publications/customs_tariff-e.html#current

_____. 2007. "Canada's New Government Invests over \$430M for Smart, Secure Borders." News release, January 12. Ottawa: CBSA. Accessed May 2, 2007. www.cbsa-asfc.gc.ca/ media/release-communique/2007/0112windsor-eng.html

Canadian Federation of Independent Business (CFIB). 2005. "Government Red Tape Cost Business \$33 Billion a Year." News release. Accessed May 30, 2007. www.cfib.ca/mcentre/mwire/releases/nat1 21205_e.asp.

Crain, W. M. 2005. *The Impact of Regulatory Costs on Small Firms*. Washington, DC: US Small Business Administration. Accessed May 2, 2007. www.sba.gov/advo/research/rs264tot.pdf

Crain, W. M., and T. D. Hopkins. 2001. *The Impact of Regulatory Costs on Small Firms: A Report for the Office of Advocacy, U.S. Small Business Administration*. Washington, DC: US Small Business Administration. Accessed May 2, 2007. www.sba.gov/advo/research/ rs207tot.pdf

Crews, C. W. Jr. 2004. *Ten Thousand Commandments: An Annual Snapshot of the Federal Regulatory State*. Washington, DC: Cato Institute.

Cross, P. 2002. "Cyclical Implications of the Rising Import Content in Exports." *Canadian Economic Observer* 15 (12), cat. no. 11-010-XPB. Ottawa: Statistics Canada. Accessed May 2, 2007. www.statcan.ca/english/ads/ 11-010-XPB/pdf/dec02.pdf

Cross P., and G. Cameron. 1999. "The Importance of Exports to GDP and Jobs." *Canadian Economic Observer* 12 (11), cat. no. 11-010-XPB. Ottawa: Statistics Canada. www.statcan.ca/english/ads/ 11-010-XPB/features.htm

Dicken, P. 2003. *Global Shift: Reshaping the Global Economic Map in the 21st Century*. 4th ed. London: Sage Publications.

Egan, M. P. 2001. *Constructing a European Market: Standards, Regulation, and Governance*. New York: Oxford University Press.

Foreign Affairs and International Trade Canada. n.d. *Balance of Payments*. Accessed April 26, 2007. www.international.gc.ca/eet/ balance-payments-en.asp

Gereffi, G. 2005. "The Global Economy: Organization, Governance, and Development." In *The Handbook of Economic Sociology*, edited by Neil J. Smelser and Richard Swedberg. 2nd ed. Princeton: Princeton University Press, Russell Sage Foundation.

Goldfarb, D. 2006. "Too Many Eggs in One Basket? Evaluating Canada's Need to Diversify Trade." *C.D. Howe Institute Commentary* 236. Toronto: C.D. Howe Institute.

Gotlieb, A. 2003. "A Grand Bargain with the US." *National Post*, March 5.

Hart, M. 2004a. "A New Accommodation with the United States: The Trade and Economic Dimension." No. 2 of *Thinking North America*, edited by Thomas J. Courchene, Donald J. Savoie, and Daniel Schwanen. *The Art of the State*, vol. 2. Montreal: Institute for Research on Public Policy.

_____. 2004b. "Is There Scope for Enhancing the Mobility of Labour between Canada and the United States?" *HRSDC-IC-SSHRC Skills Research Initiative Working Paper Series*. Ottawa: Industry Canada.

_____. 2006. "Steer or Drift? Taking Charge of Canada-US Regulatory Convergence." *C.D. Howe Institute Commentary* 229. Toronto: C.D. Howe Institute.

Hart, M., and B. Dymond. 2003. "Special and Differential Treatment and the Doha 'Development' Round." *Journal of World Trade* 37 (2): 395-415.

_____. 2006. "The World Trade Organization Plays Hong Kong." *Policy Options* 27 (2): 7-12. Montreal: IRPP.

Hart, M., and J. Noble. 2003. "Smart Borders Require Smart Regulations: The Impact of Regulatory Differences on Trade and Investment between Canada and the United States." Unpublished paper prepared for Investment Partnerships Canada.

Hodgson, G. 2004. "Trade in Evolution: The Emergence of Integrative Trade." *EDC Economics*, March. Ottawa: Export Development Canada. Accessed May 2, 2007. www.edc.ca/english/docs/Canadian_Benefits_030104_e.pdf

Jones, L., and S. Graf. 2001. "Canada's Regulatory Burden: How Many Regulations? At What Cost?" *Fraser Forum*, August. Accessed May 2, 2007. www.fraserinstitute.ca/admin/books/files/aug-forum.pdf

Kergin, M. 2002. Speech presented at the annual meeting of the Joint Industry Group, March 5, Washington, DC. Accessed May 2, 2007. geo.international.gc.ca/canam/washington/border/joint_industry_2002-en.asp

Le Roy, D. G., and K.K. Klein. 2005. "Mad Cow Chaos in Canada: Was It Just Bad Luck or Did Government Policies Play a Role?" *Canadian Public Policy* 31 (4): 381-99.

Mandel, M., et al. 2006. "Why the Economy Is a Lot Stronger Than You Think." *Business Week*, February 13.

Martin, P. 2006. "The Mounting Costs of Securing the 'Undefended' Border." *Policy Options* 27 (6): 15-18. Montreal: IRPP.

Moens, A. 2006. "Mad Cow: A Case Study in Canada-U.S. Relations." *Fraser Institute Digital Publication*, March. Accessed May 2, 2007.www.fraserinstitute.ca/admin/books/files/MadCow.pdf

Ndayisenga, F., and A. Downs. 2005. "Economic Impacts of Regulatory Convergence between Canada and the United States." *PRI Working Papers on North American Linkages* 8. Ottawa: Policy Research Initiative.

Ndayisenga, F., and Doug B. 2006 "Regulatory Expenditures and Compliance Costs Verifying the Link Using US Data." *PRI Working Papers on North American Linkages* 25. Ottawa: Policy Research Initiative.

"The New Titans." 2006. *Economist*, September 14.

Ridgeway, A. 2006. "Data Issues on Integrative Trade between Canada and the US: Measurement Issues for Supply Chains." Paper presented at the Centre for Trade Policy and Law conference "Integrative Trade between Canada and the United States: Policy Implications," December 6, Ottawa. Accessed April 26, 2007. www.carleton.ca/ctpl/conferences/documents/Ridgeway-DataIssuesonIntegrativeTradebetweenCanadaandtheUS-Paper.pdf

Robson, W. B.P., and D. Goldfarb. 2005. "Risky Business: U.S. Border Security and the Threat to Canadian Exports." *C.D. Howe Institute Commentary* 177. Toronto: C.D. Howe Institute.

Safarian, A.E. 1993. *Multinational Enterprise and Public Policy: A Study of the Industrial Countries*. Cheltenham, UK: Edward Elgar.

Sturgeon, T. J. 2006. "Conceptualizing Integrative Trade: The Global Value Chains Framework." Paper presented at the Centre for Trade Policy and Law conference "Integrative Trade between Canada and the United States: Policy Implications," December 6, Ottawa. Accessed April 26, 2007. www.carleton.ca/ctpl/conferences/documents/Sturgeon-ConceptualizingIntegrativeTrade-Presentation.pdf

Taylor, J. C., and D. R. Robideaux. 2003. "Canada-US Border Cost Impacts and Their Implications for Border Management Strategy." *Horizons* 6 (3): 47-50.

United Nations Conference on Trade and Development (UNCTAD). 2004. *World Investment Report 2004: The Shift toward Services*. Geneva: UNCTAD.

CONSTRUCTING CONSTRUCTIVE ENGAGEMENT
Jonathan T. Fried

As befits an author who brings a wealth of experience and scholarship to the task, Michael Hart, in his chapter "Canadian Engagement in the Global Economy," has presented an incisive diagnosis of the challenges that Canada faces: it is a globalized market served by global supply chains in goods and services, within which an increasingly integrated North American economy has to compete; but it also faces a United States preoccupied with security on the basis of cross-border rather than integrative rules. And the good doctor methodically reviews several symptoms of what may ail the country in addressing these challenges — including a retail trade policy too diffuse in its targets and too defensive in its posture, and a lack of focus and vision in building a more competitive North America. His prescriptions flow convincingly from his analysis: we must open Canadian trade and investment to the world and, vis-à-vis the United States, reduce the impact of the border, aggressively accelerating a process of "regulatory convergence" and building institutional capacity to implement this agenda.

Here I offer some comments and cautions respecting Hart's recommendations. Despite the title of his chapter, Hart does not offer a complete diagnosis of the challenges Canada must address to compete effectively in the twenty-first century, and thus he invites reflection on additional, related public policy priorities.

THE INTERNATIONAL CONTEXT
Economic engagement

Hart devotes the majority of his analysis to Canada's international engagement in the trade field. But, as he acknowledges in a passing reference to the International Monetary Fund (IMF) and the Organisation for Economic Co-operation and Development (OECD), the international framework for trade and investment is determined under various instruments and in forums well beyond the North American Free Trade Agreement (NAFTA) and the World Trade Organization (WTO).

The IMF, for example, is charged by its members under its articles of agreement with promoting stability and growth by fostering the macroeconomic conditions conducive to doing so. Its engagement with major industrialized and emerging economies plays an important role in reducing the likelihood of abrupt shocks to the global economy, in mitigating the impact of financial crises when they occur and in providing direction on fiscal and monetary policy — for example, regarding exchange rates — that supports a fair and level playing field for cross-border economic activity.

This agenda has long been at the centre of G7 summitry. More recently, in an effort to nurture greater co-ownership of and shared responsibility for global stability among emerging markets, the G20 group of finance ministers from developed and emerging markets — which first convened to address jointly needed improvements in international financial oversight in the wake of the Asian financial crisis of the late 1990s — has taken on an increasingly prominent role. And the OECD provides developed market economies with an important forum for drawing out best practices in macroeconomic policy and sectoral regulation.

Canada has long devoted considerable resources to supporting these institutions in their respective tasks. And these tasks are of a type that must be undertaken multilaterally. It would not be inconsistent with Hart's recommendation that priority be given to productive relations with the United States if Canada were to continue to assign high priority to a well-functioning international architecture for macroeconomic stability, rather than, as he suggests, merely sustaining its participation in these forums.

Foreign policy engagement

Similarly, as the thickening of the Canada-US border in the wake of 9/11 so starkly illustrated, threats to peace and security originating abroad can have a major impact on the functioning of the North American economy. For this reason alone, it behooves Canada to work in close partnership with the United States to curb these threats. Canada's significant commitment to Afghanistan is right for both Canada and North America; support for Haiti and for the Caribbean more generally should help to mitigate a growing immigration and refugee — as well as drug trafficking and money laundering — challenge that could otherwise reach the continent's shores; our holding of the gavel for the refugee working group in the context of the search for a lasting peace in the Middle East can contribute to solutions in the region that ultimately reduce the threat of terrorism, which could undermine a well-functioning Canada-US border. Accordingly, and as recommended by the Conference Board of Canada in volume 1 of its Canada Project report, *Mission Possible: Stellar Canadian Performance in the*

Global Economy, Canada's foreign policy footprint should be focused but significant (Hodgson and Shannon 2007).

SOME COMMENTS AND CAUTIONS
Bilateral/trilateral, regional and multilateral trade negotiations

Hart suggests that the incremental benefits flowing to the Canadian economy due to active engagement in multilateral trade negotiations and to the pursuit of various bilateral and regional trade initiatives fail to outweigh the costs (in industry and bureaucratic time, and, just as important, in attention and focus) of these undertakings. Summarizing his view, he recommends a policy of "benign neglect."

A first caution is — given that the United States and other competitors are pursuing what some have called "competitive liberalization" as a means of gaining preferred market access — that there may be good, procompetitive reasons for Canada to keep pace. Major exporters stand to lose hundreds of millions of dollars in sales because of competitors' free trade agreements (FTAs). The cumulative effect on our national economy of losing our competitive position in market after market could be significant.

Second, as a legitimate part of the policy mix, we can advance our goal of closer integration with the US by seeking FTAs with countries that already have FTAs with the US. To do otherwise risks making Canada a less desirable place from which to export from North America to certain markets and also makes Canada a less desirable investment location. In other words, matching US FTA moves is part of what Canada can do to strengthen its position on the North American platform.

More rationally, from a global supply-chain perspective, Canada and the United States could work toward a triangulation of their respective third-country FTAs. If, for example, both countries agree that imports from Israel, or from Chile or from Costa Rica, merit preferred access, then such content should be given the same preferential lower-tariff treatment as intra-NAFTA trade. More boldly, as suggested in the American Assembly report *Renewing the U.S.-Canada Relationship* (2005) and the Council on Foreign Relations Task Force report *Building a North American Community* (Council on Foreign Relations 2005), Canada and the United States might usefully examine the desirability and feasibility of a NAFTA accession agenda — in the first instance, for free trade partners in the hemisphere (particularly given the ongoing stalemate plaguing negotiation of a free trade agreement of the Americas), and ultimately for trading partners important to both countries (such as South Korea).

A third caution is that, as Hart himself notes, WTO rules underpin the bilateral trade relationship. In many areas, the Canada-US FTA and NAFTA cross-reference the General Agreement on Tariffs and Trade (GATT) and now WTO rules in such key areas as agriculture and trade remedies. In these sectors, WTO negotiations therefore provide the only avenue to further liberalization, and it is thus incumbent on Canada to devote the resources necessary to pursuing its objectives. So, too, the WTO as an institution provides an important dispute settlement forum to both countries, as demonstrated repeatedly in the course of the long-running softwood lumber dispute.

More broadly, given the transformations in global production and supply chains for goods and services that Hart identifies, active engagement in multilateral trade negotiations is the only means for Canada to address potential import substitution competition. Today, China is close to becoming the main source of US imports, despite numerous US barriers (for example, antidumping measures), substantial regulatory divergence from the US and the absence of NAFTA preferences. Canada's share of US imports fell from a high of 19.8 percent in 1996 to a low of 16.4 percent in 2006 (the figures for China are 6.5 percent in 1996 and 15.5 percent in 2006). Excluding oil and gas, Canada's share of US imports went from 20.9 percent in 1996 to 15.1 percent in 2006, whereas China's share grew from 8.6 percent in 1996 to 18.8 percent in 2006.

A further caution regarding the relative priority to be given to multilateral trade liberalization is that for Canada's service providers, third-country markets are more important than they are for Canada's producers of goods. According to the Conference Board of Canada, the US accounts for about 60 percent of Canada's service imports and exports; the remaining 40 percent is mainly accounted for by Europe and Japan, and the fastest-growing service markets are in developing countries. The WTO is the only forum for Canada to negotiate service market access with the European Union, Japan, China and India. Further, recent experience suggests that although (as Hart asserts) "most markets of interest to Canadian suppliers and investors" are fully open to international competition, the "few exceptions" (409) are still important (contrary to Hart's implication). Life insurance is a good example: Manulife and Sunlife are Canadian service export/investment leaders with a clear competitive edge in developing markets; but Vietnam, India, Indonesia, China and the Philippines, among others, are far from fully open to them, and these markets are thus the focus of considerable effort on the part of trade policy officials.

And the same is true for investment. Canadian investment capital is now being directed to markets other than the US, and foreign investment in Canada is no longer predominantly American. Indeed, as noted in a relatively recent Statistics

Canada data series on the business activities of Canadian foreign affiliates (not captured in conventional cross-border data), the contribution of this diversified activity to Canada is underestimated (Statistics Canada 2007).

The border

Hart rightly places border administration at the top of his priority list. In fact, many initiatives have been launched in the past few years to streamline and manage the regulatory requirements administered at the border (for example, electronic notification) under the 2001 Canada-US Smart Border Declaration and the 2005 Security and Prosperity Partnership (SPP) agenda. The North American Competitiveness Council (NACC) gives similar priority to border-crossing facilitation for goods and people. But Hart may understate the extent to which core security concerns of Congress and/or the US administration have driven a number of measures that run counter to border facilitation — from the Western Hemisphere Travel Initiative to new fees for the US Department of Agriculture's Animal and Plant Health Inspection Service (APHIS) inspections. Although the security establishments in both countries acknowledge that threats may arise from within as well as outside North America, the concept of perimeter security does not represent a complete answer to those who argue that two borders are better (and more secure) than one.

One of the advantages of the approach reflected in the Security and Prosperity Partnership is that the closer cooperation between Canadian and US authorities responsible for security under the Smart Border and other accords is brought together with a prosperity agenda — that is, a trade- and investment-liberalizing agenda. And having respective authorities report to the prime minister of Canada and the president of the United States (as well as the president of Mexico) provides some assurance that effective security measures will not be taken at the expense of facilitation for legitimate trade in goods and movement of businesspeople. The two governments are thus already pursuing the agenda recommended by Hart — namely, greater cooperation and information exchange, greater infrastructure and technology investments and more targeted enforcement.

Regulatory convergence

In respect of border administration and domestic regulation, Hart makes a convincing case for regulatory convergence. And, indeed, again under the SPP, governments have adopted an ambitious agenda. It is fully supported by the private sector, as reflected in the first report of the North American Competitiveness Council.

The report's initial recommendations identify specific and concrete areas for agreement over the next three years based on an assessment of mutual interest and achievability (NACC 2007).

But some caution is in order. Experience to date under the SPP confirms that the mandates of regulatory agencies are domestic. And in both Canada and the US, under sound principles of administrative law, regulatory authorities are granted independence of action, subject to judicial review. For this reason, in March 2006, the leaders of Canada, Mexico and the United States directed their "central regulatory agencies [to] complete a regulatory cooperation framework by 2007," endorsed fully by the NACC (White House 2006).

A second caution arises from the security concerns, discussed earlier, that are connected with the border. Trade in defence goods and technology is increasingly impeded by more stringent US regulations related to national-security-based export controls — for example, the International Traffic in Arms regulations under the *Trading with the Enemy Act*. With respect to border administration, harmonized regulation is but a piece of the puzzle; investigative cooperation, exchange of information and enforcement questions will also need to be studied further.

A third caution regarding regulatory convergence is related to the question of whether common regulation is always the right response. Mutual recognition has proven efficient and effective in areas ranging from electrical standards to corporate governance and audit. And such frameworks can often be negotiated more quickly than full regulatory reform. This is the approach recommended, for example, by both the Minister of Finance and the Secretary of the Treasury for liberalizing trade in equity securities, building on the earlier successful experience between the Ontario Securities Commission and the US Securities and Exchange Commission in relation to multijurisdictional prospectus offerings.

Other impediments

Hart identifies restrictions on foreign direct investment and sector-specific tariffs and subsidies as domestic impediments to Canada's global engagement. He rightly suggests that ownership restrictions may deprive a sector of the ability to raise sufficient capital to make the necessary investments to remain competitive in a North American and global context. But he does not delve deeply into the more comprehensive challenge of ensuring that the enabling sectors of transportation, telecommunications, financial services and energy — each of which provides productivity-enhancing support to every other realm of economic activity — remain competitive.

In each of these sectors, government is taking meaningful steps toward reform, but Hart does not make it clear whether he considers these steps appropriate or adequate.

For example, the Canadian government's January 2007 Convergence Policy Statement and its response to the review of ownership and related issues conducted by two parliamentary committees reflect a clear recognition of the importance of ensuring a regulatory environment that supports continued innovation in the telecommunications sector. In transportation, as well, the government's announced intentions in aviation and surface transport are forward-looking.

More generally, Hart does not examine the challenge of access to capital faced by Canadian firms beyond considering the question of foreign investment. Successive governments have analyzed Canada's capital markets with a view to identifying funding gaps and, where possible, addressing these through appropriate policy actions. This includes looking at full-spectrum financing for Canadian firms, particularly venture capital and high-yield debt (or junk-bond financing).

There is widespread agreement in Canada that the efficiency and the further development of Canada's securities markets are being obstructed by the fragmented nature of securities market regulation, which increases administrative compliance costs. In 2003, the Wise Persons' Committee established by the federal minister of finance recommended the creation of a single national regulator. Recently, the Minister of Finance has underscored the priority that the Government of Canada attaches to achieving more efficient and effective regulation and enforcement. And in December 2006, at the invitation of provincial and territorial finance ministers, the federal government agreed to join the Council of Ministers of Securities Regulation to push for a common securities regulator.

In sum, for each of these enabling sectors, a key question is how much of a constraining effect do investment restrictions, as compared with other factors, have on their international competitiveness. The Conference Board of Canada's comprehensive *Mission Possible* study, cited earlier, identifies a shortage of managerial innovation and a lack of capital intensity as major impediments; its survey of foreign multinational CEOs highlights rising labour costs, interprovincial trade barriers, a lagging physical infrastructure and a limited supplier network as concerns (Hodgson and Shannon 2007). In the most recent competitiveness ranking of the World Economic Forum, Canada was ranked low on "tax neutrality," and Canadian executives themselves cited the general level of taxation and tax regulation as the greatest barriers to doing business in Canada, although the results were based on a limited survey (Porter et al. 2007).

Further reflection on and analysis of current public policy directions, the pace of reform and the relative priority that should be given to the various policies implicated in each of these enabling sectors would be desirable.

Institutional capacity

Hart encourages the governments of Canada and the United States to "focus upon the functions that must be performed for the efficient governance of deepening integration" and to "create new institutions only where current arrangements are unsuitable" (427). He suggests a number of practical ways in which regulatory agencies can integrate a North American perspective into their work. But he follows his criticism of bureaucratically captured regulatory agendas with a series of recommendations for more bureaucracy.

First, Hart calls for the establishment of a bilateral commission "to supervise efforts to establish a more coordinated and convergent set of regulations" (428). However, the sources from which departments and regulatory agencies derive their rule-making and enforcement authority make the implementation of this recommendation challenging. These departments and agencies draw their mandates from domestic law, they are governed by regulations wholly within the four corners of the law's requirements, and they function independently of executive branch authority. Any direction to these bodies must take the form of regulation and, if necessary, amendments to governing law. Although government departments are by definition expected to carry out the government's agenda, requirements for transparency and provision of opportunity to comment, principles that both Canada and the United States adhere to, can act as a brake on the implementation of common North American approaches. The US Department of Agriculture discovered this in the process of developing rules to reopen the Canada-US border to beef and cattle trade following the discover of cases of BSE (mad cow disease) in Canada.

More fundamentally, creating a bilateral commission like the one Hart suggests would not only require legislation in each country but could also raise due process and constitutional questions, depending on the scope of authority to be delegated upward to such a body. Further legal analysis is called for. It may, in any event, be premature to propose such an institution if it is unneeded, according to Hart's own criteria. Completion of a trilateral regulatory framework this year, as called for by leaders, and its prompt implementation by the departments and agencies responsible, could well meet the stated objectives without inviting difficult legal questions.

Second, Hart recommends the establishment of a bilateral task force to develop model mutual recognition arrangements for professional accreditation. This is, in fact, the route chosen by governments for accountants, engineers and lawyers, among others; in each country, the professions were charged with developing acceptable arrangements. Given the self-regulated nature of the professions in each country, it is unclear what benefits would derive from having an outside body make recommendations, as these would come back to a table already addressing the issue.

Third, Hart proposes an independent Canada-US secretariat "with a mandate to drive the agenda and report annually to the president and prime minister on progress." In his view, such an entity could "prove critical to overcoming bureaucratic inertia" (428). An apparently separate body, styled as a joint advisory board to the president and the prime minister, "could contribute some creative drive to the development of new bilateral initiatives." Caution is again in order. Canada and the United States in their FTA, joined by Mexico in the NAFTA, consciously opted for intergovernmental, not supranational, authority. They have benefited from several independent studies, task forces and secretariats, some of which have been cited here. Ultimately, while the concept of a shared agenda is supported by sound independent analysis and advice, its implementation depends on sufficient top-level political will, authority and capacity. And political will is bolstered in democracies when public policies are responsive to the interests of stakeholders. Viewed in this light, the institutional framework provided by the SPP may well meet Hart's test for what is needed: an integrative approach to North American competitiveness that gives priority to the border and to regulatory convergence, that is premised on political leadership and, through the process of annual trilateral summits, that builds in accountability of officials for progress. Direct engagement of the private sector through the North American Competitiveness Council is likely a better litmus test of which issues are deserving of earliest attention to foster competitiveness.

REFERENCES

Council on Foreign Relations. 2005. *Building a North American Community*, May. Independent Task Force Report 53. New York and Washington, DC: Council on Foreign Relations. Accessed May 9, 2007. www.cfr.org/content/publications/attachments/NorthAmerica_TF_final.pdf

Hodgson, G., and A. P. Shannon, eds. 2007. *Mission Possible: Stellar Canadian Performance in the Global Economy.* Vol. 1 of *Mission Possible.* Ottawa: Conference Board of Canada.

North American Competitiveness Council (NACC). 2007. *Enhancing Competitiveness in Canada, Mexico, and the United States: Private-Sector Priorities for the Security and Prosperity Partnership of North America (SPP),* February. New York and Washington, DC: NACC. Accessed May 9, 2007. www.ceocoun cil.ca/publications/pdf/test_4d5f2a8ae893 32894118d2f53176d82b/NACC_Report_to_Ministers_February_23_2007.pdf

Renewing the U.S.-Canada Relationship. 2005. Statement of the 105th American Assembly, New York, February 3-6. Toronto: Canadian Institute of International Affairs; Washington, DC: Woodrow Wilson International Center for Scholars, Canada Institute; New York: American Assembly, Columbia University.

Porter, M. E., K. Schwab, A. Lopez-Claros, and X. Sala-i-Martin, eds. 2007. *The Global Competitiveness Report 2006-2007: Creating an Improved Business Environment.* Geneva: World Economic Forum.

Statistics Canada. 2007. *Foreign Affiliate Trade Statistics.* Accessed July 23, 2007. www.statcan.ca/cgi-bin/imdb/p2SV. pl?Function=getSurvey&SDDS=1539& lang=en&db=IMDB&dbg=f&adm=8&dis=2

White House 2006. "The Security and Prosperity Partnership of North America: Progress." News release. Accessed July 18, 2007. www.spp.gov/pdf/security_and_prosperity_partnership_of_north_america_statement.pdf

ENGAGE THE UNITED STATES, FORGET THE REST?
Keith Head

There are certain things that even peripheral figures in Canadian policy circles know about international trade.[1] First of all, everyone knows that Canada is too dependent on the US as a trade partner. This certainty is customarily expressed with the cliché "We shouldn't put all our eggs in one basket." Everyone also knows that Canada is "missing the boat" by failing to expand its business presence in the fast-growing markets of Asia. Furthermore, it is a matter of national pride to Canadians that we play a central role in pushing forward multilateral approaches to policy formulation; in particular, we ought to be performing life support on the "moribund" Doha Round of the World Trade Organization (WTO) negotiations. Finally, it ought to go without saying that we would contemplate no changes in trade policy that would undermine Canadian sovereignty.

In the midst of all this trade policy consensus, Michael Hart has contributed a refreshingly contrarian chapter to this volume. He decisively dismisses all of the foregoing conventional wisdom. He then boldly announces a policy agenda that is likely to be anathema to mainstream Canadian policy-makers. The points Hart makes are best seen as the starting point for a vigorous debate. While I am somewhat sympathetic to the positions he is pushing, I believe that he overstates his case.

Hart considers two big questions: With whom should we engage? And how should we do so? The answers are nested, but, for ease of exposition, let's call the first question strategic and the second one tactical. Here I provide an outline of the answers to these two questions, as Hart considers them in his chapter.

1. We should engage more broadly with the rest of the world through:
   a) global trade negotiations (Doha Round);
   b) free trade agreements (with, for example, South Korea); and
   c) ad hoc bilateral trade promotion (Team Canada missions).
2. We should pursue deeper integration with the US by:
   a) reducing the burden of the border;
   b) harmonizing regulation; and
   c) establishing new bilateral institutions to facilitate integration.

With regard to the strategic question, Hart unequivocally advocates a focus on the US: "The simple fact is that Canada's most basic economic interests have become inextricably bound up with those of the United States...The area of greatest potential is the United States. Engagement with our southern neighbour is the indispensable foundation of any Canadian policy to maximize benefits from international trade and investment." To these statements about the total effect of Canada-US integration, I cannot think of any plausible counterarguments. Over 80 percent of our exports go to the US, and the US typically provides two-thirds of our imports. We also conduct two-thirds of our service trade and foreign direct investment with the US. Economic life without the US is hard to imagine. But the issue on the table is about our efforts on the margin. Would the allocation of more resources to deeper integration with the US generate larger marginal net benefits than a similar resource allocation directed at broader integration with the rest of the world?

THE CASE AGAINST THE REST OF THE WORLD

Hart begins his argument for deeper integration with the US by demolishing the three policies that Canada would be expected to use to foster engagement with other countries: continued WTO-sponsored liberalization, proliferating free trade agreements (FTAs) and trade missions. While recognizing the value of what the WTO/GATT (General Agreement on Tariffs and Trade) accomplished in the past, Hart argues that a Canadian effort toward completing the Doha Round would have only very small marginal benefits. One reason is that, with their new assertiveness, Brazil and India seem to have pushed Canada to the periphery of the negotiation process. Hart thinks Canadian policy-makers aren't willing to put agricultural policies on the table, and he is skeptical of the agenda he sees developing countries pursuing. He also argues that the returns to FTAs with small markets are insufficient to cover the fixed costs of negotiating them. Finally, Hart dismisses Team Canada trade missions as "hoopla" and "photo ops." The conclusion we may draw from these three critiques is that the tactics Canada might use to engage with countries other than the US do not pass a cost-benefit test. I tentatively agree with Hart about Team Canada, partially agree about the new FTAs and disagree about the Doha Round.

The first component of Hart's anti-Doha argument — that Canada has become a bystander in the current negotiations — finds support in comments WTO director-general Pascal Lamy made recently in the Philippines. Announcing that "after a period of suspension, the negotiating engines are buzzing again," Lamy went on to describe who was doing the negotiating: "We don't work with the QUAD anymore. We have a new G-4 : US, EC, India, and Brazil, and G-6 with Australia and Japan" (2007). "The QUAD" is GATT-speak for the US, the European Union, Japan and Canada. Note that Canada is out of the inner quartet and not even playing in the sextet. The question I would ask is whether Canada could resume a vital role in the negotiations if our government made it a priority. If that were possible, I could see Canada helping the deal go through by setting an example on lowering agricultural subsidies and tariffs. I would also like to see Canada push for more WTO discipline on the growing use of antidumping duties (ADDs). Popular support for ADDs rests on the misconception that they are necessary to prevent predatory actions by foreign firms. The reality — as I read the evidence — is that ADDs have become a tool that legally sophisticated industries utilize to exclude foreign competitors from the market. Canadian firms have been both victims and perpetrators of ADDs. Indeed, WTO data show that Canada imposed ADDs 84 times from 1995 to 2006, but other countries imposed ADDs on Canada just 12 times. In the last decade, countries like India and Argentina have become major initiators of antidumping cases (mounting 323 and 149 cases, respectively). The proliferation of ADDs as a form of trade harassment is likely to continue, and if it does it will undermine efforts to open markets via reductions in standard duties. I would also like to see Canada push for a change in the WTO rules to compel complainants to present evidence of predatory intent by foreign firms. I predict that such evidence would not exist in most cases, and ADDs would therefore rapidly fall into disuse. While I recognize that this proposal is very unlikely to survive an attack by organized industry interests, it is important to focus attention now on ADD abuse, as neglect will almost certainly allow the problem to spread.

On the issue of FTAs, Hart is right that agreements with countries like Israel, Costa Rica and Chile are unlikely to yield high-magnitude benefits. Devoting major resources to an agreement with small countries in Central America also seems of dubious value. I draw a distinction with regard to South Korea, which should not be dismissed as a minor market. South Korea's population is 50 percent larger than that of Canada, and its economy is growing faster. While South Korea's lower average income and its remoteness from Canada decrease bilateral trade potential, I am reasonably confident that the discounted present value of future gains from trade with South Korea outweighs the opportunity cost of Foreign Affairs negotiators. As the US is also negotiating with South Korea, there is probably some additional benefit to maintaining relative parity in tariff levels.

The use of trade missions as a tool for diversifying Canadian trade probably deserves the scorn Hart heaps on it. John Ries and I (2007) recently assessed the impact of Team Canada trade missions on Canadian trade. We find that, after taking into account the pre-existing degree of trade integration, Canada's trade missions have no significant effect on bilateral trade with the visited country. Although millions of dollars in deals are announced, it seems likely that much of the trade would have happened in the absence of the mission.

In response to the recommendation that Canada pursue deeper integration with the US to the exclusion of engagement with other countries, three additional points are worth noting: first, the US is a member of the WTO, and thus one way to influence US behaviour toward Canadian goods is to pursue reforms as part of the Doha Round; second, Canada already has remarkably good access to the US market, so there may not be much low-hanging fruit to be had there; and third, about three-quarters of the world economy exists outside the US, so Canada may find that there are substantial gains to be realized from trade with other countries.

THE CASE FOR DEEPER INTEGRATION WITH THE UNITED STATES

Hart envisions three related initiatives for closer engagement with the US: "the two governments must do more to address the dated, dysfunctional and intrusive nature of border administration, the haphazard process leading to deepening regulatory convergence and the frail institutional capacity to govern accelerating integration" (406). I will now consider the pros and cons of each of these tactical proposals.

Reduce the burden of the border

Hart advocates improving management of the border so that it becomes less of an impediment to cross-border business. This may involve new infrastructure, new technology and new procedures for reducing bureaucratic hassles. Two questions need to be answered affirmatively to justify aggressive pursuit of this policy. First, does the border currently impose an undue burden? Second, is it politically feasible to materially reduce the burden? In relation to the first issue, Hart reports that nontariff border costs add 5 to 13 percent to the cost of trade. While these numbers first struck me as implausibly high, they are consistent with the well-established statistical result that provinces trade on a greater order of magnitude with other provinces than with states of similar size and proximity. With respect to the second issue, there is a large constituency of traders and travellers who would welcome a facilitation of north-south flows of goods and people. The question is which border impediments could be eliminated without setting off alarm bells over Canadian sovereignty and US security.

One clear target would be rules of origin. At present, those transporting goods across the Canada-US border must prove that the goods originated in North America before they can qualify for duty-free treatment. The NAFTA rules of origin take up 243 pages of annex 401. The rules are complex and often make it very hard for goods to qualify unless all their main parts are sourced within North America. For example, NAFTA rules do not deem a television to be North American unless its chief component, the cathode ray tube, is made in North America; this means that the tube's chief components, the cone and the glass panel, must also be North American. These rules impose a burden at the border. And more importantly perhaps, they frustrate the operation of modern trade, in which production processes are fragmented and each component is sourced from the nation with the greatest comparative advantage.

If rules of origin are so bad, why do we have them? There is an economic answer and a political answer. The economic answer is that they prevent backdoor entry into a free trade area. Suppose Canada had a most-favoured-nation (MFN) duty (the standard duty charged in the absence of an FTA) on TVs of 8 percent, but the US duty was 3 percent. An importer in Canada would be tempted to route Asia-origin TVs via US ports in order to save 5 percent on duties. This would amount to a backdoor entry, and it would incur unnecessary transport costs and transfer duty revenue away from the country that was entitled to that revenue (being the location of use). The requirement of NAFTA certificates of origin eliminates the incentive for backdoor entry. It also induces large-scale region-oriented factories to rely more on North American parts than is efficient. The North American firms that supply these inputs presumably lobbied hard to have NAFTA rules of origin be as stringent as possible. Such political pressure tactics will need to be reckoned with. However, the economic motivation for rules of origin is easily addressed: with a common external tariff (CET), backdoor entry is pointless. One might argue that it would be politically infeasible for Americans and Canadians to agree on CETs, and yet, across the Atlantic, the 25 diverse members of the European Union have agreed to CETs as part of their customs union.

Canadian and US external tariffs are, for the most part, fairly similar. They both tend to be low on most manufactured goods — except footwear, apparel and a handful of food products. In the TV example, it turns out (according to the APEC *Tariff Database* [2007]) that Canada and the US impose exactly the same 5 percent MFN duty on standard TVs. More study is needed, but it seems likely that a move to a common

Canada-US external tariff could be made with very little disruption. Mexican MFN duties tend to be considerably higher; for example, the rate on TVs is 20 percent. However, this means that Mexico would have to worry about backdoor entry via the US, not vice versa. With a Canada-US CET, we might consider limiting the NAFTA certificate-of-origin requirement to Mexico-bound goods.

I dwell on the rules-of-origin issue here — even though Hart mentions it only in passing — because I think that by addressing it we can take a concrete step toward reducing administrative hassles at the Canada-US border. Hart envisions that the next steps would involve addressing noncustoms regulations that impose a burden at the border.

Harmonize regulation

Hart writes that "regulatory divergence is tantamount to a concealed 'inefficiency tax' that citizens pay on virtually everything they purchase" (426). What is the basis for such a provocative claim? Hart points to the costs of duplicate regulations. In many cases, I believe this critique is essentially correct. For example, the CBC recently reported on a call for new safety standards for the helmets used by skiers and snowboarders. Since Canadian and American snowboarders take similar risks and their skulls respond to impacts in the same manner, I cannot think of any reason why Canada would need helmet standards distinct from those of the US. I was reassured to discover online that the Government of British Columbia accepts certification by Canadian and American standards associations for bicycle helmets. This kind of mutual recognition is the approach the EU has taken.

It seems worth noting that not all divergent regulations constitute inefficient duplication. In some cases, regulations diverge in response to divergent preferences or constraints in the two countries. For example, to comply with its Kyoto obligations, Canada might choose to impose more regulatory restrictions on emissions of greenhouse gases. Or, in deciding which drugs to approve, Canada's drug regulators might assign less importance to the interests of US-based pharmaceutical companies than the US Food and Drug Administration would. When two countries impose the same standard despite differing circumstances, it may result in a reduction in efficiency.

Hart appears to advocate for Canada to adopt US regulations unless it can justify a difference. I have a feeling this proposal would meet with considerable public opposition. The fact that many Canadians routinely travel to the US is not a direct expression of approval for US regulations any more than their penchant for holidaying in Mexico is an expression of confidence in Mexican tap water. Canadians are ultimately pragmatic, as seen, for example, in Canada's recent shift in daylight saving time dates in response to the change initiated by the US. However, they will need to be persuaded that regulatory harmonization is not just a scheme to exchange Canada's more interventionist regulatory climate for what many perceive to be a lax, probusiness regulatory climate in the US.

The case for harmonizing regulation depends in large part on establishing that regulatory divergence truly imposes significant costs on exporters. Thierry Mayer and I have addressed this indirectly by examining trade within the European Union before and after the Single Market Program (SMP) implemented from 1988 to 1992 (2000). We found that the border's negative impact on trade was slightly lower in industries characterized by standards conflict, although differences were not statistically significant. Moreover, while all border effects continued a long-standing downward trend in Europe, the border effects in industries where standards conflict was thought to be more important did not decline more quickly during the SMP. Johannes Moenius provides more direct empirical evidence on the effects of divergence in standards on trade. Using a diverse sample of 14 countries, he found that two countries that share a higher number of common standards tend to trade more. Although effects differ across industries, on average a 10 percent increase in common standards leads to about a 3 percent increase in bilateral exports. This effect supports the idea that harmonizing regulation would generate a non-negligible reduction in costs for exporters. Moenius also finds that for a given number of shared standards, use of more country-specific standards seems positively associated with manufacturing imports (2004).

The mixed evidence on how standards affect trade leaves me unsure as to how much benefit could be obtained from Canada-US standards harmonization. As neither of the two cited studies involves Canadian data, I would like to see some direct evidence of the impact of Canada-US regulatory divergence on trade between the two countries.

Establish new bilateral institutions to facilitate integration

I have little to say about Hart's last policy proposal. Presumably, in order to reduce border costs and harmonize regulations, some new bilateral commissions would be needed. The commissions would, of course, require a commitment of government resources, and the question we ought to consider is whether these resources would be better directed at promoting Canadian interests in the Doha Round or enacting a Canada-South Korea FTA. One of the less-emphasized elements of the Doha agenda is trade facilitation. A multilateral initiative to reduce nontariff costs of crossing borders might ultimately yield greater dividends for Canada, if I am correct in believing that border services in the rest of the world generally operate much more slowly and are more corrupt than those of the US-Canada border.

CONCLUSION

While I have raised a range of potential criticisms of the proposals contained in Hart's chapter, I would also like to outline our main areas of agreement. First, a small reduction in the cost of trading with the US is worth much, much more than an equivalent reduction in the cost of trading with any other partner (because of the size and proximity of the US economy). Second, increasing speed and decreasing paperwork at the border should yield significant gains; one policy that Hart and I agree on is a common external tariff with the US, which would eliminate the need for cumbersome rules of origin. Third, we ought to follow the European Union's lead in trying to find ways to achieve standards harmonization where divergent regulations lack an underlying justification.

My major disagreement with Hart is that I do not believe Canada can maximize its benefits from international trade by disengaging from the three-quarters of the global economy that resides outside the US. In particular, I would like to see Canada resume its role as an active promoter of WTO-sponsored multilateral trade liberalization.

NOTES

1   Thanks go to John Ries for offering helpful comments and furnishing some of the data reported. He bears no responsibility for any dubious assertions or unreasonable arguments expressed herein.

REFERENCES

Asia-Pacific Economic Cooperation (APEC). 2007. *Tariff Database.* Singapore: APEC.

Head, K., and J. Ries. 2007. "Do Trade Missions Increase Trade?" Unpublished paper, University of British Columbia. Available on request.

Head, K., and T. Mayer. 2000. "Non-Europe: The Magnitude and Causes of Market Fragmentation in Europe." *Weltwirtschaftliches Archiv* 136 (2): 285-314.

Lamy, P. 2007. "The Philippines' Active Involvement in the Doha Round at This Crucial Time Is Vital, Says Lamy." News release, February 23. Geneva: World Trade Organization. Accessed May 16, 2007. www.wto.org/english/news_e/sppl_e/sppl55_e.htm

Moenius, J. 2004. *Information versus Product Adaptation: The Role of Standards in Trade*, February. SSRN Working Paper Series. New York: Social Science Research Network.

OUTCOMES
HEALTH
POPULATION
AGING
ECONOMIC
SECURITY
HUMAN
CAPITAL
TRADE
AND
GLOBALIZATION
NATURAL
CAPITAL
CLIMATE
CHANGE
PRODUCTIVITY

RISING TO THE CHALLENGES OF ECONOMIC TRANSFORMATION
Wendy Dobson

The world economy is undergoing rapid interrelated changes, the likes of which we have not seen in our lifetimes. The world's two most populous economies, China and India, have joined others in integrating into trade, capital and labour markets, creating a positive supply shock with strong growth and low inflation. The speed of this integration and the sizes of the labour forces to be absorbed pose major challenges.

Canada's economy has fared relatively well, even as our relative economic clout declines. We are a major beneficiary of openness; as we are an exporter of natural resources, the terms of trade are running strongly in our favour. We are also enjoying the fruits of our efforts during the past decade to restore prudent macroeconomic policies as the cornerstone of our economic framework. We are both blessed by our proximity to the world's largest and most dynamic economy and cursed by the asymmetry and dominance of that relationship.

In this generally benign economic environment, we have an opportunity to scrutinize our policies and institutions to ensure that they sustain growth in living standards and increase our ability to anticipate and successfully respond to rapid change. However, the tendency at such times is to become complacent and by default to allow crises to force reforms at the worst possible time. The economic policies of the minority Conservative government generally move in the right direction, but some of the measures it has adopted — often for short-term political advantage — are scattershot, and they will not achieve the required response.

The project represented in this volume has a long-term focus and a rich menu of proposals for ensuring steady improvements in future economic and social well-being. My purpose is to choose a package from this menu. I begin by setting out my views on the context that influences and constrains our objectives. I then explain my choices in light of the selection criteria and evaluate the policies individually and as a package. A brief examination of the rationale and implications of policies I have not chosen follows, and I end with a discussion of the likelihood of implementation.

CONTEXT

For Canadians, the international context is deeply and inescapably influenced by proximity to the United States. Our neighbour has grown more fearful, inward-looking and internally divided in the past decade, increasing our vulnerability — a subject to which I will return in the next section. In North America and beyond, the speed and magnitude of China's emergence as a major exporter of standard-technology manufactures have been, and will continue to be, disruptive, initially creating a disinflationary supply shock. Declining prices for a wide range of consumer goods have increased the purchasing power of the world's consumers. Returns to capital have increased as production costs have declined, and strong import competition has reduced the bargaining clout of labour in the importing countries, stoking concerns about rising inequality, especially in the United States. At the same time, China's position as the assembly platform in many global supply chains means that it is also a major importer. Since 2000, its demand for oil and raw materials to feed its manufacturing machine has been an incremental factor in higher commodity prices. But the effect on consumer prices has outweighed this impact on commodity prices, and this has been a factor in the surprisingly low interest rates of recent years. India's entry has been more gradual, its liberalization more modest due to its historical ambivalence toward market forces. As higher growth rates appear to be turning into a higher potential growth trajectory, domestic political support for necessary reforms is growing.

Both countries are emerging as significant outward investors. India's largest companies are led by experienced entrepreneurs and are international forces in the information technology, steel, pharmaceutical and auto industries. Chinese government entities are major portfolio investors; China's state-owned enterprises are encouraged to invest abroad, not only to secure natural resource assets but also to reduce pressure on the exchange rate. Plans are underway to create a state investment corporation to channel about 20 percent of China's trillion-dollar foreign exchange reserves into real assets.

And there is more to come. Between 2000 and 2010, the United Nations projects that the global labour force pool (people aged 15 to 64) will grow by 665 million, nearly 40 percent of whom will reside in China and India (United Nations 2007).[1] Canada's share of this growth is a mere 1 percent. In theory, a large increase in low-wage workers in world markets is a positive-sum game in which all are better off. Living standards improve in developing countries, while developed countries move into complementary higher-productivity, higher-paying activities. But with the current abrupt transition, this has not happened. In the United States, productivity growth has been strong, but income gains have been concentrated and workers' incomes have been squeezed. At the same time, India and China are producing large numbers of skilled workers and moving rapidly to higher-value-added activities. There is general agreement that we should encourage investment in human capital, integrate immigrants and drive our flagging productivity performance to higher levels. As we go through this industrial transition, we should also be continuing to do our homework — begun a decade ago with the Organisation for Economic Co-operation and Development (OECD) Jobs Study — on more effective social safety nets as well as active labour market policies.

Rapid and ongoing change in patterns of production, employment and trade is one inescapable determinant of our policy choices. Another is a growing concern about the global commons, where consensus is forming that governments should create incentive structures for reducing pollutants and carbon dioxide emissions. It is naive to accuse the large emerging market economies of being free riders. They will most likely take action when their major customers in the OECD countries do. As well, their own problems of air, land and water pollution are creating domestic pressure to achieve energy efficiency and pollution reduction — indeed, both are compulsory targets in China's eleventh Five-Year Plan, for 2006-10 (Zhang 2006).

POLICY ANALYSIS

The purpose of this exercise is to select a five-part policy package that contributes to the future economic and social well-being of Canadians. My selection criteria are straightforward: policies should be politically and administratively feasible; they should reflect an appropriate role for government; they should be affordable and cost-effective; they should be equitable; and, as far as possible, they should maintain an external macroeconomic balance. My main operating assumption is that any package chosen from this menu will preserve Canada's fiscal and monetary prudence — that is, budget balance and price stability.

These criteria are plain, but the appropriate role for government requires brief discussion. State planning collapsed two decades ago, and since that time, governments have shifted their approach, working to create sound economic frameworks for sustained growth and appropriate incentives for markets and market-based institutions. Governments should also test market outcomes to determine whether markets are delivering growth as well as fairness, a sustainable environment and an affordable retirement for Canadians. A long-run view of Canada's policy options should recognize that markets can fail, and if they do, support for government intervention will grow. My policy package seeks to reflect an appropriate mix.

With these criteria in mind, my recommended package anticipates and responds to the changing world economy, both directly and through emphasis on strengthening human capital and productivity, and it begins to address the growing pressures on the global commons. It is made up of the following policies:

/ Trade and globalization: Improve Canada-US border administration and infrastructure

/ Health outcomes and human capital: Invest in a system of early childhood development/education (ECD/E)

/ Aging and demographic change: Improve immigration policy support and credential recognition

/ Productivity: Remove provincial sales tax (PST) on machinery and equipment purchases

/ Climate change: Begin the phased introduction of a carbon management standard to reduce greenhouse gas (GHG) emissions

I have two runners-up: in the area of trade and globalization, build institutional capacity and frameworks to improve the cross-border movement of goods and services; and in the area of natural resources, introduce a "conservation" tax and dedicate the revenues to the purchase of strategic natural capital.

What is the rationale for these five (plus two) components, and for the overall package? Before applying my criteria, I should note what is missing from the menu. First, in a smaller, open economy like ours, policy-makers should prioritize the efficient use of resources, yet Canadians allow their governments to indulge in costly overlapping policies, regulations and institutions. First among these are the persistent interprovincial trade barriers; Canada negotiates free trade agreements (FTAs) with other countries, but it has failed to create free trade among its own provinces. A second example is the existence of 13 securities and exchange commissions in Canada; this keeps the cost of capital higher than it would be if there were a single agency. A third indulgence is the prohibition on mergers among domestic financial institutions and the lack of international competition in the domestic market; this effectively denies a major industry access to sources of efficiency through innovation and economies of scale.[2]

Furthermore, there are two dogs that don't bark in the master menu. None addresses challenges of efficiency, neutrality and fairness to the Canadian tax system.

As tax experts warn, Canada's tax system needs "a heavy dose of pro-growth reform that would increase Canadians' standard of living" (Mintz 2006). Canada should be moving, as other countries are, away from taxing personal income and toward taxing consumption. Yet federal policy, with a few exceptions in the 2007 budget, has failed to do this — instead, it has reduced the GST and created and expanded special preferences. The other area of silence is Canada-US tariff policy. As Keith Head suggests in his comments on Hart, a logical next step is to negotiate a common external tariff (but not a common commercial policy) to eliminate costly rules of origin and enhance market access. These points are discussed in the next section, where I explain the rationale for my choices.

Trade and globalization: Canada in the world

Canada currently lacks a clear strategic framework for its external economic policy. When everything matters, nothing happens. We are making incremental progress on resecuring US market access, but with little vigour or leadership. A global economic strategy is indiscernible. Canada's economic position in the world needs to be viewed within the context of the priority we must accord our bilateral economic relationship with the United States,[3] so the proposals Michael Hart makes in his contribution to this volume are sensible ones, but there are broader issues to which he gives short shrift.

The Canada-US trade relationship is central to our economic well-being. Around 70 percent of this trade is intra-industry, reflecting the importance to Canadian firms of their participation in US supply chains (Beckman and Goldfarb 2007). Much technology comes from, and many knowledge industry opportunities lie in, the US market (as both the Chinese and Indian governments will readily acknowledge). Much of the flow of trade, capital and people is market-driven, but NAFTA, as an intergovernmental agreement, has brought undeniable economic benefits.[4] Cumbersome rules of origin remain, however, as do regulatory differences that make little economic sense in key industries; and obstacles to the free flow of people, capital and ideas within the North American economic space persist. The competitive challenges from China and India should be a catalyst for us to renew our efforts to remove the barriers that remain post-NAFTA and thus increase North American economic efficiency.

Another inescapable fact of North American life post-9/11 is the determination of US lawmakers to reduce the vulnerabilities of economic openness. Middle East violence, military failure in Iraq and the international proliferation of terrorism all feed a climate of fear and insularity, and in such a climate, a terrorist attack or catastrophic health event in either country could trigger a border closure. The revival of the fortunes of the US Democratic Party, which has traditionally favoured protectionism, adds to Canada's market access risks and is reminiscent of the early 1980s, when protectionist sentiments pervaded the US Congress. It remains to be seen whether the clout of key, tightly integrated auto, steel and energy industries, which rely on North American supply chains that often span both US borders, will prevail against protective and protectionist pressures in times of adversity.

Hart's proposals may be characterized as "expedited incrementalism" — they are things that need to be done sooner rather than later and that need to be pushed along by regular monitoring on the part of leaders. I agree with all of his proposals, but I have chosen expedited border administration and infrastructure development, with institutional arrangements a runner-up. Much more innovation is required to facilitate the movement of low-risk cargo and people, and large investments in border crossings are also needed. According to the selection criteria, these measures are no-brainer incremental improvements and they are politically and administratively feasible. Their benefits — reductions in business costs deriving from border measures — are large relative to their expense (which can be defrayed by private-public partnerships in infrastructure). We should also note that progress on securing market access requires the interrelation of a number of policies. For example, progress on cooperative security arrangements (not on the menu) would facilitate a border more open to the movement of goods and people. Progress on smarter regulation — based, as much as possible, on mutual recognition of domestic regulations — would reduce the need for active customs administration and release resources for other uses.[5] And regular high-level leaders' meetings would be required to push the agenda along.

Hart's exclusive focus on the bilateral relationship is understandable, but I would not go as far as he does in declaring the ineffectiveness of Canadian trade policy initiatives in the rest of the world. Although we have been marginalized at the World Trade Organization (WTO) — in part our own doing — we should surely not become a free rider. As the current round of WTO negotiations languishes for want of political will in the largest countries, Jonathan Fried and Keith Head, in their responses to Hart, make a case for initiatives with large and dynamic economies like China and India. This approach is valid and potentially important (see Dobson 2002, 2004, 2006). Indeed, if those two governments' current study of a bilateral China-India FTA ever reaches the negotiation stage, pan-Asian trading institutions will not be far behind. No trade policy expert would advocate allowing the world trading system to fragment into regional trading blocs; the best way to prevent this is through multilateral negotiations, but since these have become unwieldy and ill-focused, one alternative is to ensure cross-regional trading ties based on WTO principles, as a number of countries have already done. Canada should keep up with the United States on South Korea, although a NAFTA accession arrangement makes a lot of sense. But, as Hart argues, we should stop pursuing FTAs with small countries, since the World Bank has amply demonstrated that the benefits are negligible relative to the resources expended in such negotiations (World Bank 2004).

Finally, as Hart's chapter is the only one in this volume that looks at Canada in the world, it is unfortunate that time and space did not permit him to pay more attention to the new trade theory of global supply chains (see, for example, Trefler 2005) and offshoring, which he mentions only in passing. Hart argues that by securing and deepening North American integration, we will give Canadian firms access to global supply chains. This is probably necessary, but it is not sufficient. The evidence indicates that Canadian businesses have much to learn about offshoring in third countries to increase the efficiency of their North American operations (PricewaterhouseCoopers 2004; Scott and Ticoll 2005).

The human capital/health outcomes menu and strengthening our human capital

The major changes in the world economy require adjustments that burden some industries and their employees and benefit others. In the aging advanced industrialized countries, skills-biased technological change is one of the main reasons individuals lose their jobs and must find new ones, sometimes repeating the process several times in the course of their working lives.[6] The attraction of the early childhood development/education (ECD/E) proposals put forward in two contributions to this volume — one by Robert Evans, Clyde Hertzman and Steve Morgan, and another by Craig Riddell — is that they address a key determinant of better outcomes in people's lives in an uncertain world: give children better early-life experiences and education and they will gain the skills they need to respond to challenges and opportunities later in life.

Complementary research on health outcomes (in the Evans, Hertzman and Morgan chapter) and economic and social outcomes (in Riddell) suggests that a public good would be produced — in the form of healthier, more resilient and more able populations — that should be supported by public resources. But how much in the way of resources? Evans, Hertzman and Morgan would allocate as much as 1.5 to 2 percent of GDP over the next 10 years to reduce the ratio of Canadians reaching adulthood without the competencies they need to cope in a modern economy to less than 10 percent from over 25 percent. The authors' comprehensive system of nonprofit, community-based service delivery programs would be financed by federal-provincial transfers along the lines recommended by the Council for Early Child Development. Riddell predicts that his proposal, an early childhood education (ECE) program targeted at disadvantaged children and families, would produce high returns at the margin, because Canada currently invests a relatively small amount of public resources. But evidence of the impact of ECE is also limited and it is not clear how much displacement of voluntary private resources a universal program would entail. Jane Gaskell notes that more than 50 percent of Canada's preschool children are already enrolled in some form of child care that may or may not have an educational component.

The equity and cost-effectiveness trade-offs in these proposals are significant. The authors of both chapters agree that targeted social programs are probably more cost-effective, but such programs tend to lack broad support, which makes them politically vulnerable. Riddell provides no cost estimates, while the universal program proposed by Evans, Hertzman and Morgan would cost roughly 1.5 percent of GDP after 10 years. To illustrate in 2006 dollars, the cost of a mature program would have been more than $21 billion (nominal GDP was $1,400 billion), almost as much as federal transfers to the provinces for health and other programs ($27.2 billion) in that year. I will evaluate the fiscal implications in the next section.

First, however, a central policy issue raised in these two chapters needs informed and thoughtful public debate. Riddell, and Evans, Hertzman and Morgan provide scientific support for public sector program delivery of a public good. Yet the Conservative government in the 2007 federal budget revealed differing assumptions based on public finance and political preferences. The implementation of the Universal Child Care Benefit, from a tax policy perspective, recognizes the costs borne by parents in raising their children, and it is desirable in that it is fair. The implicit political assumption is that child care is a private good, so give parents the means and subsidize the services ($250 million in the budget). Policy is silent on what the science reveals: high-quality services produce positive outcomes; low-quality services can produce negative outcomes. Nothing is said about setting standards or regulations to ensure that the market produces positive outcomes. Can Canada afford to take a wrong turn in a policy area that has been shown to be significant to the future of our human capital? An essential adjunct to the new approach should be experimentation, with careful monitoring of the market to determine whether it delivers the goods. The experts have documented reasons for concern; the jury is out.

Immigration policy: improved economic integration

The other priority related to Canada's human capital is to get more of it. In his chapter in this volume, David Foot presents the only proposal that examines immigration policy, and so I address it here. Foot argues that Canada should rectify the labour force shortages caused by population aging by selecting skilled younger immigrants seeking better economic opportunities. He would also speed up the immigration certification process and improve immigrants' credential recognition.

Existing immigration policy is passive; it makes no attempt to match the supply of skills with the demand for them. There are other dimensions to this issue: the relative earnings of international immigrants to Canada deteriorated in the 1990s, as Serge Coulombe observes in his response to Riddell's chapter. One reason is an inappropriate emphasis in the selection process on educational qualifications rather than on skills and employability. Economists often make the mistake of inserting into their models numbers of people of labour force age without correcting for employability (determined by such factors as basic literacy and numeracy, quality of schooling and experience). Coulombe notes that Australian immigration policy selects immigrants with skills currently valued in the domestic labour market; Quebec is moving in the same direction.

Changing Canada's immigrant selection criteria costs relatively little and promises relatively high returns. But is this enough? As Don Drummond points out in his response to Andrew Sharpe's chapter on productivity, much more should be done to integrate international immigrants and their children. We do an inadequate job of absorbing immigrant children into the school system; many are unable to function in the language of instruction because they read and speak another language at home. Our attempts to involve parents in the learning process are also inadequate. This is an area where experimentation is underway, some of it funded by school boards and some of it by voluntary organizations. More is needed.

Productivity: growing the capital stock

The desirability of removing the remaining PST on machinery and equipment purchases has been extensively studied. A simple policy change is required; we simply need to act. Sharpe notes that Canada's lagging machinery and equipment investment accounts for 25 percent of the business sector labour productivity gap between Canada and the United States. If Ontario, British Columbia and three smaller provinces removed the PST on the purchase of capital goods, the marginal effective tax rates on capital would be five points lower in 2010. The cost of removing the PST on machinery and equipment in the five provinces that still impose it would not be high, since the burden of the tax is carried by consumers. The benefits relative to costs are very high, as Sharpe argues. The main barriers to action have been political: provinces fear that eliminating the PST on machinery and equipment would force them to raise taxes elsewhere. Yet the idea is popular with business, and enacting it would be an important contribution to reducing the cost of capital, which is already higher than it needs to be — in part, because of overlap and duplication in federal-provincial responsibilities that are not on the menu but continue to raise the cost of capital in Canada. Just do it![7]

Climate change: the carbon management standard

I have also selected Mark Jaccard and Nic Rivers' centrepiece proposal, a carbon management standard, as presented in their chapter in this volume. It is a prudent, flexible and innovative approach to what I accept is a threat to the global commons that requires collective action. Their policy analysis is impeccable and persuasive. Canada's voluntary approach has had almost no impact on our record as one of the world's largest emitters of GHGs in both absolute and per capita terms.

The carbon management standard is similar to the obligation and certificate-trading approach that California applies to vehicle emissions (which specifies a minimum aggregate level of zero- or low-emissions vehicles in the vehicle fleet). To Jaccard and Rivers, the issue of using the atmosphere "as a free waste receptacle" is settled. A value should be placed on its use by means of either a broad-based GHG tax or market-oriented regulations that force reductions in waste-generating activities. The authors' goal is a 60 percent reduction from today's levels by 2050. Their evaluation criteria emphasize the need for an incentive framework strong enough to change producers' and consumers' behaviour over time and to induce innovation without unduly compromising economic efficiency or international competitiveness. They also consider administrative feasibility and political acceptability in their design.

The carbon management standard is imposed on fossil fuel producers and importers, and it is phased in gradually to allow the economy to adjust. The key attribute of the Jaccard and Rivers proposal is the requirement over time for fossil fuels to have zero lifecycle GHG emissions. Producers would have to certify their own progress or face stiff financial penalties. Government monitoring would be required for at least two reasons: to verify certifications and to monitor and adjust the certification process in the face of unexpected outcomes. Jaccard and Rivers argue that this system is superior to the better-known cap-and-trade programs, because it avoids the politically difficult issue of having to allocate the permits in the first place. They also argue against a broad-based carbon tax, even though they believe it to be the more efficient means of reducing GHG emissions, because it has proven to lack political support in recent years. One reason for the unpopularity of the carbon tax is that it transfers resources from the private sector toward government; in contrast, their carbon management standard does not involve a tax and thus does not generate new revenues for the public sector.

Why should Canada act in such a draconian way in the absence of movement on the part of the United States? Gradualism helps to address the competitiveness concerns, since through this approach the phase-in can be slowed or accelerated in ways the authors discuss. In the meantime, the adoption of the incentive framework is a positive signal to innovators (a Canadian firm is a world leader in carbon capture technology, for example) who may be future technology exporters. Jaccard and Rivers emphasize that the priority is to create the incentive framework and let markets work, rather than to procrastinate because of remaining uncertainty or disagreement about instruments.

EVALUATING THE PACKAGE

As I mentioned earlier, I selected this five-part package because its components improve our ability to navigate successfully in a rapidly changing world economy by reducing risk and strengthening our assets; one part also begins to address the collective action problem in the global commons. In this section, I evaluate the package as a whole with respect to three sets of implications: first, the appropriate role of government; second, costs, benefits and fiscal impacts; and third, equity and external balance. I also explain briefly why I did not choose other proposals.

Market failure in relation to GHG emissions has been demonstrated by scientists. Collective government action is required to create a more appropriate incentive framework that prices private use of the atmosphere. The ECD/E proposals make the case that governments must deliver programs that strengthen the capabilities of the disadvantaged (and promote greater equity) when market forces deliver greater benefits to some groups than to others. Other parts of the policy package are aimed at the risks involved in failing to manage proximity to the US market, improve our productivity performance and increase human capital, but they are uncontroversial in their approach to government's role. They need to be implemented faster and more effectively.

Having made these choices, I put less weight on other valuable and well-documented proposals that rely on major public interventions, such as Evans, Hertzman and Morgan's pharmacare (entailing the transfer of billions of dollars from the private to the public sector to achieve significant overall cost savings), Nancy Olewiler's conservation plan (also entailing a major transfer of financial resources and natural capital to the public sector) and Jean-Yves Duclos' guaranteed annual income proposal. The arguments Duclos makes in his contribution to this volume are compelling, but I question whether his proposed radical changes in personal income taxation are the best we can do. A powerful case has been made by tax policy experts for moving away from personal income taxation toward consumption taxation (with refundable tax credits). Would the same resources be better expended on less interventionist or tax-distorting policies? More work is required.

In the area of fiscal impact and cost-effectiveness, improving bilateral border infrastructure will be costly, but the proposal has large benefits in the form of reduced transactions costs. Public-private partnerships are also a less-costly delivery mechanism. The proposals to remove the PST on machinery and equipment and to improve immigrants credential recognition and related programs are low-cost relative to their potential benefits. The ECD/E proposal is the most costly item in the package, but it has potentially impressive returns. Clearly, experimentation with less-costly designs is needed — such as targeted services approaches and careful monitoring of the outcomes of publicly and privately supplied programs. Finally, Jaccard and Rivers' carbon management standard has the attractive feature that it relies on a regulatory rather than a tax-based approach and so avoids transferring resources to the public sector. The authors also argue that a gradual phase-in helps to control costs, but this remains to be seen.

The third set of implications involves equity and external balance. This package has been assembled with an emphasis on efficiency concerns; even so, the ECD/E proposal (particularly if it were targeted) and the immigration proposal are fundamentally important in equipping those most at risk in a world of skills-biased technological change to adjust. External balance is addressed in this package by reducing risks of border closure or disruptions. The enhancement of competitiveness and fairness is a key factor in the selection of the immigration, ECD/E and productivity proposals, and competitiveness is taken into account in the design of the carbon management standard.

Finally, most of the proposals that I did not choose are sensible ones, such as Foot's workforce and health care policies, and Sharpe's proposals for small and medium-sized enterprise technology adoption and tax credits for job search. Others — by Jaccard and Rivers, and Duclos, Olewiler and Riddell — are linked to their major proposals discussed earlier. Still others, such as Hart's regulatory harmonization proposal, need refining, since other measures — such as mutual recognition — could achieve the desired outcome.

WHAT ARE THE PROBABILITIES OF IMPLEMENTING THIS PACKAGE?

In the short term, the probabilities are small, in part because big proposals — like those concerning ECD/E, climate change and PST reduction — are anathema to minority governments. In the longer term, these proposals should attract the support of Canadians, but not without further public debate about the role of government. The Conservative government's actions on child care and climate change reflect its preference for market-based measures over regulation or government intervention.

Despite the high level of public concern expressed about climate change in early 2007, the political calculus also seems to reflect the conviction that voters would be unwilling to pay the price of effective emissions reduction policies. Historical experience may be a guide here. In the mid-1980s, seemingly endless public sector fiscal deficits became a public concern. The economic case for spending cuts and/or tax increases was clear, but voters were initially willing to support such actions only if they were not personally affected; firing civil servants and privatizing the post office were acceptable, for example. Only after 12 years of debate and a financial crisis was an effective strategy adopted, which spread the cost widely across the population. Today, the chances of substantial political capital being spent on radical preventive actions seem small in the absence of crisis or a major change in US policies. Early childhood education will suffer the same fate: the short-term fix of a universal but modest tax benefit may be popular, but perhaps because there is no high-profile public debate that takes account of the science.

In conclusion, this package rises to the challenges Canada faces in this period of rapid global transformation. Major initiatives are balanced by relatively uncontroversial ones, and the latter gain prominence and urgency as part of the strategic agenda proposed here.

NOTES

1   If these numbers were corrected for skills and employability, they would be smaller, but the ratios would be similar.

2   The federal government indicated in *Advantage Canada: Building a Strong Economy for Canadians* its intention to deal with some issues — such as those described in my first two examples — but progress is slow (Department of Finance 2006).

3   The US accounts for more than 80 percent of the real value of Canada's exports, and nearly 60 percent of the real value of its imports.

4   Two-way merchandise trade grew significantly between 1990 and 2000 because of trade liberalization and the dynamism of the US economy; this was followed by slight declines in 2000-05.

5   This would have to be supplemented by domestic initiatives, like the 2004 Smart Regulation strategy, in order for Canada to eliminate overlap, duplication and outdated or unnecessary regulations.

6   Adjustments are also required in developing economies, but in such economies incomes are likely to be on the rise, because more productive jobs become available during liberalization and policy reform.

7   The issue was addressed in a temporary fashion in the 2007 budget through a reduction in the capital consumption allowance. This will not foster as efficient an allocation of resources as removing the PST would, but it avoids federal-provincial complications.

REFERENCES

Beckman, K., and D. Goldfarb. 2007. *Canada's Changing Role in Global Supply Chains*, March. Ottawa: Conference Board of Canada.

Department of Finance. 2006. *Advantage Canada: Building a Strong Economy for Canadians*. Ottawa: Public Works and Government Services Canada. Accessed May 28, 2007. www.fin.gc.ca/ec2006/pdf/plane.pdf

Dobson, W. 2002. "Shaping the Future of the North American Economic Space." *C.D. Howe Institute Commentary* 162. Toronto: C.D. Howe Institute. Accessed May 28, 2007. www.cdhowe.org/ pdf/commentary_162.pdf

———. 2004. "Taking a Giant's Measure: Canada, NAFTA and an Emergent China." *C.D. Howe Institute Commentary* 202. Toronto: C.D. Howe Institute. Accessed May 28, 2007. www.cdhowe.org/pdf/commentary_202.pdf

———. 2006. "The Indian Elephant Sheds Its Past: The Implications for Canada." *C.D. Howe Institute Commentary* 235. Toronto: C.D. Howe Institute. Accessed May 28, 2007. www.cdhowe.org/pdf/ commentary_235.pdf

Mintz, J. 2006. "The 2006 Tax Competitiveness Report: Proposals for Pro-growth Tax Reform." *C.D. Howe Institute Commentary* 239. Toronto: C.D. Howe Institute. Accessed May 28, 2007. www.cdhowe.org/pdf/commentary_239.pdf

PricewaterhouseCoopers. 2004. *A Fine Balance: The Impact of Offshore IT Services on Canada's IT Landscape. Executive Summary.* Toronto: PricewaterhouseCoopers. Accessed May 28, 2007. www.pwc.com/extweb/pwcpublications.nsf/dfeb71994ed9bd4d802571490030862f/35148ad1425a581b852570ca00178bf6/$FILE/fb_0404.pdf

Scott, R., and D. Ticoll. 2005. *A Fine Balance: The Buying and Selling of Canada.* Toronto: PricewaterhouseCoopers. Accessed May 28, 2007. www.itac.ca/Events/2005/05Nov TicollScottFineBalance.pdf

Trefler, D. 2005. "Twenty Years of Failed Economics and Successful Economies." In *Prospects for Canada: Progress and*

Challenges 20 Years after the Macdonald Commission, edited by David E.W. Laidler and William B.P. Robson. *C.D. Howe Institute Policy Study* 41. Toronto: C.D. Howe Institute.

United Nations. 2007. *World Population Prospects: The 2006 Revision*. Department of Economic and Social Affairs.

World Bank. 2004. *World Economic Prospects*. Washington, DC: World Bank.

Zhang, Y. 2006. *To Achieve the Goals of China's 11th Five-Year Plan through Reforms*. Beijing: Development Research Center of the State Council. Accessed May 28, 2007. www.tcf.or.jp/data/ 2006120607_Zhang_Yongsheng.pdf

DRAWING A POLICY ROAD MAP FOR CANADA
Alain Dubuc

In the third and final stage of the IRPP's Canadian Priorities Agenda (CPA) project, the judges faced an arduous responsibility. Our task consisted of selecting, from among twenty-four recommendations made by the analysts in eight areas, five policy proposals that would form the agenda most likely to improve economic and social prospects for Canadians over the next five to ten years. The task was difficult — first, because it required that choices be made and highly commendable proposals be cast aside with all the unfairness and arbitrariness that accompany any selection process. This requirement, however, as harsh as it was, matches perfectly the parameters of public debate, where the scarcity of resources forces society to set priorities and make choices in order to avoid the multiplication and dissipation of initiatives.

The judges' challenge was compounded by the need to make choices that are a logical outcome of a process of analysis and deliberation that began more than a year and a half ago. This exercise marks the last stage of this process, and it introduces new elements by combining the contributions of the judges with those of the experts who provided their analysis of specific challenges and policy proposals. But it also has to be, in my view, an extension of the debates that took place in the previous stages of the CPA project; it has to capture the spirit of those debates, and respect the various consensuses that were reached and the priorities that emerged from them. In other words, at every stage of this fascinating journey, there should be a certain degree of consistency and convergence.

These observations lead me to express some reservations about the process. The first stage of the project was expressly designed to achieve some convergence, because the twelve policy experts who were each asked to recommend three priorities subsequently engaged in discussions that led them to make trade-offs, combine some elements and reduce the number of priorities on the table. A vote was then held to establish a hierarchy of priorities and select eight issues.

This convergence effect, however, was less than assured in subsequent stages. The first reason is that each of the analysts could choose from his or her own area of expertise three measures that may not necessarily be consistent with the trade-offs and compromises achieved in the first stage of the process and may actually lead in a different direction than that intended in the original discussions. For instance, in some cases, the specialists were able to impose an ideological framework from which it was difficult to escape. Second, the fact that the six judges could then ascribe their own rationales to their policy choices may also increase the centrifugal effect since each of us reached our conclusions in isolation. Thus, the final outcome might be a set of heterogeneous choices from which it is difficult to draw a common vision or a general direction.

These considerations, coupled with a desire to respect the process set out by the IRPP, led me to approach the role of judge differently than what is conventionally the case. The traditional, almost judicial, approach would be for the judge to determine on the basis of the submitted material which of the 24 policy recommendations were most clearly expressed and most promising. While this method may appear logical and bias-free, it would nonetheless have a perverse effect in that a selection process based solely on merit and the quality of the recommendations would likely generate a set of worthy but disparate projects that, as a whole, lacked coherence and complementarity. This would not lead to the priorities agenda that the IRPP has sought to establish with this project. The risk, essentially, is that out of a concern for rules and consistency, the CPA exercise will merely produce a policy checklist, not the road map for Canada it was intended to provide.

FOUR SELECTION CRITERIA

For these reasons, I have chosen four criteria for selecting the most appropriate policy package, criteria that extend beyond each policy's intrinsic value. The first of these criteria is that the policy selected must fit within a strategic framework. My aim here is to ensure that the measures chosen are part of a constructive vision of our future and can contribute to overcoming the major challenges faced by Canada. In practice, this means that each of the policy recommendations must be assessed relative to a framework of reference, a hierarchy of priorities. Clearly, the choices made by each judge will reflect his or her own values and priorities, as was the case for the experts in the first stage and for the analysts in the second stage of the project. In the next section, I will outline the values and priorities that guided my own selections; I have attempted to align these with the ones that emerged from previous discussions.

The second criterion is related to the timeline. A time horizon is a logical component of a project such as this — a project intended to define Canada's priorities over the next five to ten years. The goal, therefore, is to select recommendations that can be integrated into a longer-term vision while setting aside measures that, interesting though they may be, are too limited in scope, are part of day-to-day public management or are so obvious that they do not warrant public debate. In other words, the chosen policies must be ambitious, and they must propel Canada into the future.

The third criterion is consistency and balance: the selected policies must have internal consistency in order to produce an agenda that provides both direction and momentum. These policies must also form a balanced package that reflects a range of widely shared concerns on which citizens can reach consensus. It seems to me that a priorities agenda is, first and foremost, a political project that advocates a vision, and that its success will depend on its ability to reflect agreements and trade-offs.

The fourth and last criterion is a combination of realism and efficiency. The issues are well summed up in the introduction to this volume: "The central theme of the project is scarcity of resources and the need for choice: the everyday reality for policy-makers is that governments have limited means at their disposal — be it revenue, manpower or political capital — and must therefore choose carefully which policies to pursue and which to leave behind. In making these choices, governments are understandably drawn to what is expedient and popular, but they should also consider the overall costs, benefits and distributional effects of various policies" (1).

A PRIORITIES FRAMEWORK

The priorities framework that I recommend reflects the fact that while Canada is a prosperous society, its success masks vulnerabilities that are a source of concern for the future. Canada's present economic strength is due in part to external factors over which it has no control and that have an element of randomness — namely, the prices of natural resources and, in particular, petroleum products. High energy prices foster strong growth, even though that growth is unevenly distributed across the country; but they also generate a significant negative side effect — an illusion of economic health. Growth in some provinces and the fiscal capacity it provides tend to obscure underlying problems and do not provide governments the incentive necessary to address significant structural issues.

In my writings, I have expressed concern about the performance of the Quebec economy and in particular the gap between Quebec and Canadian average living standards. This gap results in large part from a culture and tradition that do not encourage excellence, competitiveness and entrepreneurship, and that have led to fiscal, political and institutional choices that have stunted growth. This growth-inhibiting culture is also found in many regions of Canada, where it takes its own forms, as evidenced by numerous institutional rigidities and resistance to change in a number of key areas, such as health care for instance.

The measurable outcome is a country that is less competitive than it should be. Canada slipped from near the top of international rankings some years ago to occupy a less enviable position with respect to both productivity and living standards. In this regard, the data presented by Andrew Sharpe are very telling — in particular, his analysis of Canadian output growth per hour worked, which is consistently lower than that of the United States and places Canada in the bottom group of Organisation for Economic Co-operation and Development (OECD) member countries.

Added to this are vulnerabilities such as the fragile state of the manufacturing industry due to the double shock of the sharp rise in value of the Canadian dollar and more intense global competition. Canada's central region is particularly affected by this situation — even in sectors that were thought to be sheltered, as shown by the significant job losses in manufacturing. Canadian governments have yet to confront these issues seriously.

That is why I consider productivity growth and prosperity to be a top priority. Accordingly, this has led me to attach more importance to measures that will allow higher levels of investment, including foreign investment, and to those that will affect the determinants of prosperity: education in all its forms and for those of all ages, from early childhood to the post-secondary level; as well as innovation at all stages, from basic research to commercialization. This emphasis on economic issues must not, however, lead us to overlook social concerns. The nature of the Canadian consensus consists in seeking what Europeans would call the third way — that is, maintaining a balance between economic goals and social concerns, between a North American market-based approach and a European-style social safety net.

The concern for balance is not just a political compromise, a detour to make measures to increase competitiveness more palatable. There is an interaction between the economic and social realms. Moreover, economic and social concerns are increasingly convergent in advanced societies like ours. First, because certain promising policy areas belong in both realms — education, for example, is a cornerstone of productivity and competitiveness, and it is also a powerful tool for personal achievement and equal opportunity. Second, because supporting social development, implementing social justice measures and sustaining our health system require resources that only economic prosperity can provide. And, finally, because social progress — by ensuring greater social cohesion, by reducing the divisions caused by inequality and by improving the quality of our health and education systems as well as the quality of democratic life — is also a factor in ensuring competitiveness and attracting investment and skilled labour. Social progress is an invaluable competitive asset that helps to make us distinctive.

To this list of priorities must be added sustainable development, a source of concern for citizens and a major issue for industrialized societies, which can no longer afford to trivialize the threat posed by global warming. Fortunately, in this area as well, one can see the beginnings of convergence: the resolution of environmental issues, especially the reduction of greenhouse gas (GHG) emissions, is no longer seen only in terms of constraints and costs but also as a form of investment that can enhance economic competitiveness.

That said, converting these broad strategic orientations into policy options is not so easy, for a variety of reasons. For one thing, the analysts having made their policy choices, certain avenues were inevitably left unexplored. Furthermore, each analyst had his or her own strategy: some chose a bold approach and recommended policy measures with a quasi-experimental dimension; others chose major and very ambitious measures; and yet others deliberately focused on more concrete, circumscribed and targeted actions. As a result, judges were faced with policy proposals that are not equivalent in scope. Adding to the challenge was the fact that some of the specialists maintained very narrow ideological lines, which made it difficult to take on their recommendations without espousing their vision of society. An example can be found in the paper on health outcomes: two of the policy recommendations — for a universal early childhood development program and a national pharmacare program — made by Robert Evans, Clyde Hertzman and Steve Morgan are more in the nature of a manifesto; their implementation would turn Canada back into a 1960s-style social democratic regime.

Michael Hart's recommendations on global markets provide another example, albeit of a different nature. The author views trade with the United States as the main issue at stake for Canada in the context of globalization, and his prescriptions, while very interesting, all deal with the free flow of trade across the Canada-US border, which does not provide an opportunity to address other issues associated with globalization.

In the end, performing the judges' task was a bit like working on a puzzle, assembling a policy package from a broad range of policy recommendations on a wide range of issues by linking them to goals that were not necessarily those of their authors.

Climate change: a phased-in carbon management standard for fossil fuel producers and importers

The scientific evidence of global warming is now strong enough to force us to acknowledge a number of realities: global warming is real; there is a link between global warming and GHG emissions, particularly carbon dioxide; human intervention plays a role; and the impact of warming is significant enough to warrant state intervention to control and reduce GHG emissions. Any such intervention must be speedy and effective. Here I endorse the analysis offered by Mark Jaccard and Nic Rivers. And while there is no consensus — a term that must be used with caution in the scientific field — there is at the very least a definite convergence of studies, as shown by the work of the Intergovernmental Panel on Climate Change. Still, the need for caution must not be overlooked.

Accordingly, I believe that Canada has a duty to act, all the more so because it is one of those industrialized countries that — for reasons linked to geography, demographics and the structure of the economy — stand out because of the significance of their emissions and the limited scope of their efforts to reduce them. Delays in the fight against global warming are costly because they will result in significant environmental impacts — impacts that are expected to have major adverse effects on Canada, especially its northern regions. Delayed action means much higher costs, and by failing to fulfill its obligations, Canada risks being deprived of competitive advantages and penalized in its trade relations. As well, further delay could impair Canada's chances of being at the forefront of new technologies to reduce global warming.

On the one hand, I must admit that the need for determined action in this area was so obvious to me that it did not seem necessary to select it as a key item for the CPA. The ongoing political debate in Canada shows, however, that there is still great resistance to a sustained effort to reduce GHG emissions. The policy advanced by the Conservative government is evidence of a new determination on the part of an administration that fought hard against such a course of action yet has finally given Canada a genuine GHG reduction policy. Nonetheless, this new policy has serious shortcomings, including its relatively unambitious goals; the uneven results expected across industries, especially in the oil industry; and concerns about the effectiveness of the tools proposed to achieve these goals.

On the other hand, many Canadians find it difficult to accept that Canada is not honouring the commitments it made when it signed the Kyoto Protocol. If the

Kyoto goals were initially unrealistic for Canada, they are even less so now that we have delayed addressing GHG emissions. Our government's refusal to consider the Kyoto Protocol as dogma does not mean, however, that we have no obligation to act vigorously. That is why policies designed to reduce GHG emissions must rank high among the recommendations chosen in this project. Two sets of policy measures have been proposed in this regard: that put forward by Jaccard and Rivers, aimed directly at reducing the release of carbon into the atmosphere; and a group of very interesting measures advocated by Nancy Olewiler, designed to measure and preserve our natural capital. However, given the urgent need to act, I favour the first of these proposals.

The plan suggested by Jaccard and Rivers offers several advantages: it is a bold, results-driven approach, one that, instead of imposing ceilings, requires producers and importers of fossil energy to include in their operations a growing proportion of energy forms that do not generate GHG emissions — in short, it is an approach that runs counter to the solutions that are usually put forward. Its interest lies in the fact that it does not require governments to take on the onerous task of negotiating permits, but it does require that positive results be attained and it promotes certain avenues, such as carbon recovery in the case of coal utilization or oil sands operations. Another measure recommended by the authors and aimed at curbing emissions created by motor vehicle manufacturers and importers might be viewed as a variant of the same policy in that it is based on the same approach.

In any event, I share the view of Jaccard and Rivers' commentators, Christopher Green and James Meadowcroft, that this debate must continue in order to examine how this policy could also be applied downstream — that is, to consumers.

Human capital: an early childhood development program targeting children at risk

With this policy recommendation, Craig Riddell advocates support for early childhood development through a federal program of assistance targeted for children at risk. My reason for selecting it is twofold: first, not only does it meet a need, but the way it is formulated also seems appropriate; second, early childhood education is a cross-cutting measure that can contribute in varying degrees to the achievement of three high-priority objectives — social justice, the development of knowledge (and prosperity) and attenuating the negative effects of demographic pressures.

A child care system plays two roles. First, it helps parents reconcile work and family obligations, lessening their burden, especially that of mothers, and, as a consequence, it facilitates women's participation in the labour market. In Quebec, the establishment of a universal daycare system has contributed to a rise in women's labour force participation and to an improvement in the quality of family life. Second, such a system can, if it takes on an educational role beyond child care, provide children with learning they otherwise might not receive, for reasons linked to poverty, parents' lack of education or a dysfunctional family environment. This type of intervention, when targeted at children in their very early years — a crucial period for the acquisition of cognitive skills — contributes to their socialization, enhances their educational development and reduces the gap between them and children from more favourable environments. Over the longer term, it promotes subsequent academic success, helps to reduce the dropout rate and facilitates access to higher education.

As Evans, Hertzman and Morgan point out, a learning program for early childhood is unquestionably a very powerful tool for combatting poverty because it gives children the tools they need to reach their full potential. This fundamental social justice function also has an economic dimension: by improving educational outcomes, this policy would eventually lead to a higher-skilled population — a key factor in improving productivity growth and achieving greater prosperity. By encouraging the utilization of each individual's full potential over time, and by reducing the waste of human resources, these early interventions also become an indirect means of offsetting the negative effects of slower labour force growth — or even decline, in some provinces — on economic growth, thus softening the impact of the demographic shock.

Those are the principles at stake. They matter because these issues have been ignored in the Canadian debate. The Harper government's policy of giving monthly allowances to parents of young children was designed to give parents a choice between keeping children at home or placing them in daycare. That policy, however, simply addresses the child care aspect of the question and is of value only to families able to provide an environment that is conducive to the cognitive development of their children. It is a policy that overlooks the need to redress inequities that are rooted in the randomness of birth.

As for the approach advocated by Riddell, it seems to me that the way in which the proposed program is structured — to target children at risk — leads to an optimal use of public resources. The Quebec experience shows us that a universal scheme can have perverse effects. For example, while in principle all parents in Quebec have access to the daycare system for seven dollars a day, they can benefit from this very generous subsidy only if they manage to get into a system that still has an insufficient supply of spaces and long waiting lists. Another issue is the fact that families in which both spouses work — that is, families with higher levels of education and income — are overrepresented in the system, while families at the lower end of the socio-economic scale, who would benefit most from the program, are underrepresented. As a family policy program, the Quebec system is a success; as social policy, it is a relative failure.

The Quebec experience therefore suggests that it is better to target a specific clientele, as Riddell recommends, to avoid allocating an excessive amount of public resources to the system and to circumvent the regressive effects of the program. Targeting also ensures that the program reaches those who would benefit most from it. After all, as Riddell shows convincingly, the gains for well-to-do families are minimal or nonexistent; moreover, these families have the means to provide their children with a favourable environment.

While it is true — as Evans, Hertzman and Morgan observe — that low income is not the only indicator of inadequacy of the family environment, this is not a strong enough argument to justify a costly universal scheme as this is a very inefficient way of reaching children at risk. It would be more appropriate to develop sophisticated tools to identify vulnerable children living in unfavourable circumstances.

Productivity growth: a program for more rapid diffusion and adoption of best-practices technology

Canada's very weak productivity growth and the gap in this area between Canada and its partners, especially the United States, can be seen as this country's most fundamental economic problem. For this reason, Andrew Sharpe's proposals warrant close scrutiny. It is true, as Richard Harris notes in his comments on Sharpe's contribution, that the productivity issue does not excite public opinion because both the word and the concept generate fear, and also because Canada, thanks to the positive impact of natural resource prices, is experiencing great prosperity. Canada's current success hinders public debate and removes the pressure on decision-makers to address the country's economic shortcomings and structural weaknesses. Sharpe makes a persuasive demonstration of the significant Canada-US productivity gap and of Canada's severe lag in output-per-hour growth relative to other OECD member countries. Canada is among the countries with the slowest productivity growth precisely at a time when productivity is playing an increasingly important role in determining standards of living because labour force growth can no longer be counted on.

I share unequivocally Sharpe's view that increases in standards of living are a desirable objective, both socially and economically, for both individuals and society at large. If Canada is to maintain current levels of social services at a time when an aging population will make funding these services more challenging, it must raise the standard of living of its citizens. This will require an increase in productivity, which will in turn increase Canada's competitiveness and help its businesses face the pressures of globalization.

That said, the measures Sharpe recommends fall into the category of circumscribed actions. He advocates not broad macroeconomic policies but targeted measures aimed at addressing specific aspects of productivity growth in specific ways. The recommendation I have selected is aimed at reducing the technology gap, especially for small and medium-sized enterprises — first, because innovation is one of the determinants of productivity; and second, because Canada's innovation record is quite uneven. Canada has done very well at some stages of the innovation cycle, particularly with respect to support for academic research, which has produced excellent results and made Canada a leader in this regard. That success, however, has not been accompanied by similar results in other aspects of innovation, such as business research and development, nor has it increased the number of patents and technology transfers. This seems to suggest that greater attention must be paid to all elements of the innovation cycle, in particular the last stage — that is, converting research and development into services, processes and products. Innovation has an impact on wealth creation when it leads to commercial activity that generates jobs, investments, sales and profits.

These are the considerations that lead Sharpe to emphasize the use of the product of innovation rather than innovation itself. Instead of focusing efforts on supporting private sector research and development, he advocates support for the adoption of technological best practices and recommends that more resources be devoted to helping small and medium-sized enterprises find, adopt and adapt new technologies.

While this is a fundamental goal, I don't know whether the approach to achieving it proposed by the author — strengthening the National Research Council of Canada's Industrial Research Assistance Program (NRC-IRAP) — is the most desirable one. We may perhaps be reassured by the fact that Sharpe quotes Richard Lipsey and his colleagues Kenneth Carlaw and Clifford Bekar (2005), who claim that this is an example of a successful type of technology transfer program.

Productivity growth: remove the provincial sales tax on purchases of machinery and equipment

This recommendation is also limited in scope, but it opens the door to a wider debate. As Sharpe points out, investments in machinery and equipment are an essential contributing factor to productivity growth. He notes that Canada is ranked

20th among 28 OECD countries with respect to the share of GDP devoted to gross capital formation in machinery and equipment. The fact that Canadian governments create self-defeating barriers to investment is therefore especially counterproductive when one notes that this country has one of the highest effective capital tax rates in the world. Given this context, the provinces that still have a retail sales tax and apply it to the purchase of capital goods — Ontario, British Columbia, Prince Edward Island, Saskatchewan and Manitoba — should abandon the practice. It is bad policy. One could broaden the debate by recommending that the provinces with capital taxes (Quebec, Saskatchewan, Ontario, Manitoba, Nova Scotia and New Brunswick) either reduce or eliminate them as well since these have essentially the same impact: they increase the cost of investment and slow growth.

Such measures, while rational and self-evident on strictly economic grounds, are bound to lead to a broader discussion about the fairness of the tax system. The elimination of taxes on capital will require offsetting tax measures to avoid revenue losses, which could shift the tax burden from businesses to consumers. As Sharpe notes, this would be the case if, to offset the losses caused by the elimination of the sales tax on capital goods, the sales tax on consumer goods were raised. More generally, this recommendation would make it possible to launch a useful debate on the relative share of the tax burden borne by businesses and individuals and on the idea, not always based in fact, that business taxation should be used as an instrument for social justice — which overlooks the fact that such taxation has economic costs and that its redistributive effects are limited when the burden can subsequently be shifted to consumers.

Human capital: a policy to reduce the high school dropout rate by raising the compulsory school-leaving age to 18

The final policy measure that I selected also concerns education, the key to the future. I must admit that I hesitated between the two remaining education policies recommended by Riddell. The first of these focuses on the dropout phenomenon, the second on the establishment of a scholarship system aimed at facilitating university access for young people from low-income families who do not quite qualify academically for merit scholarships.

I ultimately chose the policy aimed at reducing the dropout rate because of the social tragedy dropping out entails, the failed hopes it creates, the social inequities it perpetuates and the economic stakes involved. A country whose labour force growth is slowing cannot rely on a supply of unskilled workers to create economic success. It cannot afford to waste human resources by accepting labour force participation rates that are too low or unemployment rates that are too high. These are clear indicators of skills mismatch and/or the inability of the labour force to adjust to the changing needs of business and economic restructuring. Dropping out has a direct impact on the ability of individuals to find jobs, and it significantly reduces their labour market prospects and their capacity to adapt during periods of rapid change and to retrain when hardship strikes.

In this regard, Canada suffers from two problems: a high dropout rate, especially in nonurban areas; and inadequate levels of literacy and numeracy (understood, in the modern sense, to mean the proficiency to function normally in society), including among the young. If we are to overcome these problems, we must ensure that the young complete their high school education. Combatting the dropout problem is the first step required to improve access to higher education and address the problem of underrepresentation of children from low-income families.

It is unclear whether the approach recommended by Riddell — raising the compulsory school-leaving age to 18 years — would be enough to dissuade the young from dropping out and looking for work, but such an outcome would be more likely if, as Riddell recommends, this measure were accompanied by more substantial investments in vocational training and better supervision for vulnerable youth.

CONCLUSION

I wish to mention here a proposal that, while not among my final choices, caught my attention. I found the policy proposed by Jean-Yves Duclos — the implementation of a universal basic income allowance — both interesting and intriguing. Such a policy would rid our income security system of many of its perverse effects, particularly with regard to work disincentives. However, the project is, in my view, too ambitious and too costly, and it entails too many uncertainties to be considered at this time.

I would also like to discuss a major policy challenge that was not among those addressed by our experts in this final phase of the CPA project. The agenda setters who were initially asked to identify the project's broad policy challenges placed in third position the idea of "achieving effective intergovernmental relations within the Canadian federation." This was not among the eight challenges ultimately selected, probably because it is more political in nature than the others, and it does not lend itself to the task of setting and assessing more specific policies.

There may, however, be a way of reinforcing the functioning of the federation that avoids political pitfalls and leads to more concrete and less controversial actions that lend themselves to consensus building — and that is to work together to establish a true internal common market in Canada.

The broader access to the US market provided by NAFTA and significant increases in north-south trade have caused an important aspect of every province's trade to be overlooked: the east-west trading axis, and the fact that trade growth in this direction, even if it is not as great as that of the north-south flows, must remain a goal. East-west trading still has strong potential, and it can provide Canadian companies with a base from which to strengthen their international competitiveness. However, Canada has not been fully exploiting this potential and has thus —by erecting barriers that hinder the movement of people, goods and capital — deprived itself of the tools that the internal market could provide. These barriers include restraints on the mobility of individual belonging to certain trades and professions (such as physicians and construction workers, in some provinces), regulations affecting certain products and provincial securities regulatory mechanisms.

The establishment of a true internal common market is undoubtedly a desirable economic objective. Alberta and British Columbia have made positive moves in this direction. But it is also an important political goal that would allow Canada to assume a more meaningful identity. Over the past 25 years, the construction of a national identity has largely rested on the development of the social union, mainly because the various elements of the social safety net embodied common values capable of defining the Canadian identity and ensuring cohesion. What might be called the social union cycle is probably nearing its end. The pendulum is now moving away from the creation of new social programs. This, and the fact that region-based allegiances are growing stronger throughout Canada, should prompt the federal government to exercise greater caution in its interventions in areas that fall under the purview of the provinces. In any event the social union cycle led the Canadian government to disperse its efforts in areas where its contribution has not been optimal and to neglect activities that are of paramount importance for the future of the country.

This should convince the Canadian government and the country as a whole to redeploy their energies, to seek other ways of developing consensus around a new nation-building enterprise. The establishment of a Canadian common market is, without doubt, a project that could give meaning and new impetus to Canada while eschewing the divisive debates that have paralyzed us in the past.

REFERENCE

Lipsey, R., K. Carlaw, and C. Bekar. 2005. *Economic Transformations: General Purpose Technologies and Long Term Economic Growth.* Oxford: Oxford University Press.

CHOOSING POLICIES TO BUILD AND SUSTAIN WELL-BEING
John F. Helliwell

SETTING THE STAGE

In the third and final phase of the Canadian Priorities Agenda, eight experts were invited to submit three policies each, and six judges were asked to individually select a five-course meal from the menu of twenty-four dishes. We judges were asked to offer reasons for our choices but not to cook anything up ourselves, either alone or in concert with our colleagues. We were permitted, and perhaps expected, to explain why we chose some policies and rejected others, leaving readers to guess what, if anything, we might have chosen in their stead. I shall try to partially fill this gap by mentioning some policy areas that might usefully have been added to the agenda — dogs that did not bark.

The gaps that seem most obvious to me relate to the human, social, economic and environmental aspects of life in twenty-first-century cities. Short- and long-term international mobility of populations is likely to continue to increase as education and income levels rise in most countries, and as travel and information exchange become cheaper. Population growth is increasingly concentrated in large cities, which are often ill-equipped to deal with the consequences of the migration decisions made by individuals and families. Many of the specific issues relate to the building and maintaining of social capital in fast-changing and increasingly diverse megacities whose complexity and physical structure make it ever harder for newcomers to develop the close ties with family, coworkers, friends and neighbours that build trust and support well-being.

To deal with such complex issues, we require a broader focus for policies and research. There are two key ways in which we could change the policy-making process to make this possible. The first is to evaluate the effects of policies by using explicit measures of subjective well-being in addition to the more usual measures of the levels and distribution of income, employment, health, education, environmental quality and crime (Helliwell 2006a). The second is to adopt a more step-by-step approach to the design and evaluation of policy alternatives, using the intermittent and partial rollout of new policies as a valuable source of experimental and near-experimental evidence.

There has been increasing, and increasingly valuable, use made in recent years of such natural experiments, as described especially in Craig Riddell's chapter in this volume. But much needs to be done to make this approach more generally applicable. For example, the common practice of covering up policy failures needs to be rejected, and policy initiatives should be designed and implemented so as to increase their value in guiding future choices. I will provide some examples.

The policies presented in this book by the experts and the evaluations provided by the discussants are supposed to build on all relevant research in the discipline from which the policies derive. Several of the expert reviews and policy proposals reflect the focus of a particular discipline — most frequently, that of economics. Some contributors rely mainly on evidence that supports their preferred policies, while others (especially Riddell) are more even-handed in their summaries of the evidence, even when it runs counter to their proposals.

THE CHOSEN PACKAGE

My preferred policy package has a long-term orientation and a twin focus. The common element is an emphasis on health and well-being — in one case, on the health and well-being of the environment; and in the other, on the health and well-being of Canadians. The environmental measures selected include three policies: an emissions tax (on the burning of fossil fuels and emissions of noxious gases), with the proceeds used to protect the natural environment; higher standards for the construction of residential and commercial buildings and for the energy efficiency of equipment and appliances; and a zero-emission standard for the manufacture of vehicles. The first proposal is drawn from Nancy Olewiler's suggestions, while the latter two are from the list proposed by Mark Jaccard and Nic Rivers.

The Olewiler proposal involves an emissions tax, the proceeds of which are to be used in a variety of ways to sustain the quality of the air and water and to protect a range of life forms on land, in the sea and in the air. The emphasis is on using limited funds to leverage the desire of landowners and others to preserve the beauty and life-sustaining capacity of the natural environment, often in areas close to where they live or work. The flexibility of the instruments to be employed encourages the development of multiple uses of given spaces, thus reducing the inevitable social costs and inefficiencies of the all-too-common "my way or no way" approach to land-use decisions.

Olewiler's proposed tax on carbon and air pollutants (CAP tax), which would be used to finance environmental protection, covers essentially the same base as the carbon management standard suggested by Jaccard and Rivers, except that it applies at the point of combustion and is extended to include other noxious emissions. Jaccard and Rivers would probably have preferred an emissions tax of the sort proposed by Olewiler, but, as veteran campaigners, they were trying to bypass previous battle-grounds. Perhaps times have changed. As David Green suggested in the general discussion, the current level of public desire to take concrete action to control emissions of greenhouse gases (GHGs) may provide new windows of opportunity to institute efficient incentives to get the job started. After all the talk, it's time to walk the walk, goes the refrain.

Fossil fuel combustion would presumably be taxed at a rate reflecting carbon content plus any related noxious gases, while noxious gases of other sorts would be taxed at a rate reflecting the damage caused. In both cases, as with taxes on smoking, the main purpose of the CAP tax would be not to raise large amounts of revenue but to limit consumption of fossil fuels and emissions of noxious gases. The carbon part of the tax would be based on carbon dioxide actually emitted as a result of combustion, thus providing a significant incentive for capturing and sequestering carbon dioxide. The same would be true for emissions of noxious gases, some of which could then be converted to saleable by-products, or at least to a more benign form.

Although there is a general presumption among economists against the ear-marking of tax revenues, using an environment-preserving tax to finance efforts to protect other parts of the natural environment is likely to have broad appeal — if any tax can ever be said to appeal to taxpayers. The CAP tax is, possibly, given the current state of public concern about the global commons, one that would acquire broad sup-port among voters, and perhaps even among those paying the tax in the first instance. The tax-paying firms would thereby acquire a whole new set of opportunities to see an economic return from investing in energy efficiency and emissions reduction.

There would be a corresponding tilt in the incentives for Canadian firms to develop efficient new technologies for these purposes, with domestic markets provid-ing a good test bed for technologies with the potential to become attractive on world markets. It is for this fundamental reason that I favour the CAP tax — decision-makers should face a set of prices that gives them the correct signals about the overall costs, including external effects, of the goods and services they buy and sell. Such taxes are an essential element of any efficient strategy for reducing GHG emissions, but they are by no means the whole story.

Jaccard and Rivers argue that taxes or similar mechanisms are the only way to make real progress in cutting GHG emissions because, they say, "individual actors will not take actions with private costs and public benefits" (Nic Rivers 2007). This is a standard assumption that economists make about how people behave — selfishly, with regard only for their financial interests. There is a wealth of psychological evidence, however, based on both experimental and real-world behaviour, that people do value the interests of others, get pleasure from helping others and enjoy finding cooperative solutions.[1] If this were not so, why would anyone use a recycling box?

As evidence for their presumption, Jaccard and Rivers report that past energy conservation guidelines and targets have not had significant effects. This evidence could instead be interpreted as showing only that the design and announcement of government targets for energy conservation are not likely to change behaviour unless they are accompanied by changes in the all-important social norms that define for each of us the right thing to do. While we may not always choose to do the right thing, these norms still matter a lot. I suspect, though only time will tell, that social norms with respect to energy consumption may well be changing, if not for the first time. If they are changing, then it will be important not just to get energy prices right, but also to make sure that a good set of energy-efficient choices is available for individuals, businesses and communities wishing to do the right thing. Exhortation alone is unlikely to have much effect, especially as governments themselves have not been at the forefront of energy conservation in those areas under their direct management. For example, the federal government has more office space than any other organization in the country. How much of that space is designed and operated according to the energy efficiency standards recommended for others? Leading by example (something more than simply using a few vehicles powered by alternative fuels) is always more effective than proposing targets for others to achieve.

A second helpful feature of the proposed energy tax is that it avoids the trust-impairing free-rider problem. People are always more willing to serve the public interest if there is some assurance that others will do the same — or, at least, that they will not take advantage of the unselfishness of their neighbours. The higher the general level of trust, the lower the pressure on the mechanism to avoid free riding; but even in a highly trusting climate, people and firms need to be given a set of environment-related costs and prices to guide their decisions.

That leads naturally to the second and third components of the environmental health package: zero-emission vehicle standards and higher energy efficiency standards for buildings and appliances (both are described in more detail in the Jaccard and

Rivers chapter). If price signals are right, why should manufacturers and builders need to meet energy standards? Would they not already be designing and delivering the energy-efficient products demanded by consumers facing higher energy prices? One possible answer is that cars and buildings are often designed to be sold to buyers who are primarily concerned with the initial price, not the subsequent operating and maintenance costs. If that is the way consumers actually make decisions — and there is some evidence that this sort of myopia is common — then producers and developers may have to be nudged to put extra resources into energy-efficient design and to inform potential buyers of the energy requirements of their products.

The second part of my package is focused on human health and well-being. There are two policies: one for providing early childhood education and one for increasing the affordability of drugs. Both of these dishes are difficult to prepare and serve. Many chefs have tried, and many smoky kitchens attest to the problems related to their design and implementation. What makes these recipes so difficult? First, they are large and expensive ventures, each involving important choices about universality versus targeting, about the scale and management of service provision and about the share of costs to be paid by final users. Second, the issues fall primarily under provincial jurisdiction. Third, there is considerable uncertainty about the best ways of delivering results.

These circumstances invite, and possibly require, combining implementation and research in a step-by-step interactive process. This would mean relatively small-scale adoption in the early years — the scale would be designed to maximize gradually gained information about what works best. The fact that different provinces would identify different target populations or communities and choose different delivery methods could pose complications, but it would also increase, in a natural way, the range of policy experiments contributing lessons for the future.

My preferred early childhood development policy would combine elements of the proposals by Craig Riddell and Robert Evans, Clyde Hertzman and Steve Morgan. Where the two proposals differ — on issues such as whether the schemes should be targeted or universal — is precisely where an experimental step-by-step strategy would be of most use. Many of the first applications would be targeted on places where needs were greatest, in the ways suggested by Riddell, but always with an eye to what would be most effective for a universal strategy. The argument for focusing especially on the early childhood years — deriving from the research reviewed by Evans, Hertzman and Morgan — is that these are the years when the social and educational environment matters most, when the brain has the greatest plasticity and when the course of the future is developing.

My second policy choice in the human well-being category, and the fifth of my five allotted choices, is a national pharmacare strategy for lowering the cost and improving the distribution of prescription drugs. In the form proposed by Evans, Hertzman and Morgan, the policy takes as its main emphasis the reduction of drug price escalation through the application of some version of the New Zealand model of centralized purchasing. New Zealand's success — in the view of Evans, Hertzman and Morgan — is due to two factors: universal coverage and a fixed budget envelope within which to negotiate drug purchases. While the authors clearly favour similar universal coverage as the goal of a national strategy for prescription drugs, their proposal entails proceeding incrementally. They recommend retaining full pharmacare for seniors and the disabled; for the whole population, they recommend adding full first-dollar coverage for drugs to treat specific health conditions within a framework that explicitly identifies and pays for only evidence-based and cost-effective treatments. Their plan also includes a separate fund to cover the costs of drug treatment for rare diseases.

Since less than 50 percent of the costs of prescription drugs in Canada are currently covered by the public health care system,[2] with the remaining amount split between individual patients and private insurance plans, the benefits of lower drug prices would be correspondingly distributed.[3]

RUNNERS-UP

Based on evidence of the education-inducing consequences of past increases in the school-leaving age, Craig Riddell suggests increasing the period of compulsory education so that it ends at age 18. My primary reason for not including this proposal in the selected set follows directly from Riddell's evidence-based approach: some provinces are already in the process of increasing their periods of compulsory school attendance, and these natural experiments will provide an even stronger evidence base to guide other provinces. Thus, it could be argued that progress of the right sort is already being made. If so, then the policy mix presented here could be judged appropriate, as the five primary choices address more urgent changes.

Riddell also suggests merit scholarships for students from low-income families, based on his review of evidence showing positive externalities from higher education. He adds the needs component to avoid the regressive effects of an entirely merit-based system and the fiscal inefficiencies of providing scholarships mainly to those who would have gone on to university in any event. Here, too, experimentation at the provincial level might help to reveal the best opportunities for extending the national scholarship system.

POSSIBLES

Evans, Hertzman and Morgan propose a standardized electronic medical record to facilitate treatment strategies, and Olewiler proposes more systematic accounting for many aspects of the physical environment. Both are worthy ideas, and progress in these directions is to some extent already implicit in the design and implementation of the selected policies.

Andrew Sharpe maintains that removing the provincial sales tax on purchases of machinery and equipment would increase real investment in capital equipment and thereby increase productivity in a cost-effective way. The arguments for this are fairly persuasive, but since such taxation falls under provincial jurisdiction, the issue is perhaps best approached as an opportunity to gain quasi-experimental evidence from independent moves of individual provinces.

The three related income security proposals of Jean-Yves Duclos are aimed at simplifying a variety of tax and transfer systems with an eye to improving equity and efficiency at the same time. Having been involved with several reform proposals over the years, starting with the 1967 report of the Royal Commission on Taxation, I am very sympathetic to Duclos' objectives. And he makes a very good case that there are many weak spots in the current patchwork. However — and here I am influenced considerably by David Green's comments on Duclos' proposals — the complexities of their design and delivery are great, and there are still many issues to resolve before a blueprint can be ready for immediate application. Reforms are never easy. Large-scale integrated reforms are the toughest of all. They are easily derailed by parties favoured by the current system, and they can quickly become a patchwork of the type Duclos is so anxious to avoid. I have slightly more faith than does Duclos that the current Canadian system is better than most, and that it is capable of being reformed piecemeal through a shrewd use of evidence and experimentation.

DON'T THINK SO

In his chapter, David Foot illustrates that while demographic projections play an essential role in setting the stage for economic and social policies, they have no clear link to particular policies. He identifies three policy areas that could be placed under increased pressure due to population aging: fine-tuning immigration policies; creating more flexible retirement options and pensions to encourage employment among those over 65; and addressing staffing requirements in the health care sector. However, none of Foot's policy suggestions is couched in specific terms or linked to research results in the policy area in question. In each of the three policy areas he mentions, the main drivers lie elsewhere — evolving demographic structures are among the slower-moving and more predictable elements (see, for example, Evans et al. 2001). For instance, shortages of some types of medical services are due more to the unexpectedly large reduction in the average workweek of primary care physicians, driven in particular by the lower number of practice hours of female doctors, who make up a rapidly growing share of the pool of general practitioners.[4] Demographic changes in the patient mix have been smaller and more predictable than gender-related changes in the supply of medical services. While the latter have probably increased individual and aggregate well-being, they have posed adjustment problems in training programs, which take many years to produce qualified doctors.

The public policy case for subsidies relies on the existence of external effects that make the total benefits from an action greater than those gained by the individual who undertakes the action. However, Sharpe presents no evidence to suggest that total gains from interprovincial migration exceed those for the migrants. And this is, above all, an area where income and employment are only part of the story, as migration is costly in human and social terms for migrating individuals and often for the communities they leave and those to which they go. For example, residents of Atlantic Canada who commute to jobs in the Alberta oil sands might be more content as commuters than they would be if they uprooted themselves and their families and moved west permanently. Sharpe also suggests converting research and development support into technology adoption support. This is another case in which evidence not yet available might support making such a change. In general, to justify subsidies, pretty solid evidence is required that net benefits will offset fiscal and administrative costs as well as the risks posed to the perceived neutrality of the tax and transfer system.

DEFINITELY NOT

Michael Hart proposes that Canada make a grand bargain with the United States, to be designed and implemented by a new federal department of North American integration. He maintains that the Canadian government could finance this continental strategy by suspending its efforts to develop trade links with other countries and its pursuit of the multilateral agreements that would improve those links. I have assessed this strategy of preferential North American integration in the past and judged it to be far inferior to a more multilaterally balanced strategy designed to leverage Canada's uniquely cosmopolitan population and overseas contacts (Helliwell 2002, chap. 3). Such a balanced strategy would support the growth of mutually beneficial trade, investment and knowledge exchange with offshore economies, where the bulk of global trade and investment growth opportunities are to be found.

Subsequent events have, if anything, increased the attractions of a global strategy as compared with a continental one. One of the unfortunate side effects of the original Canada-US Free Trade Agreement is that it provided an example for others; the world has now seen an explosion of preferential trade arrangements, each with its own rules of origin, which are increasingly cumbersome in a world where intra-industry trade at different stages of production has become the norm. This has become such a problem that some producers pay the MFN (most-favoured nation) tariff when shipping goods from Canada to the United States in order to avoid the complex procedure of measuring and reporting foreign content. How much better it would have been at the outset to invest the same amount of leadership in improving the multilateral framework connecting all the established industrial countries with each other, and especially with the faster-developing countries.

Given the existence of the North American Free Trade Agreement (NAFTA), the best strategy for managing crucial bilateral trade relations is not seeking deeper bilateral integration, as proposed by Hart, but getting the most out of established dispute resolution procedures. An object lesson in how not to proceed was provided by the 2006 Softwood Lumber Agreement, which substituted managed trade for free trade just when the United States Court of International Trade made its definitive ruling that the NAFTA regulations did apply to softwood lumber, that the US duties were invalid and that all exacted duties had to be repaid in full, with interest. Instead of waiting a few months for a highly predictable and definitive vindication in the US courts, the Canadian government inexplicably agreed to manage southbound flows of softwood lumber in a manner that only served the interests of the US industry, breaching the provisions of the World Trade Organization. By levying an export tax that rises when prices fall, Canada has ensured that its own softwood lumber producers bear the brunt of all cycles of the North American construction industry. Thus, Canadian producers are now paying export levies that exceed the duties they paid previously, and there is no chance that any of these levies will ever be returned to them in any form. And, to achieve this state of affairs, the Canadian producers had to pay almost $1 billion to the United States, most of which went directly to the very US softwood lumber producers who will benefit from the Softwood Lumber Agreement.[5]

WHAT'S MISSING?

Having reviewed twenty-four policy proposals and selected five, have I in any sense defined a possible centrepiece for a national policy agenda? I have tried to provide some semblance of coherence by adopting a well-being focus with two focal points: the health and well-being of the environment and of individual Canadians. But the five policies selected constitute only a partial list of what might have been included if such an agenda were spelled out more completely; and there are, of course, many areas in which existing Canadian policies, legal frameworks and institutions are doing a good job.

It is no accident that the selected policies do not form a properly balanced portfolio that takes due account of urgency, step-by-step experimental developments and coherence. This was almost inevitable, since we judges were offered partial menus created by eight chefs, none of whom was expected to provide a plan for the entire meal. Canadian governments, federal and provincial, address this problem by having some form of interdepartmental or supradepartmental process for designing broad policy strategies, establishing priorities and ensuring consistency among policies. So, if my policy package resembles an excerpt from the spring catalogue from Bob Newhart's Grace L. Ferguson Airline and Storm Door Company, remember that our choice was limited to the policies offered. Nonetheless, some form of all of the policies I have chosen would be strong candidates for inclusion in a wide range of full policy agendas; many of the runner-up and possible selections could well belong in a file of good ideas for current or future application.

If I were setting out to design a more integrated policy package, I would recommend (no surprise here) using well-being evidence much more broadly to assess the consequences of existing and proposed policies. This would be one way of attempting to achieve the long-sought integration of economic and social objectives.

NOTES

1   Papers reviewing some of the relevant literature on this subject are found in Huppert, Kaverne and Baylis (2005).

2   This is in contrast to the public costs of physician and hospital services, which in 2004 were 99 percent and 91 percent of the total, respectively (Canadian Institute for Health Information 2006, 16).

3   The estimated 54.4/45.6 split of 2006 prescription drug costs between the private and public sectors is illustrated in table 1 of Canadian Institute for Health Information (2007); the same table shows that of the estimated 2006 private prescription drug expenditures of $11.5 billion, $3.9 billion was paid by patients out of pocket and the rest by private insurance plans.

4   Crossley, Hurley and Jeon report a drop in average weekly work hours of general practitioners — from 45.4 hours in 1982 to 38.3 in 2003 — based on a decrease of 12 percent in average hours for male GPs and 9 percent for female GPs, as well as an increase in the share of female GPs, who in 2003 worked about eight hours less per week than their male colleagues. The authors show that these drops are not matched in other professions, most of whose members worked longer weeks in 2003 than in 1982 (Crossley, Hurley and Jeon 2007, 10).

5   This situation is documented more fully in my testimony before the Special Study on the Softwood Lumber Agreement (Helliwell 2006b).

REFERENCES

Canadian Institute for Health Information (CIHI). 2006. *National Health Expenditure Trends, 1975-2006*. Ottawa: CIHI.

_____. 2007. *Drug Expenditure in Canada, 1985-2006*. Ottawa: CIHI.

Crossley, T.F., J. Hurley, and S.H. Jeon. 2007. "Physician Labour Supply in Canada: A Cohort Analysis." SEDAP Research Paper 162. Hamilton, ON: McMaster University, Program for Research on Social and Economic Dimensions of an Aging Population. Accessed July 30, 2007. socserv.mcmaster.ca/sedap/p/sedap162.pdf

Evans, R.G., K.M. McGrail, S.G. Morgan, M.L. Barer, and C. Hertzman. 2001. "APOCALYPSE NO: Population Aging and the Future of Health Care Systems." SEDAP Research Paper 59. Hamilton, ON: McMaster University, Program for Research on Social and Economic Dimensions of an Aging Population. Accessed July 30, 2007. socserv2.socsci.mcmaster.ca/~sedap/p/sedap59.pdf

Helliwell, J.F. 2002. *Globalization and Well-Being*. Vancouver: UBC Press.

_____. 2006a. "Social Capital, Well-Being and Public Policies: What's New?" *Economic Journal* 116: C34-5.

_____. 2006b. Testimony before the Special Study on the Softwood Lumber Agreement. *Proceedings of the Senate Standing Committee on Foreign Affairs and International Trade* 7, November 22.

Huppert, F.A., B. Kaverne, and N. Baylis, eds. 2005. *The Science of Well-Being: Integrating Neurobiology, Psychology, and Social Science*. London: Oxford University Press.

Rivers, N. 2007. Presentation at the Canadian Priorities Agenda Conference, Institute for Research on Public Policy, Toronto, March 8-9.

NAVIGATING THE SHOALS: THE SEARCH FOR CANADIAN POLICY SOLUTIONS
Richard G. Lipsey

A JUDGE'S CONCERNS

I will first comment on some of the general issues involved in selecting five policy proposals from the twenty-four presented in the IRPP's Canadian Priorities Agenda (CPA) project. The analysts in the CPA project were asked to propose three specific policies for each of the eight challenges. This raises the issue of how a specific policy and a policy package are to be defined. Having identified issues of concern within their assigned areas, some analysts proposed three very specific policies, while others offered a set of interrelated ones. For example, each of David Foot's three "policies" is in fact a sub-area within the general area of population aging, and each sub-area contains a package of specific policies. It would be unhelpful to compare specific policy proposals with packages of policies, so I have tried to select specific policies, even when the analyst did not.

A second problem is that some policy concerns can be handled by a single embracing policy, while others threaten death by a thousand cuts, and the policy solution for them would involve removing a thousand causes. Because of this, no policy aimed at removing one of the thousand causes can rate as high as a policy that can solve some other whole problem, even though the issues they address may be equally important. Still, I have complied with the instructions of the project organizers and rated individual policies in such a way that the death-by-a-thousand-cuts ones have difficulty competing against the single-solution ones.

A third problem arises because some analysts have addressed political feasibility while others have not. The two approaches will produce different orderings, and both have advantages and disadvantages. On the one hand, ignoring feasibility may lead to advocating policies that have little chance of success and giving precedence to those that have a smaller payoff but a much greater chance of success. On the other hand, to dismiss a policy because it is politically difficult to achieve is to ignore some pressing issues.[1]

A fourth problem is that most authors failed to consider the fact that what looks good on paper may not fare well in practice. For example, Kathy O'Hara and

Allen Sutherland, in their comments on Jean-Yves Duclos' contribution to the project, state that Duclos "does not purport to cover in sufficient detail [quoting Duclos] 'many of the difficult issues of program design, financing, and jurisdictional division of responsibilities that must be tackled in making important policy changes.' As necessary as this might have seemed from the perspective of making this huge set of issues manageable, it is nevertheless a breathtaking statement for a public policy document aimed at agenda setting" (286).

Because responsible advocacy of specific policies requires much more detailed consideration than is possible within the confines of a single policy paper, most of the CPA presenters could do little more than they did. Thus the five policies that I selected all need further work on the details of their implementation; the policies that I put in the category "further research required," while important, all, in my opinion, require more fundamental work on their basic structures.

MAJOR ISSUES AND SPECIFIC POLICIES

Aging population

In his analysis of population aging, David Foot uses what he calls demographic transition theory (DTT) to discuss the link between population growth and stages of economic development. Because he gives no supporting references to allow readers to assess this theory, I must judge it on the evidence presented. Foot treats demographic transition as a theory when, for example, he writes that it "teaches that slower population growth is entrenched." Yet this seems to be a historical generalization based on observed demographic changes over time as opposed to a theory with behavioural underpinnings from which demographic trends are deduced. DTT summarizes the historical experience in five stages in a way that is reminiscent of W. W. Rostow's attempt to generalize historical experience into a universal theory of stages of growth (1960). The fate of Rostow's theory is a cautionary lesson about such attempts, and Karl Popper's *Poverty of Historicism* provides a more general critique (1957).

Foot's contribution does, however, give one behavioural relationship related to DTT. We are told that DTT "posits an inverse relationship between fertility and education." It is true that this relationship has been observed in less-developed countries as women achieve higher levels of education. It is not clear, however, that it is a universal behavioural constant. Also, education may be an intermediate variable standing for more basic causes, such as the increasing opportunity cost of having children, which rises as women become better educated and thus obtain more employment opportunities. As evidence of this latter conjecture, there is recent Organisation for Economic Co-operation and Development (OECD) evidence that providing better daycare facilities raises fertility rates among educated women ("How to Deal" 2007). This suggests that we should use caution in extrapolating behaviour observed in developing countries.

In discussing his first set of proposals — which he calls population policies — Foot argues that a country whose market size is decreasing experiences "diseconomies of scale in the provision of domestic output" and "gradually loses global importance from both economic and political perspectives." They may also, he suggests, have difficulty defending their sovereignty. "In contrast, countries with growing populations are likely to take over global trade and affairs, with possible detrimental effects on those with decreasing populations" (196). This leads him to ask whether population decrease can be prevented. Foot offers several proposals for slowing, if not halting, this decline that are related to immigration and a reduction in the cost of raising children.

I cannot agree with Foot's assessment that the main problem with respect to a stabilizing or declining population is determining how to slow or prevent this phenomenon. Surely, after worrying about the effects of the population explosion that elevated the world population from 1 billion to over 6 billion in two centuries, we should welcome the predicted stabilization of the world's population sometime in this century. The transition from a growing population to a stable or declining one will pose problems other than those stated in the previous paragraph, and these will require a more creative approach than trying to postpone the inevitable. I know of neither theory nor evidence to support Foot's contentions mentioned in the previous paragraph. Small countries such as the Netherlands have done well in the globalized economy. They need not worry about size if they are part of a customs union such as NAFTA, a wider economic collective such as the European Union or — at the very least — the still-influential World Trade Organization. Per capita incomes have risen rapidly in countries with effective growth policies, and this includes small nations, such as Taiwan and Singapore, and large ones, such as China and India. Also, regional political treaties such as NATO make it unnecessary for small countries to worry about being unable to defend their sovereignty.

I think the problems that are most on the public's mind with respect to current population dynamics in Canada are internal ones. Most media coverage is devoted to the problem of a growing dependency ratio (the ratio of the nonworking to the working population) and, a distant second, the problem of insufficient room at the top for the talented when the age pyramid is inverted. Neither Foot nor his commentators, Peter Hicks and Susan McDaniel, may consider these to be serious issues, but in a project directed at policy-makers, I would have liked to have seen Foot explain why he dismisses these worries — or, if he does not dismiss them, why he did not think them important enough to discuss in any detail.

Possibly, the fact that Foot chose to emphasize lifecycle theory explains why he did not stress the rising dependency ratio. According to Foot, lifecycle theory suggests that the aging population will "live off the stock of assets accumulated over their working years" (204). That contention poses problems that are too complex to consider fully here. I will merely observe that current living standards depend on current production, which (*ceteris paribus*) depends on the currently employed labour force. If retired persons seek to consume their accumulated capital, others must be willing to take it over. The old must sell their houses to people at the family formation stage and their stocks and bonds to those at the high-saving stage, and both of these groups will constitute a declining proportion of the total population. In short, what one person can do — retire and live off his or her capital — everyone cannot do. This becomes obvious when we look at the extreme case of everyone retiring at once and seeking to sell off capital to fund their purchases of the nonexistent current production.

I do not mean to argue against many of the specific policies suggested. Those that would lower the opportunity cost of raising children seem desirable because moving to a stable population would cause fewer problems than moving to a falling one. Foot argues, however, that the success of such policies will be limited by "demographic momentum"; but we do not know by how much, so we cannot even guess at the costs and benefits.

Foot's second set of proposals concerns what he calls "workforce policies." He would allow for later retirement and part-time work for elders, and a plethora of other measures, most of which seem useful to me. But he does not single out one policy that can be weighed against those advocated by the other project contributors.

His third policy set is related to health care. Although he raises many policies in his discussion, two stand out. The first is aimed at relocating health care services closer to elderly populations. The second policy is directed toward finding the staff necessary to provide health care services, especially for the elderly. Foot argues that now is the time to recruit and train the health care workforce of the future. This problem is so important, and its resolution subject to such long time lags, that it does need to be taken up with urgency now. So it is a candidate for inclusion in my package.

Climate change

Once we accept that climate change is a fact and largely caused by human action, two main areas of concern emerge: dealing with the causes and dealing with the consequences. The CPA analysts have chosen to address only the former.[2] This is regrettable, since dealing with the consequences is far more important when it comes to parochial Canadian issues. Since Canada is responsible for only a small proportion of total greenhouse gas (GHG) emissions (possibly 2 to 3 percent), eradicating its emissions would have only a small effect on the world's climate in general, and on its own in particular. But Canada will have to live with the consequences of the climate changes that are already in the works, as well as those arising from those future emissions that are inevitable, no matter how fast the world mobilizes to reduce them.

So why should we worry about reducing Canada's emissions? The prime reason is that we cannot expect the major polluters among the developing nations — such as China, India and Brazil — to act on the problem until we developed nations do. "Why," they well may ask, "should we do what those who are much richer are unwilling to do?" A secondary reason is that every reduction helps, no matter how small it is on a global scale. But if we were concerned only with our own welfare, and if what we did had no demonstration effect on others, we would spend far more on controlling the effects of climate change than on reducing our contribution to further change. Although I do not advocate such a selfish approach, I worry that far too much of our effort and resources over the next decade will go to reducing emissions and far too little to dealing with the effects.

Climate change will probably be the most important issue facing the world over the course of the twenty-first century. If a proposal to deal with its Canadian *consequences* had been among the policies presented, it would have topped my list. Since we must help to lead the way for developing nations, I still put a policy for dealing with Canadian *causes* near the top of my list.

In their contribution to the CPA project, Mark Jaccard and Nic Rivers offer these policy proposals: a phased carbon management standard for fossil fuel producers and importers; a phased zero-emission standard for vehicle manufacturers and importers; and phased building and appliance standards for energy efficiency and GHG emissions. If we are to lead the way for the rest of the world, we must adopt some such policy. But, given what I have said, I should choose the policy with the greatest demonstration effect, not necessarily the one with the greatest emissions-reducing effect. The first proposal likely passes both tests, so I have picked it, although Canada will probably adopt some variant of all three fairly soon.

The first proposal should, however, be marked for some fine-tuning in light of the commentaries offered by Christopher Green and James Meadowcroft. Green, for example, says, "Why do they include importers, and why do they limit certification to fossil fuel producers and ignore those whose activities directly generate fossil fuel emissions? In some cases, it would make more sense to move certification responsibility downstream to the power plant and pipeline levels" (109-10). Or, as Meadowcroft observes, "Most other jurisdictions have adopted...alternative designs for GHG abatement. Selecting a policy design that is different from those of other industrialized countries...could, for example, make it somewhat more difficult to engage in international emissions trading" (117). He adds, "It would be nice to see a more detailed comparison between this policy option and two others: a downstream cap-and-trade system supplemented by a downstream carbon tax (the latter applicable to the economic sectors, such as households and transport, not covered by the cap); and an upstream carbon tax (that is, one levied at the point of production or import)" (118).

The commentators have analogous qualifications concerning the other two proposals; they recommend more modifications to the zero-emission vehicle standard than to the building and appliance standards. If I were to choose the proposal that seemed closest to being workable as expounded, I would choose the building and appliance standards. But, as it has the maximum demonstration effect and largest emissions-reducing impact — assuming the details could be worked out as the commentators suggest — I have chosen the first policy.

Economic security

Jean-Yves Duclos presents a major critique of the present state of economic security in Canada. I am inclined, however, to agree with his commentators — David Green, and Kathy O'Hara and Allen Sutherland — that his strong case for some actions may be harmed by his overstatement of the present situation. For example, Green argues that Canadian worker insecurity has not increased appreciably in recent years. Also, as O'Hara and Sutherland point out, nonstandard employment may not be as serious a problem as Duclos assumes. Furthermore, the tax expenditure system has stabilized low-level incomes here much more than in the US. On another tack, O'Hara and Sutherland observe that Duclos' analysis would have been strengthened by a consideration of the extent to which the principles that he advocates are "in tension or conflict, either internally or one to the other" (278).

None of this is meant to suggest that there are no Canadian problems with respect to economic security, only that an assessment of the three measures proposed requires a full understanding of the problem. Duclos' analysis leads him to make three policy proposals: create a universal basic income for all working-age adults; reform unemployment insurance (now called employment insurance, or EI); and promote financial and human capital building among low- and middle-income Canadians. With respect to the first proposal, I do not know enough to judge whether Duclos or Green is more convincing on the issue of feasibility, but reducing the welfare wall is clearly desirable; it is a problem that has so far resisted all attempts at full resolution. I think there is enough potential in this proposal to justify more (intensive) work on it in an effort to address the concerns of Duclos' commentators; or, if this were not possible, to reconcile some of the inherent tensions and conflicts they underlined.

Turning to the second proposal, EI reform is clearly desirable. It proceeded haltingly through the 1990s, but some key aspects of it were reversed in the following decade, arguably for political purposes, illustrating the political difficulties associated with overhauling this program (for details and assessment, see Gray 2006). O'Hara and Sutherland do not think that EI is in such bad shape. They point out that the labour market is working well, but — given the current buoyant economy — this is hardly strong evidence that EI is free of serious problems. I agree with Duclos that EI does not fulfill its ostensible function and is in need of the kind of reform that he advocates. This proposal is thus included as a candidate for my policy package.

The third proposal deals with a real problem: the obstacles to asset building among low-income individuals. But here what Duclos offers is actually a package of policies — not just one. O'Hara and Sutherland single out vouchers for training and employment services as a potentially good idea but argue that these are "but one strand of what must inevitably be a multipronged effort to create robust labour market conditions" (286). There are, however, unresolved issues related to the effectiveness of each of the measures that Duclos advocates and to their appropriate mix. I therefore assign this proposal to the category of further research required.

Trade and globalization

Michael Hart makes a strong case that by far the most important issue for Canadian trade policy is, and has remained since the end of the Second World War, how to minimize impediments to the free flow of goods and services across the Canada-US border. He observes that Canada and the US do not really trade with each other, in the classic sense, as two economically separate countries exchanging goods and services; instead, they produce goods together within one more-or-less integrated economy. Anything that increases the time, money and inconvenience costs of cross-border movement has potentially major consequences for Canadian trade, employment and national income. Hence, preserving and extending cross-border access is important for Canada.

Achieving this goal requires, according to Hart, three measures: reducing further the impact of the border; increasing regulatory convergence and cooperation; and building the institutional capacity needed for the first two. Because Hart devotes the bulk of his policy analysis to these measures, I take them to be his three major proposals, despite the fact that he refers to them as only one of three "principal priorities," which are: reducing domestic impediments to Canada's engagement in the global economy; reducing the resources and efforts devoted to trade diversification; and strengthening the policy framework that governs cross-border investment and trade with the US.

Both of Hart's commentators — Jonathan Fried and Keith Head — provide important caveats related to Hart's dismissal of the value of any Canadian involvement in trade and investment issues in the rest of the world. A shift in emphasis to US-Canadian border issues need not lead to total neglect in other areas — such as trade with China and South Korea, or the Doha Round. We can still accept the overriding importance of Canada-US issues, as Hart advocates, while expending some (less, but not zero) effort in these other areas, as Fried and Head advocate. As Head puts it, "I do not believe Canada can maximize its benefits from international trade by disengaging from the three-quarters of the global economy that resides outside the US" (452).

Now consider Hart's three proposals for improving Canada-US trade flows. The value of the second proposal, regulatory convergence, is not universally agreed upon. As both commentators point out, not all regulatory divergence is inefficient, and mutual recognition of national standards has proven effective in the European Union. Furthermore, it is not clear, for example, that on pricing issues Canadian firms would be better off dealing with US law in US courts or with antidumping laws in international dispute settlement institutions. Some regulatory convergence is probably desirable, but in what areas, in what form and how much? These are questions that need further consideration before we launch concerted efforts in this direction.

Fried's comments on Hart's third proposal are penetrating: "Hart encourages the governments of Canada and the United States to 'focus upon the functions that must be performed for the efficient governance of deepening integration' and to 'create new institutions only where current arrangements are unsuitable.' He suggests a number of practical ways in which regulatory agencies can integrate a North American perspective into their work. But he follows his criticism of bureaucratically captured regulatory agendas with a series of recommendations for more bureaucracy" (442). Although institution building clearly deserves further attention, I do not yet see well-worked-out, specific proposals for changes that meet clearly defined needs and that have a good chance of being effective. So I place this proposal on my list of the many that are worthy of further consideration but not yet ready to be included in a set of policies for immediate action.

This leaves me with Hart's first proposal: reducing the impact of the border. The payoff from doing so and the cost of doing nothing are large but not obvious to the average Canadian, and this makes the effort all the more important. Not only are the costs involved significant — although difficult to measure precisely — but they are also likely to rise, if unchecked, due to increasing security concerns, a growing body of environmental regulation and elevated US protectionist sentiment. As Hart puts it, "Reducing border administration...will decrease enforcement and administrative costs for governments and compliance costs for industry, and it will reduce trade and investment disincentives" (423). I accept this as a desirable policy, although the border problems are a case of death by a thousand cuts — or at least serious harm. The policy would therefore have to include, as Hart points out, many different specific measures: "A key aspect of any initiative to ensure the more efficient and effective operation of the border is the identification of those functions within the border clearance process that can be performed away from the border or...eliminated altogether...Additionally, most customs requirements — like origin certificates — can easily be streamlined by, for example, harmonizing most-favoured-nation tariff levels" (421).

I have added this really important matter to my final list, although I have had to stretch the definition of a single policy proposal to do so.

Health outcomes

Robert Evans, Clyde Hertzman and Steve Morgan provide a detailed, cogent argument for three policies. The first is for an early childhood development (ECD) program. The authors argue, in line with much of their earlier work, that social context has far stronger effects on health status than does health care: "The experiences of early childhood become 'embedded' in the form of patterns of response to later stresses, not only as healthy or unhealthy behaviour, but also as 'learned' biological responses through the endocrine and cardiovascular systems that may support or damage health" (292). In their second proposal, they call for a major reorientation of the funding and regulation of pharmaceuticals in Canada through the introduction of a single-buyer system to control costs. Their third proposal is aimed at improving cost-effectiveness and quality of care in the health care system by introducing a standardized electronic medical record. The second two proposals have been successfully employed in other countries.

There is impressive evidence that the first proposal — for the establishment of an ECD program — is capable of solving the problem. For example, Evans, Hertzman and Morgan note that 25 percent of Canadians reach adulthood without acquiring the competencies to cope with the modern economy. There is evidence that variants of their suggested solution are working in Europe. But the fact that something works in one institutional setting does not guarantee that it will work in another. Would the policy be captured by public sector unions, which might use it to advance their own interests? Would the provinces accept the federal leadership that this policy (as well as the other two) requires? Perhaps if enough extra money were dangled along with the proposal some provinces would bite, and subsequent successes could persuade others to follow.

Concerning the second proposal, the escalation of drug costs in Canada is real, and it is exceeded only in the US. There is evidence that this escalation can be contained by a single-buyer regime — although, as commentator Raisa Deber remarks, while necessary, this may not always be sufficient for cost control. For example, a commitment is needed to buy the cheapest rather than the latest drug, which is often the most expensive. This is an easy regime to institute; the main problem is political pressure coming both from within Canada and from the powerful US drug lobby. The expected payoff from adopting this scheme is large. However, since its chances of success seem quite small to me, the expected payoff from the effort devoted to advocating this scheme is much smaller.

The third proposal, for a standardized system of electronic record keeping, is clearly feasible and not too difficult politically. There is also some evidence that it has been effective elsewhere, although Deber asserts that the value of electronic medical records is not fully supported by the data — there is debate about the size of the gains from that measure alone. Based on the evidence that I have seen, my guess is that those gains would not be insignificant and could be large.

How to prioritize these three excellent proposals? The extent of the benefits to be gained from the first is most uncertain. It remains unclear how it would work in Canada — although, if it were successful, its payoff could be great, both monetarily and in terms of social justice. However, major uncertainties linger, so I have put it on the further-research-required list. The choice between the second and third proposals should have been based on a cost-benefit analysis. I have chosen the second proposal as a candidate for my policy package because I guess that this is the one that a cost-benefit analysis would favour, but I would switch to the third proposal if such a study showed it to be the more valuable alternative.

Natural capital

Nancy Olewiler presents an excellent study of the issues surrounding the use, abuse and protection of natural capital, along with three important policy recommendations. Her first proposal is to create a conservation plan that collects data on natural capital and ecological goods and services. Second, she proposes introducing a new carbon-air pollutants tax and using the revenues generated to fund conservation initiatives. And third, she advocates the introduction of new, incentive-based policies such as tradable development rights to secure natural capital in a cost-effective manner (this last recommendation is actually a collection of policies directed at a single objective).

All three proposals should be adopted in the not-too-distant future. However, the need for action is not as urgent as it is for many of the other CPA proposals. We must first gather reliable and comprehensive information if we are to build rational policies in this area. Hence, I rank Olewiler's first proposal above the other two, although, as commentator Peter Victor points out, problems will arise in coordinating the efforts of the federal, provincial and municipal authorities. Also, the policy should do more than produce a state of the environment report — it should yield the information needed for the development of good policies for the protection of natural capital. So I have added the creation of a conservation plan to my final policy list. If this policy were adopted, it would be important to publicize its data collection function to avoid giving the impression that measuring the extent of the problem is the same as solving it. If successfully implemented, however, this policy would make the future adoption of Olewiler's other two proposals more likely.

Human capital

Craig Riddell offers a comprehensive treatment of issues related to human capital. These include identifying what human capital is and why it matters, as well as examining the factors that influence the decision to invest in it and government involvement in these decisions. Riddell also presents evidence of rates of return on human capital and describes the current state of human capital in Canada. From all this, he produces three policy proposals: introduce programs for early childhood development, raise the compulsory school-leaving age and institute a national merit-based scholarship program for low-income youths.

Looking at the first recommendation, I wonder if, with appropriate tweaking, it and the similar recommendation made by Evans, Hertzman and Morgan might be combined. Evans, Hertzman and Morgan make a strong case for the importance of early childhood influences and the ability of carefully designed programs to positively affect individual outcomes. But, as I have said, there is a large divide between things that look promising on paper and things that work well after they have been carefully drafted and introduced into a given institutional structure. I do not feel that Riddell's first proposal is advanced enough in terms of its design and empirical support to be included on my top-five policy list, but I have put it on my list (in combination with the Evans, Hertzman and Morgan recommendation) of important policies for further study.

The benefits of the second proposal are problematic. I am inclined to agree with commentator Jane Gaskell that merely raising the compulsory school-leaving age will do little for those in real need. As she observes, "Policy initiatives in relation to secondary schooling must be driven by provincial governments and produce a wider variety of secondary school programs that engage young people with different interests and needs...Research suggests that at-risk students respond to personal attention by a responsible adult, small alternative programs, culturally appropriate learning environments and relevant curriculum...The system needs to target specific groups of youth...and it must create programs that are safe, supportive and nurturing, as well as academically rich" (71). Riddell's other commentator, Serge Coulombe, points out that while "increases in the school-leaving age during the period from the 1920s to the 1970s yielded quite spectacular returns...We should not expect the same benefit today since we would not be working from the same base" (61). Furthermore, "keeping 17- and 18-year-olds at school against their will might create other problems, especially for teachers" (60). I conclude that the potential benefits from raising the compulsory school-leaving age are too uncertain, and so I have not chosen this proposal.

With regard to Riddell's third recommendation, I again agree with Gaskell — increasing access to university education is an important goal, but a system of national merit-based scholarships may not be the best approach. I have always wondered why, instead of being a creditor in an educational lending program, the state did not become a preferred stockholder in an educational venture. Students would graduate bearing the same financial obligation, but repayment would be made through the income tax system in the form of a levy of, say, 1 percent of taxable earnings. That way, repayment requirements would never constitute a crushing burden. My intention here is only to illustrate — as do the commentators in their remarks — that there may be better ways to increase access to higher education than that which Riddell proposes.

So none of Riddell's three proposals has made my top five. This reflects only on the uncertainties related to specific proposals, not on Riddell's excellent analysis of human capital issues.

Productivity

Andrew Sharpe contributes an excellent analysis of Canada's lagging productivity. While this is a serious issue, commentator Richard Harris does point out that Canadian workers do not fare as poorly in comparison with US workers as the comparative GDP data might suggest, since most of the gains from recent productivity rises in the US have gone to the top 2 percent of the income distribution (and, furthermore, Canadians do not have to worry about losing their medical insurance). However, Sharpe's other commentator, Don Drummond, explains the magnitude of the payoff that would derive from removing the gap: "Closing the difference in output per capita would lift the annual personal disposable income for the average Canadian household by $11,900 and add $108 billion per year in revenues for the federal, provincial and local governments" (390).

Of course, this could not be accomplished quickly, but the calculations still show the enormous potential financial benefits of stronger Canadian productivity growth. No other area under review comes close to this one in terms of potential gain from a solely Canadian policy. There is therefore a strong case for choosing a policy proposal from this set. The problem is that the productivity gap is a prime case of death by a thousand cuts, so dealing with it means removing a thousand causes; no one policy can achieve a high ranking, although as a package they are of critical importance. Drummond's own list, which he sets out toward the end of his commentary, and which is by no means exhaustive, illustrates amply the death-by-a-thousand-cuts aspect of the problem and the fact that many measures would be required to deal with it.

Sharpe offers three policies to deal, at least partially, with the problem: introduce measures to encourage the more rapid diffusion and adoption of new technologies by Canadian firms; abolish provincial sales taxes (PST) on the purchase of machinery and equipment; and facilitate the geographical migration of workers. Drummond and Harris maintain that the efficacy of the first policy is debatable. How important is the diffusion lag, and would further measures similar to the National Research Council of Canada's Industrial Research Assistance Program help significantly? No one can be sure. With regard to Sharpe's third recommendation, it is scandalous that it is easier for some types of workers to move among the politically separate countries of the European Union than it is for Canadian workers to move around in their own country. But powerful forces within the provinces resist the removal of the offending barriers to mobility. Yet, as important as that initiative would be as a symbol of national unity, it would not contribute substantially to total national income.

In contrast, Sharpe's second proposal to abolish the PST on machinery and equipment would seem to face no insurmountable political obstacles, and there appears to be general agreement that it is important. As a country with one of the highest costs of capital, Canada has a self-imposed disincentive to the kinds of investments that raise productivity and contribute to international competitiveness. Here is a proposal that should be adopted immediately. I have included it on my top-five list because it deals partially with the death-by-a-thousand-cuts problem and it would probably make one of the largest single contributions of the three offered by Sharpe.

MY RECOMMENDED POLICIES

My final five policy selections are:

/ Introduce a phased-in carbon management standard for fossil fuel producers
/ Reduce further the impact of the Canada-US border
/ Recruit and train the staff that will be needed to serve the needs — particularly medical — of an aging population
/ Create a conservation plan to collect data on natural capital and ecological goods and services
/ Abolish provincial sales taxes on purchases of machinery and equipment

I was allowed two runners-up, so I selected a pair of proposals that, although potentially beneficial, seemed to have a smaller chance of being implemented: reform the employment insurance system; and introduce a single-buyer program for pharmaceuticals.

Lastly, I present my list of the four proposals that I believe would benefit from further research and development. Although they address extremely important issues — more important than those addressed by some of the policies on my final list — they need more work before they can compete with my top five. The four proposals are:

/ Create a universal basic income available to all working-age adults
/ Promote financial and human capital building among low- and middle-income Canadians
/ Build the needed US-Canadian institutional capacity for further streamlining cross-border trade
/ Establish an early childhood development program

NOTES

1   For example, if I had allocated my time in the mid-1980s with an eye to what everyone believed was politically feasible, I would not have written *Taking the Initiative*, which was the first book to argue in detail the modern case for a Canada-US free trade area (Lipsey and Smith 1985).

2   Although I have not seen the brief that was given to the presenters, I have assumed from the title of the topic listed in the program that the focus was climate change in general, not just controlling its causes.

REFERENCES

Gray, D.M. 2006. "Has EI Reform Unraveled? Canada's EI Regime in the 2000s." *C.D. Howe Institute Backgrounder* 98. Toronto: C.D. Howe Institute. Accessed August 15, 2007. www.cdhowe.org/pdf/backgrounder_98.pdf

"How to Deal with a Falling Population." 2007. *Economist*, July 28.

Lipsey, R.G., and M.G. Smith. 1985. *Taking the Initiative: Canada's Trade Options in a Turbulent World*. Toronto: C.D. Howe Institute.

Popper, K. 1957. *The Poverty of Historicism*. London: Routledge and Kegan Paul.

Rostow, W.W. 1960. *The Stages of Economic Growth: A Non-Communist Manifesto*. Cambridge: Cambridge University Press.

POLICY PRIORITIES FOR CANADA: MAKING CHOICES
Carolyn Hughes Tuohy

CRITERIA FOR CHOICE

A coherent policy package for Canada in the medium term, with the purpose of enhancing the economic and social well-being of Canadians, must meet several criteria. It must balance long- and short-term payoffs. It must be supported by sound analysis and evidence. It must effectively steward public resources and provide opportunities to engage, leverage and build the capacity in the private and voluntary sectors to act in pursuit of public purpose. It must take into account the broad demographic changes shaping the population, changes that involve not only the generational make-up but also the mix of native- and foreign-born Canadians. It must not impose costs disproportionately on those least able to bear them. It must, as a whole, respond to the aspirations of residents of all the regions of Canada and engage those matters that require action at the national level. Finally, it must be capable of being expressed within the frame of an overarching policy narrative that resonates with Canadians across the country. In this introductory section, I elaborate further on each of these seven criteria as a prelude to the presentation of my choices from among the options provided within the IRPP Canadian Priorities Agenda (CPA) project.

Long-term versus short-term payoff

Most of the policy challenges identified within the CPA project have implications reaching far into the future. Some of the proposals that we judges were asked to consider would involve addressing these challenges through major policy changes that may not be feasible in the current context, for a variety of reasons. This is not to say that the proposals are not worth considering. It is important that those who are active in shaping public policy develop a repertoire of potential responses and be ready to seize windows of opportunity for their introduction and implementation.

It is also important, however, that in addition to building up a policy repertoire we act now to address the significant challenges we face — to think for the long term and act in the short term. In order to gain political support in the here and now, policies (even those directed at the long term) should have some short-term payoffs.[1] Short-term measures can also prepare the ground for action by initiating incremental changes that will shape the context in which future decisions are made. Part of this preparatory effect may be achieved by creating constituencies of support for subsequent policy initiatives.[2]

Sound analysis and evidence

The statement that sensible and effective policy must be grounded in an understanding of the relevant evidence may seem, on its face, to be unarguable. Meeting this condition, however, is far more complicated. Policy choices cannot be made through dispassionate and disinterested analysis, abstracted from the interests and world views of the participants in the process. Nonetheless, in any legitimate political system, policy advocates should be required to make their cases through persuasive analysis grounded in independently verifiable data and information. Hence, the policy options chosen in this CPA exercise must be able to withstand independent analytic scrutiny.

Stewardship and leverage

The scope and scale of the challenges faced in this project are such that they cannot be addressed by any one sector — public, private or nonprofit — acting alone. The necessary resources and understandings of the factors at play reside throughout society. In some cases, it may be appropriate for the state, taking equity and efficiency into account, to commandeer these resources through taxation or other measures. In other instances, however, such measures would require an unrealistic level of knowledge and capacity on the part of the state; and policy purposes would be better served by working with existing incentive structures to harness the potential of nonstate actors.[3] Furthermore, and especially at a historical moment when tax tolerance seems to have reached a plateau, there is a limit to how much the state can take on spending responsibilities without shedding others or finding greater efficiencies in its current operations. Accordingly, an overall package of public policies must be sensitive to demands on the public treasury and deploy public resources in ways that capitalize on the comparative advantages of the state and the private and nonprofit sectors.

That said, we must also recognize that significant policy change will almost always involve a considerable upfront blip in public spending — to pay for sweeteners that will encourage compliance with voluntary programs; to create the infrastructure necessary to implement and monitor the programs; and to deliver politically important early wins. Hence, in choosing any policy package, we must keep a close eye on its short- and long-term spending implications and ensure that its upfront draw on the treasury is politically defensible.

Demographic fit

Canada's population is relatively young in comparison with those of other advanced nations, but Canada, like most of its counterparts, projects a growing proportion of elderly persons and an increased dependency ratio in the coming decades. Among other things, this means — according to a recent Organisation for Economic Co-operation and Development (OECD) projection — that if the current policy framework remains unchanged, government expenditures could increase by 8.7 percentage points of GDP by 2050, while revenues could decrease by 1.2 percentage points (Casey et al. 2003). Absent significant policy change, the fiscal squeeze on areas of public investment, such as education, that are fundamental to fostering ingenuity and prosperity will intensify. This presents us with a dilemma: policy must respond to the needs of an aging population while also making the necessary investments in current and future prosperity.

As well, Canada is increasingly a nation of immigrants. In 2000, 19.4 percent of the population had been born outside the country — the second-highest rate in the OECD. Between 2001 and 2006, two-thirds of Canada's population growth was attributable to immigration. Absorbing this influx in ways that strengthen rather than strain the social fabric is a critical policy challenge.

Equity

Economic security is one of the specific policy objectives examined in the CPA project, and it is addressed through recommendations for an income security system that is consistent, as Jean-Yves Duclos puts it, with a society that is both just and productive. The basic value of equity — defined as the desire to ensure that the least advantaged in society are made better off, and at the very least are not made worse off, by policy change — also has broad relevance in this project. This value is ever-present in Canadian policy discourse, although it is accorded varying weight. In considering policy options in the course of this project, then, any trade-offs of equity for other policy ends need to be explicitly brought forward and examined.

Regional balance and national action

One of Canada's most distinctive characteristics is its regional diversity, reflected institutionally in a highly decentralized federal structure. Any policy agenda "for Canada" needs to be politically sensitive to regional interests and to what can properly be done at the national, as opposed to the provincial or other subnational, level. By "national" level I mean either the federal government or pan-Canadian intergovernmental arrangements.[4]

Policy narrative

It is not enough to ensure that Canadians are given a policy package with particular components that appeal to their own interests. If that package is to endure partisan change and periodic shifts in the balance of interests, it must resonate broadly with Canadians. Accordingly, it needs to be tied together by a national narrative that reflects the ways in which Canadians understand themselves as Canadians. It needs to relate to people's individual daily lives while appealing to their moral selves and their sense of community.

Tracing out such a narrative for Canada lies well beyond the scope and the mandate of my contribution to this project. But I can make a few observations. In the first place, we can identify certain narratives that have underlain public policy in Canada in the past: for example, Laurier's ringing statement that the twentieth century would belong to Canada; Trudeau's just society; and after the Second World War, the self-image of Canada as a kinder, gentler nation than its larger, more entrepreneurial, but more ruthless and (latterly) bellicose southern neighbour.[5] These traditional narratives are, however, inadequate as a frame for policies directed at some of the major challenges identified in the CPA project — notably, coping with threats to the ecosystem and creating the necessary conditions for Canada's continued prosperity.

We can identify some elements of a new narrative that would build upon past narratives and provide a frame for addressing the challenges of the future. One such element is the sense of Canada as a nation that is both favoured and at risk. Canada is richly endowed with natural resources and is a magnet for people around the world who seek a better life. It exists, however, in a world where ecological, political and economic climates are unstable and where citizens, accordingly, have an obligation to ensure that the potential of national advantages is realized. The policies associated with such a narrative need to connect with and advance the ways in which individuals experience the benefits and obligations of living in Canada. So, in putting together my preferred package from the policy options developed for the CPA project, I have kept in mind the role that these options will play within an evolving national narrative.

POLICY CHOICES

I have selected policies in three areas to form a coherent package that meets the seven criteria outlined earlier. These areas are environmental sustainability, human capital development and health care. My mandate was to select only five policy options. Nancy Olewiler's chapter presents three components of what I believe to be essentially one integrated policy. While Olewiler offers a choice of components, the resulting policy must stipulate revenue sources and revenue use, as well as methods for data collection and modelling to allow for implementation. Nonetheless, in accordance with the rules of this exercise, I accept that in selecting this package I have exercised three of my options. I then move on to select one option within the human capital category and one in health care, for a total of five.

Three policies to promote environmental sustainability

Olewiler's proposal for a tax on carbon emissions and air pollutants (a CAP tax), with revenue directed toward the protection of privately held natural capital, meets most of the outlined criteria. First, by taxing carbon emissions and thereby creating a powerful incentive for reducing them, this policy addresses a major threat to the environment, yielding substantial benefits in the long term. This is the principal benefit of the entire proposal. It also takes advantage of a window of opportunity for policy change — created by an upsurge in public concern for the environment — to build incentives for technological innovation. As entrepreneurs seize on the new business opportunities arising from this, they will begin to form a constituency of political support for policies favouring clean technologies. The policy would also confer politically important short-term benefits in that it would likely allow us to experience improvements in air quality relatively quickly. Moreover, by beginning immediately to preserve and enhance Canada's stock of ecological goods and services, the policy would demonstrate benefits in the short to medium term as part of an overall environmental strategy.

Second, Olewiler not only supports her recommendation with a careful examination of alternative policy options, but also builds into her proposal a mechanism for data collection and analysis: a federally coordinated process of establishing natural capital target models comprising environmental sustainability indicators. While this is clearly a complex modelling and data collection project, it would build upon and ultimately replace the existing environmental impact analysis process.

Third, Olewiler specifies a use for the revenues generated by her proposed CAP tax: a combination of the outright public purchase of land and the public purchase of conservation easements, which would have a similar effect on the preservation of natural capital while leaving land in private hands. The use of the funds is well suited to the source of the funds: because the intent of the CAP tax is, in fact, to reduce the production of greenhouse gases and air pollutants, revenue from it should decline over time. Earmarking this revenue for the acquisition of public rights to natural capital is thus equivalent to creating a sinking fund — that is, a fund that will be exhausted over time. It makes sense to use the tax revenue to secure benefits in perpetuity by purchasing rights upfront rather than making expenditures that will need to be supported from another revenue source when the CAP tax revenues decline. For this reason, I favour the purchase of property rights in perpetuity over the annual use of municipal tax credits to preserve natural capital. As to the actual source of funds, I would much prefer a CAP tax to a one-percentage-point increase in the GST. A CAP tax would directly target "bads" that result in environmental degradation; and its revenues could more easily be directed toward environmental benefits than could additional revenue from the GST, for which there would be many competitors. The CAP tax might also be more politically acceptable than an increase in the GST.

The relevance of the Olewiler proposals to my fourth criterion, demographic fit, is less immediately apparent. Certain demographic trends, however, suggest that there could be growing political support for a strategy such as this. David Foot claims that baby boomers are entering a phase in which many will acquire second homes at some remove from major cities; they are seeking peace and quiet and, by extension, the benefits of natural capital. Not inconsistent with this trend is the fact that a growing proportion of the population is concentrated in major urban areas, the principal loci of air pollution, and thus constitutes a strong base of potential support for antipollution policies.

The equity criterion poses a challenge for Olewiler's proposals. The CAP tax is regressive, given its insensitivity to income and ability to pay. It places a proportionately heavier burden on lower-income groups than on higher-income ones. Furthermore, taxing vehicle emissions would place a heavier financial burden on those in rural areas, who must drive greater distances to get to work and to pursue other regular activities, than it would on those in areas of greater population density, where necessities are closer at hand and there are alternative transit options. This should, however, be a transitional problem, since the tax would decline as the sources of carbon emissions and air pollutants were replaced with cleaner technologies. Furthermore, the tax could include refundable credits for low-income families, as does the GST.

Another problem related to equity is that those with low incomes would be less able to access and enjoy the areas of natural capital preserved under this policy.

Some areas purchased outright by government could be made available for limited public recreational use, but low-income individuals and families might lack the leisure time to visit these areas. Conservation easements would be much less likely to allow public access to the areas preserved; they would principally benefit those living on or adjacent to the protected private land. This suggests that in choosing between outright purchase and the purchase of easements, governments should favour the outright purchase option in areas with the greatest potential for effective public recreational use.

With regard to the criterion of regional balance and the proper national role, the Olewiler proposals face their greatest hurdle. Clearly, the costs of a CAP tax would fall differentially across industries and regions; in particular, they would be felt in the resource extraction, energy production and automotive industries concentrated in Alberta and Ontario. A new federal tax and associated spending program with such differential impacts would carry great political risk, as Olewiler recognizes with her puckish statement that a measure of success for the program would be to still have Alberta in the federation five years after the program's launch. Furthermore, the idea of purchasing public rights to natural capital with the CAP tax revenue is not an obvious fit for the federal government, given that such capital is fixed in place and likely located within the boundaries of a single province. The reality, however, is that the effects of environmental damage spill over provincial borders, thus prompting federal action.[6]

Finally, the Olewiler proposals accord very nicely with the seventh criterion: they relate a national narrative. They speak to the responsible stewardship of two of Canada's most distinctive characteristics — its energy resources and its natural beauty. They create incentives for technological innovation in a globally important field in which Canada is an important player. Together with the other pieces of my policy package (which I will discuss next), they form part of the narrative of a nation that is building upon its key assets to address pressing risks and to create a better future.

Building human capital: immigration and credential recognition

My chosen policy for building human capital comes not from Craig Riddell's contribution to this volume on that topic, but from David Foot's chapter on demographic change, buttressed by the commentaries offered by Serge Coulombe on Riddell's chapter and Don Drummond on Andrew Sharpe's chapter dealing with productivity. Riddell makes a persuasive case for the social and economic importance of human capital in presenting his proposals for investment in education; but, as Jane Gaskell observes in her comments on his contribution, those proposals are not sufficiently supported by analysis of the design issues that arise in negotiating the federal-provincial and institutional labyrinths in this field. Coulombe offers an alternative focus — a "smarter" immigration policy more closely geared to labour market demand. Interestingly, Drummond, in commenting on Sharpe's chapter, also posits such a policy as a preferable alternative to Sharpe's proposals. Fortunately for us judges — who, according to the rules of this exercise, must choose only from the options on offer — Foot has addressed the immigration issue.

He argues that, in the context of population aging and low population growth, immigration is a key to ensuring that the workforce grows at least in line with the population. Indeed, Canada's 2006 census (released after Foot's chapter was written) projects that essentially all population growth will be attributable to immigration by 2030. However, recent waves of immigration have been only imperfectly integrated into the workforce and the community. As Foot notes, unemployment rates among recent immigrants are higher than those in the general population. And as Jeffrey Reitz and Rupa Banerjee have shown, there has been a downward trend not only in employment rates but also in the relative earnings of successive cohorts of immigrants (2007, 491-9). The authors also note, referencing a Statistics Canada survey of immigrants arriving between October 2000 and September 2001, that "the lack of recognition of foreign credentials or experience is one of the most commonly reported employment problems — along with lack of Canadian job experience and official language knowledge" (Reitz and Banerjee 2007, 499). The underrecognition of foreign credentials costs the Canadian economy an estimated $3.4 to $4.9 billion annually (Alboim and McIsaac 2007, 9).

These problems are amenable to action at the national level. Foot argues for a policy requiring every occupational licensing authority in Canada "to establish a procedure that allows immigrants to apply for certification through a timely, well-defined procedure of appropriate testing to ensure that their qualifications meet the current standards of the occupation." As far as it goes, this is a worthy recommendation, but it needs to be better developed. The decision to leave the development of these certification procedures to provincial licensing authorities, as Foot recommends, has the advantage of placing policy implementation in the hands of those who have the relevant expertise, but it risks replicating the barriers to interprovincial labour mobility that plague these occupational areas more generally.

Coulombe offers an enhancement to this approach in his comments on Riddell's chapter. He suggests changing the selection criteria for immigrants to favour certain types of skill, as determined by domestic labour market demand, and he links this to the recognition of foreign credentials, as Quebec has done. He also notes that the federal Foreign Credential Recognition Program (FCRP) attempts to work with all the relevant actors — provincial and territorial governments, licensing and regulatory bodies, sector councils, employers — but, as Alboim and McIsaac argue, the FCRP is limited in size and scope, and "the challenge of integrating skilled immigrants into the labour market requires a more comprehensive and systematic approach" (2007, 12). This is an issue that would clearly benefit from the economies of scale afforded at the national level: there is no need to multiply by 14 the policy development effort in each professional group by having separate processes for each governmental jurisdiction.

A policy focused on facilitating the integration of immigrants into the Canadian labour force accords with the seven criteria I have outlined for my selection process. First, the policy has long-term benefits in that it maintains and improves productivity as the Canadian-born population ages; it also has a short-term payoff, meeting needs in areas where there is immediate high demand and where the timelines to educate the necessary workforce domestically are relatively long. One of the most telling current examples of such a need is in the health care arena. Limitations on supply, given the current stock of health care personnel and the long educational timelines, constitute a major constraint on the adoption of new and more effective policy approaches.

With regard to the second criterion — analytic support — this proposal must be given a mixed assessment. Foot and Coulombe reference compelling evidence of the problem of workforce barriers to immigrants, as well as examples of current activities that might contribute to an appropriate response. Putting effective policy into place, however, will require building in a strong data-gathering and analytic component.

When it comes to the third criterion — the effective stewardship of public funds and leveraging of private and third-sector resources — this proposal succeeds by drawing professional bodies and employers into the process of credential recognition and bringing their expertise and experience to bear.

Regarding its fit with demographic shifts, the fourth criterion, this policy is clearly a winner. It recognizes the importance of immigration as the principal source of future population growth and channels immigrants into productive engagement with the economy and society in ways that not only meet growing labour market demands deriving from population aging but also strengthen the social fabric by addressing the alienation experienced by immigrants in recent decades.

In relation to the criterion of equity, the implications of this proposal are more complex. On an individual level, ensuring that the value of each person's human capital is appropriately recognized promotes equity in the labour market. On a global level, drawing highly trained foreign workers to Canada may raise some equity concerns. However, in an increasingly interconnected global economy it is unrealistic to erect or maintain barriers to labour mobility; other mechanisms for promoting international economic development need to be considered.

With respect to the sixth criterion, that of regional balance and the proper national role, a policy that draws together federal, provincial and territorial governments, licensing bodies and employer groups under the federal aegis to address immigrant selection and foreign credential recognition seems appropriate, if complicated. All regions stand to benefit from the proposal, some because they are immigration magnets and others because they are particularly affected by population aging and in need of the relevant services — health care, in particular. Immigration is, constitutionally, an area of shared federal-provincial jurisdiction, and the argument regarding economies of scale presented earlier provides a strong rationale for action at the national level.[7]

Finally, as concerns the criterion of expression within an overarching policy narrative, a policy that facilitates the embracing of immigrants accords strongly with a narrative of Canada as a favoured nation and a destination for people around the world who seek to build a better future.

Health care: national pharmacare

A number of the policy proposals identified in the CPA exercise are at least arguably better addressed at the provincial level than the national level. The fiscal capacity of provincial governments to respond to these proposals is, however, constrained by health care costs, which are growing faster than provincial revenues and thus consuming an increasing share of provincial budgets. In their contribution to this volume, Robert Evans, Clyde Hertzman and Steve Morgan make the valid point that this crowding-out phenomenon results in large part from the deficit- and tax-reduction agendas pursued by all Canadian governments since the mid-1990s. Government spending on health care as a proportion of GDP peaked in the recession of the early 1990s, and current levels remain below that peak.[8] It is unrealistic to expect Canada's particular plateau of tax tolerance to increase appreciably in the foreseeable future. However, in at least one area, a reallocation of federal and provincial responsibilities could free up some capacity at the provincial level. Were the federal government to assume major responsibility for the fastest-growing component of health costs — out-of-hospital prescription drugs — it would relieve some pressure on provincial budgets. It would also create a framework in which Ottawa, through its purchasing power and established regulatory expertise, would be in a much stronger position to negotiate drug prices with pharmaceutical manufacturers than any provincial government.

Evans, Hertzman and Morgan propose a national pharmacare program, to be established incrementally. In the first phase, the federal government would assume half the cost (with the provincial governments) of providing first-dollar universal coverage for the most common classes of prescription drugs — such as those aimed at treating diabetes, asthma, cardiovascular diseases and depression. The program would be strictly managed to include only evidence-based and cost-effective drugs (individuals could continue to purchase alternative drugs themselves or through private insurance plans). Because drug spending in Canada is concentrated in a relatively few categories, a program of this type could quickly account for a significant proportion of total expenditure. A separate federal fund would cover drugs for rare diseases (although no rationale is given for maintaining a separate fund for this purpose). Existing provincial programs for seniors and social assistance recipients, as well as employer-based programs, would remain in place for drugs not covered by the new federal-provincial plan. Over time, as the success of the program in providing access to effective drugs was demonstrated, more drugs could be added to the national formulary. At the outset, however, these proposals would deal very cleverly at the national level both with common drugs (hence consolidating great purchasing power in a national agency) and with drugs that are rarely prescribed (although such drugs could be highly politically significant), allowing for a broader pooling of risk.

Evans, Hertzman and Morgan propose that the costs of the core program be borne "evenly" by federal and provincial governments, although they present no details on the cost allocations. This would, however, ensnare the program unnecessarily in ongoing federal-provincial negotiations. A better approach might be to convert a portion of the existing federal Canada Health Transfer (CHT) to this purpose — sufficient to fund roughly half the cost of the program[9] — and to have the federal government assume full responsibility for the program going forward. In any event, this program would likely free up some fiscal space for provincial governments. It would also be a windfall for employers and employees, opening up the possibility of a payroll tax and/or premium that would contribute to the funding of the program. Furthermore, it is not clear why the authors consider appropriate only modest co-payments limited to dispensing fees rather than more substantial, income-related deductibles or co-payments.

This policy proposal generally fares well in terms of the seven criteria that have governed my choice of policy options. First, a national pharmacare program offers both long- and short-term benefits. Over the long term, it promises to diminish a major source of fiscal pressure on provincial governments, affording them greater resources to deal with policy priorities other than health care. In the short term, it provides immediate benefits to a substantial proportion of the patient population with chronic diseases. It also creates a constituency of beneficiaries with a stake in extending the program into the future.

Second, the proposal is reasonably well supported by evidence and analysis. Evans, Hertzman and Morgan draw on the experience of a country other than Canada (New Zealand) to demonstrate the effect of public purchasing programs that incorporate cost-effectiveness criteria. (Surprisingly, given that the authors are affiliated with the University of British Columbia and are deeply engaged in BC health policy development, they do not adduce the BC experience with reference pricing for publicly covered pharmaceuticals.)[10] However, in fine-tuning the design of the program, more careful attention needs to be given to the modelling of the policy's impact on federal, provincial, employer and household budgets. The proposal also implies an ongoing capacity for identifying evidence-based and cost-effective treatment. This would presumably build on existing processes such as the Common Drug Review, but the authors do not propose a specific mechanism.

Third, regarding stewardship of public funds and leverage of other sectors, this proposal is somewhat more problematic. There is no question that a national pharmacare program along the lines proposed would transfer substantial expenditures from the private sector to the public sector. Shifting to a single-payer model should have the longer-term effect of containing price increases and hence overall drug expenditures, as it has in Australia and New Zealand; but this would require a substantial increase in the public budget for health care. Evans, Hertzman and Morgan do not identify a new source of revenue to fund this increase; but, as I noted earlier, some of the windfalls that provincial governments, employers and individuals receive as a result of this change could be captured and redirected toward funding the program (for example, through conversion of part of the CHT, through a payroll tax and/or through income-related premiums, deductibles and co-payments).[11]

With regard to the fourth criterion, demographic fit, the proposal scores a direct hit by offering a way of dealing more effectively and efficiently with one of the major sources of cost pressure on both public and private payers associated with an aging population: the cost of prescription drugs.

As for equity, the fifth criterion, this proposal goes some distance toward addressing one of the principal inequities remaining in Canadian health care — uneven coverage for prescription drugs, which leaves many low-income Canadians (other than social assistance recipients and seniors) at risk of substantial drug expenditures. Megan Coombes, Steve Morgan, Morris Barer and Nino Pagliccia (2004) have shown that the percentage of households at risk of spending more than 4 percent of their income on prescription drugs varies from zero in Saskatchewan, Manitoba and Ontario to between 5 and 8 percent in the Atlantic provinces.

Measured against the sixth criterion, regional balance and the proper national role, this proposal is also attractive. It establishes a core basket of common drugs — accounting for almost half of all drug expenditures — that would be covered on uniform terms and conditions across Canada, creating a single national entity with substantial negotiating and purchasing power. In so doing, it takes advantage of economies of scale in areas where there is likely to be little dispute about which drugs should be covered. It leaves room for provincial discretion with regard to coverage of other drugs. Admittedly, by leaving a multitude of drugs to be covered by provincial and private plans, the policy would create considerable administrative complexity. Those suffering from chronic conditions treatable with the classes of drugs covered under the national program would likely suffer from other ailments as well, and so they would be forced to obtain what they needed from several plans. Over time, however, this problem would be mitigated as drug classes migrated to the national program.

Turning to the final criterion, this proposal resonates with a national narrative of privilege, obligation and future orientation. It builds upon our image of Canada as a country sensitive to communal obligation and touches upon an iconic representation of this obligation: medicare. It redresses a major source of inequity resulting from the design of medicare (its exclusive focus on physicians and hospitals) and keeps pace with technological developments that give drugs an ever-more-central place in the health care panoply. The proposal also allows for continued experimentation at the provincial level with respect to coverage of drugs beyond the core basket.

THE ROADS NOT TAKEN

It is incumbent upon me to say something about the policy options that I have not selected. The runner-up was a national program of early childhood development, as proposed by Evans, Hertzman and Morgan and also by Riddell. Clearly, investment in child development is critical to the future of this country. It also accords very well with a forward-looking narrative of privilege and obligation. However, I am not persuaded by either of these contributions that enough is known about the design of such programs to justify adopting a national template at this time. On the contrary, the state of research evidence suggests that continued experimentation at the provincial level is most appropriate. A federal program of support for different provincial models is a possibility, and it would signal the importance of this policy area to the country as a whole; but such an option was not offered in the CPA exercise.

Policy action in two other areas of human capital development — secondary and post-secondary education — is also of great importance. However, I was persuaded by Coulombe's and Gaskell's commentaries on Riddell's chapter that more attention must be given to the intergovernmental, institutional and sociological contexts before national action is taken with respect to secondary education. In the area of post-secondary education, there is a strong rationale for action at the national level, given the mobility of highly educated individuals and the importance of higher education to national prosperity. However, I was also persuaded by the commentators that the policy option offered — a national merit-based scholarship program of student aid — should not be implemented without a root-and-branch review of the existing congeries of student aid programs at the federal, provincial and institutional levels. Canada's student aid mix is in dire need of reform;[12] concerted action must be taken involving all of these levels but, given the magnitude of the political challenges involved in such an undertaking, it is perhaps not surprising that it was not one of the options presented to the CPA judges.

Some proposals were offered as alternatives to the ones that I have selected — for example, the Mark Jaccard and Nic Rivers proposal for a carbon management system based on certificates. This is a very creative proposal with considerable promise, but, as Jaccard and Rivers themselves acknowledge, it is second best to a carbon tax, which they believe to be politically infeasible. I would place my bet, however, on Olewiler's formulation of the CAP tax and associated expenditures as the proposal that could provide a way out of this dilemma.

The Duclos proposal for a universal basic income is time-honoured and worthy. It can, however — as commentator David Green has suggested — be approached incrementally through reforms to the tax system, such as making more tax credits refundable. I proposed this earlier with respect to the CAP tax; and I have also suggested that a national pharmacare program be funded in part through income-related contributions.

I was attracted to Sharpe's proposal to harmonize the PST with the GST in the five provinces in which this has not been done. The exchange between Sharpe and Drummond, however, persuaded me that the revenue implications of this action must be better understood and agreed upon before such a proposal is implemented. Sharpe's policy proposals aimed at facilitating interprovincial migration are commendable, but, as Drummond and Richard Harris note in their commentaries on Sharpe's chapter, they are likely to have only limited marginal impact.

Finally, Michael Hart's proposals to reduce domestic impediments to Canadian global engagement are persuasive. In light of crossnational experience, however, it would appear that such action, as well as action recommended by Hart on other fronts, is likely to occur on an incremental basis in response to broad economic and geopolitical forces.[13] As for Hart's proposals for greater integration with the United States, these step into highly complex and controversial territory, and nothing less than a new Macdonald Commission would be necessary to investigate this ground and build consensus on the appropriate policy responses.

SUMMARY

I have selected a policy package for Canada that builds on key assets, that is forward-looking, that addresses a growing source of fiscal pressure while meeting an urgent need and that offers benefits in both the long and the short term — all in ways that are congruent with a national approach. A CAP tax can drive technological innovation in the energy field and position Canada to build on its status as an energy superpower by developing environmentally sustainable methods of resource extraction and energy production. Embracing new arrivals and allowing them to achieve their full potential in this country can enhance prosperity and the social harmony in which Canadians have taken such pride. A national pharmacare plan supported by contributory funding arrangements can ease the pressure of an aging population in a sustainable and equitable manner. These are policy areas in which there is a clear advantage to creating national strategies, and the policy package presented here can make an important contribution to a new Canadian priorities agenda.

NOTES

1 Or, alternatively, they should form part of a coherent policy package that contains both long-term and short-term payoffs, as I will discuss later.

2 An example of such constituencies would be new industries that emerge in response to business opportunities opened up by policy change; I will discuss this more fully later.

3 A time-honoured example of such levering is the state regulation of professions through the self-governing bodies of the professions themselves.

4 I recognize that this terminology is English Canadian usage and is disputed in Quebec.

5 In fact, the difference in professed values between the Canadian and American publics is less than this self-image would imply; and both countries show significant internal variation across regions (Inglehart, Nevitte and Basanez 1996; Policy Research Initiative 2006). However, Michael Adams, among others, has argued that the value structures of the two countries diverged over the 1980s and 1990s (Adams 2003).

6 However, a number of factors contribute to the argument that the federal government should assume such a role. Even a fairly constrained view of the federal role, such as that offered by Roger Gibbins, recognizes the appropriateness of federal action through the tax system to "provide incentives that promote environmentally friendly behaviour," as well as the legitimate federal interest in environmental "bads," such as air pollutants (and, by extension, greenhouse gases) that enter the atmosphere without respect for jurisdictional boundaries (Gibbins 2006, 87).

7 Given that Quebec currently administers its own programs for economic migrants, and in light of its particular need to incorporate French-language ability in the credential recognition process, it may be necessary to allow for a linked parallel process in that province.

8 There was a dramatic and politically disruptive fiscal swing in the area of health care from 1993 to 1998, both in real per capita terms and relative to GDP, as an unprecedented decline was followed by the beginning of a steep recovery (Tuohy 2002).

9 The basis for this conversion of the CHT would be highly contested. Using national average costs as a basis would penalize the have-not Atlantic provinces, which operate relatively slim drug coverage programs; but using province-specific costs would penalize those provinces that currently offer the most generous programs.

10 This mechanism ensures that public coverage is limited to the least costly drug in each therapeutic class while allowing individuals to purchase other drugs at their own expense.

11 Rather than taking a disease-category approach to coverage, one could do as Quebec has done and wrap a universal comprehensive public plan around existing employer-based plans, partially funding the public portion through premiums, deductibles and co-payments. This approach, however, while leveraging existing arrangements, would lack a substantial benefit of the single-payer plan: control over prices and overall costs.

12 See, for example, the recommendations in Bob Rae's review of post-secondary education in Ontario (2005, 72-86).

13 I would also like to have seen some suggestions for more appropriate ways in which governments could create what Maryann Feldman and Roger Martin call "jurisdictional advantage" for firms (2004).

REFERENCES

Adams, M. 2003. *Fire and Ice: The United States, Canada and the Myth of Converging Values*. Toronto: Penguin Canada.

Alboim, N., and E. McIsaac. 2007. "Making the Connections: Ottawa's Role in Immigrant Employment." *IRPP Choices* 9, no. 3.

Casey, B., H. Oxley, E. Whitehouse, P. Antolin, R. Duval, and W. Leibfritz. 2003. "Policies for an Aging Society: Recent Measures and Areas for Further Reform." *Economics Department Working Paper* 369. Paris: Organisation for Economic Co-operation and Development.

Coombes, M., S. Morgan, M.L. Barer, and N. Pagliccia. 2004. "Who's the Fairest of Them All? Which Provincial Pharmacare Model Would Best Protect Canadians against Catastrophic Drug Costs?" *Longwoods Review* 2 (3):13-26.

Feldman, M.P., and R. Martin. 2004. "Jurisdictional Advantage." *NBER Working Paper* W10802. Washington, DC: National Bureau of Economic Research.

Gibbins, R. 2006. "Canadian Federalism in an Age of Globalization: The Case for a New National Policy." In *Canada by Picasso: The Faces of Federalism*, edited by R. Gibbins, J. Gross Stein, and A. Maioni. Ottawa: Conference Board of Canada.

Inglehart, R., N. Nevitte, and M. Basanez. 1996. *The North American Trajectory: Cultural, Economic and Political Ties among the United States, Canada and Mexico*. New York: Aldine de Gruyter.

Policy Research Initiative. 2006. "Canada-US Relations and the Emergence of Cross-Border Regions." *North American Linkages Briefing Note*. Ottawa: Government of Canada, Policy Research Initiative. Accessed August 8, 2007. policyresearch.gc.ca/doclib/XBorder_BN_e.pdf

Rae, B. 2005. *Ontario: A Leader in Learning. Report and Recommendations*. Toronto: Queen's Printer. Accessed August 8, 2007. www.edu.gov.on.ca/eng/document/reports/postsec.pdf

Reitz, J.G., and R. Banerjee. 2007. "Racial Inequality, Social Cohesion and Policy Issues in Canada." In *Belonging? Diversity, Recognition and Shared Citizenship in Canada*, edited by K. Banting, T.J. Courchene, and F.L. Seidle. *The Art of the State*, vol. 3. Montreal: Institute for Research on Public Policy.

Tuohy, C.H. 2002. "The Costs of Constraint and the Prospects for Health Care Reform in Canada." *Health Affairs* 21 (3): 33-46.

THINK SMALL AND DO NO HARM
William Watson

JUDGING

My mother, who worked as a secretary in a law firm before raising a family, has always been disappointed that none of her children became a lawyer. She will be very impressed that one has now made judge. Not a real judge, fortunately. When I was running the editorial pages of Conrad Black's *Ottawa Citizen* in the late 1990s and we weren't quite sure whether our position on a given issue was right (and, despite what people might think of Lord Black's newspapers, there were times when we had doubts), we took comfort in knowing our editorials weren't Supreme Court decisions. If they were at all consequential, it was only over the long run and in a very indirect and marginal way. I take the same comfort here. This IRPP Canadian Priorities Agenda court has heard a number of strong arguments for several very good policies (as well as some strong arguments for several very bad policies: raising minimum wages to improve people's health, for instance), and it has had a hard time choosing among them. It is a relief, therefore, not to have the last word on exactly which, if any, policies will be adopted but rather to stop at simply commending a subset of them to Canadians for further consideration.

These days, there is much talk of bias among judges — not of the petty, corrupt variety, but rather the bias emerging from the fact that judges all went to the same law schools, read the same canon and breathed the same ideologies during their intellectually formative years. Let me now list my own policy biases, which have guided my selection of five favourites from among the twenty-four policies pitched to us (or really twenty-eight, given David Foot's six recommendations and Craig Riddell's four).

I favour small, unambitious policies with relatively certain payoffs over large, daring, imaginative, even visionary policies whose payoffs are very uncertain. Such policies often have unintended consequences and their pursuit can be rife with rent seeking — that is, searching for rewards by lobbying legislators for regulatory or fiscal privileges rather than engaging in the production of useful goods and services. In short, my preference is always for low-hanging fruit, even when it seems not as plump or inviting as fruit whose harvest may require leaning out dangerously from the top of the ladder. Jean Chrétien was widely derided as a do-nothing prime minister, albeit one whose instinct for inertia was much needed after the transformative derring-do of Brian Mulroney; but, in fact, during the Chrétien years, Canadian society made good progress over a wide range of indicators — not least, per capita GDP. Time is long. Over the years, the effects of modest incrementalism can accumulate into impressive improvements.

Like most of the other judges, I suspect, I used a scorecard to decide what I thought of the different policy proposals. Mine had four entries: the size of the problem; the likely efficacy of the proposed policy; the state of our policy-relevant knowledge in the area; and, finally, the political "flyability" of the proposed policy. This last criterion I considered the least important. We judges, operating outside the political system, should concern ourselves with a policy's inherent virtues. We should also have our eyes on the long run. If the policy must be implemented next week, political flyability is crucial. Over a longer term, it is not. One of the (regrettably few) payoffs to growing older is understanding that political acceptability changes over time. In the 1970s, I never thought Canada would negotiate a free trade agreement with the United States. But it did. In the 1980s, I never thought the federal government would get its fiscal house in order. But it did. Moreover, flyability goes both ways. A policy may be perfectly flyable; it may even be politically irresistible, as virtually any policy having to do with green matters appears to be these days. But high flyability ratings do not guarantee a policy is good. In doing my own private rankings, I therefore tried out policies both with and without consideration of flyability and in the end ignored it.

As to the first criterion, the size of the problem is obviously important. It's good to solve small problems, and if solutions are readily available, they should be implemented and the problems checked off on government's to-do list.[1] Still, all else being equal, it's better to solve a big problem than a little one. Policies aimed at solving big problems therefore get more points than those seeking more modest ends.

The efficacy of a policy is also obviously crucial. Tilting at windmills may be good for the soul, but the goal of policy is to actually get things done. If a policy isn't really of much use in bringing about even a strongly desired end, it must be marked down. That may seem obvious, but, in fact, efficacy is often neglected in modern Canadian politics; governments increasingly seem motivated by a desire to be seen to be "doing something" about perceived problems, however unlikely the "something" may be to solve the problem. In question period, the relevant minister must have a checklist of actions taken in order to demonstrate that he or she cares sufficiently about the problem of the day. At budget time, the minister of finance must have a spending line with enough zeros after the dollar sign to express appropriate concern for the problem, whether or not the money can reasonably be expected to have an ameliorative effect. "Don't just do something. Stand there" is the hardest thing in modern politics — even, apparently, for Conservatives.

A related, but not identical, concern is the state of our knowledge of the given policy area. How much do we really know about what is causing the problem we'd like to solve? And how certain are we that a policy will have the effects we'd like it to have? Of course, this reasoning can also work in reverse. There are both "known" and "unknown unknowns," to quote Donald Rumsfeld, who has been unjustly maligned for his in fact very discerning analysis of the policy-maker's informational plight.[2] If our ignorance is great and we know our ignorance is great, and the policy recommended is simply to try to reduce our ignorance — as is Nancy Olewiler's proposal for a Canada conservation audit — then that policy might well recommend itself.

With those preliminaries concluded, let me run through my ranking of the different policy areas according to the three criteria (or maybe three and a half, counting flyability); and then, after hinting broadly, I will finally reveal my preferences for the top five.

THE SIZE OF THE PROBLEM

The biggest problem, or at least potential problem, we judges were confronted with was global warming. It is, as its name suggests, not just a Canada-scale but an earth-scale phenomenon. Depending on which estimates you believe, climate change will have effects that are either relatively benign (especially in some parts of the world, such as ours) or quite disastrous. Whichever turns out to be true, everyone is disquieted at least somewhat by the prospect of human actions that have long-lived effects on the state of the entire atmosphere. None of the other policy problems we heard about had such enormous potential ramifications. All three policies Mark Jaccard and Nic Rivers proposed, therefore, got a five out of five on my scorecard for the importance of the problem they address.

I didn't plan it this way, but it turns out that most of the policies that got a four out of five in terms of importance — although they range from things like Canada-US relations to university scholarships to early childhood education — ultimately have to do with productivity, which is obviously a crucial influence on Canadian living standards in the long run. Michael Hart's policy triad of working on Canada-US border issues, improving regulatory harmonization and building Canada-US institutions deals entirely with Canada-US relations, particularly economic relations. For Canada, good economic relations with the US are crucial, have always been crucial and, despite a mysterious fall in trade ratios recently, will likely always be crucial. In economic terms, we are an appendage of the US economy, albeit a rather large appendage, and while the US would doubtless survive an appendectomy, we would not.

A number of other programs are targeted at quite serious problems. Merit-based university scholarships for low-income students address the possibility that sizable economic gains — mainly personal, but possibly also social — are to be had from tapping a so-far underdeveloped segment of society. A targeted early childhood education program would try to do the same thing. So, in a way, would Jean-Yves Duclos' proposal to move the employment insurance system to insurance principles, thus ending the permanent subsidy to part-time work — and almost-full-time unemployment — in seasonal industries.[3] David Foot's idea of boosting immigration after 2015 is aimed at smoothing demographic changes that will probably have big consequences for Canadian incomes if dependency ratios rise as much as some, but not all, forecasts suggest. (Whether, realistically, we can do much to minimize such a rise is another question.) Removing provincial sales taxes on machinery and equipment purchases might not have a big productivity payoff, but the policy does aim at closing the productivity gap with the US, which is clearly an important goal, however we choose to spend the extra output. Canadians tempted to dismiss concern for the productivity gap as crass materialism born of an excessive, American-style individualism alien to our gentler Canadian collectivist tradition should consider that the US has lower tax rates than we do and yet spends more than us in per capita terms on important social programs such as publicly funded health care. That's a clear advantage of higher productivity, and it's what makes higher productivity such an important goal, despite the average Canadian's apparent lack of interest in it.

Other policies aim at problems that strike me as being less serious. Not being able to practise a profession for which you are qualified must be a terribly frustrating experience, but I can't believe it's as widespread a problem as news reports often suggest. Digitizing medical records is long past due. It's galling, as you work your way through a medical problem in our system, to have to give your history again and again to people who record it with pen and paper, not even a tablet computer. But digitizing would improve productivity in just one sector of society, albeit an important one. The effects of other policies, even if they operated exactly as planned, would be limited. Is there really a large gap between the actual and optimal levels of interprovincial job search? If we got the work incentives for old age security recipients just right, it would certainly have an efficiency payoff, but how big would the payoff be from an economy-wide perspective?

THE EFFICACY OF POLICY

Which policies would be most likely to achieve their goals, however grand or modest those goals might be? Working on border issues would be relatively straightforward, if not always easy, our American partners being independent, occasionally obstreperous actors. Removing provincial sales tax on machinery and equipment purchases would also be reasonably simple and have generally predictable effects, even if the politics involved were difficult. Scattering health care facilities and services geographically so the growing number of older Canadians would have easier access to them isn't rocket science either.[4] That this hasn't yet been done presumably reflects a desire to minimize fixed costs in the health care system, which is a good thing to do only when time and trouble to patients are priced at zero. Letting old age security and Canada Pension Plan recipients work more and eliminating artificial disincentives for all seniors to take part-time work would probably also have a good effect without much complication. Once labour market incentives were correct, people could be counted on to adjust their behaviour accordingly. A qualification here is that not all such disincentives are artificial or inefficient. If employing part-time workers is more costly — if more workers have to be trained and more employment dossiers opened and administered — it seems only appropriate that part-time workers bear the costs.

At the bottom of the efficacy ladder are policies aimed at reducing greenhouse gas (GHG) emissions. As noted, global warming is an earth-scale problem. Canadian policy is essentially irrelevant to its outcome. We produce only 2 percent of the world's GHGs. Were we to evacuate the country and eliminate our emissions entirely, this would have no appreciable effect on the average world temperature in 2100 or 2200. Despite our country's physical vastness, our population is simply too small to be consequential. Nor, I suspect, are we decisively influential. It is often argued that although the direct effects of our actions would be minimal, we should nevertheless set a good example to persuade countries like India and China, which really could affect global temperatures in an appreciable way, to do the right thing. Surely that greatly overstates our influence in the world. If, despite high-level and high-visibility protests, Canada has not yet been able to secure the release of a lone Canadian dissident currently imprisoned in China, our chances of persuading the Chinese government to undertake a complete and wrenching overhaul of its entire economy must be zero. Moreover, in deciding what they will do, developing countries are likely to focus on our past actions, not our present ones, and argue that since we took a cavalier view of the environment during our industrialization they should be allowed to do the same. None of this is to say we can have no influence on Chinese or Indian environmental policy. But I suspect that in this effort our example will be much less effective than our money. If we pay developing countries to stop emitting GHGs, that may have an effect. But anything falling into the general category of moral suasion likely will not.[5]

Other policies I would judge unlikely to prove efficacious include encouraging an immigration burst after 2015 (the size of the burst required to change dependency ratios appreciably would greatly complicate problems of accommodation, and the result might well be unmanageable); assisting technology adoption rather than research and development (we have been trying to draw such fine distinctions in tax and technology policy for at least 40 years without fruitful effect); recognizing immigrants' credentials (which would be a good thing in and of itself, so long as the credentials were credible, but, again, it is unlikely to affect dependency ratios appreciably); providing tax credits for interprovincial job search (which would reward searches that people would have undertaken even without subsidies and would therefore cost many bucks per bang).

THE STATE OF OUR KNOWLEDGE

The concern here is how much confidence we can have that our policies will produce the desired effects. Start with an apparent paradox: the state of our knowledge about how much we know about our inventory of natural capital is very good; we know to a high degree of certainty that we know very little. Setting out to get more knowledge would therefore probably have a good payoff at the margin, though, since we are dealing with known and unknown unknowns, it is very difficult to say with any exactness how much we can spend before the value of acquired knowledge starts falling. The appropriate strategy is to make a one-time expenditure large enough to make a healthy dent in our ignorance, maybe via a royal commission, and, once that's done, to reassess how much we'd likely get from more spending. This approach argues against using an earmarked tax or making an open-ended commitment on spending.

We also know a great deal about what goes on at the Canada-US border (these are known knowns, though they were less studied and therefore less known before 9/11). Streamlining, harmonizing, digitizing, rationalizing and so on are likely to have reasonably predictable payoffs.

Moving down the scale of certainty, there has been lots of work in economics on capital and labour supply elasticities — at least some of it contradictory, unfortunately — and so we can be reasonably sure that changing taxes or regulations will have the kinds of effects and the scale of effects we think they will have. Promoting asset building at the bottom end of the income distribution gets only a middling mark in terms of the state of our knowledge: we haven't done much of that sort of policy development yet, so we don't really know what the response will be. Training more medical professionals and other health care workers will have the effects we want if those we train stay in Canada and work full-time, but our knowledge about both of those contingencies is imperfect. For instance, we do not yet have much experience with a physician population that is majority female, while the motives for emigration among medical professionals are widely and energetically disputed. By contrast, the expected effects of early childhood education are usually stated with great precision. The claim of seven dollars in eventual payback for every one dollar spent today is now a cliché in the discussion of such policies. My own suspicion, however, is that inferring the effects 20, 30 and 40 years later of what happens to a child between ages two and five is almost impossibly difficult. I'm therefore very skeptical about how much we really do know about the benefits of such policies.

Making schools better in order to reduce the dropout rate? No one would oppose such a goal. Moreover, I suspect that the truly big returns in education will come from getting dropouts back into the system rather than from lavishing more resources on our universities. But exactly how do we make schools better, given the strength of teachers' unions and education bureaucrats and the unknowable mystery that is the adolescent mind? We have been working on this problem for several decades, yet it persists.

Other policies for which it seems the knowledge base is not great are phased zero-emission standards for automobiles and phased carbon management for fossil fuel producers (do we really have an idea of the economic cost of these policies?); a post-2015 immigration burst (this would probably have large and complex effects on our society — do we really understand them?); and, finally, recognition of immigrants' credentials (do we know how many would succeed if we applied Canadian standards fairly, or what the effects of such supply increases on our economy and society would be?).

POLITICAL FLYABILITY

As I have mentioned, for a policy judge, the political acceptability of what is proposed should not be a crucial criterion. Still, it may be interesting to reflect briefly on which policies would be most popular. Green is clearly the policy colour *du jour*. Given the current mania for all things environmental, making building standards GHG-friendly and phasing in zero-emission standards for automobiles would probably be very popular — so long as the prices of houses and cars did not rise excessively and the costs to Ontario's car industry could be contained. Even my friend Terence Corcoran, editor of the *Financial Post* and a noted global warming skeptic, does not oppose regulation as a means of achieving environmental ends. By contrast, a serious carbon tax would cause problems in Alberta unless credible revenue recycling arrangements could be worked out.

Better management of the Canada-US border is also unlikely to be controversial, though building Canada-US institutions that have real power would be. And a Canada conservation audit is equally unlikely to be seen as objectionable, unless property owners fear it would result in expropriations. Removing the provincial sales tax on machinery and equipment purchases seems simple, but such an action can't be problem-free politically or it already would have been undertaken. Given the interaction between provincial and federal sales tax systems, regional jealousies could come into play. If Ottawa compensated provinces for switching over to harmonized taxation, would it also have to compensate the provinces that made the switch in the 1990s but did not receive exactly the same amount? "He got more than me!" is the standard battle cry of both six-year-olds and provincial premiers. There may also be a problem in that the policy would be perceived as benefiting business.

A targeted early childhood education program would face opposition from people who would want it to be universal. A universal basic income for all adults would provoke controversy because it would amount to welfare for life. People would also doubt, probably with good reason, that it would really supplant welfare agencies and workers, as it was designed to do. Raising the compulsory school-leaving age might be opposed by parents of nonproblem children who wouldn't want classrooms populated by large numbers of unwilling students. Teachers might also have concerns, even if the policy were coupled with attempts to make schooling more attractive to bored teenagers. Finally, an immigration surge would be opposed by the substantial number of Canadians who think accommodation has already gone beyond reasonable.

MY TOP FIVE

In the end, I decided to rank the policies without considering their political flyability (see table 1 on page 542).[6] My top five are:

/ Work on making the Canada-US border easier for nonterrorists to cross

/ Remove the provincial sales tax on machinery and equipment purchases

/ Conduct a Canada conservation audit

/ Provide merit-based university scholarships for low-income students

/ Move employment insurance (EI) to insurance principles

Taken as a group, these policies strike me as worthy, modest, relatively certain to produce the benefits at which they aim and, with the exception of EI reform, not very ambitious — which, to my mind, counts in their favour. Large-scale EI reform is always very difficult to achieve, but anyone who looks at policies solely in terms of benefits and costs is bound to conclude that EI badly needs to have *some* underlying principle.

My second five, again without considering flyability, are:

/ Scatter health facilities and services in a more user-friendly way

/ Standardize electronic medical records

/ Remove disincentives for the elderly to work part-time

/ Promote asset building at the bottom end of the income distribution

/ Let old age security and Canada Pension Plan (OAS/CPP) recipients work more

These second five are also reasonably unambitious. Scattering existing health facilities would be very costly, but if the principle were applied to new facilities, the lives of Canadians would be substantially improved. Hospitals could take lessons in this regard from Wal-Mart and other retail overachievers that profit by serving the needs of their customers, not those of their employees. As for medical records, governments are already trying to standardize and digitize them, though apparently without much success. Removing artificial disincentives for older Canadians — for all Canadians, for that matter — to work part-time is another small but sensible policy that seems worth developing, though any nonartificial disincentives (that is, any real costs) attached to taking part-time work should be retained. Promoting asset building at the bottom of the income distribution and letting OAS/CPP recipients work more also strike me as reasonable.

If we take a score of 8 out of 15 to be a passing grade, I pass fully 19 policies out of 28, which strikes me as far too many new policies. I'm also struck by the fact that most of the proposed policies are interventionist — this in an era in which, to my mind, governments are already much too interventionist. If we adopted all the policies described here, or even the ones a majority of judges favoured, what would happen to the ratio of taxes and/or public spending to GDP? I find it interesting and telling that when policy analysts hear the word "policy," they still understand it to mean "activist

The Policy Choices

TABLE 1.   POLICY RANKING

Policy	Ranking Score/5			Score/15
	Size of problem	Efficacy of policy	Knowledge base	
Work on Canada-US border issues	4	5	5	14
Remove provincial sales tax on machinery and equipment purchases	4	5	4	13
Conduct a Canada conservation audit	3	4	5	12
Create merit-based university scholarships for low-income students	4	4	4	12
Move EI to insurance principles	4	4	4	12
Remove disincentives for the elderly to work part-time	2	5	4	11
Standardize electronic medical records	3	4	4	11
Scatter health facilities/services geographically	3	5	3	11
Let CPP/OAS recipients work more	2	5	3	10
Promote asset building at the bottom end	4	3	3	10
Strengthen building standards to reduce GHG emissions	5	1	3	9
Train more health care professionals	4	3	2	9
Levy a conservation tax to fund the public purchase of natural capital	3	4	2	9
Introduce a targeted early childhood education program	4	3	2	9
Institute a universal basic income for all working-age adults	4	2	3	9
Use tradable rights to protect natural capital	3	4	2	9
Improve Canada-US regulatory harmonization	4	3	2	9
Provide comprehensive, universal early childhood education	3	3	2	8
Build Canada-US institutions	4	2	2	8
Introduce phased zero-emission standards for vehicles	5	1	1	7
Establish a national pharmacare program	3	2	2	7
Make schools better to reduce the dropout rate	3	2	2	7
Phase in carbon management for fossil fuel producers	5	1	1	7
Raise the compulsory school-leaving age	3	2	2	7
Assist technology adoption rather than research and development	4	1	2	7
Encourage an immigration surge after 2015	4	1	1	6
Offer tax credits for interprovincial job search	2	1	2	5
Recognize immigrants' credentials	1	1	1	3

intervention." Perhaps IRPP could hold a policy contest in which advocates proposed their three favourite *dis*interventions.

In any case, those policies I didn't pass are:

/ Phase in zero-emission standards for vehicles
/ Institute a national pharmacare program
/ Phase in carbon management for fossil fuel producers
/ Make schools better so as to reduce the dropout rate
/ Assist technology adoption rather than research and development
/ Raise the compulsory school-leaving age
/ Encourage an immigration surge after 2015
/ Provide tax credits for interprovincial job search
/ Recognize immigrants' credentials

I marked down the two GHG-targeting policies because they won't make an appreciable dent in the problem of global warming, even though it could be a very big problem. Also, we have little precise knowledge about the economic effects of such programs. In complaining about the Conservatives' Green Plan of 2007, Buzz Hargrove probably overstated the potential damage to his industry in particular and to the Canadian economy in general, but there is bound to be at least some damage, and the effects of large, economy-wide changes are always hard to estimate.

A national pharmacare program strikes me as a bad idea for two main reasons: first, because "national" has never been easy in modern Canada; and second, and more important, because most of the problems of Canadian health care have to do with too much government rather than too little. Monopolizing another part of the health sector can hardly help. Granted, there could be gains from bargaining with pharmaceutical companies for better prices — although the literature on why Canadian drug prices are lower than American ones already attributes significant market power to provincial government purchasers — but there would also be the inefficiencies and unfairnesses to which monopolies, especially government monopolies, are congenitally prone.

Making schools better in order to reduce the dropout rate is a laudable goal, but it's unlikely to be achieved without injecting much more competition, preferably through vouchers, into the school system. Raising the compulsory school-leaving age is subject to a related paradox. If we do improve schools, the compulsory school-leaving age is less likely to be binding. But if we aren't able to improve schools, we probably don't want more students kept in them against their will.

Tax credits for the cost of interprovincial job search are likely to be quite expensive and have very little influence on the margin at which people actually make decisions. Moreover, in the Internet age, such costs are declining rapidly.

Assisting technology adoption rather than research and development strikes me as yet another desperate attempt to fine-tune Canadian innovation in a way that produces innovation statistics that are more to the liking of academic analysts; it would not necessarily raise the living standard of anyone not working for a firm receiving the attendant subsidies. Over the last 40 years, I have no doubt, we would have been much better served by policies that were agnostic about what kinds of activity were most likely to bring about the different kinds of innovation that have been in and out of vogue and simply reduced taxes on entrepreneurship and investment in whatever form they appeared. "Lower the rate and broaden the base" is, still and always, the best policy rule for virtually all manner of taxes. If, after all our efforts, we still do not like our record of innovation, it is certainly not for want of tax gimmicks.

For its part, an immigration surge after 2015 would probably not take place on a large enough scale to do much about the country's demographics, though it might well be big enough to cause further difficulties in assimilating immigrants. Finally, recognizing immigrants' credentials, when they meet Canadian standards, is certainly something we should do, but it seems to me unlikely to have much effect on the problems posed by population aging.

One final note on the losing policies: in spite of what I regard as their substantive flaws, several do well in terms of political flyability. They would probably be popular. I hope the politicians do not notice.

And a final overall note: as someone who regularly teaches students about welfare gains, Pareto improvements, increases in consumer surplus and so on, and who invariably draws the associated diagrams and calculates the areas of resulting triangles and rectangles, it is a disappointment that almost none of the policy recommendations comes with any sort of welfare estimate attached. In the textbook world of policy choice, choosing is relatively easy: go for the biggest benefit-cost ratio available over the number of dollars you have available to spend. Of course, in the real world of policy choice, hunches and gut feelings — in short, judgment — are much more important. This sad but true fact does not mean policy recommendations cannot be informed by the best available information. Reading through the policy analyses produced in the Canadian Priorities Agenda exercise, I can only conclude that in that respect, at least, the advocates have served the process well.

This court stands adjourned.

NOTES

1   David Foot proposes that we give proper recognition — which is not the same as automatic recognition — to immigrants' credentials. My intuition is that it's simply not that big a problem: I doubt that there really are hundreds of Ph.D.s driving taxi-cabs in Canada — or, at least, Ph.D.s with degrees in useful subjects. But we should obviously provide immigrants with a fair chance to demonstrate, via exams and supplemental training, that their credentials are equivalent to Canadian credentials.

2   At a press conference held in Brussels on June 6, 2002, Rumsfeld declared, "Reports that say that something hasn't happened are always interesting to me, because as we know, there are known knowns; there are things we know we know. We also know there are known unknowns; that is to say we know there are some things we do not know. But there are also unknown unknowns — the ones we don't know we don't know" ("Rum Remark" 2003).

3   Duclos, by the way, wins the competition for the most startling graph. His figure 5, "Distribution of Marginal Effective Income Tax Rates, Quebec, 1999," which looks like a swarm of killer bees, should be reproduced on page A1 of every Quebec newspaper. For dramatic rhetorical effect, Jaccard and Rivers' graph of how actual carbon emissions went steadily up after 1990, despite repeated forecasts that this or that new green plan would bring them down, comes a close second, although I'd quibble that the actual path of emissions must have been at least slightly lower than the business-as-usual forecast in 1990: the mishmash of policies undertaken since then must have had some effect.

4   Unfortunately, the jurisdiction I'm most familiar with, Quebec, is heading in exactly the opposite direction, closing local facilities and planning two superhospitals. These will cost superbucks, and although they have been in the works for more than a decade, construction has not yet begun. Centralizing health care facilities in this way will, of course, increase the incidence of superbugs.

5   I also don't deny that reducing our own GHGs would make many of us feel better about ourselves, even if it didn't save the polar bears. But a cost-benefit analysis of national self-esteem is not easy to produce. Nor is it evident that there is a public policy problem here. While my contributing to various causes may make me feel better about myself, it's not clear why you should feel obliged to contribute to the same causes so I can feel better about myself. We can each take care of our own inner feelings with our own donations. To use economic jargon, there can be no market failure in the market for inner peace.

6   In fact, my top five list doesn't change even if flyability is considered, though when it is, the proposal of moving the employment insurance system to insurance principles ends up tied with three other policies: scattering health facilities geographically; standardizing electronic medical records; and removing disincentives for older Canadians to take part-time jobs. On further reflection, reforming EI may be more difficult politically than just a three out of five. The Chrétien government tried reforms that were less ambitious in the mid-1990s and was punished for it by Atlantic Canadian voters in the 1997 election. Doug Young, one of Chrétien's more courageous cabinet ministers, lost his seat and saw his political career end. If flyability were weighted more heavily, EI reform would not make the top five.

REFERENCE

"Rum Remark Wins Rumsfeld an Award: US Defence Secretary Donald Rumsfeld Has Won a 'Foot in Mouth' Award for One of His Now Legendary Bizarre Remarks." 2003. BBC News, December 2. Accessed August 8, 2007. news.bbc.co.uk/2/hi/americas/3254852.stm

PART III

THE IMPLICATIONS

EPILOGUE: SOME REFLECTIONS ON THE JUDGES' POLICY CHOICES

Jeremy Leonard, Christopher Ragan and France St-Hilaire

In this epilogue to *A Canadian Priorities Agenda*, we exercise our prerogative as editors and do exactly what we forbade the judges to do. Whereas the judges had to make their choices independently, without consulting one another, we examine the six policy packages as a whole in an attempt to draw out notable themes and identify areas of overlap and disagreement. We conclude by offering our thoughts about what these choices might suggest for policy-makers in Canada.

When this project was on the drawing board, we expected that the judges would base their policy selections on the evidence presented by the analysts and critics, melded with their own experience in witnessing and analyzing past policy successes and failures. We also expected their choices to be influenced by their respective views — some would say biases — about which elements are most important for Canada's economic and social well-being, and for this reason we chose a panel of judges with diverse backgrounds, perspectives and experiences. This diversity, combined with the high quality of the various proposals put forth by the analysts, led us to expect little in common among the six judges' final policy packages. But expectations are often wrong.

A RANGE OF APPROACHES TO POLICY SELECTION

We gave the judges complete liberty to use whatever frame of reference they felt was most appropriate as they pondered their choice of specific proposals for their preferred policy packages, insisting only that they explain their reasoning. Not surprisingly, there are some important differences in the approaches taken, including how much emphasis is placed on the political feasibility of specific policies. These marked differences illustrate the degree to which making policy choices is at least as much an art as it is a science.

Wendy Dobson, Alain Dubuc and John Helliwell use what might be termed a top-down technique in the sense that they first describe their own view of what

Canada's broad economic and social goals should be and then select the policies that come closest to achieving these goals. However, the specifics of the framework they use to govern their policy choices vary widely. Whereas Helliwell uses the lens of individual and societal well-being to guide his choices, Dobson focuses on the challenges and opportunities of globalization as an organizing theme and Dubuc makes his policy choices with an eye to Canada's "prosperity gap" — relative to its potential and to other countries. By using such frames of reference, these judges reveal, implicitly or explicitly, which of the eight policy challenges they believe are most pressing.

The other three judges — Richard Lipsey, Carolyn Tuohy and William Watson — take more of a bottom-up approach in the sense that they lay out their criteria for assessing specific proposals without explicitly establishing priorities among the eight challenges. Though this method may seem more objective than the top-down approach, the perspectives and biases of the judges nonetheless are revealed in their choices of criteria. For instance, in clearly stating his preference for small policy changes with relatively certain payoffs over large, visionary reforms with uncertain payoffs, Watson, echoing Donald Rumsfeld's concern over the extent of our policy ignorance, is careful to heed the "known unknowns" and the law of "unintended consequences." Important among Tuohy's criteria is the need for policies to fit into a "national narrative" that portrays a Canada that is richly endowed with natural resources and is a magnet for immigrants seeking a better life. Lipsey arguably adopts the most dispassionate approach, choosing those policies that appear to have the largest expected benefits relative to their costs, although both political feasibility and likelihood of implementation are very much part of his screening process. Overall, he keeps his cards close to his chest, revealing little of his world view apart from what can be inferred from his policy choices.

THE FINAL SELECTIONS

Despite these quite different approaches to policy selection, it is surprising how much overlap exists among the judges' final choices. Table 1 summarizes their choices and organizes the proposals in a way that helps draw out some of the themes that we will discuss later. Table 2 ranks the specific policies according to the number of judges who include each policy in their preferred package. Note that in table 2 only 22 policies are listed; in constructing this table, we combined two sets of policies the judges deemed to be roughly equivalent — the early childhood development programs

TABLE 1.   THE JUDGES' FINAL POLICY SELECTIONS

Wendy Dobson	Alain Dubuc	John Helliwell	Richard Lipsey	Carolyn Tuohy	William Watson
Carbon management standard (Jaccard-Rivers 1)	Carbon management standard (Jaccard-Rivers 1)	Carbon-air pollutants (CAP) tax to fund conservation initiatives (Olewiler 2)	Carbon management standard (Jaccard-Rivers 1)	Carbon-air pollutants (CAP) tax to fund conservation initiatives (Olewiler 2)	Reform EI to conform with insurance-based principles (Duclos 2)
Eliminate PST on machinery and equipment (Sharpe 2)	Eliminate PST on machinery and equipment (Sharpe 2)	National pharmacare program (Evans-Hertzman-Morgan 2)	Eliminate PST on machinery and equipment (Sharpe 2)	National pharmacare program (Evans-Hertzman-Morgan 2)	Eliminate PST on machinery and equipment (Sharpe 2)
Early childhood development program (Riddell 1, Evans-Hertzman-Morgan 1)	Early childhood development program (Riddell 1, Evans-Hertzman-Morgan 1)	Early childhood development program (Riddell 1, Evans-Hertzman-Morgan 1)	Canada's conservation plan (Olewiler 1)	Canada's conservation plan (Olewiler 1)	Canada's conservation plan (Olewiler 1)
Improve efficiency of Canada-US border administration (Hart 3)	Raise compulsory school-leaving age to 18 and improve programs to reduce dropout rates (Riddell 2)	Zero-emission vehicle standard (Jaccard-Rivers 2)	Improve efficiency of Canada-US border administration (Hart 3)	Tradable development rights to protect natural capital (Olewiler 3)	Improve efficiency of Canada-US border administration (Hart 3)
Improve immigrants' credential recognition (Foot 1)	Improve technology diffusion (Sharpe 1)	Stricter building and appliance efficiency standards (Jaccard-Rivers 3)	Increase training of medical personnel and relocate health care services closer to elderly populations (Foot 3)	Improve immigrants' credential recognition (Foot 1)	Merit-based university scholarships for low-income students (Riddell 3)

TABLE 2.   POLICY PROPOSALS RANKED ACCORDING TO THE JUDGES' SELECTIONS

Carbon management standard (Jaccard-Rivers 1); carbon-air pollutants (CAP) tax to fund conservation initiatives (Olewiler 2)	5
Eliminate PST on machinery and equipment (Sharpe 2)	4
Early childhood development program (Evans-Hertzman-Morgan 1, Riddell 1)	3
Improve efficiency of Canada-US border administration (Hart 3)	3
Canada's conservation plan (Olewiler 1)	3
National pharmacare program (Evans-Hertzman-Morgan 2)	2
Improve immigrants' credential recognition (Foot 1)	2
Zero-emission vehicle standard (Jaccard-Rivers 2)	1
Stricter building and appliance efficiency standards (Jaccard-Rivers 3)	1
Tradable development rights to protect natural capital (Olewiler 3)	1
Raise compulsory school-leaving age to 18 and improve programs to reduce dropout rates (Riddell 2)	1
Merit-based university scholarships for low-income students (Riddell 3)	1
Reform EI to conform with insurance-based principles (Duclos 2)	1
Improve technology diffusion (Sharpe 1)	1
Increase training of medical personnel and relocate health care services closer to elderly populations (Foot 3)	1
Tax credits to encourage interprovincial worker migration (Sharpe 3)	0
Adjust pension plans and payroll taxes to encourage employment of older workers (Foot 2)	0
Universal basic income for working-age adults (Duclos 1)	0
Promote asset building among low-income and middle-income individuals (Duclos 3)	0
Reduce impediments to foreign participation in the Canadian economy (Hart 1)	0
Reduce resources devoted to trade diversification (Hart 2)	0
Standardized electronic medical record (Evans-Hertzman-Morgan 3)	0

proposed by Craig Riddell and Robert Evans, Clyde Hertzman and Steve Morgan; and Nancy Olewiler's carbon-air pollutants (CAP) tax and Mark Jaccard and Nic Rivers' carbon management standard.

Is the distribution of the judges' selections in table 2 unusual, or is it roughly what we should expect from this exercise? In other words, with six judges each choosing five policies from an overall menu of 22 proposals, how likely is there to be much overlap in their final selections? To answer that question, imagine that the judges were making their policy selections randomly from the menu, with any individual policy as likely to be selected as the next. In this hypothetical case, the expected outcome in table 2 would translate into 14 policies with a single vote and 8 policies with two votes; we would expect to see no policies with zero votes and no policies with more than two votes. Put another way, if the judges were making their policy selections randomly, we would expect little overlap in their choices.

Table 2 reveals a considerable nonrandom element in the judges' policy choices. One policy is chosen by all but one judge, a second is chosen by four judges and three policies are chosen by three of the judges. On the one hand, such nonrandomness should be expected (and hoped for!) in this exercise, since all the judges are exposed to the same arguments and evidence regarding the effects of various policies. On the other hand, the degree of overlap in the final choices is surprising, given the diversity of the judges' backgrounds and perspectives and their often-divergent approaches to policy selection. One immediate observation here is that significant differences in perspectives on public policy need not lead to large differences in the final policy choices.

SOME OVERARCHING THEMES

What themes emerge from the judges' policy selections? We see three immediately: the need for greater environmental protection; the importance of human capital development; and the desire to pick low-hanging policy fruit.

The environment tops the Canadian Priorities Agenda

The first important theme reflected in the judges' choices (and in earlier parts of the CPA project) is the need for greater environmental protection. During the agenda-setters' meeting at the outset of the project, 10 of the 12 participants said they regarded the environment as a key challenge for Canada, and when the list of eight broad policy challenges was finalized, two of them focused on the environment. The judges' final selections display an even greater degree of consensus — all six judges choose at least one policy proposal that seeks to provide greater protection for Canada's natural environment (and Helliwell and Tuohy each choose three). Specifically, five judges (all except Watson) choose a policy aimed at reducing Canada's greenhouse gas emissions, and three judges choose Canada's conservation plan (Nancy Olewiler), a policy designed to take a careful inventory of the country's stock of natural resources in order to identify which are in the greatest need of protection.

For those judges who are persuaded of the need to reduce greenhouse gas emissions, the policy menu offered two alternatives: a carbon management standard (Jaccard and Rivers) and a CAP tax (Olewiler). While these are distinct proposals that differ in important ways, we group them together because both effectively put a price on polluting the atmosphere and create market-based incentives to reduce greenhouse gas emissions. Jaccard and Rivers state in their chapter that they actually favour a carbon tax as the optimal policy instrument for reducing greenhouse gas emissions. Concerns about its political feasibility, however, led them to propose a creative carbon management standard with tradable certificates, which approximates the effects of a carbon tax but differs significantly from the more familiar cap-and-trade approach used in some European countries (and much debated here in Canada). One essential difference between the Jaccard-Rivers and Olewiler policies is that the carbon management standard does not raise revenue for governments, whereas a central part of Olewiler's proposal is to use revenue generated from the CAP tax to fund natural resource conservation efforts.

One of the philosophical questions that the judges were confronted with on climate change is the fact that it is an "earth-scale problem," as Watson puts it, and since we produce only 2 percent of the world's greenhouse gas emissions, "Canadian policy is essentially irrelevant to its outcome" (537). Lipsey also highlights this dilemma, and argues that if we were mainly concerned with our own welfare, we would put much more policy emphasis on adapting to the domestic effects of climate change than on reducing our own emissions. Indeed, he adds that if such a proposal to deal with the domestic consequences of climate change had been on offer, it would have topped his list. Having made this point, he nevertheless includes an emissions reduction policy among his choices because of its demonstration effect on developing nations, and because he accepts the premise that every reduction helps. This last argument also motivated several of his fellow judges who saw this as a global commons issue requiring collective action, while others — like Tuohy and Dubuc — also stressed the competitiveness aspects and the desire to be at the forefront of new technologies in this area.

The second environmental policy that earns multiple votes is Olewiler's proposal for a conservation plan that would address a critical knowledge gap with respect to how much natural capital Canada has, how rapidly it is disappearing and what parts of it are most in need of protection. Thus, three of the judges (Lipsey, Tuohy and Watson) considered natural resource conservation to be an environmental priority quite separate from climate change and underscored the need for measures to ensure the sustainability of Canada's rich endowment of natural resources.

Finally, of the eight proposals that garner single votes, three pertain broadly to environmental protection (see table 2). This reflects an even deeper concern for these issues on the part of two judges. Indeed, in addition to Olewiler's CAP tax, Helliwell includes in his package Jaccard and Rivers' second and third proposals: to increase the proportion of zero-emission vehicles produced, and to strengthen building and appliance standards. And, in addition to Olewiler's CAP tax and conservation plan, Tuohy selects Olewiler's third proposal: to create a system of tradable development rights. In Tuohy's view, the three policies constitute a coherent and comprehensive package of measures that could form the basis of an overall environmental strategy.

In a way, the prominence of the environment file at all stages of the Canadian Priorities Agenda project is not all that surprising. Recent polls indicate that the environment has finally replaced health care as the top-of-mind issue for Canadians. The factors that give rise to such changes in the issues at the top of the policy agenda are both complex and circumstantial. The last time the environment garnered this kind of attention among policy thinkers in Canada was almost 20 years ago, when the Mulroney government made significant progress on reducing acid rain, eliminated the production of CFCs and played a substantial role in setting the agenda for the 1992 Earth Summit in Rio de Janeiro. However, the important economic adjustment costs and high rates of unemployment that followed first the implementation of the Canada-US Free Trade Agreement and then inflation-control measures in the late 1980s and early 1990s quickly pushed the environment into the shadows. By the mid-1990s, escalating public debt and deficits, particularly at the federal level, were the most pressing issue — although this problem turned out to be surprisingly short-lived as Ottawa quickly managed to turn persistent deficits into recurring surpluses. Ironically, it was in good measure because of this success that the spotlight again shifted to other issues. Indeed, federal cuts in transfers to the provinces (which were also cash-strapped) had an inevitable impact on social programs, and the health care system, showing the most visible cracks, became the top concern of Canadians.

Now, in the early years of the new millennium, the policy agenda is undergoing fundamental change yet again. Free trade is solidly entrenched and working well, unemployment is at a 30-year low, the deficit has been eliminated, and governments' books have rarely looked healthier. In recent years, the health care system has received large cash infusions, and although real progress on that front is slow and more difficult to achieve as population aging comes into play, health care as an issue has subsided somewhat for the time being. It is in this context, and against the backdrop of a global debate on climate change and its policy implications, that environmental protection has re-entered the Canadian policy spotlight.

Human capital development emerges as the all-purpose policy for economic and social well-being

A second challenge that figured prominently in the minds of the agenda-setters at the outset of this project was the need for more policy emphasis on human capital development, broadly defined. Indeed, there was unanimous agreement on the importance of human capital in contributing to overall economic and social well-being, and all 12 agenda-setters wanted to include it in the eight CPA policy challenges. The scope of human capital as a policy lever — and its multiple linkages to a wide range of economic and social objectives — is illustrated by the fact that 10 of the policy proposals put forward by the analysts have improving the use and/or development of human capital as one of their intended effects. The importance of human capital is echoed in the judges' final selections. All six judges include in their preferred policy packages at least one proposal directly related to human capital, and two of the judges include two such proposals.

The issue of early childhood development (ECD) was the focus of considerable attention and debate both at the CPA conference and in many of the contributions to this book. ECD is proposed as a key policy measure in the context of two different challenges. Evans, Hertzman and Morgan propose an ambitious universal ECD program as a way to improve long-term health outcomes, citing a wealth of international research suggesting that such programs lead to healthier, more productive lives. Riddell also cites evidence of the wide-ranging private and social benefits of ECD, in addition to the well-known economic gains to be derived from increased levels of human capital. His analysis, however, leads him to come out in favour of a targeted approach that would focus public resources on children at risk — that is, those likely to benefit the most.

Gauging the relative benefits of universality versus targeting is a central question in social policy. It also came up in the context of two other CPA challenges — health outcomes and economic security. The essence of the debate is well captured by Dobson's comments on the two ECD proposals: "The authors of both chapters agree that targeted social programs are probably more cost-effective, but such programs tend to lack broad support, which makes them politically vulnerable" (464).

Three of the six judges (Dobson, Dubuc and Helliwell) are convinced of the value of some kind of ECD program, and they include it in their policy packages, though they tend to favour Riddell's targeted approach. Whereas Dubuc is unequivocal on this issue, citing the unintended effects of Quebec's universal child care program as a case in point, Helliwell and Dobson call for an experimental, incremental approach, with initial targeting and careful monitoring to determine what is most effective. In addition, two other judges (Lipsey and Tuohy) mention that such a program, while not in their chosen sets of five, is nonetheless promising enough to be given serious consideration when more is known about the likely impact of different approaches. While it is clear that there are differences of opinion among the judges regarding the details of implementing an ECD program, it is equally clear that, as a panel, the judges show considerable support for the basic idea of investing in the human capital development of young children (though Watson is more ambivalent). Given the judges' differing perspectives and approaches to policy choice, this level of support is quite telling.

The proposal to improve the recognition of immigrants' employment credentials is another human capital policy whose importance is reflected by its inclusion in two of the judges' policy packages. David Foot advocates this policy in the context of mitigating the effects of an aging population, whereas Serge Coulombe highlights a similar option as an alternative to the three policies on human capital proposed by Riddell. It is more in the latter context that Tuohy and Dobson select it.

Two of the other policies that receive single votes also pertain to human capital (see table 2). Watson opts for merit-based university scholarships for low-income students and Dubuc includes Riddell's proposal to raise the compulsory school-leaving age to 18 and to improve high school programs for youths at risk of dropping out. In choosing this proposal, Dubuc draws attention to the dropout problem, which he describes as a "social tragedy," because of "the failed hopes it creates, the social inequities it perpetuates and the economic stakes involved" (483). Given that perspective, it is clear that he considers this policy to be a complement to a targeted ECD program, which he also selects, thereby supporting a two-pronged approach to human capital development.

CPA judges pick the low-hanging fruit

A third theme we see in the judges' selections is the appeal of picking the low-hanging policy fruit — the more circumscribed proposals that can be implemented and administered relatively easily and whose effects on economic outcomes over time can be predicted with reasonable confidence. We identify two policies as belonging in this basket (though other proposals, such as improving immigrants' credentials recognition, could also qualify). Andrew Sharpe's proposal to remove the provincial sales tax (PST) on machinery and equipment in those provinces where it still exists is designed to increase business investment and thereby improve real wages and labour productivity. Michael Hart's proposal to drastically streamline the clearance process for goods as well as the procedures for business travellers crossing the Canada-US border is designed to reduce costs and thus increase the gains from trade between the two countries. Not surprisingly, given his stated preference for low-hanging fruit, these two policies score highest on Watson's policy scorecard.

Four of the six judges include Sharpe's PST proposal in their policy packages, arguing that such a change is long overdue and that it is almost a no-brainer, as policy choices go. While this action on its own will not solve Canada's productivity problem — as Lipsey points out, "the productivity gap is a prime case of death by a thousand cuts, so dealing with it means removing a thousand causes"(511) — it is a simple and effective instrument, and all evidence presented by Sharpe and his critics indicates that it passes the cost-benefit test with flying colours.

Three of the six judges (Dobson, Lipsey and Watson) include Hart's border proposal in their policy packages. Hart's argument is that much of what is done at the border could be done elsewhere, in preclearance facilities, or dispensed with altogether, creating great benefits in terms of efficiency. He includes this measure as part of a broader proposal to deepen economic ties between the United States and Canada (a proposal that also includes seeking greater regulatory cooperation and building institutional capacity for further integration), but only the first element of his plan for streamlining border processes makes it into any of the judges' policy packages.

Hart's broader proposal does not leave any of the judges indifferent, however. Consistent with her view that the Canada-US trade relationship is central to our economic well-being, Dobson selects the border proposal for her package and chooses building institutional capacity as one of her two runners-up. Lipsey questions the need for regulatory convergence, but he would like to see a greater fleshing out of the institutional issues. However, three of the judges (Dubuc, Helliwell and Tuohy) specifically mention Hart's proposals for closer Canada-US economic ties as ones they would *not* include in their policy packages. Helliwell and Dubuc appear to reject outright Hart's call for a strategy of preferential North American integration at the expense of a more multilaterally balanced approach and his premise that this is the main issue at stake for Canada in the context of globalization. Dobson and Lipsey also make it clear that they do not think Canada should give up on multilateral trade agreements or on pursuing new trade opportunities in the rest of the world. Tuohy concludes that Hart's proposals for deeper economic integration with the United States "step into highly complex and controversial territory, and nothing less than a new Macdonald Commission would be necessary to investigate this ground and build consensus on the appropriate policy responses" (529). Watson, too, flags this as a controversial issue in

Canada. These reactions are probably an accurate reflection of the degree of polarization among Canadians over this question. This much was evident in the heated discussions at the CPA conference and in public debate during the 2007 North American Leaders' Summit at Montebello.

WHAT HAPPENED TO HEALTH CARE?

As we mentioned in our introduction, health care featured prominently at the CPA agenda-setters' meeting, although in the end it was the challenge of improving health outcomes in the population rather than ensuring the sustainability of the health care system that made it onto the final list of policy issues to be examined. Broaching health care from an outcomes-based rather than a system-based perspective leads to quite different policy proposals. As we already pointed out, one of the proposals by Evans, Hertzman and Morgan centres on ECD and the positive relationship between education and health outcomes. It has been known for some time that a variety of social factors have a determining effect on the health status of individuals. However, a number of CPA participants consider that this reality does not receive sufficient attention from policy-makers, who are more preoccupied with addressing ongoing and visible pressures on the health care system in the short term, often to the detriment of preventive measures.

The other two proposals by Evans and his colleagues — to implement a national pharmacare program and to develop a standardized electronic medical record — do relate directly to the health care system's operation. Evans, Hertzman and Morgan argue that a national pharmacare program, along the lines of New Zealand's, would reduce the price of prescription drugs through the workings of a single-payer system. It would also control the cost-without-benefit aspects of the current approval process for new drugs and, in turn, would lead to better access to needed drugs and better health outcomes. Another point they make is that by reducing the overall costs of the health care system, more public funds would be available for other programs, like ECD, that are likely to have a significant impact on long-term health outcomes. Both Tuohy and Helliwell select the pharmacare proposal, citing equity and social well-being arguments. Lipsey also expresses support, but he selects the proposal only as a runner-up, as he considers it is unlikely to be implemented due to political resistance. He ultimately opts for ramping up the training of medical personnel and improving the geographic allocation of health care services, as proposed by David Foot, but he nonetheless suggests that standardized electronic medical records could be quite beneficial and should be examined more closely. These last two policies also catch Watson's interest, and appear among his runners-up.

Finally, it is important to point out that the national pharmacare proposal also has its detractors. Watson describes it as a "bad idea," in terms of both its workability within our federal context and its requirement of large-scale government intervention. On this last point Dubuc agrees, arguing that its implementation "would turn Canada back into a 1960s-style social democratic regime" (477). Like the idea of a universal ECD program, the national pharmacare proposal draws cautions from even some of the supporting judges. As Helliwell points out, "Both of these dishes are difficult to prepare and serve. Many chefs have tried, and many smoky kitchens attest to the problems related to their design and implementation" (491).

THE POLICIES NOT CHOSEN

We have discussed the considerable overlap in some of the policies selected by the judges. The corollary, of course, is that several policy proposals put forward by the analysts failed to garner any support (see table 2). What does this imply in terms of the policy challenges and the specific measures involved? Interestingly, there is not a single broad policy challenge that strikes out with regard to the judges' choices, in the sense that each of the eight challenges is reflected in at least one of the policy proposals they selected. This could be taken as circumstantial evidence that the absence of a vote for any particular policy is more indicative of the judges' views on the relative effects, net benefits or political feasibility of that policy than it is of the relative importance of the broad challenge that it addresses. For instance, Sharpe's proposal to introduce tax credits to encourage interprovincial worker mobility finds no takers among the judges. But this does not indicate a lack of concern about productivity — Sharpe's recommendation to eliminate the PST on machinery and equipment receives considerable support, and Dubuc also includes Sharpe's proposal to improve the diffusion of technology in his final package. Moreover, Dubuc points directly to labour mobility as a serious problem linked to the broader issue of economic union. Both he and Dobson point out that they would like to have seen this challenge addressed as part of this project.

An important area of agreement that is not apparent in the results reported in tables 1 and 2 relates to Jean-Yves Duclos' proposed plan to replace the current patchwork of income security programs with a universal basic income and a reformed employment insurance (EI) program based on social insurance principles. The need for income security reform appears to have wide support among the judges, but Duclos' proposals simply do not make it into the judges' preferred policy packages except for Watson's — in this case, he throws his low-hanging-fruit caution to the wind and picks EI reform. Both Lipsey and Dubuc regard efforts to improve the current system as an extremely valuable pursuit, but they believe that Duclos' basic income proposal needs more work and more fleshing out before it can be considered. Dobson and Tuohy also find Duclos' arguments compelling, but Dobson is uncomfortable with some of the implications for the tax system and Tuohy questions the need for Duclos' big-bang approach. The collective view seems to be that the version of the proposal on offer is not yet an idea whose time has come. The debate surrounding Duclos' ambitious policy proposals also highlights the age-old tension between the benefits and drawbacks of comprehensive reform versus taking an incremental approach based on existing policies.

AN AGENDA FOR POLICY-MAKERS?

As we consider the seven policies that are chosen by two or more judges (see table 2), we are struck by the way this particular package of policies, taken as a whole, is balanced along a number of dimensions. First, it addresses a range of broad challenges — from greater environmental protection and better health outcomes to enhanced productivity and human capital development. Second, there is a mix of visionary policy changes (such as a national pharmacare program and a carbon management standard) and more circumscribed and pragmatic proposals (such as eliminating the provincial sales tax on machinery and equipment and improving the process for recognizing immigrants' credentials). Finally, the overall package of policies does not have any particular ideological slant. For instance, the idea of a universal ECD program has traditionally been associated with those on the political left, whereas the targeted approach favoured by the judges finds expression in many policies traditionally supported by those on the right. And while support for national pharmacare and strong environmental policies are also most often associated with those on the political left, the importance of adopting policies to enhance productivity and to reap greater gains from international trade is a position held strongly by those on the right.

It is important to circle back to the underlying theme of the CPA project, which is that the essence of good policy-making is the ability to make informed choices in the context of limited resources, striking a balance between the relative importance of various policy goals, the effectiveness of the specific policy instruments on offer and the political feasibility of implementing them. This project has done essentially that, and the exercise has produced a group of policies that, in addition to moving Canada forward with regard to economic and social well-being, could indeed have broad public appeal. While we certainly do not claim to have outlined the definitive priorities agenda for Canada, the policies at the top of the list of judges' selections have the legitimacy of surviving a thorough and arduous process and are thus worthy of consideration and debate. More important, it is our hope that the ideas, analyses and proposals contained in the pages of this volume will be valuable tools for policy-makers and politicians alike in years to come.

NOTES ON CONTRIBUTORS

Wiktor Adamowicz holds a Canada Research Chair in environmental economics. He is also a professor in the Department of Rural Economy and an adjunct professor in the Department of Economics at the University of Alberta. He obtained his B.Sc. and M.Sc. degrees from the University of Alberta and his Ph.D. from the University of Minnesota. His research interests are in developing methods that integrate environmental goods and services into economic analysis and designing policies and institutions that help capture the importance of environmental services in economic decision-making. His main research areas include environmental valuation, economic assessment of environmental changes and consumer choice modelling.

Serge Coulombe is a professor of economics at the University of Ottawa, which has been his base since 1982. He served as research adviser for the federal Department of Finance from 1991 to 1993; since 2005, he has been the senior research adviser to the chief economist at Industry Canada. His main areas of research include macroeconomics and economic growth, with a special interest, since 1993, in the study of Canadian provincial growth. He has published over 30 papers in refereed journals as well as numerous papers commissioned by organizations such as Industry Canada, Statistics Canada, the Bank of Canada, the C.D. Howe Institute and the Organisation for Economic Co-operation and Development. His current research deals with the relationship between human capital accumulation, migration, international trade and economic growth.

Raisa Deber is a professor in the Department of Health Policy, Management and Evaluation in the Faculty of Medicine at the University of Toronto. Having earned a Ph.D. in political science from the Massachusetts Institute of Technology, she has gone on to lecture and publish extensively on Canadian health policy; advise local, provincial, national and international bodies; and serve on editorial boards and review panels. She directs the Canadian Institutes of Health Research team in community care and health human resources. Her current projects include investigating the implications of the distribution of health expenditures and public/private roles in financing and delivering health services; examining where nurses and other health professionals work and the factors associated with differential "stickiness" across subsectors; and exploring issues associated with the movement of care from hospitals to home and community.

Wendy Dobson holds a Ph.D. in economics from Princeton University. She is the director of the Institute for International Business of the Rotman School of Management at the University of Toronto, where she is also a professor. A former associate deputy minister of finance in Ottawa, she has served as president of the C.D. Howe Institute, Canada's leading independent economic think tank. She is a nonexecutive director of several public companies engaged in international business, she serves as vice chair of the Canadian Public Accountability Board and she is a member of several international networks. Her research focuses on international economics and business, with a current interest in China and India in the world economy.

Don Drummond graduated from the University of Victoria, earned an MA in economics from Queen's University and joined the federal Department of Finance, where he spent almost 23 years working in the areas of economic analysis and forecasting, fiscal policy and tax policy. As associate deputy minister of finance, he was responsible for economic analysis, fiscal policy, tax policy, social policy and federal-provincial relations; he also coordinated the planning of the annual federal budgets. In June 2000, he joined the TD Bank as senior vice-president and chief economist, leading TD Economics in its work of analyzing and forecasting economic performance in Canada and abroad and of examining the policies that influence economic performance, including monetary and fiscal policies.

Alain Dubuc is a columnist for the Montreal daily *La Presse*. From 2001 to 2004, he was publisher of the Quebec City daily *Le Soleil*. He served as a business columnist for *La Presse* from 1981 to 1988 and was that paper's editorial page editor from 1988 to 2001. Dubuc holds an MA in economics from the Université de Montréal. He was the recipient of the National Newspaper Award for editorial writing in 1999 and a finalist for that prize in the same category in 1998 and 2000. He is the author of three books: *Simple comme l'économie* ("As simple as economics") (1987); *A Dialogue on Democracy in Canada* (2002), with John Ralston Saul; and *Éloge de la richesse* ("In praise of wealth") (2006), which was awarded the Prix du livre d'affaires for 2007 by Montreal's École des Hautes études commerciales.

Jean-Yves Duclos is a professor of economics at Université Laval as well as the director of the Centre Interuniversitaire sur le Risque, les Politiques Économiques et l'Emploi and network leader of the Poverty and Economic Policy international research network. His areas of research are public economics, econometrics, welfare economics, development economics and labour economics. He is a past president of the Société canadienne de science économique. Currently, he is the editor of the *Journal of Economic Inequality*, a member of the editorial board of the *Review of Income and Wealth* and a member of the executive council of the Society for the Study of Economic Inequality.

Robert G. Evans is a professor of economics and a University Killam Professor at the University of British Columbia. He is also the founding director of the Program in Population Health at the Canadian Institute for Advanced Research. His major publications include *Strained Mercy: The Economics of Canadian Health Care* (1984) and (as coeditor) *Why Are Some People Healthy and Others Not? The Determinants of Health of Populations* (1994). Evans served on the British Columbia Royal Commission on Health Care and Costs and on the Prime Minister's National Forum on Health. He was the first Canadian recipient of the Baxter International Foundation Prize for Health Services Research. His current primary research interest is integrating the large and systematic variations in health within populations into the basic models of health economics.

David K. Foot is a professor of economics at the University of Toronto and coauthor of the bestselling books *Boom, Bust and Echo: How to Profit from the Coming Demographic Shift* and *Boom, Bust and Echo: Profiting from the Demographic Shift in the 21st Century*. His interests lie in the interrelationships between economics and demographics and their implications for both private and public policies. He is a two-time recipient of the University of Toronto undergraduate teaching award and in 1992 won a 3M Fellowship for Teaching Excellence, an honour given each year to 10 university instructors from across Canada.

Jonathan T. Fried is the executive director for Canada, Ireland and the Caribbean at the International Monetary Fund. He was a senior foreign policy adviser to the prime minister of Canada and head of the Canada-US Secretariat from 2003 to 2006, advising on the full range of international issues affecting Canada, as well as secretary for cabinet committees on global affairs and on Canada-US relations; he was also the senior Canadian official responsible for coordinating the Security and Prosperity Partnership of North America. Fried previously served as associate deputy minister in the Department of Foreign Affairs and International Trade. He was also senior assistant deputy minister of finance and G7 deputy for Canada; a member of the board of directors of the Export Development Corporation; Canada's senior trade and economic policy official and chief negotiator on China's accession to the World Trade Organization; and Canada's lead lawyer for NAFTA and its side agreement negotiations.

Jane Gaskell holds an Ed.D. in the sociology of education from Harvard University and has taught at Queen's University and the University of British Columbia. She is currently a professor and dean at the Ontario Institute for Studies in Education at the University of Toronto. She has published in the areas of educational policy, secondary school reform, feminist approaches to education, school choice and the relation between education and work. Her published works include numerous articles and a book entitled *Educational Outcomes for the Canadian Workplace: New Frameworks for Policy and Research* (2004).

Christopher Green is a professor of economics at McGill University, where he has been since 1969. His interests have ranged widely over such fields as industrial organization and public finance; his current focus is climate change. In 1990, he became one of the founding members of (and the only economist with) McGill's Centre for Climate and Global Change Research. He is currently a member of its successor organization, the Global Environment and Climate Change Centre. He regularly teaches a course on the economics of climate change and conducts research on the potential of carbon-emission-free energy technologies and what it will take to stabilize climate.

David A. Green holds a Ph.D. in economics from Stanford University and is a professor of economics at the University of British Columbia. His areas of research interest are labour economics, applied econometrics and economic history. He was the recipient of the UBC Killam Research Prize in 2002 and the Harry Johnson Prize for the best article in the *Canadian Journal of Economics* in 2000. He has published many articles and is coauthor of the book *Dimensions of Inequality in Canada*, which won the Canadian Economic Association's Doug Purvis Memorial Prize in 2007.

Richard G. Harris is the Telus Professor of Economics at Simon Fraser University and program director of the Globalization Program in the Initiative on the New Economy research program TARGET (Team for Advanced Research on Globalization, Education and Technology), sponsored by the Social Sciences and Humanities Research Council. His major area of specialization is international economics — especially the economics of integration. From 1985 to 1988, he was a special adviser to the Canadian government in the negotiations leading to the Canada-US Free Trade Agreement. He has served as a consultant in the area of international economics for a number of Canadian government departments, international organizations and corporations. He has published policy-oriented books and articles on Canada-US free trade, international macroeconomics, economic growth and Canadian public policy. His current research is focused on the economic potential of a North America monetary union, North American economic integration and the interaction between human capital formation and globalization.

Michael Hart holds an MA from the University of Toronto and holds the Simon Reisman Chair in Trade Policy at the Norman Paterson School of International Affairs at Carleton University. He was previously an official in the Department of Foreign Affairs and International Trade, where he specialized in trade policy and trade negotiations. He was involved, as well, in the Canada-US free trade negotiations, the North American free trade negotiations, and various bilateral and multilateral negotiations. A founding director of Carleton's Centre for Trade Policy and Law, Hart is also the author, editor or coeditor of more than a dozen books and numerous articles and book chapters on international trade issues. His book *A Trading Nation: Canadian Trade Policy from Colonialism to Globalization* (2003) was shortlisted for the Donner Prize (public policy), the J.W. Dafoe Prize (history), the Donald V. Smiley Prize (political science) and the Purvis Prize (economics).

Keith Head obtained a BA from Swarthmore College and a Ph.D. in economics from the Massachusetts Institute of Technology. He is a professor in the Strategy and Business Economics division of the Sauder School of Business at the University of British Columbia. He holds the HSBC Professorship in Asian Commerce and teaches courses on international business management and the international economy. His research interests include multinational enterprises, international trade and economic geography. In 2007, he published a book entitled *Elements of Multinational Strategy*.

John F. Helliwell is the Arthur J.E. Child Foundation Fellow of the Canadian Institute of Advanced Research and codirector of its Social Interactions, Identity and Well-Being program. He is also professor emeritus of economics at the University of British Columbia, a member of the National Statistics Council and a research associate at the National Bureau of Economic Research. He was Killam Visiting Scholar at the Institute for Advanced Policy Research at the University of Calgary in 2005; visiting special adviser at the Bank of Canada in 2003-04; visiting research fellow at Merton

College, Oxford, in 2003; Christensen Visiting Fellow at St. Catherine's College, Oxford, in 2001; and Mackenzie King Visiting Professor of Canadian Studies at Harvard from 1991 to 1994. His books include *The Contribution of Human and Social Capital to Sustained Economic Growth and Well-Being* (2001) and *Globalization and Well-Being* (2002). He is a fellow of the Royal Society of Canada and an officer of the Order of Canada.

Clyde Hertzman is the director of the Human Early Learning Partnership and a professor in the Department of Health Care and Epidemiology at the University of British Columbia; he is also the associate director of UBC's Centre for Health Services and Policy Research. As well, he is a fellow in the CIFAR (Canadian Institute for Advanced Research) Successful Societies Program and Experience-Based Brain and Biological Development Program. He was the director of CIFAR's Population Health Program during its last five-year term, from 1998 to 2003, and a fellow in the Human Development Program, which also closed in 2003; he also held a Canada Research Chair in population health and human development. He has played a central role in creating a framework that links population health to human development, emphasizing the special role of early childhood development as a determinant of health.

Peter Hicks is currently with the Canada Public Service Agency. He has worked in policy research, strategic planning and policy development in many areas of the social policy field: education, health, employment, pensions and welfare. He was an assistant deputy minister in social policy departments and in central agencies in Ottawa before joining the Organisation for Economic Co-operation and Development in Paris, where he remained for six years. After returning Canada, in 2001, he worked at the Social Research and Demonstration Corporation, the Policy Research Initiative and the Department of Human Resources and Social Development Canada. Hicks holds a BA in economics and political science and an MA in political theory from the University of Toronto.

Mark Jaccard has been a professor in the School of Resource and Environmental Management at Simon Fraser University since 1986 — interrupted from 1992 to 1997 while he served as chair and CEO of the British Columbia Utilities Commission. He holds a Ph.D. from the Energy Economics and Policy Institute at the University of Grenoble. He is a member of Canada's National Roundtable on the Environment and the Economy and a research fellow at the C.D. Howe Institute. His coauthored book *The Cost of Climate Policy* won the 2002 Policy Research Institute award for best policy book in Canada, and his book *Sustainable Fossil Fuels: The Unusual Suspect in the Quest for Clean and Enduring Energy* won the 2005 Donner Prize. In 2007, his coauthored book *Hot Air: Meeting Canada's Climate Change Challenge* was published.

Jeremy Leonard is senior fellow, policy outreach, at the Institute for Research on Public Policy. He has been affiliated with the IRPP in a variety of research capacities since 1994 and is particularly interested in policies affecting innovation, productivity and long-term economic growth. Prior to his association with the IRPP, he was a policy analyst with the Committee for Economic Development, based in Washington, DC, and an economist with the Manufacturers Alliance/MAPI in Arlington, Virginia. He holds a BA in philosophy from the University of Pennsylvania and an MA in economics summa cum laude from McGill University.

Richard G. Lipsey, currently professor emeritus at Simon Fraser University, has held professorial posts at the London School of Economics, the University of Essex and Queen's University. He was a senior economic adviser for the C.D. Howe Institute from 1983 to 1989, and a fellow of the Canadian Institute for Advanced Research from 1989 to 2002. He has authored several widely used textbooks on economics, which have been translated into nearly 20 languages, and he has published extensively on theoretical and applied economics and economic policy. His recent coauthored book *Economic Transformations: General Purpose Technologies and Long Term Economic Growth* won the 2006 Schumpeter Prize for distinguished writing on evolutionary economics.

Susan A. McDaniel is a sociologist with active policy interests. Her research is on life course, demographic aging, generational relations, family change and the social impacts of technology. She is a fellow of the Royal Society of Canada and the recipient of many research awards. In 2002, she was awarded the University Cup by the University of Alberta for her continuing record of excellence in both research and teaching. She has been a professor of sociology at the Universities of Alberta, Waterloo and Windsor and she is currently a senior researcher at the Institute of Public and International Affairs and a professor of family and consumer studies at the University of Utah.

James Meadowcroft holds a Canada Research Chair in governance for sustainable development and is a professor in the School of Public Policy and Administration and in the Department of Political Science at Carleton University. After completing a BA in political science at McGill, he obtained a doctorate in political theory from Oxford

University. His recent contributions include work on public participation, sustainable development partnerships, planning for sustainability, national sustainable development strategies and sustainable energy policy. He is coeditor of the *International Political Science Review* and associate editor of the *Journal of Political Ideologies*.

Steve Morgan is a health economist at the University of British Columbia. He is an assistant professor in the Department of Health Care and Epidemiology and a faculty member at the Centre for Health Services and Policy Research. He studies pharmaceutical policy, health care financing and processes for promoting evidence-based decision-making; in his work he seeks to identify policies that provide equitable access to necessary care, manage expenditures for efficiency and provide incentives for valued innovation. After obtaining an MA from Queen's University and a Ph.D. from the University of British Columbia, he pursued postdoctoral training at UBC and at McMaster University's Centre for Health Economics and Policy Analysis. He holds career awards from the Canadian Institutes of Health Research and the Michael Smith Foundation for Health Research and is one of the Canadian alumni of the Harkness International Fellowships in Health Care Policy.

Kathy O'Hara holds an MBA from the University of British Columbia and an MA in public policy from the Kennedy School of Government at Harvard University. In 2006, she was appointed senior associate deputy minister of Human Resources and Social Development Canada. Prior to this appointment, she had been deputy secretary to the cabinet, machinery of government, at the Privy Council Office. She also served as assistant secretary to the cabinet, social development policy, at the Privy Council and held senior positions at Human Resources Development Canada, the Treasury Board Secretariat, Solicitor General of Canada and National Health and Welfare Canada.

Nancy Olewiler is a professor of economics and director of the graduate program in public policy at Simon Fraser University. Her areas of research include natural resource and environmental policy, ecological fiscal policy and public policy. She has published widely in academic and policy outlets. Her current work is on measuring and monetizing natural capital and the impact of environmental policy on Canadian competitiveness. From 1990 to 1995, she was managing editor of *Canadian Public Policy*. She is a resource person for the Environment and Economy Program for Southeast Asia of the International Development Research Centre and a director of BC Hydro.

Christopher Ragan holds an MA in economics from Queen's University and a Ph.D. in economics from the Massachusetts Institute of Technology. He is an associate professor in the Department of Economics at McGill University, where he has taught since 1989. His research deals mainly with the role of economic policy — most recently, the objectives and conduct of monetary policy. He has published several articles in economics journals and is the coauthor of *Economics* (12th edition), the most widely used introductory economics textbook in Canada. In 2004, he coedited *Is the Debt War Over? Dispatches from Canada's Fiscal Frontline*. He is the founding editor-in-chief of *World Economic Affairs*; for two years he had a regular column in the *National Post Business Magazine*; and in 2004-05, he served as special adviser to the governor of the Bank of Canada.

Dennis Raphael has a Ph.D. in educational theory from the University of Toronto and is a professor at the School of Health Policy and Management at York University. His over 130 scholarly publications focus on the health effects of income inequality and poverty, the quality of life of communities and individuals, and the impact of government decisions on Canadians' health and well-being. He is the editor of *Social Determinants of Health: Canadian Perspectives* (2004), coeditor of *Staying Alive: Critical Perspectives on Health, Illness, and Health Care* (2006) and author of *Poverty and Policy in Canada: Implications for Health and Quality of Life* (2007).

W. Craig Riddell is Royal Bank Faculty Research Professor in the Department of Economics at the University of British Columbia. His research interests are in labour economics, labour relations and public policy; his present research is focused on skill formation, education and training, unemployment and labour market dynamics, the evaluation of social programs, unionization and collective bargaining, and unemployment insurance and social assistance. He currently serves on the federal government's Expert Panel on Older Workers, he is chair of Statistics Canada's Advisory Committee on Labour and Income Statistics, and he is a member of the board of directors of the Centre for the Study of Living Standards and the Research Advisory Committee of Human Resources and Social Development Canada. He is also academic director of the Canadian Labour Market and Skills Researcher Network.

Nic Rivers works as a consultant to all levels of government, to industry and to non-governmental organizations on issues related to program evaluation, policy analysis and development, and economic modelling. He is also an active researcher, focusing on economic evaluation of climate change and energy efficiency policy, behavioural dynamics in energy economy models and technology policy. Articles based on his research have appeared in several economics and energy journals as well as in various popular publications. Rivers holds an MA in resource management.

Andrew Sharpe is founder and executive director of the Ottawa-based Centre for the Study of Living Standards (CSLS). Established in 1995, CSLS is a national, independent, nonprofit research organization devoted to the study of trends and determinants of productivity, living standards and economic well-being. Sharpe has held a variety of positions, including head of research at the Canadian Labour Market and Productivity Centre and chief of business sector analysis at the Department of Finance. He holds an MA and a Ph.D. in economics from McGill University and an MA in urban geography from the Université de Paris-Sorbonne. He is also executive director of the International Association for Research on Income and Wealth and founder and editor of the *International Productivity Monitor.*

France St-Hilaire is vice-president, research, at the Institute for Research on Public Policy, having joined the IRPP as research director in 1992. She currently oversees the institute's research agenda and coordinates ongoing projects in economic and social policy, including the Canadian Priorities Agenda. She is the author of a number of monographs and articles on public finance, social policy and fiscal federalism, as well as coeditor of several volumes published by the IRPP — including *The Review of Economic Performance and Social Progress* (2001 and 2002) and *Money, Politics and Health Care: Reconstructing the Federal-Provincial Partnership* (2004). She holds a graduate degree in economics from the Université de Montréal and has worked as a researcher at the Institute for Policy Analysis at the University of Toronto and in the Department of Economics at the University of Western Ontario.

Allen Sutherland is currently the director general of strategy and integration at Human Resources and Social Development Canada. As a public servant in the Government of Canada, Sutherland has held policy planning and research positions in the Privy Council Office, the Policy Research Secretariat and the Department of Foreign Affairs and International Trade. He has received degrees from the John F. Kennedy School of Government, Harvard University (MPP) and Queen's University (BA Hons).

Carolyn Hughes Tuohy is a professor emeritus in the Department of Political Science and senior fellow at the School of Public Policy and Governance at the University of Toronto. Her area of research and teaching interest is in comparative public policy, with an emphasis on social policy. Tuohy has recently served in senior academic leadership roles at the University of Toronto, including as vice-president, policy development; associate provost; and vice-president, government and institutional relations. She is a fellow of the Royal Society of Canada, and she is a member of the boards of directors of the Institute for Clinical Evaluative Sciences and the Institute for Work and Health. She is the author of *Accidental Logics: The Dynamics of Change in the Health Care Arena in the United States, Britain and Canada* (1999) and *Policy and Politics in Canada: Institutionalized Ambivalence* (1992), as well as numerous journal articles and book chapters in the areas of health and social policy, professional regulation and comparative approaches in public policy.

Peter A. Victor is an ecological economist who teaches environmental studies at York University. From 1996 to 2001, he was dean of the Faculty of Environmental Studies, and before that he spent several years as assistant deputy minister of the Environmental Sciences and Standards Division of the Ontario Ministry of the Environment. He was also a principal of VHB Consulting and Victor and Burrell Research and Consulting, where he undertook numerous influential policy-related economic studies in Canada and abroad. Victor serves on many advisory boards and committees in the public, private and nongovernmental organization sectors.

William Watson was educated at McGill University and at Yale University. He has taught at McGill since 1977, and he is now chairman of the Department of Economics. He is best known for his regular columns in the *National Post*, the Montreal *Gazette* and the *Ottawa Citizen*. From 1998 to 2002, he edited the IRPP magazine *Policy Options*, and he is currently a senior research fellow at the IRPP and research fellow at the C.D. Howe Institute. While on a leave from McGill in 1997-98, he served as editorial pages editor of the *Ottawa Citizen*. In 1989, he won the National Magazine Awards' gold medal for humour for a piece he contributed to *Saturday Night* magazine. His book *Globalization and the Meaning of Canadian Life* was runner-up for the Donner Prize for the best book on Canadian public policy published in 1998.

MARQUIS

Marquis Book Printing Inc.

Québec, Canada
2007